COST
REDUCTION
FROM

A

TO

Z

COST
REDUCTION
FROM

LINDLEY R. HIGGINS, P. E.
Associate Editor
Construction Methods and Equipment

RUTH W. STIDGER
Associate Editor
World Construction

McGRAW-HILL BOOK COMPANY
New York   St. Louis   San Francisco   Auckland
Bogotá   Düsseldorf   Johannesburg   London
Madrid   Mexico   Montreal
New Delhi   Panama   Paris   São Paulo   Singapore
Sydney   Tokyo   Toronto

530269

With affection this book is dedicated to our parents,
Kenneth and Lucille Willman

R.W.S.

and the late
Edward Roberts and Violet Moore Higgins

L.R.H.

Library of Congress Cataloging in Publication Data

Higgins, Lindley R
  Cost reduction from A to Z.

  Includes bibliographical references and index.
  1. Cost control. I. Stidger, Ruth W., date, joint author. II. Title.
HD47.5.H48   658.1'552   76-18979
ISBN 07-028765-1

1234567890 KPKP 785432109876

The editors for this book were W. Hodson Mogan and Joan Zseleczky,
the designer was Elliot Epstein, and the production supervisor
was Teresa F. Leaden. It was set in Baskerville
by University Graphics, Inc.

Printed and bound by The Kingsport Press.

INTRODUCTION

Cost Reduction from A to Z is designed to help business people locate, analyze, and reduce excessive costs in all areas of their operations.

In today's business climate—with keener competition, spiraling wages, and unstable economic conditions—the sustained controlling of costs often means the difference between profit and loss. All over the world, cost-conscious executives are taking hard looks at all aspects of their businesses with an eye toward reducing costs wherever possible. Operations, procedures, systems, and methods that seemed efficient in more buoyant business climates are now being critically reexamined to determine how cost-effective they *really* are. As a result, new concepts in plant, equipment, and managerial methods are rendering former definitions of efficiency obsolete.

Cost Reduction from A to Z is a compendium of over 600 of the best cost-controlling ideas and methods that have evolved in recent years. These techniques have been drawn from sources throughout the world—the best methods from North and South America, Western Europe, the Far East, and even behind the Iron Curtain. Within the pages of this book the business executive should find scores of useful ideas that can be directly applied to reduce costs within his or her company. Additionally, where company operations do not favor direct application, the techniques should serve as a creative springboard to launch the reader on a search for new cost-saving ideas to fit her or his particular business.

As with all books that cover a subject broadly, *Cost Reduction from A to Z* has certain limitations. Because of the sheer bulk of techniques discussed, the treatment of each subject is necessarily brief. Although more than enough information is included to give the reader a clear, concise grasp of each idea, entire books have been written on many of the techniques, and it is beyond the scope of this volume to go into such detail. Rather, it is intended that the reader will peruse the pages of the book, discover cost-controlling concepts that can be incorporated into his or her business, and then—if necessary—do further in-depth research into the subjects through more specialized books. For this purpose, *each technique includes a Suggested Further Reading list of one or more works covering the subject in detail.*

AREAS OF USE

As an aid in helping the reader easily locate all of the cost reduction techniques that the book contains in nine key business areas, all subjects include an "area of use" subheading. The nine broad areas are:

1. Psychological Motivational Management
2. Financial Motivational Management
3. Work Place Motivational Management
4. Organizational and Operational Systems
5. Paperwork Design and Flow Systems
6. Data Retention—Files and Recordkeeping
7. Materials and Equipment Management
8. Industrial Applications
9. Business and Commercial Applications

Thus, a typical entry will read:

DEEP ORGANIZATION

Areas for use in Cost Control:
ORGANIZATIONAL AND OPERATIONAL SYSTEMS
INDUSTRIAL APPLICATIONS
BUSINESS AND COMMERCIAL APPLICATIONS

Deep organization is a technique that reduces costs by lowering the number of highly skilled—and, accordingly, highly salaried—employees needed for efficient operation. A top executive concerned about the overall cost effectiveness of his company's Organizational and Operational Systems could perhaps make use of this technique. Likewise, a production vice-president might have Industrial Applications for the technique on the shop floor. The idea might also prove useful in streamlining an insurance executive's branch office—a Business and Commercial Application. Thus, all three areas of use have been listed to help each of these executives easily recognize that deep organization is pertinent to his or her particular needs.

At the same time, the area of use subheadings make it convenient for the reader to locate all techniques pertaining to one of the nine business areas without perusing the entire book. In the Index, beginning on page 493, the reader will find each of the nine areas included as part of the alphabetical listing. Under each business area, all of the page numbers are given where techniques appear that are relevant to that area. For example, an executive who is concerned about the overall cost effectiveness of paperwork in her company or department need only look up Paperwork Design and Flow Systems in the Index and she will find the page number of every technique the book contains on that subject.

The following types of material are covered in each of the nine business areas:

1. *Psychological Motivational Management.* Entries in this area are aimed at improving business efficiency by raising human productivity and offering keys to identifying redundant human activities so that duplications may be removed, reducing costs. Techniques to increase performance through understanding the human personality and methods to persuade employees to accomplish more are included. Examples:

   Behavior Control—a discussion of new psychological techniques to obtain certain desired work responses.
   Fatigue Study—an evaluation of the psychological effects of employee fatigue and how they can be overcome.
   Flextime—a method of motivating workers by permitting them the freedom of flexible—rather than rigid—working hours.

2. *Financial Motivational Management.* A broad range of methods of providing monetary or other tangible benefits in exchange for increased work performance are discussed. The importance of financial drive is evaluated against nonfinancial motivational techniques. Examples:

   Attendance Bonus—a bonus paid to employees when costs are reduced because of better work attendance.
   Bedeaux Plan—an incentive payment plan that gives employees bonuses on work time saved, comparing actual time with standard time.
   Copartnership—the involvement of workers in responsibilities and profits of the company.

3. *Work Place Motivational Management.* Sometimes called "human engineering" or "biomechanics," this area acknowledges the vital importance of the work place

and work surroundings in the level of performance achieved. Methods of increasing work output by improving atmosphere, lighting, ventilation, office layout, etc., are included. Examples:

Ergonomics—a discussion of the relationship of the worker and his or her job, with emphasis on physical and motivational efficiency of the work place.
Housekeeping—a checklist for keeping the work place clean, efficient, and safe.
Office Layout—an outline for optimum office layout, for both efficiency and employee motivation.

4. *Organizational and Operational Systems.* Office and work group cost reductions are included in this area, along with less expensive organizational systems. Operations—and systems to carry out these operations—in business offices, industrial-plant front offices, sales offices, engineering and drafting rooms, accounting offices, insurance administrative facilities, banks, etc., are discussed. Examples:

Accident Cost Control—checklists to prevent time lost through accidents.
Alternate Office Analysis Chart—a method of determining the lowest-cost office space that will satisfactorily meet company needs.
Auditing Freight Bills—guidelines for putting shipments in lower rate classifications, lowering freight costs.

5. *Paperwork Design and Flow Systems.* Paperwork design and flow methods to speed use, movement, and filing are emphasized. Samples of form design and flow layout plans are illustrated. Examples:

Correspondence Management—discusses the most efficient use of business letters, including reduction of correspondence costs.
Dyeline Payroll System—a method of reducing payroll paperwork.
Forms Design and Production—examples of efficient form design and a discussion of cost-effective production methods.

6. *Data Retention—Files and Recordkeeping.* Methods of storing and retrieving information and recordkeeping—at reduced costs—are detailed in entries marked for use in this area. Computerized methods, as well as special recordkeeping techniques for an inflationary economy, are examined. Examples:

Classification and Coding Systems—a discussion of systems used to organize items logically and efficiently.
Electronic Data Processing—cost reductions that can be realized through computerized data storage methods.
Filing and Overfiling—outlines cost-effective filing procedures.

7. *Materials and Equipment Management.* Purchasing techniques, methods to reduce materials' waste and costs, and techniques to increase equipment output are included in this area. Relationships of equipment to human labor costs are surveyed. Examples:

Capacity Studies—checklist for making maximum use of equipment.
Cash Pickup Orders—a method of reducing the paperwork costs of small orders.
Contracyclical Buying—guidelines for purchasing at lowest market levels.

8. *Industrial Applications.* Every phase of cost reduction applicable to industrial operations is labeled in this area. Pre-operational design, such as value analysis, is also included. Manufacturing, warehousing, purchasing, shipping, distribution, power generation, construction, data processing centers, and many other topics are covered. Examples:

ABC Analysis—a technique to reduce materials' costs through usage analysis.
Constraints Technique—a method for analyzing a proposed system or piece of equipment for cost effectiveness.

Cost Reduction Assessment—the evaluation of proposed cost reduction techniques to determine feasibility, effectiveness, and long- and short-term implications.

9. *Business and Commercial Applications.* Nonproduction cost reduction methods and details of their use are included in this area. Cost-saving techniques for offices, retail operations, banks, and other commercial areas are discussed. Examples:

Artificial Intelligence—the substitution of computerized equipment for human labor in decision making and reasoning.
Change-a-Word Method—a management tool to stimulate creative thinking.
Computer Security—methods to safeguard against accidental or purposeful disruption of computer facilities, and the protection of computerized information.

SELECTING MORE THAN ONE APPROACH TO A SPECIFIC PROBLEM

Although *Cost Reduction from A to Z* is arranged to help find solutions that relate directly to specific cost problems, readers will get more from the book if they check related areas. Many service-oriented businesses, for example, will find that adaptations of industrial techniques may also be made outside the factory. *Cross-referencing within each entry will help readers find these multiple possible solutions.*

Selecting more than one approach to a specific problem—called "lateral thinking" by behavioral scientists—also helps readers keep an open mind to new cost reduction methods.

ABC ANALYSIS

Area for use in Cost Control:

INDUSTRIAL APPLICATIONS

ABC analysis is a technique designed to reduce the cost of materials used in production. The method operates on the principle that the bulk of material costs are caused by only a small percentage of the parts used. In applying the technique, usage ratios are divided into three categories:

A. Materials most often used in production
B. Materials second most often used in production
C. Materials least often used in production

Efforts to find cheaper distributors, less expensive replacement items, etc., are concentrated on the A grouping. For example, if a factory makes a part that uses a specific plastic for 90 percent of its material, cotton fabric for 7 percent of its material, and adhesives for 3 percent of its material, the ABC breakdown would be:

A. Plastic, 90 percent
B. Cotton fabric, 7 percent
C. Adhesive, 3 percent

Finding the lowest-cost material would take about the same amount of time and money for any one of the three categories, but since most material costs are for category A, plastic, if all the time available for trying to cut material costs is used to find the lowest-cost plastic source, much more money will be saved than if an equal amount of time is spent on each of the three categories.

SUGGESTED FURTHER READING

Ireson, William G., and Eugene L. Grant, *Handbook of Industrial Engineering and Management,* Prentice-Hall, Englewood Cliffs, N.J., 1970.
Radke, Magnus, *Manual of Cost Reduction Techniques,* McGraw-Hill, New York, 1972.

ABILITY ESTIMATING

Areas for use in Cost Control:

ORGANIZATIONAL AND OPERATIONAL SYSTEMS
PAPERWORK DESIGN AND FLOW SYSTEMS
INDUSTRIAL APPLICATIONS
BUSINESS AND COMMERCIAL APPLICATIONS

Ability estimating is a method of statistically forecasting the performance level of employees before they are hired. This ensures hiring those who will work most efficiently, thus reducing labor costs. Former employees, teachers, or references given by the prospective employee are asked to rate the applicant on a five-point scale.

Traits commonly rated include the following:

1. Initiative
2. Technical skill
3. Reliability
4. Efficiency
5. Common sense
6. Industry
7. Resourcefulness
8. Leadership
9. Ambition
10. Tact
11. Perseverance
12. Concentration
13. Cooperativeness
14. Imagination
15. Stability
16. Ability to communicate
17. Adaptability
18. Patience
19. Aggressiveness
20. Intelligence
21. Originality
22. Accuracy
23. Loyalty

Ratings on at least four rating scales should be obtained for each prospective employee. An additional scale may be completed by company interviewers, who use their impressions of the degree these traits are present rather than actual knowledge. Ratings for all sources are then averaged for each trait.

SUGGESTED FURTHER READING

Terry, George R., *Principles of Management,* Irwin, Homewood, Ill., 1972.
Whisler, T. L., and S. F. Harper, *Performance Appraisal,* Holt, New York, 1962.

ABSENTEEISM CONTROL

Areas for use in Cost Control:

FINANCIAL MOTIVATIONAL MANAGEMENT
INDUSTRIAL APPLICATIONS
BUSINESS AND COMMERCIAL APPLICATIONS

A New York Telephone Company survey finds that absences cost U.S. businesses more than $10 billion per year. About 2 million employees are absent each day. One company participating in the survey found that absences cost about $300 per year for each person employed. Here are absence costs that can be reduced for any size of business:

1. Disrupted schedules
2. Idle machinery
3. Shipment and invoicing delays
4. Increased inventory
5. Overtime
6. Clerical costs

WHY THEY ARE ABSENT AND WHAT TO DO ABOUT IT

Absenteeism varies greatly between companies, often in direct relationship to employee turnover rates. Absenteeism and turnover frequently result from the same causes:

1. *Poor working conditions.* Bad lighting, ventilation, and plant facilities (cafeteria, restrooms, etc.) are some of the key offenders. Correcting these conditions will make coming to work more agreeable.
2. *Boredom with routine.* The most efficient approaches seem to center on giving employees more responsibility and more chance to use their initiative. A produc-

tion worker who completes a product or part of a product, for example, can feel more satisfaction about his or her work than one who screws on a nut and a bolt as the product passes by.

3. *Uneven work flow.* Pressure to finish products one day and little to do the following day creates tension, as well as partial boredom, and leads to increased absenteeism. An employee feels he or she will not be missed on slack days.

4. *Conflicts with coworkers.* Disagreements can sometimes be averted by supervisors. If workers do begin to feud, prompt and open settlement of the issues is mandatory to keep absenteeism costs down.

5. *Not enough responsibility.* Supervisory staff should make certain each employee is given responsibility according to her or his ability.

6. *Poor transportation.* Infrequent or badly operated public transportation increases absenteeism. Some companies operate buses of their own coinciding with shift changes and making runs to a central part of the city that is more easily reached by employees. Coordination of car pools, through the personnel department or through a company newsletter, is an additional way to ease this pressure.

7. *Lack of communication with supervisor.* Solving this problem depends not only on teaching the supervisor to communicate with employees, but also on his or her willingness to do so. Sensitivity training, gestalt techniques, and other systems for teaching management-employee communication essentials are recommended.

8. *No recognition for good work.* One of the strongest positive reinforcers (*see* **Behavior Control**) is praise for work well done. Lack of such praise is a key cause of absenteeism.

Bonuses for increased production and incentive plans provide improvement in work attendance because the worker's salary depends directly on what he or she produces. Bonuses tied directly to attendance and punctuality may also be effective.

Absenteeism and tardiness may drop when a chart detailing individuals absent or late for work is kept in some location likely to be seen by other employees. Such charting should be used carefully, with a small prize or bonus perhaps being offered to the worker who goes a predetermined period of time without being late or absent.

SUGGESTED FURTHER READING

Cost Control and the Supervisor, American Management Assn., New York, 1966.
Radke, Magnus, *Manual of Cost Reduction Techniques,* McGraw-Hill, New York, 1972.
Terry, George R., *Principles of Management,* Irwin, Homewood, Ill., 1972.

ACCELERATED LIFE TESTING

Areas for use in Cost Control:

ORGANIZATIONAL AND OPERATIONAL SYSTEMS

INDUSTRIAL APPLICATIONS

Accelerated life testing is a quality-control technique that inspects a product after subjecting it to conditions that rapidly simulate the item's use for the average lifetime of such a product. Without actually waiting an entire product lifetime, quality of the product can be determined for various stages of its lifetime. Use of the technique can reduce costs by detailing areas of the product that have a higher than necessary quality, allowing substitution of lower-cost materials in these areas.

SUGGESTED FURTHER READING

Ireson, William G., and Eugene L. Grant, *Handbook of Industrial Engineering and Management,* Prentice-Hall, Englewood Cliffs, N.J., 1970.
Weinberg, Sidney, *Profit through Quality,* Gower Press, London, 1969.

ACCIDENT COST CONTROL

Areas for use in Cost Control:

ORGANIZATIONAL AND OPERATIONAL SYSTEMS
MATERIALS AND EQUIPMENT MANAGEMENT
INDUSTRIAL APPLICATIONS
BUSINESS AND COMMERCIAL APPLICATIONS

Control of accident costs can be best implemented through control of individual worker behavior, since studies estimate that 85 percent of all business and industrial accidents are caused by unsafe acts of workers. The remainder are caused by unsafe equipment. Table 1 shows the types of unsafe acts, unsafe equipment, and work locations where most accidents occur, while Fig. 1 gives the accident rates in several industries.

Table 1. Common Reasons for Accidents

Acts likely to be performed unsafely	Equipment likely to be used unsafely	Likely accident locations
Lifting materials	Hand-lift trucks	Stairs
Handling materials	Cranes	Electrical outlets
	Metalworking machines	Warehouses
	Woodworking machines	Shipping departments
	Saws	
	Transmission equipment	
	Ladders/scaffolding	
	Hand tools	
	Electrical equipment	

ACCIDENT COSTS

Insurance and workmen's compensation cover some accident costs. For every $1 covered, however, an accident costs the company up to $5 more in lost working time (including time of other employees who watch or aid), lost materials, employee replacement, damaged equipment, and so on.

ACCIDENT PREVENTION

Employee awareness of safety measures is essential. This can be facilitated by safety education, including safety campaigns, posters, etc.

Accident-prone workers should be avoided when hiring, and those hired should be trained to prevent accidents or dismissed if already hired. A very small percentage of workers cause most accidents, usually as the result of personal emotional problems or psychological characteristics.

Lifting and handling materials account for about a third of industrial accidents. These can usually be prevented with correct work methods. Weight of the material handled should rest on the legs rather than the back. *See also* **Effort Control.**

Machines and tools cause accidents when improperly used and when they are in unsafe condition.

Falls are another major accident area and can usually be prevented by:

1. *Clean floors, stairs, and walkways*—spillage, dirt, and litter can increase falls.
2. *Well-maintained ladders, scaffolding, and walkways,* including railings.

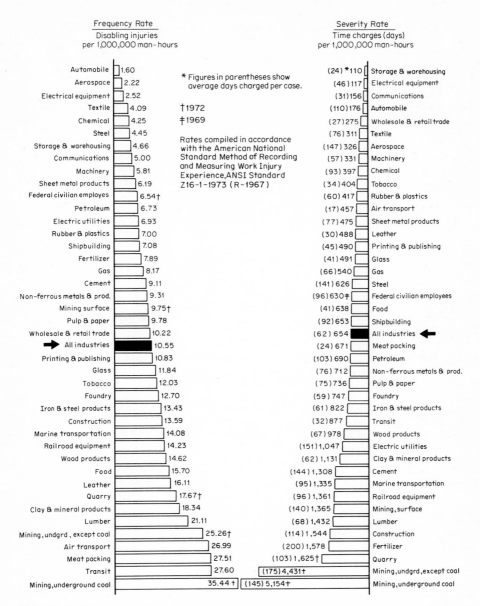

Figure 1. Accident rates in various industries. (*Accident Facts,* National Safety Council, Chicago, 1974.)

3. *Suitable shoes and boots,* with low heels and good upper-foot support. Safety shoes should be required when necessary.
4. *Safe use of ladders, scaffolding, and walkways.* Employees should use railings consistently.

Hand tools should be in good repair, and only the correct tool should be used. For example, a knife should not be used as a screwdriver.

Electrical equipment should be grounded. All wires, insulation, connections, etc., should be in good operating condition. Safety valves, fuses, fused switches, and circuit breakers should be handled only by electricians.

Keep records of job hazards and appropriate preventive measures. See also **Key-Point Safety.**

Accidents should be investigated, the cause determined, and methods of preventing similar accidents established at line-management level.

Safety gear, such as shoes, clothing, and glasses, should be *mandatory* where conditions make such gear advisable.

SUGGESTED FURTHER READING

Bittel, L. R., *What Every Supervisor Should Know,* McGraw-Hill, New York, 1974.
"Occupational Safety and Health Standards: National Consensus Standards and Established Federal Standards," *Federal Register,* vol. 36, no. 105, part 2, May 29, 1971.
Simonds, R. H., and J. V. Grimaldi, *Safety Management: Accident Cost and Control,* Irwin, Homewood, Ill., 1958.

ACCUMULATIVE TIMING

Areas for use in Cost Control:

ORGANIZATIONAL AND OPERATIONAL SYSTEMS
INDUSTRIAL APPLICATIONS

Accumulative timing is a work study technique (*see* **Work Study and Measurement**) used in obtaining more efficient work from employees, as well as in determining incentive payments (*see* **Incentive Payment Systems**). The method uses two connected stopwatches. When the first watch is stopped, the second begins automatically. The method is especially useful in multiphase work operation.

SUGGESTED FURTHER READING

ASME Work Standardization Bulletin, American Society of Mechanical Engineers, New York, 1973.
Maynard, H. B., ed., *Industrial Engineering Handbook,* 3d ed., McGraw-Hill, New York, 1974.

ACROSS-THE-BOARD SETTLEMENT

Areas for use in Cost Control:

ORGANIZATIONAL AND OPERATIONAL SYSTEMS
INDUSTRIAL APPLICATIONS
BUSINESS AND COMMERCIAL APPLICATIONS

An across-the-board settlement is an equal percentage of wages or conditions payment given to all employees in a bargaining negotiation. Use of the technique can control labor costs by increasing wages or conditions uniformly, rather than giving disproportionately high rises to some groups.

SUGGESTED FURTHER READING

Marsh, A. I., and E. O. Evans, *The Dictionary of Industrial Relations,* Hutchinson, London, 1973.
Industrial and Labor Relations, New York State School of Industrial and Labor Relations, Cornell University, Ithaca, N.Y., 1962.
Roberts' Dictionary of Industrial Relations, BNA, Washington, D.C., 1966.

ACTIVATION MOTIVATION THEORY

Area for use in Cost Control:

PSYCHOLOGICAL MOTIVATIONAL MANAGEMENT

The activation motivation theory, developed by W. E. Scott, maintains that work frustrations provide necessary variety and stimulation, reducing general employee dissatisfaction. The need to overcome the frustrations may thus be an important motivating factor. *See also* **Frustration-Aggression Motivation Theory.**

SUGGESTED FURTHER READING

Scott, W. E., "Activation Theory and Task Design," *Organizational Behavior and Human Performance,* no. 1, 1966.

ACTIVITY SAMPLING

Areas for use in Cost Control:
BUSINESS AND COMMERCIAL APPLICATIONS
INDUSTRIAL APPLICATIONS

Activity sampling is a technique for observing and recording employee activities. This shows how much time is actually spent on various aspects of a job and can be used in cutting out wasted and costly time. If, for example, an activity sampling study shows that five office workers have an hour of slack time during each day, it may be possible to eliminate one worker, redistributing his or her work among the other four.

If the results of activity sampling are to be accurate, the study must be based on enough random objective observations (usually between 500 and 1,000) to reflect actual work situations. Record observations precisely. Know how to do the work being observed, in order to recognize every step of the process.

Before beginning activity sampling, know the goal of the study—whether a particular aspect of the job is being recorded or only the employee's working and nonworking time are to be noted. Set up a system of code letters (see example below[1]) for the various phases of each job, to record each activity quickly.

A = Not present in office
N = Present, but not at work
C = Clerical work without machine
Q = Conferring about work
E = Using electric calculating machine
M = Using manual calculating machine
S = Using adding machine
T = Using typewriter
P = Using telephone

If a complete activity sampling is taken, record observations on a time sheet, detailing the amount of time spent on each aspect of work, as shown in Fig. 2, p. 12.

Combining results of the 500 to 1,000 samplings, the following can be determined from study:

1. How long a specific task, such as checking an invoice, takes.
2. Percentage of the total work day any piece of equipment is in use.
3. Percentage of time the employee actually spends working.

SUGGESTED FURTHER READING

Cemach, H. P., *Work Study in the Office,* MacLaren and Sons, London, 1969.
Maynard, H. B., *Handbook of Business Administration,* McGraw-Hill, New York, 1967.
Shrode, W. A., *Organization and Management,* Irwin, Homewood, Ill., 1974.

---

[1]Bright, B. E., "Work Study in the Office—The Application of the Ratio Delay Technique," *The Cost Accountant,* London, September 1955.

```
┌─────────────────────────────────────────┐
│ Activity Sampling Form                    │
│ Job:_____                       │
│ Employee:_____                  │
│ Observer:_____                  │
│ Date:_____Time:_____                   │
│                                           │
│ Time                                      │
├──────────┬──────────┬─────────────────────┤
│ From     │   To     │  Work Code          │
├──────────┼──────────┼─────────────────────┤
│ 9:00     │  9:05    │     C               │
│ 9:05     │  9:10    │     C               │
│ 9:10     │  9:15    │     Q               │
│ 9:15     │  9:20    │     Q               │
│ 9:20     │  9:25    │     Q               │
└──────────┴──────────┴─────────────────────┘
┌──────────┬──────────┬─────────────────────┐
│ 4:50     │  4:55    │     C               │
│ 4:55     │  5:00    │     N               │
└──────────┴──────────┴─────────────────────┘
```

Figure 2. Activity sampling form.

ACTUAL COST PRICE METHOD

Areas for use in Cost Control:

MATERIALS AND EQUIPMENT MANAGEMENT
INDUSTRIAL APPLICATIONS
BUSINESS AND COMMERCIAL APPLICATIONS

The actual cost price method is a **stock control** technique used to value goods, materials, or supplies stored. Values are determined from invoices of materials and supplies purchased, or from production cost records of inventoried goods. When such figures are available, it is a satisfactory stock valuation method.

SUGGESTED FURTHER READING

Standingford, Oliver, ed., *Newnes Encyclopedia of Business Management,* Newnes, London, 1967.

ADVERSE-WEATHER CONSTRUCTION COST REDUCTION

Areas for use in Cost Control:

ORGANIZATIONAL AND OPERATIONAL SYSTEMS
MATERIALS AND EQUIPMENT MANAGEMENT
INDUSTRIAL APPLICATIONS

Adverse weather, particularly winter weather, traditionally slows construction and raises construction costs. R. Howarth, South Devon Technical College, estimates that more construction output is lost because of bad weather than from strikes and other industrial action. Adapting working methods to adverse weather conditions, however, can save a good proportion of this output, reducing costs.

General preparations should include stocking of equipment and materials used to facilitate work during bad weather conditions. These include:

1. Portable heaters
2. Sand or gravel
3. Protective coverings such as tarps and plastic sheet
4. Sawdust
5. Antifreeze
6. Portable lighting

WORKING IN BAD WEATHER

Specific points to practice for more continuous work during bad weather are broken down by weather problems.

Snow and Frost. Be sure all motors are winterized with antifreeze and winter-weight lubricants. Engine tune-ups prior to cold weather are advised.

Concrete work can be continued during frost periods if heated water is used in mixing. Heating and mixing should be near the location of use. Curing time should be lengthened to make up for weather effects. Newly cemented areas should be protected during curing, as should newly mortared brick or block construction.

Portable mixing bays made of fiberboard provide protection for laborers from wind and facilitate work.

Scheduling should aim for exterior completion *prior* to the onset of winter, so that labor can be shifted inside during frost and snow periods.

Portable lighting can extend the winter working day as well as increase productivity and reduce accidents. Lighting can be powered by mains electricity, a portable generator, or L.P. gas.

Portable heating is needed both for labor and to warm materials, defrost ground, and dry machinery, framework, etc.

Jobs that should be saved, where possible, for the heart of winter weather include repairs, painting, interior construction and fitting, and maintenance of equipment and plant. Companies using partial prefabrication of construction components can transfer labor into the plant during inclement weather where union agreements allow it.

Rain and Damp. Protective coverings should be used over newly constructed areas, as well as on equipment. Sawdust or shavings absorb mud and water for better site movement, and sand or gravel provides equipment protection and freer movement in wet weather.

Use weatherproof glues, such as phenolic-, resorcinol-, or melamine-based products.

Spot use of portable heating may be used to dry damp areas, preventing dry rot in walls, floors, etc.

Rescheduling interior work, rather than exterior, can prevent time loss.

Dry and Hot. Allow extra drying time for paint, roofing materials, damp course, putty, etc. Alternatively, protective coverings may be used to screen out the sun and speed drying.

Wet or cover cement and brickwork to avoid too rapid drying, which may crack the materials.

Dust should also be dampened, particularly in areas where it will harm the quality of work, such as in concrete laying and painting. Vehicles should be routed away from these areas to avoid excessive dust.

Provide sun screens where possible for workers, to keep productivity at optimum levels. Avoid work that requires the worker to hold one position all day and schedule work that requires movement instead.

SUGGESTED FURTHER READING

Bricklaying in Cold Weather, MPBW Advisory Leaflet no. 8, H.M.S.O., London.
Concreting in Cold Weather, MPBW Advisory Leaflet no. 7, H.M.S.O., London.
Howarth, R., *Building Craft Foremanship,* David & Charles, Newton Abbot, England, 1972.
Protective Screens and Enclosures, MPBW Advisory Leaflet no. 74, H.M.S.O., London.
Royer, King, *The Construction Manager,* Prentice-Hall, Englewood Cliffs, N.J., 1974.
Scott, J. S., ed., *A Dictionary of Building,* Penguin, Baltimore, 1974.
Site Lighting, MPBW Advisory Leaflet no. 71, H.M.S.O., London.
Weather and the Builder, MPBW Advisory Leaflet no. 40, H.M.S.O., London.

AGE-SPAN MANAGER LOSS CONTROL

Areas for use in Cost Control:

PSYCHOLOGICAL MOTIVATIONAL MANAGEMENT
FINANCIAL MOTIVATIONAL MANAGEMENT
ORGANIZATIONAL AND OPERATIONAL SYSTEMS
INDUSTRIAL APPLICATIONS
BUSINESS AND COMMERCIAL APPLICATIONS

Age-span manager loss control is the prevention of young-manager turnover, reducing turnover and lowering costs by managerial hiring to provide a balanced age spread. Of all management staff, there will be approximately 25 percent in each of the ranges thirty, forty, fifty, and sixty years of age. This policy provides younger, newly trained managers with better possibilities for advancement and an incentive not to leave the firm after training. Additionally, it provides the company with more dynamic management.

SUGGESTED FURTHER READING

"Successful Management," *Nation's Business,* Doubleday, New York, 1964.

AIR FREIGHT

Areas for use in Cost Control:

MATERIALS AND EQUIPMENT MANAGEMENT
INDUSTRIAL APPLICATIONS

Air freight, the shipping of materials, equipment, supplies, and/or finished goods by air, can reduce costs in:

1. Marketing
2. Time
3. Inventory
4. Warehousing
5. Insurance
6. Packaging

Marketing cost reductions possible include adding sales to areas without alternate speedy freight routes, as in the case of selling perishable foods to distant markets. Equipment replacement parts, emergency material supplies, and short-lead-time goods sales can also be expanded.

Time cost reductions include saving production employee labor time when parts have been ordered to repair production equipment. The seller is paid earlier for goods shipped rapidly.

Inventory cost reductions stem from shorter lead time required for delivery of goods. For example, average safety stock of production is about 20 percent. If this minimum can be reduced to 10 percent, capital cost savings result.

Warehousing cost reductions result, since less space is required for holding smaller stocks. When warehousing can be centralized, complete storage buildings and operations (with accompanying costs) can be eliminated or leased to other firms.

Insurance cost reductions result both from a smaller amount of goods held and insured and from the lower premium rates imposed when air routes are used.

Packaging costs may also be reduced, since handling is less frequent in air transportation.

OTHER FACTORS

Air freight rates may be reduced by using air-sea or air-rail links to lessen overall time and inventory costs as well as shipment costs. For example, a Japanese firm may fly cargo from Tokyo to San Francisco, where it will be transferred to a freight train and shipped to New York.

Air freight costs can be reduced through the use of *containers*. Here, producers prepack goods in a standard-sized container to facilitate handling. Discounts of up to 10 percent are currently available for use of containers. *See also* **Containerization; Palletization.**

SUGGESTED FURTHER READING

Arbury, J. N., *A New Approach to Physical Distribution,* American Management Association, New York, 1967.
Magee, J. F., *Physical Distribution Systems,* McGraw-Hill, New York, 1967.
Murphy, G. J., *Transportation and Distribution,* Business Books, London, 1972.

ALGORITHM

Area for use in Cost Control:

ORGANIZATIONAL AND OPERATIONAL SYSTEMS

An algorithm is any technique or device that tells how to reach a specific goal. For example, in reducing the costs of a research project, the project budget is the algorithm.

SUGGESTED FURTHER READING

Beer, Stafford, and Allen Lane, *Brain of the Firm; The Managerial Cybernetics of Organization,* The Penguin Press, London, 1972.

ALTERNATIVE OFFICE ANALYSIS CHART

Areas for use in Cost Control:

ORGANIZATIONAL AND OPERATIONAL SYSTEMS
PAPERWORK DESIGN AND FLOW SYSTEMS
BUSINESS AND COMMERCIAL APPLICATIONS

An alternative office analysis chart visually compares features of several possible office locations with company needs to determine the lowest-cost space that will satisfactorily meet company needs (see Table 2, p. 16).

Looking at Table 2, although total cost is greater, only alternative office 3 provides the 10 percent growth space needed by the company in the next five years. Assuming this increased space is essential, the company may be able to rent the 500 sq ft of unneeded space for two or three years, offsetting the cost. If the additional space may not be necessary, however, other factors should be compared. Office 1 does not have a computer room, for example, but its total cost is $4,500 lower than office 2. *See also* **Strategic Space Planning.**

SUGGESTED FURTHER READING

Lock, D., ed., *Management Techniques,* Directors Bookshelf, London, 1972.

AMALGAMATION

Areas for use in Cost Control:

ORGANIZATIONAL AND OPERATIONAL SYSTEMS
INDUSTRIAL APPLICATIONS
BUSINESS AND COMMERCIAL APPLICATIONS

Amalgamation, also called *merger* (*see* **Mergers**), *absorption, combination,* and *integration,* is the combining of two or more companies. Costs can be reduced by amalgamation in the following areas:

Table 2. Typical Alternative Office Analysis Chart

Company requirements	Alternative locations		
	Office 1	Office 2	Office 3
Usable area: 4,000 sq ft	3,900 sq ft	4,200 sq ft	4,500 sq ft
Layout: 60% office	60%	65%	60%
40% open	40%	35%	35%
Facilities: Telephone	Yes	Yes	Yes
Telex	Yes	No	Yes
Computer room	No	Yes	Yes
Air condit.	Yes	Yes	Yes
700-lux illum.	Yes	Yes	No
Flexibility: 10% growth 5 years	No	No	Yes
Length of lease: 5 years	5 years	5 years	7 years
Lease cost/annual	$16,000	$19,000	$20,000
Maintenance cost/annual	$ 5,000	$ 4,500	$ 5,200
Operation cost/annual	$10,000	$12,000	$11,000
Total office cost/annual	$31,000	$35,500	$36,200

1. *Capital investment costs* can be reduced by sharing and/or optimal use of plant and equipment.
2. *Selling costs* can be reduced through wider related production of products for salesmen to offer.
3. *Distribution costs* can be reduced through centralization of warehouse and display rooms, combined transportation, etc.
4. *R&D costs* can be reduced by sharing of information previously duplicated.
5. *Advertising and public relations costs* can be reduced by the use of a single campaign as opposed to the duplication and competition of former separate campaigns.
6. *Materials cost* can be reduced through increased-volume price advantages.
7. *Administration costs* can be reduced, particularly at the top of the hierarchy structure, when separate positions are combined.

SUGGESTED FURTHER READING

Batty, J., *Management Accountancy*, MacDonald, London, 1971.

ANALYTICAL ESTIMATING

Areas for use in Cost Control:
ORGANIZATIONAL AND OPERATIONAL SYSTEMS
INDUSTRIAL APPLICATIONS

Analytical estimating is a work study technique (*see* **Work Study and Measurement**) used to estimate the time a specific piece of nonrepetitive work will take as a basis for determining incentive payments (*see* **Incentive Payment Systems**). In some industries, a data bank of estimates is established, providing a sound basis for pay rate determination and cost reduction.

SUGGESTED FURTHER READING

Industrial and Labor Relations, New York School of Industrial and Labor Relations, Cornell University, Ithaca, N.Y., 1962.

ANNUAL IMPROVEMENT FACTOR

Areas for use in Cost Control:

ORGANIZATIONAL AND OPERATIONAL SYSTEMS
INDUSTRIAL APPLICATIONS

The annual improvement factor is an agreement giving employees a percentage of costs saved or of increased productivity. For example, if employees' acceptance of a new work method saves a company $100,000 in production costs annually, employees may be given 25 percent of the cost savings, or $25,000, in bonuses.

SUGGESTED FURTHER READING

Marsh, A. I., and E. O. Evans, *The Dictionary of Industrial Relations,* Hutchinson, London, 1973.

ANTIPIRATING AGREEMENT

Areas for use in Cost Control:

ORGANIZATIONAL AND OPERATIONAL SYSTEMS
INDUSTRIAL APPLICATIONS
BUSINESS AND COMMERCIAL APPLICATIONS

An antipirating agreement, also called a no-poaching agreement, is an unwritten contract between companies forbidding aggressive recruitment of executives and/or skilled craftsmen. Turnover and training costs are reduced by use of the method.

SUGGESTED FURTHER READING

Roberts' Dictionary of Industrial Relations, BNA, Washington, D.C., 1966.

ARBITRAGE

Areas for use in Cost Control:

ORGANIZATIONAL AND OPERATIONAL SYSTEMS
INDUSTRIAL APPLICATIONS
BUSINESS AND COMMERCIAL APPLICATIONS

Arbitrage is the technique used to reduce the cost of accepting foreign currency from international trade by selling it in the market with the highest rate of exchange. Modern communications' speed is responsible for use of the technique, since such transactions can be conducted worldwide instantly.

SUGGESTED FURTHER READING

Ellsworth, P. T., *The International Economy,* Macmillan, New York, 1969.
Hanson, J. L., *A Dictionary of Economics and Commerce,* MacDonald, London, 1974.

ARSENAL CONCEPT

Areas for use in Cost Control:

ORGANIZATIONAL AND OPERATIONAL SYSTEMS
INDUSTRIAL APPLICATIONS
BUSINESS AND COMMERCIAL APPLICATIONS

The arsenal concept is a control technique that uses both public (governmental) and private (industrial or commercial) programs to solve the same cost or other problem. Although maintaining duplicate programs costs more, operational costs may be reduced (in excess of program cost increases), through improved quality of production and reserve excess capacity.

SUGGESTED FURTHER READING

Boness, A. J., *Capital Budgeting,* Longmans, London, 1972.

ARTIFICIAL INTELLIGENCE

Areas for use in Cost Control:

ORGANIZATIONAL AND OPERATIONAL SYSTEMS
MATERIALS AND EQUIPMENT MANAGEMENT
INDUSTRIAL APPLICATIONS
BUSINESS AND COMMERCIAL APPLICATIONS

Artificial intelligence is the substitution of computerized equipment for human labor in decision making and reasoning. Depending on complexity of use, artificial intelligence can both increase efficiency and reduce labor costs. For example, computers have been programmed to recognize employees' faces and/or voices as a security system link. Identity cards, guards, etc., are not needed in this case. The computer terminal identifies the employee, unlocks the door to the work area, records time of arrival and leaving, etc. Other machines have been programmed to write advertising brochures, create brand names and logos, devise sales programs, etc.

Areas not included in artificial intelligence capabilities at present include setting goals and methods of reaching goals, determining data relevance, handling exceptional situations, forming hypotheses, and creating ideas.

SUGGESTED FURTHER READING

Martin, J., and A. R. D. Norman, *The Computerized Society,* Prentice-Hall, Englewood Cliffs, N.J., 1970.
Minsky, M. L., "Artificial Intelligence," *Scientific American,* September 1966.

ASHBY APPROACH

Areas for use in Cost Control:

ORGANIZATIONAL AND OPERATIONAL SYSTEMS
MATERIALS AND EQUIPMENT MANAGEMENT
INDUSTRIAL APPLICATIONS
BUSINESS AND COMMERCIAL APPLICATIONS

The Ashby approach is the development of cybernetic equipment to amplify human intelligence in much the same way as power-generating equipment amplifies physical energy. With such intelligence amplification, work done by humans can be much more efficient, reducing labor costs. Studies indicate that such amplification can eventually reach 10,000 times, or an I.Q. of 1 million. A large intelligence amplifier will be designed in the foreseeable future to channel control of production and other industrial systems, requiring only a fraction of current human management needs. (*See also* **Cybernetics.**)

SUGGESTED FURTHER READING

Beer, Stafford, *Cybernetics and Management,* English Universities Press, London, 1959.
Brabb, George J., *Introduction to Quantitative Management,* Holt, New York, 1968.

ASSEMBLY CHART

Areas for use in Cost Control:

ORGANIZATIONAL AND OPERATIONAL SYSTEMS
MATERIALS AND EQUIPMENT MANAGEMENT
INDUSTRIAL APPLICATIONS

An assembly chart, also called a Gozinto chart, shows the flow of a product's materials and its part relationships (see Fig. 3). It can also be used to determine lowest-cost manufacturing methods, such as possible subassemblies. Layout of production lines and process scheduling can also be better controlled by using the chart.

SUGGESTED FURTHER READING

Buffa, E. S., *Modern Production Management,* Wiley, New York, 1969.

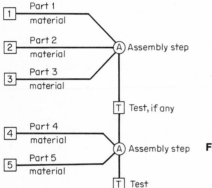

Figure 3. Typical assembly chart.

ASSEMBLY LINE BALANCING

Areas for use in Cost Control:

WORK PLACE MOTIVATIONAL MANAGEMENT
MATERIALS AND EQUIPMENT MANAGEMENT
INDUSTRIAL APPLICATIONS

Assembly line balancing is the technique of making an assembly line flow smoothly, reducing costs of wasted manpower time occurring during waiting when work does not move evenly, with each station taking the same amount of time. To do this, use *work measurement (see* **Work Study and Measurement**), breaking down all line jobs into the smallest time units used, and then assign jobs in lots as nearly equal as possible. Work should be assigned following these general rules:

1. *Line Order.* Jobs must be kept in the correct sequence.
2. *Zoning.* Some product components must use the same piece of equipment and must therefore be assembled at the same station regardless of time. Other components need work performed on different parts or sides of the same product and cannot, therefore, use the same station.
3. *Equal Work Time.* Each station should be assigned equal working time where possible.

Additionally, assembly line balancing is dependent on materials being available to all workers when needed. Complete inventory records should be maintained to help ensure a four- or five-week supply of necessary parts and materials. Layout of stored parts and materials should be keyed to the layout of the assembly line, providing the shortest possible trip from storage to line for each individual material or part (see Fig. 4).

Ordering of materials should be based on production schedules rather than on past records, and assembly supervisors should be made responsible for checking ordering and inventory control in their own production areas.

SUGGESTED FURTHER READING

Kempner, Thomas, ed., *A Handbook of Management,* Weidenfeld and Nicolson, London, 1971.
Plossl, G. W., and O. W. Wright, *Production and Inventory Control,* Prentice-Hall, Englewood Cliffs, N.J., 1967.

ASSEMBLY LINE

Component A	Component B added	Component C added	Component D added	Component E added	
					Dock
Material for component A	Material for component B	Material for component C	Material for component D	Material for component E	

MATERIALS STORAGE

Figure 4. Layout relationship of assembly line and materials storage area.

ATTENDANCE BONUS

Areas for use in Cost Control:

FINANCIAL MOTIVATIONAL MANAGEMENT
PSYCHOLOGICAL MOTIVATIONAL MANAGEMENT
ORGANIZATIONAL AND OPERATIONAL SYSTEMS
INDUSTRIAL APPLICATIONS
BUSINESS AND COMMERCIAL APPLICATIONS

An attendance bonus is a share of savings from reduced costs stemming from continual work attendance that is paid to the employee. The daily cost of absences in past years is computed, as is the average number of days each employee is absent. Employees are then paid a percent (such as 25 percent) of the amount saved for each day less than the average that they are absent. Bookkeeping costs are not a problem if bonus data can be programmed into normal computerized payroll schedules.

SUGGESTED FURTHER READING

Marsh, A. I., and E. O. Evans, *The Directory of Industrial Relations,* Hutchinson, London, 1973.
Roberts' Dictionary of Industrial Relations, BNA, Washington, D.C., 1966.

ATTITUDE SCALES

Areas for use in Cost Control:

PSYCHOLOGICAL MOTIVATIONAL MANAGEMENT
WORK PLACE MOTIVATIONAL MANAGEMENT
INDUSTRIAL APPLICATIONS
BUSINESS AND COMMERCIAL APPLICATIONS

Attitude scales measure workers' attitudes toward job placement, job satisfaction, job difficulties, their place of work, and the company for whom they work. The information used is usually obtained from questionnaires (*see* **Attitude Survey**). The scales are set up to show the amount of deviation of attitudes from a central or average value, the strength of the attitudes, and the relative importance of the attitudes as they affect the company and its production.

SUGGESTED FURTHER READING

Kempner, Thomas, ed., *A Handbook of Management,* Weidenfeld and Nicolson, London, 1971.

ATTITUDE SURVEY

Areas for use in Cost Control:

PSYCHOLOGICAL MOTIVATIONAL MANAGEMENT
WORK PLACE MOTIVATIONAL MANAGEMENT
INDUSTRIAL APPLICATIONS
BUSINESS AND COMMERCIAL APPLICATIONS

Attitude surveys are the systematic collection of attitude data, usually in the form of a questionnaire. This information is used to predict behavior, to test reactions to specific aspects of a company program or plant, or to judge the relationship between employees' attitudes and other factors. **Attitude scales** are set up from data gathered in attitude surveys. The size of the sample is an important factor, and only a sampling of 500 to 1,000 or more employees is considered an accurate base for measuring attitudes.

SUGGESTED FURTHER READING

Kempner, Thomas, ed., *A Handbook of Management,* Weidenfeld and Nicolson, London, 1971.

ATTITUDINAL STRUCTURING

Areas for use in Cost Control:

ORGANIZATIONAL AND OPERATIONAL SYSTEMS
INDUSTRIAL APPLICATIONS
BUSINESS AND COMMERCIAL APPLICATIONS

Attitudinal structuring is a collective bargaining model used to forecast employee and trade union response to various bargaining offers and conditions by determining the activities that change or form such attitudes. Use of the technique can reduce both wage costs and losses due to strikes if such employee response can be accurately predetermined.

SUGGESTED FURTHER READING

Walton, R. E., and R. McKersie, *A Behavioral Theory of Labor Relations,* McGraw-Hill, New York, 1965.

ATTRIBUTE LISTING

Areas for use in Cost Control:

ORGANIZATIONAL AND OPERATIONAL SYSTEMS
INDUSTRIAL APPLICATIONS
BUSINESS AND COMMERCIAL APPLICATIONS

Attribute listing is the listing of all attributes of a cost or other business problem to facilitate creative solution of the problem. Each attribute is evaluated and as many efficiency changes as possible are considered. For example, if attributes are listed for hiring costs, *advertising, screening, testing, interviewing techniques,* and *reference checking* may be listed. Each of these attributes is examined separately in depth and changes implemented to make the attributes as efficient as possible.

SUGGESTED FURTHER READING

Crawford, R. P., *The Techniques of Creative Thinking,* Hawthorn, New York, 1954.

ATTRITION See Hiring Freeze.

AUDITING FREIGHT BILLS

Areas for use in Cost Control:

ORGANIZATIONAL AND OPERATIONAL SYSTEMS
MATERIALS AND EQUIPMENT MANAGEMENT
INDUSTRIAL APPLICATIONS
BUSINESS AND COMMERCIAL APPLICATIONS

Auditing freight bills includes checking such bills for loopholes that put the shipment in a lower rate classification, as well as checking for mathematical errors.

Incomplete description of goods shipped is one area to audit. For example, omitting the word *portable* in the description of phonographs being shipped would raise the cost classification from 50 to 100.

Checking all freight bills may, in itself, be a costly operation. Some companies limit such audits to freight bills of $100 or more, while others use specialty auditors who check the bills in exchange for 30 to 50 percent of the cost reductions achieved.

SUGGESTED FURTHER READING

Ammer, D. S., *Materials Management,* Irwin, Homewood, Ill., 1968.

AUTOMATION

Areas for use in Cost Control:

ORGANIZATIONAL AND OPERATIONAL SYSTEMS
MATERIALS AND EQUIPMENT MANAGEMENT
INDUSTRIAL APPLICATIONS
BUSINESS AND COMMERCIAL APPLICATIONS

Automation is the substitution of mechanical power for human power in work. As the machinery used in this substitution becomes more sophisticated, even its controls are automated, replacing human control. The technique reduces costs when equipment plus operational cost is less than the cost of physical labor and needed equipment.

An example of cost reductions possible with automation can be seen in Fig. 5, where the cost of human-labor material handling cost is compared with the cost of performing the work with electrically powered equipment. Since R. W. Mallick, Westinghouse Electric Corporation, estimates that 22 percent of all U.S. labor costs are paid for materials handling, potential savings in this one area are very large indeed.

Automated equipment, while first used on heavy jobs such as lifting loads of iron or fabricating large metal components, now extends to light and very delicate work. The machines can be set to work at rates of both precision and speed that cannot be matched by human labor. In many industries and businesses, automated equipment also monitors its own performance quality, adjusting itself as necessary.

These features—speed, precision, and self-control—have been developed primarily with the use of the computer. The high-speed electronic computer and data processing machine is able to learn facts and instructions programmed or fed into its memory banks. Once programmed, it is able to remember these facts almost instantaneously and to control production equipment just as rapidly. For example, in producing steel for a

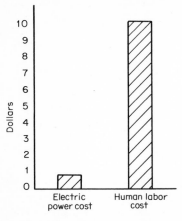

Figure 5. Comparison of human and electric power costs. Courtesy of Industrial Truck Assn., H. B. Maynard, *Industrial Engineering Handbook*, 1st ed., McGraw-Hill, New York, 1956.

bridge, the controlling computer can be programmed to quickly calculate the stresses and strains likely to occur and to correct design features, as well as producing the strength of steel required. *See also* **Electronic Data Processing.**

THE ECONOMICS OF AUTOMATION

Two factors must be considered when discussing the economic viability of automation.

First, will automating a particular type of work be cheaper? Will the cost of new equipment and the cost of its operation be less expensive than human labor using less automatic equipment?

Second, what will happen to workers displaced by automation? Will they be retrained for other work, or will they become unemployable, depressing markets for products and services and overriding the very cost advantages automation should bring? While unemployed workers from any one business or factory may not affect the overall market, collectively they surely do. Employers, as well as state and federal government agencies, can cooperate in retraining programs which are essential if automation is to be fully viable economically.

In determining the basic extent of cost reduction in proposed factory automation, the following formula may be used:

$$A \pm L = OM$$

A, or Automation Cost, is determined by adding the cost of new equipment and the estimated operating cost for the equipment's life and dividing this sum by the estimated life of the equipment.

L, or the Cost of Human Labor using current equipment, is determined by adding estimated labor costs and operating costs for the period used in *A* and dividing the sum by the number of years used in determining *A*.

OM, or the Optimal Method Cost, is the more economical of the two choices— automation or continued human labor production.

If these calculations show that automation will lower costs or increase productivity at the same cost, the next step is to resolve possible labor costs or problems.

In many industries, management will find that labor agreements prevent manufacturers' using fewer human workers even if automated equipment is installed. Some agreements even require employee approval before new equipment is installed. These factors will, of course, affect the cost savings possible with automation. Buy-out agreements may be used by management to overcome these problems. In this case, employees are granted a concession, such as optional early retirement at full retirement pay, in exchange for the lower number of employees required once automation is completed. Company retraining of displaced employees is another method used to help overcome labor union objections to automation.

On the plus side of needed labor changes, management may find that costs are further reduced as employee interest is expanded. Since one employee can operate an extended range of automated equipment, his or her productivity may increase as a result of the increased challange of the work, *in addition to* increased output from the equipment.

Floyd C. Mann, an industrial social psychologist at the University of Michigan, says that factories can also reduce labor costs with automation because less human-intense operation and the more skilled workers that are needed require considerably fewer supervisors. If each eight workers have a supervisor in a moderately mechanized operation, for example, automation may cut a whole work force from 80 to 8. At the same time, the number of supervisors can be reduced—or even eliminated entirely if the remaining employees are sufficiently skilled to be responsible to the next higher level of management.

Bonus payments, and their costs, are usually eliminated in automated plants. Since productivity is controlled by the equipment, the individual worker overseeing the machinery cannot directly increase or decrease work output, and incentive bonuses would be pointless.

Operation of automated plants 24 hours a day is more feasible than similar operations of a nonautomated plant. There is no difficulty about shift work, and bonuses for night shifts and holiday and weekend working are eliminated for the production factors of the automated operation.

COST REDUCTION OF AUTOMATION IN THE OFFICE

Automation has taken hold more slowly in the office than in the factory. Yet, its possible cost reduction impact here is potentially greater. Electronic data processing equipment is spreading through all areas of office work and markedly reducing costs where it is wisely used.

As in factories, it is necessary to determine whether work can be more economically performed by EDP equipment or by human labor. Since time-sharing programs exist, where smaller companies can rent only the share of computer facilities they need, the break-even point of automation is quickly reached in office work.

In most cases, offices that automate tend to expand data handling at a greater speed, rather than eliminating employees. This reduces the cost per item of data handled but may necessitate extensive retraining of employees to use new equipment. Government programs are available to accomplish retraining economically in some areas; computer companies or leasing firms provide training in other areas.

High-quality employees are essential to minimizing costs. Results are dependent on the accuracy of material fed into the computer.

As in plant operation, fewer supervisors are needed when office work is automated.

As automation increases, work in plants and offices tends to become more alike: increasingly, both groups control computerized equipment. This similarity may decrease labor costs somewhat, as it provides a larger common pool of available labor.

COST REDUCTION, AUTOMATION, AND MANAGEMENT

Automation is affecting management as well as workers. Not only are fewer supervisors needed when fewer workers are used. Additionally, many of the decision-making tasks of management are being taken over by computers. Melvin Ansken, professor of industrial administration at Carnegie-Mellon University, separates these into programmable and nonprogrammable decisions.

Decisions that can be programmed, reducing the need for and cost of a management person, include: inventorying, shipment, and transportation scheduling; process, batch, and item scheduling in production; ordering; and most accounting decisions. Data are programmed into the computer that will allow it to make these decisions based on maximum-profit minimum-cost criteria.

Various areas of automation are discussed specifically throughout this book, including **Cybernetics, Electronic Data Processing,** and **Systems Analysis.**

SUGGESTED FURTHER READING

Amber, G. H., and P. S. Amber, *Anatomy of Automation,* Prentice-Hall, Englewood Cliffs, N.J., 1964.

Dunlop, J. T., ed., *Automation and Technological Change,* Prentice-Hall, Englewood Cliffs, N.J., 1962.

George, F. H., *Cybernetics in Management,* Pan Books, London, 1970.

Leone, W. C., *Production Automation and Numerical Control,* Ronald, New York, 1967.

Maynard, H. B., ed., *Industrial Engineering Handbook,* 3d ed., McGraw-Hill, New York, 1974.

AVERAGE COSTS See Standard Costs.

AVERAGE PRICE METHOD

Areas for use in Cost Control:

MATERIALS AND EQUIPMENT MANAGEMENT
INDUSTRIAL APPLICATIONS
BUSINESS AND COMMERCIAL APPLICATIONS

The average price method is a **stock control** technique used to value inventoried goods and stored materials or supplies. The method averages costs of items in stock.

Costs may be weighted by the quantity of items received at a given cost. In this case, the number of items received in any one shipment is taken into the total cost of the shipment. New averages are figured for each shipment, ensuring accurate valuations.

Another variation of the method is the use of a moving average of previous shipment costs.

SUGGESTED FURTHER READING

Standingford, Oliver, ed., *Newnes Encyclopedia of Business Management,* Newnes, London, 1967.

BAISSE CLAUSE

Areas for use in Cost Control:

ORGANIZATIONAL AND OPERATIONAL SYSTEMS
PAPERWORK DESIGN AND FLOW SYSTEMS
INDUSTRIAL APPLICATIONS
BUSINESS AND COMMERCIAL APPLICATIONS

The baisse clause is inserted in on-call order contracts stating that should product prices increase, the seller has the right to renegotiate price. The purchaser can withdraw from the contract if no new price agreement is reached. The clause prevents risk for the seller and is particularly important during an inflationary economy.

SUGGESTED FURTHER READING

Radke, Magnus, *Manual of Cost Reduction Techniques,* McGraw-Hill, New York, 1972.

BANDING

Areas for use in Cost Control:

ORGANIZATIONAL AND OPERATIONAL SYSTEMS
INDUSTRIAL APPLICATIONS
BUSINESS AND COMMERCIAL APPLICATIONS

Banding is the technique of structuring wage levels, grouping together work requiring a similar degree of skill or of a similar value for each degree or rate of pay. Work value is determined through **job evaluation** methods. In broad banding, with a wide range of work included in each structured area, payroll and recordkeeping costs are reduced because of increased wage rate standardization. When banding becomes very specialized, however, pay adjustment work is increased.

SUGGESTED FURTHER READING

Marsh, A. I., and E. O. Evans, *The Dictionary of Industrial Relations,* Hutchinson, London, 1973.
Industrial and Labor Relations, New York State School of Industrial and Labor Relations, Cornell University, Ithaca, New York, 1966.

BANKING

Areas for use in Cost Control:

ORGANIZATIONAL SYSTEMS
INDUSTRIAL APPLICATIONS
BUSINESS AND COMMERCIAL APPLICATIONS

Banking is the method of not immediately paying employees for overtime or bonus work but "banking" the pay for lump payment at a predetermined time, such as the end of the year or prior to vacation. Although such labor costs are not permanently saved, of course, the employer does gain additional use of the money in the interim period.

SUGGESTED FURTHER READING

Marsh, A. I., and E. O. Evans, *The Dictionary of Industrial Relations,* Hutchinson, London, 1973.

BARTH PREMIUM PLAN

Areas for use in Cost Control:

FINANCIAL MOTIVATIONAL MANAGEMENT
ORGANIZATIONAL AND OPERATIONAL SYSTEMS
INDUSTRIAL APPLICATIONS

The Barth premium plan is an incentive payment method (*see* **Incentive Payment Systems**) used to determine wages paid by rate of production with the following formula:

Multiplicand of Hourly Wage Rate = Standard Hours of Work Produced ÷ Actual Hours Worked

Labor costs are reduced through use of the method by their payment in direct proportion to productivity.

SUGGESTED FURTHER READING

Marsh, A. I., and E. O. Evans, *The Dictionary of Industrial Relations,* Hutchinson, London, 1973.

BASING-POINT PRICING SYSTEM

Areas for use in Cost Control:

ORGANIZATIONAL AND OPERATIONAL SYSTEMS
INDUSTRIAL APPLICATIONS

The basing-point pricing system uses prices based on specified plant locations and agreed to by an entire industry as a means of controlling profit/cost ratios. Industries using the method usually have the following characteristics:

1. The industry consists of only a few large manufacturers.
2. Product weight and volume are high as compared with value.
3. Large capital investment is required.
4. Consumer locations are widely spread.
5. Fluctuations in demand are common.

Using the method, standard prices are set for each "base" plant, and standard freight rates, depending on the user's distance from the base, are specified. All manufacturers use the same base scales. This provides certain prices to manufacturers, to keep the large capital investment and other costs in variable proportion to sales.

Additionally, the method allows a company to sell at reduced costs outside its market area to obtain new customers without reducing the price to customers within its area. A customer outside the market area is quoted price and freight charges from the nearest base rather than from the manufacturer selling the products.

SUGGESTED FURTHER READING

Bannock, G., R. E. Baxter, and R. Rees, *A Dictionary of Economics,* Penguin, Baltimore, 1974.

BASS LEADERSHIP THEORY

Areas for use in Cost Control:

PSYCHOLOGICAL MOTIVATIONAL MANAGEMENT
ORGANIZATIONAL AND OPERATIONAL SYSTEMS

The Bass leadership theory involves selection and most efficient use of management personnel. Costs are reduced by increased management ability and motivation of workers.

Bass states that the management hired should be the only persons who can change employees' behavior through reinforcement principles—financial rewards, promotions, better working conditions, etc. When only managers able to do this are used, an employee/management hierarchy is set up, showing work goals and areas of responsibility. Managers discuss work goals with the individual employees they supervise, setting out rewards to be obtained once these goals are reached.

SUGGESTED FURTHER READING

Bass, B. M., *Leadership, Psychology, and Organizational Behavior,* Harper & Row, New York, 1960.

BATCH COSTING

Areas for use in Cost Control:

ORGANIZATIONAL AND OPERATIONAL SYSTEMS
INDUSTRIAL APPLICATIONS

Batch costing is the technique of separating each batch of products from other batches and computing an average cost per unit. Controls can then be more precisely applied to those batches where costs prove excessive.

SUGGESTED FURTHER READING

Goch, Desmond, *Finance and Accounts for Managers*, Pan Books, London, 1972.

BAYES THEOREM

Areas for use in Cost Control:

ORGANIZATIONAL AND OPERATIONAL SYSTEMS
INDUSTRIAL APPLICATIONS
BUSINESS AND COMMERCIAL APPLICATIONS

The Bayes theorem is a mathematical model used in decision making. Costs can be reduced by using the technique, since it can be used to predict the possibility of success in a particular area of business operation.

The theorem is:

$$P(A/B) = \frac{P(B/A)P(A)}{P(B/A)P(A) + P(B/\bar{A})P(\bar{A})}$$

where $P(A/B)$ = probability of A if B has occurred
$P(B/A)$ = probability of B if A has occurred
$P(A)$ = probability of A
$\bar{P}(A)$ = probability of result other than A
$P(B/\bar{A})$ = probability of B if A has not occurred

To apply the theorem to a business problem, terms of the problem must be translated into the mathematical model. For example, management may wish to determine the effect that a new quality control device has on production. Past records show that 80 percent of production meets quality control standards. Ninety-five percent of the products passed by quality standards meet specifications of the new device, while only 30 percent of those rejected by quality inspectors meet specifications of the device. Thus:

P/A	= probability of meeting quality standards	= 80%
P/B	= probability of meeting device specifications	= 95%
$P(B/A)$	= probability of meeting device specifications if product is passed by quality control	= 95%
$P(B/\bar{A})$	= probability of meeting device specifications if product is not passed by quality control	= 30%
$P(\bar{B}/A)$	= probability of not meeting device specifications if product is passed by quality control	= 5%
$P(\bar{B}/\bar{A})$	= probability of not meeting device specifications if product is not passed by quality control	= 70%

To determine the cost savings effect of using the device on the probability of production meeting quality standards ($P[A/B]$):

$$P(A/B) = \frac{(95\%)(80\%)}{(95\%)(80\%) + (30\%)(20\%)} = \frac{76\%}{76\% + 6\%} = 92.7\%$$

Therefore, by using the device, production meeting quality control standards can be raised from 80 percent to 92.7 percent.

The Bayes theorem can be applied to production, purchasing, and personnel problems, showing what is the most efficient decision and reducing costs.

SUGGESTED FURTHER READING

Schlaifer, R., *Introduction to Statistics for Business Decisions,* McGraw-Hill, New York, 1961.

BED AND BREAKFASTING

Areas for use in Cost Control:

ORGANIZATIONAL AND OPERATIONAL SYSTEMS
INDUSTRIAL APPLICATIONS
BUSINESS AND COMMERCIAL APPLICATIONS

Bed and breakfasting is the sale and repurchase of holdings in a subsidiary company to reduce their book value in a falling market situation and thus improve the capital gains tax loss that may be taken against future capital profits. For example, the electronics and telecommunications group, Plessey, reduced the value of its International Computer holdings by 20 percent in this way in 1974. The paper loss was written off against capital asset gains, reducing the total tax costs.

SUGGESTED FURTHER READING

Leslie, N., "Bed and Breakfast Deal," *Financial Times,* London, Sept. 10, 1974.

BEDEAUX PLAN

Areas for use in Cost Control:

FINANCIAL MOTIVATIONAL MANAGEMENT
ORGANIZATIONAL AND OPERATIONAL SYSTEMS
INDUSTRIAL APPLICATIONS

The Bedeaux plan is an incentive payment method (*see* **Incentive Payment Systems**). A bonus is paid on work time saved, as shown by comparing actual time with standard time for each job. The bonus is divided 75 percent to the employee and 25 percent to the supervisor, and it is set up on a gradually reducing scale after productivity increases to a predetermined point. Because the bonus rate decreases as productivity increases, the method can greatly reduce labor costs.

SUGGESTED FURTHER READING

Maynard, H. B., *Handbook of Business Administration;* McGraw-Hill, New York, 1967.

BEHAVIOR CONTROL

Areas for use in Cost Control:

FINANCIAL MOTIVATIONAL MANAGEMENT
PSYCHOLOGICAL MOTIVATIONAL MANAGEMENT

Since labor costs are a high percentage of any company's operating costs, it stands to reason that costs can be greatly reduced if the workers' behavior can be controlled—that is, speeded up or made more effective. Understanding of behavior and new techniques to control it have increased rapidly in the past few years, and much of this knowledge can be applied directly to industry and in offices at all levels.

Behaviorism, existential psychology, and *reality psychology* are related in their discussion of methods of controlling behavior. All three are grounded in Pavlovian theories of conditioned reflexes. Salary payment is one example of this Pavlovian behavior control. That is, to obtain a certain desired response (work), the employer rewards the worker (pays the employee). More sophisticated application of this basic technique—especially in providing nonfinancial rewards or motivation—will provide much greater control of the workers' behavior and thus more work for the money and effort expended.

EXISTENTIAL BEHAVIOR CONTROL

Abraham Maslow, an American psychologist, began studying human behavior in his undergraduate days (1929–1934) at the University of Wisconsin. From his studies, he evolved his *management theory Z,* which assumes that all workers have higher needs, no matter what their I.Q. For best management, workers should be motivated through these needs.

Every man, Maslow said, has five basic needs:

1. *Physical needs* (food and shelter)
2. *Safety needs* (a regular schedule, freedom from fear and pain, etc.)
3. *Love and belonging needs*
4. *Esteem needs*
5. *Self-actualization* (full capacity used) *needs*

As each of these needs (beginning with physical ones) is filled, the individual can be best motivated by the next one on the list. Thus, if a worker does not have enough food, promise of a salary to buy food may motivate him or her to work. But in this age of relative plenty, being made to feel part of the work group (belonging needs) or a sense of accomplishment (esteem needs) is more likely to provide motivation.

Maslow also determined that a person's attention span filters out 90 percent of his or her experience and selects 10 percent—always choosing experiences that "mean something" to, or are needed by, the individual. The successful boss-worker relationship, according to Maslow, is a *synergic* one based on mutual aid and mutual need.

From examining the needs structure, it can be seen that an authoritarian system of control in which the employer threatens to fire an unsuitable employee and uses only a salary as motivation will work only as long as the security needs of the worker are high. Once past this stage, higher needs must be filled if the worker is to achieve the most efficient results.

BEHAVIORISM

B. F. Skinner and his followers have established many practical methods for motivation through these higher needs. Again using Pavlov's operant conditioning techniques as a base, Skinner advocates motivation by reinforcing desired behavior with an immediate reward. Incentive systems and piece rate systems are financial motivation of this type; but praise by a supervisor for a job well done and promotion to a more responsible position (nonfinancial reinforcers) are just as effective. When behavior is reinforced (rewarded), Skinner says, the worker will be more likely to repeat it.

With Skinner's technique of controlling behavior through the use of reinforcers, an industry must set goals for its workers and use a series of reinforcements that will help to meet those goals. Operating contingencies must be changed if behavior is to be changed. A programmed sequence of contingencies may be needed.

In designing a behavior control program, the following are basics:

1. Survival of the company must be made important to the worker.
2. Personal reinforcers (individual praise, promotion, etc.) are more valuable than large-scale social reinforcers (company goals set out in employee newsletters, etc.). Thus, the supervisor can achieve more in this area—through his or her personal contact with workers—than can the company president.
3. Create a working environment (design contingencies) that induces workers to feel that their jobs are important to them, to the company, and to society.
4. Provide planned diversification within each job.
5. Remember that the reinforcing value of rest, relaxation, and leisure becomes weaker as work is made less compulsive.
6. Arrange effective countercontrol to involve those in authority (such as stock options, etc.).
7. Remember that even weak reinforcers become powerful when properly scheduled. The smoking habit is a good example of this. A person smokes because of the frequency of reinforcement—even though a single cigarette is not important in itself. In business, praise for work, additional responsibility, etc., provide reinforcement and should be scheduled frequently.
8. Remember that an employee will work or be idle depending on the schedule which has been reinforced.

Table 3. Seven Personality Types in Business*

Worker type	Personality traits	Job and super-visory requirements
1. Autistic	Almost babylike, discouraged	Unsuitable for industry
2. Animistic	Primitive, super-stitious	Unsuitable for industry
3. Awakening and frightened	More wide-awake, objective, but frightened of com-plexity of world	Give worker rules to obey and a sense of hierarchical security.
4. Aggressive, power-seeking	Troublesome, aggressive, angry	Use high level of supervisory tact.
5. Sociocentric	Feels secure; a joiner	Inferior worker to 3 and 4. Involve individual in group striving toward a common goal.
6. Aggressive, individualistic	Self-confident; likes to do a job his or her own way	Tell worker the goal and let her work it out. Obstructed or supervised closely, she becomes mulish.
7. Pacifist, individualistic	Self-confident; likes to do a job her or his own way	Tell worker the goal and let her work it out. She will not be obstinate if supervised too closely, but she will not do good work.

*Professor C. W. Graves, *Union College Study,* Union College, Schenectady, N.Y.

Aversive reinforcement is also used by behaviorists. This consists of applying negative reinforcements to undesirable behavior to stop it. In business, a worker might be suspended for sloppy work, reprimanded by his or her superiors, etc. Negative reinforcements are not as effective as positive ones, however, and better control of behavior will be achieved with positive reinforcements.

REALITY TECHNIQUES

A slightly different approach to behavior control is one established by Professor Clare W. Graves of Union College, Schenectady, New York. Workers are of seven basic types, according to a 14-year industrial study conducted by Professor Graves (see Table 3). When workers were slotted into these levels with supervision appropriate to their level, the study showed a 17 percent increase in production and an 87 percent decrease in employee grumbling. Turnover dropped from 21 percent to 7 percent per year.

SUGGESTED FURTHER READING

Brown, J. A. C., *Techniques of Persuasion,* Penguin, Baltimore, 1963.
Serster, Charles B., *Schedules of Reinforcement,* Appleton-Century-Crofts, New York, 1957.
Skinner, B. F., *Beyond Freedom and Dignity,* Appleton-Century-Crofts, New York, 1971.
———, *Contingencies of Reinforcement,* Appleton-Century-Crofts, New York, 1969.
Wilson, Colin, *New Pathways in Psychology,* Taplinger, New York, 1972.

BLACK BOX TECHNIQUE

Areas for use in Cost Control:

ORGANIZATIONAL AND OPERATIONAL SYSTEMS
INDUSTRIAL APPLICATIONS
BUSINESS AND COMMERCIAL APPLICATIONS

The black box technique is the use of a particularly effective control point that has no traceable reason for its effectiveness. For example, if there are three supervisors managing similar lines, but one gets better production or has lower operating costs than the others, without any special techniques or methods, he or she is the "black box" (see Fig. 6). Some unidentifiable factor in this supervisor causes workers to respond well. This

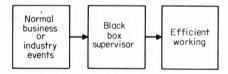

Figure 6. Black box factor.

type of employee can be actively sought in recruiting and hiring and should be placed in a responsible position for best use of the unidentifiable factor.

SUGGESTED FURTHER READING

Beer, Stafford, *Cybernetics and Management,* English Universities Press, London, 1959.

BLANK-CHECK ORDERS

Areas for use in Cost Control:

ORGANIZATIONAL AND OPERATIONAL SYSTEMS
MATERIALS AND EQUIPMENT MANAGEMENT
INDUSTRIAL APPLICATIONS
BUSINESS AND COMMERCIAL APPLICATIONS

Blank-check orders require the purchaser to give the supplier a check or bank draft for a predetermined amount—usually $500 to $1,000—to pay for small orders. Use of the method reduces costs by eliminating invoice processing for such orders. Additionally, special discounts may be obtained in exchange for the above payment.

SUGGESTED FURTHER READING

Ammer, D. S., *Materials Management,* Irwin, Homewood, Ill., 1968.

BLANKET ORDERS

Areas for use in Cost Control:

ORGANIZATIONAL AND OPERATIONAL SYSTEMS
MATERIALS AND EQUIPMENT MANAGEMENT
INDUSTRIAL APPLICATIONS
BUSINESS AND COMMERCIAL APPLICATIONS

Blanket orders are orders placed for a year's supply of a heavily purchased item but shipped and paid for in smaller lots as needed. Use of the method reduces costs by eliminating the paperwork of multiple ordering, saving buying-time labor costs, providing discounts from volume buying, and allowing shorter lead time for inventories.

SUGGESTED FURTHER READING

Ammer, D. S., *Materials Management,* Irwin, Homewood, Ill., 1968.

BLIND MAN METHOD

Areas for use in Cost Control:

ORGANIZATIONAL AND OPERATIONAL SYSTEMS
INDUSTRIAL APPLICATIONS
BUSINESS AND COMMERCIAL APPLICATIONS

The blind man method facilitates creative thinking in solving cost or other business problems. The idea is to shut the eyes and use other senses—hearing, smell, touch, taste—to work on the problem. For example, if production is slow, you might listen to the equipment at various times. The increased intensity of hearing that accompanies the absence of sight might pinpoint machines not running smoothly or not operating at all.

SUGGESTED FURTHER READING

Bittel, L. R., "How to Make Good Ideas Come Easy," *Factory Management and Maintenance,* March 1956.

BLUE MEMO METHOD

Areas for use in Cost Control:

ORGANIZATIONAL AND OPERATIONAL SYSTEMS
INDUSTRIAL APPLICATIONS
BUSINESS AND COMMERCIAL APPLICATIONS

The blue memo method refers to prediction of the profitability of a business project by computerized comparison of its projected returns and costs with those of a project of similar size and scope. *See also* **Electronic Data Processing.**

SUGGESTED FURTHER READING

Armand, R., R. Lattes, and Jacques Lesourne, *The Management Revolution,* Denoel Press, Paris, 1970.

BONUSES

Areas for use in Cost Control:

FINANCIAL MOTIVATIONAL MANAGEMENT
INDUSTRIAL APPLICATIONS
BUSINESS AND COMMERCIAL APPLICATIONS

Originally, a bonus was an "exceptional" payment—an amount paid in addition to the money due. This is the type of cost to be discussed in this section. However, modern business calls many of its incentive plans "bonuses." These payments, hinging on the standard of performance of the employee, are discussed in **Incentive Payment Systems.**

Attendance Bonus. Some firms give an employee an arbitrary amount of time off for regular work attendance. A worker who receives 15 minutes' time off for each week of full attendance can accumulate this time to use as he or she pleases.

Efficiency Bonus. When the operation of a department is made more efficient through the efforts of its employees, a bonus is sometimes given as a reward. This should not be confused with incentive plans, which provide specific bonus amounts for more efficient production. This type of bonus can be divided among the entire group responsible or can be given to an individual, such as a bonus for an employee suggestion that led to greater efficiency.

Punctuality Bonus. This payment is similar to the attendance bonus, but the payment depends on 100 percent punctuality. An arbitrarily assigned amount is used, but 15 minutes' extra pay per week of 100 percent punctuality is a common figure.

Year-End or Christmas Bonus. These payments are still widely used by smaller firms, but larger companies have generally found that the incentive power of an annual bonus is lower for the average worker than are more frequent, but smaller, bonuses. Since the employer can arbitrarily set a year-end bonus at any amount, it may discourage rather than encourage an employee if the amount is smaller than he or she anticipates or is smaller than it has been in previous years, because of poor business conditions, etc.

SETTING BONUSES

If you decide that bonuses are useful for your company, the following checklist will provide a guide in determining how much to pay:

1. Relate the amount of the bonus to the level of cost savings introduced by the individual (in case of an employee suggestion) or group.
2. Stagger the bonus according to the level of prime cost.
3. Arrange bonuses so that relatively small economies earn awards, incréasing the payment only slightly for higher levels of savings.
4. Never make a year-end bonus so large that the employee begins to count on it as a source of income. If bonuses of this size are justified, they should be tied into an incentive program that is part of the normal wage structure.

SUGGESTED FURTHER READING

Ireson, William G., and Eugene L. Grant, *Handbook of Industrial Engineering and Management,* Prentice-Hall, Englewood Cliffs, N.J., 1970.
Maynard, H. B., *Handbook of Business Administration,* McGraw-Hill, New York, 1967.
Radke, Magnus, *Manual of Cost Reduction Techniques,* McGraw-Hill, New York, 1972.

BOOSTER TRAINING

Areas for use in Cost Control:

ORGANIZATIONAL AND OPERATIONAL SYSTEMS
INDUSTRIAL APPLICATIONS
BUSINESS AND COMMERCIAL APPLICATIONS

Booster training, also called productivity training, is training to reduce the spread of productivity and accompanying costs among already employed workers. The most efficient workers are studied, their skills are analyzed, and less efficient workers are taught their methods. Particular attention is given to the psychological problem of correcting bad working habits as new methods are installed.

Work exercises may be incorporated into the training to teach the employee optimum motion and rhythm for a specific task. These may be a simple practicing of the motion and rhythm at first, to be later incorporated into practicing the movements on the job.

Each job is broken down into parts, and the employee practices each part separately until he or she becomes skilled in each aspect before the entire task is practiced.

Increased performance is scheduled first for short periods. After the employee becomes used to working harder for short periods, the length of time for maximum performance is gradually increased to 100 percent of the workday.

SUGGESTED FURTHER READING

Maynard, H. B., *Handbook of Business Administration,* McGraw-Hill, New York, 1967.

BOULWARISM

Areas for use in Cost Control:

ORGANIZATIONAL AND OPERATIONAL SYSTEMS
INDUSTRIAL APPLICATIONS

Boulwarism is the practice of making a fair wages or benefits offer, based on research and study, during labor negotiations and refusing to alter it unless new, relevant information concerning the case is presented. Named for a General Electric Company executive who first used the technique, the method can reduce labor costs by limiting wages or benefits to justified increases.

SUGGESTED FURTHER READING

Northrup, H. R., *Boulwarism,* University of Michigan Press, Ann Arbor, 1964.

BRAIN AND SKILL DRAINING

Areas for use in Cost Control:

ORGANIZATIONAL AND OPERATIONAL SYSTEMS
INDUSTRIAL APPLICATIONS
BUSINESS AND COMMERCIAL APPLICATIONS

Brain and skill draining is the attraction, by business and industry, of foreign professional persons or skilled workers. The method reduces costs by increasing professional and skilled labor pools and competitiveness for this work. Wage costs of such persons may be initially lower than domestic market levels, since most foreign professionals will be accustomed to lower salary levels in their native countries.

When adult workers enter a country fully trained, about $100,000 in taxes (from businesses and individuals) normally needed to raise and educate a professional worker are saved.

Some countries allow companies to "advertise" through their embassy offices for personnel with needed skills and professions. Immigration restrictions usually allow easy entry for persons with skills or professions in short supply.

The United States receives skilled immigrants in two main ways:

Students who enter the country to learn or further their skills.
Application of skilled foreign workers, entering under the quota or other systems of restriction.

WHAT ATTRACTS BRAINS AND SKILLS?

Factors a business or industry can use when recruiting from abroad include the following:

Salary. Individuals may earn *more* in their new country but *lower* salary levels for their new employers by increasing scarce skills in labor pools.
Advancement. The opportunity to work in a well-equipped lab or plant, with respected persons, and opportunities to try new ideas are strong drawing cards.
Personal freedom. Political freedom and freedom from religious, sexual, or racial discrimination can be used to recruit where these freedoms do not exist.
Work freedoms. Freedom from restrictions of skill or profession can be used to recruit where these freedoms do not exist.

AFTER HIRING

Once an immigrant has been recruited, the company should do its best to smooth the way with visa application assistance and help in arranging for transportation, housing, etc. A contract is generally used when the company pays transportation and/or moving expenses to provide some guarantee of equal benefits for both sides.

SUGGESTED FURTHER READING

Adams, Walter, ed., *The Brain Drain,* Macmillan, New York, 1968.
Dedijer, S., and I. Svennington, *Brain Drain and Brain Gain,* Research Policy Program, Lund, Sweden, 1967.
Thompson-Noel, Michael, "The Britons Who Vote with Their Feet," *The Financial Times,* London, Oct. 5, 1974.
"US. Brain Drain Savings," *The New York Times,* intl. ed., Paris, Apr. 11, 1967.

BRAINSTORMING

Areas for use in Cost Control:

PSYCHOLOGICAL MOTIVATIONAL MANAGEMENT
ORGANIZATIONAL AND OPERATIONAL SYSTEMS
INDUSTRIAL APPLICATIONS
BUSINESS AND COMMERCIAL APPLICATIONS

Brainstorming is a method of generating new ideas. The ideas may be for research projects, advertising, employee motivation, improved production techniques, increased sales, or any other area that requires creative thinking to increase production and sales or to lower costs.

In this technique, a group of people meet for a predetermined period of time. Groups are most effective when they are limited to about a dozen people and the time to a half-hour session.

A warm-up session of two or three minutes may be used, with participants thinking of all possible uses for an ordinary object, such as a pencil. The leader of the group then presents the problem of the meeting. Usually, this is presented in question form; e.g., "How can we increase speed of acrylic production?" or "How can we reduce clerical turnover?"

Participants are encouraged to give free rein to their imaginations, presenting any and all ideas for solving the problem that occur to them no matter how wild they seem to be. The leader writes these on a chart or blackboard until a target number (usually 100 or 150) of ideas is reached or the time allowed has elapsed. *No criticism is made of any of the ideas.*

When the primary session ends, participants discuss the ideas to see which are workable and can be developed for the company's benefit. Useful and cost-saving ideas frequently develop from these sessions that do not apply to the original problem, and care must be taken not to discard these.

Brainstorming is an especially valuable tool because of its simplicity, as well as the fact that it usually produces impressive results. No special training is needed, although it may be helpful if the group leader has attended a brainstorming session outside the company.

Dangers of the technique are inadequate follow-through and junior management misuse of the method as a vehicle for impressing their immediate superiors rather than as a means of solving problems.

SUGGESTED FURTHER READING

Baettie, O. J., and R. D. Reader, *Quantitative Management,* Barnes & Noble, Cranbury, N.J., 1971.
Hinrichs, John R., *Creativity in Industrial Scientific Research; A Critical Survey of Current Opinion, Theory, and Knowledge,* American Management Assn., New York, 1967.
Koestler, A., *The Art of Creation,* Hutchinson, London, 1964.

BRANCHING NETWORKS

Areas for use in Cost Control:

ORGANIZATIONAL AND OPERATIONAL SYSTEMS
INDUSTRIAL APPLICATIONS
BUSINESS AND COMMERCIAL APPLICATIONS

Branching networks combine the features of **program evaluation and review techniques (PERT)** and **decision trees** in that they provide several estimates of the time and path a project will take (as does PERT), as well as a decision factor and its probability (as do decision trees).

Since this technique allows alternate estimates and path examination, network diagrams are considerably more complicated than **critical path analysis (CPA)** diagrams. A chart of standard symbols used in branching network diagrams is given in Fig. 7.

An example of the branching network technique can be seen in Fig. 8. In this example, an accountant was estimating the time needed to complete a client's tax return and receive a refund.

When network diagrams show several possible courses of action, as they do in branching, a more accurate prediction of time and method required to complete the project is necessary. In Fig. 8, for example, *if* the accountant does not need to check his figures, and *if* the government processes the tax return in three weeks, the project will require four weeks, two hours, and thirty minutes from start to completion. If the sequence of steps is that of result "2," however, the project will require an additional three weeks and one day. Cost estimates can be projected and controlled with this method. In the above example, the client might feel that the cost of an extra day of the accountant's time was a worthwhile investment to ensure accuracy; or, she or he might feel that the company should chance the accuracy of the original figures, since they were computer-calculated, and might opt to save the extra day's fee.

Incoming Symbols

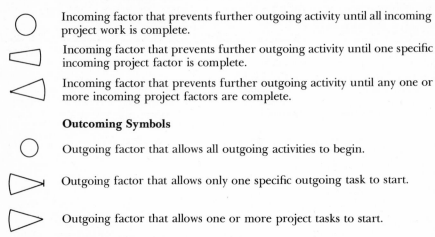

Incoming factor that prevents further outgoing activity until all incoming project work is complete.

Incoming factor that prevents further outgoing activity until one specific incoming project factor is complete.

Incoming factor that prevents further outgoing activity until any one or more incoming project factors are complete.

Outcoming Symbols

Outgoing factor that allows all outgoing activities to begin.

Outgoing factor that allows only one specific outgoing task to start.

Outgoing factor that allows one or more project tasks to start.

Figure 7. Standard branching network symbols.

Branching networks are most often used in evaluating potential research projects, including cost, time, and success factors. They can be used for almost any business evaluation, particularly very complex evaluations. Operation of the method requires thorough training, however, and the simpler, more versatile CPA method is preferred for general use.

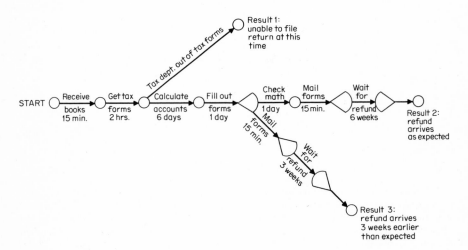

Figure 8. A branching network diagram.

SUGGESTED FURTHER READING

Beattie, C. J., H. M. Clarke, R. D. Reader, and R. V. Williams, *Branching Networks,* Management Brief OR/55/67, The Inter-Group Laboratories of the British Iron and Steel Corporation, London, 1967.

————, R. D. Reader, *Quantitative Management in R&D,* Barnes & Noble, Cranbury, N.J., 1971.

Brabb, George J., *Introduction to Quantitative Management,* Holt, New York, 1968.

Maynard, H. B., *Handbook of Business Administration,* McGraw-Hill, New York, 1967.

BREAK-EVEN ANALYSIS

Areas for use in Cost Control:

ORGANIZATIONAL AND OPERATIONAL SYSTEMS
INDUSTRIAL APPLICATIONS
BUSINESS AND COMMERCIAL APPLICATIONS

Break-even analysis is a technique used to find the point at which income and costs are the same. The method is used as the first step in determining costs at alternate levels of production, as well as in determining and controlling variable cost per production unit.

The break-even formula is:

$$BE = \frac{F \text{ (fixed costs)}}{1 - \dfrac{\text{variable cost per production unit}}{\text{selling price per production unit}}}$$

Thus, if a company has fixed costs of $50,000 per year, variable cost per production unit of $2.50, and sales price of $12.50 per unit, the *break-even point* is determined as follows:

$$BE = \frac{\$50,000}{1 - (\$2.50/\$12.50)} = \frac{\$50,000}{1 - \frac{1}{5}} = \frac{\$50,000}{\frac{4}{5}} = \$62,500$$

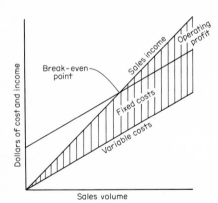

Figure 9. Typical break-even chart. (H. B. Maynard, *Handbook of Business Administration,* McGraw-Hill, 1967.)

Determination of the break-even point is necessary to be sure of profitability. Figure 9 shows a break-even chart that details the relationship of fixed costs, variable costs, sales income, break-even point, and operating profit after the break-even point is reached.

Break-even charts must be corrected periodically to reflect any changes in inventory overheads. This may be done by calculating the percentage of difference between inventories at the beginning and at the end of the period and making a similar fixed-cost change on the chart, or by adding material, labor, overhead, sales, and managerial expense for the period to determine fixed cost.

SUGGESTED FURTHER READING

Backer, Morton, and L. E. Jacobsen, *Cost Accounting: A Managerial Approach,* McGraw-Hill, New York, 1974.

Maynard, H. B., *Handbook of Business Administration,* McGraw-Hill, New York, 1967.

BRISCH CLASSIFICATION AND CODING SYSTEM

Areas for use in Cost Control:

ORGANIZATIONAL AND OPERATIONAL SYSTEMS
MATERIALS AND EQUIPMENT MANAGEMENT
DATA RETENTION—FILES AND RECORDKEEPING
INDUSTRIAL APPLICATIONS
BUSINESS AND COMMERCIAL APPLICATIONS

The Brisch classification and coding system uses a series of numbers to organize various assets and to provide abbreviated means of reference to such assets. Greater organizational control and faster reference in recordkeeping through use of the method can reduce operating costs.

Moving from left to right, each digit in a Brisch system refers to a successively narrower classification. For example, the farthest left digit refers to major divisions, while the second digit refers to sections of one of the major classifications. Each successive digit then classifies one of the major areas in the preceding digit (see Table 4).

Table 4. Typical Digit Classification in a Brisch System

1st digit	2d digit	3d digit	4th digit
	(Plant and machinery)	(Security equipment)	(Vehicles)
0—Raw materials	0—Building	0—Locks	0—Jeeps
1—Other materials	1—Production equipment	1—Fences/gates	1—Scooters
2—Parts	2—Maintenance equipment	2—Closed-circuit TV	
3—Products	3—Auxiliary equipment	3—Uniforms	
4—Plant and machinery	4—Equipment parts	4—Card scanners	
5—Spare parts	5—Maintenance tools	5—Vaults	
6—Services	6—Security equipment	6—Vehicles	
7—Office supplies and equipment	7—Shipping/ stocking equipment	7—Arms	

Using the examples shown in Table 4, a motor scooter used by a security guard to make his or her rounds inside the plant would be coded 4661:

4—Plant and machinery
6—Security equipment
6—Vehicles
1—Scooters

Further divisions might classify the scooter as to horsepower or other specifying data that could be used for maintenance referrals.

The Brisch system is commonly used because it makes it easy to memorize needed parts and because the divisions move logically from left to right. Inventory and shipping mistakes decrease with classification, and paperwork is simplified and speeded up with abbreviated references to various assets. Physical inventories can be arranged in the same sequence as the asset classification numbers, simplifying storage location and control.

SUGGESTED FURTHER READING

Brisch, E. G., and partners, *Selected Papers,* London.
Clay, M. J., and B. H. Walley, *Performance and Profitability,* Longmans, London, 1965.

BRUNSWICK LENS MODEL

Areas for use in Cost Control:

ORGANIZATIONAL AND OPERATIONAL SYSTEMS
INDUSTRIAL APPLICATIONS
BUSINESS AND COMMERCIAL APPLICATIONS

The Brunswick lens model is a technique intended to help executives make the most effective decisions through the use of three factors:

1. *Basic information* about the problem.
2. *Observed decision*—the action taken after weighing problem information.
3. *Correct decision*—the optimum decision measured against all other probable decisions.

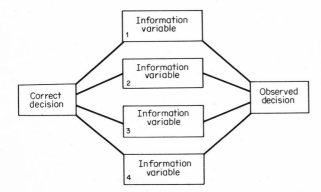

Figure 10. Brunswick lens model.

Information variables are translated into a mathematical formula as to their predictive power, various possible decisions are considered, and the optimum decision is made (see Fig. 10).

Costs can be reduced by the technique through more controlled decision making in regard to stock control, production, and personnel hiring.

SUGGESTED FURTHER READING

Brunswick, E., *Perception and the Representative Design of Psychological Experiments,* University of California Press, Berkeley, 1956.
Dudycha, L., and J. C. Naylor, *"Characteristics of the Human Inference Process in Complex Choice Behavior Situations," Organizational Behavior and Human Performance,* no. 1, 1966.

BUDDY RATINGS

Areas for use in Cost Control:

ORGANIZATIONAL AND OPERATIONAL SYSTEMS
INDUSTRIAL APPLICATIONS
BUSINESS AND COMMERCIAL APPLICATIONS

Buddy ratings are the evaluation of the performance of employees by other members of their work group as a means of appraising work and leadership levels, improving efficiency, and reducing labor costs. Each employee rates fellow workers, using a simplified method, such as the **Scott graphic rating scale,** or on a simple scale of 0 to 10. Ratings for each employee are averaged.

The method is particularly effective in evaluating leadership ability and the promotional potential of an employee, since his or her peers will naturally give higher ratings to those persons they would be most likely to willingly follow, were he or she promoted to a supervisory position.

Work performance ratings developed with the method have also been proved highly reliable, as frequently coworkers have more chance to observe specific work performance than does a supervisor who is at least partially occupied with paperwork and meetings with top management.

SUGGESTED FURTHER READING

Whisler, T. L., and S. F. Harper, *Performance Appraisal,* Holt, New York, 1962.

BUDGETARY CONTROL

Areas for use in Cost Control:

ORGANIZATIONAL AND OPERATIONAL SYSTEMS
INDUSTRIAL APPLICATIONS
BUSINESS AND COMMERCIAL APPLICATIONS

Budgetary control is the use of a budget to set cost standards and a **costing** system to check results.

Budgeting, or forecasting how money will be spent, does not necessarily mean that costs will be controlled or reduced. Budgetary control, on the other hand, has increased profits as its goal, which means reducing moneys spent. Steps used in budgetary control include the following:

1. Production and sales data and goals are set out for the purpose of establishing a budget.
2. Expenditure programs (budgets) are drawn up for production and sales, using cost control devices to limit spending.
3. Inventory levels (where applicable) are set at suitable limits.
4. Budget details are regularly evaluated against the predetermined standard figures.
5. Budget details are revised where necessary.

Some budgetary control systems use 13 periods of 28 days, since equal-length programs are desirable. Other systems use monthly or weekly measuring standards.

Budgetary control is primarily a means of looking ahead and trying to control future costs rather than waiting—as many accounting programs do—until money has been spent and can no longer be controlled. Budgetary control determines the level of efficiency possible in workers and equipment, and then seeks to limit or omit *avoidable* loss or waste up to this standard of efficiency. Operational research, cybernetics, and computerized data processing have made the system a more readily usable one.

Some of the budgetary control techniques most often used include:

1. Responsibility accounting
2. Predictive accounting
3. Participative management
4. Variance analysis
5. Flexible budgeting

All of these techniques are covered separately in more detail, but for rapid reference the following brief definitions are supplied:

Responsibility accounting is a technique used to control costs at their point of occurrence. Individual staff become responsible for controlling costs to a predetermined standard in their area of work.

Predictive accounting is a technique that uses business models in decision making. These models are used in **cybernetics, operations research,** and other quantitative cost control techniques.

Participative management involves the use of all staff thinking when drawing up and controlling budgets. The technique is intended to provide motivation for better budgetary control.

Variance analysis is a systematic checking of all cost aspects that deviate from the standard or budgetary figure to see why the cost has differed and to determine a means to control the deviation.

Flexible budgeting is a budgetary control technique that allows a variety of possible costs, the figures to change as required by business and market conditions.

The key to successful budgetary control is giving responsibility for control of spending in the areas of profit and costs to those responsible for those areas. The technique outlined above will allow a methodical control of spending according to budgeted plans.

SUGGESTED FURTHER READING

Ansoff, H. I., *Corporate Strategy,* McGraw-Hill, New York, 1974.

Backer, Morton, and L. H. Jacobsen, *Cost Accounting: A Managerial Approach,* McGraw-Hill, New York, 1974.

Herzberg, Frederic, Bernard Mauser, and Barbara Snyderman, *The Motivation to Work,* Wiley, New York, 1959.

Jones, R. L., and H. G. Trentin, *Budgeting: Key to Planning and Control,* American Management Assn., New York, 1972.

Scanlon, J. J., *"How Much Should a Corporation Earn?" Harvard Business Review,* January-February 1967.

Schoderbek, P. P., *Management Systems,* Wiley, New York, 1970.

BUDGETING

Areas for use in Cost Control:

ORGANIZATIONAL AND OPERATIONAL SYSTEMS
PAPERWORK DESIGN AND FLOW SYSTEMS
INDUSTRIAL APPLICATIONS
BUSINESS AND COMMERCIAL APPLICATIONS

Budgeting is financial planning for the business or industry. The budget serves as a review of past expenditures and profits, as well as the planning guide for purchase of materials and equipment and for the hiring of necessary labor.

Plans for expenditure (budgets) are prepared in a logical order by the accounting department working in coordination with top management.

The first step is obtaining a sales forecast for the period to be covered by the budget. This is usually a yearly period, subdivided into quarters or months.

Based on production needs to meet estimated sales, production executives next estimate costs for materials, equipment, labor, and overhead.

Managerial costs, R&D expenditures, distribution and sales costs, as well as money to be spent by other departments, are estimated and the figures submitted to the accounting department.

Once the budget is drawn up showing all estimated sales, costs, and profits, the company management will review the figures, comparing them with:

1. Past company performance
2. Current industrywide performance
3. Projected company goals

Management may change budgeted figures if they feel that one or more areas do not meet company goals, and it will then be the responsibility of those areas of the operation to produce the required result with the altered costs allowable. For example, management may consider estimated costs for new equipment to be in excess of money available. Production may be required, therefore, to keep output at the estimated level using the old equipment.

Budgeted costs are checked against actual costs to determine the need for further action as the budget period passes. *See also* **Budgetary Control.**

Budgeting in some form is necessary for even very small companies, and large firms will require accounting staff for budgeting. Used in connection with a **costing** system and long-range financial planning, budgeting should be an effective cost reduction tool.

SUGGESTED FURTHER READING

Bierman, H., and S. Smidt, *The Capital Budgeting Decision,* Macmillan, New York, 1972.
Jones, R. L., and H. G. Trentin, *Budgeting: Key to Planning and Control,* American Management Assn., New York, 1971.
Knight, W. D., and E. H. Weinwurm, *Managerial Budgeting,* Macmillan, New York, 1970.

BUFFER STOCK TECHNIQUE

Area for use in Cost Control:

MATERIALS AND EQUIPMENT MANAGEMENT

The buffer stock technique is used to maintain a reserve of needed raw materials at reduced costs. Floor and ceiling costs for the materials are determined. When the market price reaches the ceiling figure, some of the stockpiled material is sold. When it reaches the floor figure, new purchases are made.

SUGGESTED FURTHER READING

Davis, William, *Money Talks,* Coronet Books, London, 1974.
Goodman, S. R., *Effective Cost Reduction in Materials Handling,* Prentice-Hall, Englewood Cliffs, N.J., 1972.
Ireson, William G., and Eugene L. Grant, *Handbook of Industrial Engineering and Management,* Prentice-Hall, Englewood Cliffs, N.J., 1970.

BUILDING AND CONSTRUCTION COST CONTROL

Areas for use in Cost Control:

WORK PLACE MOTIVATIONAL MANAGEMENT
ORGANIZATIONAL AND OPERATIONAL SYSTEMS
INDUSTRIAL APPLICATIONS
BUSINESS AND COMMERCIAL APPLICATIONS

Traditional accounting methods for costing in building and construction for business and industry are gradually being replaced by new techniques that emphasize cost *planning*. To make such pre-bidding planning effective, careful cost control techniques have also been developed for use during the contract period.

FEASIBILITY

Once an idea for a construction project exists, the first cost control step is to study its cost feasibility. Client, architect, structural engineer, and contractors must be included in such a study. A feasibility report should be prepared at this stage including site location, estimated project cost, general details of the proposed construction including visual aids, specific details as to proposed square footage, ground specifications including safe bearing capacities, planning or zoning regulations affecting the site, cost of bringing in public utilities, and, in the case of factory construction, details of the local labor market.

BUILDING DESIGN TO REDUCE COSTS

When building a new factory or office building, or when constructing a new wing for the present plant, the first place to reduce costs is obviously through use of an economical design. What comprises an economical design? The following are general rules:

1. Keep the enclosing ratio low. The enclosing ratio measures how much wall area (including doors and windows) is needed per m^3 of gross floor area.
2. Check the number of partitions required in alternate designs, including need for load-bearing partitions versus non-load-bearing partitions.
3. Consider the effect of designs on needed heating, air-conditioning, and communication systems.
4. Some cost advantages for using multiple-story, rather than single-story, construction include the fact that foundations for a two- or three-story building differ little from those required for a single-story building. Additionally, extra stories provide insulating qualities. The need for a smaller construction site is another cost reduction factor inherent in multiple-story construction.
5. Single-story construction, on the other hand, offers lower maintenance costs, eliminates the need for stairs or elevators, and does not carry the cost premium of construction at heights.
6. Use standard-sized doors, windows, and other components.
7. Reduce the number of sizes of lumber, bricks, steel supports, and other components—even down to nails—to as few as possible.

COST ESTIMATES AND PROPOSALS

Once feasibility has been studied and the decision is made to continue, actual costs of construction must be kept as close as possible to those estimated. A method called elemental cost planning (see Table 5) is used, detailing actual costs for the 30 to 35 major building elements and comparing these costs with costs estimated for the same elements.

In the first analysis, only element-heading estimates (those in italics in Table 5) are compared. Once the architect has completed the project design, however, a complete

Table 5. Elemental Cost Analysis Form

Element	Estimated cost	Actual cost
Superstructure		
Frame		
Upper floors		
External walls		
External doors		
Stairs		
Roof		
Windows		
Internal walls		
Internal doors		
External		
Site preparation		
Drainage		
Utility work		
Internal fittings		
Electrical		
Plumbing		
Cabinetry		
Heating		
Air conditioning		
Internal finishing		
Ceiling		
Walls		
Floors		
Utilities		
Water system		
Sewer system		
Electricity		
Gas		
Ventilation system		
Heating system		
Air-conditioning system		
Elevator and/or conveyor		
Communication systems		
Security systems		

elemental cost analysis should be prepared. If several contractors are bidding on the project, ask each to prepare his portion of an analysis form.

Another method of cost estimating is *interpolation.* In this technique, a **cost analysis** for a similar building is examined, and figures are transferred to the current project's cost analysis after allowing for measurement and other construction differences. Similarity of the two projects is generally based on the following:

> Substructure
> Frame
> Number of floors
> External walls

Choice of materials may affect bids other than the one directly involved with the material. Insulation, for example, will affect the heat system required. Material choices should be determined for the most economical long-term use rather than for cheapest initial cost; and the client should be presented with options of materials along with information detailing advantages, disadvantages, and cost of each.

COST CHECKING

Cost checking should begin as soon as the bid is accepted. One successful technique of cost checking is *approximate quantities.* In this method, precise measurement of every construction factor is not necessary in order to compute what costs should be. The following are ways that approximate quantities may be used in cost checking:

1. Project measurements are based on the *standard method of measurement of building.*
2. Measurements (for cost-checking purposes only) are rounded off for simplification.
3. Standard-size doors and windows need not be figured separately, since the "wall" space in the superstructure that is not deducted will cover this cost.

The same sort of approximation is extended to other major elements: the substructure, the external site, the superstructure, etc.

If cost checking shows that original cost estimates were too low, it is better to find an alternative method of construction rather than cut out some aspect of interior finish, insulation, or furnishings. For example, PVC sewer pipe may be substituted for lead piping.

Using billings from contractors and suppliers, construction stages should be cost-checked regularly, actual sums being compared with estimates and bids. If contracts stipulate cost, variation orders must be issued if a cost change is to be made and paid for. Usually, a contingency sum is included in the client's planning for the building cost.

SUGGESTED FURTHER READING

Benson, Ben, *Critical Path Methods in Building Construction,* Prentice-Hall, Englewood Cliffs, N.J., 1970.
Cartlidge, Duncan P., *Cost Planning and Building Economics,* Hutchinson Educational Ltd., London, 1973.
Collier, Keith, *Fundamentals of Construction Estimating and Cost Accounting,* Prentice-Hall, Englewood Cliffs, N.J., 1974.

BURDEN CENTER See Cost Reduction Performance Measurement.

BURDEN COSTS See Fixed Costs.

BUY-OUT AGREEMENTS

Areas for use in Cost Control:

FINANCIAL MOTIVATIONAL MANAGEMENT
INDUSTRIAL APPLICATIONS
BUSINESS AND COMMERCIAL APPLICATIONS

In many cases, trade unions are unwilling to have production automated, because automation means fewer jobs. On the other side of the table, management requires automation to keep producing goods economically—particularly in situations where increases in demand have exceeded increases in production.

One method developed to overcome unions' objections to automation is the use of buy-out agreements. Using this system, management studies the hour differential and "buys out" the union's objections by offering a higher base rate for the same work hour (with more work being accomplished as the result of automation), larger incentive payments, or increased benefits. Taking into consideration the cost of amortizing the equipment purchased, the initial reduction of the wage bill, after the buy-out, is usually 10 to 15 percent.

SUGGESTED FURTHER READING

"Productivity: Weak Link in Our Economy," *Harvard Business Review,* January–February 1971.

CAFETERIA WAGE PLAN

Areas for use in Cost Control:

FINANCIAL MOTIVATIONAL MANAGEMENT
PSYCHOLOGICAL MOTIVATIONAL MANAGEMENT
ORGANIZATIONAL AND OPERATIONAL SYSTEMS
INDUSTRIAL APPLICATIONS
BUSINESS AND COMMERCIAL APPLICATIONS

The cafeteria wage plan is a method allowing the employee to choose his or her benefits from a selection offered. An employee may be allowed, for example, a base wage and a choice of three out of five benefits (such as medical insurance, life insurance, profit sharing, and stock options). Use of the method motivates workers both financially and psychologically, reducing labor costs.

SUGGESTED FURTHER READING

Lawler, E. E., "The Mythology of Management Compensation," *California Management Review,* 1966.

CALORIE BONUS PAYMENT

Areas for use in Cost Control:

FINANCIAL MOTIVATIONAL MANAGEMENT
INDUSTRIAL APPLICATIONS
BUSINESS AND COMMERCIAL APPLICATIONS

The calorie bonus payment gives the worker a bonus payment equal to money needed to buy a predetermined number of calories' worth of food for himself or herself and his or her dependents. The system is used to motivate workers to greater productivity, reducing labor costs, during inflationary periods. Calorie allotments specified vary, but one bonus base set a level of 16,000 calories weekly for the worker, plus an allowance to purchase 5,000 calories of food weekly for each dependent.

SUGGESTED FURTHER READING

Hanson, J. L., *A Dictionary of Economics and Commerce,* MacDonald, London, 1974.

CAPACITY PLANNING AND SCHEDULING

Areas for use in Cost Control:

ORGANIZATIONAL AND OPERATIONAL SYSTEMS
MATERIALS AND EQUIPMENT MANAGEMENT
INDUSTRIAL APPLICATIONS

Capacity planning and scheduling is a computerized technique used to make maximum use of equipment and labor, reducing the cost of downtime or slack time and overtime payments. Production data, machine and labor capacity, required delivery dates, etc., are correlated automatically, and a schedule is drawn up giving optimum use of equipment and labor. Planning is usually by stage, ranging from long-range planning where computerized evaluation of data results in a determination of capital equipment and plant additions to short-term, day-to-day labor scheduling. *See also* **Electronic Data Processing.**

SUGGESTED FURTHER READING

Orlicky, J., *The Successful Computer System,* McGraw-Hill, New York, 1974.
Plossl, G. W., and O. W. Wright, *Production and Inventory Control,* Prentice-Hall, Englewood Cliffs, N.J., 1967.

CAPACITY STUDIES

Areas for use in Cost Control:

WORK PLACE MOTIVATIONAL MANAGEMENT
MATERIALS AND EQUIPMENT MANAGEMENT

"Capacity studies" are used to determine possible economies through better use of existing machinery and equipment. The following questions should aid in the capacity study of any single piece of equipment:

1. Could the equipment use be eliminated?
2. Would the equipment be used more, or more efficiently, if it was placed elsewhere in the plant or office?
3. Are there additional jobs that could make use of the equipment?
4. Does the equipment require a full-time operator? If so, does the operator need special training?
5. Are substitute operators available for emergency use?
6. Would an incentive plan for the equipment operator lead to greater productivity?
7. Will production increase if pre-operation tasks (sorting of materials used or preparation of supplies) are carried out by someone other than the equipment operator, leaving all of the operator's time for machinery use?

SUGGESTED FURTHER READING

Cemach, H. P., *Work Study in the Office,* MacLaren & Sons, London, 1969.

CAPITAL EQUIPMENT ANALYSIS

Areas for use in Cost Control:

ORGANIZATIONAL AND OPERATIONAL SYSTEMS
MATERIALS AND EQUIPMENT MANAGEMENT
INDUSTRIAL APPLICATIONS

Capital equipment analysis evaluates potential investment in equipment to determine whether it is less costly to purchase new equipment or to continue to operate the old. Production rates, labor and fringe benefit costs, maintenance costs, downtime, etc., that can be reduced through the equipment installation are measured against the installed cost (prorated), increased power costs, lost interest on the capital investment, etc.

Several techniques are used to analyze capital investment. The **MAPI formula** is one. This method uses prepared formulas in worksheet form to compare advantages and adverse factors of both present and proposed equipment.

A second method is the **payback period technique.** Here, the company calculates the length of time a capital investment will take to pay for itself. This is done by combining savings from the proposed equipment. Choice of equipment is based on the installation with the most rapid payback period.

A third method is **discounted cash flow.** In this method, the annual return for the proposed equipment is calculated, and the investment is made only if the rate of return meets or exceeds the company standards—usually 20 to 25 percent after taxes.

SUGGESTED FURTHER READING

Ammer, D. S., *Materials Management,* Irwin, Homewood, Ill., 1968.

CAPITAL EXPENDITURE COST CONTROL

Areas for use in Cost Control:

ORGANIZATIONAL AND OPERATIONAL SYSTEMS
INDUSTRIAL APPLICATIONS
BUSINESS AND COMMERCIAL APPLICATIONS

Capital expenses—purchases of fixed assets such as buildings, land, and equipment—are an important area for cost reduction since their cost is usually large and continues to affect cost control for a long period of time.

WHICH CAPITAL EXPENDITURES?

In choosing capital expenditures geared for best results, consider two aspects of any prospective purchase:

1. Technical factors
2. Financial factors

Technical factors include the usability of the asset and its overall effect on the purchasing company. For example, in selecting production equipment, study the operation, output, quality, and quantity of work. Compare these with the same aspects of alternately available equipment.

Financial factors include purchase price, length of asset life, and inherent net profit increase.

For cost control in purchasing capital assets, add the following rules:

1. Realize at least a 15 percent rate of return.
2. Link budgets and cash flow from any capital expenditure.
3. Establish controls for purchase and use of a capital asset.

SUGGESTED FURTHER READING

Bierman, H., and S. Smidt, *The Capital Budgeting Decision,* Macmillan, New York, 1971.
Edge, C. G., *A Practical Manual on the Appraisal of Capital Expenditures,* Society of Industrial and Cost Accountants of Canada, Toronto, 1972.

CAREER TRAINEE SYSTEM

Areas for use in Cost Control:

ORGANIZATIONAL AND OPERATIONAL SYSTEMS
INDUSTRIAL APPLICATIONS
BUSINESS AND COMMERCIAL APPLICATIONS

The career trainee system is a method developed by the Japanese firm of Hitachi to deal with the cost of seasonal labor fluctuation. Temporary employees, with lower salaries, fewer benefits, and less status than regular employees, are offered a six-month work contract at the beginning of the busy season. At the end of six months, the temporary employee may be transferred to regular status, offered another six months' training contract, or terminated, depending on labor needs and/or the trainee's ability. Both salary and benefit costs are reduced during the training contract, and unemployment insurance penalties are not required, since the period of work was contracted.

SUGGESTED FURTHER READING

Azumi, K., *Higher Education and Business Recruitment in Japan,* Teachers College Press, New York, 1969.

Dore, R., *British Factory, Japanese Factory,* G. Allen, London, 1973.

CASH-AND-CARRY DISTRIBUTION

Areas for use in Cost Control:

ORGANIZATIONAL AND OPERATIONAL SYSTEMS

INDUSTRIAL APPLICATIONS

BUSINESS AND COMMERCIAL APPLICATIONS

Cash-and-carry distribution is a technique that reduces outlet servicing costs for both producers and wholesalers. Patterned on retail cash-and-carry operations, manufacturers and/or wholesalers display products, passing along to the customer some of the reduced costs in exchange for the customer's transporting the products. Outlet buyers, such as small retailers, walk through the display area, choosing merchandise, paying for it at a checkout point, and providing their own packaging and shipping. Exchanges and replacements are not generally allowed, since the purchaser is assumed to have examined the product.

Successful use of the method depends heavily on packaging and display of the products, since these act in lieu of a salesperson to present the item's advantages.

In addition to service-cost reductions, accounting costs are lowered because payment is received in cash at the time of purchase.

SUGGESTED FURTHER READING

Hoving, Walter, *The Distribution Revolution,* Washburn, New York, 1960.

Stacey, N. A., and A. Wilson, *The Changing Pattern of Distribution,* Pergamon, New York, 1965.

CASH CONTROL

Areas for use in Cost Control:

ORGANIZATIONAL AND OPERATIONAL SYSTEMS

PAPERWORK DESIGN AND FLOW SYSTEMS

INDUSTRIAL APPLICATIONS

BUSINESS AND COMMERCIAL APPLICATIONS

Cash control is prevention of improper use or theft of company cash. It is an important area for cost reduction, since cash is more easily stolen by employees than are other assets if no control system is used.

INCOMING CASH

Cash paid to the company may include checks, cash, and money orders received in the mail; sales or bills paid in person by the purchaser; and cash received by sales representatives. All steps involved in handling such cash must be controlled.

Checks and money orders received in the mail should be immediately stamped with a company "For Deposit Only" endorsement stamp. Employees opening the mail should be placed in the open where it is easy to watch for cash payments.

Payments should be recorded by the accounting department in the sales ledger and receipts, if used, issued.

Checks, money orders, and cash should be banked daily, a security service being used for transportation of funds from company premises to the bank. Where this is not possible, banking times and travel routes should be varied, and the company may use a commercial security banking bag locked to the person making deposits.

A cash ledger should be used to record all cash payments, including a separate account to deal with *bills of exchange.*

Cash sales on the premises can best be controlled by the use of automatic cash registers that record each transaction and number it. Only one person should be responsible for a cash drawer, and when this person leaves, the drawer should be removed and locked away. Cash may be checked against total sales slips for the day, as well as against the total recorded on the cash register. Cashiers sometimes steal money by "ringing short." Each time a preset amount is rung short on the register, the cashier may move one of a stack of pins to another location, may eat one of a set number of candies in his or her pocket, or may move a candy from one pocket to another. At the end of the day, the employee counts the pins or candies and removes total of the cash "rung short." Management should be on the lookout for telltale stacks of small objects near the cash drawer. The cash register should be in the open where customers can easily see the amount rung up.

Cash and checks received by sales representatives should be controlled with receipts. Discount terms may be stated on receipt forms, since improper discount allowance is the easiest way for sales reps to steal.

Bank statements should be checked against the *cash ledger.*

OUTGOING CASH

Make all payments by check. An authorized officer's signature and a second countersignature may be required on such checks. Some firms have checks printed stating, "Amount not to exceed twenty-five dollars" (or some other predetermined amount), as a further control.

In making payments, invoices should be checked and recorded in the *purchase ledger,* as should payment. An *outgoing cash ledger* is usually maintained.

Use of checks offers the best *wage payment* control. Departmental supervisors may hand out pay checks to prevent an accounting employee adding fictitious names to the payroll.

Small payments may be made from a petty cash fund, controlled through receipts and petty cash vouchers.

CASH CONTROL AND FRAUD

Teeming and lading is a fraud technique used by employees to steal cash. A check stolen by the employee is replaced by the same-size check arriving from another customer at a later date. Sometimes two or more checks are used to replace one larger one. Comparison of deposit slips and the *cash ledger* by someone other than the employee regularly handling these areas will quickly pinpoint such fraud.

A second method of employee fraud is writing a credit memo for returned goods (that were not, of course, returned) to cover the amount stolen. This is easily controlled by requiring a supervisory authorization of all credit allowances.

SUGGESTED FURTHER READING

Cost Control in Business, Dun & Bradstreet Business Library, New York, 1970.

CASH-FLO-FLATION

Areas for use in Cost Control:

ORGANIZATIONAL AND OPERATIONAL SYSTEMS
INDUSTRIAL APPLICATIONS
BUSINESS AND COMMERCIAL APPLICATIONS

Cash-flo-flation is the retention of profits to finance expansion or other capital investment intended to increase a company's profitability, rather than paying the money to shareholders as dividends. The cost of such financing is, of course, much lower than that of other means of capital financing, such as bank loans and bonds.

SUGGESTED FURTHER READING

Levinson, C., *Capital, Inflation, and the Multinationals*, G. Allen, London, 1971.

CASH PICKUP ORDERS

Areas for use in Cost Control:

ORGANIZATIONAL AND OPERATIONAL SYSTEMS
MATERIALS AND EQUIPMENT MANAGEMENT
INDUSTRIAL APPLICATIONS
BUSINESS AND COMMERCIAL APPLICATIONS

Cash pickup orders are small orders shipped or picked up and paid for with cash. Use of the method reduces costs by eliminating paperwork, including purchase orders, requisitions, receiving orders, and supplier's invoice records, for orders below a predetermined amount—usually $50 or less. Studies show that small orders of this size represent about half of all orders for small companies and about one-quarter for large firms, providing ample room for cost reduction.

SUGGESTED FURTHER READING

Ammer, D. S., *Materials Management,* Irwin, Homewood, Ill., 1968.

CENTRALIZATION

Areas for use in Cost Control:

ORGANIZATIONAL AND OPERATIONAL SYSTEMS
DATA RETENTION—FILING AND RECORDKEEPING SYSTEMS
MATERIALS AND EQUIPMENT MANAGEMENT
INDUSTRIAL APPLICATIONS
BUSINESS AND COMMERCIAL APPLICATIONS

Centralization is the concentration of control in one pivotal area. Use of the method is more apt to increase efficiency, thus lowering costs, in small to medium-sized operations. Some centralized control, however, is necessary at all levels of operation to avoid unnecessary duplication of work and costs. This is particularly true in the areas of data retention, where computerization makes centralization practical at all operational levels: in materials and equipment handling, where optimal use of such items is necessary to control costs; and in employee control and scheduling, where best use of labor is essential to good cost control.

Figure 11, p. 54, shows a typical organizational structure using centralization.

Since control of working aspects of the business, such as production and engineering, is held at the central level, cost reductions in volume purchasing, combined research and design, etc., result.

Centralization is particularly effective in reducing costs where business or industry size is not too large to allow good control at a central authority point. In very large businesses, however, most economical control may result from delegating authority to competent subordinates.

SUGGESTED FURTHER READING

Hanson, J. L., *A Dictionary of Economics and Commerce,* MacDonald, London, 1974.
Speight, H., *Economics and Industrial Efficiency,* Macmillan, New York, 1967.
Terry, G. R., *Principles of Management,* Irwin, Homewood, Ill., 1972.

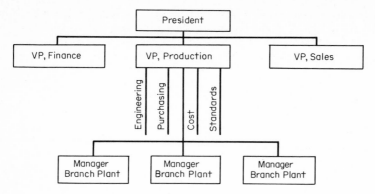

Figure 11. Typical centralized organization chart.

CERAMI'S CHECKLIST OF PRODUCT PROFITABILITY

Areas for use in Cost Control:

ORGANIZATIONAL AND OPERATIONAL SYSTEMS
INDUSTRIAL APPLICATIONS

Cerami's checklist of product profitability is used to determine whether or not a product is profitable or whether it should be dropped. The 12 items on the list are:

1. Is there an actual cash loss?
2. If this item is dropped, will costs be saved or reallocated?
3. Will customers feel the line is adequate without it?
4. Will the company have the same advertising and publicity position without it?
5. Can present stocks be sold without loss?
6. If liquidation results in tax advantages, which year is best to take it?
7. Can employees who work on the item be transferred?
8. Can vacated space be used profitably?
9. Will removal of the item improve looks or arrangement of sales displays?
10. Will price of other goods or services be cut by dropping the product?
11. Is there immediate and profitable use for freed capital?
12. Is any future development foreseen that might make the item profitable again?

SUGGESTED FURTHER READING

"Successful Management," *Nation's Business,* Doubleday, 1964.

CERAMI'S COMPETITION METHOD

Areas for use in Cost Control:

ORGANIZATIONAL AND OPERATIONAL SYSTEMS
INDUSTRIAL APPLICATIONS
BUSINESS AND COMMERCIAL APPLICATIONS

Cerami's competition method purposely establishes programs of competition between company employees and outside companies to reduce internal rivalry and in-fighting. Use of the method can increase productivity and teamwork, lowering wage and salary costs and/or increasing sales volume. Three techniques are specified by Cerami to establish such programs of competition:

1. Set up a specific opponent outside of the company and make it clear to employees that it is the competitor. Results of the competition should be posted on

bulletin boards and in company papers. Choose a competitor who is local, if possible, with nearly the same type of business, store, or company.
2. Find an area of competition best suited to your business. Total sales is often the best method.
3. Without alienating the team, find a way to reward the most productive individuals.

SUGGESTED FURTHER READING

"Successful Management," *Nation's Business,* Doubleday, New York, 1964.

CHANGE-A-WORD METHOD

Areas for use in Cost Control:

ORGANIZATIONAL AND OPERATIONAL SYSTEMS
INDUSTRIAL APPLICATIONS
BUSINESS AND COMMERCIAL APPLICATIONS

The change-a-word method facilitates creative thinking in solving cost and other business problems. Devised by G. B. Dubois, Cornell University, the technique substitutes a word in a problem statement without basically changing the meaning. For example, if the problem statement is, "We need to reduce labor costs," the statement may be changed to "We need to eliminate labor costs." This suggests the possibility of further automation to solve the problem. Or, the statement might be altered to read, "We need to change labor costs." This might suggest changing payment systems to piece rates or an incentive plan.

SUGGESTED FURTHER READING

Bittel, L. R., "How to Make Good Ideas Come Easy," *Factory Management and Maintenance,* March 1956.

CHANGE-OF-PRACTICE PRINCIPLE

Areas for use in Cost Control:

ORGANIZATIONAL AND OPERATIONAL SYSTEMS
INDUSTRIAL APPLICATIONS

The change-of-practice principle is a clause inserted in a labor agreement or contract stating that wage rates will not be changed unless working conditions, methods, or equipment are changed. Use of the clause controls labor costs by preventing additional wage-rise claims before the contract or agreement's expiration date.

SUGGESTED FURTHER READING

Marsh, A. I., and E. O. Evans, *The Dictionary of Industrial Relations,* Hutchinson, London, 1973.
Roberts' Dictionary of Industrial Relations, Bureau of National Affairs, Inc., Washington, D.C., 1966.

CHARTING

Areas for use in Cost Control:

PAPERWORK DESIGN AND FLOW SYSTEMS
DATA RETENTION—FILES AND RECORDKEEPING

Charting includes several techniques for graphically recording paperwork flow to pinpoint duplication of effort, inefficiencies, complexity, evenness of volume, etc. Types of charts generally used include the *specimen chart,* the *departmental distribution chart,* the *process chart, the multiple-activity chart, volume charts,* and *flow diagrams.*

Specimen Chart. This shows forms used in any procedure, placed in sequence on a large sheet of paper or cardboard. Frequently, notes amplifying the use of the forms are written on the chart. Since forms (invoices, orders, etc.) may be large and unwieldy, small photocopies may be used. Purpose of the chart is to show how much paperwork is connected with a single procedure, and to combine forms where possible to eliminate unnecessary paperwork.

Departmental Distribution Chart. Also called the procedure chart, the departmental distribution chart shows the office routing of a given paper. After examination, a more direct routing may result in less time spent.

Process Charting. This chart shows what work is done to the paper or form (see Fig. 12). Standard symbols (*see* **Work Study and Measurement**) are used to indicate types of activity. After examination, work steps are combined where possible to reduce costs and save time.

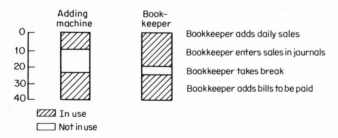

⬜1⃝ Wait to see prospect

⇨ Shown into prospect's office

① Start sales talk

② Listen to prospect's response

③ Answer prospect's questions

2⃝ Wait while prospect answers phone

④ Call prospect's attention to product

⑤ Take order

Figure 12. Process chart for a sales technique.

Multiple-Activity Chart. This chart compares the output of several employees or several pieces of equipment, or both. Its purpose is to reveal wasted time.

Figure 13 shows the activity of one bookkeeper and an adding machine. Noting the

	Adding machine	Book-keeper	
0			Bookkeeper adds daily sales
10			Bookkeeper enters sales in journals
20			Bookkeeper takes break
30			Bookkeeper adds bills to be paid
40			

▨ In use
⬜ Not in use

Figure 13. Multiple-activity chart.

amount of time the adding machine is not in use, it seems possible to have two bookkeepers share the same adding machine (see Fig. 14).

Volume Chart. These charts show activity variance by date or time of day (see Fig. 15). The purpose of the charts is to show weak points in production, sales, etc.

Flow Diagram. Also called route diagram, this chart shows where activities occur (see Fig. 16). Symbols used in process charting are also used here. The purpose of the chart is to show routing and work duplications or inefficiencies. Flow diagrams are sometimes presented in three-dimensional form with string diagrams (colored strings fixed on a scale board with pins) and scale models.

SUGGESTED FURTHER READING

Ireson, William G., and Eugene L. Grant, *Handbook of Industrial Engineering and Management,* Prentice-Hall, Englewood Cliffs, N.J., 1970.

Moon, Harry, *Office Procedures,* Milady Publishing, Bronx, N.Y., 1974.

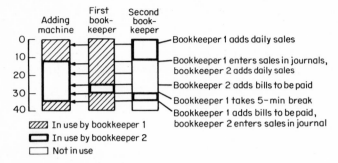

Figure 14. Revised multiple-activity chart.

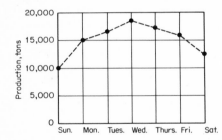

Figure 15. Volume chart (weekly production in tons).

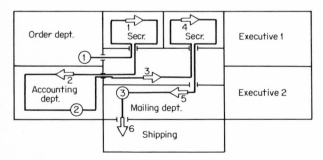

Figure 16. Flow or route diagram.

CHRONOCYCLEGRAPH TECHNIQUE

Areas for use in Cost Control:

ORGANIZATIONAL AND OPERATIONAL SYSTEMS
INDUSTRIAL APPLICATIONS
BUSINESS AND COMMERCIAL APPLICATIONS

The chronocyclegraph technique is a work study method (*see* **Work Study and Measurement**) used in obtaining most efficient (and lowest-cost) work from employees. Photographs are taken of a worker using an interrupted circuit of lighting attached to his hands, fingers, or other body parts. The flashing on and off of the light during photography records the speed (through the distance between "light on" data), direction, and path of motion of the employee's movement on the film.

SUGGESTED FURTHER READING

Maynard, H. B., ed., *Industrial Engineering Handbook,* 3d ed., New York, 1974.
ASME *Work Standardization Bulletin,* American Society of Mechanical Engineers, New York, 1971.

CIRCLE-WITH-A-POINT TECHNIQUE See Personnel Morale Building.

CIRCUIT MINIATURIZATION

Areas for use in Cost Control:

MATERIALS AND EQUIPMENT MANAGEMENT
INDUSTRIAL APPLICATIONS

Circuit miniaturization is the use of very small electronic components in circuitry to reduce maintenance costs and to increase reliability. Additionally, miniaturized components use less power. Elimination of large components and excess wiring through miniaturization has decreased component failure per hour by a factor of 1,000 in the past decade, according to David Hamilton, industrial editor for the *New Scientist.*

Miniaturization, primarily used in appliance and computer design today, can be used in transportation and freight systems, automated production equipment, communications systems, etc.

SUGGESTED FURTHER READING

Hamilton, D., *Technology, Man, and the Environment,* Faber and Faber, London, 1973.

CLASSIFICATION AND CODING SYSTEMS

Areas for use in Cost Control:

ORGANIZATIONAL AND OPERATIONAL SYSTEMS
MATERIALS AND EQUIPMENT MANAGEMENT
DATA RETENTION—FILES AND RECORDKEEPING
INDUSTRIAL APPLICATIONS
BUSINESS AND COMMERCIAL APPLICATIONS

Classification systems are those used to organize items logically, while coding systems identify each item using an abbreviation. The two systems are commonly used together to reduce costs by making it possible to find wanted items easier and faster and to simplify recordkeeping.

Main areas using classification and coding systems include:

1. Supplies (including office supplies)
2. Raw materials
3. Tools
4. Equipment
5. Plant
6. Specifications
7. Standards
8. Drawings
9. Finished products

PRINCIPLES: CLASSIFICATION SYSTEMS

In logically arranging items, the primary rule is to group similar items. For example, a library classifies books by author, title, subject, and sometimes publisher.

PRINCIPLES: CODING SYSTEMS

A coding system may be one of three basic types, or a combination of these:

1. *Numerical,* such as coding used on airline flight schedules.
2. *Alphabetical,* sometimes used for model distinctions.
3. *Symbolic,* such as "star" codings of hotels and restaurants.

Combinations are usually alphabetical-numerical, such as in federal highway codings—I81 (Interstate 81).

PRINCIPLES: COMBINED CLASSIFICATION AND CODING SYSTEMS

Combined systems use one reference to indicate both classification and code. Major combined-system types include:

Alphabetical systems—used only when small numbers of criteria are possible. For example, if three varieties each of apples, pears, and oranges are allocated for three markets, in three successive weeks, a classification coding system such as that in Table 6 might be developed. The first letter would then stand for the commodity, the second for the market, and the third for the week. Thus, "100 ABB" would mean that 100 boxes of apples were needed for Market B during the second week.

Table 6. Typical Alphabetical Classification-Coding System

Apples	A	Market	A	Week	A
Pears	B	Market	B	Week	B
Oranges	C	Market	C	Week	C

Arbitrary systems use alphabetical, numerical, symbolic, or compound classifications assigned at will.

Mnemonic systems use letter combinations that suggest the title. "ApAF" might mean *Ap*ples for Market *A* the *F*irst week, for example.

Alphabetical-numerical systems may use letters for classification and numbers for coding. For example, a type of plastic may be classified T, while numbers are assigned to different products made from it.

Numerical systems use separate digits in the number to indicate different types of classification. Thus, in the Zip Code 01236, the first digit indicates the geographical region, the second and third digits indicate subdivisions of the first region, and the fourth and fifth digits give further subdivisions. *See also* **Brisch Classification and Coding System.**

SUGGESTED FURTHER READING

Ingels, F. M., *Information and Coding Theory,* Intext Educational Publishers, New York, 1971.

CLASSIFIED WORK DISTRIBUTION ANALYSIS

Areas for use in Cost Control:

ORGANIZATIONAL AND OPERATIONAL SYSTEMS

INDUSTRIAL APPLICATIONS

BUSINESS AND COMMERCIAL APPLICATIONS

Classified work distribution analysis is a work study method (*see* **Work Study and Measurement**) used to divide employees and their work into four areas:

1. Functions
2. Activities
3. Subjects
4. Assignments

Individual employees' work is measured at random intervals in these areas and more efficient methods of work are determined. All workers are then retrained to use the more efficient work methods, decreasing labor costs.

Time standards developed from such an analysis can also be used to estimate future employee needs, determine fair wage payments, and reschedule the bulk of work in areas that will reduce costs. For example, if one function is purchase negotiation, and very little time has been spent in this area, purchasing may be costing considerably more than it would if buyers spent more time negotiating prices.

SUGGESTED FURTHER READING

Ammer, D. S., *Materials Management,* Irwin, Homewood, Ill., 1968.

COBWEB THEORY

Area for use in Cost Control:

ORGANIZATIONAL AND OPERATIONAL SYSTEMS

The cobweb theory shows visually the effects of fluctuating demand on industries that are slow in adapting production to required changes. The theory can be used in forecasting future demand to reduce wasted production costs. Basically, the cobweb theory states that in an industry with lengthy production, such as agriculture or oil, any increase in demand will disproportionately raise the selling price of the product, since no *immediate* increase in production is possible; while an increase in production initiated by such an increase in demand will bring in lower prices, since the entry of increased production on the market will cause a disproportionate falling of prices. Each change becomes progressively greater. Shown visually (see Fig. 17), the theory resembles a cobweb.

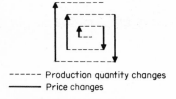

```
------ Production quantity changes
_____ Price changes
```

Figure 17. Visual representation of the cobweb theory.

Production can be timed, using the theory and charting changes as they occur, to increase production processes when prices fall, thus offering completed production when demand and prices accelerate and eliminating wasted production in the "price fall" aspect of the cycle. For example, if cattle producers are selling stock because the price is falling and they fear increased falling, obviously production will fall because there is less breeding stock. If a herd is *increased* at the point where other producers are decreasing their herds, the increased production will come to market at the optimum "price rise" point of the cycle, lowering the ratio of production cost to profit.

SUGGESTED FURTHER READING
Hanson, J. L., *A Dictionary of Economics and Commerce,* MacDonald, London, 1974.

CODING SYSTEMS See Classification and Coding Systems.

COLLECTIONS' INDEXING

Areas for use in Cost Control:
ORGANIZATIONAL AND OPERATIONAL SYSTEMS
INDUSTRIAL APPLICATIONS
BUSINESS AND COMMERCIAL APPLICATIONS

Collections' indexing is a technique developed by Brazil, used to reduce the cost of billing collections lost through changes in the rate of inflation. All commercial debts are indexed every 28 days, their amounts being adjusted to the real value of the debts at the time of purchase. Thus, if inflation increases 2 percent a month, so will the amount due from earlier billings. Inflation-increased rates are calculated by government agencies by measuring the increase in the cost of living or other index. Use of the method has resulted in prompt payment of bills to avoid indexed increases and has also reduced the cost of capital investment required by business and industry. *See also* **Index Linking; Inflation Cost Control;** and **Inflation Accounting.**

SUGGESTED FURTHER READING
Bowden, Lord, "Indexing," *The Guardian,* London, July 9, 1974.

COLUMNAR WORK SHEET METHOD

Areas for use in Cost Control:
ORGANIZATIONAL AND OPERATIONAL SYSTEMS
DATA RETENTION—FILES AND RECORDKEEPING
MATERIALS AND EQUIPMENT MANAGEMENT
INDUSTRIAL APPLICATIONS
BUSINESS AND COMMERCIAL APPLICATIONS

The columnar work sheet method is the preferred **inflation accounting** technique used to substitute purchasing power values for fixed currency values in all phases of accounting. Use of the method can reduce tax costs through revaluation of profits as well as of assets and resulting updated depreciation schedules. The technique also allows measurement of real, rather than inflated, growth, if any.

The columnar work sheet method uses converted balance sheets at the beginning and end of the accounting period as set out in the **net change method.** Additionally, it uses a converted profit and loss statement which provides a double-entry check of conversions with little extra work and cost.

The method is used as follows:

Using a work sheet, enter columns for the balance sheet at the beginning of the period, the net monetary assets account, closing items, closing journal entries, profit and loss account, and the balance sheet for the end of the period. Separate debit and credit columns may be used, or credit entries may be bracketed or made in red.

Items on the balance sheet at the beginning of the period are converted as set out in the **net change method.**

Items in the net monetary asset account are converted. This includes all cash transactions— balances, receipts, payments, etc. If such transactions occur evenly over the period, the average index figure may be used. For example, if the index was 112 at the beginning of the period and 127 at the close of the period, the conversion factor would be 7.5 percent, or half the total increase. Where transactions are not evenly distributed, conversions can be made quarterly.

Journal entries and closing items are converted to reflect purchasing power at the end of the period.

Depreciation is determined by converting cumulative asset values at the start of the year and making additions for the period, using averaged index factors. This total converted figure is then divided by the number of years in the depreciation schedule.

Stock is converted as in the **net change method.**

Converted equity interest at the close of the preceding year is entered in the balance sheets at the beginning and close of the period.

Net converted monetary liability gain (or loss) is added to the profit and loss account, crediting the figure if it is a gain and debiting it if it is a loss.

Balance sheet at the beginning of the year, net monetary assets, closing items, and journal entry columns are totaled, taking into account debit and credit entries if separate columns are not used.

These totals are entered in the profit and loss account and balance sheet at the end-of-the-year columns.

The balance of the profit and loss account column will be the retained profit for the year, if a debit balance (or loss, if a credit balance). When it is credited to the balance sheet for the end of the period, the sheet should balance.

SUGGESTED FURTHER READING

Blandon, Michael, "Adjusting the Profits with Inflation Accounting," *The Financial Times,* London, May 15, 1974.

Parker, P. W., and P. H. D. Gibbs, *Accounting for Inflation,* Phillips and Drew, London, 1974.

COMBINATION See Amalgamation.

COMBINATION METHOD

Areas for use in Cost Control:

ORGANIZATIONAL AND OPERATIONAL SYSTEMS
MATERIALS AND EQUIPMENT MANAGEMENT
INDUSTRIAL APPLICATIONS
BUSINESS AND COMMERCIAL APPLICATIONS

The combination method examines and evaluates components of three or more products or services that perform the same function and combines the lowest cost components of the three, forming a new product or service produced at reduced cost. For example, three transportation services might be examined:

1. Helicopters
2. Taxis
3. Buses

Cost components might include:

1. Fuel costs
2. Highway costs
3. Equipment costs
4. Tax costs

Table 7 shows a combination method comparison chart for these components. Combining all low-cost areas in Table 7, a new transportation service that might be

Table 7. Typical Combination Method Comparison Chart

Cost components*	Helicopter	Taxi	Bus
Fuel costs	High	Medium	Low
Highway costs	Low	High	Medium
Equipment costs	Medium	High	Low
Tax costs	High	Medium	Low

*Per passenger dollar.

suggested is a helicopter-style air bus, with low fuel, equipment, and tax costs per passenger dollar and with no need for highway costs.

SUGGESTED FURTHER READING

Radke, Magnus, *Manual of Cost Reduction Techniques,* McGraw-Hill, New York, 1972.

COMBINED DEMAND AND SUPPLY SCHEDULING

Areas for use in Cost Control:

ORGANIZATIONAL AND OPERATIONAL SYSTEMS
INDUSTRIAL APPLICATIONS
BUSINESS AND COMMERCIAL APPLICATIONS

A combined demand and supply schedule is used to project future costs of materials and future prices of products or services, based on past prices and quantities sold. Use of the technique allows purchase of materials at lowest possible cost and timing of production for most advantageous pricing. The movement of the schedule's curve is based on the principle that high prices lower the demand for a material, product, or service while low prices tend to increase demand. In a visual presentation of the schedule (see Fig. 18), supply and demand are represented by a single curve.

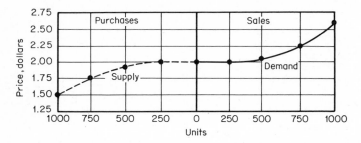

Figure 18. Typical combined demand and supply schedule.

SUGGESTED FURTHER READING

Conway, R. W., *Theory of Scheduling,* Addison-Wesley, Reading, Mass., 1967.
Hanson, J. L., *A Dictionary of Economics and Commerce,* MacDonald, London, 1974.

COMMODITY PRICE INDEXES

Areas for use in Cost Control:

MATERIALS AND EQUIPMENT MANAGEMENT
INDUSTRIAL APPLICATIONS

Commodity price indexes are control devices used to reduce the cost of materials purchasing when materials used are too diverse to apply **key parts control.**

To compile such an index, index numbers are substituted for dollar cost figures, allowing numerical classification by type of material. Base cost of the index (100) equals the unit price of each commodity at the time it is indexed. To show a material's price decrease its base of 100 may be lowered to 99.50. Overall cost reductions can be computed by multiplying the index change by the average monthly spending for that commodity. If $100,000 worth of the material is used per month, for example, with an 0.5 index reduction, cost reductions will be $500.

Such indexing will quickly show how current prices relate to those in effect when the index was begun, giving a constant check on the movement of materials costs.

SUGGESTED FURTHER READING

Ammer, D. S., *Materials Management,* Irwin, Homewood, Ill., 1968.

COMMUNICATION GRID ANALYSIS

Areas for use in Cost Control:

ORGANIZATIONAL AND OPERATIONAL SYSTEMS
PAPERWORK DESIGN AND FLOW SYSTEMS
BUSINESS AND COMMERCIAL APPLICATIONS

Communication grid analysis is a visual design technique used in planning office layout for most efficient communication. A grid (see Fig. 19), or *matrix chart* (*see* **Matrix Charts**), shows the estimated number of daily trips between departments. Optimum layout then arranges departments to minimize distance traveled by placing departments with the largest number of trips near each other (see Fig. 20).

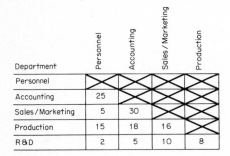

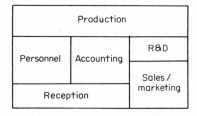

Figure 19. Interdepartmental grid analysis form.

Figure 20. Office layout determined by communication grid analysis.

Looking at Fig. 19, *accounting* makes or receives the largest number of daily trips. Therefore, it is centrally located in the layout in Fig. 20, with *sales/marketing, personnel,* and *production*—the three major communicators with the department—immediately adjacent to *accounting. Research and development,* with most of its communication shared with *production* and *sales/marketing,* is sandwiched between these two areas. *Personnel,* which communicates most often with *accounting* and *production,* is located adjacent to both. Placement of the reception area is convenient to both *sales/marketing* and *personnel,* the departments most likely to use reception facilities. *See also* **Strategic Space Planning; Office Layout.**

SUGGESTED FURTHER READING

McIntosh, D. W., *Techniques of Business Communication,* Holbrook Press, Rockleigh, N.J., 1972.

COMMUNICATION NETWORKS

Areas for use in Cost Control:

ORGANIZATIONAL AND OPERATIONAL SYSTEMS
INDUSTRIAL APPLICATIONS
BUSINESS AND COMMERCIAL APPLICATIONS

Communication networks are the organization of communication channels within a company for most effective use, reducing costs. Various network patterns are possible, and each is most effectively used in particular applications.

The Wheel. Studies show that a *wheel* communication network (see Fig. 21) makes fewer errors than the *chain* or *circle* network in problem solving. The wheel is the fastest network system, except for very simple problems, since the central position is automatically the leader of problem-solving projects, and no voting or additional organizing is needed. The wheel network requires the use of fewer written communications than chain or circle networks.

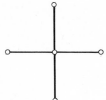

Figure 21. Wheel communication network.

Figure 22. Y communication network with extensions.

The Y. The Y network is a variation of the wheel, and offers primarily the same advantages. Extensions of the arms to include additional employees in larger organizations may slow decision making, however, as the network then becomes a combination of the wheel and chain types (see Fig. 22).

The Circle. Circle communication networks (see Fig. 23) provide difficulty in choosing a leader, thus slowing down problem solving. In very complex problems where all managers involved need to see all information, the circle is the most efficient.

The Chain. Chain communication networks (see Fig. 24) are generally slower-moving than the wheel or the Y but provide high accuracy, since each member of the chain reviews all material.

Figure 23. Circle communication network.

Figure 24. Chain communication network.

Other Networks. Other networks commonly used include the *slash* (Fig. 25), the *all-channel* (Fig. 26), and the *kite* (Fig. 27). These networks are used primarily for mathematical or statistical problem solution. High performance historically results when the central position assumes leadership using autocratic leadership techniques.

Figure 25. Slash communication network.

Figure 26. All-channel communication network.

Figure 27. Kite communication network.

SUGGESTED FURTHER READING

Applewhite, P. B., *Organizational Behavior,* Prentice-Hall, Englewood Cliffs, N.J., 1965.

Bennis, W. G., "Continuity of Leadership in Communication Networks," *Human Relations,* vol. 14, 1961.

Cohen, A. M., "Changing Small-Group Communication Networks," *Administrative Science Quarterly,* vol. 6, 1962.

COMPARATIVE ADVANTAGE TECHNIQUE

Areas for use in Cost Control:

ORGANIZATIONAL AND OPERATIONAL SYSTEMS

INDUSTRIAL APPLICATIONS

BUSINESS AND COMMERCIAL APPLICATIONS

The comparative advantage technique is the specialization of a worker or company to give the greatest comparative advantage over competing workers or firms. Thus, the machinist who can produce $150 worth of goods per hour is not used, even temporarily, in other positions that can be performed by other employees who do not effect equal output. In the same way, a company may subcontract specialized aspects of production that it cannot perform more economically itself.

SUGGESTED FURTHER READING

Ellsworth, P. T., *The International Economy,* Macmillan, New York, 1969.

Hanson, J. L., *A Dictionary of Economics and Commerce,* MacDonald, London, 1974.

COMPARATIVE AND CROSS-SECTIONAL ANALYSIS

Areas for use in Cost Control:

ORGANIZATIONAL AND OPERATIONAL SYSTEMS

INDUSTRIAL APPLICATIONS

BUSINESS AND COMMERCIAL APPLICATIONS

Comparative and cross-sectional analysis compares a cost curve of a similar product or operation to predict costs for a proposed product or operation. Proposed cost control measures can also be compared to determine the extent and effect of reductions.

SUGGESTED FURTHER READING

Shackle, G. L. S., ed., *On the Nature of Business Success,* Liverpool University Press, 1968.

COMPARATIVE ESTIMATING

Areas for use in Cost Control:

FINANCIAL MOTIVATIONAL MANAGEMENT
ORGANIZATIONAL AND OPERATIONAL SYSTEMS
INDUSTRIAL APPLICATIONS
BUSINESS AND COMMERCIAL APPLICATIONS

Comparative estimating is a **work study and measurement** technique that compares a job with similar ones already measured and gives it a similar standard time. Incentive payments may be based on the rating estimated in this way, so that labor costs are limited in proportion to productivity.

SUGGESTED FURTHER READING

Roberts, H. S., *Roberts' Dictionary of Industrial Relations,* Bureau of National Affairs, Inc., Washington, D.C., 1966.

COMPETITION ANALYSIS

Areas for use in Cost Control:

ORGANIZATIONAL AND OPERATIONAL SYSTEMS
MATERIALS AND EQUIPMENT MANAGEMENT
INDUSTRIAL APPLICATIONS
BUSINESS AND COMMERCIAL APPLICATIONS

Competition analysis is the examination and evaluation of a competitor's product or service to determine what cost reductions have been made and whether they can be applied to the company's own product or service. For example, if thinner plastic is used in a competitor's plastic bag, it would be tested to determine whether the thinner plastic is acceptable to the buyer. If so, the company may decide to use thinner material in its plastic bag.

Competition analysis includes the following techniques:

1. *Functional testing.* Does the product perform satisfactorily?

2. *Market testing.* Is the user satisfied with the product or service?

3. *Parts measurement.* How do product parts differ in the competitor's product? Are they smaller, lighter, of cheaper material than the company's product?

4. *Material identification.* What is the material in the competitor's product? What are its tolerance and other aspects?

5. *Cost determination.* What did the competitor's product cost to produce? How does the total cost compare with company production costs? How do parts costs compare with company costs?

SUGGESTED FURTHER READING

Radke, Magnus, *Manual of Cost Reduction Techniques,* McGraw-Hill, New York, 1972.

COMPETITIVE INTELLIGENCE

Areas for use in Cost Control:

ORGANIZATIONAL AND OPERATIONAL SYSTEMS
MATERIALS AND EQUIPMENT MANAGEMENT
INDUSTRIAL APPLICATIONS

Competitive intelligence, also called aggressive market research, is the use of espionage to obtain other companies' (usually competitors') proprietary methods of production, sales and marketing, research, etc., particularly where knowledge of such methods will lower costs or increase product or production efficiency. For example, a plant manager who is considering a new type of automation must know if the cost of equipment is worth the investment in increased production. Equipment manufacturers' claims may or may not be justified. But if the manager can obtain cost and production figures of a competitor already using the equipment, the answer will be clearer and a decision can be made.

Tools used by industrial spies, such as concealed microphones, telephone taps, and miniaturized cameras, are illegal under some conditions of use, while producing information by this means often is not.

INTELLIGENCE AREAS

Some aspects of management can especially benefit from competitive intelligence.

Decision Making. Advance knowledge of what competitors are doing, what they are planning, what and how much they intend to produce, equipment and methods they will use, and their marketing plans are essential to making decisions.

Research and Technological Forecasting. A company needs to know what equipment and methods will be most economical in five years' time; in 10 years'; and whether lower-cost material may be satisfactorily substituted in a product. Learning these results from a competitor's design research is less costly than operating a company research program.

Mergers. A company proposing to buy another needs to know every detail of its financial and production status, sales ratios, plans, research developments, etc.

Pricing. A company needs to know the pricing structures of competitors to ensure that it will be competitive when its product reaches the market.

Marketing and Sales Techniques. Knowing the techniques of competitors aids in planning competitive techniques.

Delivery and Service. Delivery and service patterns can be used to pinpoint possible competitor weaknesses.

SOURCES

Information can be obtained from many sources:

1. *Newspapers, trade magazines, and other publications* often provide hints of proprietary information, including data in product advertisements. Local newspapers from areas where major competitors' plants are located and in-plant newspapers and magazines may also give clues to new activities. Newspaper and magazine editors and writers may also have information that is not printed.

2. *Records of materials and equipment purchased* by competitors can provide information. The size of a material purchase, for example, may give a general idea of the status of a project.

3. *Employees working for competitors* are probably the best sources of information, particularly employees in key positions.

4. *Users of the competitor's product.* Advantages will have been explained to the purchaser during selling.

5. *Subcontractors, outside repairmen, and other persons* who have a legitimate reason to visit the competitor are good information sources. Temporary clerical personnel, including computer programmers, may be able to provide sales and cost information.

6. *Accountants, bank employees, and other outside professional agencies* may provide information on purpose or inadvertently.

7. *Manufacturers of equipment* may provide information about planned technological changes.

8. *The company's own salespeople* should be trained to listen to other salespeople's gossip, sifting out informative items and keeping quiet about their firm's proprietary information.

See also **Industrial Espionage Prevention.**

SUGGESTED FURTHER READING

International Conference on Electronics and Space, Collected Papers, Paris, 1967.
Smith, P. I., *Industrial Intelligence and Espionage,* Business Books, London, 1970.
Soule, H. V., *Electro-optical Photography at Low Illumination Levels,* Wiley, New York, N.Y., 1968.

COMPLEMENTARY DEMAND TECHNIQUE

Areas for use in Cost Control:

ORGANIZATIONAL AND OPERATIONAL SYSTEMS
INDUSTRIAL APPLICATIONS
BUSINESS AND COMMERCIAL APPLICATIONS

The complementary demand technique is a joint production and/or marketing of related goods and/or services so as to increase demand for both items while paying major marketing and sales costs for only one of the items. The method is based on the fact that when products or services are jointly demanded, such as cars and gasoline, pens and ink, or bread and butter, a company can increase sales of both by increasing sales of one. Thus, if a company produces both items, marketing and sales costs are considerably reduced on the second item by the demand effect of the marketing of the first item. For example, if a pen manufacturer produces a cartridge fountain pen *and* the ink cartridge to fill it, usual marketing and sales costs will be incurred for the pen, but demand for cartridges should increase to match demand for the pen with little or no additional marketing and sales outlay.

SUGGESTED FURTHER READING

Ellsworth, P. T., *The International Economy,* Macmillan, New York, 1969.

COMPOUND TRADING

Areas for use in Cost Control:

ORGANIZATIONAL AND OPERATIONAL SYSTEMS
BUSINESS AND COMMERCIAL APPLICATIONS

Compound trading is the extension of the variety of goods offered for sale in a single outlet. Use of the method reduces costs by accelerating the goods' turnover and sales volume, and it has grown more effective as purchasing patterns have turned toward buying more goods at one time. The technique began in retailing and is still of greatest value at this level. Greater care must be used when applying the technique to production, where diversity may mean a less efficient and thus more costly operation overall.

When considering the extension of products or services offered, the following checklist can serve as a limitations guide:

1. *Does the product require special knowledge for sales?* For example, some cosmetic items can be sold by anyone, but a product such as hair dye calls for a salesperson with some knowledge of the contents.

2. *Is the potential profit per item sufficiently high for the shelf space required?*

3. *If profit per item is relatively low, does the product turn over rapidly?*

4. *Does the item have a "pull" value to bring new traffic into the outlet?*

5. *Are stock-rotation or storage problems caused by the variety extension?*

6. *Do manufacturers' or wholesalers' terms of purchase provide financial incentives for stocking the goods?*

SUGGESTED FURTHER READING

Rickert, G. H., *Retailing Principles and Practices,* McGraw-Hill, New York, 1968.

COMPUTER SECURITY

Areas for use in Cost Control:

ORGANIZATIONAL AND OPERATIONAL SYSTEMS
MATERIALS AND EQUIPMENT MANAGEMENT
INDUSTRIAL APPLICATIONS
BUSINESS AND COMMERCIAL APPLICATIONS

Proprietary information stored in a computer and stolen, or necessary records also computerized and lost through fire or other physical destruction, are costly losses indeed. Computer security, implementing techniques and using security devices (*see also* **Security and Cost Control**), can reduce these costs.

Four areas of a computer system (*see also* **Electronic Data Processing**) are open to both physical damage and aspects of stealing information; thus they require security measures:

1. *Hardware*—computer processing unit, storage bank, and peripheral equipment such as read-out units, visual display units, and communications lines for shared computer use
2. *Software*—programs
3. *Data*—information processed by the program
4. *Data bank*—stock information

PHYSICAL SECURITY

Experts estimate that most company records will be computerized by 1980. If such data are destroyed by fire or vandalism, they will probably be impossible to replace. Prevention of such destruction, then, becomes essential.

Special vaults and cabinets are available to protect computer equipment, software, and data from fire. These items must be habitually used, however, so that physical transfer of tapes, cards, etc., may be necessary.

Most companies make duplicate recordings of vital records, which may then be stored in a shared-time operation. The shared-time service provides emergency back-up for damaged computers or peak periods, too. Companies may make exchange agreements, storing vital duplicate records for each other, thus reducing the cost of protection.

Location of the computer can aid security at no additional cost. It should not be located near areas with maximum fire risks, such as shipping rooms. The area should have adequate locks and electronic detection devices. Equipment should be in the open for easy detection of unauthorized persons, bombs, etc.

The area should not be prone to civil problems, such as bombings and riots. Areas subject to flooding, earthquakes, etc., should be avoided.

The computer room or center should be built of fire-resistant materials and materials highly resistant to impact. No windows should be used, and ventilation systems should have no external access points. A reserve ventilation system is advisable. Stand-by generators are advised for essential operations. One door should be used for normal access, with fire doors opening from the inside only.

Access control can be by electronic device, usually combined with human surveillance. Authorized personnel can be electronically identified by their handprint, their voice, or the pattern of the eye retina. A guard may search all persons, including authorized personnel.

Electronic heat, smoke, and radiation detectors can be used. Fire extinguishers should also be placed at key points.

Security lighting outside the computer center provides guards with visibility access. Electronic or infrared eyes, wires, etc., can also be used for perimeter protection.

KNOWLEDGE SECURITY

All aspects of the physical security techniques, as well as those discussed in **Security and Cost Control,** apply to the prevention of information theft by unauthorized persons. Much stolen proprietary information is taken from computers by employees, however, since they have access as well as knowledge of the equipment and programming.

As set out in **Security and Cost Control,** careful selection of authorized personnel is one of the best security methods available. The employees should be trained in security methods, and the importance of this area should be emphasized.

Employees can work in limited areas, so that the degree of knowledge available to any one person is limited. Electronic observation and eavesdropping, as well as supervisory observation, are common security controls.

No aspect of programming or information handling should be regularly controlled by one person. If a second employee regularly handles materials, changes made to illegally extract information from the computer are more likely to be observed.

Electronic sweeping devices can detect microphones or cameras placed in the computer center to transmit proprietary information outside, and the devices should be used periodically.

Computer servicemen, or other unauthorized personnel, with a valid reason for entering the center, should be watched with particular care.

Surveillance operations should also examine potential use of the computer to gain power. For example, a programmer may be able to alter personnel records to discredit coworkers, thus facilitating the likelihood of his or her own promotion through having "removed" the competition. In computerized decision-making techniques, the programmer could alter material to discredit specific members of management.

Shared-time computer operations present an additional problem, since a programmer at the computer center might devise a means of obtaining information from all subscribers' data entries.

Electronic devices to protect computers specifically are under development, and at least one American company claims to have a computer to protect the main computer. Security instructions are programmed into the unit, to provide a check of operational use of the main computer. Programming and other irregularities are reported for other checking.

SUGGESTED FURTHER READING

Hamilton, Peter, *Computer Security,* Cassell Assoc. Business Programs, London, 1972.
Post, R., and A. Kingsbury, *Security Administration,* Charles C Thomas, Springfield, Ill., 1973.

CONCEALED DISCOUNT

Areas for use in Cost Control:

ORGANIZATIONAL AND OPERATIONAL SYSTEMS
INDUSTRIAL APPLICATIONS
BUSINESS AND COMMERCIAL APPLICATIONS

A concealed discount is a reduction of the cost of materials or services offered by a supplier to a business or industry, usually in exchange for the sole right to supply the company with the material or service or because the company purchases very large quantities. The discount is kept secret to prevent other less-favored companies from asking for the same discount. *See also* **Discount.**

SUGGESTED FURTHER READING

Bannock, G., R. E. Baxter, and R. Rees, *A Dictionary of Economics,* Baltimore, 1974.

CONCEALED EMPLOYMENT CONTROL

Areas for use in Cost Control:

ORGANIZATIONAL AND OPERATIONAL SYSTEMS
INDUSTRIAL APPLICATIONS
BUSINESS AND COMMERCIAL APPLICATIONS

Concealed employment control is the elimination, through layoffs or other methods, of employees when available work falls below the level for which they are required. The technique is most often applied to industrial laborers to reduce labor costs but can be effectively used in all areas of business operations as well. Usually such elimination is in inverse order of seniority. *See also* the **New Reality Theory.**

SUGGESTED FURTHER READING

Chamberlain, N. W., *The Labor Sector,* McGraw-Hill, New York, 1962.

CONJUNCTIVE BARGAINING

Areas for use in Cost Control:

ORGANIZATIONAL AND OPERATIONAL SYSTEMS
INDUSTRIAL APPLICATIONS

Conjunctive bargaining is a labor-negotiating method in which minimal pressures are used by both labor and management, allowing a fast settlement at lower labor-cost increases than would be acceptable under more intense negotiating conditions.

SUGGESTED FURTHER READING

Chamberlain, N. W., and J. W. Kuhn, *Collective Bargaining,* McGraw-Hill, New York, 1965.

CONSORTIUM PRODUCTION

Areas for use in Cost Control:

ORGANIZATIONAL AND OPERATIONAL SYSTEMS
INDUSTRIAL APPLICATIONS
BUSINESS AND COMMERCIAL APPLICATIONS

Consortium production is the joint production of goods and/or services with several companies sharing costs of a project that is too large or complicated for a single producer. For example, North Sea oil field rigs and equipment require such joint production because of the diversity of geographical locations, construction conditions, and number of oil companies involved. Costs can be lowered through the increased efficiency and specialization possible in such joint operations, as well as through cost sharing.

SUGGESTED FURTHER READING

Ellsworth, P. T., *The International Economy,* Macmillan, New York, 1969.
Hanson, J. L., *A Dictionary of Economics and Commerce,* MacDonald, London, 1974.

CONSTRAINTS TECHNIQUE

Areas for use in Cost Control:

ORGANIZATIONAL AND OPERATIONAL SYSTEMS
MATERIALS AND EQUIPMENT MANAGEMENT
INDUSTRIAL APPLICATIONS
BUSINESS AND COMMERCIAL APPLICATIONS

The constraints technique is used to analyze factors relating to a proposed system or piece of equipment to determine whether its adoption will increase efficiency and/or reduce costs. Developed by F. J. Warburton and B. H. Walley, the method translates both absolute and relative constraints or restrictions into monetary or other terms for evaluation purposes.

Absolute constraints, such as the amount of money available for capital expansion or physical space available for a new procedure, are listed first. Alternative new procedures are checked against these, and those with absolute constraint factors are eliminated.

Relative constraints, such as effects of a noisy piece of equipment, are then rated by the following point system:

0–1	Excellent
2–3	Good
4–6	Average
7–8	Poor
9–10	Very poor

All constraining relative factors are weighted on a constraints value sheet (Fig. 28). Approximate money value is then determined for one of the relative constraints. For example, if a noisy piece of equipment is lowering employee morale and output by 10 percent, and the average hourly wage is $5, this factor costs about 50 cents an hour. If it has a point rating of 10 because of its seriousness, then each point can be converted at the rate of 5 cents an hour, transferring monetary costs to all relative constraints.

These costs are then added to absolute restraint costs, and the whole is compared with the maximum capital available to remove alternatives that are too expensive.

While constraints values are only semiscientific estimates, they do provide a means of rough cost comparison.

SUGGESTED FURTHER READING

Warburton, F. J., and B. H. Walley, *Time and Motion Study,* Longmans, London, 1961.

Relative Constraints

Proposed equipment Item_____		Operator skill required	Space	Speed	Noise	Distance	Product quality value	Deprec-iation problems	Schedul-ing problems	Total
1	Points									
	Weighting									
	Weighted points									
	$ Equivalent									
2	Points									
	Weighting									
	Weighted points									
	$ Equivalent									
3	Points									
	Weighting									
	Weighted points									
	$ Equivalent									

Figure 28. Typical constraints value sheet.

CONSULTANTS AND COST CONTROL

Areas for use in Cost Control:

ORGANIZATIONAL AND OPERATIONAL SYSTEMS
INDUSTRIAL APPLICATIONS
BUSINESS AND COMMERCIAL APPLICATIONS

A good management consultant is an expert outside the company who finds cost and other areas that need new techniques, shows company management these areas, and then helps install the recommended techniques. Areas most likely to be benefited by a management consultant include:

1. *Cross-industry knowledge.* Many industries have become highly specialized and are inbred in their use of operating techniques.

2. *Specialization.* Large consultant firms often have specialists in various business areas who make it a point to know the most economical techniques in their areas of specialization.

3. *Labor unions,* which are sometimes more willing to accept incentive payment

schemes determined by a consultant, assuming that his or her study of work methods is objective while such management decisions would be subjective.

4. *Security systems,* to prevent competitors from stealing product designs in research and/or production. These are specialty areas for some consultants.

5. *Spying.* Some consultants will infiltrate a competing company to obtain information.

6. *Subtlety.* Consultants can unobtrusively conduct surveys and studies, while similar activities by the hiring firm would be immediately noted by competitors.

7. *Production.* Consultants can often reduce unit labor costs. **Work study and measurement** is a primary technique used. New humanistic techniques used to motivate workers, such as **copartnership** or the use of **behavior control** are growing in popularity.

8. *Automation.* A specialty consultant will be aware of available equipment and its potential effect on costs.

9. *Alternate raw materials.* A specialty consultant can know new synthetic or substitute materials that offer lower-cost advantages.

10. *Stock control.* Methods of decreasing turnaround time and lowering required inventories can be determined.

11. *Negotiation.* Consultants specializing in labor negotiations can serve as objective arbitrators.

12. *Marketing strategy.* Specialist consultants can apply sound marketing techniques to the individual product, reducing overall sales costs and increasing sales.

13. *Pricing.* Consultants most effective here are those firms combining accountancy and management consultancy.

14. *EDP.* This area is a major one for specialty consultants, since few managers have a background in computer technology.

15. *Management recruitment.* Consultants can test and check on prospective management employees more efficiently than employment agencies are able to do.

CHOOSING A CONSULTANT

The following can serve as a guide in choosing a consultant:

1. Is the consultant licensed?
2. What is the consultant's business background? The educational background? Do these fit the specialty needs of the job at hand?
3. Has the consultant provided references from past clients?
4. How long has he or she been a consultant? Why did he or she enter the profession?
5. Has the consultant published books and/or magazine articles in his or her area of specialty? Is the material sound?
6. Does the consultant teach management techniques at the local college, business school, or university?
7. Is the consultant known and well thought of in his or her area of specialty?
8. Does the consultant have positive plans to help the company to achieve its cost reduction or other goals?

SUGGESTED FURTHER READING

Ansoff, H. I., *Corporate Strategy,* McGraw-Hill, New York, 1965.

CONTAINERIZATION

Areas for use in Cost Control:

ORGANIZATIONAL AND OPERATIONAL SYSTEMS
MATERIALS AND EQUIPMENT MANAGEMENT
INDUSTRIAL APPLICATIONS

Containerization is the use of standard-sized shipping modules that can be loaded with goods at the production point and delivered by one or more means of transportation without unloading and reloading. Containers generally hold one cubic meter or more, are built in sections, and are designed for reuse, as well as for easy filling and emptying. Usually, they are made of metal for durability. Container design allows easy mechanical loading and unloading for rail, sea, or road transportation. Since large quantities of goods can be handled quickly once containerized, many shipping firms provide discounts of up to 10 percent for the transportation of goods so packed. In addition, breakage costs are reduced, since goods are not rehandled; faster delivery time is implemented, cutting capital costs for excess inventories to meet lead time; and simplified recordkeeping is possible.

Studies show that distribution costs range up to 50 percent of total product cost. Of this, about 35 percent is spent for handling. With containerization and full mechanization of loading and unloading, a worker's capability to handle about 25 tons of freight per week moves to 600 tons per week, according to G. J. Murphy, Economics and Structure of Business lecturer at Lanchester Polytechnic, Coventry, England. He also estimates that as much as 75 percent of goods could be containerized if labor unions would agree to the method. *See also* **Palletization.**

SUGGESTED FURTHER READING

Magee, J. F., *Physical Distribution Systems,* McGraw-Hill, New York, 1967.

CONTRACT COSTING

Areas for use in Cost Control:

ORGANIZATIONAL AND OPERATIONAL SYSTEMS
DATA RETENTION—FILES AND RECORDKEEPING
MATERIALS AND EQUIPMENT MANAGEMENT
INDUSTRIAL APPLICATIONS
BUSINESS AND COMMERCIAL APPLICATIONS

Contract costing, also called terminal costing, applies separate **costing** to accounts pertaining to a single contract. The method is particularly useful where long-term or large-scale contracts are involved, since it details costs for that specific work against income from the contract, pointing out areas where cost reduction is needed to make the contract profitable. *See also* **Batch Costing.**

SUGGESTED FURTHER READING

Horngren, C. T., *Cost Accounting,* Prentice-Hall, Englewood Cliffs, N.J., 1972.
Lynch, R. M., *Accounting for Management,* McGraw-Hill, New York, 1967.

CONTRACT MAINTENANCE

Areas for use in Cost Control:

ORGANIZATIONAL AND OPERATIONAL SYSTEMS
MATERIALS AND EQUIPMENT MANAGEMENT
INDUSTRIAL APPLICATIONS
BUSINESS AND COMMERCIAL APPLICATIONS

Contract maintenance is the leasing of machinery and equipment maintenance. The method can reduce costs, particularly in the case of very complex or specialized equipment where use of a full-time person skilled in its maintenance and/or repair cannot be justified economically. Contract maintenance may be part of an overall lease contract or part of a purchase agreement or may be negotiated separately.

SUGGESTED FURTHER READING

Higgins, L. R., *Maintenance Engineering Handbook,* McGraw-Hill, New York, 1977.

CONTRACT PIECEWORK

Areas for use in Cost Control:

ORGANIZATIONAL AND OPERATIONAL SYSTEMS

INDUSTRIAL APPLICATIONS

Contract piecework is the system of paying a worker or group of workers a predetermined price for a specific job, regardless of the working time required. Use of the system protects the employer from excessive labor costs if the work requires more than the estimated time.

SUGGESTED FURTHER READING

Kelling, B. L., and J. A. Pendery, *Payroll Records and Accounting,* South-Western Publishing Co., Cincinnati, 1973.

Roberts, H. S., *Roberts' Dictionary of Industrial Relations,* Bureau of National Affairs, Inc., Washington, D.C., 1966.

CONTRACYCLICAL BUYING

Areas for use in Cost Control:

ORGANIZATIONAL AND OPERATIONAL SYSTEMS

MATERIALS AND EQUIPMENT MANAGEMENT

INDUSTRIAL APPLICATIONS

BUSINESS AND COMMERCIAL APPLICATIONS

Contracyclical buying is the practice of purchasing materials or supplies out of season, obtaining slack-season price concessions and reducing costs. For example, a company might purchase the current model for company automobiles as the new model is being introduced. Prices of equipment, such as electrical equipment, are also cyclical, although such cycles may not be uniform and may not match the general economic cycle.

Long-term contracts for materials to be supplied during slack periods may also be negotiated. Usual terms call for an approximate 5 percent reduction in price.

SUGGESTED FURTHER READING

Ammer, D. S., *Materials Management,* Irwin, Homewood, Ill., 1968.

CONTRIBUTION ANALYSIS

Areas for use in Cost Control:

ORGANIZATIONAL AND OPERATIONAL SYSTEMS

INDUSTRIAL APPLICATIONS

Contribution analysis is a **costing** method designed to show the amount of profit made from each product unit. *Overhead costs (see* **Overhead Cost Control***)* that would continue whether or not the product was manufactured are not charged to production costs in this technique. Instead, the method considers the *contribution* each production unit makes toward overhead and profit.

Of course, *overhead costs* still must be paid, but as these costs will not increase until full production is reached, it may be possible to sell increased volume at lowered prices. For example, assume 1,000 automobiles are manufactured by a company, selling at $3,000 each. Assume, too, that production-connected costs are $2,000, overhead is $500, and profit is $500 on each car. Until full production is reached, *overhead costs* such as rent will not increase. This means that the company can sell additional cars at $2,500 and still make $500 profit.

The technique is particularly useful in companies manufacturing several different products, because contribution analysis pinpoints production profit. Dangers of the method include possible price wars when the manufacturer lowers his price, and making customers irate who paid the full price before price cuts were made.

SUGGESTED FURTHER READING

Kelvie, W. E., and J. M. Sinclair, "New Techniques for Break-Even Charts," *The Financial Executive*, New York, June 1968.

CONTROL ACCOUNTING

Areas for use in Cost Control:

ORGANIZATIONAL AND OPERATIONAL SYSTEMS
INDUSTRIAL APPLICATIONS
BUSINESS AND COMMERCIAL APPLICATIONS

Control accounting is a technique applied to standard accounting systems to make certain that costs and other factors are tightly controlled. Controls used include **variance analysis** reports and statements, and action stimulation for **costing** and **budgetary control,** as well as organizational checks and audits, **method study,** and communications control.

SUGGESTED FURTHER READING

Backer, Morton, and L. E. Jacobsen, *Cost Accounting: A Managerial Approach,* McGraw-Hill, New York, 1964.
Moonitz, Maurice, and A. C. Littleton, *Significant Accounting Essays,* Prentice-Hall, Englewood Cliffs, N.J., 1965.

COOPERATIVE PRODUCTION

Areas for use in Cost Control:

ORGANIZATIONAL AND OPERATIONAL SYSTEMS
INDUSTRIAL APPLICATIONS

Cooperative production is a combining of manufacturers for materials buying or equipment-use sharing. While operating costs can be reduced through volume materials-buying discounts and through lower capital outlay needed for equipment purchase, the basic problem is forming a workable cooperative group of manufacturers who are not competitive. Use of the technique is more often found in materials purchase, since many types of manufacturers use the same methods to make different products.

SUGGESTED FURTHER READING

Stacey, N. A., and A. Wilson, *The Changing Pattern of Distribution,* Pergamon, New York, 1965.

COOPERATIVE PURCHASING

Areas for use in Cost Control:

ORGANIZATIONAL AND OPERATIONAL SYSTEMS
BUSINESS AND COMMERCIAL APPLICATIONS

Cooperative purchasing is combined purchasing, usually by a voluntary association of independent retailers, in order to take advantage of bulk-buying discounts. Frequently, such retailers are geographically separated, eliminating all or some of the competitive problems inherent in shared purchasing.

SUGGESTED FURTHER READING

Stacey, N. A., and A. Wilson, *The Changing Pattern of Distribution,* Pergamon, New York, 1965.

COPARTNERSHIP

Areas for use in Cost Control:

PSYCHOLOGICAL MOTIVATIONAL MANAGEMENT
FINANCIAL MOTIVATIONAL MANAGEMENT
ORGANIZATIONAL AND OPERATIONAL SYSTEMS
INDUSTRIAL APPLICATIONS
BUSINESS AND COMMERCIAL APPLICATIONS

Copartnership, also called co-ownership, is the involvement of workers in responsibilities and profits of the company. This may be effected through partial ownership plans, giving employees stock in the firm. The method was developed to give employees some rights in their employing firm without resorting to trade unionism. Current use of the method, however, is to motivate (financially and psychologically) the worker, increasing productivity and lowering labor costs. Copartnership also offers tax advantages to the employee that serve as an additional financial motivating factor.

SUGGESTED FURTHER READING

Thompson, William, *Labor Rewarded,* Burt Franklin Publishing, New York, 1971.
Vanek, J., *General Theory of Labor-Managed Market Economics,* Cornell University Press, New York, 1970.

COPYING COST CONTROL See Duplication Cost Control.

CORDER MAINTENANCE EFFICIENCY INDEX

Areas for use in Cost Control:

ORGANIZATIONAL AND OPERATIONAL SYSTEMS
MATERIALS AND EQUIPMENT MANAGEMENT
INDUSTRIAL APPLICATIONS

The Corder maintenance efficiency index is a formula that can be used to determine the efficiency of a specific maintenance or preventive maintenance program, pinpointing areas where cost reduction methods should be applied. Developed by G. C. Corder, the formula is:

$$E = \frac{K}{C + L + W}$$

where E = efficiency index
K = a constant equating E to 100 in the base year
C = maintenance labor and material cost $\div$ equipment replacement cost (these factors may be weighted to balance cash values)
L = downtime $\div$ scheduled operating time
W = percentage of scheduled production wasted because of maintenance

SUGGESTED FURTHER READING

Corder, G. C., *Organizing Maintenance,* British Institute of Maintenance, London, 1971.

CORRESPONDENCE MANAGEMENT

Areas for use in Cost Control:

ORGANIZATIONAL AND OPERATIONAL SYSTEMS
PAPERWORK DESIGN AND FLOW SYSTEMS
INDUSTRIAL APPLICATIONS
BUSINESS AND COMMERCIAL APPLICATIONS

Correspondence management is the most efficient use of letters as a management tool, and includes reducing the costs of business correspondence as well as making all letters sent more effective.

Ways of reducing correspondence costs include the following:

1. Use form letters wherever possible. This saves executive dictation time, as well as typing time.
2. Use format letters when only specific data need to be individualized. This saves executive dictation time.
3. Use up-to-date equipment, such as automatic typewriters and dictating equipment, to reduce both executive and secretarial time.
4. Keep letters simple, saying what is necessary briefly and concisely, saving both executive and secretarial time.

SUGGESTED FURTHER READING

Alldredge, Everett O., "Paperwork Management," *Cost Control and the Supervisor,* American Management Assn., New York, 1966.

COST ANALYSIS

Areas for use in Cost Control:

ORGANIZATIONAL AND OPERATIONAL SYSTEMS
INDUSTRIAL APPLICATIONS

Costs are divided into four major areas:

1. **Direct costs,** or those identifiable with a particular product or department
2. **Variable costs,** or those dependent on volume of output
3. **Fixed costs,** or those unaffected by volume of output
4. **Standard costs,** or those calculated by absorbing fixed costs into units of production

As not all costs can be classified in these categories, *mixed costs* are those combining fixed and variable costs. Two basic techniques are used in analyzing mixed costs, separating them into fixed and variable elements:

1. The **scatter graph** technique charts cost data for a number of periods, and a line is drawn midway between high and low points. *Fixed cost* is the low point; *variable cost* per time unit is the average between the two points with the *fixed cost* subtracted, divided by the number of time units used.

2. The **high-low point method** determines variable costs per unit of production by dividing the difference between the highest and lowest cost for a period by the difference between the highest and lowest measures of production or activity associated with that cost. Fixed cost is determined by subtracting the variable cost from total cost at a given point.

SUGGESTED FURTHER READING
Barclay, S. L., *Cost Analysis and Manpower,* Lexington Books, Lexington, Mass., 1972.

COST AND VARIANCE ANALYSIS

Areas for use in Cost Control:

ORGANIZATIONAL AND OPERATIONAL SYSTEMS
PAPERWORK DESIGN AND FLOW SYSTEMS
INDUSTRIAL APPLICATIONS
BUSINESS AND COMMERCIAL APPLICATIONS

Cost and variance analysis is a technique used to control costs through monthly comparison of actual with budgeted costs. A cost and variance statement (see Fig. 29) is used. These statements are prepared by supervisors for their own area of responsibility and combined for each *cost center* (*see* **Cost Reduction Assessment**) or department.

If the budget used is a *flexible budget* (*see* **Flexible Budgeting**), costs reported on the Cost and Variance Statement are compared with the fixed portion of each cost plus the percentage of standard output actually produced. For example, assume that the fixed portion of total budgeted indirect labor costs is $800, and variable budgeted indirect labor costs are $2,145, with standard production of 4,500 units. Assume further that the Cost and Variance Statement shows that production was 5,000 units, fixed indirect labor costs were $780, and variable indirect labor costs were $2,300. In comparing budgeted and actual costs, fixed labor costs are $20 below the budgeted figure; while variable indirect labor costs are $80 below the budgeted figure, since production was 111 percent of the standard production figure and $2,380 is 111 percent of $2,300.

The difference between actual and budgeted costs is expressed in a plus or minus percentage called the total cost ratio (see Fig. 29). This ratio is used to project current unit production cost for use in setting prices. Using the current-period example in Fig. 29, multiply standard labor and expense per unit ($200) by the total cost ratio (1.073). Current unit cost, then, is $214.60.

The efficiency ratio is also expressed in percentages and is the current allowance proportionate to the actual cost.

Comparison of individual budgeted and actual costs on a regular basis will show areas in need of cost reduction techniques. In Fig. 29, for example, "inside trucking" cost variances are −$110 for one month compared with −$20 for the year to date. Obviously, this area has a cost problem that needs attention.

SUGGESTED FURTHER READING
Maynard, H. B., ed., *Industrial Engineering Handbook,* 3d ed., McGraw-Hill, New York, 1974.

COST-BASED ACCEPTANCE SAMPLING

Areas for use in Cost Control:

ORGANIZATIONAL AND OPERATIONAL SYSTEMS
MATERIALS AND EQUIPMENT MANAGEMENT
INDUSTRIAL APPLICATIONS

Cost-based acceptance sampling uses a mathematical model of production to measure the costs of inspection and unacceptable-product disposition. Cost areas included are:

1. Sampling costs
2. Product-rejection costs
3. Defective-product acceptance and/or transportation costs

VARIANCES This period		NO.	ACCOUNT	Actual year to date	THIS PERIOD Ext. Budg. Allowance	Current Allowance	Actual
(100)	(150)	01	Measured Direct Labor	17,475		4,500	4,600
(100)	(50)	02	Fall Downs	1,350		350	450
5	-	03	Controllable Excess Allow.	515		140	135
(20)	35	05	Unmeasured Direct Labor	2,405		820	840
(215)	(165)		Total Direct Labor	21,745		5,810	6,025
18	16	06	Overtime Premium D. L.	50		18	-
(190)	(205)	07	Setups	2,025		490	680
5	(15)	08	Non-Standard Method	275		70	65
-	-	12	Supervision	1,500		500	500
-	-	14	Clerical	600		200	200
(36)	12	18	Material Checking	300		84	120
(5)	(20)	19	Learning	320		100	105
(110)	(20)	42	Inside Trucking	1,840		490	600
(50)	(60)	51	Inspection	710		175	225
(5)	80	52	Remake	180		70	75
(95)	(105)	62	Mtc.Machinery & Eq.	495		105	200
(468)	(317)		Total Indirect Labor	8,295		2,302	2,770
21	50	101	Shop Supplies	1,940		536	515
(12)	50	102	Power and Light	204		78	90
(10)	10	103	Heat	290		100	110
25	(20)	104	Non-durable Tools	800		210	185
24	90		Total Supplies	3,234		924	900
(659)	(392)		Total Direct Department	33,274		9,036	9,695

THIS PERIOD	PRODUCTION UNIT Standard Allowed Hours		YEAR TO DATE
5,000 Hours	PRODUCTION	STANDARD UNITS	15,000 Hours
3,500 Hours		ACTUAL UNITS	13,000 Hours
$12,500	RECOVERY	STANDARD COSTS	$32,500
$ 8,750		ACTUAL COSTS	$33,274
70%	ACTIVITY (volume) – PERCENT		86.7%
93.2%	EFFICIENCY – PERCENT		98%
107.3	TOTAL COST RATIO		101.2
March PERIOD	COST CENTER Metal Fabrication NO. 10		KEYMAN A.Smith

Figure 29. Typical cost and variance statement prepared for each cost center or department. From H. B. Maynard, *Industrial Engineering Handbook*, 1st ed., McGraw-Hill, New York, 1956.

Sampling costs include operation cost and product cost (in the case of destructive testing).

Product-rejection costs include all production and operation costs per unit minus any scrap value.

Defective products that are not caught in sampling carry the following costs:

1. Transportation to and from the customer
2. Production costs
3. Goodwill and lost future purchases costs

SAMPLE SIZE AND COSTS

The least-cost sample size is determined from comparison of costs in the model, and sampling standards are established accordingly. *Pattern search*—determination of the least-cost sample size by examining only a small number of possible sample sizes with widely diverse numbers—is used for optimum selection.

The method has achieved cost reduction per lot to 80 percent, with reductions of 40 to 50 percent being quite frequent.

SUGGESTED FURTHER READING

Lapedes, D. N., ed., *Yearbook of Science and Technology,* McGraw-Hill, New York, 1974.

COST-BENEFIT ANALYSIS

Areas of use in Cost Control:
PSYCHOLOGICAL MOTIVATIONAL MANAGEMENT
FINANCIAL MOTIVATIONAL MANAGEMENT
WORK PLACE MOTIVATIONAL MANAGEMENT
INDUSTRIAL APPLICATIONS
BUSINESS AND COMMERCIAL APPLICATIONS

In cost-benefit analysis, an attempt is made to place a monetary value on benefits provided for employees. The reason for the analysis is to decide whether the benefit is worth the amount of money spent on it. At one end of the scale, a company may wish to know what it is worth (in terms of greater production by employees as the result of financial or psychological motivation) to have a well-furnished company cafeteria. At the other extreme, a business may want to know the dollars-and-cents value of various safety programs.

Some of the intangibles that may be evaluated in this way are:

1. *Work place facilities:* cafeteria, lounge, outdoor rest areas or parks, parking lot, lighting, ventilation, medical office, library, etc.
2. *Psychological and educational facilities:* advanced training programs, college tuition refund programs, etc.
3. *Personal or family benefits:* life and health insurance, stock option rights, profit sharing, purchase benefits, safety and health programs, etc.

HOW THE TECHNIQUE IS USED

Opinion surveys are the primary means of analyzing the costs of intangible benefits. For example, if a business wants to know how much value its employees place on the company cafeteria, a survey may be taken asking how much greater salary they would need if the cafeteria were not in operation. When considering a new benefit, such as a new parking lot, the surveyors would ask employees how much less salary they would need if the company were to provide a free parking lot.

Psychological and scientific research may be used to determine the value of some intangible benefits. Studies indicating that certain types of chairs alleviate back tension may be used as a basis for evaluating office furniture, for example.

Cost-benefit analysis can help reduce costs by showing which benefits mean the most to the employee, but care must be used in not carrying it to ridiculous extremes and studying every small detail of the many benefits provided by most firms.

SUGGESTED FURTHER READING

Ansoff, H. I., ed., *Business Strategy,* Penguin, Baltimore, 1969.

COST-CONSCIOUSNESS TECHNIQUE

Areas for use in Cost Control:

ORGANIZATIONAL AND OPERATIONAL SYSTEMS
INDUSTRIAL APPLICATIONS
BUSINESS AND COMMERCIAL APPLICATIONS

The cost-consciousness technique is making sure that all employees and, particularly, management are aware of costs and the effect they have on profits, salaries, and bonuses. Employee meetings, posters, newsletters, and other forms of communication are used to create a continued cost consciousness. Employee suggestions to reduce costs are regularly requested and rewarded when used. Success of the technique depends on continued use of varied ways of presenting the facts.

SUGGESTED FURTHER READING

Cost Control in Business, Dun & Bradstreet Business Library, New York, 1970.
Wilson, Frank C., *Industrial Cost Control,* Prentice-Hall, Englewood Cliffs, N.J., 1971.

COST CURVES

Areas for use in Cost Control:

ORGANIZATIONAL AND OPERATIONAL SYSTEMS
MATERIALS AND EQUIPMENT MANAGEMENT
INDUSTRIAL APPLICATIONS
BUSINESS AND COMMERCIAL APPLICATIONS

Cost curves, also called cost lines, are visual comparisons of the amount of alternate materials, supplies, equipment, etc., that can be purchased for the same sum. In Fig. 30,

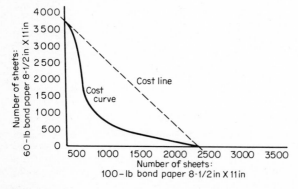

Figure 30. Typical cost curve/cost line for $25 worth of bond paper for office use.

for example, an office manager can compare the amounts of two different papers that can be purchased for $25, choosing the material that is least costly but still of acceptable quality. The cost curve shows the approximate cost saving in use—almost 40 percent in this case.

SUGGESTED FURTHER READING

Hackney, J. W., *Control and Management of Capital Projects,* Wiley, New York, 1965.
Jelen, F. C., *Cost and Optimization Engineering,* McGraw-Hill, New York, 1970.

COST EFFECTIVENESS

Areas for use in Cost Control:

ORGANIZATIONAL AND OPERATIONAL SYSTEMS
INDUSTRIAL APPLICATIONS
BUSINESS AND COMMERCIAL APPLICATIONS

Cost effectiveness is a technique used to determine the most efficient and economical method of producing a service. Alternate methods of providing the service are listed; each is costed, and the least costly method that offers the quality and type of service required is chosen. For example, if a company offers a book search service for hard-to-find or out-of-print books, it may consider the following alternate methods:

1. Stock every book as it is published.
2. Send employees to new and used bookstores to search for required books.
3. Stock book catalogs.
4. Advertise in trade journals.
5. Send inquiry forms to large used-book stores.

After costing, alternatives 1 and 2 would be eliminated, while alternatives 3, 4, and 5 would be placed in order of priority (most likely to succeed).

In addition to aiding in reduction of cost of providing services, the technique helps pinpoint service goals.

SUGGESTED FURTHER READING

Seiler, Karl, *Introduction to Systems Cost Effectiveness,* Wiley, New York, 1969.

COSTING

Areas for use in Cost Control:

ORGANIZATIONAL AND OPERATIONAL SYSTEMS
INDUSTRIAL APPLICATIONS

The techniques of determining the amount spent on particular products, processes, or services are called costing techniques. There are several major techniques of this type in general use; these include **contribution analysis; direct costing; marginal costing; opportunity costing; relevant costing.**

1. *Direct costing.* This method charges off all direct costs to products, processes, or services, leaving other costs to be written off against profits of the period in which they arise. The term is sometimes considered interchangeable with marginal costing, a term more often used in Europe than in the United States.

2. *Marginal costing.* This technique is used to separate fixed and variable elements of cost, to show cost/volume/profit relationships.

3. *Absorption costing.* All manufacturing costs, variable and fixed, are charged to production. While this practice may simplify accounting, it tends to distort income by charging fixed manufacturing overhead to the product.

4. *Relevant costing.* This technique is designed to match costs and income. Costs are carried forward as assets only when they will affect costs or income in the future.

5. *Contribution analysis.* Another costing method, contribution analysis, is designed to show the amount of profit made from each product unit.

6. *Opportunity costing.* This is a forecasting technique used to predict costs to be expected if a specific change in production is implemented.

THE COSTING SYSTEM

Use of one or more of the above costing techniques is meant to allow the user to control costs to a predetermined figure. Sometimes these figures are taken from the previous year's actual figures; sometimes they are figures set out in the company budget. In all costing methods, each cost is recorded using forms designed for the purpose. Costs are then distributed to proper areas, depending on the method used. These are regularly checked against the predetermined, budgeted figure, and corrective steps can be taken to lower the cost if it slips out of line.

Costing techniques are generally used in medium- or large-sized companies, and even here care should be taken not to make the system too detailed to be practical. Nor should such systems waste time in recording costs over which local management has no control. A local store manager, for example, should not have home office overhead costs, nor the share of them that his store has to pay, set out in his report. Use of a computer should accelerate costing, allowing prompt action by management when costs become excessive.

SUGGESTED FURTHER READING

Backer, Morton, and L. E. Jacobsen, *Cost Accounting: A Managerial Approach,* McGraw-Hill, New York, 1974.
Wright, W., *Direct Standard Costs,* McGraw-Hill, New York, 1974.

COST LADDER TECHNIQUE

Areas for use in Cost Control:

ORGANIZATIONAL AND OPERATIONAL SYSTEMS
INDUSTRIAL APPLICATIONS
BUSINESS AND COMMERCIAL APPLICATIONS

The cost ladder technique visually compares production and other costs of competing firms within the same industry (see Table 8). Although it may be difficult to obtain

Table 8. Typical Cost Ladder.

Firm	Production cost/unit
D	$2.93
A	2.80
C	2.65
E	2.41
B	2.39

such cost figures, use of the technique can be extremely helpful in judging the cost efficiency of a particular firm.

The technique is also used to forecast industry conditions. For example, if costs are not similar, firms at the top end of the cost ladder, with highest costs, are apt to be out of production shortly, unless their costs are lowered. Competing firms with lower costs may choose to expand production, on comparison of these figures, to take advantage of the increasing market from such sources.

If costs are exceptionally low, the firm involved may want to check product quality carefully, as compared with competitors' products.

A nearly horizontal cost ladder, one where costs are all nearly the same, may indicate overproduction, since any rise in costs or price drops would affect all producers.

SUGGESTED FURTHER READING

Ellsworth, P. T., *The International Economy,* Macmillan, New York, 1969.

COST-PUSH CONTROL See Inflation Cost Control.

COST RATIOS

Areas for use in Cost Control:

ORGANIZATIONAL AND OPERATIONAL SYSTEMS
DATA RETENTION—FILES AND RECORDKEEPING
INDUSTRIAL APPLICATIONS

Cost ratios, also called expense ratios, compare major cost areas with other factors. The method is used to check cost trends by comparing current ratios with those for past operational periods. Cost ratios generally used include:

1. Research and development costs to sales
2. Production costs to sales
3. Managerial costs to sales
4. Selling costs to sales
5. Capital investment to sales

Cost ratios are also used in establishing new budgets. If a company projects $100,000 in sales for the coming year, for example, various costs can be budgeted by projecting costs from past cost/sales ratios.

SUGGESTED FURTHER READING

Backer, Morton, and L. E. Jacobsen, *Cost Accounting: A Managerial Approach,* McGraw-Hill, New York, 1974.

COST REDUCTION ASSESSMENT

Areas for use in cost control:

ORGANIZATIONAL AND OPERATIONAL SYSTEMS
INDUSTRIAL APPLICATIONS
BUSINESS AND COMMERCIAL APPLICATIONS

Cost reduction assessment is the evaluation of any proposed cost reduction and the method of its achievement to determine feasibility, degree of effectiveness, and both short- and long-term effects. Such assessment is usually made by the accounting department, working with line management where cost reductions are to be applied as well as with top management.

DETERMINING ACCEPTABLE COSTS

In setting a goal by determining the acceptable level of costs:

1. Use the percentages of the company with lowest costs in your business or industry, if obtainable.

2. Use the lowest percentages of past costs achieved by your company.
3. Use a cost level that leaves net profits of about 15 percent, plus an inflationary allowance, of capital investment.
4. Average the figures secured by all three of the above methods.

The difference between "acceptable costs" and "actual costs" should be the minimum goal for cost reduction programs.

POSSIBLE COST REDUCTIONS

Determine areas, or cost centers, where needed cost reductions are feasible. Short-term reductions should be approached first, since these are most numerous and will produce the fastest and largest overall results for time and money spent:

1. **Stock control:** warehousing, materials handling, etc.
2. **Purchasing**
3. Production: all aspects
4. Research and development (*see* **Research and Development Cost Control**)
5. Sales (*see* **Sales/Operations Planning and Control**)
6. Marketing (*see* **Marketing Research**)
7. Administration

Cost reduction methods applying to all of these areas are discussed throughout the book.

COST REDUCTION VERIFICATION

Cost reduction verifications should be made periodically (usually monthly) for all programs and/or techniques in operation:

1. Comparison of costs now and one year ago
2. Comparison of costs now with last year's costs, after allowing for inflation, price changes, and personnel changes
3. Comparison of actual and target costs
4. Cost comparisons by cost center, branch, division, etc., to pinpoint high- and low-success areas

SUGGESTED FURTHER READING

Radke, Magnus, *Manual of Cost Reduction Techniques,* McGraw-Hill, New York, 1972.

COST REDUCTION IMPLEMENTATION

Areas for use in Cost Control:

ORGANIZATIONAL AND OPERATIONAL SYSTEMS
INDUSTRIAL APPLICATIONS
BUSINESS AND COMMERCIAL APPLICATIONS

The following is a simplified procedure for putting specific cost reductions to work:

1. Individual applications of the specific technique are planned.

2. The technique and all details of application for a specific area are set down in writing. Reduction goals should be included.

3. Follow-up verification of operation and degree of success of the technique should be maintained by management and accounting personnel.

4. Responsibility for physical implementation should fall to departmental management, and reports detailing such implementation should be made by them periodically.

5. Employees and line management should be invited to submit additional cost reduction ideas, and suggestions used may be rewarded with a proportion of the first year's anticipated savings.

SUGGESTED FURTHER READING

Radke, Magnus, *Manual of Cost Reduction Techniques,* McGraw-Hill, New York, 1972.

COST REDUCTION INTERVIEWS

Areas for use in Cost Control:

ORGANIZATIONAL AND OPERATIONAL SYSTEMS
INDUSTRIAL APPLICATIONS
BUSINESS AND COMMERCIAL APPLICATIONS

Cost reduction interviews are periodic individual interviews of employees by their supervisors to discuss possible ways of reducing costs. Employees are told about the interviews and their purpose a day or two beforehand to give them time to think about the problem. Suggestions that are used may be rewarded in proportion to costs saved the first year, such as 10 percent.

SUGGESTED FURTHER READING

Cost Control and the Supervisor, American Management Assn., New York, 1966.

COST REDUCTION PERFORMANCE MEASUREMENT

Areas for use in Cost Control:

FINANCIAL MOTIVATIONAL MANAGEMENT
ORGANIZATIONAL AND OPERATIONAL SYSTEMS
INDUSTRIAL APPLICATIONS
BUSINESS AND COMMERCIAL APPLICATIONS

Cost reduction performance measurement is used to evaluate and stimulate managerial effectiveness in reducing costs. This is effected in four ways:

1. Establish profit centers.
2. Evaluate individual managerial profit center contribution.
3. Set goals for future individual managerial profit center contribution.
4. Use incentives geared to companywide cost reduction.

Establish Profit Centers. The scope of each center should be clearly defined. This is usually done by dividing work by function or facility. For example, if functional divisions are used in a factory, all welding would be included in one center. Generally, profit centers should:

1. Have their own material sources.
2. Have their own markets.
3. Be operationally independent.
4. Pay costs separately from other company areas.
5. Receive income separately from other company areas.

Service areas, such as secretarial service, should be included in staff costs, since these performance costs are difficult to establish and cannot be easily applied to profit centers.

Evaluate Individual Managerial Profit Center Contributions. This can be determined by assessing:

1. Center's current profitability in currency value, rate of return on investment, and percent of sales

2. Center's growth as a percent of sales or production unit increase
3. Productivity as increase in unit output per employee or per hour, or rate of return on plant and equipment
4. Product expansion or improvement

Set Goals for Future Individual Managerial Profit Center Contribution. After examining current inputs, establish goals that incorporate increased profit, growth, sales, and productivity for each managerial head of a profit center. Methods for achieving goals at reduced costs should be detailed.

Use Incentives Geared to Companywide Cost Reduction Rather Than to the Profit Center. Successful cost reduction methods are more likely to be shared among center management under such a plan.

SUGGESTED FURTHER READING

Whisler, T. L., and S. F. Harper, *Performance Appraisal,* Holt, New York, 1962.

COST REDUCTION REPORTS

Areas for use in Cost Control:

PSYCHOLOGICAL MOTIVATIONAL MANAGEMENT
FINANCIAL MOTIVATIONAL MANAGEMENT
ORGANIZATIONAL AND OPERATIONAL SYSTEMS
PAPERWORK—DESIGN AND FLOW SYSTEMS
DATA RETENTION—FILES AND RECORDKEEPING
MATERIALS AND EQUIPMENT MANAGEMENT
INDUSTRIAL APPLICATIONS
BUSINESS AND COMMERCIAL APPLICATIONS

Cost reduction reports are used to control purchase or other costs and to measure the effectiveness of reduction efforts. Daily or weekly reports list items with cost changes: amount, reason for, and monthly cost of the change (see Fig. 31). Supplier identification, reason for change, and inventory identification may be coded to save space on the report form. Separate reports should be prepared by each cost center and/or buying group. These provide the basis for setting cost reduction goals.

Cost reduction targets should be set by management, expressed as a percentage of cost (usually 2 to 3 percent). Competition between reporting groups is often encouraged to provide psychological motivation to reduce costs. Financial incentives may be offered for the group achieving the greatest percentage of cost reduction.

SUGGESTED FURTHER READING

Ammer, D. S., *Materials Management,* Irwin, Homewood, Ill., 1968.

COUNSELING See Personnel Morale Building.

CRAWLING PEG

Areas for use in Cost Control:

ORGANIZATIONAL AND OPERATIONAL SYSTEMS
INDUSTRIAL APPLICATIONS
BUSINESS AND COMMERCIAL APPLICATIONS

The crawling peg is a Brazilian method of international monetary exchange that reduces the cost of losses through changes in inflationary rates by revaluation of

Cost–Reduction Report

Week ending _____

Department _____

Price changes

Inventory	Item	Supplier	Old price	New price	New price data	% of change	Reason for change	Monthly use (no.)	Dollar monthly cost change

L = labor cost change   N = negotiated change

M = material cost change   Q = quantity change only

D = design change   O = other

A = alternate material

Figure 31. Typical cost reduction report form.

exchange rates monthly, tied to the Wholesale Price or other index. The method offers more gradual adaptation than the snake-in-the-tunnel, free-floating method, which may fluctuate wildly from day to day based on political as well as economic factors. Yet, the crawling peg prevents losses in the purchasing-power value of monetary exchange that accrues under a fixed-rate system. *See also* **Index Linking; Inflation Cost Control; Inflation Accounting.**

SUGGESTED FURTHER READING

Wilsher, Peter, "Brazil's Cure," *The Sunday Times,* London, July 7, 1974.

CREDIT CONTROL

Areas for use in Cost Control:

ORGANIZATIONAL AND OPERATIONAL SYSTEMS

INDUSTRIAL APPLICATIONS

BUSINESS AND COMMERCIAL APPLICATIONS

Credit control is the planned use of credit, or deferred payment, as a sales tool while restricting capital investment and reducing bad-credit costs. Three basic areas are responsible for efficient credit control:

1. Credit period length
2. Credit limits and qualification
3. Credit terms

Credit Period Length. Each company will establish its own credit period limits. Generally, action for default is taken after an account is 90 days old, although most firms phrase their credit terms as "net in 30 days."

Credit Limits and Qualifications. This area is particularly important since it is much simpler and less costly to prevent bad debt costs than to regain them. New customers desiring credit should be thoroughly investigated and credit granted only to reliable accounts. A credit limit for each customer should be determined at the time of investigation, and passing this limit should trigger an immediate check of circumstances and of possible credit problems.

Credit Terms. Special terms are frequently used to facilitate prompt account payment. These include:

1. Cash discounts for prepayment or payment within a predetermined period (usually 7 or 10 days)
2. Limiting unreliable or new accounts to cash shipments
3. Charging off the debt against one the company has with the customer, if the customer is also a supplier
4. Indexing the account at the end of each 28-day period, raising the amount in proportion to inflation percentage shown on a major national index (*see* **Index Linking**).
5. Charging interest on an unpaid balance after a predetermined period (usually 30 or 60 days)

OTHER CONTROLS

If these standard credit controls do not produce payment, responsibility may be transferred to a third party before, or in place of, legal action. Debt collection companies, discount firms, and some finance companies will purchase "bad" debts for a portion of their face value (usually 50 to 65 percent). Remittances collected then become their property. It is also possible to purchase bad debt insurance.

SUGGESTED FURTHER READING

Bartels, Robert, *Credit Management,* Ronald, New York, 1967.
Bernstein, L., *How to Supervise Credit Accounts,* Beekman Publishing, New York, 1972.
Fiedler, E. R., *Measures of Credit Risk and Experience,* National Bureau of Economic Resources, Washington, D.C., 1971.

CRITICAL INCIDENT RATING See Personnel Performance Appraisal.

CRITICAL PATH ANALYSIS (CPA)

Areas for use in Cost Control:

ORGANIZATIONAL AND OPERATIONAL SYSTEMS
INDUSTRIAL APPLICATIONS
BUSINESS AND COMMERCIAL APPLICATIONS

Critical path analysis (CPA) is a name used for all **network planning and analysis,** as well as for a specific technique. In this section, CPA is discussed only as a separate technique.

A critical path diagram is a diagram of the necessary sequence of activity in a project, including times for each activity (see Fig. 32). The purpose of the technique is to aid in planning and controlling all types of projects. It differs from other techniques in that it uses *only* one estimate of the time and path a project will take.

Looking at Fig. 32, it can be seen that the shortest time in which the project can be completed is 9 months (the total of all times on the *critical path*). Delivery of construction materials is a noncritical factor until 10 days prior to the start of construction, when it moves into the critical path. Likewise, delivery of cleaning materials is a noncritical factor until 1 day prior to the start of building cleanup, when it becomes critical.

SUGGESTED FURTHER READING

Beattie, C. J., and R. D. Reader, *Quantitative Management in R & D,* Barnes & Noble, Cranbury, N.J., 1971.

Figure 32. Typical critical path diagram.

CROWN PRINCE APPROACH

Areas for use in Cost Control:

ORGANIZATIONAL AND OPERATIONAL SYSTEMS
INDUSTRIAL APPLICATIONS
BUSINESS AND COMMERCIAL APPLICATIONS

The crown prince approach is concentration of time and effort to develop one or a few management recruits for top positions, eliminating costs of advanced training and grooming of less qualified recruits who are likely to reach only line- or middle-management levels. Use of the method has received great hostility from recruits not so chosen, and it is now applied in a more subtle form than originally. For example, lists of potential company presidents among management recruits are probably no longer recorded in company records. Instead, the list is informally agreed upon, and altered, by executives responsible for developing such managers. R. K. Stolz of McKinsey & Co., Inc., for example, says that one company originally pursued management development plans for *every* employee above a predetermined salary level. On review, 90 percent of these plans were found to be inoperative—in other words, 90 percent of management development costs were wasted. Thereafter, the company concentrated time and effort on a selected list.

SUGGESTED FURTHER READING

Mann, R., ed., *The Arts of Top Management,* McGraw-Hill, New York, 1970.

CRUCIFORM CHART

Areas for use in Cost Control:

ORGANIZATIONAL AND OPERATIONAL SYSTEMS
INDUSTRIAL APPLICATIONS
BUSINESS AND COMMERCIAL APPLICATIONS

A cruciform chart visually compares cost or other strengths, weaknesses, threats, and opportunities (see Table 9, p. 94) established from various data evaluations to aid in planning the most cost-effective company strategy.

SUGGESTED FURTHER READING

Argenti, John, *Systematic Corporate Planning,* Thomas Nelson and Sons, London, 1974.

Table 9. Typical Cruciform Chart

Strengths	Weaknesses
State of industrial technology	Cost of equipment
R&D manager	Sales force
Cost of materials	

Threats	Opportunities
Economy, including inflation	Automation possibilities
Labor union demands	New markets

CUBE/ORDER INDEX

Areas for use in Cost Control:

ORGANIZATIONAL AND OPERATIONAL SYSTEMS
INDUSTRIAL APPLICATIONS

The cube/order index is a technique used to determine the least costly method of constructing storage patterns in warehouse layout. *See also* **Warehouse Layout Design.**

A cube/order index, measuring space needs and demand frequency for a product, is constructed in ascending order (see Table 10).

Table 10. Typical Cube/Order Index

Product	Cu ft required	No. orders per day	Zone	Pickup cost each	Total pickup cost
A	10,000	500	1	15¢	$ 75.00
B	12,000	350	2	20¢	70.00
C	15,000	200	3	35¢	70.00
D	50,000	600	4	60¢	360.00

The number of cubic feet required for each product is divided by daily orders for each to determine cube/order index ranking. Rankings for Table 10 are:

A500 ÷ 10,000 = 0.05
B350 ÷ 12,000 = 0.0275
C200 ÷ 15,000 = 0.0133
D600 ÷ 50,000 = 0.012

Arranged in declining order, Product A is assigned to Zone 1, Product B to Zone 2, Product C to Zone 3, and Product D to Zone 4. This allows the shortest handling requirements for the most popular and least-capacity-sized goods, reducing overall warehouse handling costs.

SUGGESTED FURTHER READING

Magee, J. F., *Physical Distribution Systems,* McGraw-Hill, New York, 1967.

CUMULATED POINTS RATING See Personnel Performance Appraisal.

CUMULATIVE SUM TECHNIQUE

Areas for use in Cost Control:
ORGANIZATIONAL AND OPERATIONAL SYSTEMS
DATA RETENTION—FILES AND RECORDKEEPING
MATERIALS AND EQUIPMENT MANAGEMENT
INDUSTRIAL APPLICATIONS
BUSINESS AND COMMERCIAL APPLICATIONS

The cumulative sum technique is the evaluation of a sequence of cost or other figures by subtracting a constant quantity from each figure and adding a running balance with each new figure. This running balance is called the cumulative sum, and can be used in many areas, including:

1. *Quality control*—continuing measurement of process and/or product performance, which allows rapid correction of problem areas before excessive poor-quality costs are incurred

2. *Sales and other forecasts*—where continued measurement allows adequate planning without unjustified and excessive costs

3. *Accounting*—pinpointing of cost areas where costs are rising and in need of control

In using the cumulative sum technique, the first step is to draw up a cumulative sum table (see Table 11). For example, suppose the accounting department wishes to study

Table 11. Cumulative Sum Table, with a Constant Factor of $2,000

Time interval	Secretarial cost	Difference from C	Cumulative sum
Jan. 1–31	$2,050	+$ 50	+$ 50
Feb. 1–28	2,200	+ 200	+ 250
Mar. 1–31	2,300	+ 300	+ 550
Apr. 1–30	1,950	− 50	+ 500
May 1–31	2,240	+ 240	+ 740
June 1–30	2,500	+ 500	+ 1,240

the cost of secretarial services, including temporary secretaries. The costs are first divided into sets, or time periods. These may be periods of one year, five years, ten years, or whatever time is necessary to provide an adequate working background. The cumulative sum formula, $S - C$ (Set − Constant factor), reflects the various sets with numerical classifications, such as S_1 and S_2. The constant factor, which may be zero, is the lowest probable common unit of the figure being evaluated. For instance, if the lowest cost in a series of costs is $50, this amount is subtracted from *all* figures in the series as a matter of convenience, eliminating the need to work with unnecessarily large figures.

A cumulative sum chart (see Fig. 33, p. 96) is drawn from the table, since visual presentation of the costs or other figures' increase or decrease is easier to evaluate.

As an accountant viewed the chart in Fig. 33, his or her first questions about secretarial costs would be:

1. Why did costs increase in January and February?
2. Why did costs drop sharply in March? Can the causes of the drop somehow be extended?
3. Why did costs increase so very rapidly in April and May? How can these costs be reduced?

A *decision boundary* should be established on a cumulative sum chart. This is the maximum variation, in original cost or other figures, that may be reached before action to control the cost or other factor is taken. For example, in the example set out above, assume that a ±10 percent decision boundary of the original figure is used. This boundary would be added to the cumulative sum chart in Fig. 33 as indicated by line *A,*

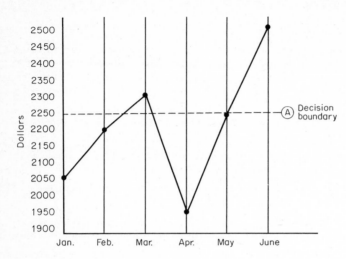

Figure 33. Cumulative sum chart.

and the accounting department would initiate action when the costs first passed the boundary on March 1. If a negative decision boundary was passed, action would also be initiated—to determine the reasons for the cost reductions and to attempt to apply them in other operational areas.

Decision boundary levels can be best determined as a percentage of the cumulative sum for previous time periods, or sets, when such figures are available, since the beginning figure in a set may not be typical.

SUGGESTED FURTHER READING

Brock, H. R., *Cost Accounting,* McGraw-Hill, New York, 1971.
DeCoster, D. T., *Accounting for Managerial Decision Making,* Wiley, New York, 1974.
Page, E. S., "Cumulative Sum Charts," *Technometrics,* 1961.
Woodward, R. H., and P. L. Goldsmith, *Cumulative Sum Techniques,* Oliver & Boyd, Edinburgh, 1964.

CUSTOMER COST ANALYSIS

Areas for use in Cost Control:

ORGANIZATIONAL AND OPERATIONAL SYSTEMS
INDUSTRIAL APPLICATIONS
BUSINESS AND COMMERCIAL APPLICATIONS

Customer cost analysis is the determination and evaluation of the cost of providing the same product or service to different groups of customers, so that marketing can be oriented toward those groups that entail the lowest costs. Costs of selling the same product or service to different types of customers vary in the following areas:

Distribution. Distribution costs vary from production to customer, including any intermediate moves such as to a warehouse or retail outlet. The fewer intermediaries involved, the lower the cost. Concentrated buying of products or services in bulk, such as cooperative purchasing directly from the producer, eliminates all intermediate distribution costs.

Geographical distribution is generally averaged, but where large markets for a product or service exist in a geographical area near the production area, cost of servicing such customers will, of course, be lower.

Handling, as well as distance, affects costs. If products can be containerized or palletized to avoid excessive handling, intermediate distribution becomes less costly. Thus, selling to customers through port A, where dockers have agreed to allow container vessels, is less costly than selling to customers through port B, where unions have prevented the use of containers.

Selling. The salesperson's time and expenses are costs that also vary from customer to customer. The size of the order is one factor, since a $500,000 order requires proportionally less time per dollar than a $5,000 order. Time spent explaining display and promotional programs is about equal for large and small customers, again providing a lower cost factor when servicing large customers.

Order Paperwork. Costs are about the same for processing invoices of all sizes, so there is a lower cost factor on large orders. Equally, customers who place large orders less frequently cost less to service than customers who place small orders very frequently.

Credit. Customers who pay invoices and/or statements promptly are less costly to service than those who must be prompted. Accounting devices can be established to screen high-cost credit customers. *See also* **Credit Control.**

COST DETERMINATION

After studying sales and accounting records, a written determination should be made of these four cost areas for each major customer group. Average cost for all groups should also be determined to provide a basis for comparison. Graphs and outline flowcharts may be helpful in establishing a visual presentation of the costs.

COST EVALUATION

Customer groups who are more costly than average to service should gradually be screened out, and both sales and marketing attempts should be aimed at the large-volume (in a few orders), fast-paying customers.

SUGGESTED FURTHER READING
Dudick, T. S., *Profile for Profitability,* Wiley, New York, 1972.

CUSUM CHARTS

Areas for use in Cost Control:
ORGANIZATIONAL AND OPERATIONAL SYSTEMS
MATERIALS AND EQUIPMENT MANAGEMENT
INDUSTRIAL APPLICATIONS

Cusum charts measure the *cumulative* deviation in cost or quality-control observations, providing more precise control than is possible with control charts where small but gradually increasing changes are less likely to be noticed. In a cost control chart (see Fig. 34), cost variations may remain within action lines. Once such variations are accumulated on a cusum chart with results as in Fig. 35, however, it is obvious that total cost excesses require action.

SUGGESTED FURTHER READING

Chatfield, C., *Statistics for Technology,* Penguin, Baltimore, 1970.
Rickmers, A. D., and H. N. Todd, *Statistics,* McGraw-Hill, New York, 1967.

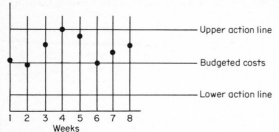

Figure 34. Cost control chart.

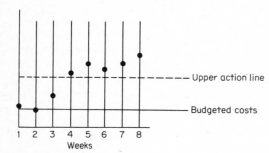

Figure 35. Cusum cost chart.

CYBERNETICS

Areas for use in Cost Control:

PSYCHOLOGICAL MOTIVATION
ORGANIZATIONAL AND OPERATIONAL SYSTEMS
INDUSTRIAL APPLICATIONS
BUSINESS AND COMMERCIAL APPLICATIONS

Cybernetics can be defined as basically scientific methods of control of problems and communication. This science is useful in almost any area of business management but particularly in psychological motivation and in reducing the costs of systems organization and operation.

WHAT CYBERNETICS ARE

Cybernetics were originally developed as a way of looking at existing problems and solution techniques—particularly in the area of communications. The new science uses mathematics to aid the interaction between men and machines and to help give the best understanding of people, their needs, and their wants. Because computers are the most efficient method of implementing cybernetic techniques to date, they are widely used in applications.

Today's cybernetics are more exact developments of trial-and-error techniques. Once management might have installed a new operation to see how it worked. Now, using cybernetics, it is possible to test the operation before going to the expense of installation. A cybernetic deduction concerning the advisability and profitability of a new installation, for example, would be reached through the following steps:

1. Observations (data) are fed into a computer.
2. The computer checks the assumptions against possible consequences.
3. The computer arrives at a deduction—or what is most likely to happen.

To put this technique into more real-life terms, suppose, for example, that you are considering installation of a new incentive plan. If you try it on the entire company's labor force, a great deal of time and money may be wasted before you know if the plan actually motivates the workers and cuts costs. If you try it on one person, it will not necessarily tell you how the majority of your workers will react to the plan. But if you use departmental groups, installing the new incentive plan in one and maintaining the old wage system in another, observation of production of the two groups will allow you to determine whether use of the incentive plan makes a significant difference in motivation and, therefore, in reducing costs.

For a large company, observation data would be fed into a correctly programmed computer and it would make the logical deduction. Thus, scientific cybernetics are really an extension of common sense, using computers or other methods to collate data and reach a logical conclusion, when the body of information is too large to be quickly handled by the human mind.

SEMANTICS AND COMMUNICATION

Lack of control in communication is, perhaps, the largest single negative factor in getting the most work from employees. It is also probably the most expensive factor. Top management may give instructions that are not clear to supervisory personnel, for example. Rather than be embarrassed by admitting they do not understand, the supervisors may try to transmit as much of the instructions as they can to the work force. We can be almost certain that the employees cannot understand these watered-down orders at all, and so the misunderstanding mushrooms down the hierarchy, slowing production and raising costs.

Semantics can be defined as making sure the common-sense meanings of communication are clear—that is, that employees understand what is being said to them whether it is about how to operate a new piece of equipment or how to update a price list in a retail store.

Semantic confusion is commonplace in the business world because the people involved do not bother to make their meaning clear. For example, if a foreman tells his workers, "Assembly of components will be paid for at the rate of 20 cents each up to the standard amount and then 25 cents each," there may be two areas of confusion. First, the worker does not know what number of units is considered *standard*. Second, he or she cannot be sure whether passing the standard means that *all* units will be paid for at 25 cents each or that *only* those assembled after the standard has been passed. If these two areas are not presented clearly, the incentive scheme—intended to motivate greater production—will fail to do its job, wasting time and money rather than reducing costs.

The best semantic use means stating communications in words that can be understood, as well as stating them completely and concisely. For instance, if a floor supervisor tells a retail salesclerk, "Your recalcitrance prevents you from making sales to nine out of ten customers," the clerk must know what "recalcitrance" means before he or she can have any understanding of the sentence.

One of the best guides to cybernetic control of communication—using words in a way that can be clearly understood—is the following checklist developed by A. E. Van Vogt and based on work of the early cyberneticist, Count Alfred Korzybski:

1. Be aware that the subject of your communication has many qualities. In making a statement about an object or an event, an individual "abstracts" only a few of its characteristics. If he or

she says the machine is noisy, this means that noisiness is one of its qualities; yet the communication does not make the listener aware of the fact that the machine also has many other qualities.

2. Date, when you communicate. Do not say, "Management believes. . . ." Rather, say, "In 1980 management believes. . . ." Since all things are subject to change, it is not practical to make a statement without attaching a date to it.

3. Use *et cetera* when you communicate. If a supervisor says, "John is a good worker," the listener should also be aware that John is many other things in addition to being a good worker.

4. Be careful not to *label*. Words like Fascist, Communist, Democrat, Republican, Catholic, and Jew refer to human beings, who never quite fit any one label.

5. Be conscious of the many-valued words one hears or speaks.

6. Learn to evaluate an event in terms of total response; nervous changes, emotional reaction, thought about the event, the spoken statement, action repressed, action taken, etc.

7. Remember that the "map is not the territory," the word is not the thing it describes. Particularly in communication about mechanical processes, it is easy to get carried away with the equipment and the process, and to forget that these only exist to serve a purpose. In the use of a computer, for example, employees can become so involved in the operation of the equipment that they forget about accomplishing goals for which the computer was purchased or rented.

8. General semantics is a discipline, not a philosophy. Its rules must be followed for clear communication, not merely considered.

ORGANIZATIONAL AND OPERATIONAL SYSTEMS AND CYBERNETICS

Because computerized methods of organizational and operational systems control are faster and less costly than other methods, business is turning to cybernetics. This cybernetic or computerized control of systems and equipment is quite simply automation. At the most basic level, automation may be a timed switch that turns on guard lights at dusk. At a more complex level, automation processes make observations and deductions, replacing the most detailed human thinking and decision making, assuming that data fed into the computer are accurate.

Cybernetic reorganization will, in the future, lead to a much greater degree of automation in factories, stores, and offices.

The primary reason for this will be the need to cut salary and wage expense as labor costs rise. While simpler jobs, such as filling a processed food package, have been fully automated for some time in most factories, the design of automated equipment can eventually replace almost every level of workers.

Automation has already made remarkable progress, and the following jobs are some of the areas where automation is already feasible and in use:

1. All storage processes can be automatic.
2. All production processes, including assembly, can be automatic.
3. All inspection can be automatic.

In addition, by 1985, all office work *can be* automated, as can many areas of management, retail sales, and maintenance.

Some of these automated methods will be electronically operated. Others will require human operators, spread over a much larger area of work than one person could handle alone. A good example of this is the electronic guard system. One person is now able to watch several areas requiring plant security control by means of a closed-circuit television camera in each location, relaying a constant series of pictures to a bank of television screens.

COMPUTERS AND CYBERNETICS

Computers are necessary to cybernetics—and will be until a more efficient means of control is devised. Once programmed correctly, computers (*see* **Electronic Data Processing**) provide a scientific and accurate means of control. In a cybernetic factory, jobs that we want completely automated to be done by a machine rather than a person will have a set of how-to-do-it instructions (a program) in a memory bank of the computer. Once this program is fed into the computer, whether the job is filing correspondence in a government office or assembling radio transistor units in a factory, the work can be repeated automatically.

DECISION MAKING

Cybernetics are also of considerable value in forecasting sales markets, economic trends, etc. Business success often depends on these factors, as does cost reduction or control. A computer programmed with all details of the worldwide energy situation, for example, could predict when oil prices might rise and by how much, the likelihood and economics of solar power within the next 10 years, and the effect that power shortages would have on the availability of a skilled work force in certain geographical areas. With this sort of knowledge of probabilities literally at management's finger tips, the opportunities for cost reduction are great. Oil purchases and storage could be planned to give the greatest economic advantage, equipment could be scheduled to phase out when new solar-operated equipment will be available, and new plants could be situated in the best location in view of the local work force needs.

PROGRAMMING FOR NATURAL LANGUAGE

Any executive who has spent some time watching a computer in operation knows that most businesses translate facts that are to be fed into the computer into mathematical equations. Computer programmers and operators have built up a certain mystique that may seem baffling to the management person who does not understand computer language and who feels he or she does not have time to learn it. Because the management person does not understand computers well, he or she may be overlooking many cost-reducing operations that the equipment can facilitate.

In fact, however, the executive does not need to learn "computerese." Newly designed equipment can be programmed to allow conversation between the executive and the computer—in the executive's own language. In addition, once a computer is programmed for natural language, further programming can be carried out in that language—that is, the executive can speak or write facts in his or her own language to be retained or used by the computer. Such a computer can deal with:

1. Experience
2. Meaning
3. Environment

For example, if a computer has been programmed with details about employment hiring and turnover, and the personnel manager checks the three top job applicants through the conversation computer, a very simple exchange might be something like the following:

Personnel Manager: "So you see, educational and experience factors are almost identical for all three. Fred is 25 and single, though, while John is 30 and married with one child. Bill is 45, married, and has two grown children, but his first 15 years of work experience were in a nonrelated field."

Computer: "Since married employees change jobs less frequently, and since John has more potential working years left than Bill, it would be best to hire John."

Of course, a computer is not needed for making this simple kind of decision, but it can handle extremely complicated exchanges, weighing all factors, almost instantaneously. Using one computer for an entire factory, or for several factories owned by the same company, also allows the observation of the business as a whole—rather than just the part that one person can know and understand. This control of the business as a single organism, rather than by local, sectional, or functional managements, grows more important as big business becomes the rule rather than the exception.

SUGGESTED FURTHER READING

Beer, Stafford, *The Brain of the Firm: A Development in Management Cybernetics,* McGraw-Hill, New York, 1972.
George, F. H., *The Anatomy of Business: An Introduction to Business Cybernetics,* Halsted Press, New York, 1974.
Jeffrey, R. C., *The Logic of Decision,* McGraw-Hill, 1965.
Korzybski, A., *Science and Sanity,* Science Press, London, 1933.
Martin, James, and Adrian R. O. Norman, *The Computerized Society,* Prentice-Hall, Englewood Cliffs, N.J., 1970.

CYBERVEILLANCE

Areas for use in Cost Control:

ORGANIZATIONAL AND OPERATIONAL SYSTEMS
INDUSTRIAL APPLICATIONS
BUSINESS AND COMMERCIAL APPLICATIONS

Cyberveillance is the constant monitoring of cost or other problems by computers that process relevant data and initiate action when the situation varies from the programmed norm.

SUGGESTED FURTHER READING

Martin, James, and Adrian R. D. Norman, *The Computerized Society,* Prentice-Hall, Englewood Cliffs, N.J., 1970.

CYCLEGRAPH TECHNIQUE

Areas for use in Cost Control:

ORGANIZATIONAL AND OPERATIONAL SYSTEMS
INDUSTRIAL APPLICATIONS
BUSINESS AND COMMERCIAL APPLICATIONS

The cyclegraph technique is a work study method (*see* **Work Study and Measurement**) used in obtaining the most efficient (and lowest-cost) work from employees. Photographs record motion and pattern of movement of lights attached to the worker's hands, fingers, or other body parts.

SUGGESTED FURTHER READING

ASME Work Standardization Bulletin, American Society of Mechanical Engineers, New York.
Maynard, H. B., ed., *Industrial Engineering Handbook,* 3d ed., McGraw-Hill, New York, 1974.

DECENTRALIZATION

Areas for use in Cost Control:

ORGANIZATIONAL AND OPERATIONAL SYSTEMS
INDUSTRIAL APPLICATIONS
BUSINESS AND COMMERCIAL APPLICATIONS

Decentralization is diversification of control. Use of the method gives tighter control, thus lowering costs, in large and/or complex organizations. Control is usually assigned by area of responsibility or by process.

SUGGESTED FURTHER READING

Speight, H., *Economics and Industrial Efficiency,* Macmillan, New York, 1967.

DECISION ACCOUNTING

Areas for use in Cost Control:

ORGANIZATIONAL AND OPERATIONAL SYSTEMS
INDUSTRIAL APPLICATIONS
BUSINESS AND COMMERCIAL APPLICATIONS

Decision accounting is a technique used to compare and choose between alternate courses of action by examining available cost data. Capital investment, operational details, pricing of production, and possible subcontracting are some of the cost areas included. Likely cost, profit, and total production results to be expected if an alternative is chosen are translated into statistical form for the comparison, so that the potential risks and gains involved can be judged.

SUGGESTED FURTHER READING

Backer, Morton, and L. E. Jacobsen, *Cost Accounting: A Managerial Approach,* McGraw-Hill, New York, 1974.
Moonitz, Maurice, and A. C. Littleton, *Significant Accounting Essays,* Prentice-Hall, Englewood Cliffs, N.J., 1972.

DECISION THEORY

Areas for use in Cost Control:

ORGANIZATIONAL AND OPERATIONAL SYSTEMS
INDUSTRIAL APPLICATIONS
BUSINESS AND COMMERCIAL APPLICATIONS

Decision theory is an **operations research** technique using complex mathematical theories to correct inaccurate forecasts. Forecasts are examined to pinpoint the error and indicate potential costs and incomes from various possible courses of action. The *best* course of action, considering the forecast errors, is then chosen. Computers are generally used for mathematical computation.

SUGGESTED FURTHER READING

Avi-Itzhak, Benjamin, *Developments in Operations Research,* Gordon Press, New York, 1974.
Cyert, R. M., and L. A. Welsch, *Management Decision Making,* Penguin, Baltimore, 1971.
Gupta, S. K., and G. M. Cozzolino, *Fundamentals of Operations Research for Management,* Holden-Day, Inc., San Francisco, 1974.

DECISION TREES

Areas for use in Cost Control:

ORGANIZATIONAL AND OPERATIONAL SYSTEMS
INDUSTRIAL APPLICATIONS
BUSINESS AND COMMERCIAL APPLICATIONS

Decision trees are an offshoot of **branching networks** and are diagrams, similar to family history charts, showing various possible decisions and the probable results of each.

They are most often used in choosing between research projects but can be used in making any business decision, including cost reduction decisions.

The method reviews the sequence of decisions already taken and, based on past action, indicates probable outcomes of several branches of future decisions. Action is then taken, using the branch the chart indicates most likely to ensure success.

In Fig. 36, a decision tree considers a hypothetical decision regarding the purchase of materials. Will the company be ahead if it buys a warehouse and stores needed

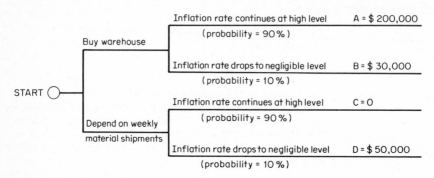

Figure 36. Decision tree.

production materials purchased now, for a future period of three years, before material prices are inflated? Or should it continue to depend upon weekly materials shipments with ever-increasing prices? If the estimated savings (assuming inflation continues at current rates for three years) are $200,000 ($A$), multiply this figure by the hypothetical 90 percent probability, obtaining $180,000. Using the same method, factor B would equal $3,000 ($30,000 × 0.10), factor C would equal 0, and factor D (the savings here are the cost of the warehouse if the decision is made not to purchase it) would equal $50,000. Factors A and B (one decision choice) equal $183,000, while factors C and D (the alternate decision choice) equal $50,000. Therefore, the company would decide to buy a warehouse.

While this technique is interesting, to accurately estimate the needed probabilities is very difficult, and only accurate probabilities assure dependability for the method.

A secondary use of the technique is as an aid to executive awareness of possible lines of action.

SUGGESTED FURTHER READING

Feller, W., *An Introduction to Probability Theory and Its Applications*, Wiley, New York, 1950.
Whitehouse, G. E., *Systems Analysis and Design Using Network Techniques*, Prentice-Hall, Englewood Cliffs, N.J., 1973.

DEDUCTIVE METHOD OF COST CONTROL

Areas for use in Cost Control:
ORGANIZATIONAL AND OPERATIONAL SYSTEMS
INDUSTRIAL APPLICATIONS
BUSINESS AND COMMERCIAL APPLICATIONS

The deductive method of cost control involves starting from a proposed cost theory and applying the theory to specific cost problems, making logical deductions. These deductions are then established as cost laws and are used to reduce and control costs in similar future cost situations.

SUGGESTED FURTHER READING

Speight, H., *Economics and Industrial Efficiency,* Macmillan, New York, 1967.

DEEP ORGANIZATION

Areas for use in Cost Control:

ORGANIZATIONAL AND OPERATIONAL SYSTEMS
INDUSTRIAL APPLICATIONS
BUSINESS AND COMMERCIAL APPLICATIONS

   Deep organization divides work by level of skill required. Skilled jobs are near the top of the organizational structure, while unskilled ones are at the bottom (see Fig. 37).

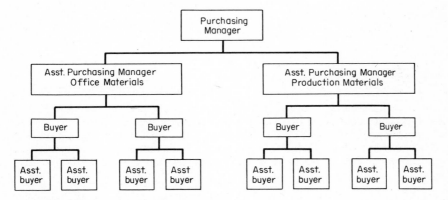

Figure 37. Typical deep organization chart.

Use of the method reduces labor costs because it lowers the number of highly skilled (and thus, highly salaried) employees needed for efficient operation.

SUGGESTED FURTHER READING

Ammer, D. S., *Materials Management,* Irwin, Homewood, Ill., 1968.

DEFERRED PAYMENT

Areas for use in Cost Control:

ORGANIZATIONAL AND OPERATIONAL SYSTEMS
INDUSTRIAL APPLICATIONS
BUSINESS AND COMMERCIAL APPLICATIONS

   Deferred payment is the paying of costs at a future time rather than at the time costs are incurred. Use of the technique reduces the real value of costs in an inflationary economy, since the value of money paid will be less at a future time.

SUGGESTED FURTHER READING

Speight, H., *Economics and Industrial Efficiency,* Macmillan, New York, 1967.

DEFICIT FINANCING

Areas for use in Cost Control:

ORGANIZATIONAL AND OPERATIONAL SYSTEMS
INDUSTRIAL APPLICATIONS
BUSINESS AND COMMERCIAL APPLICATIONS

Deficit financing is the practice of purposely budgeting more expenses than income. When such expenses are for capital improvement, such as equipment and plant, use of the method can reduce the real value of such costs in an inflationary economy, since the value of money will be less when payment is made at a later date.

Deficit financing has been traditionally used by national governments to encourage spending during recessional periods by collecting less tax money than the amount budgeted and spent to increase purchasing power and demand for consumer goods.

SUGGESTED FURTHER READING

Speight, H., *Economics and Industrial Efficiency,* Macmillan, New York, 1967.

DELIVERY ENGINEERING

Areas for use in Cost Control:

ORGANIZATIONAL AND OPERATIONAL SYSTEMS
INDUSTRIAL APPLICATIONS

Delivery engineering is setting and meeting company delivery schedules at the lowest possible cost, yet with acceptable speed and quality of labor. With the use of centralized control, all aspects of delivery are coordinated, including the following:

1. *Delivery scheduling.* Realistic delivery dates are provided to customers. Care is especially taken to see that salespeople do not advance such dates.
2. *Supplier and subcontractor* inputs are controlled to maintain production status.
3. *Production processes* are controlled to maintain schedule status.
4. *Customer feedback channels* are maintained to ensure operability of the system.

Control of suppliers and subcontractors may be implemented through use of a vendor rating list (*see* **Vendor Rating Formula**). Here, the purchasing department is provided with a list of acceptable and nonacceptable suppliers and subcontractors as regards delivery of materials or completion of work as contracted.

Scheduling of internal production can be controlled by various techniques, such as **capacity planning and scheduling,** which provides maximum production without overtime or other unnecessary costs.

SUGGESTED FURTHER READING

Murphy, George J., *Transport and Distribution,* Beekman Publishing, New York, 1972.

DELPHI METHOD

Areas for use in Cost Control:

ORGANIZATIONAL AND OPERATIONAL SYSTEMS
INDUSTRIAL APPLICATIONS
BUSINESS AND COMMERCIAL APPLICATIONS

The delphi method is using expert advice to determine when specific things can be made to happen and/or when and how events will affect specific projects. For example, a company may wish to determine the soonest possible time when a lower-cost source of power to operate equipment will be available. Several experts are chosen from areas relating to the problem, such as nuclear power, solar power, and geothermal power, for the example given above. Printed questionnaires or personal interviews may be used to obtain information relating to the project, its timing, costs, etc. Group forecasters then review data from the experts and project answers to the original questions based on all inputs, including their own experience. These projections are returned to the experts for evaluation. A consensus of opinion using all inputs is reached, so that a reasonable forecast is provided.

SUGGESTED FURTHER READING

Hoyle, Peter, *Delphi,* Fernhill House, Highland, N.J., 1967.
Smith, P. I. S., *Think Tanks and Problem Solving,* Business Books, London, 1971.
The Delphi Method III: Use of Self-Ratings to Improve Group Estimates, The Rand Corp., 1969.

DEMAND DETERMINATION

Areas for use in Cost Control:

ORGANIZATIONAL AND OPERATIONAL SYSTEMS
INDUSTRIAL APPLICATIONS
BUSINESS AND COMMERCIAL APPLICATIONS

Demand determination is a technique used to forecast what goods and/or services will be most salable to the public at a predetermined time. Use of the method reduces selling costs and eliminates the cost of wasted production that results from failing to find sufficient markets for production. While demand is determined by the consumer, affecting retail trade first, effects of demand follow the distribution of any product, eventually reaching the product's manufacturer as well as the supplier of raw materials.

In determining the demand for a specific product or service, the following should be considered:

1. Number of potential users in the market area, their average income, and their average disposable income (after taxes and basic expenses are subtracted)
2. Local and/or personality-type preferences of potential users in the market area
3. Price of the product or service related to disposable income of potential users

Thus, incomes, preferences, and prices and their relationship to each other determine demand. Several methods are used to show such relationships, including:

1. Price-elasticity concept
2. Income-elasticity concept
3. Cross-elasticity concept

The price-elasticity concept shows the relationship of demand to price. Market studies are made to determine the effects of price change on demand for products or services. The results of such studies can then be recorded in table form (see Table 12). Users are divided into types by their reaction to prices.

Table 12. Typical Price-Elasticity Table

Price of ground beef	Type users—by demand, lbs/wk			Total demand, lbs/wk
	A	*B*	*C*	
2.00	100	0	0	100
1.75	110	15	0	125
1.50	125	50	10	185
1.25	175	60	40	275
1.00	200	90	60	350
0.75	225	110	90	425

From such a table the fall in demand is measured against a rise in prices to determine the effect, which is then expressed in percentages. In Table 12, for example, a price increase of about 33 percent from 75 cents to $1 per pound results in a demand decrease of about 17½ percent, while a price increase of about 14 percent from $1.75 to $2 per pound results in a demand decrease of 20 percent. Such statistics can be extended to similar price increases on similar products or services (low-cost cuts of meat, in the case of Table 12) to forecast how consumers will react to price changes.

The income-elasticity concept shows the relationship of demand to price caused by income factors such as total income, disposable income, and size of family. In this case an algebraic formula is drawn up to show desired factors, and a price-demand schedule is drawn up to show the effects of each factor. In the case of measuring an income factor, for example, a family may spend $3 a week on beef when its income is $5,000 a year. When its income reaches $10,000 a year, it may spend 300 percent of this amount, or $9 per week, for beef. When its income reaches $20,000 per year, the percentage of demand increase for beef should fall, however, since a saturation point may be reached. Thus, formulas based on such market research will show the degree of elasticity for demand increases related to income factor increases.

The cross-elasticity concept shows that the increase or decrease in demand for one product can cause the increase or decrease in demand for related products. For example, if falling beef prices cause increased demand for steak, demand for related products such as steak knives and steak sauces will also increase. Market studies of demand for related products, therefore, can be a valuable tool in determining overall demand.

SUGGESTED FURTHER READING

Gynther, R., *Accounting for Price Level Changes,* Pergamon, New York, 1966.
Speight, H., *Economics and Industrial Efficiency,* Macmillan, New York, 1967.

DEPARTMENTAL COSTING

Areas for use in Cost Control:

ORGANIZATIONAL AND OPERATIONAL SYSTEMS
DATA RETENTION—FILES AND RECORDKEEPING
INDUSTRIAL APPLICATIONS
BUSINESS AND COMMERCIAL APPLICATIONS

Departmental costing applies separate **costing** by department to determine the need for cost reductions in specific departments and to give greater cost control.

SUGGESTED FURTHER READING

Bigg, W. F., *Cost Accounting,* MacDonald, London, 1963.

DEPRECIATION AND COST CONTROL

Areas for use in Cost Control:

ORGANIZATIONAL AND OPERATIONAL SYSTEMS
DATA RETENTION—FILES AND RECORDKEEPING
MATERIALS AND EQUIPMENT MANAGEMENT
INDUSTRIAL APPLICATIONS
BUSINESS AND COMMERCIAL APPLICATIONS

The method used to compute depreciation of plant and equipment can reduce tax costs in many cases. This is particularly true with newer techniques designed to deal with inflation.

Historic depreciation methods are based on estimating the productive hours of life of the plant or equipment and its scrap value at the end of that period. Scrap value is subtracted from original cost, and the balance is divided by the expected life (in years), resulting in an annual depreciation cost schedule. This is the *straight-line depreciation* method.

If, for tax or other purposes, a company wishes to take a greater proportion of the depreciation while the plant or equipment is relatively new, it may depreciate it on a *diminishing value schedule.* Here, for example, two-thirds of the value may be depreciated over the first half of the plant or equipment's lifetime while the remaining third is spread over the second half.

Table 13. Typical Replacement Cost
Depreciation Schedule

Year	Annual depreciation	Replacement cost
1	$ 1,000	$10,000
2	1,200	12,000
3	1,425	14,250
4	1,660	16,600
5	1,885	18,850
6	2,100	21,000
7	2,340	23,400
8	2,450	24,500
9	2,510	25,100
10	2,630	26,300
Total	$18,700	

Obsolescence and/or *deterioration depreciation* schedules may be added to the basic schedules above to account for costs of the equipment or plant during idle time or costs due to obsolescence because of probable technology changes prior to the end of the normal life of the equipment. If equipment would last for 10 years, for example, but new processes are likely to make it useless in 7 years, the total cost may be depreciated in 7 years.

Table 14. Typical Inflation Accounting
Depreciation Schedule

Year	Annual depreciation	Inflated cost
1	$ 1,000	$10,000
2	1,150	11,500
3	1,320	13,200
4	1,520	15,200
5	1,750	17,500
6	2,010	20,100
7	2,310	23,100
8	2,650	26,500
9	3,050	30,500
10	3,510	35,100
Total	$20,270	

Replacement cost depreciation is a Dutch method in which the depreciation value is varied periodically to account for increased costs of equipment. If a machine costs $10,000 in 1975 and has a life of 10 years, depreciation would be $1,000 the first year. If it would cost $12,000 to replace the equipment in 1976—because of inflation, technological advances, etc.—depreciation is $1,200 the second year. Table 13 shows how replacement cost depreciation schedules can increase in a 10-year period.

Table 13 shows that total depreciation allowed with this method would be almost twice the cost of the original machinery. While some accountants argue that such tax cost allowances are not fair, others maintain that such allowances are needed for future capital expansion because of rapidly rising equipment costs stemming from inflation, technology changes, etc.

Inflation accounting depreciation schedules (*see* **Inflation Accounting**) reflect changes in the value of equipment or plant due to inflation. Thus, if a piece of equipment costs $10,000 and has a life of 10 years, assuming an annual inflation rate of 15 percent, total depreciation will be $20,270 (see Table 14).

SUGGESTED FURTHER READING

Bigg, W. F., *Cost Accounting,* MacDonald, London, 1963.
Depreciation Guide, Commerce Clearing House, Dept. of Commerce, Washington, D.C., 1973.
Wilsher, P., "Has Brazil Really Cured the Money Disease?" *The Sunday Times,* London, July 7, 1974.

DESKILLING

Area for use in Cost Control:

ORGANIZATIONAL AND OPERATIONAL SYSTEMS

Deskilling is the technique of dividing work into much simplified parts and assigning one part to each employee. In the office, this may mean that one employee examines orders and passes them on to the shipping department, another clerk types the invoices for the goods, and a third worker addresses the envelopes and mails the invoices. The dangers of the technique are boredom and a lack of pride in the work, since no whole task is completed by any one employee. However, in large firms employing great numbers, the technique ensures simplified tasks for which little or no training is required. Because of the simple nature of the work, rhythm and speed increase. The technique may save equipment time, since the employee using the equipment will do so continuously. *See also* **Skilling.**

SUGGESTED FURTHER READING

Cemach, H. P., *Work Study in the Office,* MacLaren & Sons, London, 1969.

DIMINISHING PRODUCTIVITY THEORY AND EVALUATION

Areas for use in Cost Control:

ORGANIZATIONAL AND OPERATIONAL SYSTEMS
INDUSTRIAL APPLICATIONS
BUSINESS AND COMMERCIAL APPLICATIONS

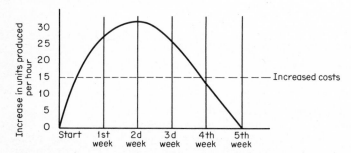

Figure 38. Typical diminishing productivity chart.

The diminishing productivity theory states that when any varying factor, such as labor or machine efficiency, is increased through application to any fixed factor, such as the materials or equipment used in production, the variable-factor output will eventually decrease. Since increased efficiency costs money, as in the use of incentive schemes, it is necessary to evaluate the rate of increase and to withdraw costs before the increases diminish to a point where the scheme becomes uneconomic. For example, an incentive plan motivates workers to increase production output. Figure 38 shows a typical chart of diminishing productivity.

Looking at Fig. 38, we can see that the incentive scheme increases production rapidly at first, reaching an economic level by the end of the first week. By the end of the second week, production is still increasing, but the rate of increase has slowed while the cost of increase remained stable. Ideally, the incentive plan would offer bonus payments for increased production only to the point where costs for such increases were lower than the value of the increase (midway between weeks 3 and 4 in Fig. 38). At this point, incentives should be lowered to lower the costs of increased production as it begins to diminish. Thus, such an incentive scheme might be scheduled as that in Table 15.

Table 15. Typical Decreasing-Return Bonus Schedule

Increased units of production*	Bonus payment each
0–5	5¢
6–10	6¢
11–15	7¢
16–30	10¢
31–35	7¢
36–45	6¢
Over 45	5¢

*In addition to a predetermined base production output.

SUGGESTED FURTHER READING

Dudick, Thomas S., *Profile for Profitability, Using Cost Control and Profitability Analysis,* Wiley, New York, 1972.

DIRECT COSTING

Areas for use in Cost Control:

ORGANIZATIONAL AND OPERATIONAL SYSTEMS

INDUSTRIAL APPLICATIONS

This **costing** technique charges off all direct costs to products, processes, or services, leaving other costs to be written off against profits of the period. Data are recorded on forms, analyzed, and used in managerial decisions. The separated fixed and variable costs are included in any income statement, and **fixed costs** are generally written off as period costs and are not carried forward to a future period.

Some opponents of direct costing feel that not all fixed costs can be charged to production units, since some part of the benefit of such costs may carry forward into new periods. Costs that are not at least indirectly traceable to production units should not be charged against production, they contend. Costs, such as those for service for equipment, are of this type, since it is impossible to say how long this service will contribute benefits. Such costs will become increasingly important as automation increases, replacing labor costs, and it seems likely that methods used to charge expense will include these costs in some manner.

SUGGESTED FURTHER READING

Tipper, H., *Controlling Overhead,* American Management Assn., New York, 1966.

DIRECT COSTS

Areas for use in Cost Control:

ORGANIZATIONAL AND OPERATIONAL SYSTEMS

INDUSTRIAL APPLICATIONS

Direct costs are those identified with cost centers (*see* **Cost Reduction Assessment**), such as a particular department or process, or those that can be identified with production of a specific product. *See also* **Overhead Cost Control.**

SUGGESTED FURTHER READING

Dickey, R. I., *Accountant's Cost Handbook,* Ronald, New York, 1960.

DISCOUNT

Areas for use in Cost Control:

ORGANIZATIONAL AND OPERATIONAL SYSTEMS

INDUSTRIAL APPLICATIONS

BUSINESS AND COMMERCIAL APPLICATIONS

Reducing costs through the use of a discount involves paying less in return for prompt payment, usually within 3 to 7 days of the date of an invoice. Terms of discount, if any, are allowed by the supplier. Thus, maximum cost reduction via the method requires purchasing from suppliers with the best discount terms, provided their original price does not offset the discount.

Discount may also apply to a reduction in required payment when goods are sold within the trade, by a wholesaler to a retailer (a *trade discount*); to a bill of exchange purchased for less than the face value because of risk or term factors; and to goods whose selling price has been reduced because of stock age, obsolescence, or other factors.

SUGGESTED FURTHER READING

Bierman, H., *Financial Accounting,* Macmillan, New York, 1965.

Speight, H., *Economics and Industrial Efficiency,* Macmillan, New York, 1967.

DISCOUNTED CASH FLOW

Areas for use in Cost Control:

ORGANIZATIONAL AND OPERATIONAL SYSTEMS

INDUSTRIAL APPLICATIONS

BUSINESS AND COMMERCIAL APPLICATIONS

Discounted cash flow is a technique used to determine the cost/profitability ratio of capital investment. Use of the method involves three steps:

1. *Determine total cost of the capital investment,* subtracting estimated annual net returns for the first 7 to 10 years.
2. *Adjust capital costs and net returns to show taxes paid,* leaving net cost and returns after tax figures.
3. *Using a discounting factor equivalent to current interest rates, discount cash returns annually* to determine the cost/profitability ratio after taxes and lost interest on the capital expenditure have been considered.

For example, if a company requires a 22 percent return, and a capital investment of $50,000 with an annual net cash flow of $15,000 is proposed, the discounted present value of such income over the life of the equipment (10 years) would be calculated. Using a 22 percent discount rate table (see Table 16), which shows the return spaced evenly over each year, the total discounted present value of the investment is $62,850 (see Table 17). Since this amount exceeds the cost of the capital investment, the expenditure would be approved.

SUGGESTED FURTHER READING

Ammer, D. S., *Materials Management,* Irwin, Homewood, Ill., 1968.
Wright, M. G., *Discounted Cash Flow,* McGraw-Hill, New York, 1973.

Table 16. Present Value of Future Payment of $1 at 22%

Year	Present value
1	$0.901
2	0.731
3	0.593
4	0.482
5	0.391
6	0.317
7	0.258
8	0.209
9	0.170
10	0.138

Table 17. Discounted Present Value; Annual Net Cash Flow of $15,000, Discount Rate 22 Percent

Year	Present value
1	$13,515
2	10,965
3	8,895
4	7,230
5	5,865
6	4,755
7	3,870
8	3,135
9	2,550
10	2,070
Total	$62,850

DISINTEGRATION

Areas for use in Cost Control:

ORGANIZATIONAL AND OPERATIONAL SYSTEMS
MATERIALS AND EQUIPMENT MANAGEMENT
INDUSTRIAL APPLICATIONS

Disintegration is the subcontracting of very specialized processes to firms specializing in these areas when operational costs can be reduced by doing so. The technique is especially effective for smaller manufacturers who cannot afford to support limited and/or specialized work areas which are, nevertheless, essential to some phase of their operation.

SUGGESTED FURTHER READING

Dunlop, J. T., and V. P. Diatchenko, *Labor Productivity,* McGraw-Hill, New York, 1964.
Speight, H., *Economics and Industrial Efficiency,* Macmillan, New York, 1967.

DRAWBACK

Areas for use in Cost Control:

INDUSTRIAL APPLICATIONS
BUSINESS AND COMMERCIAL APPLICATIONS

A drawback is the repayment of import duty costs when the item is reexported. For example, if gemstones are imported for mounting in a piece of jewelry and reexported, the drawback would refund import duty costs paid, in countries using the method.

SUGGESTED FURTHER READING
Ellsworth, P. T., *The International Economy,* Macmillan, New York, 1969.

DRUCKER'S COMPULSORY AGED EMPLOYMENT TECHNIQUE

Areas for use in Cost Control:
ORGANIZATIONAL AND OPERATIONAL SYSTEMS
INDUSTRIAL APPLICATIONS
BUSINESS AND COMMERCIAL APPLICATIONS

Drucker's compulsory aged employment technique would use right-to-work programs for employees now forced to retire, to reduce the costs of social security and other pensions. The method, as seen by Peter F. Drucker, will probably be instigated by unions and government, and will reduce costs for younger employees and companies. Reduced pensions would be available for workers unable or unwilling to work after 65. The primary problem of the technique would be overcoming promotional slowdowns that it would cause.

SUGGESTED FURTHER READING
Drucker, P. F., *The Practice of Management,* Harper & Row, New York, 1954.

DRUCKER'S RESPONSIBILITY THEORY

Areas for use in Cost Control:
PSYCHOLOGICAL MOTIVATIONAL MANAGEMENT
ORGANIZATIONAL AND OPERATIONAL SYSTEMS
INDUSTRIAL APPLICATIONS
BUSINESS AND COMMERCIAL APPLICATIONS

Originated by Peter F. Drucker, the responsibility theory states that if an employee is given as much responsibility as he or she can handle, the employee will be motivated to maximum work performance, reducing labor costs.

SUGGESTED FURTHER READING
Drucker, P. F., *The Practice of Management,* Harper & Row, New York, 1954.

DUAL LABOR MARKET METHOD

Areas for use in Cost Control:
FINANCIAL MOTIVATIONAL MANAGEMENT
INDUSTRIAL APPLICATIONS
BUSINESS AND COMMERCIAL APPLICATIONS

This system offers employment to disadvantaged or retarded workers by establishing a dual wage scale. Handicapped or retarded persons are paid a lower wage than are normal employees, until such time as they can be trained or brought up to standard production levels. For jobs that require little mental activity, it is possible to hire a retarded person at a lower rate of pay, giving him the opportunity to support him or herself and saving salary costs for the employer at the same time.

SUGGESTED FURTHER READING
The Economic Journal, vol. 83, no. 330, June 1973.

DUPLICATION COST CONTROL

Areas for use in Cost Control:

ORGANIZATIONAL AND OPERATIONAL SYSTEMS
MATERIALS AND EQUIPMENT MANAGEMENT
INDUSTRIAL APPLICATIONS
BUSINESS AND COMMERCIAL APPLICATIONS

Duplication and copying are major cost areas that can be reduced in a number of ways:

1. *Limitation* of mechanical copying. Authorization for duplication of all types should be required.

2. *Selection* of method of duplication. Costs per copy are more important than equipment costs if a good volume of copying is required.

3. *Leasing or buying decisions* may be based on original equipment costs. Generally, expensive equipment should be leased, since modern rapid design changes and improvements in duplicating equipment offer the probability of only a short useful life for equipment.

4. *Servicing,* if likely to be expensive, provides another reason for leasing with an all-in agreement to provide prompt repairs and/or replacement service in the event of a breakdown.

5. *Waste control* includes maximum utilization of paper and other supplies, as well as of operator time.

Knowledge of various duplicating methods is also important in controlling duplication costs.

Photocopying. Xerox machines and other photocopiers are the fastest and easiest to use, but these qualities often lead to overuse. For example, secretaries may copy letters rather than making carbons, adding several cents to the cost of each letter mailed.

Postage costs can be reduced, however. If a branch office needs 15 copies of a sales report, the home office can send one copy, which is then duplicated by the branch operation.

Legal records, canceled checks, etc., can be photocopied for business use, allowing the company to retain the original material.

Offset Litho. For moderately large numbers of copies, offset litho is an extremely versatile method. Plastic (to 5,000 copies) or metal plates (over 5,000 copies) are photographed from camera-ready copy.

A small offset press can be used to print letterheads, envelopes, brochures, price lists, training material, employee bulletins, newspapers, etc.

Stencil and Spirit Duplication. These low-cost machines reproduce typed stencils or master copies. Limited numbers of moderate-quality copies can be printed at a very low cost and are suitable for company distribution.

Minor Equipment and Supplies. Small items of copying equipment that can be used to reduce duplication costs include:

1. Carbon sets for letters and forms, to allow multiple-copy preparation without the insertion of carbon paper
2. Carbon-free copy paper, a pressure-sensitive paper imprinted from the pen or typewriter's pressure on the original copy above it

3. Stencils
4. Rub-off letters, also called *transfer lettering,* that have the appearance of professionally set type
5. Rubber stamps
6. Preprinted labels

SUGGESTED FURTHER READING

Chambers, H. T., *Copying, Duplicating, and Microfilm,* Beekman Publishing, New York, 1972.
Gardiner, A. W., *Typewriting and Office Duplicating Processes,* Hastings House, New York, 1968.

DYELINE PAYROLL SYSTEM

Areas for use in Cost Control:

PAPERWORK DESIGN AND FLOW SYSTEMS
ORGANIZATIONAL AND OPERATIONAL SYSTEMS
DATA RETENTION—FILES AND RECORDKEEPING
BUSINESS AND COMMERCIAL APPLICATIONS

The dyeline payroll system is an automated payroll method for nonfluctuating payrolls that reduces labor and costs. Typed master payroll sheets are photographed onto foil and dyelined by machine into payroll checks and stubs. Changes are made by cleaning the section of foil involved and reapplying new figures. In payrolls where amounts, including tax deductions, are stable from pay period to pay period, no other records need be kept.

SUGGESTED FURTHER READING

Pendery and Fuller, *Clerical Payroll Procedures,* South-Western Publishing Company, Cincinnati, 1970.

EARLY-WARNING SYSTEM

Areas for use in Cost Control:

ORGANIZATIONAL AND OPERATIONAL SYSTEMS
DATA RETENTION—FILES AND RECORDKEEPING
INDUSTRIAL APPLICATIONS
BUSINESS AND COMMERCIAL APPLICATIONS

The early-warning system gives management warning of impending cost or other economic problems through a series of controls built into the accounting operation. The method can be programmed for operation by a computer and an automatic warning provided when costs—related to output, pricing, or profits—pass a danger point. The method is patterned on military defense warning systems and allows examination of all cost aspects—materials, labor, overhead—as well as pricing and profit, before problems relating to these aspects become effective.

SUGGESTED FURTHER READING

Roberts, H. S., *Roberts' Dictionary of Industrial Relations,* Bureau of National Affairs, Inc., Washington, D.C., 1966.

ECONOMIC-BATCH REORDERING QUANTITY

Areas for use in Cost Control:

ORGANIZATIONAL AND OPERATIONAL SYSTEMS
INDUSTRIAL APPLICATIONS
BUSINESS AND COMMERCIAL APPLICATIONS

Economic-batch reordering quantity shows the least costly ordering point, considering the buyer's paperwork cost of ordering, storage costs, and bulk-buying discounts. Both most economical size and frequency of order are determined by multiplying the annual value of a particular product used and the cost of paperwork involved in ordering by 2 and dividing the total by the cost of storage of these goods. Calculations are made for various sizes of orders, and the most economical-sized order is used.

Allowance for inflation factors may be added to the formula by multiplying the annual product cost, plus the cost of paperwork involved in ordering, by 2 and dividing the total by the cost of storage minus the cost of annual inflation (10 to 15 percent of the annual cost of the goods).

SUGGESTED FURTHER READING

Cyert, R. M., and L. A. Welsch, *Management Decision Making,* Penguin, Baltimore, 1971.

EDGE-PUNCHED CARD PROCESSES

Areas for use in Cost Control:

ORGANIZATIONAL AND OPERATIONAL SYSTEMS
PAPERWORK DESIGN AND FLOW SYSTEMS
DATA RETENTION—FILES AND RECORDKEEPING
MATERIALS AND EQUIPMENT MANAGEMENT
INDUSTRIAL APPLICATIONS
BUSINESS AND COMMERCIAL APPLICATIONS

The edge-punched card process uses cards with a coded set of indentations punched by hand around the edge of the cards as a means of sorting various data such as payroll records, production statistics, and file indexes. The punched cards (see Fig. 39)

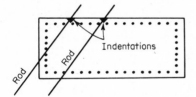

Figure 39. Typical edge-punched card with coded indentations.

are passed over a series of rods which are placed through a row of holes punched at the top edge of the cards. When the rod for a specific classification passes through, the indentation allows the card to fall away, so that all cards with a specific code are automatically sorted into one stack.

SUGGESTED FURTHER READING

Longman, H. H., *How to Reduce Office Costs,* Anbar Publications, London, 1967.

EFFICIENCY AGREEMENT

Areas for use in Cost Control:

ORGANIZATIONAL AND OPERATIONAL SYSTEMS
INDUSTRIAL APPLICATIONS

An efficiency agreement is a contract between labor and management in which management agrees to give workers a portion of reduced costs stemming from improved work methods or technological changes and in return labor promises to cooperate with such changes. Such changes often result in decreased human labor, so that overall costs are reduced, even though individual employees' wages are increased.

SUGGESTED FURTHER READING

Roberts, H. S., *Roberts' Dictionary of Industrial Relations,* Bureau of National Affairs, Inc., Washington, D.C., 1966.

EFFORT CONTROL

Areas for use in Cost Control:

PSYCHOLOGICAL MOTIVATIONAL MANAGEMENT
ORGANIZATIONAL AND OPERATIONAL SYSTEMS
INDUSTRIAL APPLICATIONS
BUSINESS AND COMMERCIAL APPLICATIONS

Effort control is the development of rhythmic work methods that will increase work efficiency and reduce labor costs. The technique uses **Labanotation,** developed by Rudolf Laban, or work measurement (*see* **Work Study and Measurement**) as developed by Taylor to establish the basic motions a worker uses. These motions are recorded and studied, and the worker is selected by motion type and/or trained to use rhythmic, more effective motions to increase work output.

PERSONNEL CHOICE AND EFFORT CONTROL

Selection of employees naturally inclined toward the rhythm best suited to a specific task is one aspect of effort control. For example, a carpenter who must repeatedly make strong, fast, and direct motions with his or her hands should be naturally inclined toward this type of movement. Tests have been devised to measure these factors, but observation of the way a prospective employee walks, sits, handles a hammer, etc., can give a rough idea of his or her movement type. A sensitive, well-coordinated movement and sustained effort are needed for electrical-component assembly work, on the other hand, and a person given to strong, quick movements would probably work less efficiently in this area than would a worker with natural inclinations toward flexible, sensitive motions. Additionally, when the worker's nature is suited to the motion involved in his or her work, the work will be more satisfying to the worker.

EFFORT TRAINING

Workers, particularly those inclined toward a type of motion, can be trained to perform motions of that type more effectively. General training should start with the eight basic motions (slashing, pressing, wringing, punching, gliding, flicking, dabbing, and floating) and their relationship to time, weight, and space. Specific jobs are then divided into these motions, and the worker is shown how to combine the necessary motions rhythmically and without wasted effort. In ironing clothes, for example, the basic effort required is gliding, since the heat of the iron presses out the wrinkles. However, the average person presses down hard on the iron, wasting a great deal of effort. The same motion is used in sanding a piece of wood with an electric sander. Here, too, a strenuous pressing motion may force the sander down, actually damaging the wood, as well as wasting the worker's effort. On the other hand, using no pressure at all will result in a minimal amount of smoothing.

In effort training, exercises are developed that allow the worker to practice moving from one basic motion to another in rhythm. In turning a control and pushing a machine part back, for example, the worker will use first a wringing motion and then a

Table 18. Common Motions Divided by Basic Motion Types

Basic motion type	Common motions
Pressing	Crushing, cutting, squeezing
Slashing	Throwing, beating, digging, whipping, chopping
Wringing	Pulling, turning, stretching, plucking
Dabbing	Patting, shaking, tapping
Gliding	Smoothing, rubbing, smearing, smudging
Flicking	Counting, flapping, flipping, jerking
Punching	Pushing, jabbing, beating

pressing (away) motion. Weight and strength exerted should not be broken between the two motions but should be practiced by the worker until one continuous movement is achieved.

SUGGESTED FURTHER READING

Laban, R., and F. C. Lawrence, *Effort,* MacDonald, London, 1965.

EFFORT RATING

Areas for use in Cost Control:

PSYCHOLOGICAL MOTIVATIONAL MANAGEMENT
FINANCIAL MOTIVATIONAL MANAGEMENT
ORGANIZATIONAL AND OPERATIONAL SYSTEMS

Effort rating is a **performance rating** (technique) used to measure employee work speed compared with standard speed. Skill is considered an integral part of the speed measurement and is not evaluated separately. Effort rating used as a basis for incentive payments reduces costs by limiting payment to the proportion of work accomplished.

SUGGESTED FURTHER READING

Presgrave, Ralph, *The Dynamics of Time Study,* McGraw-Hill, New York, 1945.

ELECTRONIC DATA PROCESSING

Areas for use in Cost Control:

WORK PLACE MOTIVATIONAL MANAGEMENT
ORGANIZATIONAL AND OPERATIONAL SYSTEMS
DATA RETENTION—FILES AND RECORDKEEPING
MATERIALS AND EQUIPMENT MANAGEMENT
BUSINESS AND COMMERCIAL APPLICATIONS
INDUSTRIAL APPLICATIONS

Electronic data processing is the storage or computation of information by electronic, mechanical means—using a computer. Computerization of data retention systems and other procedures is one of the most important and one of the least understood basics of cost reduction. The executive has no need to fully understand most of the technical details. A basic understanding of how computers work and a good knowledge of the ways to save money using them are the facts he or she needs to know. This section outlines such information, while the Suggested Further Reading will give new sources if the reader wishes to know more. Refer also to related subjects in the book: **Ashby Approach; Critical Path Analysis; Cybernetics; Heuristic Methods; Program Evaluation and Review Technique; Programmed Instruction.**

THE MAIN COMPONENTS

It is important to realize that the computer does *not* think for itself. It can make decisions if programmed correctly (*see* **Cybernetics**). It *can* solve problems—including cost problems—if it is given the parameters of the problem. In addition, the cost of solving the problem can be less in dollars spent and will almost certainly be less in terms of time spent.

Any computer has three main components (Fig. 40):

1. Ability to read (input)
2. Ability to remember (process)
3. Ability to write (output)

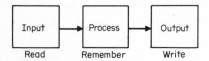

Figure 40. Computer components.

The reading or input unit translates information about a specific problem into a numerically coded form acceptable to the machine. Such information may be punched in digital form on a card or recorded on a magnetic tape. Once the input unit recognizes the pattern or code, it electronically passes the signals on to the processing, or remembering, unit. The processing unit has a data storage section, a data control section, and an arithmetical section. It will electronically relate new signals to information already stored in its data banks, with the control unit sorting through for data related to the current problem. Next, the processing unit electronically passes possible solutions and their probable outcomes to the writing or output unit. The output unit then deciphers the reply in a written form (see Fig. 41).

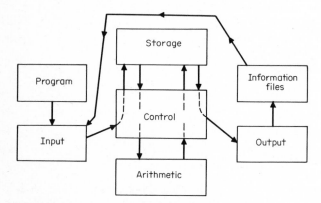

Figure 41. Computer operation sequence.

These units do nothing that cannot also be done manually by a clerk, but the computer achieves its results almost instantaneously and error-free.

HOW TO USE A COMPUTER

Few executives will be interested in learning to operate a computer themselves; the EDP department will handle actual computer operation. Two general rules are advisable, however, for obtaining the most effective use of the computer:

1. Keep the data processing department aware of the company and its problems, as well as of the fact that the use of the computer is to aid the company. This will prevent a close-knit clique, completely absorbed in methods rather than in useful results.

2. Control of EDP seems best handled by a steering committee of top management. The data processing manager reports to this committee, which is responsible for all computer progress, costs, and results. Terms of control reference generally include:
   a. Setting objectives for data processing, and their achievement
   b. Examining and approving long-term data processing plans
   c. Approving priorities
   d. Approving proposed feasibility studies
   e. Approving all systems definitions
   f. Monitoring progress
   g. Suggesting organizational changes needed
   h. Reviewing project success

The steering committee can be kept up to date in the following ways:

1. The data analyst in charge of each project prepares a very short weekly summary of factors affecting development.
2. The data analyst draws up an overall plan of the project, including costs, problems, etc., so the committee can follow its progress as it moves along.

COMPUTERS AND MISTAKES

Because computerized data processing operates so rapidly and on such a large volume, mistakes can be extremely costly. Overall, however, manual data processing errors are more frequent and more costly than EDP system errors.

Output from a computer can be wrong for four reasons:

1. Wrong input
2. Program deliberately altered to produce false results
3. Previous undetected program (input) error
4. Hardware (equipment) malfunction

Wrong input is frequently called "garbage in—garbage out." If a person feeding information into the computer makes a mistake (unless the error is illogical enough to be caught by a program's input checks), it will probably get through the system. Use of both a programmer and a verifier will keep this occurrence at a minimum. Using top-quality employees here will result in cost savings.

Program alteration opens doors to larceny possibilities, especially if only a few people in the company understand how the computer works. As a check, an auditor should see and approve any new system, and programmers may be required to make duplicate programs.

Previously undetected program errors, while wasting time, are usually caught because the program answers are so absurd.

Hardware failures are increasingly rare because of many internal checks being built into computers. Largest hardware failure problems are whole computerized files being destroyed by an inefficient computer operator inadvertently or by a fire that destroys the storage unit.

COST-REDUCING APPLICATIONS

Some of the many ways a computer can save company costs are now discussed.

Integrated Management Information Systems. Keeping management informed via EDP means that:

1. A continuous flow of data is translated into significant and understandable information reports, while superfluous material is sifted out.
2. The output indicates alternative courses of action on the basis of this information and the probable results of each.
3. The system gives complete flexibility.

Billing, Payments, and Recordkeeping. Billing, invoicing, and payments can be computerized by feeding required data (purchases, sales, etc.) into the hardware. Personnel records and payroll payments are typical applications.

Inventory Control. Costs of stock shortages, overstocking, throughput, stock holding, and operation can be cut with computerization. Stock is recorded in the computer, which follows stock use and automatically provides orders, invoices, shortage reports, etc. Inventory-servicing levels should improve under computerization. At the same time, production delay costs caused by stock shortages should be eliminated. The computer can also calculate optimum stock levels, reducing stocking costs.

Production and Work Control. Improved delivery dates, reduced stock expenditure, reduced labor costs, and a more completely utilized factory or office can result from feeding production into the computer. A computer can break down a sales forecast, product by product, into component units, assemblies, price of parts, and raw materials. Once this information is processed and compared with material on hand, the computer can provide an answer as to net requirements of each element, as well as translating the requirements into economic manufacturing batches and ordering the needed material from vendors.

The computer can also plan the best flow of work—whether on the plant floors or in the office. It can give statistics about product loading or increased number of employees needed, and it can call the executive's attention to imbalance between workload and capacity through processing of work schedules, to individual project status, to route lists, etc.

Translation. Operating in a worldwide economy requires more translation from one language to another. Although computers cannot catch every literary nuance, they can be used satisfactorily for translating scientific and business material.

Operations Research. Calculations used in any research can be speeded by processing them through a computer. Results are not only almost instantaneous but also extremely precise. *See also* **Operations Research.**

Models. Computer processing is useful for any model that needs analysis regularly, such as market demand for a specific product or service. The computer's ability to handle a large volume of information economically means more analysis in less time and at less dollar cost than comparable manual processing. *See also* **Models.**

Business Gaming. Training through the use of business games or simulation is accelerated by use of the computer, giving experience in making business decisions. A typical game might give a description of a business situation complete with cost, quality, and goal data. Using the computer, a manager can learn to solve such problems quickly and economically. *See also* **Gaming.**

Teaching Machines. Training of all employees can be facilitated through programmed instruction. With the computer assessing the answers to test questions, the employee learns immediately whether his reply is right or wrong and avoids being sidetracked to an incorrect area of study.

Critical Path Analysis. The **critical path analysis (CPA)** technique, also known as **program evaluation and review technique (PERT)** or **network planning and analysis,** is used in planning and controlling a project. Detailed control, on a major project at least, is almost impossible without a computer. The technique is used in planning projects which require the combination of resources at different points in time. Related events and activities are drawn on a network and individual items are analyzed. Estimates of total time and a plan for the sequence of work are then established (see Fig. 42).

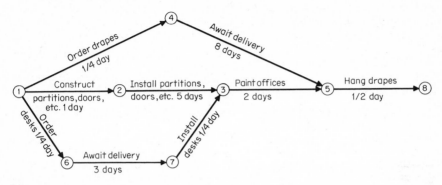

Figure 42. Critical path network: remodeling an office.

Company Files and Records. All company files and records can be transferred to the computer's data bank if desired. Space savings and flexibility of handling are some of the cost reduction features.

HOW MUCH COST REDUCTION FROM COMPUTERS?

Computerized data processing can save money, but the reader will want to know how much he or she can expect to save. Many variables affect this figure: efficiency of the computer used, ability of the data processing staff, etc. An accepted rule of thumb, however, is that efficient computerized data processing can save 10 percent or more. Since according to Fritz Machlup, professor of economics at Princeton University, the U.S. spends 29 percent of its gross national product on information, the savings can be considerable.

Choosing the least expensive but most effective means of computerizing a data retention system depends on the company's individual organization and operation, but the following checklist provides some questions the reader should ask:

1. What are the alternatives—to lease, buy on contract, or purchase outright?
2. If leasing a computer, are the maintenance, insurance, cost of training staff, and programming aid costs included?
3. What is the period of lease? Can it be altered?
4. Does the company have unlimited use of the hardware, or is it limited to x number of hours?
5. Are allowances made for downtime?
6. If the computer is purchased, what is the cost of the contract? Can the computer be traded in later for a new model? Will the manufacturer train the purchaser's engineers?
7. Who pays for transporting the computer to its site?

Optimum use of the computer can include multiple shifts. Direct savings the company can expect from computerization, in addition to this, include:

1. Cost of equipment replaced
2. Reduction of clerical staff

3. Reduction of overtime
4. Reduction of space costs
5. Reduction of supervision
6. Reduction of information transfer costs

Indirect savings include:

1. Ability to produce work faster
2. Ability to handle a larger volume of work
3. Flexibility

COMPUTER TERMS

Rather than listing each computer term separately, the following short glossary will provide basic terms and their definition:

Access time. Time needed to move information from the data bank to the computer's computation function.
ADP. Automated data processing.
Analytical method. Choosing computer systems that will accomplish needed tasks at an economically probable figure.
Computer. A machine with certain logical properties which enable it to process data, to a speed of 40,000,000 operations per second.
Data bank. Computer-storage units of information that can be drawn on to solve problems.
Data processing. Starting with a given piece of information and putting it into another form (sorting, reorganizing, translating, or calculating) or drawing certain conclusions from it.
Direct-access memories. Information always connected to the central processing unit of a computer.
EDP. Electronic data processing.
Feedback. Control mechanisms that amplify or hold back a system to bring it to a stable nature.
Hardware. Computer equipment.
Input equipment. Devices used to feed information to a computer.
Linear programming. A mathematical technique that seeks out the minimum of a linear function of a set of variables subjected to restrictions or standards which are also linear.
MICR. (Magnetic ink character recognition.) Common machine language for computerized handling of checks, including transit number field, bank number field, and amount field. Checks can be handled at the rate of 2,000 per minute in this system, which generates and transmits electrical impulses to a computer for reading and sorting while performing mathematical calculations, including statement tabulation.
Multiprogramming and multiprocessing. Simultaneous use of computer resources for several programs.
Software. Programs needed to operate computer systems.
Systems analysis for EDP and ADP. A study designed to aid decision makers in investigating alternative ways of achieving effectiveness and cost control considerations.
Three-plan model. Computer equipment program that allows 224 constraints and 253 variables.
Time sharing. Simultaneous use of computer resources by several operators or companies.

SUGGESTED FURTHER READING

Armand, R., R. Lattes, and J. LeSoume, *The Management Revolution,* Denoel Press, Paris, 1970.

Baughn, W. H., and C. E. Walker, *The Bankers Handbook,* Dow Jones-Irwin, New York, 1966.
McRae, T. W., *The Impact of Computers on Accounting,* Wiley, New York, 1964.
Van Horne, James C., *Financial Management and Policy,* Prentice-Hall, Englewood Cliffs, N.J., 1971.

EMPLOYEE PERFORMANCE RECORD

Areas for use in Cost Control:

ORGANIZATIONAL AND OPERATIONAL SYSTEMS
PAPERWORK DESIGN AND FLOW SYSTEMS
INDUSTRIAL APPLICATIONS
BUSINESS AND COMMERCIAL APPLICATIONS

The employee performance record is an efficiency evaluation technique used to reduce labor costs. In this method, the supervisor appraises each employee's performance daily in several areas, which may include work output, reliability, cooperation, amiability, initiative, responsibility, use of equipment, comprehension, use of work methods, coordination, mathematical performance, physical condition, mental condition, and work checking.

A form is designed to make evaluation as simple as possible. A single form may incorporate daily appraisals for a month or a week (see Fig. 43). Ratings usually are by brief recorded observations of either a positive or a negative nature.

Employee Performance Record							
Performance trait	Date	Positive rating			Negative rating		
		A	B	C	C	B	A
Equipment use	11/1/76			cleaned Type writer			
					Desk messy		

Figure 43. Typical employee performance record format.

Primary use of the method should include supervisory improvement of problem areas. At regular intervals, the supervisor should review the performance records and discuss their contents with the employee, pointing out both commendable performance and areas where the employee should strive for improvement.

SUGGESTED FURTHER READING

Whisler, T. L., and S. F. Harper, *Performance Appraisal,* Holt, New York, 1962.

EMPLOYEE-PROBLEM-SOLVING METHOD See Personnel Morale Building.

ENVIRONMENTAL IMPROVEMENT COST CONTROL

Areas for use in Cost Control:

ORGANIZATIONAL AND OPERATIONAL SYSTEMS
INDUSTRIAL APPLICATIONS
BUSINESS AND COMMERCIAL APPLICATIONS

Environmental improvement has become required in many areas, with laws demanding costly cleanup of air, water, land, etc., used by industry. While such improvement *is* mandatory, and will become increasingly so in the future, costs of these programs can be reduced by using the most effective methods per dollar spent and by taking advantage of available government financing or grants to complete projects of this type. This section discusses various types of pollution and available ways to reduce the cost of eliminating such pollution.

WATER POLLUTION

Permanent United States federal water pollution legislation was first passed in 1956, and state legislation of varying strength supports this.

United States water pollution control will cost industry nearly $1 billion per year, plus an additional $200 million in increased operating costs, experts predict. Two billion dollars more will have to be spent on thermal pollution control for cooling of water used to generate electricity.

CONTROLLING WATER POLLUTION AT REDUCED COST

The following are suggested ways of reducing the cost of water pollution control:

1. *Include pollution control techniques when production processes are designed.* Both equipment and operational costs are lowered when pollution treatment is just one step of the production process.

2. *Use U.S. federal grants* for "research and projects to prevent pollution of water by industry." About $10 million a year is currently available.

3. *Implement use of U.S. federal or state funds available* to construct municipality sewage treatment centers and sewage collection, treatment, and disposal. About 30 percent of the cost of the project can be recovered, and the center can sometimes provide industrial water pollution treatment.

4. *Use pollution treatment equipment as a tax write-off or as an investment tax credit.* Additionally, some states exempt such equipment from property taxation and from state sales tax at time of purchase.

5. *Implement R&D projects* to see if any beneficial materials can be reclaimed from waste water during treatment.

6. *Companies may join together* voluntarily or through government-enforced effluent taxes to establish a water pollution treatment system. In either case, the company's payment depends on the degree of its pollution but overall costs are reduced, since they are shared.

7. *Temporary pollution permits are granted by some states* and will ensure freedom from large fines and/or suits (up to $10,000 in Vermont, for example). A charge for pollution may be fixed for the period of the permit. Such temporary permits are intended as breathing space to give the individual company time to plan and construct water pollution treatment equipment.

AIR POLLUTION

Transportation is the largest source of air pollution (over 40 percent) in the United States; fuel combustion in stationary sources accounts for more than 20 percent, and industrial processes emit almost 14 percent.

Total investment necessary to control air pollution in the United States is about $5 billion. Cost to industry averages about 1 percent of annual production.

CONTROLLING AIR POLLUTION AT REDUCED COST

1. *If soot, carbon, etc., is not controlled, the company should attempt to purchase land where it is apt to fall,* since some state and federal courts have found such emissions an act of trespass and have awarded damages.

2. *Material recovery systems can be implemented with air pollution control devices to reduce costs.* For example, California law restricts emission of fumes from auto spray painting. Equipment developed to stop such emissions recovers particles of the plastic-based paint for additional use.

3. *Use U.S. federal grants* available for research relating to fuels and vehicles. For private industry, these take the form of contracts to design, develop, and/or construct devices or methods to prevent air pollution by transportation. Grants cannot currently exceed $1.5 million each.

4. *Purchase and use equipment with the fewest possible air pollution problems.*

5. *Obtain temporary state permits* to emit air pollutants when necessary. Federal fines for violation of U.S. standards may be up to $25,000 per day for the first offense and to $50,000 per day of violation for succeeding offenses. Imprisonment may be up to two years per day for either. Violation of state air-quality laws may be punished by the *federal* government with fines up to $10,000 per day of violation.

SOLID WASTES

Over 4 billion tons of solid waste is produced annually in the U.S. Federal guidelines have been established, but state and local laws generally determine the cost and required extent of solid waste pollution control.

CONTROLLING SOLID WASTE POLLUTION AT REDUCED COST

The following are suggested ways of reducing the cost of solid waste pollution control:

1. *Share disposal systems with other companies in the area.*

2. *Recycle materials* where economically feasible.

3. *Use scavenger or spoils services* where possible, as they will use the waste, perhaps paying a small amount to remove it.

4. *Compaction of industrial solid wastes reduces bulk,* reducing transportation and handling costs of disposal.

CONTROLLING RADIATION POLLUTION AT REDUCED COST

While cost of radiation pollution control is often predetermined by required shielding, transportation, restrictions, etc., some methods of reducing radiation pollution control costs are available and include the following:

1. *Location of operation site* can determine the number, and therefore the cost, of safeguards required. Remote areas need fewer safety features.

2. *Operations that can be carried out jointly can reduce cost of shielding, etc.* For example, ten medical clinics may construct one X-ray treatment center and share costs for necessary radiation pollution control devices.

3. *Liability for damage from radiation pollution* has a tremendous cost potential that makes effective control, however expensive, much less costly in the long run than an accident that might otherwise occur.

NOISE POLLUTION

Most governmental controls of noise pollution are local, but the U.S. government issued enforceable federal standards for occupational exposure in 1969. Serious costs may stem from the employer's liability to an employee whose hearing is permanently damaged or destroyed by occupational noise pollution.

CONTROLLING NOISE POLLUTION AT REDUCED COST

The following are suggested ways of reducing the cost of noise pollution control:

1. *All phases of operation that produce excessive noise* should be isolated in one or more soundproofed areas of the factory.

2. *Effective noise pollution control in urban offices* can be accomplished at little or no cost by choosing office locations on upper floors and in buildings well removed from airplane flight patterns, heavy rail or truck transportation routes, etc.

3. *When building new office or plant facilities,* materials effecting sound control can be used for walls, dividers, etc., at little or no increased cost over conventional materials.

4. *Location of noisy manufacturing operations, transportation routes, etc.,* should be away from densely populated areas, lowering the effects of noise pollution at little or no additional cost.

5. *A low-level constant noise,* such as piped-in music, may reduce the effect of exterior noise pollution by distracting employee attention.

SUGGESTED FURTHER READING

Brown, R. P., and D. D. Smith, *Marine Disposal of Solid Wastes,* Bureau of Solid Waste Management, Washington, D.C., 1970.
Clean Water for the 1970's, U.S. Federal Water Quality Administration, Washington, D.C., 1970.
Environmental Law, Grad, F. P., Matthew Binder, New York, 1971.
Industrial Waste Guide to Thermal Pollution, U.S. Federal Water Pollution Control Administration, Washington, D.C., 1968.
Murphy, *Financial Protection Against Atomic Hazards,* Atomic Industrial Forum, Inc., Columbia University, 1957.
U.S. Clean Air Amendments, Government Printing Office, Washington, D.C., 1970.

EQUAL-PRODUCT CURVE

Areas for use in Cost Control:

ORGANIZATIONAL AND OPERATIONAL SYSTEMS
MATERIALS AND EQUIPMENT MANAGEMENT
INDUSTRIAL APPLICATIONS

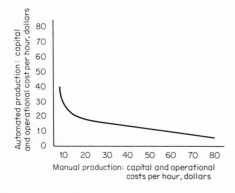

Figure 44. Typical equal-product curve for producing 50 product units per hour.

An equal-product curve is a visual method of comparing cost or other factors of two production methods, each producing the same output (see Fig. 44). In Fig. 44, for example, production costs for 50 units per hour by automated and manual production are compared, showing that allowing for both capital and operational costs, cost per unit is about 80 cents using automated methods while cost per unit is $1.60 using manual production techniques.

SUGGESTED FURTHER READING

Chamberlain, N. W., The Firm: Micro-Economic Planning and Action, McGraw-Hill, New York, 1965.
Speight, H., Economics and Industrial Efficiency, Macmillan, New York, 1967.

ERGONOMICS

Areas for use in Cost Control:

PSYCHOLOGICAL MOTIVATIONAL MANAGEMENT
WORK PLACE MOTIVATIONAL MANAGEMENT
ORGANIZATIONAL AND OPERATIONAL SYSTEMS
INDUSTRIAL APPLICATIONS
BUSINESS AND COMMERCIAL APPLICATIONS

Ergonomics is the study of the relationship of the worker and his or her job, in order to fit the job to the employee by increasing work efficiency and lowering fatigue, thus reducing labor costs. Use of the method combines techniques from many areas including work study, psychology, physiology, and engineering to accomplish these goals.

Equipment, furniture, and work places are studied with the object of fitting their design and characteristics to worker needs. For example, switches on a piece of equipment may be designed for easiest manipulation by the operator. Switch labeling will be planned for easiest reading. Size, position, shape, color, labeling, safety features, operating capacity, etc., will all be determined by the workers' physical, physiological, and psychological limitations.

Lighting systems, noise control, ventilation, etc., will also be planned to prevent employee fatigue and to heighten his or her productive efficiency.

Aspects of worker/job relationships commonly studied and used in ergonomics include:

1. Individual worker capacities: physical
2. Individual worker capacities: mental
3. Physiological limitations of the worker
4. Capacity for monotony
5. Skills assessment
6. Effects of age on skills and/or coordination
7. Effects of noise on physiological aspects of work
8. Effects of noise on psychological aspects of work
9. Effects of temperature variance on efficiency
10. Effects of lighting variance on efficiency
11. Effects of ventilation on efficiency

Analysis of these various aspects is used to design work methods, equipment, and place, to increase employee efficiency, and to reduce worker fatigue. *See also* **Fatigue Study.** Steps followed in analyzing worker/job relationships may include:

1. Determine relationship goal.
2. Define alternate methods of reaching the goal.
3. Choose the method best suited to increasing worker efficiency.
4. Where possible remove work factors that cause fatigue or decrease efficiency.

SUGGESTED FURTHER READING

McCormick, E. J., Human Factors Engineering, 3d ed., McGraw-Hill, New York, 1974.
Shepherd, Roy J., Men at Work: Applications of Ergonomics to Performance and Design, Charles C Thomas, Springfield, Ill., 1974.

ESCALATION CLAUSES

Areas for use in Cost Control:

ORGANIZATIONAL AND OPERATIONAL SYSTEMS
MATERIALS AND EQUIPMENT MANAGEMENT
INDUSTRIAL APPLICATIONS

Escalation clauses are contract additions that provide price changes to adjust for unforeseen costs. They are used in most long-term contracts to protect the seller. The buyer should carefully define areas of escalation, limiting changes to basic costs, to reduce overall cost increases that will result from the use of such a clause. Escalation clauses should permit price changes based on *industrywide* materials or labor cost changes rather than on the seller's *internal* costs, for example. A maximum increase, usually 10 to 15 percent of the original price, should also be specified.

SUGGESTED FURTHER READING

Ammer, D. S., *Materials Management,* Irwin, Homewood, Ill., 1968.

EVOLUTIONARY OPERATION (EVOP)

Areas for use in Cost Control:

ORGANIZATIONAL AND OPERATIONAL SYSTEMS
MATERIALS AND EQUIPMENT MANAGEMENT
INDUSTRIAL APPLICATIONS

Evolutionary operation (EVOP) is a system of continuous recording and evaluation of production detail used to maintain output and reduce production costs. Data relating to raw materials, equipment, processing details and times, employee output, etc., are continuously monitored and cycled via a feedback loop for evaluation by management. As data are studied, each factor is improved in performance to the maximum degree possible while each cost is reduced as much as possible, providing an "evolutionary" selection of optimum methods.

Success of the method depends on the quality of continual data recording and evaluation as means of spotting and ejecting problems or cost rises that may gradually enter production processes.

SUGGESTED FURTHER READING

Clay, M. J., and B. H. Walley, *Performance and Profitability,* Longmans, London, 1965.

EXCLUSIVE DEALING

Areas for use in Cost Control:

ORGANIZATIONAL AND OPERATIONAL SYSTEMS
INDUSTRIAL APPLICATIONS
BUSINESS AND COMMERCIAL APPLICATIONS

Exclusive dealing is the limitation of sale of manufactured products to specific predetermined outlets to reduce sales, distribution, and servicing costs for the manufacturer and to provide exclusivity of products handled for the retailer. The method can successfully reduce such costs when outlets in suitable locations and with adequate markets are used. Legal problems in the restrictive trade area can arise. Manufacturers sometimes justify the practice, however, by stating that exclusive dealing is necessary to provide the customer with adequate service, as in the case of an automobile dealership. Other products, such as some perfumes, use exclusive dealing methods without such justification, however.

SUGGESTED FURTHER READING

Bannock, G., R. E. Baxter, and R. Rees, *A Dictionary of Economics,* Penguin, Baltimore, 1974.

EXECUTIVE PERFORMANCE APPRAISAL See In-Basket.

EXECUTIVE PROGRAMS

Areas for use in Cost Control:
ORGANIZATIONAL AND OPERATIONAL SYSTEMS
DATA RETENTION—FILES AND RECORDKEEPING
MATERIALS AND EQUIPMENT MANAGEMENT
INDUSTRIAL APPLICATIONS
BUSINESS AND COMMERCIAL APPLICATIONS

Executive programs, also called supervision programs, are multi-access operating systems used to control various individual programs and operating procedures in a computer system. Use of the method increases working efficiency of the computer, reducing processing costs per item, and also reduces human programming errors, reducing overall operating costs.

In an executive program, standard general-purpose self-processing routines are built into the computer equipment or "hardware." Functions used by the programmer are interpreted and carried out by this underlying multi-access operating system, the executive program. This program allows processing of two or more different pieces of work at the same time. Mechanics of the program require minimal equipment additions to allow simultaneous reading, computing, and outputting of data. In this way, the computer uses all three of its major capabilities at the same time, saving wasted time of two abilities while the third is in use. The executive program coordinates the operation according to built-in priorities and rules. The processor is switched, by the executive program, back and forth among several programs depending on ability availability. For example, assume two programs are being run, each requiring a total of 10 minutes. The first requires the computer's reading ability for 70 percent of its running time and output for the remaining 30 percent. The second program uses the computer's reading ability 10 percent of its running time, printing (output) ability 10 percent of the time, and computing ability 80 percent of the time. Figure 45 shows how such work might be scheduled by the executive program.

The white areas in Fig. 45 show free computer time in the three skill areas that remains *even while programs 1 and 2 are being processed.* Other programs, or parts of programs, requiring these skills can be processed at the same time as 1 and 2. If these were added, all computer skills would be in full use and work output would be maximized. In actual practice, of course, all processing in one area need not be done at the same time. The computer can stop at any point, such as when partially through the reading of program 1, and later resume processing with no time loss. Decisions as to when to interrupt one program to provide optimal overall operating efficiency of the computer is the job of the executive program.

SUGGESTED FURTHER READING

Cuttle, G., and P. B. Robinson, *Executive Programs and Operating Systems,* American Elsevier, New York, 1970.

Rosen, S., *Programming Systems and Languages,* McGraw-Hill, New York, 1967.

Wilkes, M. V., and R. M. Needham, "The Design of Multiple-Access Computer Systems," 2 parts, *Computer Journal,* May 1967 and February 1968.

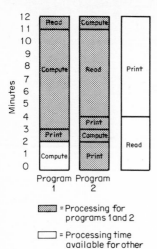

Figure 45. Simultaneous processing of two computer programs by an executive program.

EXECUTIVE TIME CONTROL

Areas for use in Cost Control:

ORGANIZATIONAL AND OPERATIONAL SYSTEMS

INDUSTRIAL APPLICATIONS

BUSINESS AND COMMERCIAL APPLICATIONS

Executive time control is the reduction of cost of management through more efficient use of executive time.

INTERRUPTIONS

One of the biggest problems in making the best use of executive time is how to eliminate interruptions. Planning and reading are particularly difficult if there are interruptions every few moments. At the same time, it is essential for other members of the company to be able to communicate with the executive.

The best way of dealing with this problem is to set aside a two-hour period each day, perhaps 11 A.M. to 1 P.M., when the executive is not to be disturbed. This leaves time early in the morning and after lunch for employees to present problems. The 11-to-1 time is generally good, because some of the regular staff will be lunching during that period.

A less satisfactory solution is for the executive to regularly work for a couple of hours after the staff has gone for the day.

DELEGATION OF RESPONSIBILITY

The best method of conserving executive time is to delegate all routine work to subordinates. The problem, however, is hiring subordinates capable of such responsibilities and training them to carry out the work. If the executive spends a good part of the day discussing the pros and cons of every task with her or his subordinates, she or he might as well have done the jobs.

Both university training in management decision making and intercompany managerial training programs are necessary to overcome this problem. The executive should also let subordinates know he or she expects them to be responsible for duties delegated to them, as junior managerial staff tend to think their superiors want and expect constant questioning.

CONTACTS WITH OTHER PEOPLE

Various studies of executive time show that over half of each working day is spent in contact with other people—meetings, telephone calls, contact with individual staff members, etc. With this amount of time "spent," it is difficult to find needed time for planning, reading technical or business literature, and thinking creatively.

Solution of the problem means setting aside time regularly for this planning, reading, and creative thinking. If necessary, find a location away from the office for these activities.

Keep meetings and conferences to a minimum time by coming to the point, dealing with it, and returning to other work. Many meetings tend to turn into social affairs, wasting business time.

Schedule regular times to deal with subordinate problems and questions.

Organize communication, using brief, written communication where possible, since verbal conversations have a greater tendency to become "chatty." Telex messages, for example, are much less expensive than telephone calls, take less of the executive's time, and provide a record of the communication. In addition, use of the Telex requires the executive to think out the problem *before* starting the communication, rather than thinking it out piecemeal during an expensive long-distance telephone call.

Written communication is easier to analyze for value of content than is verbal communication. Briefly look through carbon copies of correspondence for the past week. What percentage deals with cost reduction? What percentage deals with planning? With quality control? Such a study will show areas that need more attention.

Studying copies of written communication of subordinates will pinpoint those employees who are ready for advancement and more responsibility.

FINANCIAL PROBLEMS

Best use of time depends on limiting executive handling of financial problems to responsibility areas. Company presidents, for example, will be concerned with planning for profitability, but collections, liquidity, etc., should be dealt with by the head of the accounting department.

TECHNICAL PROBLEMS

In the same way, technical aspects of the firm should be distributed according to executive function. Top-level executives generally will oversee R&D (after the program is set by the head of R&D), purchasing *policy* discussions, pricing methods, trade relations policy, budgeting, plant working conditions, and staffing of senior positions. Department heads, of course, are responsible for technical problems within their departments, and supervisory personnel should handle line technical matters such as optimum equipment and material use.

SOCIALIZING

Some business is necessarily conducted in social atmospheres, but three-hour business lunches, excessive trade conferences and meetings, as well as the time required to travel to and from these events, are executive time-wasters. Careful evaluation should be made of social/business events to be certain that the business matter deserves the amount of time that will be required. If a social event does require business representation, care should be taken to send only the executive who can do the company the most good. There is no point in junior staff going along unless they are required for a specific reason. Top executives are not always the best business representatives at social events. The managerial person who will have contact in the future with other persons attending is the one who should attend.

SUGGESTED FURTHER READING

Humble, John, *Improving the Performance of the Experienced Manager,* McGraw-Hill, New York, 1973.
McNulty, N. G., *Training Managers,* Harper & Row, New York, 1969.

EXPERT-KNOWLEDGE APPROACH

Areas for use in Cost Control:

ORGANIZATIONAL AND OPERATIONAL SYSTEMS
DATA RETENTION—FILES AND RECORDKEEPING
MATERIALS AND EQUIPMENT MANAGEMENT
INDUSTRIAL APPLICATIONS
BUSINESS AND COMMERCIAL APPLICATIONS

The expert-knowledge approach eliminates the need for a programmer when producing some computer software items by using a bank of expert knowledge that can apply to multiple problems. This knowledge falls into three main types:

1. *Problems*—includes a structured set of relations between domain entities.
2. *Operations*—includes rules determining when to apply operations or transformations to specific problems.
3. *Specialization*—specific application of expert knowledge to individual problems.

Use of the technique allows automatic software production, without a programmer, particularly in inventory and data processing applications.

SUGGESTED FURTHER READING

Lapedes, D. N., ed., *Yearbook of Science and Technology,* McGraw-Hill, New York, 1974.

EXPONENTIAL SMOOTHING

Areas for use in Cost Control:

ORGANIZATIONAL AND OPERATIONAL SYSTEMS
INDUSTRIAL APPLICATIONS
BUSINESS AND COMMERCIAL APPLICATIONS

Exponential smoothing can reduce the costs of business forecasting by increasing the accuracy of such forecasts. The technique gives greater weight to recent trends when forecasting through use of a *smoothing constant* factor. For example, in calculating a simple average, figures are used at their usual 1/1 value. In exponential smoothing, however, older figures are valued at a lower figure, while later figures are given a value ratio of over 1. For example, if weekly sales figures have been $68,000, $72,000, $76,000, $74,000, $77,000, and $83,000, the average of the six weeks' sales is $75,000. Yet this figure would not provide an accurate forecast, since the later weeks show an increasing trend. The last figure is multiplied by a smoothing constant. The smoothing constant is expressed as a percentage figure—the higher the figure, the more wieght given to the last figure.

$$\$83,000 \times 40\% = \$33,200$$

The five earlier figures are averaged separately and multiplied by the percentage remaining from 100 percent after the smoothing constant has been subtracted (60 percent in this case):

$$\frac{\$68,000 + \$72,000 + \$76,000 + \$74,000 + \$77,000}{5} = \$73,400 \times 60\%$$

$$= \$44,040$$

These two factors are then added:

$33,200
 44,040
─────────
$77,240

The result is an *exponentially smoothed* sales forecast of $77,240 weekly, which gives more weight to recent sales trends.

Various percentage rates may be used as the smoothing constant, and determination of an accurate percentage may be made by examination of past sales records. If these are not used, a trial-and-error method may be adopted until an accurate percentage is determined.

SUGGESTED FURTHER READING

Argenti, John, *Management Techniques,* G. Allen, London, 1970.

EXTERNALITY TECHNIQUE

Areas for use in Cost Control:

ORGANIZATIONAL AND OPERATIONAL SYSTEMS
INDUSTRIAL APPLICATIONS
BUSINESS AND COMMERCIAL APPLICATIONS

The externality technique makes use of methods, programs, etc., developed by a competitor to reduce costs. For example, a manufacturer may cite a settlement favorable to the competing company when conducting labor negotiations, hoping to reduce labor costs in the settlement. Or a department store may actively recruit employees from a competitor with an especially good training program, reducing its own training costs.

SUGGESTED FURTHER READING

Bannock, G., R. E. Baxter, and R. Rees, *A Dictionary of Economics,* Penguin, Baltimore, 1974.

FACTORING

Areas for use in Cost Control:

ORGANIZATIONAL AND OPERATIONAL SYSTEMS
INDUSTRIAL APPLICATIONS
BUSINESS AND COMMERCIAL APPLICATIONS

Factoring is the selling of invoices to reduce collection and bad debt costs and to provide additional capital. Frequently, banks own all or are part owners of the factoring companies that buy the invoices. The technique is used for both national and international collections.

SUGGESTED FURTHER READING

Davis, William, *Money Talks,* Coronet Books, London, 1974.
Ellsworth, P. T., *The International Economy,* Macmillan, New York, 1969.

FAIL SOFTLY SYSTEM

Area for use in Cost Control:

ORGANIZATIONAL AND OPERATIONAL SYSTEMS

A fail softly system is a computer system designed to remove or reroute the necessary portion of a workload when a single piece of the system's equipment becomes inoperable, reducing the costs and problems created by such failures. Programs are written to provide switching of work from one unit to another, to use separate and still available files, to use alternate terminals, etc. Thus, an entire operation is not halted by a single equipment breakdown as it would be if a fail softly system were not incorporated into the programming.

SUGGESTED FURTHER READING

Martin, J., and A. R. D. Norman, *The Computerized Society,* Prentice-Hall, Englewood Cliffs, N.J., 1970.

FATIGUE STUDY

Areas for use in Cost Control:

PSYCHOLOGICAL MOTIVATIONAL MANAGEMENT
WORK PLACE MOTIVATIONAL MANAGEMENT
ORGANIZATIONAL AND OPERATIONAL SYSTEMS
INDUSTRIAL APPLICATIONS
BUSINESS AND COMMERCIAL APPLICATIONS

Fatigue study details and evaluates fatigue variables to determine how to reduce them, reducing unit production costs at the same time.

Worker fatigue is generally caused by one or more of the following:

1. *Poor working conditions,* including factors of noise, lighting, ventilation, temperature and humidity, and physical equipment design

2. *Job demands,* including physical and psychological demands

3. *Workers' physical and psychological condition*

Measurement of such fatigue can be obtained by one or more of three methods:

1. *Observation and statistical measurement* to determine the degree of fatigue in a given performance area, such as hand-eye coordination

2. *Comparison of actual fatigue factors* with variables previously measured, including greater amounts of time required to complete a given task once an undesirable level of fatigue is reached

3. *Mechanical measurement,* using various electronic and other instruments designed to measure fatigue

Reduction of fatigue, and thus reduction of production costs per unit, may be implemented in several ways:

Improving Work Conditions. Better lighting, ventilation, physical equipment or furnishings design, colors used, and noise control are examples of improvements in physical working conditions that can reduce fatigue.

Efficient Use of Motion. Reduction of physical energy through controlled physical patterns of work. *See also* **Motion Study.**

Overtime Limitation. Regular and steady overtime increases fatigue, lowering production as well as adding disproportionate costs to production. Limiting overtime to a set proportion of the standard workweek serves to reduce such fatigue.

Hiring Suitable Employees. Workers should be neither over- nor underqualified, for minimization of fatigue. A college graduate, for example, would be bored and quickly fatigued by a monotonous, minimal job, while an underqualified worker would be fatigued by the pressures of a job demanding more than his or her capabilities.

Efficient Scheduling and Use of Rest Breaks. Rest-period schedules should be developed to provide fatigue relief but not of a frequency or duration to break a normal work cycle.

Psychological Motivation. Employees who are satisfied with their jobs and working conditions are less subject to fatigue.

SUGGESTED FURTHER READING

Barnes, R. M., *Motion and Time Study,* 2d ed., Wiley, New York, 1961.
Florence, Philip S., *Use of Factory Statistics in the Investigation of Industrial Fatigue,* AMS Press, Inc., New York, 1973.

FIEDLER MODEL OF LEADERSHIP EFFECTIVENESS

Areas for use in Cost Control:

PSYCHOLOGICAL MOTIVATIONAL MANAGEMENT
ORGANIZATIONAL AND OPERATIONAL SYSTEMS

The Fiedler model of leadership effectiveness states that workers are best motivated by a leader through:

1. Good work relationship between employee and supervisor
2. Authority structure that gives the leader the power to reward and/or punish employees
3. Organization of work and work methods suited to the type of workers involved

As in other leadership models, costs are reduced through increased worker performance.

SUGGESTED FURTHER READING

Fiedler, F. E., *A Contingency Model of Leadership Effectiveness,* Academic, New York, 1964.

FILING AND OVERFILING

Areas for use in Cost Control:

PAPERWORK DESIGN AND FLOW SYSTEMS
DATA RETENTION SYSTEMS

Reducing the cost of any filing system involves:

1. Establishing a clear, concise filing system
2. Filing only those items that may be needed for business purposes

Establishing a Filing System. Basically, two methods are used. In the first, all items are filed alphabetically in one central file. This is particularly suitable in smaller companies where multiple files create more work than they save.

In larger firms, however, some type of multiple filing system is necessary. These may include:

1. *Division by department,* with each area filing its own paperwork alphabetically.

2. *Duplicate divisional filing,* with one copy of all material filed centrally and a second copy filed in the department's own file. Such duplicate filing can be justified only if clerical personnel in both departmental and central offices are housed some distance apart and both must constantly refer to filed material. Often, even this situation can be avoided by using an office and plant layout that facilitates using only one filing system (see Fig. 46).

3. *Division by subject area,* with alphabetical filing in each. This includes separation into types of transaction. Invoices are filed in one place, for example, while orders are filed in another.

Alphabetical filing generally proves more economical and efficient than filing by date, since a customer's name is a more certain point of reference than a date that may or may not be remembered correctly.

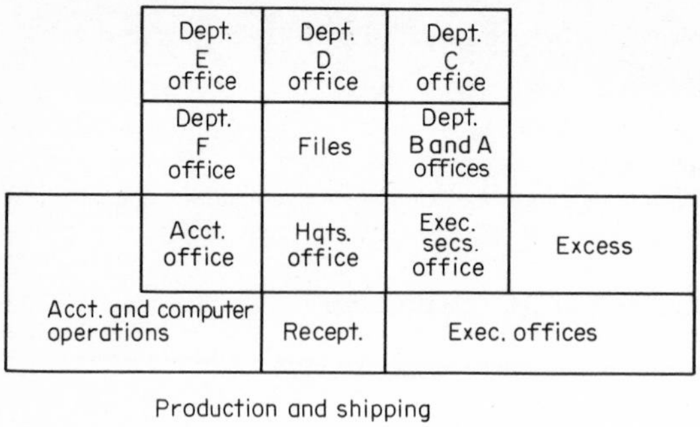

Dept. E office	Dept. D office	Dept. C office	
Dept. F office	Files	Dept. B and A offices	
Acct. office	Hqts. office	Exec. secs. office	Excess
Acct. and computer operations	Recept.	Exec. offices	

Production and shipping

Figure 46. Office layout for central filing.

Limiting Filing. Many firms waste time and money by overfiling. Items that do not need to be kept include:

1. Memos later put into letter or agreement form.
2. Letters and papers with only a temporary value, such as a bid for a government contract. If the firm does not get this bid, no one will ever refer to it again.
3. First or working drafts that are later duplicated in a finished form.
4. Routine letters of congratulation or thanks.
5. Printed matter fastened to a letter or paper that should be filed.

The key here is to make certain that someone has the authority to throw such items away. Without such authority, a secretary is apt to file everything that comes across his or her desk rather than take a chance.

FILING EQUIPMENT

Filing equipment will eventually be replaced by computerized storage of necessary information. When this happens, the letter, invoice, or order can be coded for entry in data banks at the time it is prepared. In the meantime, however, conventional systems vary. Good points to look for when choosing a system include:

1. Filing space at a convenient height. Some cabinets have file drawers at arm and shoulder level, leaving floor-level space for storage of seldom-used material.

2. Pull-out horizontal racks, rather than narrow drawers, facilitate paperwork identification and handling.

3. Filing equipment designed for use at seated height. Large companies with clerical staff who do nothing but file invoices, orders, etc., each day will especially find this type of system economical.

It is a mistake to purchase the cheapest possible equipment, since it is a one-time cost. Rather, buy the equipment that will allow staff to file material as quickly and easily as possible, since the cost of their labor is the major expense of filing.

SUGGESTED FURTHER READING

Cost Control and the Supervisor, American Management Assn., New York, 1966.

FILING CLASSIFICATION SYSTEMS

Areas for use in Cost Control:

DATA RETENTION—FILES AND RECORDKEEPING
INDUSTRIAL APPLICATIONS
BUSINESS AND COMMERCIAL APPLICATIONS

Filing classification systems include alphabetical, numerical, geographical, subject area, and chronological classifications. Costs are reduced by using the system or systems best suited to a particular operation. In invoice files, for example, classification may be by account name, invoice number, or shipment date, depending on company policy.

Alphabetical classification generally uses customer name, filing data alphabetically beginning with *A*. Decisions must be made as to whether to file abbreviated names, such as Mt. Olympus Tile Company, as if the abbreviation were fully written out, or to follow the abbreviated lettering. Names beginning with *Mc, Mac,* or *O'* should be filed following the entire sequence of lettering.

Numerical classification files *one* type of form, such as invoices, in numerical sequence. A different file must be maintained for each type of form used.

Geographical classification files data by address of the company concerned. Government departments are widest users of this method, using filing by geographical areas for property tax records, deeds, zoning data, etc.

Subject classification files data by subject matter. The technique is useful for research projects, including market research, but it is not generally suitable for other business and industrial applications.

Chronological classification files data by date. The system is seldom used by itself, but is often combined with alphabetical classification. For example, a sales file may contain folders for each account, filed alphabetically by customer name. Within each folder, correspondence and other data may be filed chronologically.

SUGGESTED FURTHER READING

Bassett, E. D., *Business Filing and Records Control,* South-Western Publishing Company, Cincinnati, 1963.

Place, I. M., and E. L. Popham, *Filing and Records Management,* Prentice-Hall, Englewood Cliffs, N.J., 1966.

FIXED COSTS

Areas for use in Cost Control:

ORGANIZATIONAL AND OPERATIONAL SYSTEMS

INDUSTRIAL APPLICATIONS

Fixed costs are those generally unaffected by quantity of output. They usually have a time, rather than a use, function; these are such costs as monthly rentals and weekly cleaning costs. Fixed costs are sometimes called period costs and burden costs. Fixed costs may be determined by budget appropriations or by investment needs for future operation.

SUGGESTED FURTHER READING

Sowell, Ellis, *Theories and Techniques of Standard Costs,* University of Alabama Press, 1973.

FLEXIBILITY LEADERSHIP

Areas for use in Cost Control:

PSYCHOLOGICAL MOTIVATIONAL MANAGEMENT

ORGANIZATIONAL AND OPERATIONAL SYSTEMS

Flexibility leadership is based on the idea that successful leadership is dependent on a supervisor's sensitivity to workers and their goals and his or her ability to motivate employees to accomplish their goals via increased or more efficient work production. Good use of various means of communication between supervisor and subordinate is essential to the success of the technique. **Sensitivity training** is used for managerial education in this area.

SUGGESTED FURTHER READING
Tannenbaum, R., I. R. Weschler, and F. Massarik, *Leadership and Organization,* McGraw-Hill, New York, 1961.

FLEXIBLE BUDGETING

Areas for use in Cost Control:
ORGANIZATIONAL AND OPERATIONAL SYSTEMS
PAPERWORK DESIGN AND FLOW SYSTEMS
INDUSTRIAL APPLICATIONS
BUSINESS AND COMMERCIAL APPLICATIONS

Flexible budgeting is a **budgetary control** technique that allows a variety of possible outputs and their costs, the figures to change as required by business and market conditions. The method is most useful when such changes require additional expenditure and production cannot wait for time-consuming supplementary budget authorization.

Such flexible budgets can be drawn to show how costs and profits may vary by rate of production (see Table 19).

Table 19. A Flexible Budget

	Production, number of units, in millions					
	10	20	30	40	50	60
Price per unit	$ 20	$ 19	$ 18	$ 17	$ 16	$ 15
Sales, in millions of $s	$200	$380	$540	$680	$800	$900
Fixed costs, in millions of $s	$ 30	$ 30	$ 30	$ 30	$ 30	$ 30
Semifixed costs, in millions of $s	40	40	50	50	60	60
Variable costs, in millions of $s	60	90	150	220	260	300
Total costs, in millions of $s	$130	$160	$230	$300	$350	$390
Profit, in millions of $s	$ 70	$220	$310	$380	$450	$510

In addition, flexible budgeting must provide supplementary budgets where changing conditions require different expenditures. Budgeted standards must also be checked frequently, perhaps every three months, and changed when needed. Both of these aspects of the technique are more easily implemented by keeping careful records of labor or material price changes.

SUGGESTED FURTHER READING
Bunge, Walter R., *Managerial Budgeting for Profit Improvement,* McGraw-Hill, New York, 1968.
Willsmore, A. W., *Business Budgets in Practice,* Pitman, New York, 1973.

FLEXTIME

Area for use in Cost Control:
PSYCHOLOGICAL MOTIVATIONAL MANAGEMENT

Flextime, also called flexible working hours, is the use of variable working hours, allowing the employee to determine, within set boundaries, his or her own working hours. Usually a core time of 10 A.M. to 4 P.M. is required, and the additional two hours a day may be worked whenever the employee likes. Use of the technique can reduce labor costs by motivating employees to increase productivity.

SUGGESTED FURTHER READING

Roberts, H. S., *Roberts' Dictionary of Industrial Relations,* Bureau of National Affairs, Inc., Washington, D.C., 1966.

FLOWCHARTS See Procedure Charts.

F_0 FORECASTS

Areas for use in Cost Control:

ORGANIZATIONAL AND OPERATIONAL SYSTEMS
INDUSTRIAL APPLICATIONS
BUSINESS AND COMMERCIAL APPLICATIONS

An F_0 forecast, also called planned projection, shows the cost and other factors that will result from any business operation if company strategy operates as it has operated historically. By comparing F_0 forecasts with budgets and other goals, the company can determine areas needing strategy change to reduce costs and/or increase efficiency. The method also identifies historical factors that have affected major company trends.

In F_0 forecasting, historical, current, and projected levels calculated include the following:

1. Percentage of market held
2. Price increases, annual (percentage)
3. Costs increases, annual (percentage)
4. Overhead increases, annual (percentage)
5. Productivity change
6. Tax rate change

These percentages are then applied to monetary figures to forecast costs for any specified period.

SUGGESTED FURTHER READING

Argenti, John, *Systematic Corporate Planning,* Thomas Nelson and Sons, Ltd., London, 1974.

FOLLETT PHILOSOPHY

Areas for use in Cost Control:

PSYCHOLOGICAL MOTIVATIONAL MANAGEMENT
ORGANIZATIONAL AND OPERATIONAL SYSTEMS
INDUSTRIAL APPLICATIONS
BUSINESS AND COMMERCIAL APPLICATIONS

The Follett philosophy, developed by Mary Parker Follett, recommends the use of work as a constructive part of workers' goals and relationships, which both enriches the individual worker's life by giving him or her more job satisfactions and increases work efficiency, reducing labor costs. The Follett philosophy is based on the following principles, which can be applied to work situations:

Conflict can be constructive. When conflict, such as labor negotiation, is used to find solutions that are beneficial for both sides, it becomes constructive rather than destructive. To achieve this, both sides should identify their needs, stating them openly. Such needs are broken into parts and examined, and then suggestions for achievement of the needs are set out by both sides.

Order-giving and supervision should be limited to the minimum necessary to achieve work goals. Orders, when given, should be phrased in a way to obtain cooperation rather than resentment. Employees should be trained to know their work and take responsibility for it without excessive order-giving and supervision.

Power over other employees should be avoided and efforts made to achieve power with others. Employees should assume power and responsibility equal to their capacity.

Workers must share company objectives to obtain maximum efficiency. While a supervisor may tell a worker the department goal is 600 units, this will mean little unless the worker wants the department to reach this goal. Then he or she will put extra effort into achieving this goal. Employee sharing in policy making, goal setting, and financial gains is suggested as a means of involvement.

Knowledge, "expert" advice, etc., are considered for the effect they will have on overall company operations. Experts are not used because they are considered "experts," nor rejected because the manager does not like the experts' looks. They are used where they can benefit the company and its goals as a whole.

Training of persons who are interested in the quality of their work in known management techniques can improve the efficiency of the organization. These techniques must then be applied to work throughout the company.

SUGGESTED FURTHER READING

Pollard, H. R., *Developments in Management Thought,* Heinemann, London, 1974.

FOLLOW-THROUGH

Areas for use in Cost Control:

ORGANIZATIONAL AND OPERATIONAL SYSTEMS
INDUSTRIAL APPLICATIONS
BUSINESS AND COMMERCIAL APPLICATIONS

Establishing new cost reduction techniques sounds good to the responsible executive. But how do you know that it really works? And how can you be sure that it is continually used once the method is installed? The answer is follow-through. This technique is divided into two main areas:

1. Evaluation of a newly installed cost reduction technique
2. Enforcement of use of the technique

Evaluation. Methods of measuring the effectiveness of a cost reduction technique vary depending on the method, but the following cover major areas:

Office Cost Reduction Technique Evaluation. Checking the efficiency of most clerical techniques means evaluating the level and smoothness of paperwork flow. Date of backlogged (and unanswered) correspondence, number of unanswered items of correspondence, backlog (by date) of unfiled items, and backlog of uncompleted bookkeeping, order, or billing forms are the major yardsticks to be used. For example, if a travel bureau took 6 weeks to answer an average mail inquiry prior to implementing the new technique, has this figure now been cut to an acceptable time lag?

Stock Control Technique Evaluation. Questions to be asked in following through include:

1. Does the system show the total cost of new shipments, items used or sold, and current stocks quickly and conveniently at any given moment?

2. Does the technique show the individual or department that has used or subtracted items from inventory?

Filing System Evaluation. Follow-through in this area would mean a check to see if the new method keeps files in a central location, limits items filed to needed items, has cross-referencing to make finding a multi-entry faster and easier. Physically, is the system a convenient height and depth? And functionally, is filing up to date or more current than under the previous technique?

Production Evaluation. New cost reduction systems in production can be measured by checking to see whether:

1. Production time is less.
2. Material costs are smaller.
3. Production quality is better.

In evaluating cost reduction systems in *any* area, use the following basic measures:

1. Plan installation of the new technique and a measuring technique together.
2. Use a minimum of objective measurements.
3. Measure the "working employees'" production apart from that of supervisory labor.

Enforcement. A cost reduction system is without value if it is not used. It becomes necessary, then, to make sure that the new technique is followed. The essential steps in enforcing use of a new cost reduction technique include:

1. Make sure all supervisory staff understand all aspects of the technique thoroughly, and that they know it is to be in constant use.

2. Make sure employees understand all areas of the technique that affect their work. Generally, it is best to instruct them in the complete technique so they understand why it is being used as well as how it affects them personally. Instruct workers that the technique is to be used at all times.

3. Set up an inspection system making sure that the system is in use. Middle management may perform these inspections in areas related to their specialized field, or supervisors can be asked to inspect alternating departments where they have a working knowledge.

SUGGESTED FURTHER READING

Cost Control and the Supervisor, American Management Assn., New York, 1966.
Higgins, L. R., and L. C. Morrow, *Maintenance Engineering Handbook,* 3d ed., McGraw-Hill, New York, 1977.

FORCED-CHOICE RATING See Personnel Performance Appraisal.

FORCED DISTRIBUTION SYSTEM

Areas for use in Cost Control:
ORGANIZATIONAL AND OPERATIONAL SYSTEMS
INDUSTRIAL APPLICATIONS
BUSINESS AND COMMERCIAL APPLICATIONS

The forced distribution system is a simplified method of evaluating employee performance to show areas where efficiency can be increased to reduce labor costs. Each employee is rated in two areas: work performance and promotability.

In work performance rating, the employee is ranked on a five-point scale. Each supervisor distributes his or her subordinates on this scale as follows:

1. Best work performance: 10%
2. Good work performance: 20%

3. Satisfactory work performance: 40%
4. Low work performance: 20%
5. Worst work performance: 10%

Employees are rated as to promotability on a three-point scale:

1. Very promotable
2. Possibly promotable
3. Unlikely to be promotable

SUGGESTED FURTHER READING

Whisler, T. L., and S. F. Harper, *Performance Appraisal,* Holt, New York, 1962.

FORMS DESIGN AND PRODUCTION

Areas for use in Cost Control:

PAPERWORK DESIGN AND FLOW SYSTEMS
BUSINESS AND COMMERCIAL APPLICATIONS

Forms design and production reduces costs when properly carried out by increasing the efficiency of all required paperwork. Specific examples of well-designed forms are given in many specialized areas of this book; this entry presents the basic principles needed in designing and producing all types of forms.

Forms usually are designed by a combination of accident and practical experience. The printer may complain that there is not room for a specific column, for example, or the busy department head may decide to use an old form as the pattern rather than take the time to design a new one. The following checklist provides the principles of form design; not only can it be used in creating new forms, but forms in current use may be checked against it.

FORM DESIGN CHECKLIST

1. Are forms standardized, using one masthead, one layout style, one typeface, etc.?
2. Can forms be combined for more efficient use and lower printing costs?
3. Use brief form titles.
    mize data that the form will contain in the sequence they will be used, as a guide to body layout.
5. Layout should move in the sequence that work will be performed, from the top left of the page to the bottom right.
6. Figures to be added or subtracted should be placed in vertical columns, one under the other.
7. Figures to be multiplied or divided should be placed horizontally, one beside the other.
8. Vertical spacing should match that of the machines used to complete the form.
9. Horizontal spacing should allow ⅛ inch per letter or figure.

Production of forms is as important as their design. The following checklist provides the principles of form production:

FORM PRODUCTION CHECKLIST

1. Paper or card stock should be chosen for being the most economical that is suitable for use. Multiple-use forms should be printed on card stock. Forms seen by customers should be printed on good-quality paper. Office-use-only forms should use paper adequate for needed handling and filing.

2. Use standard international sizes:

74 by 105 mm	$2\frac{7}{8}$ by $4\frac{1}{8}$ in*
105 by 148 mm	$4\frac{1}{8}$ by $5\frac{7}{8}$ in*
148 by 210 mm	$5\frac{7}{8}$ by $8\frac{1}{4}$ in*
210 by 297 mm	$8\frac{1}{4}$ by $11\frac{3}{4}$ in*
297 by 420 mm	$11\frac{3}{4}$ by $16\frac{1}{2}$ in*

*Approximate figures.

3. For fewer than 25,000 copies of a single form, use offset printing.

4. For fewer than 5,000 copies, use plastic photographed plates rather than the more expensive metal plates used when printing forms by offset.

5. For more than 25,000 copies of a single form, letterpress printing should be cheapest.

6. For offset printing, prepare the form in a camera-ready style, or ask the printer to have an artist do this.

7. For letterpress printing, provide the printer with copy and a rough layout.

8. Choose form makeup according to use:

Glued in pads
Glued in sets with carbon copies
Perforated
Serially numbered

9. Check a proof copy or the camera-ready artwork before the form is printed, correcting any errors with a nonreproducing or light-blue-leaded pencil.

SUGGESTED FURTHER READING

Elfenbein, Julien, *Handbook of Business Form Letters and Forms,* Monarch Press, New York, 1971.
Kish, J. L., *Business Forms: Design and Control,* Ronald, New York, 1971.

FORMS FLOW CONTROL

Areas for use in Cost Control:

PAPERWORK DESIGN AND FLOW SYSTEMS
INDUSTRIAL APPLICATIONS
BUSINESS AND COMMERCIAL APPLICATIONS

Once forms are properly designed, further cost reduction can be effected by better forms flow control. To check your current forms flow control, sketch the office layout and draw a line indicating how each form moves through the office. If it zigzags back and forth, better control is needed.

Another method of checking forms flow control is to compare the time employees actually spend putting information on a form or using it with the time the form spends traveling around the office. At least 75 percent of the total should be *working* rather than *traveling* time.

Office layout should be planned to facilitate smooth forms flow. Invoice typists, for example, may be arranged so that completed invoices can be handed to the clerk checking them without either the typist or the clerk getting up at all.

Some offices can utilize a mechanical paper flow system by setting up a moving belt, similar to a small assembly line, for transportation of paperwork (see Fig. 47).

When movement of forms cannot be instantaneous, it is preferable to have periodic movement, rather than letting a whole day's paperwork accumulate in one employee's "out" basket. The employee may move these forms to their next work location or an internal mail service may be used.

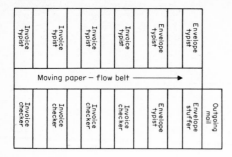

Figure 47. Possible office layout for mechanical transport of forms.

Forms and other paperwork should be timed so as to avoid peak and lax periods. The following are some methods of doing this:

1. Salaries should be paid at times of the month not coinciding with invoicing, bill collection, etc. Banking and income tax rulings make the 5th or 6th of each month suitable days for monthly salaries. Twice-monthly checks on specified dates are preferable to biweekly salaries that constantly change dates.

2. Customers can be billed on an alphabetical cycle, with letters A–D invoiced the 10th of each month, E–K invoiced the 15th of each month, etc. Some firms bill 13 times a year by working on a 28-day alphabetical cycle, which moves the billing date forward each month.

3. Routine work, such as forms filing, should be stockpiled for off-peak periods.

SUGGESTED FURTHER READING
Kish, J. L., *Business Forms: Design and Control,* Ronald, New York, 1971.
Urwick, L. F., *The Pattern of Management,* University of Minnesota Press, Minneapolis, 1970.

FORWARD MARKETING See Futures.

FREIGHT CLASSIFICATION CHANGES

Areas for use in Cost Control:
ORGANIZATIONAL AND OPERATIONAL SYSTEMS
MATERIALS AND EQUIPMENT MANAGEMENT
INDUSTRIAL APPLICATIONS
BUSINESS AND COMMERCIAL APPLICATIONS

Freight classification changes refers to obtaining authorization to lower freight classifications of a particular material or product to reduce transportation costs. The shipper applies to the common carrier and the government agency regulating rates, specifying reasons why the product or material deserves special classification and lower rates. The technique is most likely to be successful for relatively new products, or for products recently converted to new materials, since fewer classification precedents will exist for these. Thus, one product, such as a wastebasket, may have multiple classifications depending on the material used (weight), space required (dimensions and stackability), value of the product, durability, etc.

SUGGESTED FURTHER READING
Ammer, D. S., *Materials Management,* Irwin, Homewood, Ill., 1968.

FREIGHT EQUALIZATION

Areas for use in Cost Control:
MATERIALS AND EQUIPMENT MANAGEMENT
INDUSTRIAL APPLICATIONS

Freight equalization is the practice of obtaining an allowance when purchasing a standard-priced material that will equalize the material shipment cost with that of the seller's competitor located geographically nearer the buyer (with accompanying lower freight costs). Use of the method reduces overall costs of such materials when purchasing them from distant companies.

SUGGESTED FURTHER READING
Ammer, D. S., *Materials Management,* Irwin, Homewood, Ill., 1968.

FREIGHTLINER SYSTEM

Area for use in Cost Control:
INDUSTRIAL APPLICATIONS

The freightliner system is a method of rail shipment that combines regularly scheduled freight trains between major cities and the use of preloaded containers that are mechanically placed on flat cars designed for their use. At rail destinations, containers are loaded onto trucks mechanically. Costs are reduced by the lower amount of handling required, particularly on medium- and long-haul runs, but for greatest savings quantity of shipment must be adequate to fill a container. *See also* **Containerization.**

SUGGESTED FURTHER READING
Magee, J. F., *Physical Distribution Systems,* McGraw-Hill, New York, 1967.

FRINGE BENEFITS COST CONTROL

Areas for use in Cost Control:
FINANCIAL MOTIVATIONAL MANAGEMENT
ORGANIZATIONAL AND OPERATIONAL SYSTEMS
INDUSTRIAL APPLICATIONS
BUSINESS AND COMMERCIAL APPLICATIONS

The cost of fringe benefits has been estimated at as much as 25 percent of the costs of labor; the average cost, at about 15 percent (see Table 20). Fringe benefits are an expanding cost area as labor seeks increased and nontaxable benefits in addition to increased salaries. Clearly, then, with such large sums being spent, the area of fringe benefits offers considerable room for application of cost reduction methods.

Vacations. Vacations are usually the most expensive fringe benefit, averaging 8½ percent of labor costs for executives, 7½ percent for salaried employees, and about 6 percent for hourly employees.

While cutting vacation expense is a difficult task, some firms have experimented with a *vacation incentive plan.* Using this method, an employee is given a base vacation (usually one week) and then earns additional vacation time by meeting increased production scale ratings. Thus, if an employee's production is increased by 10 percent, averaged over a yearly period, he or she will receive a second week's paid vacation (in addition to wage incentive payments where operative). A 20 percent increase in productivity might earn four weeks' paid vacation overall, and so on.

Table 20. Comparison of United States and United Kingdom Companies' Fringe Benefits as a Percentage of Payroll[1]

Country	0–5%	5–7½%	7½–10%	10–12½%	12½–15%	15–17½%	17½–20%	20–25%	25–30%	30–35%	35–40%	40%+
U.S.A.	2.5%	—	10.0%	20.0%	10.0%	12.5%	22.5%	5.0%	10.0%	2.5%	—	5.0%
U.K.	0.7%	2.6%	21.8%	31.9%	18.6%	7.2%	5.8%	6.2%	2.9%	1.3%	0.3%	0.7%

[1]*Enquiry into Fringe Benefits*, Glasgow University Department of Social and Economic Research, Glasgow, Scotland.

Holidays. Costs due to absenteeism before and/or after a holiday have been reduced by some firms through *holiday insurance plans.* Using this method, employees are paid for a holiday *only* if they work the day before and the day following.

Tardiness and production slump are best controlled by supervisory attention. Some firms find that more frequent, shorter breaks alleviate pre- and post-holiday restlessness, bringing production levels back to normal.

Paid Sick Leave. Various control systems are in use, including:

1. Predetermined allowable number of sick days per year; usually, one per month, not to exceed 10 per year. Some firms allow accumulation of sick days from year to year, but most do not. U.S. civil service employees may accumulate up to 60 sick days.

2. Paid leave only on provision of a doctor's certificate.

3. No pay for the first one to four consecutive days, followed by full pay for a predetermined time. This method is usually in connection with a group insurance policy so that the only cost to the company is the insurance premium. Employee income is protected during a long-term illness, yet single "sick days" are less frequent when the employee is not to be paid.

Insurance: Medical, Hospitalization, and Life. Costs can be reduced by offering the employee a selection of plans. For example, an employee with a starting salary of $15,000 may be offered a choice of three of the five following items:

1. Full medical coverage
2. Full dental coverage
3. Full hospitalization coverage
4. $10,000 life insurance
5. $100-deductible medical and hospitalization

Depending on the employee's personal situation, the choices will vary. For example, a single man or woman will probably be less interested in life insurance than will a married employee, while full medical, dental, and hospitalization coverage may be quite appealing to him or her.

Another common method is to share insurance coverage costs with the employee, deducting his or her portion from the pay check.

Retirement Plans. Costs can be reduced through fairly rigorous eligibility requirements. For example, an employee may become eligible for retirement plans only after a predetermined period of employment (this may be as much as five years) and within a predetermined age bracket.

The company may share retirement plan payments with employees as a means of reducing costs, but this method has the disadvantage of requiring some return of money to the employee who leaves the firm prior to retirement.

Severance Pay. Reduction of such costs depends mainly on two areas of control:

1. Careful hiring of employees so that a department is not overstaffed, and hiring of a quality employee to prevent the need to dismiss workers
2. Precise limitations for collection: length of service, cause of job loss, etc.

Moving Expenses. Cost reduction can best be effected through limitations in the form of a company policy. For example, all moves paid by the firm may be made through a moving company with which the firm has an annual contract at a reduced rate. In addition, since the company, rather than the employee, is the mover's client, billings are more likely to be controlled. Specification should be made as to allowable methods of travel if the company pays transportation for the new employee and his or her dependents. Mileage by car is the usual method, although tourist-class air fares may be allowed for long-distance traveling.

If temporary housing expenses are paid while the employee looks for a new home, maximum cost and time limits should be set. These may be graduated by employment level. Very large companies may own a few housing units for temporary housing purchases, which can provide a sound capital investment in addition to reducing temporary housing costs.

Automobiles and Driving Expenses. Generally, three methods are used for automobile provision:

1. Company ownership
2. Leasing
3. Employee allowance

Leasing is generally considered the least expensive method, as well as the least troublesome, since no capital expenditure is required and since the leasing firm is responsible for insurance and maintenance.

Most firms pay employees a fixed mileage rate to cover operational costs, but such costs may be reduced by requiring that local gasoline and oil purchases be made at a specific station located near the business site. All billings for such expenses come directly to the firm, where they are checked for authorization signatures, amounts, etc.

An alternate method is to compute the mileage an employee is expected to travel, and to pay a lump sum to cover operating expenses. Use of this method is probably the best means of ensuring that costs are actually business expenses, but estimation of mileage to be traveled may prove difficult for employees whose business travel does not follow a predetermined route.

Profit Sharing and/or Stock Options. Costs may be reduced by limiting such plans to employees with predetermined seniority or status, but care should be taken to calculate possible motivational benefits and to weigh these against the cost of more inclusive plans.

Further Education. Costs are best reduced by limiting such payment to college or technical education related or helpful to the employee's work, or to an area of work within the company. In addition, tuition and/or book payments should be reimbursed *after* the employee has satisfactorily completed the class. College-grade cards of a predetermined level or an instructor's statement may be used for this purpose. Amounts reimbursed may be limited to the equivalent of fees charged by government-operated schools or universities, or limited to a percentage of total fees, sharing the cost with the employee.

Meals at work are frequently subsidized, with some firms providing free meals. Usually a contractual agreement is signed with a commercial or industrial food-catering firm, with the company providing kitchen and cafeteria space and equipment, allowing low-cost meals, since rent, utility, and equipment overheads have been removed. Acquiring maximum service and food quality for minimum expenditure can best be achieved by random sampling of operations of two or three reputable firms being considered.

In some cases, costs can be reduced further by hiring a food service manager who will oversee the operation without a catering firm. Such an employee will be more likely to provide quality and economical service, since he or she will have a more long-term interest in the operation.

Food operation costs carry the benefit of keeping employees on the premises and may easily be offset by saved tardiness.

FRINGE BENEFIT VISIBILITY

In addition to reducing fringe benefit costs, the company can get maximum value for its expenditures by making sure employees regularly know the value of their benefits. This can be achieved with the use of a personal fringe benefit report. Such reports may be issued periodically (usually quarterly) and can be printed out quite economically through computerized standard fringe benefit cost data. Figure 48 shows a sample personal fringe benefit report form, which can be modified as needed.

SUGGESTED FURTHER READING

Coffin, R., and M. Shaw, *Effective Communication of Employee Benefits,* American Management Assn., New York, 1971.
Hettenhouse, G. W., "Cost Benefit Analysis of Executive Compensation," *Harvard Business Review,* July–August 1970.

PERSONAL FRINGE BENEFIT REPORT

Name ___Frank Reed___

Department ___Marketing___   Date Dec. 31. 1976

Listed below are the values of your XYZ Company fringe benefits for the year to date:

Vacation pay	$1,250.25
Holiday pay	532.30
Medical insurance	240.90
Hospitalization insurance	635.10
Dental insurance	105.05
Life insurance	56.15
Sick pay	540.20
Automobile	1,830.50
Retirement plan contribution	250.00
Profit sharing	350.00
Stock options	225.00
Educational	260.75
Other (specify moving, housing, etc.)	. . .
Total	$6,276.20

Figure 48. Sample personal fringe benefit report form.

FRUSTRATION-AGGRESSION MOTIVATION THEORY

Area for use in Cost Control:

PSYCHOLOGICAL MOTIVATIONAL MANAGEMENT

The frustration-aggression motivation theory states that job frustration creates aggressive activity. Thus, an employee who finds a barrier to his or her work goals may do one of three things:

1. Try to reach the goal in new ways.
2. Decide not to work toward any goal at all.
3. Substitute more easily achieved goals.

If he or she decides not to work toward any goal, or becomes hostile in attempts to reach the unattainable goal, the work will be adversely affected. It is, therefore, important to establish a system of attainable goals with suitable rewards to maintain labor efficiency and lower its costs.

According to W. H. Eaton, an industrial psychologist, work frustrations can be divided into seven major areas:

1. Work-group unimportance
2. Lack of contact (and approval or disapproval) from company ownership

3. Lack of position advancement
4. Lack of a defined work role
5. Rapidly changing work conditions and technology
6. Isolation of work from social community
7. Economic work insecurity

SUGGESTED FURTHER READING

Dollard, J., W. Doob, N. E. Miller, O. H. Mower, and R. R. Sears, *Frustration and Aggression,* Yale University Press, New Haven, 1939.

Eaton, W. H., "Hypotheses Related to Worker Frustration," *Journal of Social Psychology,* no. 35, 1952.

FULL-LINE FORCING

Areas for use in Cost Control:

ORGANIZATIONAL AND OPERATIONAL SYSTEMS
INDUSTRIAL APPLICATIONS
BUSINESS AND COMMERCIAL APPLICATIONS

Full-line forcing is forcing the consumer to buy two or more products in a line of products to obtain the one he or she wants. For example, four cakes of eye shadow may be packed together, with no single cakes available. In Europe, film is commonly sold including processing. The method ensures sales of products or services that might or might not otherwise be purchased from the same company and also reduces sales, packaging, and distribution costs per product and/or service unit.

SUGGESTED FURTHER READING

Bannock, G., R. E. Baxter, and R. Rees, *A Dictionary of Economics,* Penguin, Baltimore, 1974.

FULL-LOAD VEHICULIZATION

Area for use in Cost Control:

INDUSTRIAL APPLICATIONS

Full-load vehiculization is a method of reducing transportation charges by filling a tractor/trailor unit with goods for one destination. The unit can be sealed by the customs department for overseas transport and driven on and off the ship, saving dock loading and unloading costs.

SUGGESTED FURTHER READING

Dover, Victor, *The Shipping Industry,* MacDonald, London.

FUNCTIONAL ANALYSIS

Areas for use in Cost Control:

ORGANIZATIONAL AND OPERATIONAL SYSTEMS
BUSINESS AND COMMERCIAL APPLICATIONS

Functional analysis groups similar functions in **procedure study** to increase efficiency and reduce labor costs of clerical procedures. The person performing the analysis works from a typical procedure study flow process chart (Fig. 86) and groups motions and activities together where possible on an activity classification chart (Fig. 49). Functions are then combined or eliminated (Fig. 50).

SUGGESTED FURTHER READING

Clay, M. J., and B. H. Walley, *Performance and Profitability,* Longmans, London, 1965.

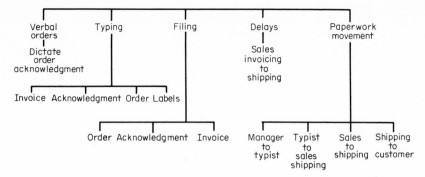

Figure 49. Typical activity classification chart, system under study.

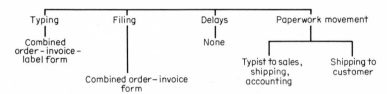

Figure 50. Typical activity classification chart, after functional analysis.

FUNCTIONAL ORGANIZATION

Areas for use in Cost Control:

ORGANIZATIONAL AND OPERATIONAL SYSTEMS
MATERIALS AND EQUIPMENT MANAGEMENT
INDUSTRIAL APPLICATIONS
BUSINESS AND COMMERCIAL APPLICATIONS

Functional organization is the division of work and responsibility by function to reduce costs and increase efficiency. One top-line manager oversees managerial staff who are responsible for the economical operation of the function of their areas (see Fig. 51). Within each functional area, specialized functions may also exist (see Fig. 52).

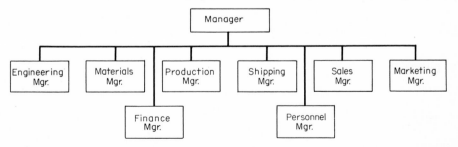

Figure 51. Typical functional organization chart.

Functional organization reduces the cost of specialized labor by limiting its use to the areas of specialty. For example, a technological forecaster in the marketing department is not expected to join group meetings reporting advertising returns, as he or she might be in a different type of organization. Instead, the use of time will all be related to technological forecasting. Employees operating equipment generally use the same piece

Figure 52. Specialized function division in functional organization.

of equipment continuously, improving their efficiency. A typist does not, for example, periodically use the calculator to help the accounting department. At managerial levels, dividing work by function also increases efficiency, because the employee is or becomes a specialist in his or her field. For example, a buyer who purchases only plastic materials will be better able to survey available materials, prices, etc., obtaining the lowest-cost material needed at a required level of quality, while a buyer purchasing several types of materials cannot develop such a specialized knowledge.

SUGGESTED FURTHER READING

Ammer, D. S., *Materials Management,* Irwin, Homewood, Ill., 1968.

FUNCTION ANALYSIS SYSTEM TECHNIQUE See Value Analysis.

FUNDING

Areas for use in Cost Control:

ORGANIZATIONAL AND OPERATIONAL SYSTEMS
INDUSTRIAL APPLICATIONS
BUSINESS AND COMMERCIAL APPLICATIONS

Funding is the conversion of short-term debt to long-term debt. Financing costs can be reduced in two ways:

1. Long-term debt interest rates are usually lower than short-term debt interest rates.

2. In an inflationary economy, the debt's full amount will decrease considerably in real value, proportionate to the length of time in which the debt is paid.

SUGGESTED FURTHER READING

Bannock, G., R. E. Baxter, and R. Rees, *A Dictionary of Economics,* Penguin, Baltimore, 1974.

FUTURES

Areas for use in Cost Control:

ORGANIZATIONAL AND OPERATIONAL SYSTEMS
INDUSTRIAL APPLICATIONS
BUSINESS AND COMMERCIAL APPLICATIONS

Futures are present contracts for future delivery of commodities purchased. The technique can reduce costs of needed materials and supplies if the user can accurately estimate the future market price and stop short of this amount in negotiations.

SUGGESTED FURTHER READING

Goss, B. A., *The Theory of Futures Trading,* Routledge and Kegan, Boston, Mass., 1972.

GAMING

Areas for use in Cost Control:

ORGANIZATIONAL AND OPERATIONAL SYSTEMS

INDUSTRIAL APPLICATIONS

BUSINESS AND COMMERCIAL APPLICATIONS

Gaming is an **operations research** technique using mathematical formulas to forecast probable actions of customers, competitors, etc., in controlling costs. For example, a company may wish to determine the highest possible price a customer will pay for a product. Or it may wish to determine the lowest-quality materials a customer will accept in a specific product.

Large numbers of business games or exercises have been developed, but the most useful ones include:

AMA Game. One of the earliest games, developed by the American Management Association in 1956, was a computerized game similar to a noncomputerized game called the "Andlinger Exercise," developed by McKinsey & Co. The AMA Game uses five teams of three to five players each. Each team represents a "company" and invents a hypothetical product to be sold in competition with the other teams. Business decisions are made in each "quarter" of simulated operation—usually 20 quarters to a game. These decisions include:

1. Product sales price
2. Marketing budget
3. Rate of production
4. Plant capacity
5. R&D budget
6. Market research budget

Three to nine quarterly decisions are required.

IBM Game. In this game, three hypothetical firms compete against one another. The market is divided into four geographical areas with each "company" located in one of the areas. Game procedure is like the AMA Game from this point.

INTOP. This game was developed by the University of Chicago for study of international trade. Three to 15 "companies" are chosen with four to seven members each. Each company's home office is in Lichtenstein, and the companies operate in one, two, or all of the following places:

1. United States
2. EEC
3. Brazil

Each company manufactures four grades of two products. Production management, best plant size, cost factors, scheduling, and financing decisions are made in the course of "play." Import and export taxes, shipping problems, etc., are included.

Carnegie Tech Game. This game simulates the packaged detergent industry. Thirty to 50 simulated months and 300 decisions are used. Each company sells three products in four geographical areas.

Daedalus. A British game, it allows for the manufacture of a variety of products from one basic raw material, before proceeding along usual gaming-procedure channels.

Quintain. This game was developed by Howard Farrow, Ltd., London, and simulates problems in the construction industry. Invitation to bid and bidding procedures are practiced by "players," as well as the usual production and marketing decision making. Predetermined economic factors, such as interest rates, flow of work, and labor markets, change during the game.

Wage Negotiation. This game was developed by the British Oxygen Staff College. "Players" practice wage negotiation on both company and labor union "teams." Precedent within the industry, economic state of the country and company, company policy, cost of living, increased production, other benefits paid, and cost and price status are the factors considered in negotiation.

SUGGESTED FURTHER READING

Avi-Itzhak, Benjamin, *Developments in Operations Research,* Gordon Press, New York, 1971.
Cyert, R. M., and L. A. Welsch, *Management Decision Making,* Penguin, Baltimore, 1971.

GANTT RESERVED-TIME PLANNING CHART

Areas for use in Cost Control:

ORGANIZATIONAL AND OPERATIONAL SYSTEMS
PAPERWORK DESIGN AND FLOW SYSTEMS
MATERIALS AND EQUIPMENT MANAGEMENT
INDUSTRIAL APPLICATIONS
BUSINESS AND COMMERCIAL APPLICATIONS

A Gantt reserved-time planning chart is an early visual technique used to schedule the workload of equipment and/or employees to ensure maximum use (see Fig. 53).

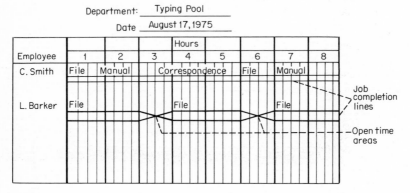

Figure 53. Gantt reserved-time planning chart.

Equipment or employees are listed to the left of a horizontal strip, which represents a period of time, such as a day. Planned work is scheduled by filling in the chart. When the work is completed, a line is drawn under the entry. Slack time is visually obvious to the supervisor, who can add to the schedule until all time is utilized. *See also* **Charting.**

SUGGESTED FURTHER READING

Bittel, L. R., *What Every Supervisor Should Know,* McGraw-Hill, New York, 1974.

GEARING

Areas for use in Cost Control:

ORGANIZATIONAL AND OPERATIONAL SYSTEMS
INDUSTRIAL APPLICATIONS
BUSINESS AND COMMERCIAL APPLICATIONS

Gearing, also called *leverage,* is evaluation of the cost of borrowing company profits to further increase profits and of the risk of not being able to meet usual dividend payment levels, to determine the least costly and most satisfactory source of money for this purpose.

SUGGESTED FURTHER READING

Argenti, John, *Systematic Corporate Planning,* Thomas Nelson and Sons, London, 1974.

GESTALT TECHNIQUES

Areas for use in Cost Control:

PSYCHOLOGICAL MOTIVATIONAL MANAGEMENT
INDUSTRIAL APPLICATIONS
BUSINESS AND COMMERCIAL APPLICATIONS

Gestalt techniques are behavior-adapting methods that help the manager or worker to develop his or her own problem-solving capacity, increasing efficiency and responsibility and thus lowering labor costs. *Gestalt,* a German word meaning "to see the whole," uses various methods of helping the individual to see different aspects of a work or other problem so as to be able to understand the whole situation and to do something positive to solve the problem. For example, most production speed problems can be viewed from at least two points of view:

Management's view, which sees the worker as lazy, unmotivated, and not willing to work as fast or as efficiently as he or she can.
Labor's view, which sees management as making an excessive profit from their work.

By using Gestalt techniques, both groups can see the other's point of view, easing the implementation of a productivity-increasing plan agreeable to both. Some of the techniques include:

Role-Playing. Members of both groups take turns pretending to be members of the other group, saying what they would do to solve the problem, how they would increase production, etc.

Physical Awareness. Gestalt psychologists have discovered that work and other problems are constantly shown through physical symptoms. Thus, if a worker says that constant headaches keep him or her from working efficiently, what he or she really means is that another person is so upsetting that it causes him or her to have a headache. If this occurs only at work, it may be the supervisor. Management can then study the supervisor's method of handling employees, which is probably holding back production. In physical-awareness exercises, participants express awareness of their physical condition at *this moment,* such as, "*Now,* my head hurts. *Now,* my back aches and feels tired."

Mental Awareness. Increased awareness increases efficiency by focusing the worker's attention on the matter at hand, such as how to increase production. If he or she is aware of this problem, without the mind wandering off on several different tracks, the worker can concentrate on the problem, solving it more quickly. In this way, supervisors may watch their workers for signs of a lack of awareness—looking absently into space, nervously drumming on a desk, or frowning at nothing in particular, for example. Such signs show decreased awareness of the present, the *now;* and as the worker's mind dwells on past misjustices or hypothetical future glories, it is impossible for him or her to concentrate on producing effectively the work to be done now.

Exercises that teach the worker to become accustomed to concentrating on the present may be practiced regularly. For example, the worker may verbally make observations about a coworker to the supervisor, being careful to *always* speak about the present.

Intervention. The supervisor asks workers *what* they are doing and *how* they are doing it, focusing their attention on current work.

Directness. All employees speak directly to one another, never using the third person. One worker does not complain about another's work to the supervisor in this technique, but instead tells the other worker directly of his dissatisfaction. This increases the employees' sense of responsibility to their coworkers, as well as to management.

Statements, Not Questions. In this technique, no questions are used. Instead, they are rephrased as statements. Rather than asking a supervisor, "Why didn't you tell me how to do that?" for example, a worker might rephrase the question, saying, "I need to know about that." The technique removes "hidden" innuendos of blame or inference among workers, allowing them to concentrate on the work at hand.

SUGGESTED FURTHER READING

Fagan, J., and I. L. Shepherd, eds., *Gestalt Therapy Now,* Harper and Row, New York, 1971.

Perls, Frederich, R. H. Hefferline, and Paul Goodman, *Gestalt Therapy,* Dell, New York, 1965.

GOLDEN HANDSHAKE

Areas for use in Cost Control:

ORGANIZATIONAL AND OPERATIONAL SYSTEMS
INDUSTRIAL APPLICATIONS
BUSINESS AND COMMERCIAL APPLICATIONS

The golden handshake is making a payment to an executive when dismissing him or her because of a lack of work. Use of the technique can reduce administrative costs by reducing overall salary expense, even though the one-time golden handshake payment may be quite high, depending on position and tenure.

SUGGESTED FURTHER READING

Hanson, J. L., *A Dictionary of Economics and Commerce,* MacDonald, London, 1974.

GORDON TECHNIQUE

Areas for use in Cost Control:

ORGANIZATIONAL AND OPERATIONAL SYSTEMS
INDUSTRIAL APPLICATIONS
BUSINESS AND COMMERCIAL APPLICATIONS

The Gordon technique is a method used to facilitate creative thinking in solving cost or other business problems that was developed by W. J. J. Gordon of Arthur D. Little, Inc. The technique resembles **brainstorming** except that group participants are not told the exact nature of the problem, so as to avoid hasty decision making and egocentric involvement in the problem. The group leader introduces a subject aligned to the problem, and this subject is discussed and ideas are established. Later in the session, these ideas are evaluated in relation to the basic problem. For example, if the problem is finding a low-cost material to substitute for steel in underwater construction, the leader may introduce the "effects of salt water on metal" as the initial subject. This would naturally lead to discussion of how sea water affects other materials. Next, an element suggesting the strength of various materials might be discussed, to involve those materials strong enough for construction purposes.

SUGGESTED FURTHER READING

Whiting, C. S., "Operational Techniques of Creative Thinking," *Advanced Management,* October 1955.

GOZINTO CHART See Assembly Chart.

GREEN STAMP TECHNIQUE See Prize Incentives.

GROUP DECISION MAKING

Areas for use in Cost Control:

PSYCHOLOGICAL MOTIVATIONAL MANAGEMENT
ORGANIZATIONAL AND OPERATIONAL SYSTEMS
INDUSTRIAL APPLICATIONS
BUSINESS AND COMMERCIAL APPLICATIONS

Group decision making is the motivation of workers to increase productivity and job satisfaction by their participation in company operational decision making. The method is one aspect of job democratization. Content of problems to be solved is said to be relatively unimportant so long as workers feel that the required decisions are meaningful. Motivation stems from the workers' feelings of involvement in the decision and consequent extended efforts to reach goals determined by the decision. Some experts, such as Likert, feel that decisions do not have to be unanimous in order to motivate the entire involved group, while others, such as Maier, feel that unanimous group decision is responsible for motivation.

SUGGESTED FURTHER READING

Davis, L. E., and J. C. Taylor, *Design of Jobs,* Penguin, Baltimore, 1972.
Likert, P., *New Patterns of Management,* McGraw-Hill, New York, 1961.
Maier, N. R. F., *Problem-Solving Discussions and Conferences,* McGraw-Hill, New York, 1963.

GROUP INTERVIEW

Areas for use in Cost Control:

ORGANIZATIONAL AND OPERATIONAL SYSTEMS
INDUSTRIAL APPLICATIONS
BUSINESS AND COMMERCIAL APPLICATIONS

The group interview is used to reduce time and costs of communicating necessary identical information to several employees. Auren Uris, in *The Efficient Executive,* says the method is most effective when:

1. Total interview time is proportionate to group size—usually about five minutes per employee.
2. Interview content is limited to facts and fact-finding.
3. Personal response is encouraged, with at least one response from each person being interviewed.

SUGGESTED FURTHER READING

Uris, Auren, *The Efficient Executive,* McGraw-Hill, New York, 1957.

GROUP TECHNOLOGY

Areas for use in Cost Control:

ORGANIZATIONAL AND OPERATIONAL SYSTEMS
MATERIALS AND EQUIPMENT MANAGEMENT
INDUSTRIAL APPLICATIONS

Group technology is the grouping of small lots of similar parts for mass production. Use of the technique reduces costs through the application of flow-line or mass production costs even to small numbers of products. All similar processes of such a group are performed together. For example, if three plastic products are all based on a similar-sized plastic disc, this base piece will be produced for all three products in one run. Or if all products in a group require drilling, all will be processed together.

Flow-line layouts are flexible ones when used in group technology. Machines are grouped by the technology required for the group of parts being processed, but these may be used in a variety of sequences.

Use of the method can be increased by designing products to contain similar technological processing steps where feasible.

Classification and/or coding (*see* **Classification and Coding Systems**) of technological aspects of each part manufactured will serve as a guide for grouping in future production. Such classification may be by material, design feature (such as shape), technological processes required, machines used, dimensions, and quantities to be produced.

Studies show that use of group technology reduces costs to the following degrees:

Capital	40%
Operation	50%
Inventory	50%
Labor	60%
Transportation	80%

SUGGESTED FURTHER READING

Burbidge, J. L., *An Introduction to Group Technology,* Turin International Center, 1969.
Lawson, H., and A. O. Putnam, "Group Technology," *Metalworking Economics,* June 1971.

GUARANTEE TECHNIQUE

Area for use in Cost Control:

PSYCHOLOGICAL MOTIVATIONAL MANAGEMENT

The guarantee technique is the use of a promise to persuade an employee to try a new work method or piece of equipment that can increase efficiency and/or reduce costs. For example, if a clerk is unwilling to use a new faster electronic calculator instead of a manual model, the supervisor may promise that the manual model can be used if the clerk tries the new machine for a week and still does not like it. Of course, it is essential that the clerk be thoroughly trained in how to work the new calculator so that dislike is not just a mask for lack of operating knowledge.

SUGGESTED FURTHER READING

Bittel, L. R., *What Every Supervisor Should Know,* McGraw-Hill, New York, 1974.

GUIDED INTERVIEWING See Personnel Attitude Measurement.

HAWTHORNE TECHNIQUE

Areas for use in Cost Control:

PSYCHOLOGICAL MOTIVATIONAL MANAGEMENT
ORGANIZATIONAL AND OPERATIONAL SYSTEMS
INDUSTRIAL APPLICATIONS
BUSINESS AND COMMERCIAL APPLICATIONS

The Hawthorne technique is the dividing of workers into small groups and is based on an experiment at Chicago's Western Electric Company that showed employees work most efficiently under such small-team conditions. Use of the method can reduce labor costs by increasing productivity.

SUGGESTED FURTHER READING

Dunlop, J. T., and V. P. Diatchenko, *Labor Productivity,* McGraw-Hill, New York, 1964.
Speight, H., *Economics and Industrial Efficiency,* Macmillan, New York, 1967.

HEAT RECOVERY AND COST CONTROL

Areas for use in Cost Control:

ORGANIZATIONAL AND OPERATIONAL SYSTEMS
MATERIALS AND EQUIPMENT MANAGEMENT
INDUSTRIAL APPLICATIONS
BUSINESS AND COMMERCIAL APPLICATIONS

Heat recovery in office and industrial locations can be implemented by several techniques, from the use of adequate insulation and draft excluders to the use of new mechanical equipment. Several newly developed items in this last category are particularly effective and have reduced heating costs as much as 50 percent. These include:

Electrical zone control equipment—individual temperature control of multiple areas from one master control unit, ensuring that heat is used only when and where necessary.
Recycled water or steam heating—cycling of industrial water or steam *after* production use, for heating purposes.
Waste incineration—systems that use heat from incinerated wastes for plant heat. Some plant installations have proved self-supporting once equipment is installed. In one new town in England heat and hot water are provided to several office blocks and an entire housing estate from the incineration of garbage collections.
Room heat conditioners remove heat from stale air as the air is extracted and add it to fresh incoming air. Operational costs per unit are about the same as those required for one 60-w light bulb.
Heat pumps transfer heat from the outside air into a building, providing about 2 kw of heat for each kw of electricity used in average winter weather conditions.
A *heat recovery wheel* is a motor-driven wheel heat exchanger that removes heat from exhaust air, returning it to the heating system, reducing fuel consumption by up to 50 percent.
Modular ceiling panels recover heat from lighting and exhaust air, recycling it into the building's heating system.

See also **Solar Power.**

SUGGESTED FURTHER READING

Chapman, A. J., *Heat Transfer,* Macmillan, New York, 1974.
Manser, J., "Designs to Cut the Fuel Bill," *The Financial Times,* London, Aug. 12, 1974.

HEDGING

Areas for use in Cost Control:

ORGANIZATIONAL AND OPERATIONAL SYSTEMS
INDUSTRIAL APPLICATIONS
BUSINESS AND COMMERCIAL APPLICATIONS

Hedging is the practice of buying needed materials or supplies for the future at the current price, protecting oneself from price movements by a speculative sale to a dealer, also for future delivery. Thus, the purchaser pays or reserves from the dealer the difference between the price paid and the price at delivery time. The technique reduces costs by compensating for any price loss or gain.

SUGGESTED FURTHER READING

Burnham, T. H., and G. O. Hoskins, *Elements of Industrial Organization,* Pitman, London, 1965.
Nicholson, T. A., *Optimization in Industry,* Aldine, Chicago, 1972.

HERZBERG'S TWO-FACTOR THEORY OF MOTIVATION

Area for use in Cost Control:
PSYCHOLOGICAL MOTIVATIONAL MANAGEMENT

Herzberg's two-factor theory states that two kinds of work factors exist:

1. *Motivating Factors*—those that are aimed at reaching work goals
2. *Dissatisfaction Factors*—those that meet employee needs through avoidance of unpleasant conditions or situations

Motivating factors include work recognition, achievement, completion, advancement, responsibility, and increased pay.

Dissatisfaction factors—unpleasant areas to be avoided because they do not necessarily provide any job satisfaction even when completed—include work problems with company policy, supervisors, salary, and adverse working conditions.

Thus, employees need to resolve dissatisfaction factors if deterioration of work quality and speed are to be prevented, but improvement in these areas is apt to result from achievement of motivating factors.

SUGGESTED FURTHER READING

Herzberg, F., B. Mausner, and B. B. Snyderman, *The Motivation to Work,* Wiley, New York, 1959.

HEURISTIC METHODS

Areas for use in Cost Control:
PSYCHOLOGICAL MOTIVATIONAL MANAGEMENT
ORGANIZATIONAL AND OPERATIONAL SYSTEMS
DATA RETENTION—FILES AND RECORDKEEPING

Heuristics are generalized rules used where precise data are not possible because of expense or other difficulties. Thus, in programming a computer for decision making or automation control, it is possible to reduce costs by using these generalized rules that can cover many situations, if precise data control is not needed. Heuristics are especially useful in areas such as sales forecasting and marketing studies. They may also be used in simulated problem solving to provide the best approaches to a cost problem, selecting from many feasible alternatives.

Normal language programming is used in heuristics, since mathematical equations are specific rather than generalized. Applications of heuristics are informal decisions, whether made by an individual or by a computer, stemming from the general rules provided.

SUGGESTED FURTHER READING

Borko, H., *Computer Applications in the Behavioral Sciences,* Prentice-Hall, Englewood Cliffs, N.J., 1962.
Feigenbaum, E. A., and J. Feldman, *Computers and Thought,* McGraw-Hill, New York, 1963.
George, F. H., *Cybernetics in Management,* Pan Books, London, 1970.

HIGH-LOW POINT METHOD

Areas for use in Cost Control:

ORGANIZATIONAL AND OPERATIONAL SYSTEMS
INDUSTRIAL APPLICATIONS

The high-low point method is a **cost analysis** technique (*see also* **Overhead Cost Control**). **Variable costs** per unit of production are separated from **fixed costs** by dividing the difference between the highest and lowest cost for a period by the difference between the highest and lowest measure of production or activity associated with that cost (see Table 21).

Table 21. Variable Cost Calculation in High-Low Point Method

		Equipment hours	Cost
Highest cost:	November	20,000	$700
Lowest cost:	June	12,000	450
		8,000	$250

$$\text{Variable cost} = \frac{\$250}{8{,}000} = \$0.03125 \text{ per equipment hour}$$

Fixed cost is determined by subtracting the variable cost from total cost at a given point.

SUGGESTED FURTHER READING

Fremgen, J. M., *Accounting for Managerial Analysis,* Irwin, Homewood, Ill., 1972.
Wood, E. G., *Costing Matters for Managers,* Cahners Publishing Company, Boston, 1974.

HIRING FREEZE

Areas for use in Cost Control:

ORGANIZATIONAL AND OPERATIONAL SYSTEMS
INDUSTRIAL APPLICATIONS
BUSINESS AND COMMERCIAL APPLICATIONS

A hiring freeze is the temporary elimination of any new hiring in an attempt to reduce labor costs when cost/profit ratios are not satisfactory. Employees are expected to absorb additional work created by retirements, illnesses, or vacancies. The method may reduce labor costs for a short time, but it is not a suitable long-term solution to labor cost problems, since some departments will experience heavier vacancy rates than others, creating unequal and, in some cases, impossible workloads.

SUGGESTED FURTHER READING

Horwitz, Ralph, *Realities of Profitability,* Pan Books, London, 1973.
Speight, H., *Economics and Industrial Efficiency,* Macmillan, New York, 1967.

HISTOGRAMS

Areas for use in Cost Control:

ORGANIZATIONAL AND OPERATIONAL SYSTEMS
INDUSTRIAL APPLICATIONS
BUSINESS AND COMMERCIAL APPLICATIONS

Histograms are statistical diagrams showing changes in figures—such as increases and/or decreases in income, production, or other areas—during a certain historical period; they are used in such cost control areas as budgeting and forecasting. Table 22 shows a typical histogram.

SUGGESTED FURTHER READING

Standingford, Oliver, ed., *Newnes Encyclopedia of Business Management,* Newnes, London, 1967.

Table 22. Histogram of Production Increases for 110 Companies for the Calendar Year 1974

Decrease (%)	Increase (%)	No. of companies
Over ½, less than 1		2
0 or over, less than ½		1
	0 or over, less than ½	6
	½ or over, less than 1	13
	1 or over, less than 1½	16
	1½ or over, less than 2	24
	2 or over, less than 2½	35
	2½ or over, less than 3	10
	3 or over	3

HORIZONTAL INTEGRATION

Areas for use in Cost Control:

ORGANIZATIONAL AND OPERATIONAL SYSTEMS
INDUSTRIAL APPLICATIONS
BUSINESS AND COMMERCIAL APPLICATIONS

Horizontal integration is the linking of similar businesses to reduce costs and/or increase efficiency (see Fig. 54). For example, a woolen mill may purchase synthetic fabric mills and cotton fabric mills, since the same equipment and staff can be used in many areas of all three operations, and since the market for all three is similar. Bulk purchasing, exchange of personnel, and combination of marketing operations are some of the operational areas that can secure reduced costs.

Figure 54. Horizontal integration.

Care must be taken to avoid horizontal integration to an extent that conflicts with antimonopoly laws.

SUGGESTED FURTHER READING

Batty, J., *Corporate Planning and Budgetary Control,* MacDonald, London, 1970.
Burnham, T. H., and G. O. Hoskins, *Elements of Industrial Organization,* London, 1965.

HOUSEKEEPING

Area for use in Cost Control:

WORK PLACE MOTIVATIONAL MANAGEMENT

Good housekeeping in an office or production facility can reduce costs because it:

1. Increases safety of the facility.
2. Keeps needed materials and supplies neatly at hand, saving searching time.

Initiating a thorough housekeeping program involves setting periodic checks, inspections, and reorganizations, as well as training employees in methods that will ensure continued good housekeeping.

HOUSEKEEPING CHECKLIST[1]

Walls and Ceilings
  1. Do you prohibit hanging of pipes, rags, wire, and other supplies on walls and ceilings?
  2. Do you provide a bulletin board for calendars, posters, and cartoons, so that employees will not place them on the walls?

Floors
  3. Is the danger of throwing scrap, parts, wire, nails, and other material on floors and platforms impressed upon workers?
  4. Are floors vacuum-cleaned or swept daily or, if necessary, more than once a day?
  5. Are floors washed regularly?
  6. Would a nonslip floor coating pay for itself by reducing slipping hazards?
  7. Do you need an exhaust system to remove dust or sawdust?
  8. Are oil and grease spots sanded immediately?
  9. When greasy, oily parts are removed from machines, are they placed on paper or sawdust, rather than directly on the floor?
 10. Is the floor kept wet and slippery in spots by oil spillage or drippage, or by water leaks?
 11. If so, have you tried to correct the cause by:
     a. Making repairs?
     b. Teaching good maintenance techniques?
     c. Installing oil pans, drip pans, and splash guards, or improving your present pans and guards?
 12. Wherever possible, are chips, shavings, and other refuse caught in containers as they are produced?

Aisles
 13. Are aisles sufficiently wide to permit easy flow of traffic?
 14. Are aisles clearly marked with painted lines?
 15. Are aisles kept free of materials and finished items?
 16. In piling materials, is care taken not to have ends jutting out into the aisles?

Work Areas
 17. Is there sufficient space around machines, benches, and other equipment for safe, uncrowded work?
 18. Are work areas clearly marked off with painted lines?
 19. Are machines, benches, tables, and other items of equipment arranged in an orderly manner?
 20. Do workers have racks or other holders in which to keep tools and parts so that they will not throw them carelessly on the floor?
 21. Do you plan production carefully so that there is no need for unusually large amounts of work materials or finished items in work areas at any one time?
 22. Have you told workers to draw minimum amounts of needed materials and supplies, to avoid cluttering work areas?
 23. Are excess materials returned promptly to the storeroom?
 24. When tools no longer are needed, are they returned promptly to the supply room?
 25. Do you provide containers or portable equipment for work-in-process?

[1]*Cost Control and the Supervisor,* American Management Assn., New York, 1966.

HOUSEKEEPING PROCEDURES

Once a check of conditions is completed, the following procedures will aid in housekeeping on a regular basis:

1. Make sure there is a convenient storage place for everything—tools, supplies, and employees' personal belongings. Most often used items should be kept at easy-to-reach heights, and contents of shelves and drawers should be clearly labeled.
2. Heavy cleaning should be carried out on a regular schedule—every month, perhaps. Floor and wall scrubbing are good starting points, but if this has not been done for some years, repainting or varnishing may be necessary. Windows, as well as room contents (desks, filing cabinets, etc.), should also be scrubbed regularly.
3. Usually, industrial housekeeping calls for servicing equipment on a preventative maintenance basis at specified intervals. The length of the interval will depend on the condition of the equipment and the amount of use it receives.
4. Insist that employees maintain the area, once heavy housekeeping is completed. It is just as easy to return tools and supplies to their correct storage places, saving time when next someone wants the items.

SUGGESTED FURTHER READING

Higgins, L. R., and L. C. Morrow, *Maintenance Engineering Handbook,* 3d ed., McGraw-Hill, New York, 1977.

HUMAN ACCOUNTING

Areas for use in Cost Control:

ORGANIZATIONAL AND OPERATIONAL SYSTEMS
INDUSTRIAL APPLICATIONS
BUSINESS AND COMMERCIAL APPLICATIONS

Human accounting is an experimental technique that estimates the dollar value of workers, including their productivity and, in business, their effect on customer relations. Such values for personnel, using current work methods, are then compared with estimated values using proposed new work methods, to see which method is the least costly.

A typical way of measuring the value of personnel is to draw up a Monetary Value Scale (see Tables 23 and 24), rating specific jobs in the following areas:

1. Intelligence
2. Work skills
3. Training/education
4. Leadership abilities
5. Cooperative attitude
6. Initiative
7. Ability to communicate
8. Experience in work area

Job characteristics are rated on a hypothetical scale. In Tables 23 and 24, the base monetary value is taken from the top weekly starting pay for the job being rated—$200 in the case of the management trainee and $210 for the machinist. Monetary values are assigned to individual characteristics depending on their effect on the total value of the job. Very high intelligence is a positive value for a management trainee position, for example, while it would be a drawback for a machinist, who would probably be overqualified for, and bored with, the work.

Specific employees, when being valued, are rated using the monetary value scale for their job. In addition, recruiting, hiring, and training costs must be determined, preferably by job type. Customer goodwill value should also be estimated and added. This figure is the sale value of the firm above liquidity figures.

Table 23. Sample Management Trainee Monetary Value Scale

Job: Management Trainee

	Very high	High	Average	Below average	Low
1. Intelligence	$30	$25	$15	$10	$5
2. Work skills	20	15	10	8	6
3. Training/education	30	15	10	8	6
4. Leadership abilities	30	25	15	10	5
5. Cooperative attitude	20	15	10	8	6
6. Initiative	30	25	15	10	5
7. Ability to communicate	30	25	15	10	5
8. Experience in work area	10	8	7	6	5

Table 24. Sample Machinist Monetary Value Scale

Job: Machinist

	Very high	High	Average	Below average	Low
1. Intelligence	$ 5	$10	$15	$10	$ 5
2. Work skills	40	30	20	10	5
3. Training/education	30	25	20	15	10
4. Leadership abilities	10	15	20	15	10
5. Cooperative attitude	30	20	15	10	5
6. Initiative	20	15	10	8	6
7. Ability to communicate	15	12	10	8	6
8. Experience in work area	40	30	20	10	5

These sets of valuations are then added together to determine the monetary value of an employee and of the entire work force.

Such figures are, of course, estimations. However, they provide a standard of measurement in comparing total personnel value and its effects on production and/or sales at a later time with new methods of operation.

SUGGESTED FURTHER READING

Alexander, M. O., "Investments in People," *Canadian Chartered Accountant,* July 1971.
Pyle, W. C., "Accounting System for Human Resources," *Innovation,* no. 10, 1970.

HUMAN FACTORS ENGINEERING

Areas for use in Cost Control:
PSYCHOLOGICAL MOTIVATIONAL MANAGEMENT
WORK PLACE MOTIVATIONAL MANAGEMENT
INDUSTRIAL APPLICATIONS

Human factors engineering is motivation of workers in efficient use of equipment and tools. One human factors engineering expert, N. Jordan, suggests that management consider such motivation a necessary source of power for best use of employees, in much the same way that electricity is the power necessary to operate some kinds of equipment. Thus, by "plugging" workers "into" those aspects of mechanized work designed to use machines as an extension of people and their abilities, rather than using people in a mechanical way, management secures worker-equipment cooperation, which increases productivity and reduces labor costs.

Definite responsibilities that require human work are assigned to each worker when human factors engineering techniques are used. Employees are trained in methods of machine control and shown that their skill in operation is responsible for the degree of success in the use of the machinery. Work challenges, such as the completion of one phase of production, are included in each job. The work setting, whether factory or office, is modified to motivate workers in efficient use of machinery. Primarily, this means adapting equipment and tools for comfortable use. If the machinery requires the worker's being seated, the seat should be adjusted to fit the worker's size. In the same way, operational controls should be designed for easy reach and use. Lighting, ventilation, noise control, etc., should be implemented at human standards, rather than solely at equipment operational standards.

SUGGESTED FURTHER READING

Davis, L. E., and J. C. Taylor, *Design of Jobs,* Penguin, Baltimore, 1972.

Jordan, N., "Allocation of Functions between Man and Machines in Automated Systems," *Applied Psychology,* vol. 47, 1963.

Sheppard, H. L., and N. Q. Herrick, *Where Have All the Robots Gone?* Upjohn Institute, New York, 1971.

HYGIENE FACTORS

Areas for use in Cost Control:

PSYCHOLOGICAL MOTIVATIONAL MANAGEMENT
FINANCIAL MOTIVATIONAL MANAGEMENT
WORK PLACE MOTIVATIONAL MANAGEMENT

Hygiene factors are job-context aspects, such as work payment, job security, and optimum working conditions, that reduce job dissatisfaction, thus reducing labor costs through increased productivity.

SUGGESTED FURTHER READING

Herzberg, F., B. Mausner, and B. Snyderman, *The Motivation to Work,* Wiley, New York, 1969.

HYPNOSIS

Areas for use in Cost Control:

PSYCHOLOGICAL MOTIVATIONAL MANAGEMENT
ORGANIZATIONAL AND OPERATIONAL SYSTEMS
INDUSTRIAL APPLICATIONS
BUSINESS AND COMMERCIAL APPLICATIONS

Hypnosis is the practice of placing a person in a trance of varying degrees of depth so that he or she will be open to suggestions made. Costs are reduced by persuading the employee to produce more while under hypnosis. For business and industrial use, the technique can at present be divided into two primary areas:

1. *Suggestibility,* where a light trance may be consciously or unconsciously produced in an employee and his or her motivation increased by suggestions from a supervisor, coworker, etc.

2. *Experimental hypnotic techniques,* dealing with means of training employees more rapidly, of reducing physical fatigue during work, etc.

SUGGESTIBILITY

Suggestibility is really an informal use of hypnotism. Playing on the employee's openness to suggestion, for example, a supervisor may say, "That was a fine job you did last week, John. Do you think we can beat our own production record this week?" A light trance may have been induced subconsciously by repetitive noises or music, or by the soothing sound of the supervisor's voice strengthening the motivational power of such a remark (although not as much as the suggestion would strengthen motivation if given in a full, deep hypnotic trance). When productivity is increased by this method, cost per unit is of course reduced.

A light trance (although it may be called "attention-focusing" or given some other name) may be produced in a training session by repetition. For example, some companies have used taped foreign language lessons with rhythmic repetitious presentation of material that produces a light trance, leaving the employee more open to the suggestion that he or she will learn the material. The same effect is achieved when a motion-rhythm cycle is introduced in an industrial training class. The instructor may show trainees a motion-rhythm cycle of machine operation, for example, and they will practice the movement as the instructor repeats the instruction rhythmically—"One—press, two—press, three—press," etc. In this light-trance state, the trainee is more open to suggestion, and his or her training is likely to proceed more rapidly than without it, reducing training costs.

HYPNOTISM

Still largely in experimental stages, *hypnotism* has achieved some interesting results that can reduce business and industry costs. Comparison of results should be evaluated on three levels:

1. Performance in the normal state
2. Performance in the hypnotic state
3. Performance with posthypnotic suggestion

The *normal state* is the employee's usual level of performance.

In the *hypnotic*, or deep-trance, state, the employee may be able to increase his or her performance level by 30 to 60 percent.

Using *posthypnotic suggestion*, it is possible to increase performance *temporarily* by 20 to 40 percent.

Most experiments using posthypnotic suggestion produce diminishing results. Performance that improves 40 percent will eventually work its way back to normal at the end of about one week. Some psychologists believe this period can be extended with practice and repeated use.

What practical uses can be made of hypnotism by business and industry? Table 25 provides some guides. In general, the deeper the trance, the more use business and industry might make of the method. Performance of easier tasks is usually increased to a greater degree than performance of complicated tasks. Some psychologists feel that increased performance is due to relaxation of muscles, since when tense these draw off energy. Thus, the deeper the trance, the larger the increase in performance; and the more recent the posthypnotic suggestion, the greater the increase in performance.

Emotional blocks and anxieties that lower work performance, cause excessive absence and tardiness, etc., can also be removed by hypnotism in some cases. As with increased motivation, posthypnotic suggestions removing these factors are only temporarily successful under present methods and would need repetitious administration.

Boring, routine work tasks may be carried out at a higher level of motivation, since simplest tasks are the most easily reinforced.

Unpleasant physical conditions necessary to a particular task, such as extreme heat or cold, might be temporarily negated under hypnosis, particularly if the worker was one of the 20 percent belonging to the deep-trance susceptibility group.

Table 25. Hypnotic Susceptibilities of Workers by Percent

Susceptibility	Likely business and industrial applications	Approximate percent of workers
Not susceptible	None	15
Suggestible	Slightly increased motivation, some training reinforcement	15
Light trance	Increased motivation, training reinforcement, increased posthypnotic work performance to 20%	25
Medium trance	Marked increase in motivation, rapid training, increase in posthypnotic work performance to 30%, less physical discomfort in work	25
Deep trance	Extreme increase in motivation, very rapid training, increase in posthypnotic work performance to 40%, near imperception to physical discomforts in work	20

IMPLEMENTATION

Some psychologists suggest application of hypnotism in business and industry through self-induced trances. An employee is trained in self-hypnotism and is told how to suggest increased performance, decreased tiredness, etc., to herself or himself. Perhaps application would be more widespread if financial incentives accompanied increased performance. Self-hypnosis is a currently operable method, and subjects have achieved many of the same results using it as in hypnosis by another person. Results include age-regression and recall, posthypnotic suggestions acted out, and performance improvement.

SUGGESTED FURTHER READING

Eysenck, H. J., *Sense and Nonsense in Psychology,* Penguin, Baltimore, 1972.
Weitzenhoffer, A. M., *Hypnotism: An Objective Study in Suggestibility,* Wiley, New York, 1973.

IEMOTO

Areas for use in Cost Control:

PSYCHOLOGICAL MOTIVATIONAL MANAGEMENT
ORGANIZATIONAL AND OPERATIONAL SYSTEMS
INDUSTRIAL APPLICATIONS
BUSINESS AND COMMERCIAL APPLICATIONS

Iemoto is a Japanese system that involves strengthening the feeling of kinship and responsibility to the employer among a group of workers and extending such feelings to social groupings. The feeling is developed to such a strength that workers have beaten and even killed a coworker for attempting to leave the group or even for being legitimately absent at a crucial time because of illness. The employing company, management, and workers form a relationship similar to a family grouping, with the traditional Oriental respect for ancestors being given to the company and to management. Company songs, pledges, exercise classes, etc., are all practiced regularly before or after working hours, and company interests are put ahead of family and personal needs. Use of the method reduces turnover costs and raises productivity. While some part of the success of Iemoto is certainly due to the Japanese willingness to hold work authority in high regard, use of side tools such as company songs and social gatherings does intensify employee kinship feelings, subsequently reducing turnover and production costs.

SUGGESTED FURTHER READING

Hsu, F., *Iemoto: The Heart of Japan,* Schenkman Publishing, Cambridge, Mass., 1974.
Komiya, Ryutaro, *Post-War Economic Growth in Japan,* University of California Press, Los Angeles, 1966.

IMITATIVE PATTERNING

Areas for use in Cost Control:

ORGANIZATIONAL AND OPERATIONAL SYSTEMS
INDUSTRIAL APPLICATIONS
BUSINESS AND COMMERCIAL APPLICATIONS

Imitative patterning is the adaptation of another company's organizational pattern because it has been proved successful. When used, care must be taken to ensure that all phases of the pattern, including feedback and other control systems, are copied. A typical cost reduction area, for instance, might be copying General Motors' profit-accountable product division organizational pattern.

SUGGESTED FURTHER READING

Mann, R., ed., *The Arts of Top Management,* McGraw-Hill, New York, 1970.

IMPRESSIONISTIC METHOD See Personnel Attitude Measurement.

IMPREST SYSTEM

Areas for use in Cost Control:

ORGANIZATIONAL AND OPERATIONAL SYSTEMS
DATA RETENTION—FILES AND RECORDKEEPING
INDUSTRIAL APPLICATIONS

The imprest system is a method of replacing depleted inventories. Invoiced orders are duplicated, and, using these to determine quantities, goods shipped are replaced on a one-to-one basis in the inventory periodically. Use of the method can reduce costs, since replacement is automatic and requires no additional paperwork. In addition, branch inventories are not required, since they will automatically stand at predetermined normal figures after each periodic replacement. Inventory levels are usually determined by sales records, with a margin allowed for safety.

SUGGESTED FURTHER READING

Brown, R. G., *Decision Rules for Inventory Management,* Holt, New York, 1967.
Wentworth, F. R. L., ed., *Physical Distribution Management,* Gower Press, London, 1970.

IN-BASKET

Areas for use in Cost Control:

ORGANIZATIONAL AND OPERATIONAL SYSTEMS
INDUSTRIAL APPLICATIONS
BUSINESS AND COMMERCIAL APPLICATIONS

The in-basket technique is a method of executive performance appraisal that uses a test to simulate executive work factors. It reduces costs by pinpointing weak performance areas, which can then be corrected; by aiding in the selection of new executives; by aiding promotion of staff personnel to managerial level; and by training management trainees.

The in-basket test presents the employee with hypothetical work problems he or she might expect to find in his or her "In" basket. As the employee deals with these problems, the appraiser judges on:

1. Independent action taken
2. Speed and amount of work
3. Consultation with others
4. Behavior patterns, such as tact, courtesy, and control of others

SUGGESTED FURTHER READING

Frederiksen, N., "Factors in In-Basket Performance," *Psychological Monographs*, no. 22, 1962.

INCENTIVE PAYMENT SYSTEMS

Areas for use in Cost Control:

FINANCIAL MOTIVATIONAL MANAGEMENT
INDUSTRIAL APPLICATIONS
BUSINESS AND COMMERCIAL APPLICATIONS

Incentive payments can be one of the greatest cost cutters available if properly designed and implemented, because they encourage a worker to produce more in return for larger payments. Since the basic costs for each worker remain static, the margin of profit advances more rapidly than do extra payments made on an incentive basis. Incentive payment systems can be devised for almost any working group—industrial or clerical. Such systems are almost always used in some form in setting a wage scale for salespersons. Basically, the various incentive systems now in use can be divided as follows:

1. *Individual incentive systems*
   a. Piece rates
   b. Premium bonuses
2. *Group incentive systems*
   a. Group piecework
   b. Group bonuses
      (1) Direct workers
      (2) Indirect workers
3. *Profit sharing and copartnership*

INDIVIDUAL INCENTIVE SYSTEMS

Piece Rate Systems. When employing a piece rate system, the worker's wages are calculated solely on the number of pieces or product items produced. The rate is set, after time and work study, by management, at what is considered a fair amount for the time it normally takes to produce each product. Of course, labor unions may disagree about what is a fair rate, and negotiations may be held to determine the rate.

Advantages of the systems are that:

1. The person who works harder can earn more.
2. Supervision costs are minimal.
3. There is more intensive use of equipment.
4. Labor costs can be more readily predetermined.

5. The total wage per worker is higher. Thus, there is lower employee dissatisfaction and turnover, and total cost per production unit tends to be lower.

Disadvantages are that:

1. Inspection costs are high.
2. Disputes are likely when units are rejected, since workers are not paid for these.
3. Spoilage costs may be high.

Differential Piece Rate Systems. These methods use more than one rate of pay per item produced for the same work. The first of these plans was originated by F. W. Taylor and is probably the best known.

1. *The Taylor differential piece rate system* pays a lower rate to the slower worker and a higher rate to those who exceed the standard level of output. Once an employee exceeds the standard, or average, production, he or she is paid the *higher rate* for all production, including that completed before reaching the standard. Thus, if the lower rate is 20 cents and the higher rate is 25 cents, actual pay for a day's work may vary as in the following example:

   Standard number of items produced per day: 130
   Worker A produced 127 items. Compensation for the day: $25.40
   Worker B produced 132 items. Compensation for the day: $33.00

   If this is extended to a one-week period, it is seen that Worker A earns $127, compared with the $165 earned by Worker B.

2. *The Merrick differential piece rate system* provides three levels of compensation, but as a worker reaches a new level, the goods already produced are not compensated at the next higher step. The formula used for rate of pay is as follows:

   Base rate: Production up to 83% of standard
   2d rate: Production from 83% to standard
   3d rate: Over standard production

   If the base rate is 18 cents, the second rate 23 cents, and the third rate 26 cents, Worker A given in the Taylor plan above would earn:

108 items (83% of standard) @ 18¢	$19.44
19 items @ the 2d rate of 23¢	4.37
Total daily earnings	$23.81

   Worker B, also given in the Taylor plan example, would earn:

108 items @ 18¢	$19.44
22 items @ 23¢	5.06
2 items @ 26¢	.52
Total daily earnings	$25.02

Premium Bonus Systems. In any of the premium bonus systems, the worker earns a set hourly wage plus a bonus on any saving in previously determined time. Trade unions prefer these systems, usually, because they provide a guaranteed minimum wage yet offer a chance of exceptional earnings for the employee who wants to work hard.

The Halsey-Wise sharing payment system offers the worker 50 percent of the time saved over the predetermined standard production time. In this system, the formula looks as follows:

Standard job time	48 hours
Standard hourly rate	$5
Standard employee wage	$240

But if an employee can do the job in 40 hours rather than 48, he or she will earn more money, as shown in the following example:

Rate of pay for hours used
    (40 × $5) $200

Bonus (time saved ÷ 2)

$$\frac{8 \text{ hours} \times \$5}{2} \quad = \quad \underline{20}$$

Total employee wage $220

Of course, the company cost is cut $20 in the above example, just as the worker's salary is increased by $20 (on an hourly-wage basis)—both resulting from the fact that the bonus payment caused the employee to work faster than he or she normally would have done.

The Rowan system is based on much the same principle as the Halsey-Wise system, except that it uses the percent of time saved as a base. Standard hourly rates are paid for the time used, with a bonus figured on the percent of time saved. Using the same example as in the Halsey-Wise system:

Rate of pay for time used
    (40 hours × $5) $200

$$\text{Bonus} = \frac{\text{hours saved}}{\text{hours scheduled}} \times \frac{\text{actual wage}}{1}$$

or

$$\frac{8}{48} \times \frac{\$200}{1} \quad = \quad \underline{33.33}$$

Total employee wage $233.33

GROUP INCENTIVE SYSTEMS

Group Piecework Systems. These are virtually the same methods used for individual piecework systems, except that the rates are divided among the department responsible for production. Rates are usually divided in a way that gives skilled employees a larger cut of the overall production payment.

Group-Bonus Systems for Direct Workers. In these systems, production can be directly traced to a group of employees, and bonuses paid for production exceeding the standard are "shared out" among the workers in a predetermined fashion.

The Priestman method is a typical example. In this system, a production standard is set to cover an entire department or other group. If production exceeds this standard, a bonus equivalent to the percent over standard is paid, e.g.:

Standard	100 units of production
Actual production	130 units
Bonus	30%

The Scanlon plan pays employees of a department or company a proportion (usually 50 to 75 percent) of the savings resulting from production over a predetermined standard figure. Standards are set by committees, which include members of the labor force as well as management. Generally, the method has been used in small or medium-sized firms in an attempt to make the firm's employees feel more a part of the company. Some companies have combined share-outs of profits with share-outs of labor savings. When profits fall, however, instead of rising, the system then becomes a deterrent to labor motivation rather than an incentive. Operation of the system by committee has not always proven entirely satisfactory.

Group-Bonus Systems for Indirect Workers. Bonuses are much more difficult to figure for indirect workers, since their work is not so easily measured. But the reasons for installing incentive systems are just as valid for this group as for production employees, and some general guidelines can be given.

Clerical Workers. A standard can be based on completing a volume of work according to a predetermined time schedule. If all work scheduled is completed on time, a small set bonus is paid—perhaps equal to an hour's extra pay per week. Work can be graded, with higher rates going to employees who do the more difficult, higher-graded work. Bonuses can also be paid on the number of policies typed, the number of invoices handled, etc.

Foremen and Supervisors. Bonuses for foremen and supervisors are usually dependent on the output of the supervisor's employees. Both production output and savings on cost of production (labor and materials) should be used in figuring the bonus.

Management. Bonuses to management are generally based on departmental efficiency, with an assigned standard of performance used as the base.

PROFIT SHARING AND COPARTNERSHIP

Profit sharing is a system that pays employees a part of their employer's profits. The method of dividing profits among shareholders or between owner and employees is set out in advance—usually stated in percentages, since the dollar amount of profits may vary from year to year. This percentage cannot be changed by the employer once the terms are agreed upon, unless the employees agree to a new schedule. There are four general types of profit sharing systems: profit sharing alone, share ownership, copartnership, and deferred payment plans.

Profit Sharing Alone. Using this method, employees receive a percentage of profits after working expenses, taxes, capital investment, reserves, etc., have been subtracted. In one common method, shareholders are paid a 5 to 6 percent dividend, with production and office employees receiving one-half the remaining profit. One-tenth of the remaining profit goes to management; four-tenths goes to investors.

Participation by the worker usually starts after one to three years of employment. Such funds are generally divided on the basis of the employee's salary. Average payment from profit sharing is about 6 percent of an individual employee's earnings.

The money may be paid in cash or credited to a savings account. Some firms pay attractive interest rates on profit sharing funds left with the company.

Share Ownership. This system pays profits to employees by giving them shares of stock in the firm. If employees own company stock, the reasoning goes, they will be more interested in the firm's problems and in its success. Stock ownership and cash profit sharing payments are combined by many companies.

An alternative plan allows employees to buy shares of company stock through payroll deductions, with the firm contributing an amount equal to the salary withheld. In these cases, stock cannot always be cashed in at will by employees, but must be held until they retire or leave the firm. Some companies pay the market value of such stock when employees leave; others pay the par value.

Copartnership. Using this method, more than cash and stocks are given to employees. They are given wider participation in the business. They may serve on work committees and production committees and may vote at annual meetings. A few firms even provide for employee shareholders to be represented on the board of directors. In such systems, only long-term employees with a minimum number of shares of stock can be nominated for directorships.

Deferred Payment Plans. Some profit sharing systems place the employee's share of the profits in retirement annuities or trust funds. Large companies, particularly, have turned to this method of satisfying labor union demands for lifetime security for the employee. In some firms, employees contribute a percentage from their salaries, which is matched or even quadrupled by company profits.

VALUE AND LIMITATIONS OF PROFIT SHARING

Profit sharing has not generally stimulated greater production or effort, perhaps because it is not a frequent or readily tangible reward. Another reason for this is that profits rely on many factors in addition to employee effort—market conditions, management efficiency, etc. The real value of profit sharing is in winning the employees' good will and subsequent lower turnover and fewer operational problems stemming from personality differences.

Tax advantages in profit sharing plans make them attractive in some countries. In the United States, for example, firms in high tax brackets actually pay about 15 percent of money given employees through profit sharing. The remaining 85 percent comes from funds that would otherwise have had to be paid as taxes.

SUGGESTED FURTHER READING

Eisenberg, Joseph, *Cost Controls for the Office,* Prentice-Hall, Englewood Cliffs, N.J., 1968.
Radke, Magnus, *Manual of Cost Reduction Techniques,* McGraw-Hill, New York, 1972.

IN-COMPANY INSURANCE

Areas for use in Cost Control:

ORGANIZATIONAL AND OPERATIONAL SYSTEMS
MATERIALS AND EQUIPMENT MANAGEMENT
INDUSTRIAL APPLICATIONS
BUSINESS AND COMMERCIAL APPLICATIONS

In-company insurance is the technique of establishing an in-house insurance company to insure some or all of the firm's risks only, reducing the overall premium costs. "Premiums" are "paid" by the company to the insurance division—to itself, in effect—and value of the insurance coverage is returned to operating funds if the loss occurs. In addition to insurance cost reductions, the method is used to gain tax advantages. For example, reserve funds can be accumulated by the in-house insurance company without tax deductions. The in-house insurance company can also place risks too large for the company to absorb with reinsurance brokers without paying the additional fee costs to an intermediate insurance broker. *See also* **Reinsurance.**

SUGGESTED FURTHER READING

Lewis, Keith, "Saving on Insurance Costs," *The Financial Times,* London, July 8, 1974.

INDEXED CONTRACTS

Areas for use in Cost Control:

ORGANIZATIONAL AND OPERATIONAL SYSTEMS
INDUSTRIAL APPLICATIONS
BUSINESS AND COMMERCIAL APPLICATIONS

Indexed contracts are those which tie payment to the Cost of Living or other index as a means of reducing the cost of losses incurred by changes in the rate of inflation. Thus, if a contract is signed to sell goods to a customer in three months, and the rate of inflation decreases the real value of the agreed selling price, the indexed contract will require the customer to pay a price equivalent to the real value at the time the contract was signed. The method is particularly useful in long-term contracts, where the future prices of raw materials, labor, etc., cannot be accurately predicted. *See also* **Index Linking; Inflation Accounting; Inflation Cost Control.**

SUGGESTED FURTHER READING

Brittan, Samuel, "Economic Viewpoint," *The Financial Times,* London, July 11, 1974.

INDEX LINKING

Areas for use in Cost Control:

ORGANIZATIONAL AND OPERATIONAL SYSTEMS
DATA RETENTION—FILES AND RECORDKEEPING
INDUSTRIAL APPLICATIONS
BUSINESS AND COMMERCIAL APPLICATIONS

Index linking is a technique used to reduce erosion costs of inflation and including industrial or business and commercial applications. In using the method, a monetary or other financial base is determined and the purchasing value of the money or other financial asset is later rated against this base. If, for example, a dollar is rated as the index base in a given year and the next year it takes $1.20 to purchase the same amount of goods, the index value of the dollar will then have moved to 120. Under such a system, $120 worth of profits at an index of 120 would pay taxes on only $100. Rent of $1,000 would automatically move to $1,200, and wages of $10,000 would automatically increase to $12,000.

Such *money indexing* ties interest rates for loans to the purchasing value of money, with maximum rates generally controlled by the government. **Inflation accounting** is used to reflect the purchasing value of profits, rather than their paper value, reducing tax costs for business areas adversely affected by inflation and adding tax costs to businesses (such as property development) that benefit from inflation. Index linking is a necessary feature of a workable inflation accounting system.

Both index linking and inflation accounting have been developed and refined by Brazil as a means of living with inflation. Annual revaluation of fixed assets and a working capital reserve fund are provided, allowing up to 20 percent annually for profit exemption from taxes. Prices, wages, rent, money rates, etc., are all readjusted according to the base for each index and its current worth in real rather than paper terms.

SUGGESTED FURTHER READING

Perkins, J. E. B., "How the Brazilians Learned to Live with Inflation," *The Guardian,* London, June 18, 1974.

INDIFFERENCE CURVES

Areas for use in Cost Control:

ORGANIZATIONAL AND OPERATIONAL SYSTEMS
INDUSTRIAL APPLICATIONS
BUSINESS AND COMMERCIAL APPLICATIONS

Indifference curves are visual comparisons of consumer demand used to forecast future markets, thus reducing marketing and sales costs. In the use of the method, the company's product or service is compared with an average of competing products or services. Curves are drawn to show all possible points at which consumers may become indifferent to the compared products or services (see Fig. 55), depending on the consumers' income, product price, and consumers' need or desire for the product. Additional curves drawn to the right of the original curve represent greater degrees of satisfaction than preceding curves, extending the range of measurement of consumer indifference.

A consumer preference line is drawn to illustrate the predicted purchase pattern. In Fig. 55, for example, if consumers like pears and apples equally well and have an average of 40 cents to spend on fruit, the purchase pattern line shows that the second level of consumption is the indifference point.

SUGGESTED FURTHER READING

Hanson, J. L., *A Dictionary of Economics and Commerce,* MacDonald, London, 1974.
Speight, H., *Economics and Industrial Efficiency,* Macmillan, New York, 1967.

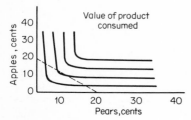

Figure 55. Typical indifference curve chart.

INDIRECT METHOD See Personnel Attitude Measurement.

INDIVISIBILITY

Areas for use in Cost Control:
ORGANIZATIONAL AND OPERATIONAL SYSTEMS
MATERIALS AND EQUIPMENT MANAGEMENT
INDUSTRIAL APPLICATIONS

Indivisibility is the method of dividing human and/or equipment work into the smallest operable (most specialized) unit possible to reduce training, work movement, and wasted-time and material costs. The technique is more successfully operated in a large factory where greater specialization is possible because of the greater volume of work available. For example, it is easier and less costly to teach a new employee to repeatedly add one part to the assembly of a product than to teach her or him to assemble the entire product alone.

In the use of equipment, the smallest piece of machinery that can complete a given task is used, allowing for any multiple use of the machinery by other production operations in the same factory.

SUGGESTED FURTHER READING

Dunlop, J. T., and V. P. Diatchenko, *Labor Productivity,* McGraw-Hill, New York, 1964.
Speight, H., *Economic and Industrial Efficiency,* Macmillan, New York, 1967.

INDULGENCY PATTERNING

Areas for use in Cost Control:
PSYCHOLOGICAL MOTIVATIONAL MANAGEMENT
INDUSTRIAL APPLICATIONS
BUSINESS AND COMMERCIAL APPLICATIONS

Indulgency patterning is the deliberate management practice of not structuring or supervising work too formally so that the resulting lenient atmosphere will motivate workers to increased production and reduced labor costs.

SUGGESTED FURTHER READING

Kornhauser, A. W., *Psychology of Labor-Management Relations,* University Microfilms, Ann Arbor, Mich., 1966.

Roberts, H. S., *Roberts' Dictionary of Industrial Relations,* Bureau of National Affairs, Inc., Washington, D.C., 1971.

INDUSTRIAL EQUATION TECHNIQUE

Areas for use in Cost Control:

ORGANIZATIONAL AND OPERATIONAL SYSTEMS
MATERIALS AND EQUIPMENT MANAGEMENT
INDUSTRIAL APPLICATIONS

The industrial equation technique is the increasing of behavior and resource efficiency through combined knowledge and the greatest possible international market application (sales and/or use) to reduce production costs as much as possible. Such increased efficiency reduces costs in many areas when the equation is applied to specific industrial problems.

Resource Alteration. Although industry often accommodates itself to the natural allocation of resources by locating near the source, it can sometimes reduce material costs through resource alteration. For example, the United States has a very small natural allocation of tin. Yet, vast mines of it exist—above ground and imported only once. The low melting point of the material makes it largely reclaimable, and large amounts of available outdated equipment, including obsolete dies, are regularly recycled in quantities.

Development of synthetic materials, such as plastics and nylon fibers, is another example of resource alteration. Using this method, materials not located in a particular area—natural fibers—are replaced with fiber substitutes made from available natural materials—oil—at the same or reduced cost.

Performance and Cost Ratios. This area is the basis for all mass production savings. When the maximum number of uses and/or users for a given product are found and its invention and production cost are divided by this number, scale economies are seen. In the same way, when the performance ratio of a relatively low-cost material is increased economically, such as by adding relatively inexpensive glass fiber to plastic to increase its performance per pound of weight, the cost factor in relation to the performance factor drops.

Tools to Make More Tools. Reduced costs also result when industrial tools are used to build more tools, creating greater production capacity and the accompanying economies of scale. In the same area, new cost-reducing production uses can be found for tools. Closed-circuit television banks, originally used for security purposes, for example, are now being used to allow multiple-area supervision of production work by a single supervisor, reducing labor costs. The various advances in automation can also be included in this area, referring back to the original principle of increasing the number of consumers for a specific product as a stimulus to finding optimal performance and cost levels.

SUGGESTED FURTHER READING

Meller, James, ed., *The Buckminster Fuller Reader,* Penguin, Baltimore, 1972.

INDUSTRIAL ESPIONAGE PREVENTION

Areas for use in Cost Control:

ORGANIZATIONAL AND OPERATIONAL SYSTEMS
MATERIALS AND EQUIPMENT MANAGEMENT
INDUSTRIAL APPLICATIONS

Industrial espionage prevention is the making secure of proprietary information. Costs can be reduced since information of this type lost through espionage to competitors negates much of the value of findings from expensive research and work methods programs, product design, and use of proprietary systems. A company security system of this type is needed primarily because laws in most countries do not provide protection from, or reimbursement for, such losses. Unless trade secrets are specifically tied to patents or licensing agreements, little legal recourse is available. And when information is stolen in one country for use in another, even less control is possible. Prevention of such costly loss, then, is best initiated at the source: the company that has developed proprietary methods, designs, or other information.

PREVENTING INFORMATION LEAKS

Since it is less costly to prevent information leaks than to lose valuable material *and* have to find the source of the leak, an information security system should be established. This may be connected with normal, physical security precautions but should not be left to a contracted guard service whose sole experience may be in physically protecting plant and equipment.

Information leaks always require a person, and usually that person is an employee. Competitors' intelligence operatives may acquire the information without the employee knowing it, or they may pay the employee to provide information. Additionally, a competitor may hire a key employee at a larger salary to acquire information.

Screening. Screening employees as to intelligence risks is the best preventative measure. *Screening* is often necessary at all levels since clerical employees may have considerable access to proprietary information. It is a serious mistake to assume that information is safe because "such employees probably don't understand its value."

Employees may also be planted by competitors to serve as espionage agents. False qualifications and references are used and may be difficult to "break."

Some types of people are more susceptible to espionage than others because factors in their pasts or personal lives leave them open to blackmail. Persons who have been or are members of subversive political parties, alcoholics, drug addicts, homosexuals, etc., fall into this category. While such persons may be well qualified, their skills should be carefully weighed against the possibility of a competitor blackmailing them for espionage purposes. For example, if an employee is known to be homosexual by employees and friends, competitors have no way of using that fact to blackmail the individual. Employee political inclinations, known or unknown, however, may affect government contracts given to the company, if not the possibility of intelligence espionage.

Qualifications should be carefully checked, as should references, particularly those of previous employers. Hiring should be done in-company where possible, since employment agency checking may not be verified. Additionally, some employment agencies have provided information about vacancies, applicants, and new employees to competing firms. Social security credentials, driver's license, passport, and other forms of identification should also be checked. Firms with particularly sensitive information may wish to use lie detector tests, run fingerprint checks, etc. Applicants for top management positions are sometimes thoroughly investigated by a private investigation agency, determining marital, financial, political, and religious status and examining friends, hobbies, education, etc. Psychological tests are frequently used to measure personality, stability, and other characteristics.

Temporary personnel, often hired through temporary agencies, are particularly poor security risks since there is no practical way to screen such personnel. It is better to be short-handed than to take such risks if the employee will have any possibility of access to proprietary information.

Records. Once an employee is hired, all information obtained during screening should be placed in his or her file for future reference. Such records can be useful in finding the source of an information leak should one occur.

Training. Employees should be made aware of espionage techniques that may be used to inadvertently obtain information from them, including:

1. *Eavesdropping* on business conversations in public places such as bars, restaurants, and theaters. Referring to proprietary information should absolutely be avoided in such locations.

2. *Customer conversations,* particularly with sales representatives and technical personnel, may provide information leaks for the competition's benefit. Product benefits should be explained without the inclusion of technical information where possible. Needless to say, this is not always possible if sales are to be made, and the area offers difficulties that are not easy to control.

3. *False inquiry* for information may be made by industrial spies posing as journalists, government inspectors, etc. Credentials should be carefully checked, particularly when inquiries are telephoned.

4. *News releases,* including company newspapers, should never include proprietary information.

5. *Advertisements,* including personnel ads, should where possible exclude information that would be useful to industrial spies.

6. *Conversations* at trade fairs, conventions, etc., should be especially guarded.

7. *Printed and typed material, including copies,* should be carefully controlled.

8. *Outside repairmen, subcontractors, sales representatives, etc.,* should be accompanied by a reliable and knowledgeable employee at *all* times. This is particularly important in the repair or installation of computers and photocopying equipment.

FINDING AN INFORMATION LEAK

Once an information leak takes place, costs go up. Still, the leak must be discovered to prevent further costly losses. Most employees responsible for information leaks fall into one of several categories:

1. *Plants*—clerical or research staff planted by a competitor to obtain specific information. References and qualifications are often too well established to screen out the employee at hiring, so all relatively new employees with access to proprietary information should be considered when an information leak occurs.

2. *Consultants* hired for special work can also be industrial spies. References should be thoroughly checked and information access should be limited in accordance with specific assignment.

3. *Financially disturbed employees* with severe financial problems.

4. *Bribable employees*—employees with character weaknesses, such as drinking, drug addiction, and fondness for expensive cars.

5. *Mentally troubled* employees are often more open to bribes and pressures.

6. *Dissatisfied employees* who feel they are underpaid and/or not sufficiently appreciated.

7. *Extremists,* who enjoy violence and may be determined to undermine capitalism.

8. *Ex-employees,* who may feel it their duty to provide a new employer with information, or who may be angry at having been fired or laid off. Laws provide minimal protection in this area, but it is often difficult to prove which parts of an ex-employee's knowledge belong to his or her former employer.

Suspected spies have sometimes been caught by use of a *counterespionage* technique. A call is placed to the suspected "spy" at his or her office, with the caller pretending to be a representative of the competitor's espionage team. The reaction of the "spy" is used to determine guilt or innocence.

IMPLEMENTING INTELLIGENCE SECURITY

In addition to personnel control, other control devices and techniques are important to the security of proprietary information:

1. *Physical security* of offices and plant is essential. Unauthorized persons should never gain admittance, and repairmen or other temporary visitors should be accompanied by a reliable employee at all times.

2. *Material to be printed,* whether news releases, brochures, house magazines, or press interviews, should be carefully reviewed and proprietary material removed.

3. *Computer operations* should use special security controls to prevent removal of information.

4. *Photocopying* should be performed for all departments by one or more reliable employees with no other assignments. All copies should be authorized and accounted for by management.

5. *Microfilmed* material should be carefully controlled.

6. *Private security firms* may be used to check for mechanical spying equipment, such as wire taps and bugs, *after* their own references are thoroughly checked.

7. *Microphones and hidden cameras* may be used to "watch" employee activities.

8. *Counterspies* may be planted by management in its own staff to learn about employee activities.

9. *Papers* containing information should be mutilated by methods such as shredding before they are discarded in wastebaskets or waste areas. This includes not only final drafts of such material, but also executive memos, doodles, notes, first drafts, etc.

10. *Carbon paper and carbon typewriter ribbon* use should be controlled when strategic material is typed.

SUGGESTED FURTHER READING

International Conference on Electronics and Space, Collected Papers, Paris, 1967.
Walsh, T. J., and R. J. Healy, *Protecting Your Business against Espionage,* American Management Assn., New York, 1973.

INDUSTRIAL INTELLIGENCE See Competitive Intelligence.

INDUSTRIAL SPY METHOD See Personnel Morale Building.

INFLATION ACCOUNTING

Areas for use in Cost Control:
ORGANIZATIONAL AND OPERATIONAL SYSTEMS
DATA RETENTION—FILES AND RECORDKEEPING
MATERIALS AND EQUIPMENT MANAGEMENT

INDUSTRIAL APPLICATIONS
BUSINESS AND COMMERCIAL APPLICATIONS

Inflation accounting is the substitution of real or purchasing power values for fixed currency values in all aspects of accounting. The technique is used to bring taxable profits, depreciation, tax allowances, etc., back into line with their real values as opposed to the decreased false values reflected when historic accounting methods are used during an inflationary period, reducing costs in all areas to purchasing power costs. For example, using inflation accounting, taxable company earnings in purchasing power terms would average 15 percent less than their monetary figure. Table 26 gives a breakdown by industry.

Table 26. Taxable Company Earnings Changes with Inflation Accounting[1]

Property	+310%	Light electronics, etc.	−15%
Entertainment, food service	+40	Tobacco	−15
Breweries	+35	Food manufacturing	−20
Stores	+5	Office equipment	−25
Food retailing	+5	Oil	−25
Publishing	−10	Household goods	−35
Construction	−10	Packaging/paper	−35
Building materials	−10	Shipping	−40
Installment purchase	−15	Engineering (heavy)	−40
Banks	−15	Textiles	−50
Chemicals	−15	Electronics	−50
Wines/spirits	−15	Automobiles	−60

[1]Blandon, Michael, "Adjusting the Profits with Inflation Accounting," *The Financial Times,* London, May 15, 1974.

In the same way, inflation accounting makes better preparation for equipment replacement by allowing a larger percentage of the actual value of depreciation, as compared with the monetary value. For example, if a $10,000 piece of equipment is depreciated over a period of 10 years, and inflation averages 15 percent per year, $40,000 will be needed to replace the equipment. With historic accounting methods, only $10,000, or $1,000 annually, would have been depreciated, still assuming a 10-year depreciation schedule. With inflation accounting, $23,310 would have been allowed.

Inflation accounting methods as used in Canada, Brazil, and Israel generally make allowance for changes in the value of currency only, although related techniques such as the Dutch **replacement cost accounting** depreciates assets by replacement cost of the investment, providing allowances for technological advancements as well as for inflation.

Many Western countries have provisional or absolute accounting standards for inflation accounting purposes. Companies in countries without such standards may choose to use the basic principles of those standards already in use as a means of comparison.

CONVERSIONS TO CURRENT PURCHASING POWER

Figures are converted by linking them to an index—usually a retail price index, since this best reflects changes in the purchasing power of currency. In all accounting steps, figures are multiplied by the index at the end of the accounting period and then divided by the index at the time of the purchase—or at the beginning of the period, in the case of profit indexation. Assume that a piece of equipment cost $10,000 and was purchased when the index was 105. At the end of the accounting period, the index is 120. The inflation-adjusted cost of the asset for that period is:

$$\$10,000 \times 120 \div 105 = \$11,428$$

Depreciation, on a 10-year scale, would then be $1,143 for this annual period.

If, at the end of the following year, the index is 135, the inflation-adjusted cost of the asset will be:

$10,000 × 135 ÷ 105 = $11,885

Depreciation for the second year would be $1,189.

Conversions of this type apply to three accounting processes:

1. Balance sheet at the start of the accounting period
2. Balance sheet at the close of the accounting period
3. Profit and loss statement for the accounting period

Balance Sheet at the Start of the Accounting Period. Conversion of figures includes those for monetary items, nonmonetary items, and equity interest.

Monetary Items. Outstanding accounts due, cash, and outstanding accounts owed may be balanced and converted *for the accounting period.* The items can be converted separately where balance sheet format requires this.

Nonmonetary Items. These include depreciation, fixed assets, and stock. Fixed assets are converted in the same way as the depreciation examples already provided. Stock figures are converted for the accounting period.

Equity Interest. Both liabilities and assets are converted for the accounting period. Converted liabilities are subtracted from converted assets, or equity interest.

Profit and Loss Statement for the Accounting Period. Studies show that taxable income may be lowered by 50 to 60 percent in some industries after conversion (see Table 26). Five basic conversions are required:

1. Transactions for the accounting period
2. Stock at the start of the accounting period
3. Stock at the end of the accounting period
4. Total depreciation for the accounting period
5. Retained monetary asset losses

Transactions for the Accounting Period. These include sales, purchases, and expenses. If transactions occur evenly over the period, the average index for the period can be used. For example, if the index is 135 at the end of the period, but the average of the index for the period was 127, purchases of $100,000 would be converted as follows:

$100,000 × 135 ÷ 127 = $106,100

This reflects the fact that, although materials or other purchases cost $100,000, the real money value of their cost was $106,100.

If transactions are periodic in nature, conversions can be by weighted average, or transactions can be converted for each 28-day period or for each quarter. This plan may be particularly useful if the company makes a large proportion of its purchases or other transactions early in the annual period.

Stock at the start of the accounting period will have been converted for the balance sheet at the beginning of the accounting period, and this figure can be used.

Stock at the end of the accounting period is converted by applying an average index for the period. Gross profit and cost of stocks sold during the period are not converted from historic figures. Instead, converted figures for other areas are added and subtracted as applicable, producing gross profit and cost of stock figures that have been inherently converted.

Total depreciation for the accounting period is determined by multiplying individual assets by the index at the close of the accounting period and dividing it by the index at the time of the asset's purchase. This figure is divided by 10 (or other depreciation time scale) to produce current depreciation per asset.

Retained monetary asset losses are those stemming from decreasing-value cash or other monetary assets held during the accounting period. Assuming the index at the close of the period is 135, and that it was 120 at the beginning, losses on monetary assets of $100,000 can be determined by the following formula:

$$\$100,000 \times \left(\frac{135 - 120}{120} \right) = \$12,500$$

Monetary assets accumulated evenly during the year will not be subject to the same figures. If $300,000 in monetary assets is held at the end of the period, beginning assets are subtracted and an averaged index formula is applied:

$$\begin{array}{r} \$300,000 \\ -100,000 \\ \hline \end{array}$$

$$\$200,000 \times \left(\frac{135 - 127.5}{127.5} \right) = \$11,765$$

Total losses on retained monetary assets in this example during one period are $24,265, then, and are entered as losses, resulting in lower taxation.

CONVERSION ANOMALIES

The net realizable value of stock or nonmonetary assets should be considered before conversion figures are used. Where net realizable value has been used in historical accounting, this is converted to current purchasing power figures. Generally, the lower of cost or net realizable value is used as the base for conversion.

USE OF CONVERSIONS

Two methods are available for the use of conversions for inflation accounting: the net change method and the columnar work sheet method.

The **net change method** uses converted balance sheets at the beginning and close of the accounting period but does not convert the profit and loss statement. Converted profits or losses are determined by subtracting equity interest at the start of the period from the figure at the end of the period and adding dividends accrued. The method does not adequately show purchasing power gain or loss of profits/losses, and the second method is preferred.

The **columnar work sheet method** uses a converted balance sheet at the beginning and end of the accounting period, as well as a converted profit and loss statement. Double-entry accounting inherent in the method provides a check of conversions with little extra work or cost.

In both methods, converted figures may be updated with annual index changes in subsequent years to avoid the necessity of conversion of the original figures.

MAKING THE MOST OF INFLATION ACCOUNTING

The purchasing power of figures in business and industry tells the real story of a company's success or failure. For example, a dividend payment may seem to be rising when increased from 50 to 55 cents a share. But if the annual inflation rate is 15 percent, the purchasing power of the dividend will actually have declined to 47.5 cents.

Tax savings due to lower purchasing power of profits or purchasing power value of capital gains are an essential value of the method, as is adequate depreciation.

Growth also should be measured in terms of purchasing power. For example, if $50,000 of profits are retained for capital investment, an annual inflation rate of 15 percent can shrink the purchasing value of this asset to $42,500, if the investments are not made by the end of the first year. By the same token, assets, once acquired, will increase in value.

SUGGESTED FURTHER READING

Bacher, M., "Valuation Reporting: A Real-Life Example," *Financial Executive,* January 1973.
Blandon, Michael, "Adjusting the Profits with Inflation Accounting," *The Financial Times,* London, May 15, 1974.
Brittan, Samuel, "Living with Inflation—The Key Points," *The Financial Times,* London, May 13, 1974.
Farmer, R., "Inflation Accountancy and the Buyer," *Purchasing Journal,* June 1973.
Lafferty, Michael, "How Shares React to Inflation Accounts," *The Financial Times,* Oct. 9, 1974, London.
Parker, P. W., and P. M. D. Gibbs, *Accounting for Inflation,* Phillips and Drew, London, 1974.
U. K. Accounting Standards Committee, *Document ED8,* H. M. Printing Office, London, 1973.

INFLATION COST CONTROL

Areas for use in Cost Control:

FINANCIAL MOTIVATIONAL MANAGEMENT
ORGANIZATIONAL AND OPERATIONAL SYSTEMS
MATERIALS AND EQUIPMENT MANAGEMENT
INDUSTRIAL APPLICATIONS
BUSINESS AND COMMERCIAL APPLICATIONS

While methods to deal with inflation-connected costs are often methods that can be used in all aspects of business cost reduction, some of them are especially important in an inflationary spiral. To make best use of these methods, we must first understand what inflation is and some of the factors that cause it.

The original concept of inflation was that a complete loss of confidence in currency occurred, resulting in astronomical prices and probably complete monetary collapse. Since World War II, a new trend—recently much accelerated—has set in. This is creeping inflation, a continual and gradual rise in wages and prices. Labor union leaders and businessmen argue about which comes first, higher prices causing higher wages, or higher wages necessitating higher prices.

Inflation was once considered a separate element of the economy—something that happened all by itself. But J. M. Keynes's theories—widely accepted today—argue that the level of employment and various monetary factors (including prices) combine to fire inflation. An example of this principle in action was the American scene during World War II. Unemployment fell sharply as young men were drafted into the armed forces, incomes rose, and consumer goods production fell. This combination of events pulled prices up—and was called the "inflationary gap"—the amount incomes exceeded planned spending. Keynes suggested raising taxes to absorb this gap, in an effort to keep prices more even and slow inflation. Keynes also stressed the relationship among prices, productivity, and costs in the shape of the money wage level. Looking at the following examples of this relationship, we can see what happens when the various elements are not balanced.

National production		$1,000,000,000,000
Export surplus	$ 66,000,000,000	
Government expenditures	500,000,000,000	
	$566,000,000,000	566,000,000,000
Balance of goods remaining		$ 434,000,000,000

Individual income		$1,000,000,000,000
Taxes	$333,000,000,000	333,000,000,000
Balance consumers have to spend		$ 667,000,000,000
Balance of goods remaining		434,000,000,000
The inflationary gap		$ 233,000,000,000

Looking at these examples, we can see that the consumers have $233 billion to spend, but no goods or services remain for them to buy. If they save the total amount, the inflationary problems will be postponed, at least. If not, an inflationary gap develops.

Individual income for which there are no goods	$233,000,000,000
Savings	146,000,000,000
The inflationary gap	$ 87,000,000,000

Any amount not saved ($87 billion, in this example) will have to be absorbed in some way. Left as it is, economists have shown that prices will rise to absorb it (a 20 percent increase). Once prices go up 20 percent, workers will demand pay increases to match, and the whole spiral will start again.

Another possible solution would be raising taxes to absorb the $87 billion; or the government could lower national spending by that amount, freeing goods for individual purchase. Importing an additional $87 billion worth of products might also serve to hold inflation back. Other methods have been tried. The American government, when first encountering creeping inflation in 1933, met the situation by issuing new money not backed by gold as it had been before that time. The government felt this step was necessary to maintain full employment and meet increasing costs.

TRADE UNIONS AND INFLATION

Before setting out individual ways in which a company can meet inflation-connected costs, it is important to consider the trade unions' role. Many economists feel that trade union policies are at the heart of the creeping inflation problem, since the current trend is for unions to demand wage increases in excess of increased production. Lewis's law, named by economists for the American labor union leader, states that we have unionism, and we desire full employment and stable prices. The three cannot exist concurrently, economists say, but any two can:

1. Unionism and full employment (with inflation)
2. Unionism and stable prices (without full employment)
3. Stable prices and full employment (without unionism)

Economists may accept these three choices, but both business and government frequently try to control all of the elements to allow a country to have all three variables—unionism, full employment, and stable prices.

In 1959, for example, United States Senator O'Mahoney introduced a plan to check inflation: he proposed a price control that would check pricing policies, ensuring price reductions when productivity increased to balance increased prices where production is stable or falls. The bill did not pass.

Recent intervention by most governments, with wage and price controls, have not been very effective in controlling inflation, either. In fact, government policies can add to the inflationary cycle, particularly if a government guarantees full employment by buying goods not otherwise purchased. Under such circumstances, unions do not hesitate to ask for big wage increases, and business does not hesitate to give them. A good example of this is the building industry in Britain. Inflation has pushed the average cost of a modest two- or three-bedroom home to $25,000, while the average salary is less than

$4,000. Clearly, the average worker cannot afford to rent or buy this property. Thus, the government buys the property and rents it at a loss—perhaps $12 a week. But, as it cannot afford to buy and subsidize the vast amounts of housing needed, building slows down and housing becomes crowded and scarce. When a situation of this type continues for any length of time (and wages are being controlled by the government, which prevents their reaching the level of housing costs), a recession or depression will eventually occur to bring prices down.

Business methods of dealing with trade union influences on inflation have not historically been very effective either. Economists say that business often tends to forget that trade unions have become political in nature, rather than economic, as they first were. If trade unionists can be shown that their wage demands would bankrupt a company, the economists say, the unions will lower their demands. Many business executives would question the truth of this statement, and the situation becomes even more exaggerated in those countries with nationalized businesses, where the union tends to feel that the country can pay workers anything demanded through raising taxes or prices.

CONTROLLING INFLATION-CONNECTED COSTS

What can the individual business executive do to control inflation-connected costs in his company? Generally, these costs can be divided into two areas: labor costs and material costs—with labor costs being the more important, since the primary cost in most businesses is salaries.

INFLATION-RELATED LABOR COST CONTROL

Replace manpower with machinery as soon as machinery is economical. Take into consideration that machinery cost, once paid, will remain stable, whereas manpower cost will increase 10 to 15 percent per year. Thus, a machine that will cost $10,000 a year to buy and operate over a period of five years will save $17,156 over the salary cost of a $10,000-a-year employee whose annual wages will have risen to $16,105 at the end of five years if only a 10 percent annual salary increment is given.

Use minimum-wage or lower-cost minority-group labor wherever possible, hiring bright individuals and offering thorough training. While some countries now theoretically require equal pay for all ages, sexes, and races, the fact is that there may be a minimum wage, but beyond the base figure, pay is almost always subjective—particularly when the earnings are in the form of a salary.

Table 27. Comparative Wages[1]

White men	$168/week
Minority men	$123/week
White women	$103/week

[1]U.S. Bureau of Labor Statistics, 1971.

Women are the obvious choice for many jobs. In smaller, nonunion businesses, women will usually work for a lower salary than men with the same educational and social backgrounds. It is, of course, illegal to pay women less than men for the same work. It is not illegal to hire women when the salary offered is too low to attract male workers.

Political minorities, particularly political refugees from Eastern European countries, have proved very satisfactory employees for some businesses. One Midwestern American plant, while paying refugees the standard hourly wage, found that they turned out considerably more work than their coworkers. Although these newly arrived persons often did not yet speak English well, fellow refugees would bring them to the plant personnel office and later would help them learn the on-line job. Company loyalty among this group was strong, the firm found; the strikes, slowdowns, etc., were actively fought against by this group.

Part-time workers, whether students, semiretired persons, or housewives, can provide an inexpensive source of labor. McDonald's hamburger chain, for example, keeps its wages low by hiring many minimum-wage part-time students for the body of its work force. When this type of worker is being hired, it is important that the job be one that has a set formula of work. Good training is essential.

Switch as many workers as possible to a productivity-related pay standard. Piece rate and other incentive pay schemes are described in the entry **Incentive Payment Systems**; they are well worth investigating as a means of getting more work for your money.

Make sure work is efficiently organized, since it is likely that fewer employees could do the same amount of work. A good example of this can be seen by looking at the British production records during an emergency three-day working week declared by the government early in 1974. In a majority of firms limited to normal operating hours on only three days of each week (60 percent of the normal working week), production remained at 80 to 90 percent of normal. Businessmen explained this by saying that workers put extra effort into their jobs; but the truth is that employees organized their work better and worked nearer their actual capacity because they feared their jobs would be lost if production dropped too drastically. And there seems to be no reason why, if near-normal production could be accomplished with 60 percent of the normal labor time, normal operations should not be more efficient, eliminating excess employees.

Eliminate overtime payments wherever possible. Sometimes it is essential to get an order out, and overtime cannot be avoided. But it is only common sense to keep wage costs to straight time whenever possible. Many businesses operate on a constant overtime schedule. Table 28 shows the difference in operating costs of a typical firm, with total production costing an additional 31 percent where overtime is regularly used.

Table 28. Comparison of Production Costs Using Straight-Time versus Overtime Payment Methods

	Company A		Company B	
	Hours	Cost	Hours	Cost
Hours of work required	400		400	
Hours straight time @ $4/hr.	200	$ 800	400	$1,600
Hours @ time and a half	150	$ 900		
Hours @ double time	50	$ 400		
Total cost of production		$2,100		$1,600

Help the employee produce more, through better training, better human relations programs, and a better work atmosphere. Complete details of cost reduction methods in these areas are also contained in this book.

Discourage union wage increases that exceed production increases, minus any capital expenditures needed to increase productivity. In the bargaining, this should be your primary goal. Approach the union representatives as a political entity, on the basis that if labor can increase production, management will give an increased wage in return. As the first part of this section sets out, one of the causes of inflation is wages increasing faster than production. From 1947 through 1969, U.S. production rose an average of 3.2 percent per year, while compensation increases averaged 5.1 percent annually. In 1970, U.S. production dropped 0.09 percent, but wages increased 7.1 percent, boosting inflation and causing the government to institute wage and price controls.

Locate, when possible, in economically depressed or low-wage areas to take advantage of low-cost labor. The Honeywell plant in Phoenix, Arizona, in 1973, for example, paid some of its skilled workers less than $3 an hour. In the Chicago area, such labor would have cost $5 or more an hour. Phoenix employees were satisfied with the wage scale, because the Honeywell plant paid the best overall wages in the area. Managerial costs for the same plant were proportionately lower, too, usually running little more than half the salaries for comparable jobs in Chicago, New York, and Los Angeles. Lower salaries also mean lower costs in building and maintaining the plant and lower cost of property (thus, lower taxes). When choosing a geographical location, you must be sure, however, that workers are available in that area who are as skilled as necessary or easily trainable.

INFLATION-CONNECTED MATERIAL AND OVERHEAD COSTS

The other side of the inflation-connected cost problem is money spent on materials and overhead with always increasing price tags. Parts, equipment, rent, utilities—all increase steadily with creeping inflation. But there are steps you can take to control and reduce your costs.

Work out the point where purchase price increases exceed storage costs for every major material used. Assuming material costs will rise on the average of 15 percent per year, and considerably more for some materials, decide which you can afford to buy now and store for future use. In the case of small, easily stored items (small parts for the factory and typewriter ribbons and pens for an office), you can probably afford to buy and store several years' supply. Materials made of paper or based on oil (such as plastics and synthetics) should be given special consideration, since they are likely to increase much more than 15 percent a year in cost.

Contracts to purchase materials may provide you with economy plus the advantage of having the materials' manufacturer keep the goods until you want them. But more and more contracts carry an inflationary clause raising your costs as inflation spirals.

Buy equipment primarily for quality and simplicity. Equipment, replacement parts, and repair labor will probably rise at 15 percent per year, and an additional 5 percent spent now on quality can mean good savings if fewer than normal repairs or replacements are required.

Check prices of imported materials, and use these where quality and cost make them the better choice.

Shop around, checking prices of smaller materials manufacturers as well as the major firms. Smaller companies may have no labor union, less overhead, and tighter control that can allow them to sell their product at a more reasonable price.

Consider producing your own materials. If your company wants to expand, producing your own materials is a natural direction to go. Management will already be oriented toward the type of materials needed, making the expansion smoother and more likely to succeed.

Determine whether the quality of materials used in your product can be lowered without hurting sales potential.

Determine whether alternative materials would lower the cost of producing your product without hurting sales potential. Greatly inflated oil prices, for example, will push plastic and synthetic fabric and material prices up. Natural materials may now be less costly, although just the opposite was recently true.

Your own research and development may be beneficial, if the company is large enough to afford a good department of this type. If gasoline and electricity are major expenses for your firm, for example, a scientific and economic investigation of solar power for use in 10 years' time may eventually save you large sums.

Borrow money now for investment in good-quality equipment and plant. If you will need new equipment or additions to your plant in the near future, you may be ahead to borrow the money now—at a lower interest rate than will probably be available in the future—and purchase these items before their prices rise even further. At the same time, consider your outmoded equipment. Although its value may have depreciated to nil on company books, inflationary prices may have pushed real value up. If so, sell the outmoded equipment and reinvest in needed materials or equipment.

SUGGESTED FURTHER READING

Ball, R. J., and Peter Doyle, *Inflation,* Penguin, Baltimore, 1972.
Hagger, A. J., *The Theory of Inflation: A Review,* Melbourne University Press, 1964.
Hague, D. C., *Inflation,* Macmillan, New York, 1962.
Johnson, H. G., *Essays in Monetary Economics,* Allen and Unwin, London, 1967.
Stidger, R. W., "Coping with Inflation," *World Construction,* New York, January 1975.

INFORMATION AGREEMENTS

Areas for use in Cost Control:

ORGANIZATIONAL AND OPERATIONAL SYSTEMS
INDUSTRIAL APPLICATIONS
BUSINESS AND COMMERCIAL APPLICATIONS

Information agreements are the intercompany exchange of data about prices to be charged or bids to be made, production levels, or other information (see Table 29) that can reduce or control operating costs. Generally, exchange of information used to reduce or control operational costs, such as customer credit experiences, production costs (as a point of performance comparison), work standards exchange, etc., are not illegal; while information exchanged about prices to be charged, bids to be made, etc., are more likely to be considered in violation of antitrust laws.

Table 29. Information Exchanged in Information Agreements

Individual firm's information	Industrywide information
Customer credit experience	Price agreements
Competition espionage	R&D exchange
Production prices to be charged	Cost comparisons
Production data	Work standards exchange
Distribution data	Costing methods
Costs	Trade association data
Bids	Governmental statistics
Turnover	Research agency data
	International comparisons

SUGGESTED FURTHER READING

O'Brien, D. P., and D. Swann, *Information Agreements, Competition, and Efficiency,* St. Martin's, New York, 1968.
Peacock, C. D., "The Law of Open Pricing in the United States and Britain," *International and Comparative Law Quarterly,* vol. 19, 1967.

INFORMATION THEORY

Areas for use in Cost Control:

ORGANIZATIONAL AND OPERATIONAL SYSTEMS
INDUSTRIAL APPLICATIONS
BUSINESS AND COMMERCIAL APPLICATIONS

Information theory is a relatively new **operations research** technique that uses complex mathematical formulas to develop cost reduction and efficiency control data from information in operational business documents. Calculations are computerized. Specialized operating procedure knowledge is necessary to use the technique, as is knowledge of computer programming and operation.

SUGGESTED FURTHER READING

Brinckloe, W. D., *Managerial Operations Research,* McGraw-Hill, New York, 1969.

IN-PLANT TRAVEL-TIME REDUCTION

Areas for use in Cost Control:

WORK PLACE MOTIVATIONAL MANAGEMENT

INDUSTRIAL APPLICATIONS

Since time is money, excess in-plant travel time is an obvious area for cost reduction. Poor supplies planning and confusion about procedures are the major causes of wasted time spent moving about the plant, and these are the first problems to solve to reduce costs.

Supplies Planning. Wherever possible, commonly needed supplies should be at hand or within a few steps. Since few production areas have great amounts of storage space near the production area, some companies have set up a large closet-type storage area for each supervisor. These cabinets, with shelves and/or drawers, are periodically restocked with small tools, supplies, and commonly used forms. Exact contents, of course, depend on the phase of production supervised and the materials needed. The cabinets can be self-service, or for better control the supervisor can dispense supplies.

Procedures Knowledge. Another method of reducing costs is to make certain that all employees know any procedure that affects them. If a certain form must be filled out, for example, the employee should have that form at hand for completion, rather than having to stop midway through the procedure to go to the office for a form. In the same way, a thorough knowledge of procedures will ensure that an employee can assemble all needed tools and materials at one time, saving hours wasted moving around the plant.

Other Methods. In very large plants, some companies have found a mechanized method of in-plant travel advisable. Motorized golf carts are one system, and moving walkways much like an escalator are another. These methods are particularly useful in transporting tools and supplies from one area of the plant to another.

SUGGESTED FURTHER READING

Cost Control and the Supervisor, American Management Assn., New York, 1966.

INPUT-OUTPUT

Areas of use in Cost Control:

ORGANIZATIONAL AND OPERATIONAL SYSTEMS

INDUSTRIAL APPLICATIONS

BUSINESS AND COMMERCIAL APPLICATIONS

Input-output, also called the Maptik Component Input-Output Service, is a simplified model of possible alternate economies used to control costs of materials and labor used in proposed goods and services and to analyze possible markets and profits to be made from such goods and services. Developed by Samson Science Corporation, a business trend specialty group, the model follows the flow of all materials, products, and services between industries, suggesting alternate items not used that might be more effective or reduce costs. Individual proposed products or services can then be examined in the context of these data and the most economical materials, as well as suitable end markets, can be determined.

Quantum Science Corporation has developed a complete set of tables from input-output techniques, providing for electronics, computer, and technological areas componentized data that can be applied block by block to applicable industries. Cost of such a componentized service is lower since data structuring is not done for a specific project but is maintained for specialized areas of business and industry.

SUGGESTED FURTHER READING

Bjerram, C. A., *Forecasts 1968–2000 of Computer Developments and Applications,* Parsons and Williams, Copenhagen, 1974.

George, Frank, *Models of Thinking,* Schenkman, Cambridge, Mass., 1972.

INSPECTION CENSUS

Areas for use in Cost Control:

ORGANIZATIONAL AND OPERATIONAL SYSTEMS
INDUSTRIAL APPLICATIONS

An inspection census is the listing of all specific inspection or testing tasks, and the cost of each, as a means of determining needed quality checks not being performed and/or eliminating the cost of duplicated quality checks. Data to be obtained from an inspection census include:

1. Work areas
2. Number of inspectors
3. Specific inspection tasks
4. Work methods used; inspection measurement standards
5. Cost of specific inspection tasks
6. Use of inspections in future discussions

The final report is usually listed, with the most costly inspection tasks first, in descending order to aid in cost identification and reduction.

SUGGESTED FURTHER READING

Juran, J. M., ed., *Quality Control Handbook,* McGraw-Hill, New York, 1962.

INTEGER PROGRAMMING See Mathematical Programming.

INTEGRATION See Amalgamation.

INTEGRATIVE BARGAINING

Areas for use in Cost Control:

ORGANIZATIONAL AND OPERATIONAL SYSTEMS
INDUSTRIAL APPLICATIONS
BUSINESS AND COMMERCIAL APPLICATIONS

Integrative bargaining is a collective bargaining model used to forecast employee and trade union response to various cost or other problem solutions for common benefits offered in negotiation. If such employee response can be accurately predetermined, use of the technique can reduce both increased wage costs and losses that might result from industrial actions.

SUGGESTED FURTHER READING

Walton, R. E., and R. McKersie, *A Behavioral Theory of Labor Negotiations,* McGraw-Hill, New York, 1965.

INTERCOMPANY COOPERATION

Areas for use in Cost Control:

ORGANIZATIONAL AND OPERATIONAL SYSTEMS
INDUSTRIAL APPLICATIONS
BUSINESS AND COMMERCIAL APPLICATIONS

Intercompany cooperation is the pooling of ideas, knowledge, techniques, etc., among competitors for the purpose of lowering costs to the individual company, since costs are shared. In some areas, such as the standardization of parts, intercompany cooperation is operating well. In others, such as joint R&D programs, methods need to be found to overcome intercompany rivalries if costs and gains are to be shared. *See also* **Information Agreements.**

SUGGESTED FURTHER READING

Bloom, G. F., "Productivity: Weak Link in Our Economy," *Harvard Business Review,* January-February 1971.

INTERFIRM COMPARISONS

Areas for use in Cost Control:

ORGANIZATIONAL AND OPERATIONAL SYSTEMS
INDUSTRIAL APPLICATIONS
BUSINESS AND COMMERCIAL APPLICATIONS

Interfirm comparisons are the comparisons by one company of its predetermined key figures with like figures of others in its own industry as a means of pinpointing areas where cost reduction techniques are needed. Because companies do not want to give figures to their competitors, the method is most successfully applied where an association or other trade body compiles industry-average figures, guaranteeing confidentiality to all participants. Such comparisons show a company its strengths and give it industry-average targets for which to aim, as well as diagnosing trouble spots.

Key figures used in interfirm comparisons include:

1. Profit/Capital Invested ratio
2. Profit/Sales ratio
3. Sales/Capital Invested ratio
4. Fixed Assets/Capital Invested ratio
5. Sales/Inventory ratio
6. Production Cost/Sales ratio
7. Administrative Cost/Sales ratio
8. Marketing Cost/Sales ratio
9. Current Liabilities/Sales ratio

SUGGESTED FURTHER READING

Wood, E. G., *Costing Matters for Managers,* Cahners Publishing Co., Boston, 1974.

INTERIM BUDGETING

Areas for use in Cost Control:

ORGANIZATIONAL AND OPERATIONAL SYSTEMS
DATA RETENTION—FILES AND RECORDKEEPING
INDUSTRIAL APPLICATIONS
BUSINESS AND COMMERCIAL APPLICATIONS

Interim budgeting is the updating of a budget, or preparation of a new budget, before the budget period has expired. The technique provides greater cost control when economic or market conditions have changed and costs must be reduced or increased to meet current needs. *See also* **Budgeting.**

SUGGESTED FURTHER READING

Hanson, J. L., *A Dictionary of Economics and Commerce,* MacDonald, London, 1974.
Speight, H., *Economics and Industrial Efficiency,* Macmillan, New York, 1967.

INTERNAL-MOTIVATION JOB DESIGN

Areas for use in Cost Control:

PSYCHOLOGICAL MOTIVATIONAL MANAGEMENT
ORGANIZATIONAL AND OPERATIONAL SYSTEMS
INDUSTRIAL APPLICATIONS
BUSINESS AND COMMERCIAL APPLICATIONS

Internal-motivation job design is the creation of specified work that motivates through its own nature. Requirements for such work are that it:

1. *Provide feelings of responsibility and achievement.* The employee must realize the purpose of the work, that it is his or her own work, and that he or she is responsible for its successful completion. Generally, individualized work promotes this feeling, whereas teamwork divides responsibility.

2. *Be of a worthwhile nature.* The employee should feel that his or her work is of value to society, or to some aspect of society.

3. *Provide feedback as to the success or failure of the employee's work.* This may take the form of praise and/or constructive criticism so long as *regularly scheduled* feedback channels are operated rather than sporadic ones. This means that the supervisor should criticize or praise *every* completed unit of work.

Use of internal-motivation job design can increase work satisfaction, increase productivity, and lower absenteeism and turnover, while reducing labor costs.

SUGGESTED FURTHER READING

Blood, M. R., and C. L. Hulin, "Alienation, Environmental Characteristics and Worker Responses," *Journal of Applied Psychology,* vol. 51, 1967.
Davis, L. E., and J. C. Taylor, eds., *Design of Jobs,* Penguin, Baltimore, 1972.
Hackman, J. R., and E. E. Lawler III, "Employee Reactions to Job Characteristics," *Journal of Applied Psychology,* vol. 55, 1971.

INTERNATIONAL LAW AND COST CONTROL

Areas for use in Cost Control:

ORGANIZATIONAL AND OPERATIONAL SYSTEMS
INDUSTRIAL APPLICATIONS
BUSINESS AND COMMERCIAL APPLICATIONS

As more businesses and industries become involved in international trade, a greater importance is attached to cost effects of international law. At present, only specific agreements between countries are legally binding. However, the trend is toward international agreements extending to such a large percentage of the world as to make them enforceable in most cases. International Monetary Fund, International Finance, and other international agreements are examples of this. Through the United Nations' Commission on International Trade Law, first established in 1968, the following trends affecting costs emerge:

1. *Discriminatory trade restrictions, including taxes on imports from one country but not those of another, are generally not used* except in cases where such restrictions are justified by imbalance of trade. The Permanent Court of International Justice has made rulings that add strength to this trend, but trade agreements between countries are still used. Such a trend has generally reduced taxation costs in trading abroad.

2. *International groups have encouraged the passage of laws protecting foreign investment, including payment of profits, withdrawal of investment, and exchange control.* Such protection is usually not extended if monetary reserves of the country in which the investment is held are affected, or when the temporary "national good" conditions, such as are enforced during a revolution, prevent withdrawal of such funds. Incoming investment has been encouraged by most countries unless such investment places an adverse proportion of national economic power in foreign hands. As the trend grows, increased protection against partial or complete loss of international capital investment costs seems likely.

3. *International commodity agreements are aimed at stabilizing commodity prices through balance of supply and demand,* and this movement may become international law, excluding national needs to restrict production for protection against an unbalanced economy. Commodity futures trading, now being used for speculative as well as industrial purposes, may also be regulated both nationally and internationally in the years to come. This would provide some insurance against increased costs of imported raw materials.

4. *Quantitative import restrictions may be abolished,* reducing some raw material costs of materials now restricted.

5. *Environmental controls on industry, and the resulting costs, appear to be moving in much the same direction as national policies. See also* **Environmental Improvement Cost Control.**

SUGGESTED FURTHER READING

Starke, J. G., *Introduction to International Law,* Butterworth, London, 1972.
United Nations' Resolution of December 17, 1966: International Trade Law Commission.
U.S. Department of State Bulletin on Development, Washington, D.C., Aug. 24, 1970.

INTERPERSONAL NETWORK ADVERTISING

Areas for use in Cost Control:
PSYCHOLOGICAL MOTIVATIONAL MANAGEMENT
ORGANIZATIONAL AND OPERATIONAL SYSTEMS
INDUSTRIAL APPLICATIONS
BUSINESS AND COMMERCIAL APPLICATIONS

Interpersonal network advertising is a low-cost sales technique developed from **motivation market research** findings. Community, social, or other group leaders are persuaded to purchase the product or service to be advertised and to communicate that fact directly (through personal contact) and/or indirectly (through advertising) to the groups they lead. The method is especially effective when used for groups of products or services (such as beauty salon services, air conditioners, and central heating) by trade associations or similar groups. Usual sales costs are considerably reduced if the target market is motivated to buy through interpersonal network advertising. American executives purchase air conditioning for their cars, for example, because the company owner has it. Women purchase hair care because television and movie stars do, and because community social-group leaders do.

SUGGESTED FURTHER READING

Martineau, Pierre, *Motivation in Advertising,* McGraw-Hill, New York, 1957.
Stacey, N. A., and A. Wilson, *The Changing Pattern of Distribution,* Pergamon, New York, 1965.

INTRAORGANIZATIONAL BARGAINING

Areas for use in Cost Control:

ORGANIZATIONAL AND OPERATIONAL SYSTEMS
INDUSTRIAL APPLICATIONS
BUSINESS AND COMMERCIAL APPLICATIONS

Intraorganizational bargaining is a negotiating model used to forecast labor union response to bargaining offers and utilizing behavior that will secure approval of such offers. Use of the technique can reduce both increased labor costs and losses due to industrial action if such labor union response is accurately predetermined.

SUGGESTED FURTHER READING

Walton, R. E., and R. McKersie, *A Behavioral Theory of Labor Negotiations,* McGraw-Hill, New York, 1965.

INTUITIVE PLANNING

Areas for use in Cost Control:

ORGANIZATIONAL AND OPERATIONAL SYSTEMS
INDUSTRIAL APPLICATIONS
BUSINESS AND COMMERCIAL APPLICATIONS

Intuitive planning is a Japanese technique for long-range planning and forecasting based on pragmatic, intuitive methods and very specialized study, contrasted with Western statistical and scientific forecasting techniques. Intuitive planning can reduce costs primarily by determining, in the design stages, alternate materials that are more economical in a proposed product and by transfer of technology, ideas, and markets to previously unrelated areas.

SUGGESTED FURTHER READING

Smith, P. I. S., *Think Tanks and Problem Solving,* Business Books, London, 1971.

INVENTORY CONTROL See Stock Control.

INVERSE BONUS TECHNIQUE

Areas for use in Cost Control:

FINANCIAL MOTIVATIONAL MANAGEMENT
ORGANIZATIONAL AND OPERATIONAL SYSTEMS
INDUSTRIAL APPLICATIONS
BUSINESS AND COMMERCIAL APPLICATIONS

The inverse bonus technique reduces materials or other waste by reducing bonus payments for each item of wastage. The technique was developed in the tannery industry, where skins were frequently ruined through careless cutting. Here, a bonus schedule was established determined by the percentage of cuts to total number of hide skins, with a predetermined percentage of the bonus removed for each wasted skin. The technique can be applied to cut business output wastage as well as being used in industrial incentive plans. In sales, for example, a bonus may be paid and a percentage of the payment removed if predetermined sales quotas are not reached. In offices, inverse bonuses might apply to meeting work schedules.

SUGGESTED FURTHER READING

Neal, A. W., *Industrial Waste,* Business Books, London, 1971.

INVERTED PYRAMID TECHNIQUE See Personnel Morale Building.

INVERTED TAKE-OVER

Areas for use in Cost Control:

ORGANIZATIONAL AND OPERATIONAL SYSTEMS
INDUSTRIAL APPLICATIONS
BUSINESS AND COMMERCIAL APPLICATIONS

Inverted take-over is the acquisition of a large company, usually one losing money, by a smaller company to give the smaller company a means of entry to the stock exchange without applying for it (if the larger company belongs) and/or to reduce tax costs by offsetting the smaller company's profits against the larger firm's losses. Such acquisitions may also give the smaller company other assets, such as plant, equipment, and labor pools at a lower-than-market cost.

SUGGESTED FURTHER READING

Hanson, J. L., *A Dictionary of Economics and Commerce,* MacDonald, London, 1974.
Robicheck, A. A., and S. C. Myers, *Optimal Financing Decisions,* Prentice-Hall, Englewood Cliffs, N.J., 1965.

INVESTMENT FURNISHING

Areas for use in Cost Control:

ORGANIZATIONAL AND OPERATIONAL SYSTEMS
INDUSTRIAL APPLICATIONS
BUSINESS AND COMMERCIAL APPLICATIONS

Investment furnishing is purchasing and using antique office furniture with good investment potential. Costs are reduced since the cost may be more than offset as the value of the furnishings rises. Successful use of investment furnishing depends on purchasing furniture that is still classified as secondhand, and therefore is relatively inexpensive, but which will soon be classified as antique, carrying a constantly increasing value. Auctions are the primary sources of such articles at low cost, including rolltop desks, partners' desks (a large writing table with drawer and pedestal base designed for two persons sitting opposite), board room tables and chairs, bookcases, and other chairs. Good-quality wood (which may need refinishing to bring the item to full value), such as mahogany, sound leather-topped tables, desks, and chairs, and marble-topped tables are factors that should mean a more rapid increase in the articles' value.

SUGGESTED FURTHER READING

Field, J., "The Executive's World: Furniture with Investment Appeal," *The Financial Times,* London, July 23, 1974.

JOB DESIGN

Areas for use in Cost Control:

PSYCHOLOGICAL MOTIVATIONAL MANAGEMENT
ORGANIZATIONAL AND OPERATIONAL SYSTEMS
INDUSTRIAL APPLICATIONS
BUSINESS AND COMMERCIAL APPLICATIONS

Job design is the detailing of tasks, methods, and roles in jobs to increase productivity and worker job satisfaction while decreasing absenteeism and turnover rates—all of which reduce labor costs. Both physical and psychological motivational aspects of job content are specified. Physical work specification generally uses *work study* techniques (*see* **Work Study and Measurement**) for optimum results. Psychological job aspects are not so easy to specify, however. Basically, techniques that motivate employees and/or help them meet the needs of rapidly changing technologies are used. Such techniques are discussed in more detail separately, but they include:

1. *Job Enlargement*—the expansion of work duties. Employees are motivated through increased interest in the broader scope of work, greater responsibility, pride in seeing a piece of work through from start to completion, and greater involvement with company objectives. *See also* **Job Enlargement.**

2. *Human Factors Engineering*—the motivation of workers to greater productivity in their use of machines in their work. *See also* **Human Factors Engineering.**

3. *Job Enrichment*—motivation through psychological growth while working. This may include providing increased numbers of work challenges and responsibilities to make best use of an employee's abilities. *See also* **Job Enrichment.**

4. *Job Loading.* Two types of motivators are possible here: *horizontal job loading,* or motivation to do essentially meaningless tasks; and *vertical job loading,* motivation by increased responsibility and achievement. Vertical job loading reduces labor costs through increased productivity, and care should be taken to limit use of job loading to this aspect of the technique. *See also* **Vertical Job Loading.**

5. *Internal-Motivation Job Design*—planning work that motivates by its nature—such as providing feelings of responsibility and achievement because the work is of a worthwhile nature—and providing feedback to be sure workers know that their achievements are recognized. *See also* **Internal-Motivation Job Design.**

6. *Group Decision Making*—motivating through worker participation in operational decision making for the company. *See also* **Group Decision Making.**

JOB DESIGN COST CONTROL

While most executives know that best use of job design can often save labor costs, too little effort has been expended to compare actual long-term costs of jobs that have evolved and with costs of jobs that have been designed. Three basic methods can be used for such comparison:

1. *Determine capital investment in the working force by calculating the start-up cost for this area.* Recruiting, hiring, and training costs should be included, as should break-in time. An estimated figure per worker can then be obtained by dividing the cost

by the original number of employees. Turnover reduction savings stemming from job design can be compared with the answer.

2. *Recruiting, hiring, and training costs can be calculated for each type of job.* Once again, such figures show cost reductions possible with lower turnover.

3. *Increased productivity from job design can be measured with production records.* Such work should be measured for a break-in time of about six months after the job design changes have been implemented. Although production will fall off initially, as workers learn new aspects of the job, it should increase well above beginning levels in a short period of time.

Work cost factors to be considered when designing jobs include:

1. *Efficiency.* Will the newly designed job increase productivity? How much?
2. *Training.* Can a new employee be trained quickly and economically for the newly designed job?
3. *Management.* Does the job require less supervision than previously?
4. *Materials.* Will the worker waste materials during the training program?
5. *Quality.* Will the new job design improve product quality?
6. *Personnel.* Will the new job design decrease absenteeism and turnover?
7. *Versatility.* Will the new job design provide back-up labor for other jobs?

By placing a dollar value on each of these, the estimated value of *Efficiency* (1), *Management declination* (3), *Quality* (5), and *Versatility* (7) can be measured against *Training costs* (2), *Materials wastage cost* (4), and *Personnel absenteeism and tardiness costs* (6) to give a rough idea of the monetary value of job design. *See also* **Human Accounting.**

JOB DESIGN AND AUTOMATION

Automation, and other technological changes, will have major effects on job design, the company using labor, and workers. An employee will expect to hold a series of jobs in his or her lifetime, rather than planning a single career. This means that training will become an increasingly important factor, and that job design must consider training and retraining as extensions of the work specified. Adaptability will be an increasingly sought-after employee characteristic.

In all aspects of automation, job design must take into account the importance of the working place and facilities, i.e., the equipment, and the relationship of employees to this work environment. Task specification must then be made considering the environment and employee team as a whole.

Automation, of itself, may lead to increased productivity and motivation, since monotonous work is usually automated, leaving the more challenging, complex work for humans. The remaining tasks, however, are interdependent rather than individualistic, and job design must implement this factor into its task specification.

Since equipment costs and downtime costs are greatly increased with automation, job content specification must be geared to the most rapid restoration of the system possible. Rather than using steady task inputs, such as adding one piece to an assembled part, automated job content specification will call for erratic effort as required by the system. Commitment of employees to company goals will be motivated through self-regulation and planning methods, giving the individual worker or team of workers more autonomy.

CURRENT TRENDS AND JOB DESIGN

Job design is most successful when it reflects the ideas and ideals of the day. Current social trends that affect job content specification include:

1. Desire for greater social significance and/or product utility value
2. Increasing strength of psychological motivation over financial motivation
3. Need for involvement through work
4. Need for continued learning and growth through work
5. Need for variety and challenge in work
6. Need for the structure provided by basic work standards and feedback of worker effort in meeting these standards
7. Desire for working autonomy, individually or as a work group
8. Need for two-way communication between workers and management

Such trends should be considered in job design and gradually absorbed into the specifications of work, methods, and working relationships.

SUGGESTED FURTHER READING

Chadwick-Jones, J., *Automation and Behavior,* Wiley, New York, 1969.
Crozier, M., *The World of the Office Worker,* University of Chicago, 1971.
Davis, L. E., and J. C. Taylor, eds., *Design of Jobs,* Penguin, Baltimore, 1972.
Myers, M. S., *Every Employee a Manager,* McGraw-Hill, New York, 1970.
Pyle, W. C., "Human Resource Accounting," *Financial Analysts Journal,* September–October 1970.
Sheppard, H. L., and N. Q. Herrick, *Where Have All the Robots Gone?* Upjohn Institute, New York, 1971.

JOB ENGINEERING

Areas for use in Cost Control:

PSYCHOLOGICAL MOTIVATIONAL MANAGEMENT
ORGANIZATIONAL AND OPERATIONAL SYSTEMS
INDUSTRIAL APPLICATIONS
BUSINESS AND COMMERCIAL APPLICATIONS

Job engineering is the technique of shaping work to fit a reliable employee's personality by altering work location, methods, equipment, responsibilities, etc., rather than hiring an employee to fit predetermined job aspects. The method can reduce labor costs—particularly when the labor market is tight and reliable workers are at a premium—through increased productivity stemming from greater job satisfaction.

SUGGESTED FURTHER READING

Mandell, M. M., *The Selection Process,* American Management Assn., New York, 1964.

JOB ENLARGEMENT

Area for use in Cost Control:

PSYCHOLOGICAL MOTIVATIONAL MANAGEMENT

Job enlargement is the expansion of work responsibilities to provide better work satisfaction. Enlargement provides greater variety for the employee, as well as giving him or her a greater sense of attainment when the work is completed, easing the work frustrations that occur when work is very simplified, and providing greater motivation. Care should be taken to enlarge work duties only to the degree of an employee's capacity, however, since too much responsibility may be as frustrating as too little.

SUGGESTED FURTHER READING

Davis, L., and A. Cherns, *A Quality of Working Life,* Free Press, New York, 1975.
King-Taylor, L., *Not for Bread Alone,* Cahners Publishing Co., Boston, 1973.

JOB ENRICHMENT

Areas for use in Cost Control:

PSYCHOLOGICAL MOTIVATIONAL MANAGEMENT
ORGANIZATIONAL AND OPERATIONAL SYSTEMS
INDUSTRIAL APPLICATIONS
BUSINESS AND COMMERCIAL APPLICATIONS

Job enrichment adds factors to the job that will enrich the employee's work by offering psychological growth. Use of the method can increase productivity, lower absenteeism, and lower turnover rates, lowering the accompanying costs as well.

In using job enrichment, the following are typical methods of application:

1. Choose jobs that need performance improvement because of monotony of work, etc., such as repetitive assembly work or typing of form letters.

2. Managerial staff then conducts a **brainstorming** session for possible changes that will enrich the job. Generally, these will follow **vertical job loading** lines.

3. Decide on specific changes to adopt vertical loading factors, such as having a typist do a rough draft of a form letter to be typed or giving an assembly worker a complete unit to assemble rather than having the worker simply add one part.

Although efficiency may drop temporarily as the employee becomes familiar with the new aspects of the job, and although some hostility from supervisors may be encountered originally, studies show that the method may increase performance by as much as 80 percent.

In addition to the above, the method pinpoints employees who have been hired for a job that requires less than their maximum ability. These employees can be moved into more challenging positions where they will provide a greater asset for the company.

SUGGESTED FURTHER READING

Davis, L. E. and J. C. Taylor, eds., *Design of Jobs,* Penguin, Baltimore, 1972.
Herzberg, F., "One More Time: How Do You Motivate Employees," *Harvard Business Review,* vol. 46, 1968.
Vroom, V. H., *Work and Motivation,* Wiley, New York, 1964.

JOB EVALUATION

Areas for use in Cost Control:

FINANCIAL MOTIVATION
INDUSTRIAL APPLICATIONS
BUSINESS AND COMMERCIAL APPLICATIONS

Job evaluation is a means of establishing equal pay for equal work. Each job is individually analyzed to find out what it requires of the employee, and then the jobs are compared to establish a comparable rate of pay for similar skills. Cost savings can be high if jobs are properly evaluated and if those evaluations are used, since only an employee able to do the job will be hired once duties are clearly defined.

Factors to be considered when evaluating a job include:

1. Job duties, including physical activities
2. Intelligence needed to do the work
3. Special skills or aptitudes required
4. Special educational background needed
5. Experience required
6. Social aspects (night shifts, dirty working conditions, etc.)

7. Safety and health risks
8. Age of employee required
9. Supervision required
10. Job hours
11. Suitable wages

METHODS OF JOB EVALUATION

Job Ranking. In this system, work is compared by a supervisory employee and jobs are arranged in the order of their difficulty or their value to the firm. This is one of the poorer methods, since few employees will be thoroughly familiar with the requirements and duties of all jobs. Opinion as to the value of any job is extremely subjective when this method is used.

Job Classification. Job variations are expressed in different grades (see Table 30), and a range of salaries for each grade is combined with years of service to evaluate job worth. While this method is preferred to job ranking alone, it offers little or no leeway for proper compensation of an exceptional individual whose worth may far exceed the grade in which his job is automatically placed.

Table 30. Grading Work

Area	Job level	Type of work done	Job title	Job grade
Policy making	Executive	Coordination	President	9
	management	Policy	Vice president	8
Coordination	Senior	Coordination	General Mgr.	7
	management	Policy	Senior Mgr.	6
Linking	Junior	Coordination	Dept. Head	5
	management	Communication	Superintendent	4
General labor	Skilled	Enforcing	Supervisor	3
		General Labor	Craftsman	2
Automatic	Semiskilled	Automatic	Machinist	1
Restricted	Unskilled	Restricted	Sweeper	0

Point Method. For some years, this has been the most popular method of job evaluation. Job characteristics are classified according to skill, effort, job conditions, and responsibility. Each classification has a number of arbitrarily assigned points, and the total of the employee's points in all categories decides his or her pay rating (see Table 31).

Factor Comparison. This method is similar to the point system, but a monetary value is fixed for each factor rather than awarding points (see Table 32).

Castellion Method. This system, started by Dr. Lucian Cortis, is a form of the point method but emphasizes decision making. Each job is broken down as to the types of decisions made, their difficulty, their frequency, and the consequence if an error occurs. Each decision-making factor is assigned a point value. A comparison of point values is used to create a companywide scale of pay.

This method offers proportionately greater rewards to managerial personnel and takes very little notice of adverse working conditions, such as unsocial hours or dangerous jobs. Particularly where trade unions are involved, employee opposition to using the plan is likely to be met.

Table 31. A Typical Rating Scale for the Point Method

Rating points	Skill required	Effort required	Responsibility required	Job conditions
4	High degree	High degree	High degree	Unsocial working hours, dangerous, and/or dirty working conditions in an extreme degree
3	Moderately heavy	Moderately heavy	Moderately heavy	Moderately bad
2	Average	Average	Average	Average
1	Below average	Below average	Below average	Good
0	None	None	None	Excellent

Table 32. Typical Factor Comparison Scale

Value	Skill required	Effort required	Responsibility required	Job conditions
$12/wk	High degree	High degree	High degree	Unsocial working hours, dangerous or dirty working conditions in extreme degree
$9/wk	Moderately heavy	Moderately heavy	Moderately heavy	Moderately bad
$6/wk	Average	Average	Average	Average
$3/wk	Below average	Below average	Below average	Good
$0/wk	None	None	None	Excellent

Time Span. This system analyzes the period of time from making a decision until the results of the work are scrutinized for adequacy. A scale of pay is set up, with the most money going to those jobs with the longest time spans. In other words, the less frequently an employee's work needs to be checked by his or her superior, the greater his pay.

Guide-Chart Profile. Devised by Dr. E. N. Hay, this method (see Table 33) rates three factors—know-how (education/experience), problem solving, and responsibility (accountability)—dividing them into eight levels each. The problem-solving factor is multiplied by the know-how factor to give a fourth rating emphasizing decision making. Pay scales are then based on the points earned.

Job Ranking. In this method—now less popular than in the past—jobs are compared with each other, rather than the different work elements being compared. Job descriptions are prepared and are arranged in a hierarchal order with those of most importance to the company receiving top classifications. Usually, each depart-

Table 33. Typical Guide-Chart Profile

Point value	Know-how	Problem solving	Responsibility
8	Advanced degree, heavy experience	Executive level	Executive level
7	Advanced degree, moderate experience	Very heavy	Very heavy
6	Degree, heavy experience	Heavy	Heavy
5	High school, heavy experience	Moderately heavy	Moderately heavy
4	High school, some experience	Moderate	Moderate
3	High school, no experience	Below average	Below average
2	Grade school, some experience	Minimal	Minimal
1	Grade school, no experience	None	None

ment is ranked by a supervisor or shop steward, since he or she should, in theory, be most aware of the importance of each job. After this step, departmental lists are combined.

Disadvantages include the fact that, using this system, it is very difficult to obtain unbiased ratings. Abilities and problems, such as dangerous working conditions, may not be given any consideration.

Job Grading. In this system, a specific job area is graded according to the level of responsibility and skill required. Two major examples of this job classification system in use are the U.S. public service and the British Institute of Office Management (IOM) Clerical Job Grading and Merit Rating Scale.

The U.S. public service system is divided into two parts: a General Schedule (GS) for professional and scientific service, clerical, and administrative positions (ratings from 1 to 18, advancing in complexity); and a Crafts, Protective, and Custodial Schedule (CPC) with four grades. All GS ratings exceed CPC ratings in the evaluation scale.

Job ranking and job grading are not much used in modern circumstances because job values are so subjectively assigned, rather than taking required skills, abilities, and working situations into account.

OTHER PURPOSES

Work evaluation serves many purposes in addition to determining a pay scale.

Training. Once a company analyzes its jobs, it becomes relatively easy for the investigator to see what training programs are needed and how much capacity each training class requires. It should also be simple to tell if training can be carried out on-the-job in an apprentice-type program, or whether career-oriented classes are needed.

Advancement. Only when a job is clearly defined is it possible to see opportunities to promote employees. Along with this aspect, managerial appraisal of any employee is made simpler if the basics of the job are clearly set out as they are in job evaluation methods.

Organization. By the very act of evaluating all of a company's jobs, the work and work schedules will become more clearly organized. Such evaluation defines areas of responsibility.

SUGGESTED FURTHER READING

Hay, E. N., *AMA Handbook of Wage and Salary Administration,* American Management Assn., New York, 1950.
Lytle, C. W., *Job Evaluation Methods,* Ronald, New York, 1954.
Patterson, T. T., *Job Evaluation,* Beekman Publishing, New York, 1972.

JOB PRESSURE AND COST CONTROL

Areas for use in Cost Control:
PSYCHOLOGICAL MOTIVATIONAL MANAGEMENT
FINANCIAL MOTIVATIONAL MANAGEMENT
ORGANIZATIONAL AND OPERATIONAL SYSTEMS
INDUSTRIAL APPLICATIONS
BUSINESS AND COMMERCIAL APPLICATIONS

Recent studies show that excessive job pressures add many costs, including higher wage demands as well as turnover and absenteeism problems, and that increased pressure does not necessarily increase production. By reducing job pressures to an acceptable level—for both management and labor—these costs can be reduced.

WHAT IS JOB PRESSURE?

Vernon E. Buck, University of Washington, says that job pressure contains three basic elements:

1. *Conflicting forces or incompatible demands.* For example, a supervisor may tell the worker that production goals *must* be met; but if the equipment in use is not capable of production at such a speed, the worker will feel job pressure.

2. *One or more induced demands.* Here, demands are made on the worker or manager by other elements. For example, if the manager's wife or husband demands that he or she obtain a 30 percent raise, this will cause work pressure unless it is time for a sizable raise and unless the manager knows that the raise will be easily obtained.

3. *Own and induced forces, recurrent or stable overtime.* These are long-lived demands. For example, if a management trainee of 23 decides he or she will do anything necessary to be a company vice president by age 35, pressure will gradually build as the years pass, becoming unbearable if the goal is not attainable and if the manager will not accept a more realistic objective.

REDUCING EXCESSIVE JOB PRESSURE

Several areas can be emphasized when reducing excessive job pressures and the resulting costs.

Communications should be improved. Employees should know why extra production is needed, and their ideas about how to accomplish goals should be sought. Worker involvement in goal setting and profit sharing is ideal for reducing these pressures. *See also* **Productivity Bargaining and Agreements.**

Benefits and wages should be competitive within the industry. Workers or managers not receiving wages and benefits comparable to those offered by competing firms are likely to be subjected to excessive pressures by their families, which will affect their work adversely.

Work should be structured to provide variety and challenge wherever possible. A worker or manager who is challenged by the work itself will work harder and faster, and excessive pressure tactics will not be needed. Even in repetitive work, employees should be encouraged to present new ideas and rewarded if these are successfully implemented.

Work should fit individual goals. Workers and managers whose work satisfies individual needs or has the potential of doing so are less likely to feel job pressures.

Supervisors who are considerate and fair alleviate job pressures. This is basic psychology. The supervisor who rides rough-shod over an employee alienates the employee and probably lowers production. On the other hand, the supervisor who can enlist employee cooperation can effectively increase output. Studies also show that workers are likely to pattern their behavior on that of their supervisors. Thus, consideration and cooperation become "catching," relieving job pressures.

Group ties alleviate job pressures. While unions have accomplished this to some extent for workers, it is more important to provide group ties for the company as a whole as a means of lightening job pressure. Involvement techniques such as **productivity bargaining and agreements** and **job enrichment** are specific examples.

SUGGESTED FURTHER READING

Brehm, Jack W., *A Theory of Psychological Reactance,* Academic, New York, 1966.
Kahn, R. L., D. M. Wolfe, R. P. Quinn, J. D. Shoek, and R. A. Rosenthal, *Organizational Stress: Studies in Role Conflict and Ambiguity,* Wiley, New York, 1964.
Kornhauser, Arthur, *Mental Health of the Industrial Worker,* Wiley, New York, 1965.
Likert, Rensis, *New Patterns of Management,* McGraw-Hill, New York, 1961.
Whyte, W. F., *Men at Work,* Dorsey and Irwin, Homewood, Ill., 1961.

JOB ROTATION

Areas for use in Cost Control:

PSYCHOLOGICAL MOTIVATIONAL MANAGEMENT
ORGANIZATIONAL AND OPERATIONAL SYSTEMS
INDUSTRIAL APPLICATIONS
BUSINESS AND COMMERCIAL APPLICATIONS

Job rotation varies an employee's work duties and decreases boredom by moving the person from one type of work to another. Costs can be reduced through increased productivity motivated by these factors. *See also* **Work Structuring.**

SUGGESTED FURTHER READING

Maher, J. R., ed., *New Prospectives in Job Enrichment,* Reinhold, New York, 1971.

JOB SATISFACTION FORECASTING

Areas for use in Cost Control:

PSYCHOLOGICAL MOTIVATIONAL MANAGEMENT
FINANCIAL MOTIVATIONAL MANAGEMENT

Job satisfaction forecasting is the technique of finding and hiring an employee who can be satisfied by the available job. Costs are reduced by using the method, since employee motivation and satisfaction are achieved more easily in such circumstances. Use of the technique involves testing for intelligence and attitudes (*see also* **Personnel Testing**) and eliminating persons whose I.Q.'s are too high or too low or whose attitudes are maladjusted. Standard scales of average suitable I.Q.'s, such as the Fryer Occupational Intelligence Standards Scale, are available.

Family stability, financial needs, life adjustment, and emotional stability, as well as needed skills or abilities, should be considered when predicting the likelihood of an employee's satisfaction with a specific job.

SUGGESTED FURTHER READING

Fisher, V. E., and J. V. Hanna, *The Dissatisfied Worker,* Macmillan, New York, 1931.
Fryer, D., "Occupational Intelligence Standards," *School and Sociology,* no. 16, 1922.

JOINT DEMAND See Complementary Demand Technique.

KEIR'S COST RULE OF THUMB

Areas for use in Cost Control:

ORGANIZATIONAL AND OPERATIONAL SYSTEMS
BUSINESS AND COMMERCIAL APPLICATIONS

Keir's cost rule of thumb is a guide developed by Jack Keir, Certified Life Underwriter, to the approximate economical level of costs of insurance companies for each $1,000 in new business:

Office salaries	$1.40
Supervisors' salaries	.90
Supervisors' incentives	1.35
Office expense	2.35
Sales and promotion	.40
Recruiting	.30
Training	.30
Financing losses	.50
Total	$7.50

Costs should be limited to these amounts to ensure optimum profitability.

SUGGESTED FURTHER READING

Keir, J. C., *The Life Insurance Sales Handbook,* Prentice-Hall, Englewood Cliffs, N.J., 1971.

KEY PARTS CONTROL

Areas for use in Cost Control:

MATERIALS AND EQUIPMENT MANAGEMENT
INDUSTRIAL APPLICATIONS

Key parts control is the reduction of materials costs by control of the 10 to 15 percent of the number of different items purchased that account for 80 to 90 percent of all costs. Careful price records are maintained of all price changes for these items, and the greatest amount of price negotiation time, etc., is expended on controlling the relatively few items that make up the bulk of spending. Ideally, the method is computerized, with price changes programmed into the system as they occur. In this way, lowest prices for key parts can be obtained at any given time.

SUGGESTED FURTHER READING

Ammer, D. S., *Materials Management,* Irwin, Homewood, Ill., 1968.

KEY-POINT SAFETY

Areas for use in Cost Control:

ORGANIZATIONAL AND OPERATIONAL SYSTEMS
PAPERWORK DESIGN AND FLOW SYSTEMS

MATERIALS AND EQUIPMENT MANAGEMENT
INDUSTRIAL APPLICATIONS
BUSINESS AND COMMERCIAL APPLICATIONS

Key-point safety is a job analysis technique used to reduce accidents and their costs. The supervisor analyzes each job by listing the safety problems and employee preventative steps on a key-point safety planning card (see Fig. 56). A copy of the card is given to

(Company Safety Slogan)		
Job: Offset press operation		
Job Planning	Hazard	Safety Precaution
Run press	Teeth and movement of press drum in motion	Stop press to remove paper caught in drum

Figure 56. Key-point safety planning card.

the employee performing the job and the points listed are discussed. For ongoing jobs, cards should be posted at the work site and discussion of safety measures should be held regularly. *See also* **Accident Cost Control.**

SUGGESTED FURTHER READING

Bittel, L. R., *What Every Supervisor Should Know,* McGraw-Hill, New York, 1974.

KINETOGRAMS

Areas for use in Cost Control:

ORGANIZATIONAL AND OPERATIONAL SYSTEMS
MATERIALS AND EQUIPMENT MANAGEMENT
INDUSTRIAL APPLICATIONS

Kinetograms are photographic records that show the motion path of work. Periodically flashing lights are fastened to the worker's hands to register speed acceleration, distance, and direction movements. Results are studied and analyzed to develop motion efficiency, reducing labor production costs per unit. *See also* **Motion Study.**

SUGGESTED FURTHER READING

Mundel, M. E., *Motion and Time Study,* Prentice-Hall, Englewood Cliffs, N.J.

KINETOGRAPHY See Labanotation.

KOTLER'S COST AND PROFIT FORMULAS

Areas for use in Cost Control:

ORGANIZATIONAL AND OPERATIONAL SYSTEMS
INDUSTRIAL APPLICATIONS

Kotler's cost and profit formulas are used to predict product costs and the profits which are needed to plan new product programs and to eliminate uneconomical production. Developed by Dr. Philip Kotler, Professor of Marketing at Northwestern University, the formulas relate profits to costs.

The profit formula is:

$$Z_{i,t} = (P_{i,t} - c_{i,t})Q_{i,t} - F_{i,t} - A_{i,t} - D_{i,t}$$

where $Z_{i,t}$ = company i's profits in year t

$\quad\quad P_{i,t}$ = company i's average product price in year t

$\quad\quad c_{i,t}$ = variable unit cost of company i's product in year t

$\quad\quad Q_{i,t}$ = company i's units of product in year t

$\quad\quad F_{i,t}$ = fixed manufacturing and selling costs for company i's product in year t

$\quad\quad A_{i,t}$ = advertising and promotion costs for company i's product in year t

$\quad\quad D_{i,t}$ = distribution and sales force cost for company i's product in year t

Next, total industry sales are estimated, using the following Kotler formula:

$$Q_t = Q_0 (1 + g)^t \left(\frac{P_0}{P_t}\right)^{eP} \left[\frac{A_t}{.4_0(1 + g)^t}\right] \left(\frac{Y_t}{Y_0}\right)^{eY}$$

where Q = total market demand

$\quad\quad g$ = annual growth rate of demand

$\quad\quad P$ = average industry price

$\quad\quad Y$ = average income per capita

$\quad\quad e$ = elasticity parameter

$\quad\quad t$ = time subscript for year

$\quad\quad 0$ = subscript for the values of the variable at time o.

The company's share of this total industry sales figure is then determined, using the Kotler formula:

$$s_i = \frac{M_i}{\Sigma M_i} Q$$

where $\quad s_i$ = company i's market share

$\quad\quad M_i$ = company i's marketing effort

$\quad\quad Q$ = total market demand

Thus, if company i spends \$100,000 a year on marketing efforts, while company j spends \$50,000, and there are no other competitors:

$$s_i = \frac{\$100,000}{\$100,000 + \$50,000} = \frac{2}{3}$$

Company i should have $\frac{2}{3}$ of the total market demand. These formulas can be applied to every product in the company line and relationship of anticipated profits and costs determined, as well as a forecast of the market share the company should enjoy.

Computerization of the process is essential for broad product lines, since this process can be easily updated, giving regular and periodic forecasts.

Pricing changes, product modifications or eliminations, and profit maximization (including necessary cost controls) can all be facilitated through use of the formulas.

SUGGESTED FURTHER READING

Kotler, Philip, *Marketing Decision Making: A Model-Building Approach,* Holt, New York, 1971.
———, *Marketing Management,* Prentice-Hall, Englewood Cliffs, N.J., 1972.
Kuehn, A. A., and D. L. Weiss, "Marketing Analysis Training Exercise," *Behavioral Science,* January 1965.

LABANOTATION

Areas for use in Cost Control:

ORGANIZATIONAL AND OPERATIONAL SYSTEMS
INDUSTRIAL APPLICATIONS
BUSINESS AND COMMERCIAL APPLICATIONS

Labanotation, also called kinetography, is a method of recording work movements to develop rhythmic work methods that will increase work efficiency and reduce labor costs. Developed by Rudolf Laban, the technique forms the basis for **effort control,** which has shortened the time required to complete a specific task by as much as 80 percent.

Notations of motion are recorded in the system using a combination of basic symbols. The basic symbol is shown in Fig. 57. Any motion is recorded with one vertical movement (exertion) and/or one horizontal movement (control). Recorded motions of a worker performing a task are compared with suitable motions for that task. If they are incorrect, the worker's effort is being wasted.

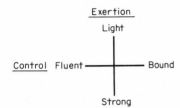

Figure 57. Basic Labanotation symbol.

For example, if a worker is using a hammer, the most effective motion is:

Strong/Fluent

If, however, his or her motion is recorded as:

Light/Bound

it becomes obvious that the worker's efforts are not as efficient as they should be, and that if someone shows the worker the correct motion, work output can be increased.

Time duration can be added to the recording system. Figure 58 shows the basic symbol with timing of the work motion added.

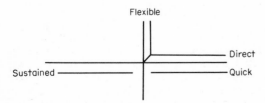

Figure 58. Labanotation symbol with time indication additions.

In the example of using a hammer, a recording of

would indicate that the worker is producing long, drawn-out motions. By changing the timing of the motion to a faster, shorter pace,

work output can be increased.

A series of eight fundamental symbols represent the most common work motions. These are shown in Fig. 59.

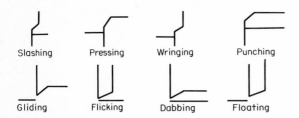

Figure 59. Eight fundamental Labanotation symbols.

SUGGESTED FURTHER READING
Laban, R., and F. C. Lawrence, *Effort,* MacDonald, London, 1965.

LAGS TECHNIQUE

Areas for use in Cost Control:
ORGANIZATIONAL AND OPERATIONAL SYSTEMS
MATERIALS AND EQUIPMENT MANAGEMENT
INDUSTRIAL APPLICATIONS
BUSINESS AND COMMERCIAL APPLICATIONS

The Lags technique is a method of reducing costs of materials bought internationally when it seems likely that the country from which they are purchased will have a lower-value currency in the future. The currency devaluation may stem from an announcement predicting a trade deficit, high unemployment, etc. Goods are ordered and shipped, but the purchasing company withholds payment as long as possible from a credit standpoint, so long as the currency value is decreasing. When the invoice is paid, the currency to make payment costs less, in effect reducing the cost of the materials. *See also* **Leads Technique.**

SUGGESTED FURTHER READING

Bailey, Peter, and David Farmer, *Purchasing Principles and Techniques,* Pitman, New York, 1968.

Davis, William, *Money Talks,* Coronet Books, London, 1974.

LAST-IN, FIRST-OUT METHOD

Areas for use in Cost Control:

MATERIALS AND EQUIPMENT MANAGEMENT

INDUSTRIAL APPLICATIONS

BUSINESS AND COMMERCIAL APPLICATIONS

The last-in, first-out method is a **stock control** technique used to value inventoried goods and stored materials and supplies. It uses the cost of the first shipment of items received as the value of all items.

Although not much used in the past, since values would be reduced if market costs were to fall, inflation has tended to encourage use of the technique. It is simpler to operate than the *first-in, first-out* method since for valuation purposes no check is needed of the quantity used.

SUGGESTED FURTHER READING

Goodman, S., *Effective Cost Reduction in Materials Handling,* Prentice-Hall, Englewood Cliffs, N.J., 1972.

Hobbs, J. A., *Control over Inventory and Production,* McGraw-Hill, New York, 1973.

LATERAL THINKING

Areas for use in Cost Control:

PSYCHOLOGICAL MOTIVATIONAL MANAGEMENT

ORGANIZATIONAL AND OPERATIONAL SYSTEMS

INDUSTRIAL APPLICATIONS

BUSINESS AND COMMERCIAL APPLICATIONS

Lateral thinking is a method of restructuring patterned or sequential thought in problem solving. It is a method developed by Edward de Bono and used in his *PO* system of creative problem solving (*see* **PO**).

SUGGESTED FURTHER READING

de Bono, Edward, *Lateral Thinking,* Penguin, Baltimore, 1973.

———, *PO: Beyond Yes and No,* Simon & Schuster, New York, 1972.

LAW OF DIMINISHING UTILITY

Areas for use in Cost Control:

ORGANIZATIONAL AND OPERATIONAL SYSTEMS

INDUSTRIAL APPLICATIONS

BUSINESS AND COMMERCIAL APPLICATIONS

The law of diminishing utility determines the exchange value of any production or operation by the marginal cost of production. This cost is the amount needed to manufacture the most expensive unit. Thus, the price of the product is determined by the highest costs, including a satisfactory profit. If the price drops below this point, production cannot continue. If it rises above this point, additional manufacturers will produce the item and competition will force the price down.

SUGGESTED FURTHER READING

Koch, J. V., *Industrial Organization and Prices,* Prentice-Hall, Englewood Cliffs, N.J., 1974.

LEADS TECHNIQUE

Areas for use in Cost Control:

ORGANIZATIONAL AND OPERATIONAL SYSTEMS
MATERIALS AND EQUIPMENT MANAGEMENT
INDUSTRIAL APPLICATIONS
BUSINESS AND COMMERCIAL APPLICATIONS

The leads technique is a method of reducing costs of materials bought internationally. For example, if an upcoming political or economic situation makes it likely that the country from which materials are purchased will have a higher-value currency when the purchases are made, the currency is purchased with as much "lead" time—at the lower rate—as possible. This money—then of more value—is paid at the time of purchase, in effect reducing the cost of materials purchased. *See also* **Lags Technique.**

SUGGESTED FURTHER READING

Bailey, Peter, and Daniel Farmer, *Purchasing Principles and Techniques,* Pitman, New York, 1968.
Davis, William, *Money Talks,* Coronet Books, London, 1974.

LEASED TRANSPORTATION

Areas for use in Cost Control:

ORGANIZATIONAL AND OPERATIONAL SYSTEMS
MATERIALS AND EQUIPMENT MANAGEMENT
INDUSTRIAL APPLICATIONS
BUSINESS AND COMMERCIAL APPLICATIONS

Leased transportation is the leasing of transportation as opposed to the use of a common carrier. Cost reductions are largely due to the fact that rates for such chartered transportation are not regulated by the government. Thus, the user pays only for the movement of goods and does not have to indirectly subsidize common carrier routes unable to pay their own way but mandatorily operated.

Quantity of shipment must be adequate to fill the vehicle used and to keep it busy during the time leased. Joint use of trucks by several suppliers is often a means of chartering delivery service for smaller operations.

Schedules can also be tailored to a supplier's needs when transportation is chartered, while common carriers have a general and usually slower schedule. In addition, special packing and handling are more easily used in chartered transportation, where there is only one customer to please.

SUGGESTED FURTHER READING

Ammer, D. S., *Materials Management,* Irwin, Homewood, Ill., 1968.

LEASING

Areas for use in Cost Control

ORGANIZATIONAL AND OPERATIONAL SYSTEMS
MATERIALS AND EQUIPMENT MANAGEMENT
INDUSTRIAL APPLICATIONS
BUSINESS AND COMMERCIAL APPLICATIONS

Leasing equipment, tools, and office and/or production space can reduce costs that would be incurred if these items were purchased, under certain conditions. These opportunities for saving include:

1. *Tax advantages.* These are a major cost-saver in leasing, since leasing costs are deductible as operating expense.

2. *Capital* that would be invested in items if purchased rather than leased can be used for other purposes.

3. *Technological changes* can make such items obsolete very quickly in some industries. If new equipment is needed every two or three years, leasing will cost less than buying.

4. Most lease contracts include *maintenance,* saving the user the cost of repairs. However, such repairs and maintenance must be carried out promptly by the lessor or this factory becomes a burden rather than a saving.

5. *Short-term* or *seasonal* needs for items and personnel can often be met at a lower price by leasing, including both equipment rental and manpower rental via temporary employment agencies.

SUGGESTED FURTHER READING

Mead, H., and G. Mitchell, *Plant Hire for Building and Construction,* Newnes-Butterworths, Sevenoaks, Kent, England, 1972.
Vanburgh, H. D., "When It Pays to Lease Equipment," *Cost Control and the Supervisor,* American Management Assn., New York, 1966.
Wolfman, Bernard, *Federal Income Taxation of Business Enterprise,* Little, Brown, Boston, 1971.

LEAST-COST FACTOR COMBINATION

Areas for use in Cost Control:

ORGANIZATIONAL AND OPERATIONAL SYSTEMS
MATERIALS AND EQUIPMENT MANAGEMENT
INDUSTRIAL APPLICATIONS
BUSINESS AND COMMERCIAL APPLICATIONS

Least-cost factor combination is a method used to evaluate the least costly of several alternative ways of producing a predetermined amount of goods or services. Cost factors involved in the various ways are determined. For example, if 5,000 tabulations are to be

Table 34. Typical Least-Cost Factor Combination

Alternative methods to make 5,000 tabulations	Costs			
	Clerical labor ($4/hr)	Computer programmer ($7/hr)	Computer ($100/hr)	Total method cost
A	$200.00	—	—	$200.00
B	$100.00	$3.50	$ 50.00	$153.50
C	—	$7.00	$100.00	$107.00

A = 100% clerical labor @ 100 tabulations/hr

B = 50% clerical labor @ 100 tabulations/hr and 50% computerized tabulation
    @ 5,000 tabulations/hr

C = 100% computerized tabulation @ 5,000 tabulations/hr

made, clerical labor may cost $4 an hour, computer programmers may cost $7 an hour, and the use of computer equipment may cost $100 an hour. A comparison table showing the costs for alternative methods of accomplishing the work is then drawn up (see Table 34) and the least costly method of producing the goods or service can be determined. Success depends on the accuracy of the cost inputs for the alternative methods.

SUGGESTED FURTHER READING

Samuelson, P. A., *Economics,* McGraw-Hill, New York, 1973.

LEEPER THEORY

Areas for use in Cost Control:

PSYCHOLOGICAL MOTIVATIONAL MANAGEMENT
INDUSTRIAL APPLICATIONS
BUSINESS AND COMMERCIAL APPLICATIONS

The Leeper theory states that specific actions accompany emotions. Thus, by creating certain emotions or emotional conditions, specific actions, such as increased pace of work, can be effected. For example, if a person is made angry, the accompanying motions can be those of hitting. If the person is made sad, the motion may be to cry. For business purposes, the worker may be made curious, and the accompanying motion will be to solve the problem, complete a piece of work, etc., in order to rapidly satisfy curiosity.

By organizing employee emotions with challenging treatment by supervisors and using challenging working conditions, then, worker motivation and efficiency are improved.

SUGGESTED FURTHER READING

Leeper, R. W., "A Motivational Theory of Emotion," *Psychological Review,* vol. 55, 1948.
Pribram, K. H., *Adaptation,* Penguin, Baltimore, 1969.

LETTER WRITING AND COST CONTROL

Areas for use in Cost Control:

PSYCHOLOGICAL MOTIVATIONAL MANAGEMENT
ORGANIZATIONAL AND OPERATIONAL SYSTEMS
PAPERWORK DESIGN AND FLOW SYSTEMS
MATERIALS AND EQUIPMENT MANAGEMENT
INDUSTRIAL APPLICATIONS
BUSINESS AND COMMERCIAL APPLICATIONS

Effective letter writing can reduce costs by motivating the receiver, by persuading him or her to act promptly (on deliveries, bill payments, and order solicitation), by obtaining sales interviews at a cost lower than that for a personal "first call," and by promoting company goodwill. In many cases, a letter can be more effective than a costly personal visit or a telephone call because it provides a written record of information to be conveyed that can be studied at the receiver's leisure and retained for future reference. Further, it reduces the amount of time spent on nonessential conversation.

The first step in effective letter writing is to gear the style and contents to the person who will receive it. Technical terminology should be avoided, for example, when writing to someone who will not understand such writing well. Contents should be limited to information that the reader will want or need to deal with the matter presented, but needed information should be complete.

The letter should use positive rather than negative phrasing to help hold the reader's interest and to help persuade him or her to have a positive attitude about the subject of a letter.

If possible, the lead of the letter should suggest a benefit for the reader. Why should he or she choose this product over others available? What can it do for the reader that other products cannot do?

LANGUAGE AND LETTER WRITING

In writing effective letters, use language that makes your meaning clear to the reader. Old-fashioned flowery phrases or obsolete terms should be avoided. A refresher study of a grammar textbook may be useful if grammar rules are not well fixed in your mind. Use as few words as possible to convey the exact meaning. Long adjectives added to look impressive may deter or confuse the reader, not impressing him or her at all.

Maintain positive language throughout the letter, and omit superlatives that may sound phony.

POLITENESS IN LETTER WRITING

Letters, even those written to complain, are more effective when they are polite. Special care should be taken not to imply unimportance in the reader. If a branch manager is being reprimanded for a drop in store sales, for example, there is no need to imply that he is stupid with sentences like, *Perhaps you haven't noticed the current sales volume of your branch.*

Instead, be honest about the problem: *We need to find a way to bring your branch's sales volume up to par. Please stop by my office at 10 a.m. on the 4th, to discuss it.*

LETTER CONTENT

The *salutation* is the first part of the letter. The reader's name should be used if you know it.

References, if used, follow the salutation. These should be used primarily when the subject is a numbered document, such as an order or invoice.

The *body* of the letter should open positively, calling attention to a benefit for the reader when possible.

Avoid trite openings referring to previous correspondence, the weather, or other nonessential data.

Table 35. Typical Opening Statements to Catch the Reader's Interest

Type	Typical statement
Factual	Four hundred pages an hour can be copied with Model XYZ.
Curiosity	The XYZ model was developed to help power the first moon flight.
New products	The XYZ is different from any other type of copier. It can. . . .
Special prices	At ¾ of the usual price, the XYZ can be yours.
Special offer	With each XYZ, a month's supply of paper will be included.
Challenge	The XYZ dares your office copier to match its performance.
Ego buildup	You'll appreciate the quality of the XYZ model.
Question	Have you seen the new XYZ model in use?

The success of many letters depends on arousing and holding the reader's interest. This may be accomplished with presentation of facts; arousing his or her curiosity; humor; building up the reader's ego; presenting new products, offers, or prices; presenting a challenge; or asking a question. Table 35 gives a typical interest-opener for each of these types.

The *closing* of an effective letter persuades the reader to agree with the writer and to act positively in the way the writer wants. Several effective closing methods can be used, including *choice, special benefit,* and *action* closings. Table 36 presents some typical closings of these types.

The *farewell greeting* of the letter may be *Sincerely yours, Yours truly,* or, for a warmer feeling, *Cordially.* Be sure your name is typed in the space below your signature to provide your correspondent with accurate spelling.

Table 36. Typical Closings of Effective Letters

Type	Typical closing
Choice	Would you prefer to pay the balance of your account now, or to spread it over an additional 90 days index-linked?
Special benefit	Our usual policy is payment within 30 days, but because you are a regular customer, you may spread payment, index-linked, over 90 days if you wish.
Action	Give me a call when you receive this letter to let me know how you wish to make your payments.

SPECIALTY LETTERS

Specific business problems call for specialized approaches. These specialty letters may include sales letters, order and complaint acknowledgments, and collection letters.

Sales Letters. Any letter sent to a customer should be used to "sell" him or her on the company and its products in addition to other purposes, such as order acknowledgment. Letters sent to suppliers, branch personnel, or others should also incorporate "selling" the value of the company as a motivational tool.

Direct sales letters require special attention. All coupons or inquiries should be answered promptly and any questions asked should be carefully answered. If enclosures, such as sales brochures, are used, the letter should point out parts of the enclosure that are of special interest to the reader.

The close of a sales letter should make action easy and/or set the scene for a personal call by a member of the sales staff.

A sales letter should be followed up with a second letter or a telephone call if satisfactory results are not obtained with the first try.

Order Acknowledgment. Order acknowledgments should express thanks, welcome new customers, and confirm *exact* data of the order. Delivery date, credit terms, discounts, and special offers should be mentioned. If goods will be shipped separately, or if the order will be incomplete, this should be stated, along with the estimated date for completion of delivery.

In some cases, the customer will be at fault for an incomplete order because not enough data were included in her or his order. Special tact should be used in wording a request for this missing information to avoid making the customer feel foolish.

Order acknowledgments are useful as subsidiary sales tools. When acknowledging a machine order, for example, enclose an order form for spare parts, materials used by the machine, maintenance service, etc.

Complaints. Before writing letters in response to complaints, make sure you determine the truth. Is the complaint justified or not?

If the complaint *is* justified, apologize and make whatever restitution is possible—refund, replacement, etc. Do not try to place the blame on an individual or department or make a fuss about the restitution. Do answer as quickly as possible. Do thank the complainant for bringing the matter to your attention, and do try to resell him or her on the quality of your company and/or its products.

If the complaint is not justified, explain the situation as tactfully as possible, using only positive language.

Collection Letters. Collection letters are the most difficult. Some of these can be averted by using thorough credit checks for new accounts and limiting the amount of credit, depending on these checks. Letters welcoming new accounts are advised to further "sell" the customer on your company.

Letters rejecting applications for credit, however, require the use of tact. The following example is a credit rejection that should not alienate the customer:

> *We were pleased to receive your credit application, and hope we can open an account for you in the future. Because of credit restrictions in the economy, we would like to discuss your credit application personally before proceeding. Why not stop by my office soon, so I can explain company policy.*

Seldom will the customer with a poor credit rating come into the office, yet the letter should not anger him or her, preventing future *cash* sales.

Handling of overdue bills depends on the reasons for late payment. These may include thoughtlessness; payment withheld due to a customer complaint; shortage of cash; absence of cash; and terms that were promised by the salesperson but not authorized.

Stickers or "payment please" cards may be used with second requests for overdue accounts. Telephone calls are also effective in some cases. If these do not produce results, follow-up letters may be used, geared to the customer's emotional response. If the customer is personally known to a salesperson, it is worthwhile to try to determine from him or her which approach would be most likely to work. Such letters may be based on fear, pride, fair play, humor, or urgency.

Fear is the strongest of these. The letter may suggest that the debtor's credit will be stopped, that his or her credit rating will be ruined, and that the debtor will be taken to court for collection. But these should not be openly mentioned while any other method is available. Instead, phrase fear-based letters tactfully:

> *Mr. Smith, your XYZ salesman, has promised that you intend to pay your overdue materials account, and I want to help him in backing you. If your check is received by the 5th, I will stop the court action authorized by the credit department head.*

Pride is another strong emotion that can be used in collecting overdue accounts. For example:

> *You have paid your account promptly for the past five years, and frankly we are puzzled by the current delay.*
>
> *You haven't answered my earlier letters, but I'm sure you want to continue to have our respect as a responsible customer. The enclosed envelope will bring your check to us, maintaining the good business relationship we've enjoyed for so long.*

Fair play may include meeting the customer halfway:

> *We were sorry to hear about your store fire, and we will be glad to arrange a spread of payments to help you through this difficult time. Monthly payments of $50 each, with the unpaid balance index-linked to protect against inflation, will be agreeable to us for paying the overdue amount. . . .*

Urgency can be used if the customer feels any responsibility toward your company, or if it applies to benefits he or she may earn:

> *Company policy requires inclusion of accounts past 90 days in the weekly city computer credit check. This would tie your credit rating drop into computers nationwide. But you can avoid this problem if you mail your check now. . . .*

SUGGESTED FURTHER READING

Elliot, Simon, *Elliot's Quick Guide to Letterwriting,* Cahners Publishing Co., Boston, 1972.
Gilbert, M. B., *Letters That Mean Business,* Wiley, New York, 1973.

LEVERAGE See Gearing.

LEWIS METHOD TO CONTROL LOSING OPERATIONS

Areas for use in Cost Control:

ORGANIZATIONAL AND OPERATIONAL SYSTEMS
INDUSTRIAL APPLICATIONS
BUSINESS AND COMMERCIAL APPLICATIONS

The Lewis method to control losing operations uses the following steps to determine the financial position of a company or branch that is losing money:

1. Book value or present capital investment
2. Probable loss from liquidation
3. Subtract No. 2 from No. 1 (cash recovery)
4. Federal income tax recoveries
5. Replacement costs avoided if liquidated?
6. Add No. 3, No. 4, and No. 5 (total cash recovery)
7. Total profit of business now
8. Total profit of business after operation in question is liquidated
9. Subtract No. 8 from No. 7 (difference in profit)
10. Divide No. 9 by No. 6 (rate of return if liquidated or cost of capital if operation is continued)

SUGGESTED FURTHER READING

"Successful Management," *Nation's Business,* Doubleday, New York, 1964.

LIGHT-PEN ORDERING

Areas for use in Cost Control:

ORGANIZATIONAL AND OPERATIONAL SYSTEMS
MATERIALS AND EQUIPMENT MANAGEMENT
INDUSTRIAL APPLICATIONS
BUSINESS AND COMMERCIAL APPLICATIONS

Light-pen ordering is a computerized system used by branch stores or plants to order retail stock or raw materials from central stocks. The system eliminates most labor and paperwork required in conventional ordering systems, reducing costs and speeding delivery of goods. A *light-pen* readable label describing the product or material is fastened to the storage or display shelf. To reorder, labels are electronically scanned and the quantity required is entered on a keyboard connected to a cassette tape recorder. The tape contents are stored in the telephone or other public communications network and transmitted at the request of the central computer (depending on its workload distribution), and goods are automatically shipped for arrival at the branch location within 24 hours of order placement. An additional advantage is that most order processing can be carried out at night, since personnel are not required for intermediary steps.

SUGGESTED FURTHER READING

Brown, D., "Branch Ordering Systems," *Computer Executive,* April 1973.

LIKERT MODIFIED THEORY OF MANAGEMENT

Areas for use in Cost Control:

PSYCHOLOGICAL MOTIVATIONAL MANAGEMENT
ORGANIZATIONAL AND OPERATIONAL SYSTEMS

The Likert modified theory of management uses worker participation in work place and work-structuring systems. Motivation is accomplished by worker participation in operational decisions. Such involvement reduces costs by encouraging the employee to accept greater responsibility, complete more work, etc."

SUGGESTED FURTHER READING

Likert, R. A., *A Motivational Approach to a Modified Theory of Organization and Management,* Wiley, New York, 1959.

LINE AND STAFF SYSTEM

Areas for use in Cost Control:

ORGANIZATIONAL AND OPERATIONAL SYSTEMS
INDUSTRIAL APPLICATIONS

The line and staff system is an organizational and operational system similar to the **military system,** where each employee has one supervisor, except that each manager has functional and/or departmental managers. The method can reduce costs, particu-

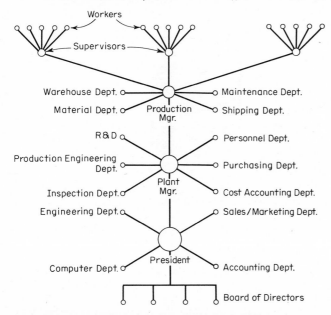

Figure 60. Typical line and staff organization chart.

larly in large organizations where line executives cannot be responsible for all functions because of the complexity and size of the operation, yet the responsibility for performance moves up the line as in the military system. Figure 60 shows a typical line and staff system organizational chart.

SUGGESTED FURTHER READING

Maynard, H. B., ed., *Industrial Engineering Handbook,* 3d ed., McGraw-Hill, New York, 1974.
Robertson, S. A., *Engineering Management,* Blackie, Glasgow, 1967.

LINEAR DECISION RULE

Areas for use in Cost Control:

ORGANIZATIONAL AND OPERATIONAL SYSTEMS
INDUSTRIAL APPLICATIONS
BUSINESS AND COMMERCIAL APPLICATIONS

The linear decision rule is a quadratic method of reducing labor, hiring and layoff, overtime, and inventory costs. **Cost curves** are constructed for each of the areas. These are combined as the total cost function, shown in relation to total production, and the levels of labor required for lowest cost per production unit are determined. Using sales and production forecasts, the number of employees needed, without having to work overtime and without excess hiring causing lost training costs and layoff costs, can be estimated. Inventory costs can be reduced through this optimum use of labor to shorten the lead time required.

SUGGESTED FURTHER READING

Buffa, E. S., *Modern Production Management,* Wiley, New York, 1969.
Holt, C. C., F. Modigliani, J. F. Muth, and H. A. Simon, *Planning Production, Inventories, and Work Force,* Prentice-Hall, Englewood Cliffs, N.J., 1960.

LINEAR PROGRAMMING See Mathematical Programming.

LINE-STAFF ORGANIZATION

Areas for use in Cost Control:

ORGANIZATIONAL AND OPERATIONAL SYSTEMS
INDUSTRIAL APPLICATIONS
BUSINESS AND COMMERCIAL APPLICATIONS

Line-staff organization is a structural technique used to obtain the most efficient business operation through the use of line management to make decisions and give direct orders while staff management contributions are only advisory. Costs can be reduced through more closely defined responsibility for management.

SUGGESTED FURTHER READING

Rhenman, E., L. Stromberg, and G. Webster-Lund, *Conflict and Cooperation in Business Organizations,* Wiley, New York, 1970.

LIVING-IN

Area for use in Cost Control:

ORGANIZATIONAL AND OPERATIONAL SYSTEMS

A cost reduction expert uses the living-in technique by temporarily becoming part of the organization he or she intends to study. Coworkers are not told that this is an expert. At the end of a period of study, the expert suggests cost reductions that can be applied. Although fairly effective, the technique requires several months' use for best results.

SUGGESTED FURTHER READING

Haire, M., ed., *Modern Organizational Theory,* Wiley, New York, 1959.
Sayles, L. R., and G. Strauss, *Human Behavior in Organizations,* Prentice-Hall, Englewood Cliffs, N.J., 1966.

LOCALIZATION

Areas for use in Cost Control:

ORGANIZATIONAL AND OPERATIONAL SYSTEMS
INDUSTRIAL APPLICATIONS

Localization is the intensification of an industry in one geographical area. An area with reasonable land and labor costs, accessible to material supplies and markets, is chosen. Further cost reductions can result from availability of needed specialized processes, a pool of labor skilled in needed industry trades, and shared marketing, training, and financing resources.

Governments may tend to discourage localization, however economical it may be for the industry, since use of the method makes the area of localization dependent on the industry involved.

SUGGESTED FURTHER READING

Speight, H., *Economics and Industrial Efficiency,* Macmillan, New York, 1967.

LOCATIONAL ORGANIZATION

Areas for use in Cost Control:

ORGANIZATIONAL AND OPERATIONAL SYSTEMS
MATERIALS AND EQUIPMENT MANAGEMENT
INDUSTRIAL APPLICATIONS
BUSINESS AND COMMERCIAL APPLICATIONS

Locational organization is the division of work and responsibility by their geographical location to reduce costs and increase efficiency by the banding together of work in close physical proximity. The system is especially applicable in companies with several production or service locations. Thus, a corporate officer may be the superior for several functional managers of the same level in different locations (see Fig. 61).

Figure 61. Typical locational organization chart.

Cost reductions may result from this method through the familiarity of locational management with local materials, production, shipping, and other problems; but care is advised, since specialization and bulk purchasing advantages are lost.

SUGGESTED FURTHER READING

Ammer, D. S., *Materials Management,* Irwin, Homewood, Ill., 1968.

LOW-COST AUTOMATION

Areas for use in Cost Control:

ORGANIZATIONAL AND OPERATIONAL SYSTEMS
MATERIALS AND EQUIPMENT MANAGEMENT
INDUSTRIAL APPLICATIONS

Automation is equipment, usually computerized, that wholly or partially replaces human labor. Many such applications reduce costs in specialized areas, such as **numerical control production,** used where complex or short-run specialized parts are manufactured without special tooling. These areas are discussed separately. However, several general industrial automation techniques reduce labor costs by increasing work efficiency and speed yet are relatively inexpensive to install.

Transfer of materials and parts within a plant can be automated to reduce handling costs. *Conveyors* are the primary method available. Movement of conveyers should be timed to coincide with the time required by each worker to perform tasks (preferably mechanized) on the material or part.

Work operations may include full or partial automation of work processes along the conveyor line. In partial automation, equipment controls are mechanized so that the worker's pushing of one control performs several work steps at once. For example, several pins may be positioned and placed at once. Total automation uses complete mechanization of all work steps in a particular process. The work may be controlled by one worker or by a computer that monitors the process.

In manual equipment operation, *digital indicators* may be used to decrease operator setup time. Control indicators, such as dials, gauges, etc., should be located for rapid and easy reading. In automated units, a computer may monitor such indicators, making changes as needed.

Pressure, temperature, and liquid flow are some additional processes that can be automated (converted to mechanical or other action) at relatively low cost. Fluidic equipment, using air or fluids as signals, is one method of control. Electronic signals are another.

Inspection, as well as production, can be mechanized and corrective action applied mechanically where necessary.

SUGGESTED FURTHER READING

Hamilton, D., *Technology, Man, and the Environment,* Faber, London, 1973.

LOW-PROFIT-AREA REDUCTION

Areas for use in Cost Control:

ORGANIZATIONAL AND OPERATIONAL SYSTEMS
INDUSTRIAL APPLICATIONS

Low-profit-area reduction is the elimination of production, factories, branches, etc., where profits fall below a predetermined level. Money from the sale of such operations may be reinvested in more profitable areas, or plant and equipment may be used for more profitable production.

SUGGESTED FURTHER READING

Dudick, T. S., *Profile for Profitability,* Wiley, New York, 1972.

LUMP HIRING

Areas for use in Cost Control:

ORGANIZATIONAL AND OPERATIONAL SYSTEMS
INDUSTRIAL APPLICATIONS
BUSINESS AND COMMERCIAL APPLICATIONS

Lump hiring is the practice of using the *lump*—self-employed-labor-only subcontractors (often, individuals rather than a group of workers). Use of the technique reduces labor costs because payment recordkeeping is simplified since no tax or other deductions are withheld, and since no fringe benefits, such as medical insurance, pension plans, profit sharing, etc., are paid. In some cases, tax advantages may reduce costs further. The method began in the construction industry but spread to other industries in the mid-1970s as a way for both employer and employee to avoid governmental control of wages.

SUGGESTED FURTHER READING

Marsh, A. I., and E. O. Evans, *The Dictionary of Industrial Relations,* Hutchinson, London, 1973. "The Lump," *Building,* June 14, 1974.

MACROECONOMIC COST CONTROL

Area for use in Cost Control:

ORGANIZATIONAL AND OPERATIONAL SYSTEMS

Macroeconomic cost control includes all methods of controlling production, consumption, and other costs of an entire community, state, or nation. Such controls are often initiated by governmental action, but they have a definite effect on individual firms, since operational costs are passed along in the form of taxes and since policies may affect individual firms' production or other costs. Business and industry may affect the direction and/or degree of governmental macroeconomic cost control through lobbies, geographical location of plant, voting, degree of cooperation with voluntary governmental policies, etc. *See also* **Microeconomic Cost Control.**

SUGGESTED FURTHER READING

Conrad, J. W., *Inflation, Growth, and Employment,* Prentice-Hall, Englewood Cliffs, N.J., 1964.

MAINTENANCE EFFICIENCY INDEX See Corder Maintenance Efficiency Index.

MANAGEMENT ACCOUNTING

Areas for use in Cost Control:

ORGANIZATIONAL AND OPERATIONAL SYSTEMS
PAPERWORK DESIGN AND FLOW SYSTEMS
INDUSTRIAL APPLICATIONS
BUSINESS AND COMMERCIAL APPLICATIONS

Management accounting is the presentation of accounting data in the best way to help management establish operational policies and methods. For the executive, it is making use of accounting data in controlling costs and other factors of the operation.

A management accounting plan includes:

1. Setting and defining business and cost goals
2. Delegating responsibility for meeting these goals to specific individuals within the organization
3. Measuring the success or failure in reaching those goals

Management accounting reports current company performance, usually in production quantity or monetary terms. Such figures may be presented in graph or chart form. Their purpose is to give management current performance data to use as a basis for decision making.

Comparisons are especially important—comparisons of various years' sales or production figures, for example. Such comparisons, however, must be adjusted to allow for seasonal differences, longer months, and other abnormal factors.

Reports should be limited to data that management can actually use in decision making, rather than including every record in the accounting department thrown into one or more massive reports.

Design of such a report (see Fig. 62) can be guided by inclusion of the following factors:

1. Date of report
2. Period covered by the report
3. Employee preparing report
4. Areas of content and/or a table of contents
5. Keys or other necessary terms of reference
6. Introduction, if needed
7. Body data
8. Conclusions and recommendations when requested
9. Appendices for supporting detail where required

May 20, 1976

Report covers calendar sales year January 1, 1977, to December 31, 1977.

Report prepared by: Keith Singer
                                Accounting Department Supervisor

Sales of Imported Goods

Month	Food	Clothing	Giftware	Total
January	$1,230	$2,003	$ 980	$4,213
February	1,305	1,430	950	3,685
March	1,290	1,310	910	3,510
April	1,350	1,809	1,200	4,359
May	1,507	1,750	1,325	4,582
June	1,410	1,506	2,810	5,726
July	1,341	1,225	1,410	3,976
August	1,425	1,304	2,200	4,929
September	1,520	1,906	1,650	5,076
October	1,600	1,325	950	3,875
November	1,710	1,040	1,020	3,770
December	1,850	1,834	2,001	5,685
Total	$17,538	$18,442	$17,406	$53,386

Figure 62. Typical report to management.

An example of the use of reports following such a format can be seen in Fig. 62, where a tabulation of sales of imported goods is presented to management to aid in determining quantities of goods to be purchased for the coming year. Seasonal trends are obvious, as are overall trends.

SUGGESTED FURTHER READING

Greene, W. C., *Case Problems in Managerial Accounting,* Holt, New York, 1964.

MANAGEMENT BY ANTICIPATION

Areas for use in Cost Control:

ORGANIZATIONAL AND OPERATIONAL SYSTEMS
MATERIALS AND EQUIPMENT MANAGEMENT
INDUSTRIAL APPLICATIONS
BUSINESS AND COMMERCIAL APPLICATIONS

Management by anticipation is a system used to control cost and other business problems by focusing attention on anticipated situations rather than basing decisions for the future on data about past performance, as most management systems do. Designed by Geoff Wood, Director of the Center for Innovation and Productivity, Sheffield Polytechnic, England, management by anticipation includes looking at potential production bottlenecks, upcoming sales quotas and programs, upcoming budgets, etc., and finding solutions that anticipate the problems to solve them *before* they happen.

SUGGESTED FURTHER READING

Wood, G., "Look Ahead," *The Financial Times,* London, July 12, 1974.

MANAGEMENT BY CONSENT

Areas for use in Cost Control:

PSYCHOLOGICAL MOTIVATIONAL MANAGEMENT
ORGANIZATIONAL AND OPERATIONAL SYSTEMS
INDUSTRIAL APPLICATIONS
BUSINESS AND COMMERCIAL APPLICATIONS

Management by consent is a method of reducing costs and increasing operational efficiency through cooperative management by workers and executives. In most decision areas, use of the method requires consultation with employees. Productivity can be increased through additional motivation.

SUGGESTED FURTHER READING

Marsh, A. I., and E. O. Evans, *The Dictionary of Industrial Relations,* Hutchinson, London, 1973.
Roberts, H. S., *Roberts' Dictionary of Industrial Relations,* Bureau of National Affairs, Inc., Washington, D.C., 1971.

MANAGEMENT BY EXCEPTION

Areas for use in Cost Control:

ORGANIZATIONAL AND OPERATIONAL SYSTEMS
INDUSTRIAL APPLICATIONS
BUSINESS AND COMMERCIAL APPLICATIONS

Management by exception requires that only "exceptional" or unplanned-for work factors be referred to management. Normal factors are handled by a predetermined set of rules, plans, budgets, etc. Costs are reduced through the decrease of management detail, as well as through the increased efficiency of using a well-planned operating procedure. Although the technique was first designed for industrial use, it is easily applicable in all commercial areas.

SUGGESTED FURTHER READING

Bittel, L. R., *Management by Exception: Systematizing and Simplifying the Managerial Job,* McGraw-Hill, New York, 1964.

MANAGEMENT BY OBJECTIVES (MBO)

Areas for use in Cost Control:

ORGANIZATIONAL AND OPERATIONAL SYSTEMS
INDUSTRIAL APPLICATIONS
BUSINESS AND COMMERCIAL APPLICATIONS

Management by objectives (MBO) is a means of setting profit, cost reduction, expansion, or other goals by involving the employee in all areas of goal setting which affect the worker, effectively creating a work challenge. Additionally, employees will have a better understanding of the goal and the methods used to reach it, improving their efficiency.

Related to behavioral science techniques (*see* **Behavior Control**), the method assumes that workers will work more responsibly when they are involved in establishing company and personal work goals.

Each manager meets with his or her subordinates to discuss goals, possible methods to achieve the goals, and controls to make certain that the methods work. Key problems and possible improvements are identified and debated, and the best methods to reach the goal are chosen. Such discussions operate at all managerial levels, with each level discussing problems and solutions with both supervisors and subordinates. The feedback from one group to another serves as a control of effectiveness.

Figure 63 shows the various management levels that may discuss a single problem, such as the degree of automation needed to increase productivity by 10 percent annually. The materials, equipment, and assembly managers will first discuss goals and methods with the vice president of production. Next, they discuss goals and methods with their supervisors. Using feedback from this meeting, they discuss problems and implications with the vice president. In turn, supervisors discuss goals, methods, problems, etc., with workers.

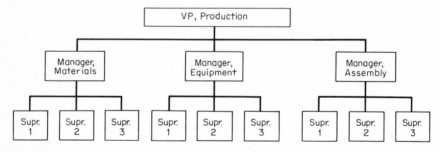

Figure 63. Management chart for MBO.

As decided methods are implemented, follow-up discussions are held to measure results against goals and to modify action where necessary. Paperwork and performance standards should be minimized in using the system, to keep the cost of the method down.

SUGGESTED FURTHER READING

Humble, J. W., *Management by Objectives,* McGraw-Hill, New York, 1970.

MANAGEMENT EXCHANGE

Areas for use in Cost Control:

PSYCHOLOGICAL MOTIVATIONAL MANAGEMENT
ORGANIZATIONAL AND OPERATIONAL SYSTEMS
BUSINESS AND COMMERCIAL APPLICATIONS

Management exchange is a temporary trading of managers by several companies to promote management's learning new methods of cost reduction and other business techniques. Working temporarily in a new firm, managers see their company's cost or other problems from a fresh viewpoint, learn other firms' techniques for dealing with problems, and learn more about their industry as a whole.

Some industries have conducted management exchanges for a fairly lengthy period of time. For example, more than 20 companies in Belgium exchanged senior management representatives for a period of 10 months. In this program, representatives were assigned to firms outside their own industry for a wider view of business problems. Other programs use a shorter exchange period.

Another variation is a temporary department exchange within a single company, to provide management with an increased knowledge of other areas of their own firm. In a Nigerian management exchange program, department heads worked temporarily with other department heads to solve cost and other problems.

Temporary management shifts to different levels of responsibility have also proven effective. For example, in a London exchange, top management serving temporarily with middle management found that vaguely worded company policies caused a disproportionate amount of time to be spent on work organization. Exchange by level of responsibility usually moves top management to lower levels as a means of keeping them in touch with lower levels, but a day or two in a more senior position can also give a management trainee or line supervisor a new appreciation and better understanding of top management.

Exchange programs may be arranged within companies, between companies (at their own volition), and by consultants, colleges, etc. Harvard Business School, M.I.T.'s Sloan School of Management, and Arthur D. Little and Co. are some of the American founders of the exchange projects. Belgium's Fondation Industrie—Université has arranged several international exchanges.

SUGGESTED FURTHER READING

Humble, John, ed., *The Experienced Manager*, McGraw-Hill, New York, 1973.
Ludwig, Steven, "Why 21 Firms Swapped Managers," *International Management,* August 1970.

MANAGEMENT HUSBANDS AND WIVES

Areas for use in Cost Control:

ORGANIZATIONAL AND OPERATIONAL SYSTEMS
INDUSTRIAL APPLICATIONS
BUSINESS AND COMMERCIAL APPLICATIONS

Management husbands and wives can affect their partners' work performance (and therefore the value received by the firm for his or her salary), management turnover, and willingness to accept transfers. To hire managers whose partners have attitudes that facilitate performance is to reduce costs and increase efficiency. Areas where costs are directly or indirectly affected by management husbands and wives include:

Mobility. In many businesses and industries it is essential that management go where they are most needed. Too many companies have spent time and money developing a young manager, only to have him or her refuse advancement that requires a move to a new location. The reason is often that the marriage partner does not want to move. The manager may then leave the company, and new costs are incurred in recruiting, hiring, and training a replacement; or he or she may continue at the low-level job, wasting a good portion of the training cost.

The time to assess potential problems in this area is prior to or at hiring. Recruitment advertising, for example, may state the fact that a management trainee will be moved after the initial training period. This point should be emphasized again during interviewing, with the applicant being sounded out as to the attitudes of both himself or herself and the partner toward job mobility.

When more senior management is being hired, the applicant's background should be examined for mobility, if he or she will be asked to transfer. If there is no record of past location changes, careful discussion of attitudes toward job mobility should be developed.

One study, conducted by J. M. and R. E. Pahl, showes that wives most favorable to job mobility are those without a college education and age 35 or under. Factors considered most important in encouraging the wife to react favorably toward a job move were improved work activity for her husband, increased pay or status resulting from the move, and good educational facilities for their children in the new area.

Turnover. Ironically, the same characteristics that make a manager's partner a cost liability in the question of job location changes make him or her an asset in retaining a manager in his or her present company. Older partners, or more highly educated ones with careers of their own, are more inclined to encourage the manager to stay where he or she is, particularly if job and salary are satisfactory. Studies show that few managers actively seek other jobs unless there are problems at work. If other jobs are offered, of course, they will be considered.

Partners may encourage active job seeking (and for the company, costly turnover) if the manager's work entails duties they find disagreeable. These may include excessive travel, long hours, and social obligations. Work duties likely to cause problems of this nature should be emphasized in recruiting and hiring and both the manager and his or her partner's attitudes toward them evaluated.

Performance. Costs of lost work performance stemming from managerial partner attitudes are perhaps the greatest area of potential saving. Again, screening at hiring is preferable. For current employees, a revetting of partner attitudes is suggested prior to promotion.

The attitudes most likely to aid work performance depend largely on the duties of the manager. If the position requires frequent travel, evening and weekend work, or heavy client entertaining, only partner cooperation will ensure best performance. Some companies prefer partners with work or civic and social interests of their own, to decrease demands on the manager's time, yet not a career the partner would be reluctant to leave if the manager were transferred.

Attitudes toward the manager's work as a tool to family success should also be considered. Most companies prefer partners who encourage managers to work hard but who do not push for advancement at an impossible pace.

Nagging partners have always been frowned on as being sources of bad temper at work, but one top woman construction executive recently suggested that supervisors with nagging husbands or wives perform best, because they rid themselves of their frustrations by attacking their work aggressively.

SUGGESTED FURTHER READING

Berlew, D. E., and D. T. Hall, "The Socialization of Managers: Effects of Expectations on Performance," *Administrative Science Quarterly,* 1966.

Gans, H. J., *The Levittowners,* Penguin, Baltimore, 1967.

Glaser, B. G., *Organizational Careers,* Aldine, Chicago, 1968.

Helfrich, M. L., *The Social Role of the Executive's Wife,* Bureau of Business Research, Ohio State University, 1965.

Kemper, T. D., "Reference Groups, Socialization and Achievement," *American Sociological Review,* 1968.

Pahl, J. M. and R. E., *Managers and Their Wives,* Penguin, Baltimore, 1971.

MANAGEMENT RECENTRALIZATION

Areas for use in Cost Control:

ORGANIZATIONAL AND OPERATIONAL SYSTEMS
INDUSTRIAL APPLICATIONS
BUSINESS AND COMMERCIAL APPLICATIONS

Management recentralization is the reduction of need for management, and the accompanying costs, through reorganization to increase supervisory efficiency and restructuring of jobs, increasing individual responsibility. The theory behind the method is that business has followed Parkinson's law—paperwork flow, committee activities, etc., expand to fill executive time not used for real responsibilities.

Decreases in specialization and enlargement of job duties are a primary technique used in management recentralization. An executive has a primary job, such as sales manager, for example, but also supervises other areas aligned with his or her abilities and interests.

SUGGESTED FURTHER READING

Mann, R., ed., *The Arts of Top Management,* McGraw-Hill, New York, 1970.
Parkinson, C. N., *Parkinson's Law,* Houghton Mifflin, Boston, 1957.

MANAGERIAL GRID

Areas for use in Cost Control:

PSYCHOLOGICAL MOTIVATIONAL MANAGEMENT
ORGANIZATIONAL AND OPERATIONAL SYSTEMS

The managerial grid is a leadership model to motivate workers with use of:

1. Supervisory concern for employees
2. Managerial concern with increased production

Costs are reduced most when a manager rates very high in both areas of the grid (see Fig. 64) and increases production while cutting working time through motivation of

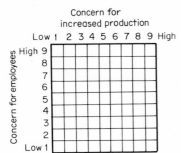

Figure 64. Blake and Mouton's managerial grid.

employees. A two-stage training process increasing, first, managerial abilities and then organizational capability has been developed for use once managerial employees are rated on the grid.

SUGGESTED FURTHER READING

Blake, R. R., and J. S. Mouton, *The Managerial Grid,* Gulf, Houston, Tex., 1964.

MAPI FORMULA

Areas for use in Cost Control:
ORGANIZATIONAL AND OPERATIONAL SYSTEMS
MATERIALS AND EQUIPMENT MANAGEMENT
INDUSTRIAL APPLICATIONS

The MAPI formula is a technique developed by the Machinery and Allied Products Institute to measure possible cost reductions to be realized from installation of new equipment. Both equipment and operating advantages and adverse factors are listed (see Fig. 65) and the totals are compared.

SUGGESTED FURTHER READING
Ammer, D. S., *Materials Management,* Irwin, Homewood, Ill., 1968.

Equipment Analysis

Equipment item _____
Date _____ Plant location _____

Present	*Proposed*
Equipment specs _____	Equipment specs _____
Salvage value _____	Installed cost _____
Age _____	Expected life _____

Adverse Factors

Present

Labor cost reductions with new equipment _____

Capital cost, prorated annually _____

Interest, capital investment _____
Total _____

Proposed

Increased operating costs _____

Lost capital interest @ 10%

Total _____

Operating Factors

	Present	Proposed
Quality variance	$_____	$_____
Production variance	_____	_____
Labor costs	_____	_____
Fringe benefit costs	_____	_____
Maintenance costs	_____	_____
Downtime costs	_____	_____
Space requirement costs	_____	_____
Power costs	_____	_____
Insurance costs	_____	_____
Tax costs	_____	_____
Other	_____	_____
Totals:	_____	_____

Figure 65. Sample MAPI formula work sheet.

MARGINAL COSTING

Areas for use in Cost Control:

ORGANIZATIONAL AND OPERATIONAL SYSTEMS
INDUSTRIAL APPLICATIONS

This technique is used to ascertain costs for increased production or sales. Fixed and variable elements of costs are separated to show cost/volume/profit relationships. Thus, production of 10,000 units would have a lower cost per unit than production of 100 units. Breakdown of costs at a proposed volume will provide needed data for pricing decisions, as well as give estimated profit per unit.

Marginal costing is essential in determining the profitability of a potential order, allowing a management decision as to whether to increase production or turn down the order.

SUGGESTED FURTHER READING

Hart, H., *Overhead Costs,* Heinemann, London, 1973.

MARGIN OF SAFETY

Areas for use in Cost Control:

ORGANIZATIONAL AND OPERATIONAL SYSTEMS
INDUSTRIAL APPLICATIONS
BUSINESS AND COMMERCIAL APPLICATIONS

The margin of safety technique is used primarily to determine the *need* for cost reduction, as well as the need to increase selling price per unit. Use of the method determines the difference between actual sales and the *break-even point* (*see* **Break-Even Analysis**). If this "margin of safety," usually 20 to 50 percent, is not satisfactory, variable or fixed costs should be reduced and/or the sales price should be increased.

The formula used to determine the margin of safety is:

MS = total sales − break-even point

Thus, if a company has total sales of $125,000 and a break-even point of $80,000, its margin of safety is $45,000, or 36 percent.

MS = $125,000 − $80,000 = $45,000 (36%)

SUGGESTED FURTHER READING

Backer, Morton, and L. W. Jacobsen, *Cost Accounting: A Managerial Approach,* McGraw-Hill, New York, 1964.
Gremgen, J. M., *Accounting for Managerial Analysis,* Irwin, Homewood, Ill., 1972.

MARKET RESEARCH

Areas for use in Cost Control:

ORGANIZATIONAL AND OPERATIONAL SYSTEMS
INDUSTRIAL APPLICATIONS
BUSINESS AND COMMERCIAL APPLICATIONS

"Market research" is the identification of potential customers for the producer's goods and/or services, as well as the evaluation of the extent of these markets. Use of the technique reduces sales costs, since with its use products or services are designed for and aimed at specific suitable markets determined by market research, as are subsequent advertising campaigns.

Three general areas of market research include:

1. Basic market research
2. Industrial market research
3. Consumer market research

Basic market research studies potential demand for a specific product or service. Estimates may be broken down geographically, by age group, by sex, or by other criteria. Predictions are based on past demand, current availability, and trends that may affect such demand—population and economic trends, for example. Interviews and questionnaires are used. *See also* **Mathematical Statistics.**

Industrial market research uses much the same methods but limits its market predictions to those for products or services that will be used by manufacturing companies. Estimates are usually broken down by type of industry, as well as by geographical location.

Consumer market research predicts market size and strength for products or services used by individuals. Consumer preferences and habits are studied, using personal observation, questionnaires, and personal interviews. Breakdowns are usually by geographical area, age, social status, economic status, and sex.

Success in all three areas depends on suitable access to relevant statistics, as well as to current investigations. Because trained specialists are required for use of the method, market research is expensive to use. Proportionately greater cost reductions can be achieved through its use, however, in finding new markets for old products, as well as in determining potential markets for new products.

SUGGESTED FURTHER READING

Distributive Trades EDC, *The Future Pattern of Shopping*, H.M.S.O., London, 1971.
Seibert and Wills, eds., *Marketing Research*, Penguin, Baltimore, 1972.
Wilson, A., *The Marketing of Professional Services*, McGraw-Hill, New York, 1973.

MATERIAL UTILIZATION

Areas for use in Cost Control:

ORGANIZATIONAL AND OPERATIONAL SYSTEMS
MATERIALS AND EQUIPMENT MANAGEMENT
INDUSTRIAL APPLICATIONS

Material utilization is the efficient use of raw materials to reduce waste, thus lowering costs. Primary methods include efficient material selection, efficient handling and use, standardized materials practices, and administrative controls.

Efficient material selection includes choosing the lowest-cost material of an adequate quality for production, *after* considering the availability of needed grades, sizes, etc.

Efficient handling and use can be facilitated through production with correctly designed and maintained tools and equipment. Dies, for example, must be carefully checked to avoid waste from stampings. Oil leaks, rusty pipes, etc., can also ruin raw materials. Production shortcuts, such as not cleaning equipment between runs, increase the amount of spoiled and wasted raw material, and the savings created by the shorter production time should be carefully measured against increased waste costs.

Standardized materials practices in the handling and storage of materials, such as practices designed to protect materials from the weather when necessary, can also reduce waste costs.

Administrative controls are needed to determine many facets of waste economies. For example, in a short run of a specific product, waste costs may be excessive, and it would be more economical to refuse the order. Waste material must also be examined for reuse. For instance, in some cases if waste cuttings are *increased* in size, they can be reused, while minimal cuttings are discarded. In such a case, the first waste should be increased for eventual optimal use of the material. *See also* **Material Waste Control.**

SUGGESTED FURTHER READING

Grad, F. P., *Environmental Law: Sources and Problems,* Matthew Bender, New York, 1971.
Neal, A. W., *Industrial Waste,* Business Books, London, 1971.

MATERIAL WASTE CONTROL

Areas for use in Cost Control:

ORGANIZATIONAL AND OPERATIONAL SYSTEMS
MATERIALS AND EQUIPMENT MANAGEMENT
INDUSTRIAL APPLICATIONS

Material waste control methods reduce business and industry wastage from practices already in operation, thus reducing operating costs. Control is applied to the following areas:

1. *Raw material quality.* Inspections of raw materials prior to production can eliminate faulty material that would waste processing labor and other materials if unchecked. Raw material standards should be specified to aid in the inspection process.

2. *Material handling efficiency,* including equipment and methods that will not damage materials in storage or in intra-plant transit.

3. *Plant and equipment layout* should be designed for efficient material use, including good machine setup and maintenance practices.

4. *Employee training* to maximize efficient production and minimize waste.

5. *Automation waste* should be measured against human waste in production as an additional factor in determining the degree of automation to be used. One fish-processing plant using automated fileting equipment, for example, returned to human labor fileting when fish prices rose more rapidly than labor costs, since human-labor fileting produced 10 percent more salable pounds of fish than did automated equipment.

6. *Sturdy packing* to protect incoming materials and outgoing products.

When determining the amount of waste and methods to control it, the following statistics should be established:

1. Weight and/or volume of wastes
2. Source of wastes
3. Type of wastes
4. Value of wastes
5. Later use of wastes, if any

Monthly comparisons of such waste inventories are an excellent tool in calling attention to the problem.

Potential use for scrap material and wastes should be determined where possible. **Recycling** techniques are being developed for many types of wastes, providing reuse of dwindling supplies of raw materials as well as cost reductions. Recovered wastes may be reused in the same production operation if possible, or they can be sold to other processors or recycled if this is more economical. *See also* **Material Utilization.**

SUGGESTED FURTHER READING

Ammer, D. S., *Materials Management,* Irwin, Homewood, Ill., 1974.
Neal, A. W., *Industrial Waste,* Business Books, London, 1971.

MATHEMATICAL PROGRAMMING

Areas for use in Cost Control:

ORGANIZATIONAL AND OPERATIONAL SYSTEMS
INDUSTRIAL APPLICATIONS
BUSINESS AND COMMERCIAL APPLICATIONS

Mathematical programming is an **operations research** technique used to translate a company's resources into mathematical equation form to make it possible to choose optimum uses of such resources. Variations within the technique include *linear, integer, quadratic, separable,* and *transportation programming.*

To translate resources into equations, use the following example: A production manager knows that product A requires 4 pounds of plastic to produce it, while product B requires 2 pounds of plastic. There are 200 pounds of plastic in stock. This is translated to 0.5A + 0.25B of total stock, which must not exceed 200 pounds. The company employees 125 men who work 40 hours per week each, or a total of 5,000 hours per week. Product A requires 100 man-hours to produce, while product B requires 240 man-hours; or, 100A + 240B must not exceed 5,000.

Next, cost and price equations are added. Product A can be sold for \$150, while product B can be sold for \$400, and labor costs are \$5 an hour, or 150A + 400B − 5L.

Using these equations, the best mix of product A and product B production is computed. In this case, the equations show that best use of company resources—plastic, labor, and potential selling price—call for manufacturing four B products for each A product. The technique can also be used to test product mix under hypothetical circumstances, such as increased plastic purchases, additional employees, etc.

Computers are generally used in operating the technique because of the complexity of the equations, and only large companies with very complex resources will find the needed time and equipment expense worthwhile in the present state of the technique development. Up to 10 percent of operating costs have been saved in some operations, but annual mathematical programming budgets may cost as much as \$1 million, with single program runs costing \$1,000 each or more.

Linear programming, the most important of the variations, uses the techniques on resources that have a linear relationship, such as stable production cost per unit at or above a predetermined figure.

SUGGESTED FURTHER READING

Armand, R., R. Lattes, and J. Lesourne, *The Management Revolution,* Denoel Press, Paris, 1970.

Van Horne, James C., *Financial Management and Policy,* Prentice-Hall, Englewood Cliffs, N.J., 1971.

MATHEMATICAL STATISTICS

Areas for use in Cost Control:

ORGANIZATIONAL AND OPERATIONAL SYSTEMS
INDUSTRIAL APPLICATIONS
BUSINESS AND COMMERCIAL APPLICATIONS

Mathematical statistics, an **operations research** technique, is used to clarify confusing cost or other figures. Employing one of several methods (see below), an executive uses statistics relating to his or her area of responsibility to pinpoint operational cost and other problems and to correct them.

Methods used in the technique include the following:

1. *Experiments design*—to reduce research costs by determining the minimum number of experiments required to prove the results.

2. *Technological forecasting*—to predict future trends, markets, costs, etc.

3. *Stock control*—to determine the most economical level of stocks.

4. *Random sampling*—to reduce costs of information by making observations according to some predetermined pattern, such as checking every fourth factor, rather than examining each factor. The technique is most often used in **market research,** but it can be effectively applied to other areas as well.

5. *Sequential analysis*—to reduce quality-control costs by determining the minimum number of inspections of items produced needed to provide acceptable quality, and implementing such a system.

6. *Statistical quality control*—to reduce costs in designing the most efficient quality-control program by statistically determining acceptable limits of quality standards.

7. *Variance analysis*—a mathematical evaluation method used to reach conclusions from complex cost or other figures.

See also **Sequential Analysis; Stock Control; Technological Forecasting; Variance Analysis.**

SUGGESTED FURTHER READING

Chu, Kong, *Quantitative Methods for Business and Economic Analysis,* Intext Educational Publishers, New York, 1969.

MATRIX CHARTS

Areas for use in Cost Control:

ORGANIZATIONAL AND OPERATIONAL SYSTEMS
MATERIALS AND EQUIPMENT MANAGEMENT
INDUSTRIAL APPLICATIONS
BUSINESS AND COMMERCIAL APPLICATIONS

Matrix charts are a visual means of comparing interrelated factors in determining the lowest cost possible or other optimum decisions to be made. In drawing a matrix

Trips per day by \ Trips per day to	Production	Accounting	Sales	Shipping	Personnel
Production	×	5	0	2	7
Accounting	2	×	3	3	1
Sales	10	15	×	2	2
Shipping	15	10	2	×	2
Personnel	8	2	2	3	×

Figure 66. Typical matrix chart.

chart, various factors are run vertically and horizontally, with the intersecting point showing the effect of one on another. For example, if a company wishes to determine the number of trips made between departments so that such intercompany travel time and cost can be reduced when a new plant is designed, a matrix chart (see Fig. 66) will allow rapid comparison.

The information in Fig. 66 has been reorganized in Fig. 66A to list total trips by department. The company can then determine that the production department should be most centrally located, since the most trips are made to and from it. Since sales and shipping account for most of these trips, they should be given best access to the department.

Department	To other departments	From other departments	Total
Production	14	35	49
Accounting	9	32	41
Sales	29	7	36
Shipping	29	10	39
Personnel	15	12	27

Personnel, on the other hand, accounts for the fewest trips. Most of these are to or from production. If the department is given fairly good access to production, costs for time spent going to or from other departments will be minimized.

A *plus and minus technique* can be combined with matrix charts to compare various factors, such as the costs of alternate materials. In Fig. 67, for example, alternate

Materials	A	B	C	D	E
A	×	−	+	−	−
B	+	×	+	−	−
C	−	−	×	−	−
D	+	+	+	×	−
E	+	+	+	+	×

Figure 67. Matrix chart using plus and minus cost comparisons.

materials are given a *plus* rating when they cost more than the material against which they are compared, and a *minus* rating when they cost less. Looking at Fig. 67, material E is the only material, then, that costs less than each of the other four. *See also* **Charting.**

SUGGESTED FURTHER READING

Chatfield, C., *Statistics for Technology,* Penguin, Baltimore, 1970.
Chu, Kong, *Quantitative Methods for Business and Economic Analysis,* Intext Educational Publishers, New York, 1968.

MCGREGOR'S THEORIES X AND Y

Areas for use in Cost Control:
PSYCHOLOGICAL MOTIVATIONAL MANAGEMENT
ORGANIZATIONAL AND OPERATIONAL SYSTEMS
INDUSTRIAL APPLICATIONS
BUSINESS AND COMMERCIAL APPLICATIONS

McGregor's theories X and Y are two theories of managerial effectiveness developed by Douglas McGregor, late professor of industrial management at Massachusetts Institute of Technology.

Theory X is the traditional concept of why workers behave as they do; it is commonly used by management as the basis for its handling of employees to increase productivity and reduce costs. The following are assumptions made by theory X about employee behavior:

1. The average human being has an inherent dislike of work and will avoid it if she or he can.

2. Most people must be coerced, controlled, directed, and threatened with punishment if they are to achieve top production efficiency.

3. The average worker prefers to be directed, wishes to avoid responsibility, and has relatively little ambition. He or she wants security above all.

Theory Y is a more modern set of assumptions about worker behavior and how to increase productivity, based on human engineering studies:

1. The use of physical and mental effort in work is as natural as rest or play.

2. External control and punishment are not the only means of motivation.

3. Commitment to objectives is a result of the association of rewards with their achievement. The most important rewards are those satisfying the need for self-respect and personal improvement.

4. The average human can learn to accept and seek responsibility.

5. The capacity to use a relatively high degree of imagination, ingenuity, and creativity in the solution of organizational problems is widely distributed in the population.

6. Modern industry only partially uses human potential.

In evaluating the two theories, it can be seen that applying the assumptions of theory Y to the limitations of theory X, an individual supervisor can best increase productivity and decrease costs by combining the worker's needs with those of the company or department.

SUGGESTED FURTHER READING

Bittel, L. R., *What Every Supervisor Should Know,* McGraw-Hill, New York, 1974.
McGregor, D., *The Human Side of Enterprise,* McGraw-Hill, New York, 1960.
Pugh, D. S., ed., *Organizational Theory,* Penguin, Baltimore, 1971.

MEASUREMENT FOR COST CONTROL

Areas for use in Cost Control:

ORGANIZATIONAL AND OPERATIONAL SYSTEMS
INDUSTRIAL APPLICATIONS

Measurement of various costs is an essential step in understanding and reducing costs. Areas to be measured include the following:

1. *Material Yields.* These all are best measured using invoices which specify materials as well as quantity. Processing waste should be calculated as a percentage of the total and subtracted from invoiced amounts.

2. *Direct Labor.* This may be measured by cost per production unit, by standard labor-hour, or by machine-hour.

3. *Indirect Labor.* Measurements for supervision, clerical labor, etc., are usually budgeted controls, determined by level of activity.

4. *Indirect Expense.* Measurement of office supplies, small tools, etc., is also budget-controlled.

5. *Overheads.* Measurement of interdepartmental production overheads, including such items as rent, interdepartmental equipment, building depreciation, etc., is budget-controlled according to the level of activity.

6. *Sales Costs.* These can be measured as a percentage of unit selling price, or they can be budgeted according to level of activity.

SUGGESTED FURTHER READING

Maynard, H. B., ed., *Industrial Engineering Handbook,* 3d ed., McGraw-Hill, New York, 1974.

MEASURE OF ECONOMIC WELFARE (MEW) See Net Economic Welfare.

MEMOMOTION

Areas for use in Cost Control:
ORGANIZATIONAL AND OPERATIONAL SYSTEMS
MATERIALS AND EQUIPMENT MANAGEMENT
INDUSTRIAL APPLICATIONS

Memomotion is the automatic, periodic, sequential recording, with a camera, of work motions for subsequent observation and analysis to develop increased motion efficiency and to reduce costs. Shots are usually spaced from 0.5 second to 4 seconds over a long period of time to develop adequate sampling. The technique is particularly useful for slow-motion, nonrepetitive, or long-cycle jobs. *See also* **Motion Study.**

SUGGESTED FURTHER READING

Mundel, M. E., *Motion and Time Study,* Prentice-Hall, Englewood Cliffs, N.J., 1971.

MENSUALIZATION

Areas for use in Cost Control:
PSYCHOLOGICAL MOTIVATIONAL MANAGEMENT
ORGANIZATIONAL AND OPERATIONAL SYSTEMS
INDUSTRIAL APPLICATIONS

Mensualization involves transferring hourly or piece rate workers to a monthly salary basis to motivate workers through increased status. In addition to the cost reductions through increased productivity it secures, labor union negotiations and terms are generally more favorable for management when salary is paid on a monthly basis, since overtime and productivity payments are not stressed.

SUGGESTED FURTHER READING

Galenson, W., *Comparative Labor Movements,* Prentice-Hall, New York, 1952.
Marsh, A. I., and E. O. Evans, *The Dictionary of Industrial Relations,* Hutchinson, London, 1973.

MERGERS

Area for use in Cost Control:
ORGANIZATIONAL AND OPERATIONAL SYSTEMS

While mergers in the 1930s were necessitated by economic pressures, today many companies find that costs can be cut and profits increased by merging, or joining, with one or more of their competitors. Reasons why mergers are increasing in popularity include the following:

1. Competition is narrowed.

2. Some expense factors, such as R&D, computerization, and management cost, drop per dollar of sales in a larger, merged company.

3. Key skilled staff are gained by the combination of two or more firms.

4. Methods, patents, and specialized know-how are acquired.

5. Governmental policy of forcing or holding back the economy is more easily met by a large company than a small one.

FINDING A PARTNER

Within the next few years, at least 2 percent of all businesses will merge with another company. Once the decision is made, the problem becomes one of finding a company that will offer the greatest cost savings and financial gains through the merger. The following checklist gives seven factors by which to judge a prospective partner:

1. Does the company product or service relate to or duplicate that of your own firm?

2. If the firm has fewer than 100 employees, will the owner remain with the merged business? In a company of this size, the owner is usually the "success element."

3. Has the company grown steadily, with a minimum of $75,000 income per year?

4. Does the firm have a core of young, vital management that will remain with the merged company?

5. Is the firm public or private? And if it is public, what proportion of shares are held by the owner?

6. Does the price of the company generally meet the following rule of thumb?

   Company assets $= \frac{2}{3}$ of price

   (Manufacturing-company assets may be a slightly higher percentage, while companies selling services may have assets equaling less than $\frac{2}{3}$ of the selling price.)

7. Have profits increased steadily? Valuation is sometimes figured by multiplying gross profit by 5 for manufacturing firms and gross profit by 3 for service industries.

SUGGESTED FURTHER READING

Bull, George, ed., *The Director's Handbook,* McGraw-Hill, London, 1969.

MERITOCRACY

Areas for use in Cost Control:

ORGANIZATIONAL AND OPERATIONAL SYSTEMS
INDUSTRIAL APPLICATIONS
BUSINESS AND COMMERCIAL APPLICATIONS

"Meritocracy" is the giving of power to those executives with the most intelligence and with capability in dealing with cost or other business problems.

SUGGESTED FURTHER READING

Nelson, R. R., M. J. Peck, and E. D. Kalachek, *Technology, Economic Growth, and Public Policy,* Rand Corp. and Brookings Institution, Washington, D.C., 1967.

MERIT RATING

Areas for use in Cost Control:

FINANCIAL MOTIVATIONAL MANAGEMENT
ORGANIZATIONAL AND OPERATIONAL SYSTEMS

Merit rating is a system of appraising the efficiency and quality of individual employees' work, ranking them on a predetermined scale. Wage payments are sometimes determined by the worker's merit rating, reducing wage and salary costs to match the proportion and quality of work done. *See also* **Job Evaluation.**

SUGGESTED FURTHER READING

ASME Work Standardization Bulletin, American Society of Mechanical Engineers, New York.
Maynard, H. B., ed., *Industrial Engineering Handbook,* 3d ed., McGraw-Hill, New York, 1974.

MERRY-GO-ROUND METHOD

Area for use in Cost Control:

INDUSTRIAL APPLICATIONS

The merry-go-round method is a nonstop rail shipment technique first used to move coal from mines to end users. Rail cars are preloaded at the production site. At the delivery point, the train slows down and goods or raw materials are automatically pushed onto a carrying system that uses moving belts to transport goods or materials to the buyer's storage point. Costs are reduced by reduced handling.

SUGGESTED FURTHER READING

Magee, J. F., *Physical Distribution Systems,* McGraw-Hill, New York, 1967.
Murphy, G. J., *Transportation and Distribution,* Business Books, London, 1972.

METHOD ANALYSIS

Areas for use in Cost Control:

ORGANIZATIONAL AND OPERATIONAL SYSTEMS
PAPERWORK DESIGN AND FLOW SYSTEMS
BUSINESS AND COMMERCIAL APPLICATIONS

Method analysis is an investigative technique used to assess the efficiency of design, flow, and use of forms in an office operation. The technique reduces cost by pinpointing unneeded or unwieldy forms, forms overlapping in purpose, misuse of forms, and/or awkward and repetitious form flow. It is generally used as the second step in **organization and methods (O&M) analysis.**

SUGGESTED FURTHER READING

Frank, H. E., *Organization Structuring,* McGraw-Hill, New York, 1971.
Prentice-Hall Editorial Staff, *Handbook of Successful Operating Systems and Procedures,* Prentice-Hall, Englewood Cliffs, N.J., 1964.

METHODS CHANGE MEASUREMENT

Areas for use in Cost Control:

ORGANIZATIONAL AND OPERATIONAL SYSTEMS
PAPERWORK DESIGN AND FLOW SYSTEMS
DATA RETENTION—FILES AND RECORDKEEPING
INDUSTRIAL APPLICATIONS
BUSINESS AND COMMERCIAL APPLICATIONS

Changing operational methods *can* reduce costs, but it can also increase costs. Measurement of methods change is needed to make certain that only changes that are an improvement are used. These include:

1. *Models, mock-ups, trial runs.* This technique measures a change before it takes place by trying the new system under hypothetical conditions.

2. *Comparison testing.* In this method, work to be changed is measured both before and after the change. For example, number of units of office work not completed, average age of unanswered or unfiled correspondence, and distribution of not completed work might be checked both before and after the change in methods.

3. *Duplication checking.* A record is kept of individuals and departments handling each unit of work. If the same work must be gone over by two or more persons, the change in methods has not eliminated duplication and requires revision.

4. *Work flow checking.* A *flowchart* (*see* **Charting**) is prepared to show the flow of work. If flow overlaps or backtracks, the change of method should be revised to control these elements.

Managerial staff should plan to evaluate every methods change as a matter of course. Performance of all activities in the new method should be measured, using quantitative measurements of the basic elements.

SUGGESTED FURTHER READING

Valentine, R. F., "How to Tell Whether a Methods Change Is Really Paying Off," *Cost Control and the Supervisor,* American Management Assn., New York, 1966.

METHODS ENGINEERING

Areas for use in Cost Control:

ORGANIZATIONAL AND OPERATIONAL SYSTEMS
MATERIALS AND EQUIPMENT MANAGEMENT
INDUSTRIAL APPLICATIONS

Methods engineering is the evaluation of current work methods as a basis for improving or changing these methods for more efficient use. *Work study* (*see* **Work Study and Measurement**) and **Methods Study** are used for this analysis. Use of methods engineering can increase productivity, reduce labor costs per unit, and reduce material and capacity waste, reducing costs.

METHODS ENGINEERING GOALS

Specific methods engineering objectives include the following:

Greater Operator Efficiency. In this area, operator motion is studied, and changes are made in the work method to decrease unnecessary movement, conserving operator energy. Several methods of motion study can be used, including **predetermined motion time systems (PMTS)** and **Labanotation.** Work place layout is also studied and redesigned to reduce operator movement in working.

Greater Material Efficiency. Here, causes of material waste are pinpointed and corrected.

Human Labor/Equipment Balance. The most economical combination of human labor and automated equipment is determined. This will vary from industry to industry, depending on required skills, and within an industry, depending on the economic situation at the time. For example, in recent years, increasing labor union strength has forced wage levels up more rapidly than productivity has increased. With such a trend, there is a good case for converting as much work as possible to equipment-oriented methods.

Optimal Equipment Scheduling. Once purchased, equipment can be economical only if it is fully used. Methods engineering includes scheduling of work to ensure optimum use of equipment. If excessive equipment has been purchased, and increased production in its area is not economically viable, such equipment is sold or converted for another purpose.

Quality Control. Waste of materials and labor is eliminated through quality control (*see* **Quality Survey**).

Preventive Maintenance is used to ensure minimal downtime of equipment, as well as minimal lost operator time (*see* **Preventive Maintenance**).

Skill Structuring. Here, the skills required for each aspect of work are studied and employees are used only for work requiring their specific skills. If setup can be done by a less skilled employee, for example, the operator is scheduled onto other work requiring his or her skills during setup. In other words, human skills are not wasted on work a less skilled person could do. It must be remembered, however, that this reduces costs *only* if there is other work available for the more skilled worker. It is not economical to pay a less skilled employee to set up while the operator watches from the sidelines.

Simplification and Standardization. These are two key goals in methods engineering. Use of standard parts and materials allows cost reduction inherent in bulk purchases, for example. Simplification, whether of product design or the work method itself, reduces labor time and cost per unit. Equipment costs are also reduced when new jigs, dies, etc., are not needed frequently.

Standards Control. Reasonable standards in costs, time, etc., are established, and systems to ensure meeting these standards are added. Control factors such as **incentive payment systems** are based on standards setting.

ORGANIZING METHODS ENGINEERING

Organization of methods engineering will depend on the size of the company, as well as the number and type of products manufactured. Generally, however, the following departments should be part of the methods engineering organization:

1. *Control*—design, materials, planning, production, quality control, time study, and inspection departments
2. *Engineering*—design, production, and maintenance engineering departments
3. *Supportive*—accounting, data processing, purchasing, and marketing departments

In larger firms, methods engineering will be a specific department serving as a control link between plant manager and operations. In smaller companies where management wears several hats, the plant manager or the head industrial engineer may also act as head of methods engineering. It is essential that the person in charge of methods engineering be familiar with all its aspects, even though specialized attention to each may be accomplished departmentally.

Operational organization of methods engineering is broken into three major areas:

1. Human labor
2. Materials usage
3. Equipment usage

Human labor may be further divided into four areas:

1. *Economics*—wage levels and plans
2. *Physical*—motion study and conservation
3. *Social*—the role of labor
4. *Psychological*—motivation and cooperation

APPLICATION OF METHODS ENGINEERING

Human Labor. Human labor is perhaps the most difficult company asset to control. It is also the most important, since it accounts for the largest percentage of production costs in most industries.

Economics. A primary problem in negotiations with labor unions is finding a way to show that living standards can be increased only by improved productivity. As inflationary trends in the 1970s show, wage increases from $100,000 to $150,000 do not improve the workers' lot if only $100,000 worth of goods are manufactured. Instead, prices expand to meet increased wages. On the other hand, if productivity expands at about the same rate as wages, everyone gains real values. It makes sense, then, to key payment systems to productivity. To raise living standards, control inflation, and obtain maximum profitability for the company, this is an ideal control. Productivity bargaining, which encourages employee participation and productivity-linked payment, is an important way to reach labor with this important message (*see* **Productivity Bargaining and Agreements**).

If incentive plans are to effectively increase productivity, lowering labor costs per unit, an accurate and fair accounting system is necessary. In fact, some experts say that the worker's knowledge of his or her wages being based on a fair-return method with careful bookkeeping serves more effectively as a motivator than the thought of increased "rewards" for increased output.

Ideally, employees participate in establishing incentive plans. In any case, such payment systems must be "sold" to workers, just as products are marketed to customers, because worker cooperation is needed to ensure the success of such systems.

Incentive systems may profitably include payment for cost reductions, such as lower material wastage, as well as payment for increased output.

Physical Aspects of Human Labor. In methods engineering, their consideration is sometimes called human engineering (*see* **Human Factors Engineering**). Generally it aims to evaluate the human body at work in the same way equipment would be analyzed. Efficiency (or lack of it) in motions is studied, capacities of the human body over periods of time are analyzed, and causes for variations in the degree of physical performance in identical conditions are determined.

These evaluations are used to improve work layout and the motions used in work methods. Additionally, they should be used when setting new personnel-hiring standards. For example, if such analysis shows that workers with mechanical skill ratings above a specific level are more productive than employees with lower ratings, all job applicants should be tested for mechanical skills and new hires should be limited to those passing the acceptable level. Mechanical tests may include those for physical strength, mechanical aptitude, coordination, etc.

Physiological tests are also commonly used, since the biological capacity of the body affects work performance.

Social Factors. Evaluation of social factors is an increasingly important aspect of methods engineering, since the individual worker's social status (especially within the company) affects both the quantity and the quality of his or her work. For example, a production worker who does not fit in or who is not accepted by coworkers will not produce to capacity. A supervisor who is not accepted can adversely affect the productivity of his or her entire department. Meeting these social needs through methods engineering means involvement of employees in work decisions, operations, and profits.

In addition, a working social code should be established. Responsibility should be clearly defined, for instance, so that supervisors do not blame subordinates for their own errors. Fair treatment and payment of all workers, in return for performance, are the basis of such a code.

Psychological Factors. Here, the methods engineer's goal is to select the right person for a specific job. On the job, job pressures (*see* **Job Pressure and Cost Control**) should be minimized.

Selection of employees is particularly important. Job descriptions and specifications provide a list of skills needed, and applicants can be tested in these areas to make sure they have the necessary qualifications. Emotional stability, personality, attitudes, and learning capacity are less easily measured but are just as important in obtaining maximum employee performance. For example, hiring a male supervisor who feels that women are inferior is bound to adversely affect work performance of employees if he is required to supervise women employees. At the same time, a female supervisor can be effective only if male subordinates have an open attitude toward working for a woman.

It is important not to hire overqualified applicants. A typist with a broad, educated background and a high I.Q., for example, will probably be bored and will not stay in the job long, increasing turnover costs. An assembly line worker with a college degree may be absent a disproportionate amount of time because of boredom. Qualified workers, but those who will find the job a challenge, are better choices economically.

Materials Usage. Waste of materials is one of the largest and most unnecessary costs in manufacturing. For analysis in methods engineering, waste can be broken into two areas: production material waste and overhead material waste.

Production material waste includes raw materials used in manufacturing processes. As supplies of raw materials decrease in availability and increase in cost, conservation of materials becomes more important in economic production.

Value of specific raw materials used should be determined by the methods engineer and his or her attention directed first to the most costly and widely used materials. For example, if $300,000 worth of plastic is used per month, while $25,000 worth of wood is used, first attention should be given to obtaining the most efficient use of plastic.

Waste may be caused by several factors, including the following:

1. Loss due to poor recordkeeping
2. Loss due to inefficient handling
3. Loss through inadequate storage, allowing heat or weather elements to ruin materials, for example
4. Lack of requisitioning control
5. Inefficient equipment or work methods in production
6. Employee pilferage
7. Outside theft of materials
8. Fire, or other disaster effects

Techniques to control costs in these areas are discussed separately throughout the book.

Raw material waste control can also be implemented through design by substitution of lower-cost materials where these have satisfactory performance and other qualities. Platforms for oil drilling are a good example. Early designs used expensive and short-supply steel throughout. Later, lower-cost concrete was partially or wholly substituted.

The material now used may be available in lower-cost grades or finishes that will not affect performance. These should be considered wherever possible.

Overhead material waste includes excessive use of electricity or other power sources for both production and operations, such as plant heating and lighting. Equipment left running during breaks and overnight, little or no supervision of lighting and heating, and uneconomical sources of power are common causes of waste.

Increased supervision of lighting, heating, and equipment operation can be easily implemented through line management.

A larger cost reduction can result from using the most economical sources of power (*see* **Power Cost Reduction**), or using power more efficiently through increased building insulation, limiting the power supplied to equipment to that required, etc. Building systems may incorporate heat recovery features that extract heat once power is used in production or that return a percentage of heat normally lost in ventilation. Experimental design has allowed economical use of solar and water power in some operations. As oil, electricity, and other power costs accelerate, such alternate sources are more likely to be developed and made economically viable.

Equipment Usage. Efficient use of equipment is primarily a matter of production planning, including the following areas:

1. *Process planning*—a complete description of each manufacturing process— length of the cycle, individual equipment time, worker time, etc.

2. *Equipment design*—design or adaptation of equipment to perform work at maximum efficiency.

3. *Plant layout*—arrangement of departments for work and flow efficiency.

4. *Payment planning*—determining incentive payments to achieve maximum use of equipment.

5. *Scheduling*—also called *forward loading*—to provide a continuous flow of work to and from all pieces of equipment. This includes scheduling of materials and labor, as well as equipment.

Techniques used in these specific areas are discussed separately throughout the book.

Accounting, marketing, data processing, and purchasing departments, as well as the various production departments, should be involved in methods engineering equipment utilization decisions.

Equipment Measurement. This is an important aspect of methods engineering used to evaluate equipment performance. Recording precise details of equipment use can show which brands are performing best, as well as the exact cost of each machine's operation, to pinpoint areas where cost control is needed. For example, if a piece of equipment cutting thread is not accurately set, the fractions can add up to a large loss over a period of time. Measurement can also show where rescheduling of equipment is necessary for optimum use.

Measurement may be by direct observation, by mechanical equipment, or by automatic devices. Direct observation requires that the observer check or otherwise indicate performance on a report. Mechanical measurement equipment can be added to production equipment, with the operator pushing the control as part of his or her work cycle. Fully automated counting or measuring devices are attached directly to the equipment being checked.

Measurements, once evaluated, then form the basis for equipment modifications, changes, or rescheduling to increase efficiency.

SUGGESTED FURTHER READING

Avery, Michael, *Methods Engineering,* MacDonald, London, 1962.
Davis, L. E., and J. C. Taylor, *Design of Jobs,* Penguin, Baltimore, 1972.
Maynard, H. B., *Industrial Engineering Handbook,* 3d ed., McGraw-Hill, New York, 1974.
Nadler, Gerald, *Work Design,* Irwin, Homewood, Ill., 1970.

METHOD STUDY

Areas for use in Cost Control:

INDUSTRIAL APPLICATIONS
BUSINESS AND COMMERCIAL APPLICATIONS

Method study is another name for the *work study* technique of examining ways in which work is done (*see* **Work Study and Measurement**).

MICROECONOMIC COST CONTROL

Areas for use in Cost Control:

ORGANIZATIONAL AND OPERATIONAL SYSTEMS
INDUSTRIAL APPLICATIONS
BUSINESS AND COMMERCIAL APPLICATIONS

Microeconomic cost control includes all methods of controlling research, production, marketing, sales, and other costs of an individual company. *See also* **Macroeconomics Cost Control.**

SUGGESTED FURTHER READING

Chamberlain, N. W., *Microeconomic Planning and Action,* McGraw-Hill, New York, 1965.

MICROFILMING

Areas for use in Cost Control:

ORGANIZATIONAL AND OPERATIONAL SYSTEMS
DATA RETENTION—FILES AND RECORDKEEPING
MATERIALS AND EQUIPMENT MANAGEMENT
INDUSTRIAL APPLICATIONS
BUSINESS AND COMMERCIAL APPLICATIONS

Microfilming is the copying of data to be retained (such as sales and inventory records and correspondence files) on film to reduce the cost of storing, handling, and access. The method can reduce costs when space used for filing is needed for production or other purposes, when space rent is extremely high, and when files are kept for a very long time. Access costs can be reduced if the system is properly indexed.

In deciding whether microfilming will reduce costs in a particular application, the following factors should be estimated at current monetary values:

1. *Annual cost of current filing space versus projected annual cost of microfilming space and supplies*
2. *Annual depreciation of microfilming equipment versus annual depreciation of filing equipment*
3. *Estimated cost of access per item in the filing system versus estimated cost of access per item in microfilming*

For example, if office space rents for $30 per sq ft per month, a bank of files 10 ft by 3 ft will cost $10,800 annually. If a 100-ft roll of microfilm costs $4 and holds 2 cu ft of filing, the data will require 75 rolls of film if files are 5 ft high, at a total cost of $300. Storage space for 75 rolls of film is minimal, not exceeding 1 sq ft or $360 annually.

Microfilming recorder and reader, with maintenance, may cost about $3,000, or about $600 annually depreciated over a five-year period. Filing equipment may cost about $1,200, or $240 annually depreciated over five years.

Average length of time to find a filed item in the current system is 10 minutes, and average wage per hour is $4, for an average cost per item of 67 cents. Approximately 20,000 referrals to the files are made annually. If even one minute can be trimmed from average access time with microfilming, a cost reduction of nearly $1,400 would occur.

Summarizing possible cost comparisons in this example:

	Microfilming	Filing
Annual space cost and supplies	$ 660	$10,800
Annual equipment depreciation costs	600	240
Annual access costs	12,000	13,400
Total annual estimated costs	$13,260	$24,440

Cost of microfilming, cost of filing materials, and lost income from nonproductive use of filing space may also be calculated and evaluated.

SUGGESTED FURTHER READING

Stevens, G. W., *Microphotography,* Wiley, New York, 1968.

MICROMOTION STUDY

Areas for use in Cost Control:

ORGANIZATIONAL AND OPERATIONAL SYSTEMS
MATERIALS AND EQUIPMENT MANAGEMENT
INDUSTRIAL APPLICATIONS

Micromotion study is the observation and analysis of motions that are too rapid or small for normal *motion study* techniques, and the development of increased motion efficiency with the accompanying reduction of labor costs per unit. Such rapid or small motions are recorded by a 16-mm camera, with most rapid motions filmed at speeds to 64 frames per second. Single frames, arresting motion, are then used as a basis for observation and analysis using standard **motion study** techniques.

SUGGESTED FURTHER READING

Barnes, R. M., *Motion and Time Study,* 2d ed., Wiley, New York, 1961.
Sprieght, W. R., and C. E. Myers, eds., *The Writings of the Gilbreths,* Irwin, Homewood, Ill., 1967.

MILITARY SYSTEM

Areas for use in Cost Control:

ORGANIZATIONAL AND OPERATIONAL SYSTEMS
INDUSTRIAL APPLICATIONS

The military system is an organizational and operational system patterned on traditional military hierarchy patterns in which each employee below the level of company president has only one supervisor. Because the system is so simple, and because responsibility can be so precisely placed, the method can reduce costs as compared with more awkward and/or complex systems *provided* key positions do not break down.

For all except the smallest firms, in the military system of organization companies are divided into work areas or departments (see Fig. 68). The flow or responsibility moves upward, with the employee in each position held accountable for those positions above him or her on the chart.

SUGGESTED FURTHER READING

"Military Staff," *Encyclopedia Britannica,* London, 1974.
Robertson, S. A., *Engineering Management,* Blackie, Glasgow, 1967.

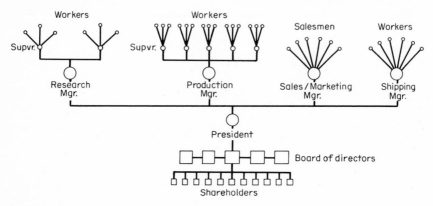

Figure 68. Typical military system organization chart.

MIND DEVELOPMENT

Areas for use in Cost Control:

PSYCHOLOGICAL MOTIVATIONAL MANAGEMENT
ORGANIZATIONAL AND OPERATIONAL SYSTEMS
INDUSTRIAL APPLICATIONS
BUSINESS AND COMMERCIAL APPLICATIONS

Mind development is a technique used to solve cost and other problems through altering the executive's state of consciousness and through the use of his or her subconscious. The method involves the executive subconsciously conversing with people about cost or other problems that need to be solved. It uses "targeting" intuition—focusing it on specific issues. Intuitive "glimpses" are analyzed and used. Such intuitive movement is especially encouraged by reducing stress and tension, so that personnel are operating in a totally relaxed state.

SUGGESTED FURTHER READING

Allen, Audrey, "Managing by Intuition," *Sales Management,* New York, May 27, 1974.
Esposito, Stewart, *Mind Development,* American Management Assn., New York, 1974.

MINIMAX PRINCIPLE

Areas for use in Cost Control:

ORGANIZATIONAL AND OPERATIONAL SYSTEMS
INDUSTRIAL APPLICATIONS
BUSINESS AND COMMERCIAL APPLICATIONS

The minimax principle determines decisions by selecting the choice with the smallest maximum possible loss. Costs can be reduced by the technique since possible losses are minimized. In some cases, use of the method prevents possible large gains.

SUGGESTED FURTHER READING

Schlaifer, Robert, *Introduction to Statistics for Business Decisions,* McGraw-Hill, New York, 1961.

MNEMONIC TECHNIQUES

Areas for use in Cost Control:

INDUSTRIAL APPLICATIONS
BUSINESS AND COMMERCIAL APPLICATIONS

Mnemonic techniques are systems used to make remembering easier. When used in training, such systems can reduce training time and costs. In working conditions, they can be used to reduce work time and costs. The various techniques include:

Loci Method. This involves imagining that various items to be remembered are in specific and different locations. To remember the item, the person visualizes its location.

Analytic Substitutions. In learning numbers, the numbers are changed into sounds, sounds into words, and words into sentences. The method is especially useful in remembering parts and other numbers. *S* or *Z* usually stand for zero; *T, D,* or *TH* for one; *N* for two; *M* for three; *R* for four; *L* for five; *J, CH,* or *SH* for six; *G, K, Q,* or *C* for seven; *F* or *V* for eight; and *B* or *P* for nine. In remembering a part number 26339, for example, a sentence would be constructed using the alphabet code for the first letter of each word, such as, *Now Sharon's mother makes bread,* or *Never change my market price.*

Rhyming. Rhyming can be used to memorize numbers or facts.

Organizing. This is mentally dividing material into areas to be used. For example, a long number may be divided into groups of two or three numbers which will be easier to remember. While 023619482 would be difficult to remember, 023-619-482 is relatively easy to recall.

SUGGESTED FURTHER READING

Norman, D. A., *Memory and Attention,* Wiley, New York, 1969.

MOBILE OFFICES

Areas for use in Cost Control:

ORGANIZATIONAL AND OPERATIONAL SYSTEMS
INDUSTRIAL APPLICATIONS
BUSINESS AND COMMERCIAL APPLICATIONS

Mobile offices are prefabricated units that can be moved under their own power or with another vehicle.

Even when plushily furnished, such units cost considerably less per square foot than conventional office space. Not only is construction done in-factory at lower hourly labor cost than under on-site construction, but the units require no capital expenditure for land.

Uses include the following:

1. *Traveling Sales Office*—used by sales reps for both business and entertaining of clients on "home ground." In addition, units can convert to sleeping quarters at night, saving hotel costs.

2. *Recruiting Personnel.* Units offer ample space for testing several applicants at once, interviews, etc., and are easily moved from college to college or city to city.

3. *Conference Rooms.* Most models offer space for conferences of 12 to 15 persons. Such units are flexible in that they can be used near the home office, moved to clients' plants or offices, or driven to trade fairs, conventions, etc.

4. *Temporary Space.* In areas without zoning permission for new industrial or office construction, authorities may grant permission for temporary facilities for up to five years. One mobile unit is designed for stacking, with an outside stairwell quickly erected, providing modular offices that can quickly be taken apart and moved to new sites as needed.

5. *Training Centers.* Larger mobile units make ideal classrooms for training programs. These can be moved from branch to branch for use in such areas as insurance sales training or from plant to plant for the training of industrial personnel.

6. *Professional Offices.* Units equipped as dentists' and doctors' offices are in use, particularly in rural areas and developing nations where one professional person serves a large geographical area.

SUGGESTED FURTHER READING

Manser, Jose, "Take the Office to Work," *The Financial Times,* London, July 8, 1974.

MODELS

Areas for use in Cost Control:

ORGANIZATIONAL AND OPERATIONAL SYSTEMS
INDUSTRIAL APPLICATIONS
BUSINESS AND COMMERCIAL APPLICATIONS

Models are **operations research** hypothetical mathematical constructions used to examine how a change in circumstances might affect a complicated business situation. Models can reduce costs because their use allows a company to compare costs of several methods of operation without really making the changes. **Simulation** and mathematical models are the two types generally used. *See also* **Mathematical Programming; Simulation.**

In model construction, business factors such as profits, fixed costs, and depreciation are translated into operating equations. The technique requires a trained mathematician, and a computer should be used to speed calculations.

Some companies have constructed models of their markets, fixed costs, and operating expenses, but the technique can be applied to any area involving decision making.

SUGGESTED FURTHER READING

Cyert, R. M., and L. A. Welsch, *Management Decision Making,* Penguin, Baltimore, 1971.
Devlin, K. J., *Aspects of Constructability,* Springer-Verlag, New York, 1974.

MODULE TRAINING

Areas for use in Cost Control:

ORGANIZATIONAL AND OPERATIONAL SYSTEMS
INDUSTRIAL APPLICATIONS
BUSINESS AND COMMERCIAL APPLICATIONS

Module training is a work training technique that divides the teaching of work skills into specialized areas or modules. Employees are taught only those modules that specifically apply to their job, a practice that decreases time spent and cost of the training.

SUGGESTED FURTHER READING

Marsh, A. I., and E. O. Evans, *The Dictionary of Industrial Relations,* Hutchinson, London, 1973.

MONEY INDEXING See Index Linking.

MONTE CARLO

Areas for use in Cost Control:
ORGANIZATIONAL AND OPERATIONAL SYSTEMS
INDUSTRIAL APPLICATIONS
BUSINESS AND COMMERCIAL APPLICATIONS

Monte Carlo is an **operations research** technique and a form of **simulation** used to analyze a business situation that has been complicated by one or more random factors. The technique reduces costs by pinpointing needed operational changes, such as fewer employees and less equipment.

For example, a public transportation company might want to analyze the length of time customers must wait to catch a bus. At least 100 samplings would be taken, with someone recording the number of persons waiting at a bus stop in a predetermined time limit, such as five minutes. The numbers recorded will be of a random pattern, such as 10, 9, 13, 8. The next step is to subtract the number of persons who boarded buses during that period. If, on the average, 8 persons boarded the bus each period while, on the average, 11 persons moved to the bus stop, bus service obviously is not frequent enough for that time of day.

Production schedules, including equipment breakdowns, capacity of retail sales-clerks, and loading and unloading capacities, are only a few of the areas that can be analyzed. For simpler applications, the technique can be applied manually, but for very complex applications a computer should be used.

SUGGESTED FURTHER READING

Cyert, R. M., and L. A. Welsch, *Management Decision Making,* Penguin, Baltimore, 1971.
Sivazlian, B. D., and Larry E. Stanfel, *Optimization and Techniques in Operations Research,* Prentice-Hall, Englewood Cliffs, N.J., 1974.

MOTION STUDY

Areas for use in Cost Control:
ORGANIZATIONAL AND OPERATIONAL SYSTEMS
MATERIALS AND EQUIPMENT MANAGEMENT
INDUSTRIAL APPLICATIONS

Motion study is the detailing of motions involved in a job, with the goal of using such motions efficiently, increasing production speed, and decreasing production costs per unit. It is aligned with **predetermined motion time systems** in that PMTS uses detailed studies of motions during the work cycle to apply standard times.

Motion study was first developed by Frank Gilbreth, who determined that all motions can be broken down into 18 fundamental motions, which he called Therbligs (an anagram of his own name). For simplicity in labeling controls, he also devised a symbol and color chart to indicate the various Therbligs. The American Society of Mechanical Engineers has added four basic motions to the Gilbreth lists, but without symbols or color. Table 37 compares the Gilbreth and the ASME fundamental motion charts.

Table 37. Basic Human Motions

Motion name	Therblig number	Identity color	Identity symbol	ASME motion name
Search	1	Black	⊂⊃	Search
Find	2	Gray	⊂◯⊃	—
Select	3	Lt. gray	→	Select
Grasp	4	Red	∩	Grasp
Hold	5	Gold ocher	⊥∩⊥	Hold
Transport loaded	6	Green	⌣∩	—
Position	7	Blue	9	Position
Assemble	8	Violet	#	—
Use	9	Purple	U	—
Disassemble	10	Lt. violet	#	Disengage
Inspect	11	Burnt ocher	◯	Examine
Pre-position	12	Pale blue	⚲	Pre-position
Release load	13	Carmine	⌢	Release load
Transport empty	14	Olive	⌣	—
Rest to overcome fatigue	15	Orange	⌇	Rest to overcome fatigue
Unavoidable delay	16	Yellow	⌒o	Unavoidable delay
Avoidable delay	17	Lemon yellow	∟o	Avoidable delay
Plan	18	Brown	⏚	Plan
—	—	—	—	Reach
—	—	—	—	Move
—	—	—	—	Change direction
—	—	—	—	Balancing delay

Gilbreth's studies developed several basic principles to increase motion efficiency which are set out in Table 38. These principles were later condensed into six basic rules for motion economy:

1. Use minimum movement.
2. Use simultaneous movement.
3. Use natural movement.
4. Use rhythmical movement.
5. Use habitual movement.
6. Use symmetrical movement.

"Minimum movement" usually means an area equal to two semicircles, one vertical and one horizontal, the radius the length of the worker's forearm from fingertip to elbow when the elbow is positioned at the edge of the work place. "Maximum movement" is an area equal to similar vertical and horizonal semicircles with radius equal to the length of the full arm.

Table 38. Gilbreth's Motion Principles

---

*Two hands should begin motions simultaneously where possible.
*Two hands should complete motions simultaneously where possible.
*Two hands should not be idle simultaneously except in rest periods.
*Hand motions should be confined to lowest satisfactory classifications:
    1. Finger motions
    2. Finger and wrist motions
    3. Finger, wrist, and forearm motions
    4. Finger, wrist, forearm, and upper-arm motions.
    5. Finger, wrist, forearm, upper-arm, and shoulder motions.
*Motions of the arms should be in opposite and symmetrical directions, made simultaneously.
*Materials and tools should be placed for best sequence of motions.
*Continuous curved motions are preferable to sharp, sudden changes of direction.
*Free, loose movements are faster and more accurate than restricted ones.
*Natural rhythm of motion increases efficiency.
*Momentum aids efficiency.
*Hands should not do work that can be performed by other parts of the body.
*"Drop deliveries" are most efficient.
*Gravity feed bins should deliver material to the assembly point.
*Tools and materials should be located as near the work point as possible.
*Materials, tools, and equipment should have pre-positioned work stations.
*Mechanical devices should replace "hold" motions.
*Height of work place should allow alternate standing and sitting positions.
*Chair height and design should implement good worker posture.
*Finger motion load should be equalized with finger motion capacity.
*Small tools should be designed for as hard a surface as possible.
*Equipment controls should be placed for the least possible body motion and the greatest mechanical advantage.
*Sliding of small objects is faster than carrying.
*Full hook grasps are faster than pressure grasps.
*Tools handled most frequently should be placed closest to the work point.

SUGGESTED FURTHER READING
Barnes, R. M., *Motion and Time Study,* 2d ed., Wiley, New York, 1961.
Sprieght, W. R., and C. E. Myers, eds., *The Writings of the Gilbreths,* Irwin, Homewood, Ill., 1969.

MOTIVATION-HYGIENE THEORY

Areas for use in Cost Control:
PSYCHOLOGICAL MOTIVATIONAL MANAGEMENT
FINANCIAL MOTIVATIONAL MANAGEMENT
WORK PLACE MOTIVATIONAL MANAGEMENT
INDUSTRIAL APPLICATIONS
BUSINESS AND COMMERCIAL APPLICATIONS

The motivation-hygiene theory identifies those factors that motivate workers and those factors that diminish job satisfaction and performance. The theory was developed by Frederich Herzberg, based on his now famous study of industrial engineers and accountants. Later studies verified the validity of these findings. Criteria used in determining the factors were governed by several rules to prevent occasional moods or emotions from turning up in the study as motivators or diminishers. These include:

1. Recorded sequences include an event or series of events.
2. A time span is identified for all events.
3. Events recorded are to take place during a period of strong feeling about the job, and the event should affect these feelings.

THE MOTIVATORS

Five primary factors were identified by means of the study as strong work motivators:

1. Achievement
2. Recognition
3. Work itself
4. Responsibility
5. Advancement

These factors motivated the workers psychologically and, in some cases, financially. In addition, the motivating factors are all connected with satisfying needs for work and personal growth.

To motivate employees to increased efficiency, reducing labor costs, then, it is necessary to give them opportunities for growth in these areas.

THE DIMINISHERS

The factors that diminish job satisfaction, called hygiene factors by Herzberg, are:

1. Company policy and administration
2. Supervision
3. Salary
4. Interpersonal relations
5. Working conditions

Herzberg found that these factors could diminish job satisfaction because they could necessitate avoiding unpleasantness. Instead of allowing the worker to grow, they forced him or her to adapt to their structure.

Thus, to aid motivation, it is important to minimize the pressures from these diminishing factors. For example, an employee should receive only necessary supervision. If he or she is capable of working without any supervision, this should be arranged. Or, working conditions should not restrict the employee's efforts to do a job well. For instance, if a piece of equipment is operated more efficiently by a worker in a position or height other than standard, he or she should not be forced to operate it in the standard position.

Diminishing aspects of salary stem primarily from a situation where the salary is wholly inadequate for maintaining a satisfactory quality of life. Once this point is passed, the salary level ceases to create diminished work satisfaction and becomes less important altogether.

SUGGESTED FURTHER READING

Herzberg, F., "Motivation-Hygiene Concept," *Personnel Administration,* January–February 1964.

———, B. Mausner, and B. Snyderman, *The Motivation to Work,* Wiley, New York, 1959.

MOTIVATION MARKET RESEARCH

Areas for use in Cost Control:

PSYCHOLOGICAL MOTIVATIONAL MANAGEMENT
ORGANIZATIONAL AND OPERATIONAL SYSTEMS
INDUSTRIAL APPLICATIONS
BUSINESS AND COMMERCIAL APPLICATIONS

Motivation market research reduces sales and marketing costs by learning *why* specific products are purchased, in addition to the **market research** knowledge of *what* products are purchased *where* and *when*. Clinical psychology techniques such as projections and depth interviews are used for understanding the reason why one product is chosen in preference to a competing product. The technique can be used by manufacturers and by retailers.

SUGGESTED FURTHER READING

Martineau, Pierre, *Motivation in Advertising,* McGraw-Hill, New York, 1957.
Stacey, N. A., and A. Wilson, *The Changing Pattern of Distribution,* Pergamon, New York, 1965.

MS 70

Areas for use in Cost Control:

ORGANIZATIONAL AND OPERATIONAL SYSTEMS
INDUSTRIAL APPLICATIONS
BUSINESS AND COMMERCIAL APPLICATIONS

MS 70 is a management system developed by John Argenti. The system is based on understanding social, technological, economic, and political trends and is used in reducing costs through control of objectives, decisions, creativity, communications, and human relations.

Argenti states that successful management must include the following steps:

1. Deciding what to do
2. Deciding how to do it
3. Telling subordinates what to do
4. Checking the results

Additionally, the company must have a hierarchical structure of agreed seniority.

An important aspect of checking results is the checking of the supervisor's results as well as those of the subordinate.

Trends of the seventies that affect managerial control through MS 70 include:

1. *Universality.* Trends in all areas have become universal in nature. Although some countries may be moving more slowly, eventually there will be few differences.

2. *Communications volume, use of visual communications, and personalized communications are increasing.* This means that business control, including cost control, will be judged by international standards. It also ties the management hierarchy closer together.

3. *Computer usage.* Computers will be used for decision making as well as for operational calculations.

4. *Information.* Volume of data in all areas of business is increasing rapidly.

5. *Education and training.* Because behavior changes are accelerating, education and training will be needed throughout the executive's lifetime, rather than only prior to the beginning of his or her career.

6. *The Rate of Change.* This trend will continue to accelerate.

7. *Variety.* Consumers will demand increased variety.

8. *Size.* Large organizations will become larger, but there will also be many new small organizations.

9. *Social Attitude.* Organizations will be forced to accept a role of social responsibility.

10. *Quantification.* Business problems will be translated into mathematical formulas for more scientific control.

11. *Specialization.* The number of specialists will continue to increase.

12. *Authority Conflicts.* Centralization of power will lead to authority conflicts, strikes, trade union power, high turnover, and lower productivity.

13. *Affluence.* Increasing affluence will cause financial incentives to become less important while psychological motivation becomes more important.

14. *Automation.* Increases in automation and mechanization will accelerate.

15. *Decisions.* Complexity and size of decisions will increase, as will extent of results from business decisions.

Using the 15 trends, an executive modifies the four steps Argenti says are necessary in management, as well as modifying the company hierarchy, to give optimum control of cost or other business problems.

SUGGESTED FURTHER READING

Argenti, John, *A Management System for the Seventies,* Davlin Publications, Los Angeles, 1972.

MUTUAL STRIKE AID

Areas for use in Cost Control:

ORGANIZATIONAL AND OPERATIONAL SYSTEMS
INDUSTRIAL APPLICATIONS
BUSINESS AND COMMERCIAL APPLICATIONS

Mutual strike aid, also called employer strike insurance, is the contribution of specific amounts of money by competing firms for use if one of the companies is subject to a strike. Use of the method can reduce costs since it may help an employer to withstand the effects of a strike long enough to bargain for lower wage increase costs than originally sought by the employees.

SUGGESTED FURTHER READING

Hitsch, J. S., Jr., "Strike Insurance," *Industrial and Labor Review,* vol. 22, no. 3, 1969.

NEGATIVE INDUCTION TECHNIQUE

Areas for use in Cost Control:

PSYCHOLOGICAL MOTIVATIONAL MANAGEMENT
FINANCIAL MOTIVATIONAL MANAGEMENT
WORK PLACE MOTIVATIONAL MANAGEMENT

The negative induction technique conditions a worker to respond positively to one factor of work that can reduce costs or meet other company goals, and at the same time it suppresses his or her interest in another factor of the work which does not satisfactorily meet company goals. For example, assume that a company has a very high tardiness rate that is accompanied by exorbitant costs. It may then wish to condition employee promptness (a positive response) while decreasing tardiness (a negative response).

Promptness is then presented attractively on a number of subsequent occasions. The employees might be given a free breakfast if they arrive 30 minutes prior to work, or a monetary bonus may be given for each successive day's promptness, or a portion of the time saved may be given as a "time-off" bonus. These positive actions will gradually condition the employees' behavior and prompt arrival at work will become a habit, replacing the old (unrewarded) habit of tardiness. In extreme cases, a negative conditioner, such as a pay deduction, may be applied to tardy employees to further reinforce the conditioning. *See* **Behavior Control.**

SUGGESTED FURTHER READING

Eysenck, H. J., *Sense and Nonsense in Psychology,* Penguin, Baltimore, 1972.

NET CHANGE METHOD

Areas for use in Cost Control:

ORGANIZATIONAL AND OPERATIONAL SYSTEMS

DATA RETENTION—FILES AND RECORDKEEPING

MATERIALS AND EQUIPMENT MANAGEMENT

INDUSTRIAL APPLICATIONS

BUSINESS AND COMMERCIAL APPLICATIONS

The net change method is one of two major **inflation accounting** techniques used to substitute purchasing power values for fixed currency values in all phases of accounting. Use of the method can reduce taxes through revaluation of profits as well as assets and also of resulting depreciation schedules.

The method uses converted balance sheets at the beginning and close of each accounting period but does not convert the profit and loss statement. Converted profits or losses are determined by subtracting equity interest at the start of the period from the figure at the close of the period and adding accrued dividends.

Conversions are determined using the retail price or other index. Specific types of asset conversion include:

Plant and/or Property. The index base is its figure at the time the property was purchased. Thus, if the retail price index was 110 when such property was obtained, all investments are computed from this base rather than from 100.

To convert the value, the cost is multiplied by the index at the close of the accounting period and divided by the index at the time of purchase. For example, if a plant addition cost $100,000 at the time of purchase (when the index stood at 110), and at the end of three years the index is 142, conversion of the current value would be as follows:

$100,000 \times 142 \div 110 = $129,091

Depreciation is then determined by dividing the converted value by the number of years in the depreciation schedule.

Equipment. Equipment, which is acquired more often than plant and property, should be converted using cumulative conversions to make allowance for additions for each period. Once annual additions and subtractions are made and the annual total is converted, this converted figure can be carried forward to the following year, where the same process will be followed.

For example, if $100,000 worth of equipment was purchased for a new plant when the index was 110, and the following year $10,000 worth of equipment was added with an index of 125, the $100,000 would be converted at 125, while the $10,000 would be converted at the average index (117.5), assuming the equipment was purchased evenly throughout the year:

$100,000 ×   125 ÷ 110 = $113,636
+$ 10,000 × 117.5 ÷ 110 =   <u>10,682</u>
                      $124,318, Total converted value

The following year, the cumulative converted balance would be carried forward, converted by the index change, and new equipment value converted at the average index change for the period.

Fixed Interest. Interest from investments is converted by multiplying it by the index at the end of the period and dividing by the index at the beginning of the period.

Equity Investments. Equity investments are converted by multiplying them by the index at the end of the accounting period and dividing this result by the index at the time of acquisition.

Stock. Stock is converted by multiplying the stock acquired during the period by the average index during that period and dividing by the index at the beginning of the period. Previously held stock is converted for the whole period, as cash held would be. *See also* **Inflation Accounting.**

Monetary Assets and Liabilities. These are converted in the same way as fixed interest, set out above.

Once all balance sheet items for start and close of the period have been converted, assets are added and liabilities are subtracted, giving the net converted assets. Difference between net converted assets (equity interest) at the beginning and close of the period is the converted retained profit. By adding converted dividends paid, converted gross profit is determined.

SUGGESTED FURTHER READING

Parker, P. W., and P. H. D. Gibbs, *Accounting for Inflation,* Phillips and Drew, London, 1974.
Stidger, R. W., "Inflation Accounting," *World Construction,* New York, May 1975.

NET ECONOMIC WELFARE

Areas for use in Cost Control:
ORGANIZATIONAL AND OPERATIONAL SYSTEMS
DATA RETENTION—FILES AND RECORDKEEPING
MATERIALS AND EQUIPMENT MANAGEMENT
INDUSTRIAL APPLICATIONS
BUSINESS AND COMMERCIAL APPLICATIONS

New economic welfare (NEW), also called measure of economic welfare (MEW), is a technique used to adjust costs to reflect negative aspects. For example, if new material costs of plastic used in a specific product are 20 cents, and the costs of a negative factor such as the equipping and operation of facilities to prevent environmental pollution from the production of that plastic are 2 cents, then the NEW raw material cost totals 22 cents. Even if environmental controls are not used, cost remains at or even exceeds 22 cents, since some adjustment is necessary to indicate all factors affecting the economy. If, for example, no environmental controls are used when the plastic is produced, and it costs 6 cents to later clean up the polluted air, water, etc., caused by its production, the NEW raw material cost increases to 26 cents.

SUGGESTED FURTHER READING

Nordhaus, W., and J. Tobin, *Is Growth Obsolete?* Columbia University Press, New York, 1972.
Samuelson, P. A., *Economics,* McGraw-Hill, New York, 1973.

NET PRESENT VALUE

Areas for use in Cost Control:

ORGANIZATIONAL AND OPERATIONAL SYSTEMS
INDUSTRIAL APPLICATIONS
BUSINESS AND COMMERCIAL APPLICATIONS

Net present value is a technique used to determine the cost/value ratio of proposed capital investments in deciding whether such investments should or should not be made. The technique is especially effective for multiple-stage investments or in comparing alternate investments.

To use the method, use the capital interest rate, applying the discount factor (*see* **Discounted Cash Flow**) to annual cash flows, returning them to the net present value, or the cash figures at the beginning of the project. Net present values for all investments are added and should be greater than the capital cost of the project if the investment is to be made.

SUGGESTED FURTHER READING

Argenti, John, *Management Techniques,* Davlin Publications, Los Angeles, 1969.

NETWORK PLANNING AND ANALYSIS

Areas for use in Cost Control:

ORGANIZATIONAL AND OPERATIONAL SYSTEMS
INDUSTRIAL APPLICATIONS
BUSINESS AND COMMERCIAL APPLICATIONS

Network planning and analysis is used in planning and controlling a complex cost or other problem or a project. Any such problem or project has a sequence of actions, each step dependent upon completion of earlier steps. Timing of each step and the sequence of required action—the *critical path*—determine how long the entire project will take (*see* **Critical Path Analysis**). Other side activities or spin-offs of the project may be planned, but it is the *critical path* that must be completed. Through planning and analysis of the network of activities, it may be possible to shorten the critical path, speeding completion of the project and cutting costs.

In network planning and analysis the following aspect of the project should be considered:

1. Setting out the *critical path*
2. Determining the timing of separate aspects of the project when various noncritical phases become critical
3. Determining the time required for each phase of the project
4. Determining the cost effect of reducing the time required for various phases of the project

A good number of network planning and analysis techniques have been developed. Major techniques are **branching networks, decision trees, critical path analysis** (CPA), **program evaluation and review technique** (PERT), **PERT/cost,** and **resource allocation,** which are discussed in detail separately.

Branching Networks. These are used primarily for research projects. The technique is an offshoot of *critical path analysis,* but it additionally provides for alternative network sequences to be used when one sequence cannot be definitely predetermined. Use of the method is generally limited to personnel highly trained in *branching networks.*

Decision Trees. These are used primarily in choosing between projects. A *branching network* chart, similar to a family history tree, is drawn up showing various possible decisions and their probable results. Using this method, it is possible to compare the cost of automating production now, automating in five years, and continuing current production methods indefinitely.

Critical Path Analysis (CPA). This is a term used to cover all of network planning and analysis, as well as a specific technique. CPA differs from other methods, particularly PERT, in that it uses only one estimate of the time and path a project will take.

Program Evaluation and Review Technique (PERT). This technique uses three estimates of the time for each project—an optimistic time, a pessimistic time, and a likely time. A more precise estimate of project completion can be made using PERT.

PERT/Cost. This ratio projects cost estimates in a network system much like the critical path method. This technique gives management an idea of what costs will be incurred and when. As the project proceeds, further calculations will permit watching and controlling day-to-day operating costs.

Resource Allocation. This plan uses *graphic calculations, linear programming,* or *simulation* to decide resources for each aspect of a project.

Results from using network planning and analysis are impressive, with some companies cutting project time in half. Training courses of two weeks or so are sufficient for capable use of the technique.

The technique is best applied to very complex projects. Diagrams (see Fig. 69) can be prepared manually or data can be fed to a computer for fast results.

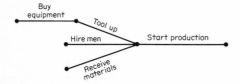

Figure 69. Network analysis.

SUGGESTED FURTHER READING

Battersby, A., *Network Analysis,* Macmillan, New York, 1967.
Beattie, C. J., and R. D. Reader, *Quantitative Management in R&D,* Barnes & Noble, Cranbury, N.J., 1971.
Bull, George, ed., *The Director's Handbook,* McGraw-Hill, London, 1969.

NEW REALITY THEORY

Areas for use in Cost Control:

ORGANIZATIONAL AND OPERATIONAL SYSTEMS
INDUSTRIAL APPLICATIONS
BUSINESS AND COMMERCIAL APPLICATIONS

The new reality theory reduces costs by maintaining professional staff at only the current need level. Such employees are suspended during slack periods, reducing overhead. Depending on the degree of organization, layoffs may be applied first to less efficient workers, rather than by inverse seniority, as union agreements usually require for the general labor force.

SUGGESTED FURTHER READING

Townsend, Robert, *Up the Organization,* Fawcett, New York, 1971.

NONDESTRUCTIVE TESTING

Areas for use in Cost Control:

ORGANIZATIONAL AND OPERATIONAL SYSTEMS
MATERIALS AND EQUIPMENT MANAGEMENT
INDUSTRIAL APPLICATIONS

Nondestructive testing is checking production for unacceptable flaws without ruining the tested product, using such tests as x-ray, temperature flow patterns, magnetic fields, sound waves, liquid penetrating dye and ultraviolet light, and eddy currents. Nondestructive testing reduces costs, since the tested product is not destroyed and can be sold.

SUGGESTED FURTHER READING

Bittel, L. R., *What Every Supervisor Should Know,* McGraw-Hill, New York, 1974.
Juran, J. M., and F. M. Gryna, Jr., *Quality Planning and Analysis: From Product Development through Usage,* McGraw-Hill, New York, 1970.

NONDIRECTIVE INTERVIEWING See Personnel Attitude Measurement.

NO OFFICE TECHNIQUE

Areas for use in Cost Control:

ORGANIZATIONAL AND OPERATIONAL SYSTEMS
MATERIALS AND EQUIPMENT MANAGEMENT

The no office technique is the use of computer terminals at home to eliminate the need (and cost) for an office. Current use of the method is limited to salesmen who transmit needed records and orders by computer and to technical personnel who use home terminals as auxiliary work locations. Some companies are beginning to experiment with complete office replacement by home terminals, however. Work results will be communicated to a central location by computer, and supervisors can audit work both through examination of incoming computer inputs and through visual and audio examination through dialed telecommunications with the employee.

SUGGESTED FURTHER READING

Martin, J., and A. R. D. Norman, *The Computerized Society,* Prentice-Hall, Englewood Cliffs, N.J., 1970.

NO-POACHING AGREEMENT See Antipirating Agreement.

NUCLEAR POWER

Areas for use in Cost Control:

ORGANIZATIONAL AND OPERATIONAL SYSTEMS
MATERIALS AND EQUIPMENT MANAGEMENT
INDUSTRIAL APPLICATIONS

Nuclear power is currently the most economical and viable alternate power source, compared with power from fossil sources—oil, coal, and gas—which have increased dramatically in cost and which are, furthermore, in relatively short supply for long-term planning. Even at current stages of development, electricity generated by nuclear reactors is produced at competitive prices. Increased use, as in all types of mass production, should further reduce costs. Smaller nuclear power plants may solely power large industrial complexes.

Most economical of various nuclear reactors are the fast-breeder types which can eventually produce more fissile nuclei (the source of power obtained) than they use, conserving the uranium, which is converted into plutonium, which fuels the reactor. Regular breeder reactors are refueled with several tons of uranium approximately every two years, while fast-breeder reactors can double inventories of plutonium in 10 to 20 years.

Safety of nuclear power, particularly when it is eventually adapted to individual industrial-complex installations, is an important factor in cost considerations, since the company or companies producing nuclear power for their own industrial use will presumably be financially responsible for damage costs related to any accident. The danger is not that of a nuclear explosion, since reactor design uses fissile material too dilute for such an eventuality. A nonnuclear explosion, however, could damage vital shielding, releasing the vast amounts of radioactivity accumulated in the fuel charge.

Some reactor designs use a triple protection system—fuel cladding, reactor vessel and cooling circuits insulation, and building insulation—to decrease such possibilities, while other designs use only the first two. Fuel cladding is particularly susceptible to leaking, which puts the bulk of protection in the latter case on the insulating qualities of the reactor vessel and cooling circuits. Gas-cooled reactors, which use less power from radioactivity itself, and prestressed concrete pressure vessels seem to offer the best protection combination in this area.

American industries already involved with light-water nuclear reactors for civil purposes include Westinghouse and General Electric. Gulf General Atomic is similarly concerned with high-temperature reactors. At this point, at least, installation and operation costs to these industries are reduced through government subsidies of research, construction, operation, and accident insurance. Insurance economics for industrial coverage at present involves commercial coverage of about 1 part to 7 parts of U.S. government coverage, with the stipulation that industrial insurance premiums are repaid if no damage claims are paid. The U.S. law that determines this plan is due for renewal in 1977, when it may be modified.

SUGGESTED FURTHER READING

Nucleonics Week, McGraw-Hill, New York.
Power and Research Reactors in Member States, International Atomic Energy Agency, Vienna.
Understanding the Atom, Atomic Energy Commission, Washington, D.C.

NUMERICAL CONTROL PRODUCTION

Areas for use in Cost Control:

ORGANIZATIONAL AND OPERATIONAL SYSTEMS
MATERIALS AND EQUIPMENT MANAGEMENT
INDUSTRIAL APPLICATIONS

Numerical control production, also called continuous path production, is the use of computer-controlled equipment to produce specialized and/or complex parts without costly special tooling, test runs, etc. Parts can be sculptured by a cutter, a milling wheel, etc., and controlled by a computer programmed with the part's design. The technique is also used to eliminate the possibility of human error in cutting or working precise and strategic parts. Positioning of work is immediate and precise in such a system, and precision is exact. Additionally, equipment is used up to 20 percent more of the time than when manually controlled.

SUGGESTED FURTHER READING

Martin, J., and A. R. D. Norman, *The Computerized Society,* Prentice-Hall, Englewood Cliffs, N.J., 1970.

NUMERICAL RATING See Personnel Performance Appraisal.

OBJECTIVE RATING

Areas for use in Cost Control:

PSYCHOLOGICAL MOTIVATIONAL MANAGEMENT
FINANCIAL MOTIVATIONAL MANAGEMENT
ORGANIZATIONAL AND OPERATIONAL SYSTEMS

Objective rating is a **performance rating** technique used to measure employee work speed and tempo with an adjustment for job difficulty factors such as the use of foot pedals, heavy weight handling, and eye-hand coordination. Measurements are made for each aspect of the job against numerically expressed standard goals. When the technique is used as the basis for incentive payments, wages rise when the rating exceeds the standard goal. This limits wage costs to the proportion of work accomplished.

SUGGESTED FURTHER READING

Maynard, H. B., ed., *Industrial Engineering Handbook,* 3d ed., McGraw-Hill, New York, 1974.

OCEAN MINING

Areas for use in Cost Control:

ORGANIZATIONAL AND OPERATIONAL SYSTEMS
MATERIALS AND EQUIPMENT MANAGEMENT
INDUSTRIAL APPLICATIONS

Ocean mining, a new source of raw materials, offers possible reductions in the cost of raw materials as land supplies grow shorter and more expensive.

The extent of possible cost savings on raw materials can be estimated from Table 39, which shows the probable supplies of some materials available from ocean bed and surface deposits.

Three ocean mining problems are of primary importance:

1. Development of technology
2. Political aspects
3. Environmental effects

Development of technology. Decreasing mineral and other land supplies and accompanying increased costs, including vast oil price increases, have added incentives for producing a technology that will make ocean mining economically viable. Costs and problems vary with respect to the location of materials in the ocean bed.

Underwater oil and gas drilling are the most advanced at this time, with offshore drilling, floating platforms, semisubmersible platforms, etc. The floating units can be moved; they provide workers' living quarters, equipment, and work space, as well as supporting the drilling rig.

Because nations are only now beginning to divide areas of the ocean bed, division can be influenced by industry management now to further reduce the future cost of materials.

International law has historically provided freedom of the *surface* of the seas, excluding territorial limits (200 miles, at present); but several new methods of dividing the ocean bed for mining and/or agricultural purposes (including fishing and fish-farming) have been proposed. These proposals include:

The continental-shelf concept. This method, set out in the Geneva Continental Shelf Convention, Article VI, states that "where the continental shelf is adjacent to the

Table 39. Estimated Ocean Bed Surface Deposits and Known Global Deposits of Mineral Resources

Mineral resource	Estimated ocean bed surface deposits*		Approximate known global deposits†	
	Tons, millions	Estimated length of supply at present rate of use, years	Tons, millions	Estimated length of supply at present rate of use, years
Aluminum	43,000	1,130	1,170.00	31
Cobalt	5,200	260,000	2.18	110
Copper	7,900	925	308.00	36
Gold	5	5,500	0.01	11
Iron	207,000	480	100,000.00	240
Lead	1,300	370	91.00	26
Manganese	358,000	43,400	800.00	97
Nickel	14,700	15	147,000.00	150
Petroleum	12,000‡	6	60,000.00§	31

*United Nations' "Survey of Oceanbed Mineral Resources."
†U.S. Bureau of Mines' report, "Mineral Facts and Problems."
‡*Offshore* petroleum only.
§Estimated weight.

territories of two or more states whose coasts are opposite each other . . . in the absence of agreement, and unless another boundary line is justified by special circumstances, the boundary is the median line, every point of which is equidistant from the nearest points of the base lines from which the breadth of the territorial sea of each state is measured. . . ." Using this method, countries owning small islands may expand their holdings with very little coastal land. Both the French and the British hold islands that would give them ocean bed rights that are nowhere near their countries, for example.

International law, including decisions of the International Court of Justice, has upheld this division of the ocean bed to the limit of extending full national sovereignty to continental shelves.

Common domain. Countries without coastlines naturally object to division of the ocean bed in any way that does not give them an equal share. One proposal of the International Law Commission of the United Nations limited coastal territorial rights by depth of water, with suggested depths ranging from 200 to 500 meters. With mining at 1,000-meter depths already possible, coastal states found these limits unsatisfactory.

Proposals have also been made to divide nonterritorial waters proportionately among all nations.

Global leasing. A third proposal is the leasing of nonterritorial areas by a global agency, such as the United Nations. Moneys earned from the mining rights would be returned to the various economies via research grants for improved technology or other benefits. Without a truly universal global administering agency, however, such powers might prove difficult to regulate and enforce.

Trench division. Ocean bed rights extending from coastal areas to the great ocean trenches have also been proposed.

After a division decision is finally reached, various national and regional proposals will divide each country's share of the ocean bed. The resulting policies will have a vast influence over raw material costs for the future. Will companies be able to buy or lease at a very low cost or for a very long period the mineral rights *before* ocean mining becomes a major source of raw materials? If so, the company holding such leases or rights will eventually have the same material cost advantages that developing industries controlling iron, oil, and other land resources have had.

SUGGESTED FURTHER READING

Friedmann, W., *The Future of the Oceans,* George Braziller, New York, 1971.

LaQue, F., "Deep Ocean Mining: Prospects and Anticipated Short-term Benefits," *Pacem in Maribus,* 1970.

Proceedings from the Symposium on the International Regime of the Seabed, Rome, 1970.

Wenk, E., Jr., "Map of Ocean Floor Resources," *Scientific American,* September 1969.

OFFICE COMMUNES

Areas for use in Cost Control:

ORGANIZATIONAL AND OPERATIONAL SYSTEMS
MATERIALS AND EQUIPMENT MANAGEMENT
INDUSTRIAL APPLICATIONS
BUSINESS AND COMMERCIAL APPLICATIONS

Office communes are fully equipped offices established by a company, trade association, or government and shared by a group of companies to reduce operating costs. For example, one office commune established in Burbank, California, provided individual company facilities for about 12 companies at $6,000 a year each, compared with the approximate $60,000 per year that experts estimate individually established offices would cost each user.

Office commune costs are most efficiently reduced when user companies are in related but not competitive fields. This allows the joint use of specialized equipment and services such as management information data. In addition to office space and furnishings; secretarial, photocopying, Telex, accounting, warehouse, and distribution facilities are shared.

SUGGESTED FURTHER READING

Paulden, S., "Office Communes," *The Financial Times,* London, Aug. 12, 1974.

OFFICE CONCEPT

Areas for use in Cost Control:

ORGANIZATIONAL AND OPERATIONAL SYSTEMS
INDUSTRIAL APPLICATIONS
BUSINESS AND COMMERCIAL APPLICATIONS

The office concept is the viewing of each major job as an *office,* with a group of responsibilities and authorities that are quite separate from the worker who *holds* the office. Thus, duties and authority accompanying a specific job are carried out more effectively, improving overall efficiency and lowering labor and other costs. Scope of the position should be defined and should not be altered without organizational reasons, so that more precise attention is allowed to job parts. For example, an executive magazine editor who happens to enjoy proofreading does not waste his or her expensive time doing so using the office concept because the *office* is too senior for that sort of duty. Instead, he or she concentrates on the responsibilities of the job or office—such as planning and making industry contacts.

SUGGESTED FURTHER READING

Mann, R., ed., *The Arts of Top Management,* McGraw-Hill, New York, 1970.

OFFICE LANDSCAPING See Panoramic Office Planning (POP).

OFFICE LAYOUT

Areas for use in Cost Control:

WORK PLACE MOTIVATIONAL MANAGEMENT
ORGANIZATIONAL AND OPERATIONAL SYSTEMS
INDUSTRIAL APPLICATIONS
BUSINESS AND COMMERCIAL APPLICATIONS

Office layout can reduce costs through improved work flow (see Fig. 70), increased use of space per square foot, and work place motivation. Good office layout provides sufficient space for work and needed materials storage, sufficient movement to decrease boredom, freedom from distractions, and good physical conditions such as good lighting, ventilation, and heating and satisfactory furnishings and decoration.

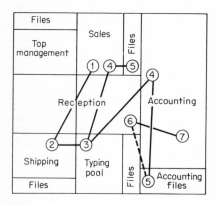
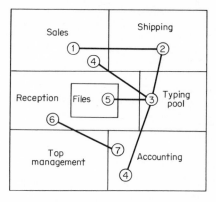

Figure 70. Comparison of work sequence flow in two office layouts.

Working Space. Large companies often establish space allotted per employee according to employee grade or status. An area of 5 ft by 5 ft may be allowed for a typist, for example, while middle managerial staff merit office space of 10 ft by 14 ft. The working areas should allow space for a desk, chair, and other equipment as needed. Aisles between desks in typing pools or other multiple-employee offices should be 4 ft wide or more in busy areas, 3 ft wide or more in fringe areas.

Open offices for subordinate employees have become popular with management, because supervision is easier. Other advantages include less overall space needed; easier heating, lighting, and ventilation; and greater layout flexibility. Filing cabinets and 3- or 4-ft wall dividers may be used to separate work areas and to help control noise factors.

Work areas should be arranged to give an even flow of work in sequence. *See also* **Charting; Working Conditions Improvement.**

Desk size should be standardized. All typists' desks may be 4½ by 2½ ft, for example, while supervisors' desks are 5 by 2½ ft. Two-pedestal desks offer additional filing space with no extra cost in floor space. L-shaped desks are particularly useful for employees using various types of equipment.

Chairs should be adjustable, and should be adjusted to the correct height and position for individual employees.

Actual use of the desk-top work area should be arranged to keep current work in front of the employee, work to be done to the right, and outgoing work to the left. The telephone should be placed to the left, while the back of the desk should hold reference materials. Layout would be reversed for a left-handed employee.

Layout of desks, files, etc., should depend on work sequence and flow, as should general office layout (see Fig. 71). Such layout should pass work smoothly from one

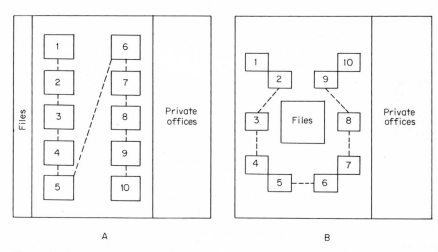

Figure 71. Comparison of interoffice layout.

station to the next. In example A, work flow is logical but involves a long walk from clerk 5 to clerk 6. Needed files may be a considerable distance from any clerk. In example B, distance between clerks in the work sequence is short, and no clerk has more than a few feet to walk to centralized files.

1. Order is received.
2. Order is processed and shipped.
3. Invoice is typed.
4. Copies of invoice to accounting and sales.
5. Invoices are filed.
6. Payment is received.
7. Payment is recorded.

Lighting. Both natural and artificial light should be available. Reflection and glare can be reduced with tinted window glass and absorption colors in decorating. Indirect lighting provides more even distribution when reflected from a light-colored ceiling.

Heating. Temperature should be maintained at an even 65 to 68° for best work. New heating methods are being developed to reduce costs of traditional gas- or oil-fired systems. Solar heating and air conditioning are already in operation in some office buildings. Generally, a screen of piped water is placed on the building roof, heated by the sun, and channeled through the building. As such systems develop, costs will be lowered; but already solar heating cost is comparable to other forms of costs in some installations.

Distractions. Internal noises, such as equipment noise, talking, and telephones, can be controlled through use of sound-absorption material for floors, ceilings, area dividers, etc. Individual offices are advised for very noisy operations. External sound, such as highway noise, can be controlled by sound-absorption material and double doors and windows.

Aesthetics. Motivation is strongly affected by office decoration. Cheerful, warm colors such as yellows are especially good. Bright accessories in red and orange are effective. Use of lighter colors will aid lighting if window space is minimal. Furniture, flooring, draperies, etc., should be chosen for aesthetic reasons as well as functional ones.

SUGGESTED FURTHER READING

Saphier, M., *Office Planning and Design,* McGraw-Hill, New York, 1968.

OFFICE MACHINERY AND EQUIPMENT

Areas for use in Cost Control:

WORK PLACE MOTIVATIONAL MANAGEMENT

MATERIALS AND EQUIPMENT MANAGEMENT

By 1985, all office work *could* be handled by computerized equipment. But as recently as 1970, at least 75 percent of U.S. paperwork was still handled by electromechanical or manual methods. As systems are automated or brought up to date, it is important to know which types of office machinery and equipment can save costs.

The starting point when considering any new office machinery or equipment (including computerized methods) should be to compare present costs with projected costs (see Table 40). Current operational costs include clerical salaries, current equipment depreciation (if any), repairs, value of office space used, and cost of supplies. New-equipment operation costs include depreciation of equipment, operator's wages, equipment repairs, value of office space used, and cost of supplies. Additionally, it is necessary to consider whether the present equipment or speed of operation can be used and still meet company needs.

If a new piece of automated equipment can, for example, triple the production of a single clerical worker, salary paid will be greatly reduced and equipment cost can be considerably greater. The overall savings, however, must be great enough to make a changeover to new equipment and the resulting new methods of operation worthwhile.

Table 40. Comparison of Current and New Equipment Use Costs

Current operation (with current equipment)	Projected operation (with new equipment)
Clerical salary	Operator's salary
Equipment depreciation	Equipment depreciation
Equipment repairs	Equipment unkeep
Value of office space	Value of office space
Supplies used	Supplies used
Speed of operation	Speed of operation
	Expansion of production possibilities

The following checklist provides a guide to newer types of office equipment that may reduce costs:

1. *Typewriters.* Noiseless machines, electric typewriters, flat-bed typewriters, Vari-typers, wide-carriage machines, and automatic typewriters are available. At the most up-to-date end of the scale, computerized typewriters can now lay out and type business forms and letters dictated directly into the computer with no human operation. A predetermined business vocabulary must be used.

2. *Dictating Equipment.* Centralized dictation systems have been devised, using the telephone system to link an executive directly to a dictating machine. The operation is said to double the average number of words per typist.

3. *Duplicating and Reproduction Equipment.* Flat-bed and rotary stenciling equipment, simplified offset lithographic processes, automatic typesetting, electronic scanners, photocopying, and microfilming systems are available. Cost depends primarily on the quality, quantity, and speed of duplication desired.

4. *Addressing Equipment.* Metal plates and waxed stencils have largely been replaced by computerized printout equipment that automatically prints any number of copies of an address list on gummed labels.

5. *Calculating Equipment.* Hand-operated and electrical models are still used, but computerized models that print results on dials offer speed and economy. Miniaturized models are especially popular, are low in original cost, and use very little office space.

6. *Adding Equipment.* Listing machines with full keyboards, 10 keys, and 12 keys are being replaced by computerized models. Some of these relay stock or other information to the central computer as well as adding figures.

7. *Accounting Equipment.* Includes computerized printout calculators and adding-listing machines.

8. *Punched-Card Machines* are mechanized processes for sorting and/or tabulating information.

9. *Electronic Data Processing Equipment.* See **Electronic Data Processing** for complete detailing of equipment to automatically store data, transfer them, and solve problems with them.

SUGGESTED FURTHER READING

Hollingdale, S. H., and G. C. Tootill, *Electronic Computers,* Penguin, Baltimore, 1965.
Schuh, J. F., *Principles of Automation,* Macmillan, New York, 1966.
Wilsing, W. C., *Office Machines,* Irwin, Homewood, Ill., 1974.

OFFICE MECHANIZATION AND AUTOMATION

Areas for use in Cost Control:

ORGANIZATIONAL AND OPERATIONAL SYSTEMS
MATERIALS AND EQUIPMENT MANAGEMENT
BUSINESS AND COMMERCIAL APPLICATIONS

Office mechanization and automation reduce costs through faster work and the ensuing labor savings. For greatest cost reduction, equipment should be in use the maximum possible time each working day. To calculate possible economies, cost of the use of any equipment can be spread over average workloads for a seven-year period. For example, if an automatic typewriter costs $1,000 and is used approximately 20 hours per week for 7 years, the prorated cost of the machine will be slightly more than 14 cents an hour. At the same time, if the machine doubles the output of a $5-an-hour typist using a standard typewriter with an hourly machine cost of about 5 cents an hour, the saving per typed page should amont to more than 37 cents (see Table 41).

Possible cost reductions should be calculated for all equipment being considered for use to provide a basis for comparison and choice. *See also* **Automation.**

Table 41. Comparison of Typing Costs for 10 Manuscript Pages

Standard typewriter × 1.5 hours	$ .125
Typist × 1.5 hours	7.50
Total cost	$7.625
Per-page cost	$ .76
Automatic typewriter × 0.75 hour	$ .106
Typist × 0.75 hour	3.75
Total cost	$3.856
Per-page cost	$ .39

SUGGESTED FURTHER READING

Dunlop, J. T., ed., *Automation and Technological Change,* Prentice-Hall, Englewood Cliffs, N.J., 1962.

OFFICE METHODS RESEARCH (OMR)

Areas for use in Cost Control:
ORGANIZATIONAL AND OPERATIONAL SYSTEMS
PAPERWORK—DESIGN AND FLOW SYSTEMS
DATA RETENTION—FILES AND RECORDKEEPING
MATERIALS AND EQUIPMENT MANAGEMENT
INDUSTRIAL APPLICATIONS
BUSINESS AND COMMERCIAL APPLICATIONS

Office methods research (OMR) is the use of a research team to develop more efficient and/or lower-cost work methods, in much the same way that a production research team develops new products or new production methods or alters current methods to lower costs and/or increase efficiency.

Beginning OMR. Choose researchers who know and understand office work, who are creative, and who take the initiative in a work situation. These employees may be promoted from within the company, since they will have a good understanding of existing conditions and methods. Choice of male or female researchers should depend on areas ministered to by OMR, as well as on the ability of the individual. If employees who will ultimately use the new methods developed by OMR are primarily female, for example, women OMR executives may be able to install the new methods more easily.

Establishing OMR. A competitive spirit may be established in industrial companies where production and office cost reductions are compared by percentage of overall reduction. Contests, posted notices of comparisons, and comparisons published in the company newspaper or magazine are a few effective ways to establish a competitive spirit.

Research employees should *sell* new work methods to line management rather than force the issue.

Office equipment and forms should be studied, as well as work methods, and redesigned when efficiency can be increased or costs reduced by this means.

Research that establishes a time-saving method for one office does not necessarily indicate that the same method will save time and costs in any similar office. The method should be adapted and refined for each new installation. Such adaptation may save more time than the original new method, in which case it should be introduced in the refined version to the first office.

Basic research of existing methods should be carried out and changes made before work measurement techniques, such as checking standard times, are used. For example, if a section of a company's files are to be transferred to computer data banks, measurement of current filing methods is a waste of time and money.

Using machines of various, rather than standardized, makes can help the OMR employee keep abreast of new and cost-reducing equipment. If nothing but brand R typewriters have been used in an office for several years, for example, and brand S develops a fully automatic machine, it may be some time before trade advertising or other methods bring news of the development. The company that uses several makes of equipment, on the other hand, will be more likely to receive early demonstrations of improved machines.

Methods Review. Before tackling individual methods problems, a detailed review of all office procedures should be carried out by the OMR staff, including:

1. Problems of each work process.
2. Equipment specifications and records.
3. Forms specifications.
4. Work specifications for all jobs.

Problems of each work process should be detailed in written form. These can include bottlenecks such as where there is just one mimeograph machine when all insurance agency sales records for six districts must be produced during a single two-hour period.

Equipment specifications and records are checked to see how they relate to problems. For example, are there other machines in the office that can be used to duplicate the six sets of sales records? Can the Xerox also be used? Are any of the districts small enough to use carbon copies made on a typewriter?

Forms specifications are reviewed and changes that will increase efficiency or reduce costs are initiated. In the example above, if the insurance company districts are small enough (10 or fewer salespeople), the sales report form can be redesigned in a Redi-set format, eliminating all need for any mimeographing other than one master list at agency level.

Work specifications for all jobs should also be checked. For example, if all district sales records are combined into one agency sales record, broken down by salesperson and district, there will be only one form to prepare and one form to mimeograph. Additionally, this method allows both salesperson and district comparison of performance. Increased competitive spirit can provide motivation for increased sales.

In reviewing these areas, the following factors should be considered:

1. Cost of the method
2. Work steps required and the length of time each takes
3. Work flow
4. Number of employees, related to overtime required, slack time, etc.
5. Equipment used and its cost compared with labor saved
6. Office organizational structure
7. Value of each work sequence compared with its cost

Work Sequence Specification. Once the review is completed, a written work sequence specification should be prepared setting out minimum acceptable work in each sequence, method of work to be used, and the cost. For example, if letters are opened by a clerk, scanned for content, passed on to secretaries, scanned for content, and finally passed on to the addressee, a great deal of time and money are being wasted. For very senior executives, it may be necessary for the secretary to screen incoming mail. For other employees, letters should be delivered directly to the persons addressed. Letters addressed to a department or the company in general will still need to be screened by a competent person. A sequence specification in such a case would be written as follows:

1. Incoming letters addressed to the company president are delivered to the president's secretary for screening.

2. Incoming letters addressed to other employees are delivered directly to each.

3. Letters not addressed to individuals are delivered to head clerk X for screening and distribution.

Harold Longman, chief O&M officer for Unilever for 20 years, states that most office work can be broken into three parts:

1. Sorting
2. Summarizing
3. Reproduction

By identifying the primary element in a given task and eliminating all but the basic necessary work in this area, the task can be simplified and its cost reduced. In the example above setting out the handling of incoming mail, the basic work element is sorting. In the revised work method, interim sorting steps and unrelated summarizing (reading of the material by employees unqualified to pass judgment on the contents) are eliminated.

Installation of New Methods. Once new work methods are created, they should be tested in operation before being installed throughout the office. If possible, the OMR employee should check the method personally to make sure it increases work efficiency and/or reduces costs.

Operational details of the new method must be explained to employees expected to use them, with special training sessions where required. OMR staff should be on hand during the first days of operation to answer questions and aid supervisory personnel in the changeover from old to new work methods.

Follow-up. Periodic follow-up review of new work methods should determine:

1. Amount of improved work efficiency
2. Decrease in time used
3. Reduction in labor costs
4. Possibilities for further improvement of the method

SUGGESTED FURTHER READING

Longman, H. H., *How to Cut Office Costs,* International Publications Service, New York, 1972.

OFFICE ORGANIZATION

Areas for use in Cost Control:

ORGANIZATIONAL AND OPERATIONAL SYSTEMS

INDUSTRIAL APPLICATIONS

BUSINESS AND COMMERCIAL APPLICATIONS

Office organization is the planning of work location and flow for the most efficient operation. Costs can be reduced by choosing the most suitable type of organization and the most effective installation of such a system.

Office organization type should be determined by work or production needs. Three types of organization should be considered:

1. Centralization
2. Decentralization
3. Network organization with central control

Centralization. In this office organization technique, one large central office serves all departments of the business or industry. Typists, stenographers, clerks, etc., form a single work pool, drawn on by departmental employees as needed.

Advantages of the technique include:

1. Need for fewer employees, since work can be more evenly distributed
2. Closer and simpler supervision of clerical work
3. Office layout and conditions designed for optimum work production
4. Optimum use of complex office equipment, such as automatic typewriters and computers
5. Less duplication of filing and recordkeeping

Disadvantages for the technique include:

1. Work priorities must be assigned, seldom pleasing everyone.

2. Centralized employees seldom become familiar with all phases of operations, requiring more supervisory assistance.

3. Employee boredom is apt to be greater, because centralized operations lend themselves to specialization with one employee typing all invoices, one typing all purchase orders, etc.

Decentralization. This technique is more convenient from the individual executive's point of view because it provides each work area or department with its own office staff. Employees are less apt to be bored and they learn more about their particular department than centralized employees. On the other hand, work is more likely to be duplicated, more employees are needed, complex equipment is not economical since there are fewer employees to use it, and good supervision may not be possible.

Network Organization with Central Control. This technique combines the advantages of both centralization and decentralization. Area or departmental offices are maintained, but files, training, and complex equipment are located centrally with area employees scheduling use of these facilities as required.

SUGGESTED FURTHER READING

Mills, G., and O. Standingford, *Office Organization and Methods,* Pitman, New York, 1972.

OPEN-DOOR TECHNIQUE

Areas for use in Cost Control:

PSYCHOLOGICAL MOTIVATIONAL MANAGEMENT
ORGANIZATIONAL AND OPERATIONAL SYSTEMS
INDUSTRIAL APPLICATIONS
BUSINESS AND COMMERCIAL APPLICATIONS

The open-door technique is the encouragement of all employees to present their work problems and/or grievances to any company executive, bypassing intermediate supervisors where desired. Use of the technique can reduce costs by decreasing the necessity for labor union activity in settling grievances, through increased status motivation, and through more complete managerial awareness of operational problems at all levels.

SUGGESTED FURTHER READING

Marsh, A. I., and E. O. Evans, *The Dictionary of Industrial Relations,* Hutchinson, London, 1973.
Roberts, H. S., *Roberts' Dictionary of Industrial Relations,* Bureau of National Affairs, Inc., Washington, D.C., 1966.

OPEN-END PRICING

Areas for use in Cost Control:

ORGANIZATIONAL AND OPERATIONAL SYSTEMS
MATERIALS AND EQUIPMENT MANAGEMENT
INDUSTRIAL APPLICATIONS

Open-end pricing is the sale of goods without specification of a price. Usually the sale is a contractual one guaranteeing the buyer specified quantities of a product or material; but the seller is protected from possible losses due to increased cost of materials or labor needed to produce the goods. The method operates to the advantage of the seller and should be implemented where possible with goods to be sold. As a buyer, a company should avoid open-end pricing whenever possible, since it offers no control of materials' costs.

SUGGESTED FURTHER READING

Ammer, D. S., *Materials Management,* Irwin, Homewood, Ill., 1968.

OPERATING PROCEDURES CHECKING

Areas for use in Cost Control:

ORGANIZATIONAL AND OPERATIONAL SYSTEMS
INDUSTRIAL APPLICATIONS

When checking operating procedures to make sure they are efficient and low-cost, the following checklist of questions prepared by the American Management Association, New York, is a sound guide.

MATERIAL

1. Can cheaper material be used without impairing quality?
2. Can lighter-gauge material be used advantageously? Heavier-gauge?
3. Can standard stock parts be purchased?
4. Can some use be found for scrap and rejected parts?
5. Is material received in the most economical length? Size? Weight?
6. Is it utilized to the fullest?
7. Should we change from "make" to "buy," or from "buy" to "make"?

DESIGN

1. Can a part be eliminated completely? Partly?
2. Will it help to change tolerances? Specifications?
3. Can design be changed to make fabrication easier? Cheaper?

SEQUENCE

1. Is every operation necessary? Can part of an operation be eliminated?
2. Is every operation performed at the right time? In the right place? In the right way?
3. Is the plant layout the best that can be obtained?
4. Can operations be combined? Separated?

5. Is it economical to use conveyors to move materials?
6. Would change in lot size help?
7. Can inspection be made a part of operations?
8. Can operations be performed while material is in transit?

TOOLS, GAUGES, EQUIPMENT, AND WORK PLACE

1. Is the machine the best type for the job? Can it be improved? Is it in good condition?
2. Is it running at the right speed?
3. Would it be economical to make it automatic?
4. Are the machine controls conveniently located? Are they easy to use? Are they safe? Can they be made automatic?
5. Must the operator continue holding controls after the machine starts for safety's sake or merely because controls are made that way?
6. Is material received and disposed of in suitable containers? Delivered to point of use? Is there any unnecessary handling?
7. Are tools and materials pre-positioned in proper sequence?
8. Is it necessary to use clamps? If so, are clamps quick-acting?
9. Is it easy to locate parts in a fixture?
10. Can automatic feed be used?
11. Is disposal automatic?
12. Are tools and fixtures the best that can be designed for the job?
13. Can combination tools be used?
14. Are proper gauges quickly available? Easy to use?
15. Can parts be made in multiples? One at a time? With another part?
16. Is the work place properly laid out?

OPERATOR

1. Can operator perform work either sitting or standing?
2. Does operator do unnecessary positioning? Holding? Reaching? Bending?
3. Is operator properly performing the job? Would further instruction help?
4. Will it help to change to a taller operator? A shorter one? A more dexterous one?
5. Is material handling by operator reduced to a minimum?
6. Are both hands productively occupied?
7. Is the work balanced between the two hands?
8. Can work now being done by the hands be relieved by foot devices? Automatic devices? Holding jigs? Indexing fixtures?
9. Are operators on similar jobs using the same methods?

SUGGESTED FURTHER READING

Cost Control and the Supervisor, American Management Assn., New York, 1966.

OPERATING SYSTEMS

Areas for use in Cost Control:

ORGANIZATIONAL AND OPERATIONAL SYSTEMS
DATA RETENTION—FILES AND RECORDKEEPING
MATERIALS AND EQUIPMENT MANAGEMENT
INDUSTRIAL APPLICATIONS
BUSINESS AND COMMERCIAL APPLICATIONS

Operating systems are partially automated computer control systems which allow organization and application of computers by manufactured devices. Human operation is reduced, lowering both the likelihood of costly errors and the direct labor costs. Fully automated operating systems are in developmental stages and should be available soon.

Operating systems are particularly useful for jobs where setup time is disproportionate to running time. For example, if it takes the programmer 10 minutes to set up a one-minute mathematical run, 9 of every 10 minutes of computer time are used inefficiently. By programming automated equipment to set up this type of job, which it can do almost instantaneously, efficiency of computer use can be increased by perhaps 80 percent or more.

When more unusual or complex programs require intervention by a programmer, the operating system is used to check correct sequence of processing or job priority, optimum use of tapes, etc. Time restraints may be implemented by the operating system, program errors are trapped, and the computer operator is given instructions for unautomated work to be done.

Multi-access, the sharing of several processing units for multiple jobs, can also be precisely scheduled and implemented by the operating system.

Operating systems are written by systems writers. These permanent programs become part of the hardware, or equipment, and all subsequent software is subject to their basic operating rules.

Three basic types of operating systems are used:

1. Batch operating systems
2. Multi-access operating systems
3. Real-time operating systems

Batch Operating Systems. Here, a "batch" of work is given to the computer. The operating system automatically assigns processing priorities, and each item is processed separately and automatically in order. Results are usually provided in line-printed hard copy.

Multi-access Operating Systems. Several users requiring different programs share a computer. The system processes on a basis of the user's equal share of the time available, automatically switching programs, as well as providing security of information stored in the data banks.

Real-Time Operating Systems. These allow multiple use of one program. For example, 1,000 stockbrokers may have access to a program that provides current stock quotations.

ADVANTAGES OF OPERATING SYSTEMS

Operating systems of all three types offer several advantages, including:

1. *Speed*—decisions as well as use are faster when controlled by the computer.
2. *Complexity* is handled more accurately and more rapidly by the computer.
3. *User error is checked* by the computer.

COST FACTORS OF OPERATING SYSTEMS

The most important cost factor is that more work can be processed through the computer using an operating system than through one relying on human control, lowering the cost per item. If a company has ample work to make full use of the system, this is the economical choice. If, however, work is minimal, the permanent program hardware costs may offset the processing savings. Additionally, very complex operations or those requiring security will be more efficient with operating systems' use, even when maximum use of the computer is not required. Martin Warwick, International Computers, estimates that an operating system works up to 10,000 times faster than a human processor.

SUGGESTED FURTHER READING

Baecher, H. D., "The Impact of Multiaccess," *Computer Bulletin,* March 1968.
Cuttle, G., and P. B. Robinson, eds., *Executive Programs and Operating Systems,* American Elsevier, New York, 1970.
Proceedings of the A.C.M. Symposium on Operating Systems Principles, Gatlinburg, Tenn., May 1968.
Rosen, S., *Programming Systems and Languages,* McGraw-Hill, New York, 1967.

OPERATIONAL TESTING

Areas for use in Cost Control:

ORGANIZATIONAL AND OPERATIONAL SYSTEMS
INDUSTRIAL APPLICATIONS
BUSINESS AND COMMERCIAL APPLICATIONS

Operational testing is a quality-control technique that measures equipment or worker performance during actual operations. Use of the technique reduces costs by pinpointing unacceptable aspects of the operation, which can then be corrected. The method is considered more satisfactory than equipment and labor testing under hypothetical conditions which may not duplicate all aspects of the actual process.

Testing should be limited to factors needed to acquire predetermined significant operational data.

SUGGESTED FURTHER READING

Weinberg, Sidney, *Profit through Quality,* Cahners Publishing, Boston, 1970.

OPERATIONS COSTING

Areas for use in Cost Control:

ORGANIZATIONAL AND OPERATIONAL SYSTEMS
DATA RETENTION—FILES AND RECORDKEEPING
BUSINESS AND COMMERCIAL APPLICATIONS

Operations costing applies separate **costing** to each type of operation when cost/profit relationships are shown for services rather than products. For example, if a company provides a delivery service, cost/profit per pound-mile will be determined. The method can detail types of deliveries with too high a cost ratio necessitating cost reduction or service charge increases.

SUGGESTED FURTHER READING

Brock, H. R., *Cost Accounting: Theory and Practice,* McGraw-Hill, New York, 1971.

OPERATIONS RESEARCH (OR)

Areas for use in Cost Control:

ORGANIZATIONAL AND OPERATIONAL SYSTEMS
INDUSTRIAL APPLICATIONS
BUSINESS AND COMMERCIAL APPLICATIONS

Operations research (OR), also called operational research and management science, is the scientific analysis and solution of cost and other problems. OR generally becomes a worthwhile investment in companies that employ 500 or more workers. When OR techniques are understood and correctly applied, cost reductions can be large, as OR redefines activities and resources and pinpoints those needing change for more economical operation.

The following list contains OR techniques:

1. **Cybernetics** is a technique (usually electronically controlled) used to control operations, processes, machines, etc.

2. **Decision theory** uses complex mathematical theories to correct inaccurate forecasts.

3. **Decision trees** use network diagrams to show various possible decisions and their cost outcomes. The most economical outcome is chosen and adopted.

4. **Economic-batch reordering quantity** and retailing cost control calculate the most economical-sized lot of materials or goods to order from a supplier.

5. **Gaming** uses mathematical formulas to forecast probable actions of customers, competitors, etc.

6. **Information theory** uses mathematical formulas to develop cost reduction and information plans.

7. **Mathematical programming** translates a company's resources into mathematical equation terms to choose the optimum uses of such resources. Variations within the technique include *linear, integer, quadratic, separable,* and *transportation programming.*

8. **Mathematical statistics** are used to clarify confusing cost or other figures. Methods used in this technique include *experiments design,* **technological forecasting, stock control,** *random sampling, regression analysis,* **sequential analysis,** *statistical quality control,* and **variance analysis.**

9. **Models** are the construction of hypothetical mathematical operations to determine how a planned change will affect the whole operation.

10. **Monte Carlo** is a form of simulation used to analyze a business situation that has been complicated by one or more random factors.

11. **Network planning and analysis** is used to schedule and control a complex task using **critical path analysis, program evaluation and review technique (PERT), PERT/Cost, resource allocation, branching networks,** and **decision trees.**

12. **Portfolio selection** is used to choose new markets or products by translating advantages and disadvantages into mathematical equations.

13. **Process control** includes several computerized methods for controlling complicated production or operational procedures.

14. **Production control** includes several methods of scheduling for optimum production, including **simulation, critical path analysis, heuristic methods,** and **mathematical programming.**

15. **Replacement control** is used to determine the best time to replace equipment, tools, plant, and employees by forecasting expenses connected with these factors, the term of their useful life, etc.

16. **Simulation** is the representation of possible results from alternate operational methods to determine whether they could do as good a job or better than current methods at a lower cost.

17. **Stock control** is used to determine optimum stock levels needed by considering such factors as work flow, transportation and distribution, costs of storage, and quantity of materials or products used or needed.

18. **Technological forecasting** uses mathematical equations to predict future trends and markets.

19. **Utility theory** is used in determining the size of a potential risk and assessing the impact of that risk on a specific operation.

SUGGESTED FURTHER READING

Cyert, R. M., and L. A. Welsch, *Management Decision Making,* Penguin, Baltimore, 1971.

Sivazlian, B. D., and Larry E. Stanfel, *Optimization Techniques in Operations Research,* Prentice-Hall, Englewood Cliffs, N.J., 1974.

OPPORTUNITY COSTING

Areas for use in Cost Control:

ORGANIZATIONAL AND OPERATIONAL SYSTEMS
INDUSTRIAL APPLICATIONS

Opportunity costing is a forecasting technique used to predict costs *if* a specific change in production is implemented. Use of the method consists of determining what else could be done with an asset. This is used to determine the opportunity cost of the asset. For example, equipment may be used only half time, producing $20,000 in profits annually, yet have a book value of $30,000. If only half-capacity production of the product manufactured by the equipment is salable, then its "opportunity cost" is the amount of profit that can be made on this volume of production ($20,000 in this case). If, however, production can be doubled to full capacity and all production sold, the opportunity cost, or real value, of the equipment will be doubled to $40,000.

SUGGESTED FURTHER READING

Wood, E. G., *Costing Matters for Managers,* Cahners Publishing Co., Boston, 1974.

OPPORTUNITY COST METHOD

Areas for use in Cost Control:

ORGANIZATIONAL AND OPERATIONAL SYSTEMS
MATERIALS AND EQUIPMENT MANAGEMENT
INDUSTRIAL APPLICATIONS
BUSINESS AND COMMERCIAL APPLICATIONS

The opportunity cost method reduces operating costs by showing how to increase use of company equipment, plant, employees, and other assets.

Use of the method involves considering each asset and determining new or extended uses for it (*see also* **Brainstorming**). For example an employee who scored very well on intelligence and aptitude tests may be used by the company in the mailroom simply because he or she applied for that position or because that position was open. How might his or her abilities be better used by the company?

Or, a department head may want to purchase a piece of equipment worth $3,000 that will be used only two hours a day, saving six hours of manual labor. What alternate equipment could be purchased for the same sum that would save more labor?

In another case, a production employee is asked to give a prospective management employee a tour of the shop. The tour requires an hour and the cost was figured at $5.25, the production worker's wages. Since the production worker's hourly output of $120 worth of goods was lost, cost should have been calculated at $125.25 and a different employee, perhaps a higher-salaried one with lower measurable output, should have been used to conduct the tour.

SUGGESTED FURTHER READING

Argenti, John, *Management Techniques,* Darvin Publishing, Los Angeles, 1969.
Wood, E. G., *Costing Matters for Managers,* Cahners Publishing Co., Boston, 1974.

OPTICAL FIBER COMMUNICATIONS

Areas for use in Cost Control:

ORGANIZATIONAL AND OPERATIONAL SYSTEMS
MATERIALS AND EQUIPMENT MANAGEMENT
INDUSTRIAL APPLICATIONS
BUSINESS AND COMMERCIAL APPLICATIONS

Optical fiber communications are the transmission of telephone calls by light impulses through tiny hairs of glass fibers. Each strand is capable of carrying several thousand calls, television programs, etc., at one time, and as many as 100 strands would use approximately the same space as one conductor in a heavy power cord. Fewer repeaters are required in the method than in current methods, reducing operating costs as well as requiring minimal space.

The method is in advanced experimental stages for interoffice trunk and loop systems, as well as for conventional telephone communication use.

SUGGESTED FURTHER READING

Lapedes, D. N., ed., *Yearbook of Science and Technology,* McGraw-Hill, New York, 1974.

OPTIMUM REACTION RATE METHOD

Areas for use in Cost Control:

ORGANIZATIONAL AND OPERATIONAL SYSTEMS
INDUSTRIAL APPLICATIONS

The optimum reaction rate method limits personnel hiring and training costs to an optimum level by hiring and training the same percentage of the planned recruiting figure as the actual percentage of predicted sales that are achieved. For example, assume that hiring and training costs are budgeted at $10,000 and sales are forecast at $500,000. If actual sales are $400,000 (80 percent of the forecast figure), hiring and training costs are limited to 80 percent of the budgeted sum, or $8,000. If, however, actual sales reach $600,000 (120 percent of the forecast figure), hiring and training expenditures are increased to 120 percent of the budgeted sum, or $12,000.

Inventories needed can be adjusted in the same way, ensuring that only adequate stocks for the current level of sales are maintained.

SUGGESTED FURTHER READING

Buffa, E. S., *Modern Production Management,* Wiley, New York, 1969.
Magee, J. F., and D. M. Boodman, *Production Planning and Inventory Control,* McGraw-Hill, New York, 1967.

OPTION

Areas for use in Cost Control:

ORGANIZATIONAL AND OPERATIONAL SYSTEMS
INDUSTRIAL APPLICATIONS
BUSINESS AND COMMERCIAL APPLICATIONS

The option is a contract that allows the purchaser to buy materials or supplies (exercise the option) at a predetermined price or to withdraw if the price is too high when the contract is due. The technique reduces costs because it allows the purchaser to acquire the needed materials at a good price or to reject the materials if the price on the open market has fallen lower than the contract price and to pay only the small option commission.

SUGGESTED FURTHER READING

Bain, J. S., *Industrial Organization,* Wiley, New York, 1968.

ORGANIZATION AND METHODS (O&M) ANALYSIS

Areas for use in Cost Control:
ORGANIZATIONAL AND OPERATIONAL SYSTEMS
PAPERWORK DESIGN AND FLOW SYSTEMS
DATA RETENTION—FILES AND RECORDKEEPING
MATERIALS AND EQUIPMENT MANAGEMENT
BUSINESS AND COMMERCIAL APPLICATIONS

Organization and methods (O&M) analysis is the evaluation of office work methods and organization and the determination of the use of these to create the most efficient, lowest-cost system. Work methods, procedures, processing, analyzing, data storage, accounting, paperwork, and office research are some of the areas that can be analyzed using O&M techniques.

All aspects of work are usually analyzed by O&M personnel *by department;* that is, a specific work area is evaluated and suggestions for cost reductions and other improvements in the area's work methods and organization are made. For example, O&M might recommend aspects within a work area that could be automated.

WHO SHOULD CARRY OUT O&M ANALYSIS?

For best results, personnel should be professionally trained in O&M techniques. Business management associations, technical colleges, and some universities offer periodic seminars to teach the methods.

Smaller companies may hire a consultant specializing in O&M, but larger firms generally find it worthwhile to train and use their own O&M staff to ensure continuing improvement. In some cases, a department head requests analysis as a special service, and its cost is charged against that department. In other companies, mandatory and periodic O&M analysis is the rule.

O&M analysts should have a good working knowledge of business in general, as well as of their company's activities. Methodical and well-organized persons are particularly recommended for training. At the same time, creativity and imagination can prove extremely helpful in solving problems determined by the analysis.

WHAT AREAS USE O&M?

Major areas that are most likely to benefit from O&M include:

Work methods. Ways of working that were once satisfactory may be uneconomical now. For example, filing was once suitable for most data retention applications, but today microfilming may be a cost-saving and desirable method.

Procedures. These too may require alteration, since new methods may make it possible to eliminate some procedures.

Forms may be updated and simplified for more economical use.

Office equipment should be evaluated and updated where economical. *See also* **Office Mechanization and Automation.**

Work study and measurement can lead to improved method adoption.

Wasted time and materials can be reduced.

THE O&M ANALYSIS

Although the analysis will vary depending on the organizational area or work method being studied, a basic outline that can be applied to all projects is:

1. Determine the goals of the analysis.
2. Collect all relevant data.
3. Analyze the data.
4. Draw conclusions from the data.
5. Determine possible improvements in organization and/or methods.
6. Propose alternative improvements.
7. Decide, with work area head and/or personnel, on alternate improvement to be used.
8. Implement improvement.

In all of these steps, several factors may be compared:

1. Cost efficiency compared with other company- or industrywide standards
2. Work accomplishment compared with other company- or industrywide standards
3. Customer response to work done by the department or area being examined as compared with such attitudes toward other areas of the company or industry
4. Current work and cost performance compared with earlier work and cost performance
5. Quality of work compared with work quality in other departments or companies

O&M Goals. Objectives are primarily to find more efficient work methods and to reduce operating costs. These should be expressed precisely for any project, however. Particularly important in the company as a whole is the elimination of duplicated or overlapping work performed by more than one department, each quite ignorant of the other's activities. Few businesses can match governmental offices in the need for improvements in this area. For example, in tabulating the federal U.S. expenditures for school lunch and related programs in 1968, it was found that 34 departments allotted money. None of these know the precise amount or qualifications of moneys spent through each of the others, nor, in most cases, the names of other departments involved. The federal budget made allotment by department, not detailing all expenditures made in this area. Efficient planning to make sure that some expenditures were not duplicated and others completely missed would seem to be nearly impossible in such cases. Organizational and work method goals are the first step needed to implement more efficient operation—in private business as well as in governmental offices.

O&M Data Collection. Once goals are established, all relevant data must be collected. Cost, technical, and operational information should be included. Methods of obtaining these data may include:

1. Management interviews or discussions with work area supervisors
2. Worker interviews or discussions with employees within the work area
3. Analysis of department reports—operational, accounting, and technical
4. Personal observation of work methods, flow, and procedures
5. Random sampling of work methods

Specific information will vary depending on the work area, but in general the following types of information should be recorded.

1. Job content of each worker and manager; duties and responsibilities
2. Relationship and overlap with other work areas or departments
3. Work flow: path, time, cycle, etc.

4. Work quantity
5. Work quality
6. Costs
7. Work performance times
8. Equipment available; capacity of each item and degree of its use
9. Work place conditions and layout
10. Forms used; their content and design
11. Files used

Analyzing O&M Data. As information is collected, the first step in analysis is to note details that seem to indicate inefficiencies or work overlap. Later, in studying each aspect of the information, inefficiencies can be noted in detail. Overall operation will be examined for unnecessary steps, duplication of effort, costly procedures where cheaper ones will do just as well, etc. For example, in noting that the head of a department has a private secretary who has less than a full day's work to do, the need for a more efficient method of performing the work is listed as a needed improvement.

Procedure charts are frequently used to analyze data. These illustrate the information, making inefficiencies visual, and provide an excellent supplement to **procedure study.**

Possible Improvements. In analyzing data, possible improvements will suggest themselves. These should be carefully noted for later evaluation. **Brainstorming** and other creative thinking techniques may be used to suggest possible improvements, too. Prior knowledge of the work area, discussion with departmental management and workers, and encouraging their suggestions for improvement are other fruitful sources of new ideas.

Proposals and Decisions. Alternate improvements should be proposed in written form for careful evaluation. Such proposals should detail how the change would work, as well as its effect on costs, employees, and equipment. Charts and graphs should be used where these will make the proposed improvement easier to understand. These factors are compared and the best alternatives chosen.

Implementing O&M Proposals. Implementation of O&M proposals is the responsibility of the manager of the work department, but he or she can be aided a great deal by the O&M staff. The first step is to make sure that both managers and workers thoroughly understand the new work methods or organizational changes— why they are better as well as how they will operate. Work procedures should be prepared, and made available to all workers, in written form.

Periodic checks should be made, following a change, to make certain that the new work method is being used and that some employees have not added remnants of the old method from habit. If these holdovers are found, retraining in the new method is necessary.

Checks should also catch further economical refinements in the new work method that are obvious only when it has been put into action.

SUGGESTED FURTHER READING
Neuschel, R. F., *Management Systems in Profit and Growth,* McGraw-Hill, New York, 1976.

ORGANIZATION BY PRODUCT

Areas for use in Cost Control:
ORGANIZATIONAL AND OPERATIONAL SYSTEMS
MATERIALS AND EQUIPMENT MANAGEMENT
INDUSTRIAL APPLICATIONS
BUSINESS AND COMMERCIAL APPLICATIONS

Organization by product divides work and responsibility by product or service to increase efficiency and reduce costs. One functional manager supervises employees, whose work is assigned by product or service (see Fig. 72).

Cost advantages from organization by product stem from the degree of specialization and increased efficiency of each employee. For example, if a production manager is responsible for only one product or group of similar products, he or she can devote a great deal more time to reducing production costs for that product and will also be more familiar with all aspects of the production process and related problems.

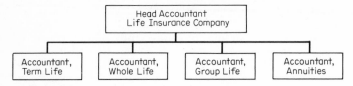

Figure 72. Typical organization by product chart.

SUGGESTED FURTHER READING

Ammer, D. S., *Materials Management,* Irwin, Homewood, Ill., 1968.

OUTPUT BUDGETING

Areas for use in Cost Control:

ORGANIZATIONAL AND OPERATIONAL SYSTEMS
INDUSTRIAL APPLICATIONS
BUSINESS AND COMMERCIAL APPLICATIONS

Output budgeting allocates money to be spent by productivity goal, to provide easier appraisal of cost efficiency. Thus, the costs of materials, labor, etc., for a specific output—such as 5,000 units of product A or 1,000 typed letters—are budgeted, rather than the traditional method of budgeting all labor costs, all material costs, etc. Actual costs are compared with budgeted costs in the same goal areas, and the effectiveness of each goal, costwise, can be quickly determined.

Historical output cost figures are also used to predict costs that would be required in expanded production.

SUGGESTED FURTHER READING

Williams, Alan, *Output Budgeting,* H.M. Printing Office, London, 1967.

OUTPUT COSTING

Areas for use in Cost Control:

ORGANIZATIONAL AND OPERATIONAL SYSTEMS
DATA RETENTION—FILES AND RECORDKEEPING
MATERIALS AND EQUIPMENT MANAGEMENT
INDUSTRIAL APPLICATIONS
BUSINESS AND COMMERCIAL APPLICATIONS

Output costing, also called single costing, applies separate **costing** to each unit of goods or services produced. In a dairy, for example, each quart of milk would be costed by element of cost. The technique shows the proportion of cost for each element, pinpointing areas in need of cost reduction for greatest profitability. For example, if labor is 20 percent of the total cost of producing a quart of milk, while labor is 40 percent of the total cost of producing a pint of cottage cheese, cost reduction techniques such as automation may be needed in cottage cheese production.

SUGGESTED FURTHER READING

Davis, H. S., *Productivity Accounting,* University of Pennsylvania Press, 1955.

OVERHEAD COST CONTROL

Areas for use in Cost Control:

ORGANIZATIONAL AND OPERATIONAL SYSTEMS

INDUSTRIAL APPLICATIONS

Industrialization has created new cost areas in addition to traditional material and labor costs. Buildings, equipment, and plant are examples of such *overheads,* as are indirect material, labor, and expense costs. Some economists have tried to handle these expense items by including overheads in the cost of each unit of production as a basis for pricing. More modern views, however, conclude that prices are determined by competition, and that cost reduction is necessary in order to make a profit. Ideally, pricing is based on a combination of these two lines of thought; competition does determine price to some extent, but the actual cost of production (including overheads) must be taken into consideration. The area of overhead costs is a particularly important area for cost reduction, as overhead costs will become a larger proportion of total production cost as automation expands.

TYPES OF OVERHEAD COSTS

Direct costs are those identified with a particular process or department or those that can be identified with production of a specific product.

Variable costs are those that alter directly in proportion to volume of output and other measures of activity, such as production lot size, utilization of plant, and continuity of production. Costs that have a use rather than a time function generally are variable costs.

Fixed costs are costs generally unaffected by quantity of output. They usually have a time rather than a use function.

Standard costs are calculated by absorbing fixed costs into units of production.

These four types of costs are more complicated than they seem at first glance. In a company with a guaranteed wage for production workers, for example, these labor costs may be categorized as fixed costs. When materials, such as a sand quarry, are bought for planned future use in production, their cost may be called a variable cost.

COST ANALYSIS TECHNIQUES

Not all costs can be neatly placed in one category. To determine fixed and variable components that may be contained in one cost, two basic techniques have been developed:

The **scatter graph** technique charts cost data for a number of periods and a line is drawn midway between high and low points. *Fixed cost* is the low point. *Variable cost* per time unit is the average between the two points, once the fixed cost is subtracted and the remainder is divided by the number of time units used.

The **high-low point method** determines variable costs per unit of production by dividing the difference between the highest and lowest cost for a period by the difference between the highest and lowest measure of production or activity associated with that cost. Fixed cost is determined by subtracting the variable cost from the total cost at a given point.

OVERHEAD COST CLASSIFICATION

Overheads should be broken into functional classification for best cost control. Main overhead classifications are:

1. Administrative overheads
2. Production overheads
3. Sales overheads
4. Distribution overheads

Administrative costs are sometimes separated into *general administrative* costs and *functional overhead* costs.

CONTROLLING OVERHEAD COSTS

Control of overhead costs means defining cost limits and staying inside these limits. Cost reduction can be effected by cutbacks on the part of the person who will do the spending, by sharing of equipment and/or services from other work areas of the company, and by exterior cost cutting of a proposed expenditure.

Fixed costs can be controlled, as well as variable costs. Suggestions for areas of cost reduction include:

1. *Equipment output should be analyzed* as to production cost per manufactured unit and percentage of equipment utilization. Such studies might show a good case for renting equipment on a production/cost basis rather than owning it outright; or they might show underuse, correctable by rearranging labor schedules.

2. *Rearrange recordkeeping to change fixed costs to variable costs* wherever possible, since these can more readily be related to output units.

3. *Use standards of equipment operation,* to include reduced costs stemming from use of more efficient equipment.

4. *Use profitability standards,* with full use of current equipment.

Specific examples of *overhead cost reduction* in practice include:

1. Determine whether plant and office layouts make optimum use of floor space. If not, rearrange areas toward this goal.

2. Determine whether equipment in office or plant is used to its fullest. If not, rearrange schedules for optimum use of equipment.

3. Determine whether plant improvements, such as better insulation, easy-care flooring and walling, etc., would cut overhead costs.

4. Check equipment and plant maintenance programs to determine if care keeps them in optimum working order.

5. Check utility cost control planning. Are electricity, gas, water, telephone, supplies, and mail service used in a conservative manner?

SUGGESTED FURTHER READING

Bierman, H., Jr., and T. R. Dyckman, *Overhead Cost Accounting,* Macmillan, New York, 1971.
Burns, T. J., *Behavioral Aspects of Accounting Data,* Ohio State University Press, Columbus, 1970.
McRae, T. W., *Analytical Management,* Wiley, New York, 1970.

OVERSTAFFING

Area for use in Cost Control:

ORGANIZATIONAL AND OPERATIONAL SYSTEMS

Having more staff than is really needed is one of the most common money wasters. By thoroughly analyzing staff size and applying suitable reductions, it is estimated that the average business can save 10 to 50 percent of its staff cost.

But overstaffing is also one of the most difficult costs to control. Supervisors are hesitant to cut staff, since it reduces their area of responsibility and makes remaining employees grumble as a larger share of the workload falls on their shoulders. Trade unions oppose staff cuts and sometimes go on strike when cuts are made.

Often, overstaffing is caused by hiring the number of persons needed to do the work during peak loads. In normal working situations, the staff then may have a great deal of free time.

Another cause of overstaffing is a reduction in the workload. If orders or sales fall, or if faster, automated equipment is introduced, fewer staff will be needed.

At the same time, it is essential not to cut staff to the point of undermanning, which may mean delays in production, order filling, etc.

To reach a happy medium—the right-sized staff—the following checklist will provide a guide:

1. *Establish the time needed for each job,* such as filling an order or typing an invoice. Multiply this by the average number of such jobs to be done each day. Thus, if typing an invoice takes 5 minutes and 1,200 invoices are produced per day, on an average, a total of 100 hours of typing work per day should be required. Allowing time for breaks, 14 typists should be able to complete the daily workload.

2. *Check job procedures to make sure they are economical.* Are unnecessary steps included? Would doing the job a different way save time? Can rearrangement of the office or plant save time?

3. *Peak loads can best be handled by doing essential work first,* asking staff to work harder, controlling vacation schedules, and using overtime when it becomes absolutely necessary. Temporary employees may also be hired to handle surplus work.

SUGGESTED FURTHER READING

Cost Control and the Supervisor, American Management Assn., New York, 1966.

OWN RISK TECHNIQUE

Areas for use in Cost Control:

ORGANIZATIONAL AND OPERATIONAL SYSTEMS
INDUSTRIAL APPLICATIONS
BUSINESS AND COMMERCIAL APPLICATIONS

The own risk technique is the company assumption of risks below a predetermined amount on transportation, storage, or other aspects of materials and supplies. The maximum of risk assumed by the company is the point where receipt from such claims exceeds the cost of processing applications for them. For example, if $10 worth of office supplies are lost in transit or stolen from the warehouse, cost of applying for insurance payment and processing such payment when received will exceed the value of the goods and payment.

SUGGESTED FURTHER READING

Longman, H. H., *How to Cut Office Costs,* International Publications Services, New York, 1972.

PACE RATING

Areas for use in Cost Control:

PSYCHOLOGICAL MOTIVATIONAL MANAGEMENT
FINANCIAL MOTIVATIONAL MANAGEMENT
ORGANIZATIONAL AND OPERATIONAL SYSTEMS

Pace rating is a **performance rating** technique used to measure employee work tempo and speed for a specific type of work done. Pace rating, used as a basis for incentive payments, reduces costs by limiting payment to the proportion of work accomplished.

SUGGESTED FURTHER READING

Maynard, H. B., ed., *Industrial Engineering Handbook,* 3d ed., McGraw-Hill, New York, 1974.

PACKING REUSE TECHNIQUE

Areas for use in Cost Control:

MATERIALS AND EQUIPMENT MANAGEMENT
INDUSTRIAL APPLICATIONS
BUSINESS AND COMMERCIAL APPLICATIONS

The packing reuse technique is the specification of containers or cartons for materials purchased that can be reused to ship goods to the company's own customers, reducing packaging costs. Container size and the material used in its construction are the two primary areas of specification.

SUGGESTED FURTHER READING

Ammer, D. S., *Materials Management,* Irwin, Homewood, Ill., 1968.

PAIRED COMPARISONS See Personnel Performance Appraisal.

PALLETIZATION

Areas for use in Cost Control:

ORGANIZATIONAL AND OPERATIONAL SYSTEMS
MATERIALS AND EQUIPMENT MANAGEMENT
INDUSTRIAL APPLICATIONS

Palletization is the prepacking of wooden platforms with cartons of goods for shipment. Design of the pallets allows one operator using a forklift to load or unload goods that would ordinarily require several workers, saving labor costs. The method is similar to **containerization,** but the pallet is a smaller module than the container, requiring less capital cost for equipment. It is more suitable for smaller shipments. In addition, handling equipment, such as forklifts, will probably be in operation before palletization, eliminating capital costs, while containerization requires more specialized heavy-duty equipment. Decreased inventories owing to faster shipment of palletized goods is another cost reduction resulting from use of the method.

Pallets do not offer protection from weather as containers do, but plastic covers can be used where needed.

SUGGESTED FURTHER READING

Magee, J. F., *Physical Distribution Systems,* McGraw-Hill, New York, 1967.
Murphy, G. J., *Transport and Distribution,* Business Books, London, 1972.

PALLET POOLS

Areas for use in Cost Control:

ORGANIZATIONAL AND OPERATIONAL SYSTEMS
MATERIALS AND EQUIPMENT MANAGEMENT
INDUSTRIAL APPLICATIONS

Pallet pools are organized multiple-use operations to share the use of transportation pallets. Some transportation companies operate their own pallet pools for use in or on their vehicles and/or rail cars; but commercial pools exist, too, providing temporary rental of pallets. Use of pallet pools, particularly during peak periods, can greatly reduce the capital costs that would be required if they were purchased by individual companies. *See also* **Palletization.**

SUGGESTED FURTHER READING

Wentworth, F. R. L., ed., *Physical Distribution Management,* Gower Press, London, 1970.

PANORAMIC OFFICE PLANNING (POP)

Areas for use in Cost Control:

WORK PLACE MOTIVATIONAL MANAGEMENT
ORGANIZATIONAL AND OPERATIONAL SYSTEMS

Panoramic office planning (POP), also called office landscaping, is the arrangement of offices to increase employee motivation via a more pleasant work place and to increase interoffice communication efficiency. POP office arrangement generally falls into three areas:

1. Environmental (working conditions)
2. Communication and work flow
3. Flexibility

Environmental. Typical factors added to improve the working place include:

1. Open glass wall areas, to avoid shut-in feelings

2. Sound-absorption wallboard, window panels, divider panels, and ceilings

3. Localized air-conditioning and heat control

4. Carpeting

5. Well-designed and attractive furniture

6. Good lighting

7. Attractive color plans

8. Office arrangement to provide a pleasant view

9. Fewer status symbols, such as partitioned offices

10. Scattered, rather than rigid, desk arrangement

Communication and Work Flow. Amount of communication and work flow between departments should be analyzed and the layout arranged to facilitate this flow. *See also* **Communication Grid Analysis.** In POP arrangements, which are more often open, a minimum area of 50 by 100 ft should be allocated for each department.

Flexibility. Sound-absorbing screens and panels are frequently used in POP arrangements to provide some privacy in an open layout. These are easily rearranged, providing greater flexibility than partitioned offices. Underfloor power grids for electricity and telephone services provide needed flexibility for easy rearrangement of work areas.

COSTS OF POP

Studies show that POP arrangements require less space than partitioned arrangements but more space than open, conventionally organized arrangements. Construction, heating, and air-conditioning costs are lower in POP arrangements both because partitions are not used and because insulation is facilitated through carpeting, acoustical panels, and generally newer, more power-conservation-oriented construction.

Improved productivity through increased employee satisfaction with the working place is, however, the primary means of reducing costs with POP.

SUGGESTED FURTHER READING

Lock, D., ed., *Management Techniques,* Director's Bookshelf, London, 1972.

PARAMETER ANALYSIS

Areas for use in Cost Control:

ORGANIZATIONAL AND OPERATIONAL SYSTEMS
INDUSTRIAL APPLICATIONS
BUSINESS AND COMMERCIAL APPLICATIONS

Parameter analysis is a technique used to determine when specific events can be made to happen, as well as when and how events will affect specific projects, based on the extension of current trends. Thus, if a company wishes to determine how reducing the quality (and cost) of a material in one of its products will affect the sales and profits for that product, current trends in minimum-quality acceptability will be traced statistically and extended. Future effects are forecast using these figures.

SUGGESTED FURTHER READING

Smith, P. I. S., *Think Tanks and Problem Solving,* Business Books, London, 1971.

PARTICIPATIVE MANAGEMENT

Areas for use in Cost Control:

PSYCHOLOGICAL MOTIVATIONAL MANAGEMENT
FINANCIAL MOTIVATIONAL MANAGEMENT
ORGANIZATIONAL AND OPERATIONAL SYSTEMS
INDUSTRIAL APPLICATIONS
BUSINESS AND COMMERCIAL APPLICATIONS

Participative management is a **budgetary control** technique that uses the thinking of all staff in drawing up and controlling budgets. The technique provides both financial and psychological motivation for better cost control. Executive meetings, suggestion plans, and committee problem assignment are used to encourage participation. Since employees are allowed to suggest cost control ideas, such goals seem more personal to them, and they work harder at implementing them. In addition, financial rewards are frequently given for good budgetary control ideas.

Degrees of staff involvement must, of course, vary at different levels. Not all employees can sit in on a budget meeting, for example. But it is important that all *key* employees be involved in both budget planning and budget control. These employees, in turn, will present budget ideas for their work area to subordinates, asking for their opinions and ideas.

A system for employee participation should include the following steps:

1. *Set up a hierarchy of communication.* Key employees attend the executive meeting, for example, and then present the problems informally to their subordinates. Suggestions are received at all levels and carried back to a second key-employee meeting for further discussion and possible implementation.

2. *Delegation of work* should be practiced wherever possible to encourage a sense of participation.

3. *Cost control objectives can also be stated in written form,* with employees participating by submitting written suggestions.

SUGGESTED FURTHER READING

Herzberg, Frederic, Bernard Mauser, and Barbara Snyderman, *The Motivation to Work,* Wiley, New York, 1959.

PARTICLE ANALYSIS

Areas for use in Cost Control:

ORGANIZATIONAL AND OPERATIONAL SYSTEMS
MATERIALS AND EQUIPMENT MANAGEMENT
INDUSTRIAL APPLICATIONS

In particle analysis, product designs are drawn to scale on graph paper with 1-mm squares, and each square is examined to see if that part of the product can be eliminated. Particles not affecting the product's function are hypothetically removed and the resulting redesigned skeletal product is examined for acceptability and economy of production. The technique is particularly useful for products using materials that are rapidly decreasing in supply and increasing in cost, such as copper, when even the smallest reduction in product part size can eventually mean sizable cost reductions.

SUGGESTED FURTHER READING

Radke, Magnus, *Manual of Cost Reduction Techniques,* McGraw-Hill, New York, 1972.

PAYBACK-PERIOD TECHNIQUE

Areas for use in Cost Control:

ORGANIZATIONAL AND OPERATIONAL SYSTEMS
MATERIALS AND EQUIPMENT MANAGEMENT
INDUSTRIAL APPLICATIONS

The payback-period technique is used to evaluate potential capital investments by calculating the length of time such investments will take to pay for themselves. Annual savings from each investment are divided into the purchase price, and the equipment with the fastest payback period is purchased, reducing capital costs. For example, if proposed equipment A will save $40,000 in labor and fringe benefit (F.B.) costs and $3,000 in tax and insurance costs and sells for $350,000, while proposed equipment B will save $60,000 in labor and fringe benefit costs and sells for $525,000, calculations will be as follows:

Proposed equipment A:

Labor and F.B. savings	$40,000
Insurance savings	3,000
	$43,000

$$\frac{\text{Price of } \$350,000}{\$43,000} = 8.14 \text{ years (payback period)}$$

Proposed equipment B:

$$\frac{\text{Price of \$525,000}}{\text{Labor and F.B. saving of \$60,000}} = 8.75 \text{ years (payback period)}$$

Thus, proposed equipment A has the fastest payback period.

SUGGESTED FURTHER READING

Ammer, D. S., *Materials Management,* Irwin, Homewood, Ill., 1968.

PAYMENT TERMS NEGOTIATION

Areas for use in Cost Control:

ORGANIZATIONAL AND OPERATIONAL SYSTEMS
MATERIALS AND EQUIPMENT MANAGEMENT
INDUSTRIAL APPLICATIONS
BUSINESS AND COMMERCIAL APPLICATIONS

Payment terms negotiation can sometimes be used to reduce materials and goods purchase costs for items that are industry-priced. For example, steel tubing prices are determined by the steel industry and cannot be reduced. The supplier will sometimes agree to very generous terms, such as 8 percent reduction for prompt payment, as a means of attracting business.

SUGGESTED FURTHER READING

Ammer, D. S., *Materials Management,* Irwin, Homewood, Ill., 1968.

PAYROLL ANALYSIS

Areas for use in Cost Control:

ORGANIZATIONAL AND OPERATIONAL SYSTEMS
PAPERWORK DESIGN AND FLOW SYSTEMS
INDUSTRIAL APPLICATIONS
BUSINESS AND COMMERCIAL APPLICATIONS

Payroll analysis consists of periodic checks of actual wage and salary costs, which can then be measured against budgeted wage and salary costs. Weekly analysis records provide a constant system of cost checks and controls. Such records (see Fig. 73) should be prepared at the same time that pay checks are prepared to implement the control system at lowest cost.

SUGGESTED FURTHER READING

Maynard, H. B., ed., *Industrial Engineering Handbook,* 3d ed., McGraw-Hill, New York, 1974.

PAYROLL COST CONTROL

Areas for use in Cost Control:

ORGANIZATIONAL AND OPERATIONAL SYSTEMS
PAPERWORK DESIGN AND FLOW SYSTEMS
DATA RETENTION—FILES AND RECORDKEEPING
INDUSTRIAL APPLICATIONS
BUSINESS AND COMMERCIAL APPLICATIONS

Payroll Summary

Variance	99	Account	Ex. B. Allow		Cur' Allw.		Actual	
		Cost ctr: *Metal Fabrication*						
		Keyman:						
(25)	01	Measured dir. lab.			1125		1150	
(25)	02	Fall down			87		112	
1	03	Cont. ex. allow			35		34	
	04	Band cut (credit)						
(5)	05	Unmeasured d'l.			205		210	
18	06	Overtime (dir. lab.)			18		—	
	11	Executive						
—	12	Supervision			125		125	
	13	Misc. oper. ind.						
—	14	Clerical			50		50	
	16	Overtime (ind. L.)						
	34	Service						
	35	First aid						
(25)	42	Inside trucking			125		150	
	43	Outside trucking						
(12)	51	Inspection			44		56	
(21)	52	Remake			18		39	
	61	Mtc. land. & B.						
(24)	62	Mtc. mach. & eq.			26		50	
(48)	07	Set ups			122		170	
—	08	Non-std. method			17		17	
(6)	09 18	Unc. exc. allow Mat'l checking			24		30	
(2)	19	Learning			25		27	
	59	Def. prod. uncon.						
	9314	Exper. & devel.						
(174)		Total payroll			2046		2220	
		Less 93 P. & L.						
		Net 99 expense						

	% Act.	Unit *Hours*	Produced 875	Budgeted 1250	% Act. 70	
10	Cost ctr.	Act. hrs.		Cost ctr.		10
	Week ended		3/15			
	Comments					

NOTE: *Parentheses mean budget variance losses*

Figure 73. Typical weekly payroll summary. From H. B. Maynard, *Industrial Engineering Handbook,* 1st ed., McGraw-Hill, New York, 1956.

Payroll costs are best reduced through various means of simplification, some of which are applicable to limited types of payrolls. Basic simplifications include:

1. *Fewer paydays.* From the company point of view, costs are greatly reduced if the employees are paid monthly rather than weekly, since there is then much less paperwork. Although employees may object to monthly payment in some cases, most salaried employees can adjust their personal budgeting to the system without difficulty. Hourly employees, or those with incentive payments that fluctuate, may require more frequent payment since the impact of the bonus for extra effort should follow the extra work as closely as possible to ensure maximum motivational effect. Tax deductions and records are also more economically handled at monthly rather than weekly intervals.

2. *Staggered payment.* By staggering paydays or payweeks, accounting employees' workload is leveled over the entire working period and fewer payroll employees are needed to handle "peak" loads. Additionally, companywide morale is less likely to be affected by a mass pay period. For example, if everyone is paid at noon each Friday, the period of time just prior to payment is apt to have low work output in anticipation of payment, while the afternoon working time will have even lower work output as employees anticipate leaving work to enjoy their salary. Staggered paydays spread and weaken this effect.

3. *Pay by check,* since checks provide an additional record of payment when canceled and eliminate handling of cash. Larger companies have found computerization of payroll effective, particularly for salaried employees.

4. *Transparent-window pay envelopes* avoid the cost of typing the employee's name a second time.

5. *Limited pay and incentive scales* reduce the amount of time required to calculate total payment.

6. *Time clocks should be used only to record overtime,* eliminating the additional paperwork requirements under normal working conditions.

7. *Form design* should emphasize saving of machine time used in payroll preparation and should incorporate multiple forms in a carbon-set style to reduce form recording.

See also **Dyeline Payroll System.**

SUGGESTED FURTHER READING

Longman, H. H., *How to Cut Office Costs,* Anbar Publications, London, 1967.

PERFORMANCE RATING

Areas for use in Cost Control:

PSYCHOLOGICAL MOTIVATIONAL MANAGEMENT
FINANCIAL MOTIVATIONAL MANAGEMENT
ORGANIZATIONAL AND OPERATIONAL SYSTEMS

Performance rating is a technique that combines several methods of work comparison to establish the particular ranking of individual employees. The ranking may be used as the basis for **incentive payment systems,** motivating the employee financially and reducing labor time and costs; and it can be used competitively to psychologically motivate the employee.

Methods of performance rating compare work performance with accepted work standards statistically as well as by supervisory judgment of work. Specific techniques include **time rating, effort rating, pace rating, synthetic leveling,** and **objective rating.**

Establishment of rating standards is the most difficult part of performance rating, and care should be taken to establish standards by averaging data taken from a sampling of 500 to 1,000 or more cases.

SUGGESTED FURTHER READING

Maynard, H. B., ed., *Industrial Engineering Handbook,* 3d ed., McGraw-Hill, New York, 1974.
Mundel, M. E., *Motion and Time Study,* Prentice-Hall, New York, 1955.

PERIOD COSTS See Fixed Costs.

PERPETUAL INVENTORY

Areas for use in Cost Control:

ORGANIZATIONAL AND OPERATIONAL SYSTEMS
DATA RETENTION—FILES AND RECORDKEEPING
MATERIALS AND EQUIPMENT MANAGEMENT
INDUSTRIAL APPLICATIONS

The perpetual inventory system is used to reduce inventory costs. A record card is used for each material stored, indicating the running balance of the material on hand, material withdrawals, material deliveries, and the point of reorder (see Fig. 74).

| Material: _____ Commodity Index: _____ |||||||
| Point of reorder:_____ |||||||
Date	Item	Amount withdrawn	Amount delivered	Amount on order	Balance in stock

Figure 74. Typical perpetual inventory record card.

Withdrawals are recorded, and when the balance in stock reaches the point of reorder, orders are automatically placed. All entries are documented by requisitions, purchase orders, etc., so that the possibility and cost of materials theft are lowered. Thus, the system is especially useful in controlling more valuable inventories, including production materials.

SUGGESTED FURTHER READING

Ammer, D. S., *Materials Management,* Irwin, Homewood, III., 1968.

PERSONNEL ASSESSMENT

Areas for use in Cost Control:

ORGANIZATIONAL AND OPERATIONAL SYSTEMS
INDUSTRIAL APPLICATIONS
BUSINESS AND COMMERCIAL APPLICATIONS

Personnel assessment is the evaluation of long-term employee needs to reduce the cost of obtaining and training such workers. Using long-term company growth and profit goals as a starting point, the number of employees and special skills required are estimated. The firm's ability to fill these spots internally, the degree of outside recruitment required, and special training needs are also assessed. For every projected budget, projected personnel requirements should be determined. Detailed reports of the number of hourly, clerical, and managerial employees required for each proposed project should accompany other planning reports, such as proposed profits, as a matter of course.

SUGGESTED FURTHER READING

Mann, R., ed., *The Arts of Top Management,* McGraw-Hill, New York, 1970.

PERSONNEL ATTITUDE MEASUREMENT

Areas for use in Cost Control:

PSYCHOLOGICAL MOTIVATIONAL MANAGEMENT
ORGANIZATIONAL AND OPERATIONAL SYSTEMS
INDUSTRIAL APPLICATIONS
BUSINESS AND COMMERCIAL APPLICATIONS

The way an employee feels toward his or her work and his or her employer (his or her attitude) affects both the quality and the quantity of work. If this attitude is improved, the quality and the amount of work will also improve, reducing costs. Personnel attitude measurement techniques are those used to pinpoint employee attitudes that are negative or below the norm, so that they can be improved; or, if they cannot be improved, so that the employee can be replaced.

Methods of personnel attitude measurement include the *impressionistic method, nondirective interviewing, guided interviewing, questionnaire study,* **Attitude Scales, Attitude Survey,** and the *indirect method.* All methods use some form of sampling, usually *random sampling,* as the first step.

The Impressionistic Method. The impressionistic method uses random observation of employee behavior and attitudes and provides a means of preliminary survey to locate trouble areas. Because the method is subjective, and not statistical, specific results are impossible to obtain. The appraiser usually records the general impression of what he or she sees, such as, "Assembly employees were complaining among themselves about the new assembly line speed and breakdown."

Nondirective Interviewing. Nondirective interviewing, also called unguided interviewing, measures employee attitude via a free discussion. The employee determines the content of material discussed, while the appraiser listens to and encourages presentation of the employee's views and ideas. The appraiser is careful to make the employee feel comfortable and to not argue, give advice, or display authority. Questions are asked only to make the employee feel at ease or to move the conversation to areas not discussed. The appraiser lets the employee know that his or her attitudes are important to the company. A small tape recorder may be used to record the interview, since note-taking might make the employee uncomfortable.

The appraiser should not pass judgment on employee comments but only record them. If an employee has difficulty expressing an attitude because of fear of the appraiser's or company's disapproval, the appraiser should encourage freedom in speaking.

Guided Interviewing. Guided interviewing is an interview that directs specific questions to measure employee attitudes. The appraiser asks questions but does not offer peripheral comments.

A *closed-type guided interview* uses questions that can be answered by "yes" or "no," but the appraiser scores answers on a scale of 1 to 5 depending on the strength of the reply.

Questions are aimed at determining employee satisfaction or dissatisfaction with wages, work, supervisor, coworkers, working place, hours of work, job security, chance for advancement, etc.

Questionnaire Study. Questionnaire study is best suited for quantity measurement of attitudes, since it requires less personal contact and time spent per employee by the appraiser. Questions covering subjects listed in "Guided Interviewing" (above) are prepared in written form, with five multiple-choice answers: "Very satisfied," "Satisfied," "Unsatisfied," "Very unsatisfied," and "Don't know."

Attitude Scales and Attitude Surveys. These measure attitudes against a predetermined standard. These standards, or scales, are generally developed by one of the following methods:

1. Scaled-item methods
2. Rating-scale methods
3. Criterion-group methods
4. Osgood Semantic scale method
5. Guttman scale method

The *scaled-item method* divides attitude statements into general subject areas, such as statements about working conditions. Individual statements on each area are arranged in order, ranking from *very satisfied* to *very unsatisfied*. Duplicate or unmeaningful statements are removed, leaving a scale of attitude statements against which future attitude statements can be measured.

Rating-scale methods are "do-it-yourself" attitude measurement techniques. The appraiser asks the employee to mark his or her degree of satisfaction or dissatisfaction with a particular value on a scale with a high of 100 percent and a low of 0.

Criterion-group methods use a written test measuring satisfaction or dissatisfaction with value areas. Resulting attitudes are measured against standard attitude scales, such as the *Likert Scale* or the *Error-Choice Scale*.

The *Osgood Semantic scale method* measures an employee's attitudes from responses to a series of polar terms such as "good—bad," "helpful—harmful," etc. Answers may be rated on a scale of four, six, or eight points.

The *Guttman scale method* uses a cumulative assessment scale. The employee's responses will be positive until reaching a point of dissatisfaction within a given value area. Thereafter, all responses will be negative until a new value area is introduced, because attitude statements build from one another.

The Indirect Method. *Indirect methods* measure employee attitudes without their knowledge of the goal of the test or interview. Word-association tests and picture and story completion devices are examples. The technique was developed to overcome employee hesitancy about revealing actual attitudes.

SUGGESTED FURTHER READING

Guilford, J. P., *Psychometric Methods,* McGraw-Hill, New York, 1954.
Krech, D., R. S. Crutchfield, and E. Z. Ballackey, *Individual in Society,* McGraw-Hill, New York, 1962.

PERSONNEL INTERVIEWING

Areas for use in Cost Control:

ORGANIZATIONAL AND OPERATIONAL SYSTEMS
INDUSTRIAL APPLICATIONS
BUSINESS AND COMMERCIAL APPLICATIONS

Personnel interviewing techniques are one area that can reduce turnover and other labor costs through the selection of the most suitable employees for specific jobs (*see also* **Personnel Testing**). *Selection interview* techniques aid in measuring prospective employees, and should be supplemented by references and application forms, as well as testing.

Personnel interviews are also used for determining current employee attitudes toward jobs, working conditions, wages, etc. Such interviews are sometimes conducted during studies of motivational methods but are more often conducted when an employee leaves the company, in the form of a *separation interview* or *debriefing*.

A third type of personnel interview is the *counseling interview,* usually conducted by an employee's immediate supervisor to make the employee aware of a work or personal problem that is damaging his or her work performance.

Selection Interviewing. Once data from application forms and basic tests have screened wholly unsuitable job applicants, various stages of *Selection Interviews* begin. The applicant may be interviewed from one to 10 times, depending on company policy. To keep costs at a reasonable level, the average applicant should be interviewed only by the personnel department manager in charge of the job area and by the immediate supervisor to the job position. In higher-level hiring, the applicant will also be interviewed by the department head or the next highest managerial-level person.

Selection interviews have two main purposes:

1. To obtain information about the applicant.
2. To evaluate such information as a basis for hiring or rejection.

The interview also serves as a method of testing the personality relationship between applicant and his or her potential supervisor.

Information about the applicant, if not provided by the application form, should include the following:

1. Age
2. Education
3. Work experience
4. Marital status and family status
5. Work goals
6. Wage required
7. Personal habits and goals
8. Financial status
9. Working habits
10. Work accomplishments
11. Personal accomplishments

Supplementing information acquired from personality testing, the interviewer should rate the following personality characteristic of applicants:

1. Aggressiveness
2. Alertness
3. Ability to present ideas verbally and/or in writing
4. Intelligence
5. Personality
6. Self-confidence
7. Tact
8. Sociability

SUGGESTED FURTHER READING

Anderson, R. C., "The Guided Interview as an Evaluation Instrument," *Journal of Educational Research*, no. 48, 1954.

Bellows, R. M., and M. F. Estep, *Employment Psychology: The Interview,* Rinehart, New York, 1954.

Bolster, B. I., and B. M. Springbitt, "The Reaction of Interviewers to Favorable and Unfavorable Information," *Journal of Applied Psychology,* June 1964.

PERSONNEL MORALE BUILDING

Area for use in Cost Control:

PSYCHOLOGICAL MOTIVATIONAL MANAGEMENT

Personnel morale is the employees' feeling of belonging and acceptance in the work group, as well as the sharing of work goals and respect for these work goals. Good work morale among personnel reduces costs because it eliminates time spent in grumbling or bickering and because coordinated group effort, possible only with good morale, means more rapidly completed, better-quality work. Building personnel morale requires a channeling of employee energy in ways that contribute to work-group cooperation. Generally, this can best be done by providing work goals for the group, by making observation of progress toward such goals visible through charts or other visual aids, and by making sure the work group understands the value (social, technical, financial) of the work.

Prior to attempts to improve morale, measurement techniques should be used to determine present status (*see also* **Personnel Morale Measurement**). If morale is found to be low, techniques that may be used to build morale include:

1. Industrial spy method
2. Sociometry application
3. Expert approach
4. Counseling
5. Employee problem-solving method
6. Vertical round-table technique
7. Inverted-pyramid technique
8. Circle-with-a-point technique

The *industrial spy method* uses an expert unknown to the workers, planting him or her in their group as an ordinary employee. He or she gains acceptance of the group to learn their problems and complaints and draws up a report of morale status as well as suggestions for morale improvement and opinions as to the cause of low morale.

Sociometry application involves the regrouping of employees to fit patterns shown in *sociograms* (*see* **Personnel Morale Measurement**). If a clique, or inner group, has formed, for example, these workers may be separated into one unit. If an informal leader has developed, he or she and workers who named him or her may be separated into a new work group.

The *expert approach* involves an "expert" touring the work premises, talking to personnel, and making general observations. He or she may recommend group meetings, safety or other campaigns, posters, employee social activities, etc., as a means of uniting employee groups. While these methods usually cause a temporary lift in morale, they will improve morale permanently only if the expert is able to identify problems causing low morale and to remove them.

Counseling improves morale by acting as a means of communication between employees and management. Employees are encouraged to discuss any work problems with counselors and are paid their usual wages for the time spent. The counselor may be able to help the employee immediately to solve problems, or management may need to change the factors causing low morale. The counselor is also useful in pointing out work goals and progress to work groups.

The *employee problem-solving method* is quite similar to the *counseling technique* except that with its use the group supervisor keeps abreast of current problems in the work group and attempts to remove, with whatever management help is needed, sources of low morale.

The *vertical round-table technique* builds morale by bringing together personnel at a vertical level, especially management personnel, to discuss poor-morale causes and to decide how to correct such causes. Problems are divided into three areas:

1. *Worker personality or human nature problems*—personality difficulties among workers and employee dislike of specific operational methods, such as use of time clocks.

2. *Industrial problems*—shortages of needed quality materials, rising labor costs, etc.

3. *Company problems*—lack of suitable supervisors, need for working place improvement, etc.

The *inverted-pyramid technique* improves morale through a series of interviews, using first individual interviews, then interviews of pairs of employees, then interviews with four employees, and finally reducing total-work-group interviews. Morale problems are discussed and resolved in each interview.

The *circle-with-a-point technique* improves morale through conducting regularly scheduled (weekly, monthly) meetings of all levels of management to discuss and resolve morale problems. The technique is most effective in small companies where limited numbers of management staff prevent use of the *vertical round-table technique*.

SUGGESTED FURTHER READING

Gordon, O. J., "The Factors in Human Needs and Industrial Morale," *Personnel Psychology,* no. 8, 1955.
Gurion, R. M., "Industrial Morale," *Personnel Psychology,* no. 11, 1958.
Yuzak, R. P., *The Assessment of Employee Morale,* Ohio State University Press, 1961.

PERSONNEL MORALE MEASUREMENT

Area for use in Cost Control:

PSYCHOLOGICAL MOTIVATIONAL MANAGEMENT

Personnel morale measurement is used prior to **personnel morale building** to determine current status of work-group cooperation, goals, goal progress, and group values participation. Techniques used for personnel morale measurement include:

1. Sociometry
2. Giese and Ruter Morale Measurement
3. Bernberg Morale Measurement

Figure 75. Sociogram. **Figure 76.** Leadership formation in a sociogram.

Sociometry, also called the "nominating technique," measures morale by asking each employee to name the coworker he or she feels would make the best supervisor. A *sociogram* chart is then drawn up with each work-group member represented by a circle (see Fig. 75). An arrow runs from each employee to the coworker he or she names.

Factors to be considered when studying a sociogram include:

1. Was the foreman chosen by the majority of the group, or was another employee chosen, making him or her the informal leader? (See Fig. 76.)

2. Does the sociogram indicate cliques, or closed groups, within the group that may damage overall morale? (See Fig. 77.)

3. Does the sociogram indicate paired workers who may isolate themselves from the group, diminishing morale? (See Fig. 78.)

Figure 77. Clique formation in a sociogram.

Figure 78. Pairing formation in a sociogram.

Giese and Ruter morale measurement determines the current status of morale in correlation with the operable degree of five work factors:

1. Productive efficiency
2. Error efficiency
3. Turnover
4. Absenteeism
5. Tardiness

When absenteeism is high, for example, morale is low.

Bernberg morale measurement determines probable morale by correlation with the operable degree of four work factors:

1. Absences
2. Tardiness
3. Number of annual medical department visits
4. Merit rating

SUGGESTED FURTHER READING

Bernberg, R. E., "Socio-psychological Factors in Industrial Morale," *Journal of Social Psychology,* no. 36, 1952.

Giese, J. W., and H. W. Ruter, "An Objective Analysis of Morale," *Journal of Applied Psychology,* no. 19, 1946.

Moreno, J. L., "Foundation of Sociometry," *Sociometry Monographs,* no. 4, Beacon Press, Boston, 1943.

Yuzak, R. P., *The Assessment of Employee Morale,* Ohio State University Press, Columbus, 1961.

PERSONNEL PERFORMANCE APPRAISAL

Areas for use in Cost Control:

ORGANIZATIONAL AND OPERATIONAL SYSTEMS
PAPERWORK DESIGN AND FLOW SYSTEMS
INDUSTRIAL APPLICATIONS
BUSINESS AND COMMERCIAL APPLICATIONS

Personnel performance appraisal techniques reduce costs by measuring efficiency of work, so that needed improvements can be observed and implemented. Employee areas that should be regularly evaluated include:

1. Work speed
2. Work quality
3. Abilities and training
4. Earnings related to output
5. Punctuality
6. Absenteeism
7. Improvement and advancement

Such evaluations may be made by supervisory personnel, coworkers, or the employee. For cost reduction purposes, supervisory evaluation is most often used, although planned self-evaluation programs may also lead to improved work performance and resulting lower costs.

Major types of evaluation systems include the following:

1. Cumulative points rating
2. Critical incident rating
3. Ranking
4. Numerical rating
5. Standard scales rating
6. Paired comparisons
7. Forced-choice rating

Cumulative Points Rating. The appraiser checks listed work characteristics that apply to the employee being appraised. Scoring is based on total number of items checked, and the employee's performance is compared with the performance of other personnel doing the same work.

Critical Incident Rating. The appraiser decides which work factors are most important in each job and scales them by importance. Employee performance of these factors is rated in a manner similar to cumulative points rating.

Ranking. One or more appraisers list all employees in the order of their quality of performance, from high to low, for each work factor.

Average rank is calculated for each employee. The technique should not be used for evaluating groups larger than 50 employees.

Numerical Rating. Graphic scales are used by the appraiser, who then rates each employee on the 1-to-9 scale in each work area. Total score is the average of individual ratings.

Standard Scales Rating. Also called man-to-man comparison scales. The appraiser rates individual work performance as compared with predetermined standards among departmental workers. Care must be taken to keep the scale confidential.

Paired Comparisons. The appraiser compares each employee's work with the work of every other employee by checking the best worker on a pair chart.

A *paired-comparison matrix* (see Fig. 79) is prepared by placing an × in the box of the preferred employee of each pair. The total number of ×'s gives the proportion of time an employee's work is preferred over other workers'.

Forced-Choice Rating. This technique can be used to evaluate the following:

1. Leadership
2. Supervisory ability
3. Interests

	Taylor	White	Hickman	Jones	Prichard	Davis	Smith	Reed	Knowles
Taylor				×					
White	×		×	×	×				
Hickman	×			×	×				
Jones									
Prichard	×			×					
Davis	×	×	×	×	×				
Smith	×	×	×	×	×	×			×
Reed	×	×	×	×	×	×	×		×
Knowles	×	×	×	×	×	×			
Proportion of times preferred	7/8	1/2	5/8	1	3/4	3/8	1/8	0	1/4

Figure 79. Typical paired comparison matrix.

4. Attitudes
5. Empathy
6. Sensory ability

Characteristics of the highest- and lowest-quality performance in a particular area are set out in brief form. This pair of values, and an additional pair of values relating to another facet of the work, are set out together to provide more choice for the appraiser. A fifth, neutral characteristic is sometimes added. The forced-choice items then appear in the following form:

Sloppy
Conscientious
Careful
Wasteful

The appraiser chooses the adjective that he or she feels best suits the employee's performance. Scoring gives points to characteristics from the highest-quality performance.

SUGGESTED FURTHER READING

Guilford, J. P., *Psychometric Methods,* McGraw-Hill, New York, 1954.
Rothaus, P., R. B. Morton, and P. G. Hanson, "Performance Appraisal and Psychological Distance," *Journal of Applied Psychology,* no. 49, 1965.
Zavala, A., "A Development of the Forced-Choices Rating Scale Technique," *Psychological Bulletin,* no. 63, 1965.

PERSONNEL PLANNING

Areas for use in Cost Control:

ORGANIZATIONAL AND OPERATIONAL SYSTEMS
INDUSTRIAL APPLICATIONS
BUSINESS AND COMMERCIAL APPLICATIONS

Personnel planning reduces lost operational time costs by hiring and training employees so that they are ready to begin work as soon as the vacancy occurs. The following steps are included:

1. *Study company plans for future operations.* What new products will be made? What special skills will be required of employees making these products? What new services will be offered? What special skills will be required of employees in this area? How many employees can be retrained from other areas? How many new employees will be needed, and in which areas?

2. *Study the rate of company retirements and turnover.* Which areas are most affected? How many new employees will be needed in each? When will they be needed?

3. *Consider possible business changes.* Will the standard workweek be shortened? If so, when? How many employees will such a move require?

4. *Consider possible technological changes.* Will automation affect the number of workers required? If so, how and when?

5. *Set up criteria* based on past experience, testing, reference, etc., for personal traits that are most inherent in successful employees, and use these as a guideline in hiring.

6. *Develop training programs,* particularly in those areas where outside education is not adequate.

Develop hiring and training goals in writing, and maintain records to ensure completion of targeted figures.

SUGGESTED FURTHER READING

Argenti, John, *Management Techniques,* G. Allen, London, 1970.

PERSONNEL REFERENCE ASSESSMENT

Areas for use in Cost Control:

ORGANIZATIONAL AND OPERATIONAL SYSTEMS
INDUSTRIAL APPLICATIONS
BUSINESS AND COMMERCIAL APPLICATIONS

Many companies rely heavily on an applicant's references or recommendations in employee selection. Successful analysis of references can cut hiring and turnover costs by providing an added assurance that the person hired is capable of performing the work. But care must be taken to obtain an accurate reference, since the new employer has no real way of knowing whether the reference is presenting an honest picture of the applicant.

For most accurate results, assessment of a reference should be made considering the reliability of the recommendation source, including the following factors:

1. *Personal acquaintance with or knowledge of the applicant.* Preferably, the source will have been the applicant's immediate supervisor and will have direct knowledge of his or her abilities and working habits.

2. *Writing or verbal ability* of the reference source to express his or her opinion of the applicant's working ability and habits.

3. *Sincerity of source.* Some sources are reluctant to say anything damaging, or they may provide falsely favorable data to get rid of a poor employee. Other sources may be vindictive if an employee decides to leave and may give an unjustified poor report of abilities.

SUGGESTED FURTHER READING

Goheen, H. W., and J. N. Mosel, "Validity of the Employment Recommendation Questionnaire: II—Comparison with Field Investigations," *Personnel Psychology,* no. 12, 1959.
Tiffin, J., and E. C. Nevis, *Industrial Psychology,* Prentice-Hall, Englewood Cliffs, N.J., 1965.

PERSONNEL TESTING

Areas for use in Cost Control:

ORGANIZATIONAL AND OPERATIONAL SYSTEMS
INDUSTRIAL APPLICATIONS
BUSINESS AND COMMERCIAL APPLICATIONS

Personnel testing techniques are those using tests and other statistical devices to select and place personnel. Costs can be greatly reduced by the techniques, since employees correctly selected and placed for positions change jobs less frequently (eliminating very high turnover costs) and are able to do a more effective job. Indeed, since wages and salaries are still the most expensive "cost" item for many companies, these techniques can be the most important cost savers available.

Great numbers of *statistical employment* techniques are available, but those generally felt to be the most effective are detailed here:

Mental Ability Tests. These tests are usually short screening devices taking less than ½ hour for use early in the job application procedure.

The *Aptitude Test* is a 15-minute mental ability measurement test developed for industrial and business white-collar or managerial applicants.

Otis Self-Administering Tests of Mental Ability were some of the earliest developed (1922). One group measures mental ability of high school graduates or applicants with some college training, while a second group measures mental ability of applicants who have not completed high school. They are most effective for lower-level jobs but are generally less acceptable today with increased general levels of education.

The *Thurstone Test of Mental Alertness* gives both quantitative and verbal mental ability measurements from a 20-minute test. It is most effective in screening clerical and/or sales applicants.

The *Wonderlic Personnel Test* is a 12-minute abridgment of the higher-series Otis tests. Questions used are those measuring the potential level of ability of an employee, and the test is often considered more accurate than the longer Otis tests. It may be used to test manual laborers as well as white-collar applicants, but it is most effective in selection of clerical employees.

Mechanical Aptitude Tests. These tests measure physical adeptness and perception of spatial relationships, as well as mechanical knowledge.

The *Bennett Test of Mechanical Comprehension* uses a series of pictures as the basis for questions about mechanical information. Since different tests are used for women, trade school applicants, and engineering applicants, the company should check the legality of such tests in its state or country before using them.

The *Minnesota Paper Form Board Test* uses 64 geometrical forms cut into five pieces each. Several assembled forms are offered as possible copies of the original. The applicant chooses the assembled form believed to correlate with the pieces.

The *Minnesota Mechanical Assembly Test* requires applicants to reassemble a series of 33 disassembled simple mechanical items; it requires about one hour to complete.

The *Minnesota Spatial Relations Test* uses 58 geometric shapes which have been cut from each of four large boards. The applicant places cutouts in the correct places as rapidly as possible; accuracy counts equally with speed.

Sensory Ability Tests. These give statistical evidence of the ability of the physical senses—color vision, hearing, etc. Because of the nature of sensory ability, tests use devices other than paper-and-pencil tests.

Vision Tests. The *Ishihari Test* measures color blindness through a series of cards with designs made of one color of dots and background dots of a second color. Cards measure normal vision and red, green, or total color blindness.

The *Ortho-Rater* is an instrument that measures perception of depth and color blindness, as does the *Sight-Screener*.

The *Snellen Chart* measures approximately the ability to see distant items by means of a chart of rows of letters that gradually diminish in size.

Hearing Tests. The *audiometer* is an instrument that measures degree of sensitivity to various sound frequencies. Each ear is tested and a chart, called an *audiogram,* is prepared to compare the potential employee's hearing with the norm.

Motor Ability Tests. The devices measure degree of motor coordination.

The *Crawford Small Parts Dexterity Test* measures motor coordination by timing the applicant's ability to place pins in holes with a tweezers and add a metal collar over the pin, as well as ability to thread small screws into holes by hand and tighten them with a screwdriver.

The *Minnesota Rate of Manipulation Test* measures motor coordination by timing the applicant as he or she places 58 round blocks into a board having 58 holes and then turns each block and replaces it.

Personality Tests. Although the applicant's personality will play a major part in his or her success or failure on a particular job, devising tests that can accurately measure qualities needed for success is a difficult matter. The tests are useful, however, in screening out obvious misfits and hostile or disturbed personalities.

The *Activity Vector Analysis* classifies personality types through a test using 81 descriptive words. The applicant marks all adjectives which have been used by others in describing him or her in one column and all adjectives the applicant applies to himself or herself in a second column. Adjectives measure four personality areas—avoidance, amiability, sociability, and aggressiveness. The test requires little time and the tester needs no special skills.

The *Bernreuter Personality Inventory* measures dominance, confidence, neuroticism, self-sufficiency, sociability, and introversion tendencies in the applicant via a 125-item true-and-false test.

The *Guilford-Zimmerman Temperament Survey* measures the applicant's activity level, sociability, objectivity, emotional stability, restraint, thoughtfulness, friendliness, personal relations, masculinity, and ascendance. Caution should be used where laws forbid use of prejudicial testing, since masculinity traits are measured.

The *Minnesota Multiphasic Personality Inventory (MMPI)* measures the applicant's tendency toward paranoia, social introversion, hypomania, hypochondria, depression, psychasthenia, hysteria, schizophrenia, psychopathic deviation, and masculinity/femininity balance with a test of 550 statements to be classified as "true," "false," or "cannot say." As in the Guilford-Zimmerman Survey, caution should be used when testing in areas with legal test restrictions.

The *Rorschach Test* uses an applicant's reaction to 10 standardized ink blots to measure personality and emotional tendencies. The technique requires a highly trained administrator if it is to be useful.

The *Thematic Apperception Test (TAT)* measures an applicant's conflicts, drives, and inhibitions through his or her reactions to a series of pictures. Skilled administration of the test is necessary.

Interest Tests. Measurement of the applicant's interests can indicate whether he or she will be interested in doing a specific type of work. Interest tests ask questions about the applicant's interests, correlating the results with the job available through a set of keys for types of occupation.

The *Kuder Preference Record* measures interest in clerical, outdoor, mechanical, computational, scientific, persuasive, musical, artistic, literary, and social service areas by having the applicant choose one of three listed activities he or she would most enjoy in a series of such choices.

The *Strong Vocational Interest Blank* measures interests in different types of occupations, as well as measuring masculinity, interest maturity, occupational level, and specialization level. Separate questionnaires are used for men and women, and caution should be used where legal testing controls exist.

SUGGESTED FURTHER READING

Gross, M. L., *The Brain Watchers,* Random House, New York, 1962.
Guion, R. M., *Personnel Testing,* McGraw-Hill, New York, 1965.
Hoffman, B., *The Tyranny of Testing,* Crowell-Collier, New York, 1962.

PERT/COST

Areas for use in Cost Control:

ORGANIZATIONAL AND OPERATIONAL SYSTEMS
INDUSTRIAL APPLICATIONS
BUSINESS AND COMMERCIAL APPLICATIONS

Program evaluation and review technique/cost (PERT/Cost) projects cost estimates in a network system much like **critical path analysis (CPA)** to give management some idea of what costs a project will incur, and when. The technique predicts what project completion will cost, depending on such factors as numbers of workers used and amount of material and supplies provided. It can also project how much more a project will cost if completion is advanced; and how much less it will cost (if any) if completion is delayed. Additionally, the calculations of *cost for each step or phase of the project* facilitate negotiations for loans in time to prevent work delays and operating cost control.

SUGGESTED FURTHER READING

Deverell, C. S., *Business Administration and Management,* Gee & Co., London, 1966.

PHEROMONE MOTIVATION

Area for use in Cost Control:

PSYCHOLOGICAL MOTIVATIONAL MANAGEMENT

A technique in the experimental stages, pheromone motivation involves the use of scents that control reactions (pheromones) to motivate workers to greater productivity, decrease turnover, create greater job satisfaction, etc., thus reducing costs in these areas. The pheromones are chemical secretions of the body with a scent that can regulate behavior other than that of the person secreting the chemical. For example, in a riot situation, the substance secreted will further incite aggression. In the same way, other moods can be induced. Experimenters indicate that real or artificially produced pheromones might be sprayed into a working atmosphere or applied through a ventilating or air-conditioning system to induce a desired attitude toward work. Primary experimenters in pheromone motivation include: the U.S. Army Research Labs; R. Michael, Maudsley Institute of Psychology; and B. Keverne, Cambridge.

SUGGESTED FURTHER READING

Owen, L., "Nostril Power," *The Guardian,* London, June 29, 1974.

PLANNED MAINTENANCE See Preventive Maintenance.

PLANNED PROJECTIONS See F_0 Forecasts.

PLANT LAYOUT

Areas for use in Cost Control:

WORK PLACE MOTIVATIONAL MANAGEMENT
ORGANIZATIONAL AND OPERATIONAL SYSTEMS
INDUSTRIAL APPLICATIONS

Sound plant layout is the most economic arrangement of manufacturing work places and equipment. Plant layout requirements that particularly affect costs include:

1. Unified operation of the entire plant, including work flow
2. Minimum materials handling
3. Optimum use of space and equipment
4. Human-oriented arrangement to motivate workers
5. Versatility for expansion or change

Three basic types of layout may be considered:

1. *Material layout.* Materials are the focal point here, and workers come to the materials bringing tools, equipment, and other pieces of material. In this system, material handling is reduced, but equipment and employee movement is increased. The system has become more popular in recent years, since by means of it workers have more variety in their jobs and skilled employees can move easily from one product to another.

2. *Process layout.* In this system, plant layout is determined by function. For example, all painting is completed in one area. The method provides more complete use of equipment and is more adaptable for product changes than are other systems.

3. *Product layout.* Here, each type of product is constructed in one area or production line. Work is performed sequentially. The system reduces costs by reducing material handling and by reducing labor costs due to job specialization and simplification. Supervision of workers in such a consolidated unit is simplified, as is the paperwork needed for control.

All the three types are suitable in different situations.

Material location layout is most efficient for limited production, high material movement costs, and limited-equipment production. Examples of operations suited to material location layout are denture making, on-site building construction, and airplane manufacture.

Process layout is best used for operations using hard-to-move and/or expensive equipment, operations with a multiplicity of products, and products manufactured seasonally. Examples of operations suited to process layout include food processing and wine manufacture.

Product layout is most efficient for extensive production and standardized-design assembly. Examples include radio assembly and costume jewelry manufacture.

Often, efficient plant layout combines elements of all three types. An example is automobile manufacture. The main assembly is in one location (material location layout); but individual parts are processed by type of work, such as painting (process location); and smaller unit assembly, such as fenders, bumpers, and lights, is on a production line (product layout) basis.

Factors that determine how plant layout is most effective include the following:

1. *Materials.* Raw materials—how they are used, the quantity used, and the steps of use—are considered in establishing the most efficient layout.

2. *Equipment.* Sequence of use, size, and operational time of equipment must be considered.

3. *Employees.* Layout should follow the sequence of labor, providing adequate ventilation, lighting, and noise control. Equipment should be placed for greatest employee efficiency in operation.

4. *Work flow.* Work should follow the simplest route possible to reduce handling costs.

5. *Storage.* Areas must be provided for permanent or temporary storage of materials, equipment, and completed production.

6. *Flexibility.* Layout should allow method or production change as required.

Of these areas, materials and work flow are the most important to cost-saving plant reduction. If only one product is manufactured, materials and work flow can follow the sequence of work quite easily. If several products are manufactured, however, a decision must be made as to whether to use a layout that repeats equipment, dividing production into separate areas for each product; or whether work is best completed by process, grouping products that use similar equipment, work sequence, operations, and materials. Degree of similarity and volume of production are the primary determining factors. Similar operations lend themselves to grouping, as do small-volume production steps that are not sufficient to require an employee's full working time. Specialized

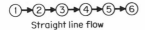
Straight line flow

Zig–zag flow

U–shaped flow

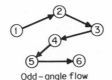
Odd–angle flow

Circular flow

Figure 80. Basic flow patterns. From H. B. Maynard, *Industrial Engineering Handbook,* 3d ed., McGraw-Hill, New York, 1974.

production methods, however, should be set out separately from multiproduct operations in order to ensure efficient work flow.

Work flow patterns should be planned for minimum movement of materials, equipment, and labor, allowing sufficient space for work. Basic flow patterns (see Fig. 80) include:

1. Straight line
2. Zigzag
3. U-shaped
4. Circular
5. Odd angle

Arrangement should be in sequence wherever possible to eliminate duplication of movement. Once sequence flow is established, the area size required for each production phase must be decided. An activity-relationship flow diagram (see Fig. 81) can then be translated into a space-relationship flow diagram (see Fig. 82) to determine the relative area needed for each production step.

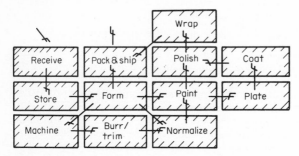

Figure 81. Typical activity-relationship flow diagram. From H. B. Maynard, *Industrial Engineering Handbook,* 1st ed., McGraw-Hill, New York, 1956.

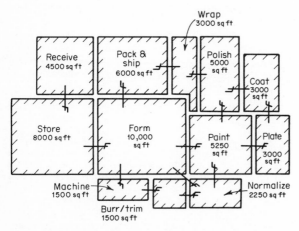

Figure 82. Typical space-relationship flow diagram. From H. B. Maynard, *Industrial Engineering Handbook,* 1st ed., McGraw-Hill, New York, 1956.

Proposed layouts may be compared by using the following checklist to determine the most effective operation with the lowest cost.

1. Does the layout reduce handling or labor (time spent) costs?
2. Does it increase speed of production?
3. Does it save space?

4. Does it reduce waste materials?
5. Does it reduce accidents?
6. Does it improve motivation?
7. Does it decrease maintenance and/or housekeeping?

SUGGESTED FURTHER READING

Maynard, H. B., ed., *Industrial Engineering Handbook,* 3d ed., McGraw-Hill, New York, 1974.

PO

Areas for use in Cost Control:

PSYCHOLOGICAL MOTIVATIONAL MANAGEMENT
ORGANIZATIONAL AND OPERATIONAL SYSTEMS
INDUSTRIAL APPLICATIONS
BUSINESS AND COMMERCIAL APPLICATIONS

PO is a creative problem-solving technique, based on science and mathematics, developed by Edward de Bono. The system is concerned with finding new concepts to handle cost and other problems rather than with processing already known data and/or concepts.

De Bono says that in conventional thinking, there are three intellectual stages in the average person's life:

1. Birth to five years—the age of "Why?"
2. Five to ten years—the age of "Why not?"
3. Ten to seventy-five years—"the age of "Because."

The second stage, "Why not?" is the only creative, problem-solving stage, he says, and principles learned here should be extended into later years for creative problem solving.

The first step in using PO is to look at new ideas without basing their worth on conventional standards or changing current ideas to find more workable ones.

The sequence of thinking and acting on a problem often becomes a trap, according to De Bono. In considering any sequence of steps in solving cost problems, the following factors apply in using PO:

1. Each step in conventional problem solving may be correct while the whole may be wrong.

2. A step or idea in solving cost problems *may* have been right at some particular time in the past yet be wrong today. For example, at one time storage costs were avoided by carrying the base-required inventory; yet, today, storage costs may be more than offset by savings on cost of materials due to the current rate of inflation.

Such patterned or sequenced thinking requires a new way of thinking if the pattern or sequence is to be broken. *Lateral thinking,* or restructuring such thoughts rather than building on already known thoughts, is the basic process in using the PO system.

Instead of finding fault with a new idea, PO encourages discussion of good points of a new idea as well as modifications that could improve it further. In PO, a new idea, no matter how ridiculous it seems, is not rejected but is considered from all angles.

In PO, ideas that seem ridiculous are called *intermediate impossibles* and are used in the following instances:

1. *A ridiculous idea occurs.* Instead of rejecting it immediately, try to use it as a basis for other ideas. For example, you may wish you could hire labor for the same price your firm paid in the 1930s. This is, of course, a ridiculous idea. But instead

of rejecting it, consider *why* you were able to hire labor at such costs. Rent was less expensive, as were food and clothing. If the company provided homes or lower-priced goods, then perhaps lower-cost labor would still be possible today.

2. *Do not reject other people's ideas that seem absurd.* Again, try to build on the idea. Suppose your secretary looks at materials cost for production and says, "If only we had bought a three years' supply of those last year!" The idea seems ridiculous, but consider future prices. If inflation rates continue to grow, it may be wise to buy a three years' supply of the materials today.

3. *At times, you may want to set up your own "intermediate impossible."* To do this, reverse any problem you have, and consider it from that difficult aspect.

A second step in PO is randomly connecting problems with seemingly unrelated words to create problem solution ideas. For example, consider the problem of finding a new transportation product in connection with the word *clock*. Clocks, PO reasoning might go, follow the movement of the sun. Perhaps the product can be powered by the sun. Or, clocks make a *tick-tock* sound. Perhaps the product could operate as quietly as a clock. Clocks usually have alarms; perhaps the transportation product could have an alarm that rings if the vehicle comes within a predetermined distance of another vehicle and is in danger of a collision.

In another example, the problem may be trade union pressures for higher wages. You may choose a word such as "soap" to create ideas. Soap cleans things; thus, perhaps if working conditions were cleaned and improved, wage demands would not be so high. Soap dissolves in water; thus, wage claims may dissolve if watered down by company benefits.

From these examples, you can easily see that the important thing is not *which* words to apply to your particular problem, but to use illogical words at random *to bring outside elements and new modes of thinking to your problem.*

The third step in PO puts the first suggested solution to a cost problem to one side, no matter how good it seems, while additional new solutions are considered.

For example, a trade union may say, "We need a 15 percent wage increase to meet the rising costs of living. That's only fair." Putting aside the offered solution of raising wages, alternate solutions should be considered. Is there, perhaps, a way to lower the cost of living? Or is there a way to give a better day's work for the improved wages?

These three steps are the basis of using PO as a tool for creative thinking, solution of cost and other problems in new ways, and avoidance of stagnant and patterned or structured action in business. Use of the technique can be effective in special PO brainstorming sessions, as well as in individual problem solution. *See also* **Brainstorming.**

SUGGESTED FURTHER READING

de Bono, Edward, *Lateral Thinking,* Penguin, Baltimore, 1973.
———, *PO: Beyond Yes and No,* Simon & Schuster, New York, 1972.

POOLING OF WORK

Areas for use in Cost Control:

INDUSTRIAL APPLICATIONS
BUSINESS AND COMMERCIAL APPLICATIONS

For some tasks requiring special skills, such as typing, taking shorthand, and calculating, it may be possible to reduce costs by maintaining an employee labor pool to deal with the jobs as they arise. Thus, a salesperson who spends most of his or her time out of the office will not use the costly full-time services of a secretary but will more economically use a stenographer from the pool for the few weekly hours of dictation. Table 42 shows advantages and disadvantages of pooling.

Table 42. Advantages and Disadvantages of Using Pools[1]

Advantages	Disadvantages
Fewer work peaks.	Loss of personal relationship with employer.
Priorities judged on departmental basis.	Employees do not learn new skills.
Operators continuously employed on one task.	Needs to refer back to using department.
Higher equipment utilization.	Departments use pool as scapegoat for own shortcomings.
Better opportunity to set standards and introduce incentives.	Many persons dislike the impersonality of working in a pool.
Greater flexibility and less difficulty with holidays and absences.	

[1]Cemach, H. P., *Work Study in the Office,* MacLaren & Sons, London, 1969.

Although less common than in office use, pooling can reduce costs in industrial applications. Operation of special skill pools, such as welding, oiling, and electrical work, can be an economical means of sharing costs among departments. General labor pools, including day laborers, are also common and can reduce costs when used to supplement regular labor staff during peak periods. In this way, if the shipping department needs extra men for 5 to 10 days each month, the grounds maintenance department may be able to use the same employees for the remainder of the time.

SUGGESTED FURTHER READING

Cemach, H. P., *Work Study in the Office,* MacLaren & Sons, London, 1969.

POPULARITY STORAGE

Areas for use in Cost Control:

MATERIALS AND EQUIPMENT MANAGEMENT
INDUSTRIAL APPLICATIONS
BUSINESS AND COMMERCIAL APPLICATIONS

Popularity storage is a stock control technique that places the most frequently used and/or the most easily moved materials, supplies, or goods nearest the point of issue. Priorities and storage positions are assigned to goods in the following order:

1. Most often issued, most easily moved items
2. Less frequently used, less easily moved items
3. Out-of-season items
4. Out-of-date items
5. Excess stock items

SUGGESTED FURTHER READING

Standingford, Oliver, ed., *Newnes Encyclopedia of Business Management,* Newnes, London, 1967.

PORTER MOTIVATION STUDIES

Area for use in Cost Control:

PSYCHOLOGICAL MOTIVATIONAL MANAGEMENT

Five studies in motivation based on the *Maslow theory of motivation* were conducted by L. W. Porter at the University of California, providing guidelines for effective motivational management.

Study 1 detailed bottom- and middle-level management personal rankings of the importance of various needs. Each need was rated from a minimum of one point to a maximum of seven. The study, conducted in three separate companies, showed that various levels of management have different levels of needs. First-line management, such as supervisors, have more unsatisfied security and esteem needs than do middle management. Self-actualization needs are not well satisfied at any level of management.

Study 2 ranked more than 6,000 top managers' and executives' needs. Self-actualization needs were found to be the least satisfied.

Study 3 measured need importance of the sample used in Study 2, and found that more top executives than lower-level managers felt self-actualization needs were important.

Study 4 measured need fulfillment and importance, comparing low, middle, and top management. Line management had more unfulfilled needs than did other groups, particularly esteem and self-actualization needs.

Study 5 measured need fulfillment and importance, comparing various-sized companies. Lower-level management was found to be more satisfied in small companies than in large companies, while top-level management was more satisfied in large companies than in small companies.

SUGGESTED FURTHER READING

Porter, L. W., "A Study of Perceived Need Satisfactions in Need-Fulfillment as a Function of Job Level," *Journal of Applied Psychology:* Basic Study, no. 45, 1962; Study 1, no. 46, 1962; Study 2, no. 47, 1963; Study 3, no. 47, 1963; Study 4, no. 47, 1963.

PORTFOLIO SELECTION

Areas for use in Cost Control:

ORGANIZATIONAL AND OPERATIONAL SYSTEMS
INDUSTRIAL APPLICATIONS
BUSINESS AND COMMERCIAL APPLICATIONS

Portfolio selection is an **operations research** technique used to choose new markets or products by translating advantages and disadvantages into mathematical equations to analyze possible risks and probable returns. The technique reduces costs by selection of potential areas with the lowest-cost/highest-profit margin. Use of a computer makes the technique a costly one, but cost advantages can be great if market estimates are accurate.

SUGGESTED FURTHER READING

Cyert, R. M., and L. A. Welsch, *Management Decision Making,* Penguin, Baltimore, 1971.

POSITIVE-ANSWER METHOD

Area for use in Cost Control:

PSYCHOLOGICAL MOTIVATIONAL MANAGEMENT

The positive-answer method is the phrasing of a question in such a way that the person answering must reply affirmatively. The technique can be used in motivating employees, training employees, conducting sales, etc. In employee motivation, the goal may be the completion of work normally requiring six hours in only five hours. The supervisor might ask the employee questions about the details of stepping up the work. For example, one question might be, "Will you need to have the stock room send in more supplies?" As the employee answers affirmatively, he or she assumes that the work will be done more rapidly and unconsciously steps up the level of output. The method is used in **programmed instruction** training systems, where the employee must answer each question positively to proceed to the next step because that correct response forms the basis of new information learned for the next question.

SUGGESTED FURTHER READING

Newman, W. H., and C. E. Summer, *The Process of Management,* Prentice-Hall, Englewood Cliffs, N.J., 1967.

POSTAL COST CONTROL

Areas for use in Cost Control:

ORGANIZATIONAL AND OPERATIONAL SYSTEMS
INDUSTRIAL APPLICATIONS
BUSINESS AND COMMERCIAL APPLICATIONS

Postal cost control can be implemented in several ways, including:

Rates knowledge. It is essential that all mail room personnel be aware of available postage rates. Special bulk mailing, printed material, book, and other commercial rates offer substantial savings.

Choice of rate class. Discriminating between urgent and nonurgent mail and choice of suitable class can also reduce postage costs. For example, in overseas goods shipments, can such shipments be sent surface? Or do they need to be sent airmail? Where airmail, first-class, and second-class domestic rates are offered, is the item nonurgent, allowing use of a lower rate? How do various rates actually affect handling?

Packaging. Special packaging can reduce rates in many cases. For example, unsealed, easily opened packages of books may be mailed at a rate reduced further than normal parcel or book rates in some countries.

Grouping. Mailing items from all departments to one branch or company in a single item reduces postage costs through decreased envelope weight and uses decreased per-ounce rates for larger packets. On a smaller scale, invoices and statements of account may be enclosed together.

Authorization. Care should be taken to screen out unstamped personal letters mailed by employees. Secretaries, clerks, and others may frequently place personal bill payments and letters in outgoing mailboxes. This practice should be discouraged, because of both postage and mail-room handling costs.

Intercompany mail delivery and pickup should be scheduled on a minimum acceptable basis, with mail being delivered once after each public delivery to the company and once later in the day to facilitate interoffice messages. Delivery and pickup should be simultaneous. Late-afternoon pickup can be eliminated by having secretaries drop mail as they leave the office.

SUGGESTED FURTHER READING

Radke, Magnus, *Manual of Cost Reduction Techniques,* McGraw-Hill, New York, 1972.

POWER COST REDUCTION

Areas for use in Cost Control:

ORGANIZATIONAL AND OPERATIONAL SYSTEMS
MATERIALS AND EQUIPMENT MANAGEMENT
INDUSTRIAL APPLICATIONS

Power costs, which have doubled and, in some cases, quadrupled in recent years, offer many possible areas for cost reduction, including:

Power selection. Alternate power types should be carefully examined *before* any new installation comes on line, and the most economical, yet acceptable, choice should be made. Oil, gas, coal, and electricity are the traditional sources of power, but new installations of nuclear, geothermal, solar, and other types of power are being developed and are economically viable in some locations.

Plant and equipment design. Efficient use of power should be a major consideration when designing or choosing plant and/or equipment. Insulation, glass area restriction, wall and floor layout, etc., can restrict heat loss in the factory itself. Hot water or steam used in production processes can frequently be circulated to provide heat and/or power for the interior of the plant, and at least one plant powers the facility with heat from scrap burning.

Equipment pipes, fittings, etc., should also be designed for efficient use of power. Good maintenance of such equipment is essential to ensure optimum use of power.

Equipment may be designed to accumulate and store power during off-peak power periods, when special lower rates are usually available.

Employee power use. Employees should be encouraged to reduce power use and costs wherever possible. Posters should be visible providing power costs in terms the workers can understand. For example, one might read, "To operate this machine for one day, power costs are $_____." Supervisors should watch for and correct obvious power wastage, such as lights on when not needed during the daytime and machines left switched on when the operator is absent. Heating and lighting may be regulated by master controls for most efficient power use.

See also **Heat Recovery and Cost Control; Nuclear Power; Solar Power.**

SUGGESTED FURTHER READING

Radke, Magnus, *Manual of Cost Reduction Techniques,* McGraw-Hill, New York, 1972.

PPBS

Areas for use in Cost Control:

ORGANIZATIONAL AND OPERATIONAL SYSTEMS
INDUSTRIAL APPLICATIONS
BUSINESS AND COMMERCIAL APPLICATIONS

PPBS (Planning, Programming, Budgeting System) is a technique used to control investment costs. Developed by the U.S. Department of Defense, the system uses mathematical programming to identify investment cash flow, control investment time phasing, and budget investments. By use of this technique, overall investment costs are balanced to make sure that all investment areas are included in the program on the basis of their priorities. In areas where projects overlap, investment costs are shared rather than repeated.

SUGGESTED FURTHER READING

Joint Economic Committee, U.S. Congress, *The Planning—Programming—Budgeting System,* Government Printing Office, Washington, D.C., 1967.
Kovick, David, ed., *Program Budgeting, Program Analysis of the Federal Budget,* Harvard, Cambridge, Mass., 1965.

PREDETERMINED MOTION TIME SYSTEMS (PMTS)

Area for use in Cost Control:

ORGANIZATIONAL AND OPERATIONAL SYSTEMS

Predetermined Motion Time Systems (PMTS) use a work measurement chart of standard times for standard jobs, or for specific motions within jobs (*see also* **Work Study and Measurement**). On this chart, such activities as grasping a tool with the hand and turning at a 45° angle are listed as to time required. To determine the total time for an assembly job, add together the separate times from the PMTS chart. Usually, a company draws up its own chart of times for jobs, such as those of spot welders and assemblers.

This technique reduces costs in work study, since times are taken from the chart rather than being taken by a person on the floor or in the office, timing the job with a stopwatch. The system is also known as Work Factor and Methods Time Measurement.

SUGGESTED FURTHER READING

Cemach, H. P., *Work Study in the Office,* MacLaren & Sons, London, 1969.
Richards, M. D., and W. A. Nielander, *Readings in Management,* South-Western Publishing Co., Cincinnati, 1967.

PREDICTIVE ACCOUNTING

Areas for use in Cost Control:

ORGANIZATIONAL AND OPERATIONAL SYSTEMS
PAPERWORK DESIGN AND FLOW SYSTEMS
INDUSTRIAL APPLICATIONS
BUSINESS AND COMMERCIAL APPLICATIONS

Predictive accounting is a **budgetary control** technique that uses business models in decision making. Such models are the executive's assumption, based on certain factual records, of what can be expected in an upcoming budgetary period. Two types of models can be used:

The first are *mathematical models,* built from accounting department information including material cost sheets, invoices, profit and loss statements, forecasts, balance sheets, labor costs, maintenance costs, and other cost records. To use this technique, all cost facts, as well as predicted sales, are set down in black and white, and the managerial staff use these figures as a basis for decision making.

A second type of predictive model uses only cost records. This *historical model* uses past cost figures alone as the basis for future decisions.

By analyzing such models, the executive can see what will probably happen in the future, and this allows him or her to make necessary changes in planning and production, keeping costs to the minimum necessary.

SUGGESTED FURTHER READING

Welch, D. T., *Budgetary Control,* MacDonald, London, 1969.

PREMIUM PAYMENT TECHNIQUE

Areas for use in Cost Control:

FINANCIAL MOTIVATIONAL MANAGEMENT
ORGANIZATIONAL AND OPERATIONAL SYSTEMS
INDUSTRIAL APPLICATIONS

The premium payment technique is a form of incentive payment in which the worker contracts for a specified payment in exchange for a specified level of productivity, in effect choosing both his or her own rate of work and rate of payment (see Table 43). Work rates and payments are graded and a specific production must be maintained for two or more weeks before payment can be advanced to a higher level (before a new contract can be effected).

Table 43. Typical Premium Payment Contract Chart

Units produced per hour	Payment per hour	Units produced per hour	Payment per hour
Over 100	$2.00	Over 180	$4.40
110	2.25	190	4.75
120	2.50	200	5.25
130	2.75	210	5.75
140	3.00	220	6.25
150	3.35	230	6.75
160	3.70	240	7.25
170	4.05	250	7.75

Thus, if a worker contracts to produce 200 units per hour at a payment of $5.25 per hour, he or she must produce 210 units an hour—the next volume level—continually for two weeks before his or her hourly rate is increased to a new contract level of $5.75.

Use of the technique reduces costs by limiting payment to output, and it also increases productivity through financial motivation.

SUGGESTED FURTHER READING

Marsh, A. I., and E. O. Evans, *The Dictionary of Industrial Relations,* Hutchinson, London, 1973.

PRE-PRODUCTION PLANNING

Areas for use in Cost Control:

ORGANIZATIONAL AND OPERATIONAL SYSTEMS
MATERIALS AND EQUIPMENT MANAGEMENT
INDUSTRIAL APPLICATIONS

Pre-production planning applies cost reduction methods to all proposed capital investment. Materials to be used, equipment, labor, and work methods—all of the proposed expenditures in the product design—are mocked up and subjected to available cost reduction techniques and the optimum alternative is chosen in each case.

Capital expenditures where PPP can best be applied include:

1. *Organizational changes.* Labor may be less costly if organized functionally, for example.
2. *New labor requirements versus automation.*
3. *Proposed equipment costs.*
4. *Proposed plant costs.*
5. *Proposed management costs.*
6. *Design.* Product quality, materials, and packaging costs may be reduced.

Several methods of applying cost reduction techniques before capital is spent have been developed, including:

1. Managerial training
2. Cost reduction specialization
3. Laissez-faire
4. Operational standards
5. Project evaluation

Managerial training. In this method, management at all levels receives formal training in cost reduction techniques through business school courses, lectures, conferences, and use of cost reduction manuals. Effectiveness is high, since it applies to all areas of operation.

Cost reduction specialization. Teams can identify areas for cost reduction and can inform management of methods available. If management as a whole is not involved, however, *application* of cost reduction techniques may never happen.

Laissez-faire. Laissez-faire is everyone doing his or her "best." This method, although commonly used, is seldom effective, since management may not know many basic cost reduction methods, and since cost reduction is carried out piecemeal rather than in an organized fashion.

Operational standards. These do little good in PPP, since cost reduction should be based on proposed standards, not past ones.

Project evaluation. This combines managerial training with **pre-production purchase analysis.** Capital return, marketability, maximum cost control, etc., can be applied to various alternate projects and the best choice demonstrated. New employees needed, organizational changes, new plant and equipment, plant layout changes, managerial changes, and materials and packaging changes and their costs are all areas that should be considered for each alternative project.

Such changes should be weighed in view of change permanency, flexibility, and coordination with other plant operations, in addition to initial cost factors.

SUGGESTED FURTHER READING

Clay, M. J., and B. H. Walley, *Performance and Profitability,* Longmans, London.

PRE-PRODUCTION PURCHASE ANALYSIS

Areas for use in Cost Control:

ORGANIZATIONAL AND OPERATIONAL SYSTEMS
MATERIALS AND EQUIPMENT MANAGEMENT
INDUSTRIAL APPLICATIONS

Pre-production purchase analysis is used to reduce the cost of production during the product's design stage. Here, materials and engineering managements follow all design work, including drawings and mock-ups, and offer suggestions for incorporation into the design that would lower production and materials costs. For example, a material already used on other products may be substituted to give standardization cost benefits. Or an alternate, less costly material may be suggested. Manufacture of two parts combined into one, for instance, can greatly reduce equipment costs if the change is made before dies are produced.

SUGGESTED FURTHER READING

Ammer, D. S., *Materials Management,* Irwin, Homewood, Ill., 1968.

PRESENTATIONS COST CONTROL

Areas for use in Cost Control:

PSYCHOLOGICAL MOTIVATIONAL MANAGEMENT
ORGANIZATIONAL AND OPERATIONAL SYSTEMS
INDUSTRIAL APPLICATIONS
BUSINESS AND COMMERCIAL APPLICATIONS

Effective presentation of new ideas, work methods, and products is an essential area of cost reduction. If the worker is to use a new time and labor cost-saving technique, for example, he or she must:

1. Be able to understand how it works.
2. Want to use it.

To accomplish this, the method must be presented effectively. That is, the necessary information must be clearly and accurately given, often in a very limited period of time, and those receiving the information should be persuaded to understand its value and to feel excited and interested in it.

Care should be taken to avoid patterning the presentation on the classroom situation. Although information is being offered, a presentation is not a lecture or a test, and if it is given in this manner, the new work method or other material may cause resentment rather than win cooperation.

Consider the audience and their position. Do they know anything about this new technique? Have they read about it? Have they seen a similar system in operation?

Determine how you want the presentation to affect the audience. Do you want the viewers to be able to operate such a supervisory system the next day? Or is the presentation a first step, intended to arouse the audience's interest in the use of such a system?

Next, list all of the points you want to make in sequence and set a tentative time limit for each, depending on its importance.

From this written presentation sequence, the actual presentation develops. Management should be aware of the basic rules for effective presentation:

1. The presentation should be in logical order and information should be given as concisely as possible still allowing a clear understanding.

2. The speaker should establish himself or herself as a person similar to those in the audience, rather than taking on a teaching or superior attitude.

3. Start at the lowest audience level of knowledge of the subject. If all know the basics, do not bore the listeners by repeating these. Do not start at too advanced a point, or nothing will be learned.

4. Arouse interest by showing the audience why your information is important to them personally. For example, a closed-circuit supervisory bank can save their constant movement from work area to work area; it can let them observe many work areas at once, increasing efficiency and increasing any financial incentives paid to management.

5. Always keep yourself in the audience's shoes. Explain things you would need and want to know if you were in their position.

6. The presentation is more effective if it is in story form. For instance, "About two weeks ago, John suggested we adapt the closed-circuit security system for supervisory use. Bill agreed that it would be worth investigating, since he figured he walked six miles a day moving from work area to work area to supervise. . . ."

7. Provide the basics; detailed demonstration and practice should be scheduled separately. For example, each supervisor would need to practice operating closed-circuit controls, but this should be done individually so as not to consume the group's time.

8. Vary presentation methods. Use visual aids, demonstrations, and question periods to break up the speaking part of the presentation.

9. Limit the length of the presentation. The psychological *attention curve* starts at a low point which rises slowly for about 10 minutes. It rises more rapidly during the next 10 minutes, then drops quite rapidly during the third 10 minutes. After this comes another short spurt of attention. If longer sessions are required because of the volume of material to be presented, breaks should be provided. Forty-minute sessions, followed by 10-minute breaks, are the maximum.

10. Use leaders to keep audience interest, such as, "After the coffee break, we'll have an interesting demonstration of the system."

11. Involvement of the audience may be facilitated through questions and jokes. The audience should be given something connected with the presentation that they can keep. A diagram of the system would be one example. Shareholder product "gift" packs at annual meetings are another example.

12. Use several people to present material for variety, and make sure they can speak effectively. Those most adept at presentations should provide the bulk of the material.

13. Practice the presentation at least once.

14. Use a suitably sized room. Empty space is depressing and ineffective.

15. Place the presentation areas away from distractions, such as open windows or office working areas.

16. Use suitable lighting, ventilation, and sound systems.

SUGGESTED FURTHER READING

Jay, A., *Effective Presentation,* Management Publications, London, 1970.

PRESENT VALUE FORMULA

Areas for use in Cost Control:

ORGANIZATIONAL AND OPERATIONAL SYSTEMS
INDUSTRIAL APPLICATIONS
BUSINESS AND COMMERCIAL APPLICATIONS

The present value system measures and evaluates potential investment alternatives, including tangible and intangible assets. Current cash flows are compared with increased assets when new investments are made in the following manner:

$$\text{Present value of investment} = \frac{\text{cash inflows} - \text{cash outflows}}{\text{economic life of investment}}$$

Thus, if a new piece of equipment costs $10,000 but will provide $50,000 extra profits over a seven-year period, the present value formula would look like this:

$$\text{PV(I)} = \frac{\$50,000 - \$10,000}{7} = \$5,714$$

In using the technique to reduce costs, the company accepts only those investments with a positive present value.

SUGGESTED FURTHER READING

Boness, A. J., *Capital Budgeting,* Longmans, London, 1972.
Mao, James, *Quantitative Analysis of Financial Decisions,* Macmillan, New York, 1969.

PREVENTIVE MAINTENANCE

Areas for use in Cost Control:

ORGANIZATIONAL AND OPERATIONAL SYSTEMS
MATERIALS AND EQUIPMENT MANAGEMENT
INDUSTRIAL APPLICATIONS

Preventive maintenance, also called planned maintenance, is the periodic inspection, repair, and upkeep of machinery and equipment *before* a breakdown occurs.

Preventive maintenance reduces overall maintenance costs, as well as downtime costs that may stem from breakdowns, since repairs, etc., can be carried out during slack operating periods.

Predetermined standards are established for all equipment parts and for maintenance methods, such as lubrication, part replacement, and inspection, as are predetermined schedules for inspection, maintenance, and necessary repairs for each piece of equipment. Using past performance records, work and frequency of such needed maintenance can be estimated to determine an approximate schedule. For example, if a piece of equipment has six parts with an overall life of 3 months, then one part will fail about every 2 weeks. Time required for each repair, including disassembly, part replacement, inspection, etc., may be 3 hours (1 hour for part replacement, 2 hours for inspection, testing, etc.), or a total of 18 hours each 3 months if all parts are replaced as they fail. But if all six parts are replaced at one time, each 2¾ months, assuming 1 hour labor for each part replaced and 2 hours to inspect and test the entire assembly, total labor time is reduced to 8 hours—a saving of 10 hours.

Except in plants operating around the clock, routine parts replacement, lubrication, accident maintenance, etc., can be performed during off hours, eliminating operator waiting time and lost production costs. Even in 24-hour operations, more equipment will be idle during night shifts and weekend hours. After comparing increased maintenance costs (due to premium maintenance labor costs during these times) with production costs savings, many preventive maintenance activities may be scheduled for slack periods.

Some factories replace equipment components with spare parts during slack hours—a rather quick operation, leaving the inoperable part for repair during normal working hours. Although this method reduces both premium maintenance labor costs and downtime costs, it necessitates a large stock of spare parts. The capital investment required for such a stock should be measured against possible savings from use of the method.

Inverse bonus payments (*see* **Inverse Bonus Technique**) are used successfully in some preventive maintenance programs. Here, maintenance workers receive a bonus which is reduced inversely in proportion to the amount of downtime.

Authorization is an important factor in reducing preventive or other maintenance costs. Authorization procedures should be built into overall control and scheduling procedures of such a program, including planning and authorization of capital projects.

All maintenance costs must be promptly recorded and charged to appropriate cost centers, equipment accounts, etc.

SUGGESTED FURTHER READING

Higgins, L. R., and L. C. Morrow, *Maintenance Engineering Handbook,* McGraw-Hill, New York, 1977.

PRICE REDEMPTION CLAUSES

Areas for use in Cost Control:

ORGANIZATIONAL AND OPERATIONAL SYSTEMS
MATERIALS AND EQUIPMENT MANAGEMENT
INDUSTRIAL APPLICATIONS

Price redemption clauses are contract additions that allow periodic renegotiation of prices. They protect the seller from possible losses due to increased costs, particularly in long-term contracts, although price increases are not tied to increased costs. The clause can also protect the buyer, since long-term production costs may be reduced, particularly when volume of output is greatly increased.

The price redemption clause was originally used in military purchasing but has now extended to all areas of business. Price renegotiation commonly occurs once a year—or oftener in an inflationary economy.

SUGGESTED FURTHER READING
Ammer, D. S., *Materials Management,* Irwin, Homewood, Ill. 1968.

PRICE TAGGING

Areas for use in Cost Control:
ORGANIZATIONAL AND OPERATIONAL SYSTEMS
MATERIALS AND EQUIPMENT MANAGEMENT
INDUSTRIAL APPLICATIONS
BUSINESS AND COMMERCIAL APPLICATIONS

Price tagging is a technique aimed at cutting costs of small office or industrial materials that are often wasted by employees. Office supplies, such as pens, stationery, and special forms, are often used for other than their intended purpose. Stationery may be used for scratch purposes, for example. Small industrial items, such as safety goggles and oil and oil cans, are often handled carelessly and discarded before they are past a useful life.

By marking the cost for each item at the employee pickup point and making sure that all employees know that operating costs are charged to each department, a firm can reduce improper use and waste for such items, saving money. Price tagging will automatically caution the secretary not to use expensive letterheads for first-draft copies, for example.

The technique is especially effective if employees share in the profits through an incentive plan, since they can then see that wasted materials mean less pay in their pockets.

SUGGESTED FURTHER READING
Cost Control and the Supervisor, American Management Assn., New York, 1966.

PRIZE INCENTIVES

Areas for use in Cost Control:
PSYCHOLOGICAL MOTIVATIONAL MANAGEMENT
FINANCIAL MOTIVATIONAL MANAGEMENT
ORGANIZATIONAL AND OPERATIONAL SYSTEMS
INDUSTRIAL APPLICATIONS
BUSINESS AND COMMERCIAL APPLICATIONS

Prize incentives, also called the green stamp technique, are the use of prizes to motivate employees to increase productivity and to attend work regularly and promptly. Point values are assigned for various elements of productivity increase, attendance, and promptness. These are accumulated by the employee and can be exchanged for prizes. The method provides a short-term incentive that is not as readily absorbed into his or her standard of living, causing less resentment than monetary incentives in case the work fails to achieve the bonus for one period. Additionally, the prizes are usually shared by the workers' families (who should be made aware of the plan), who then become enforcement factors in motivating the employees' higher output and better rate of attendance and promptness.

Prize values (purchased wholesale by the company) are about 50 percent under the accumulated point value to allow the company to pay any gift or other tax on the prize, providing a strong psychological advantage in giving the worker "tax-free" merchandise.

The system has been most extensively used in Australia for industrial productivity increases, on-time transportation and distribution operations, sales increases, work attendance, and work promptness. Prize ranges are extensive, but home appliances and package vacations are especially popular.

SUGGESTED FURTHER READING
Gilling-Smith, D., "Giving Prizes as a Spur," *The Financial Times,* London, Aug. 20, 1974.

PROBLEM ANALYSIS

Areas for use in Cost Control:
ORGANIZATIONAL AND OPERATIONAL SYSTEMS
PAPERWORK DESIGN AND FLOW SYSTEMS
DATA RETENTION—FILES AND RECORDKEEPING
MATERIALS AND EQUIPMENT MANAGEMENT
INDUSTRIAL APPLICATIONS
BUSINESS AND COMMERCIAL APPLICATIONS

Problem analysis is a technique used to determine the cause of cost or other problems, in order to prevent their recurrence. The method is implemented by listing the various factors of the problem, as well as *all* possible causes for each factor. Causes are then tested mentally to determine the most likely of them. For example, assume that the cost of manufacturing plastic sheet has risen sharply in six of a company's ten plants, while production cost has remained stable in four factories. A list of factors concerning the problem includes the following:

1. Three of the six increased-cost plants are on the East Coast of the United States. The remaining three are on the West Coast. The four stable-cost plants are in the Appalachian area.
2. Costs have increased in the last 30 days.
3. No cost increase in raw materials has occurred for 60 days.
4. No labor union agreement has been signed recently.
5. Negotiations for a new labor union contract have been under way for three months.

A list of possible causes includes:

1. One of the East Coast plants has an addition under construction.
2. Raw materials producers are located near to the four Appalachian area plants.
3. Informal slowdowns have been put into practice to add pressure to labor negotiations in some areas.

By examining the possible causes, it can be seen that construction at one plant would not affect costs at six plants. In addition, raw materials suppliers have always been located nearer the Appalachian area plants. This leaves the third possible cause, which did not affect Appalachian area plants because the area was so economically depressed that workers refused to jeopardize their jobs through an informal work slowdown.

One of the primary advantages of the technique is that its use prevents spending money on other than the real cause of the problem.

SUGGESTED FURTHER READING
Argenti, John, *Management Techniques,* Davlin Publications, Los Angeles, 1969.

PROCEDURE AGREEMENTS

Areas for use in Cost Control:
ORGANIZATIONAL AND OPERATIONAL SYSTEMS
INDUSTRIAL APPLICATIONS
BUSINESS AND COMMERCIAL APPLICATIONS

Procedure agreements are contracts between employers and trade unions agreeing on a course of action to be taken during a labor dispute. Usually, a number of procedural negotiation steps are established. While these are being followed, the union agrees not to strike and the employer agrees not to hold a lockout. Use of the technique can reduce costs if the additional time provided allows avoidance of a strike.

SUGGESTED FURTHER READING

Grant, J. V., and G. Smith, *Personnel Administration and Industrial Relations,* Longmans, London, 1969.

PROCEDURE CHARTS

Areas for use in Cost Control:

ORGANIZATIONAL AND OPERATIONAL SYSTEMS
PAPERWORK DESIGN AND FLOW SYSTEMS
DATA RETENTION—FILES AND RECORDKEEPING
BUSINESS AND COMMERCIAL APPLICATIONS

Procedure charts present procedure data visually and are used to accompany **procedure study** in determining the most efficient and economical office procedures to be used in specific applications. There are three types of procedure charts:

1. Classification charts
2. Description charts
3. Flowcharts

Classification charts show information by type of work, including operation, check, transport, file, and delay. Other symbols, or variations of the basic five, may be used in specific charts. For example, the operation symbol might be annotated with an *A* to indicate the accounting operation. The five basic symbols, as used by the Institute of Administrative Management, are shown in Fig. 83.

Operation   Check   Transport   File   Delay

Figure 83. Classification chart symbols.

Description charts show information by connection of boxes containing descriptions of the information. These may be used to show various steps in a work method, possible choices in a work method, individual worker responsibility in a work method, etc. Figure 84 gives a description chart which shows that worker *A* has two options in dealing with work material in a work process (sorting pamphlets for the company library): to file the material or to discard it.

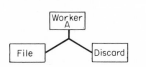

Figure 84. Typical description chart.

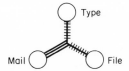

Figure 85. Typical flow procedure chart.

Flowcharts link various steps in a work process, and line symbols indicate the type of action. Solid lines are used to indicate work or document flow and alternatives. Figure 85 shows a *flowchart.* Here, the vertical barred line indicates that more than three reports are typed in a work process. Three of these may be mailed to the home office, or all of them may be filed for future reference, depending on the report. The V'd branch shows this alternative.

SUGGESTED FURTHER READING

Bull, George, ed., *The Director's Handbook,* McGraw-Hill, London, 1969.
Webster, W. A. R., *Handbook of O & M Analysis,* Business Books, London, 1973.

PROCEDURE MAPS

Areas for use in Cost Control:

ORGANIZATIONAL AND OPERATIONAL SYSTEMS
PAPERWORK DESIGN AND FLOW SYSTEMS
DATA RETENTION—FILES AND RECORDKEEPING
BUSINESS AND COMMERCIAL APPLICATIONS

Procedure maps are visual constructions showing documents used in a work procedure, arranged in order, to analyze the procedure and improve its efficiency. Costs can be reduced by elimination or simplification of individual documents in a specific procedure.

Documents are fastened to a wall or board in order of use and are connected by colored tape to indicate the flow of work. Document content, duplication, and overlaps are particularly easy to identify. The latter may then be eliminated by document combination.

SUGGESTED FURTHER READING

Bull, George, ed., *The Director's Handbook,* McGraw-Hill, London, 1969.
Webster, W. A. R., *Handbook of O & M Analysis,* Business Books, London, 1973.

PROCEDURE STUDY

Areas for use in Cost Control:

ORGANIZATIONAL AND OPERATIONAL SYSTEMS
BUSINESS AND COMMERCIAL APPLICATIONS

Procedure study transfers **method study** techniques (*see also* **Work Study and Measurement**) to observation and analysis of clerical procedures to develop increased efficiency, and so to reduce labor costs. **Procedure charts,** for example, are adapted, showing the flow of work in a given procedure and using flow-processing charting symbols (see Fig. 86). **Functional analysis** methods are used to group similar work functions in the procedure, thus reducing the amount of time required to complete it. For example, the dictation step shown in Fig. 86 may be eliminated by using a standard acknowledgment form. If this form can be mimeographed, typing of individual acknowledgments can also be eliminated. If a combination order-invoice form is used, separate invoice typing can be avoided. If perforated address labels can be grouped with this form, later addressing can also be avoided.

SUGGESTED FURTHER READING

Clay, M. J., and B. H. Walley, *Performance and Profitability,* Longmans, London, 1965.

PROCESS ANALYSIS

Areas for use in Cost Control:

ORGANIZATIONAL AND OPERATIONAL SYSTEMS
MATERIALS AND EQUIPMENT MANAGEMENT
INDUSTRIAL APPLICATIONS

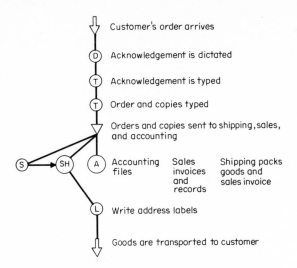

Figure 86. Typical procedure study flow process chart.

Process analysis is the examination and evaluation of product design at all stages to introduce less costly work processes where possible. Similar products, including their production costs, form one basis for comparison at each stage of evaluation. New and proposed process costs should be estimated prior to use and be compared with costs of existing production techniques.

SUGGESTED FURTHER READING

Radke, Magnus, *Manual of Cost Reduction Techniques,* McGraw-Hill, New York, 1972.

PROCESS CHARTS See Procedure Charts.

PROCESS CONTROL

Areas for use in Cost Control:

ORGANIZATIONAL AND OPERATIONAL SYSTEMS

INDUSTRIAL APPLICATIONS

Process control is an **operations research** technique used to control complicated production or operational procedures. Several computerized methods of the technique include:

1. Adaptive control
2. Data recording
3. Direct digital control
4. Evolutionary control

Adaptive Control. This method uses a computer to forecast small operational changes that will improve production. The computer is also used to determine the precise nature of the changes, which are then implemented.

Data Recording. This is computerized recording and/or analysis of factory operations.

Direct Digital Control. This is computerized operation of work normally done by human controllers. Computerized work is much cheaper, particularly in a large firm.

Evolutionary Control. This method uses a computer to make small operational changes in production or operation methods, and then to analyze the changes. If costs or time are saved or production increased, the changes are maintained.

SUGGESTED FURTHER READING

Wicks, C. T., and G. A. Yewdall, *Operational Research,* David & Charles, London, 1971.

PROCESS COSTING

Areas for use in Cost Control:

ORGANIZATIONAL AND OPERATIONAL SYSTEMS
DATA RETENTION—FILES AND RECORDKEEPING
MATERIALS AND EQUIPMENT MANAGEMENT
INDUSTRIAL APPLICATIONS

Process costing applies separate **costing** to each "process" or stage of manufacture to pinpoint excess wastes, to average unit costs over a period of time, and to separate the costs of main and by-products.

SUGGESTED FURTHER READING

Bigg, W. F., *Cost Accounting,* MacDonald, London, 1963.

PRODUCT ELIMINATION SYSTEM

Areas for use in Cost Control:

ORGANIZATIONAL AND OPERATIONAL SYSTEMS
INDUSTRIAL APPLICATIONS

The product elimination system is a method used to evaluate products and eliminate from production those that are disproportionately costly or weak. Weak-product costs include the following, which should be considered when deciding whether or not to retain the item in the company mix:

1. Lost customer confidence in the company's products
2. Disproportionate advertising costs
3. Disproportionate public relations costs
4. Disproportionate sales costs
5. Disproportionate management costs
6. Price adjustment costs due to frequent price fluctuations of leader sales attempts
7. Excessive inventory costs
8. Disproportionate production costs due to short runs
9. Loss of development of a more salable "replacement" product

PRODUCT EVALUATION

To eliminate weak-product costs, all products in a company's line should be evaluated regularly. After examination, each product should be maintained, modified for better performance, or eliminated, depending on its profitability, volume of sales, and sales potential.

An evaluation system should be formally established and followed, and should include these steps:

1. An evaluation board is created consisting of representatives from accounting, marketing, and sales as well as top management.

2. Minimum sales objectives are determined for each product in the company mix, to be sure that each is carrying its own weight.

3. Accounting representatives develop cost and income figures for each product.

4. Sales representatives develop sales volume figures for each product.

5. Marketing representatives evaluate marketing problems and then "cost" each product.

6. Top management reviews these reports, rating products that show performances below the preset objectives per product.

7. Top management makes product modification or elimination plans for products not performing satisfactorily.

MANAGERIAL PRODUCT RATING

One efficient method of managerial product rating is Philip Kotler's *product retention index*. A rating of 0 to 10 is given the product in relation to each of the following:

1. Future sales potential
2. Future sales potential if product is modified to meet market needs
3. Probable positive effect of market strategy modification on sales
4. Executive time saved by product elimination
5. Potential of alternate production opportunities
6. Product income after direct costs
7. Effect of product on remainder of line

ELIMINATION

If, after evaluation, the decision is made to eliminate a product, phasing-out plans must be made and implemented. **Network planning and analysis** techniques such as **program evaluation and review technique (PERT)** may be used to establish precise time controls. Phasing out must take into consideration the amounts of raw materials already on hand for production, inventories of the product, and what special prices and services should be offered to customers purchasing the last of the product. Additionally, production management should report on alternate uses for the production equipment, area, and/or unused raw material supplies.

As timing of the phase-out develops, both management and workers on the product must be scheduled to other work.

SUGGESTED FURTHER READING

Kotler, Philip, "Phasing Out Weak Products," *Harvard Business Review,* March–April 1965.

PRODUCTION CONTROL

Areas for use in Cost Control:

ORGANIZATIONAL AND OPERATIONAL SYSTEMS
INDUSTRIAL APPLICATIONS
BUSINESS AND COMMERCIAL APPLICATIONS

Production control is an **operations research** technique that includes several methods of work scheduling for lowest costs/highest production: **simulation; critical path analysis; heuristic methods; mathematical programming;** and **models.**

Based on **technological forecasting** of data predicting future markets and **stock control** giving current production status, one or more of the methods above are used to determine relationships between production rate, product stocks on hand, equipment and manpower needed, and material, labor, and overhead costs. Schedules are then established, via one of the above methods, to give the desired production at the lowest possible cost.

SUGGESTED FURTHER READING
Wicks, C. T., and G. A. Yewdall, *Operational Research,* David & Charles, London, 1971.

PRODUCTION STUDY

Areas for use in Cost Control:
ORGANIZATIONAL AND OPERATIONAL SYSTEMS
MATERIALS AND EQUIPMENT MANAGEMENT
INDUSTRIAL APPLICATIONS

Production study is the continuous examination of a production operation, for a minimum of one shift, as a means of evaluating standard times, determining new standard times, or checking other aspects of production. Use of the method can pinpoint bottlenecks or too liberal standard times and thus reduce labor costs.

Production study is related to **work study and measurement.** Both are aimed at reducing costs. However, production study is oriented in checking to assure that:

1. Standard times are not overly generous.
2. Quality is being maintained, as well as standard production time.
3. Possible production changes that result in time improvement are implemented.

Production ratings are recorded each 30 seconds, using a stopwatch and continuing without pause for a period that may vary from one shift to several days, depending on the length of the work cycle. At the end of the study, working time is totaled, excluding waiting time, rest periods, and other nonmeasured factors. Average rating is determined from this figure.

SUGGESTED FURTHER READING
Barnes, R. M., *Motion and Time Study,* 2d ed., Wiley, New York, 1961.
Maynard, H. B., ed., *Industrial Engineering Handbook,* 3d ed., McGraw-Hill, New York, 1974.

PRODUCTIVITY BARGAINING AND AGREEMENTS

Areas for use in Cost Control:
PSYCHOLOGICAL MOTIVATIONAL MANAGEMENT
FINANCIAL MOTIVATIONAL MANAGEMENT
ORGANIZATIONAL AND OPERATIONAL SYSTEMS
INDUSTRIAL APPLICATIONS
BUSINESS AND COMMERCIAL APPLICATIONS

Productivity bargaining is a form of labor negotiation basing wage or salary increases and other employee benefit increases, such as shorter working hours, on increments in productivity. Use of the method can reduce labor costs by limiting increased wages and benefits to a proportion of productivity gains. To make the technique work satisfactorily from management's point of view, industrial relations executives must implement *productivity agreements* once the bargaining has been successfully concluded.

WHAT PRODUCTIVITY BARGAINING INCLUDES

Productivity bargaining includes giving workers advantages in exchange for their use of work methods or equipment that increases work efficiency, reducing wage costs per production unit. This may result in higher wages for more work in the same time or in the same wages for less working time while more goods or services are produced. It may also result in agreements to retrain and/or transfer workers whose present working methods are not economical. The benefits given workers are tied directly to increased productivity.

Basically, three types of agreements are sought by management in productivity bargaining:

1. *Package agreements,* involving changes in work methods for an entire factory or office.

2. *Partial agreements,* involving one department or work area, such as parts assembly or computerized accounts billing.

3. *Framework agreements* within an industry, allowing individual agreement in plants or branches based on a more general constitutional-style industrywide agreement that serves as a guide.

THE MECHANICS OF PRODUCTIVITY BARGAINING

The actual use of productivity bargaining involves three major steps:

1. Drawing up a productivity agreement to present during negotiations
2. Negotiations during a productivity bargaining session
3. Combining productivity bargaining results with operational systems

Drawing Up the Productivity Agreement. This first step is the most essential to the success of productivity bargaining as a tool of inflation control, since content of the agreement will have as much effect as or more effect than negotiation in persuading labor to accept a benefits-productivity link. Valid objections that will be raised by labor should, ideally, be anticipated by management and resolved *before* the agreement is proposed.

Communication of the need for a benefits-productivity link should be inherent in both planning the agreement and the agreement itself. If the agreement is to serve as an alternative to government controls of wages or increasing unemployment from tighter inflation credit controls, this fact should be clearly stated in the agreement.

If a governmental wage control is already in effect, limiting wage increases to a specific increase, such as 5 percent annually, the fact of increased productivity may be used to justify higher increases to the government. Again, this should be clearly stated.

In addition, it is often necessary to show—in facts and figures—that a company cannot remain competitive at home and/or abroad, providing work stability, and still provide increased worker wages or benefits *unless* productivity is also increased.

Possibilities for increasing productivity should be discussed with labor leaders as well as among management. Labor involvement in finding ways to solve this mutual management-labor problem will facilitate cooperation at the negotiating stage. Additionally, labor is very familiar with the nuts-and-bolts part of everyday production and may have some extremely practical and valuable ideas about how to increase productivity if they are asked.

Objectives for the degree of productivity increase attainable should also be discussed by both labor and management, since attainment of such goals depends upon both. Typical objectives discussed may include unit-cost reduction possibilities, greater use of plant and equipment through shift work or better scheduling, decreased use of overtime to increase productivity per dollar of labor cost, etc., using methods that will increase the individual worker's take-home pay or shorten his or her working week in exchange for using the more productive work method.

Both labor and management should formally express a commitment to analyzing and solving agreed-upon problems and reaching agreed goals at this point, to make sure the eventual agreement has a good chance of acceptance.

Joint productivity committees are established next to carry out a thorough analysis of productivity problems and goals. Often, use of an entirely new committee, with no members from previous negotiations of whatever type, provides the most satisfactory approach. Members already too committed to previous ideas or older types of negotiation cannot act as objectively in finding mutually satisfactory ways of increasing productivity and worker benefits.

Information about company functions must be provided to *both* labor committee members and management members, since a thorough evaluation of increased productivity possibilities cannot be made with only partial knowledge of the situation.

Joint proposals for increasing productivity should be invited. These should follow naturally if other steps have used a joint labor-management involvement approach.

Evaluation of proposals is the next step. Each proposal should be translated into understandable model form to show precise costs per production unit, time per production unit, etc., that can be saved by use of a specific method. Each factor must be weighted according to its importance. For example, if method A will increase production (using the same facilities) by 5,000 units per day at the same cost per unit, this is very important only if there is a sound market that can be developed to buy the increased production. If no such potential market exists, method B, which decreases unit production costs of current production levels by 20 percent per unit, is much more important and deserves greater consideration.

Negotiations During a Productivity Bargaining Session. Negotiations during agreement production involve determination of what return labor can expect in exchange for attainment of increased productivity goals. In work method changes that will result in reduced labor costs per production unit, labor may be given increased wages. This increase is usually expressed as a percentage of the cost savings *after* an allowance is made for the capital investment required to implement the increase in productivity. This often averages 50 to 75 percent of the after-investment cost saving.

When increased output with the same per-unit cost is the result of a productivity increase, wage gains may be expressed as a percentage of increased profits that will result from increased sales. Additionally, working hours may be shortened, with take-home wages remaining stable, in proportion to time saved per production unit.

Retraining or other disposition of workers displaced by new work methods must be determined at this stage. Management should remember that this return to labor benefits the company as well, since it can result in the acquisition of needed skills in short supply.

Conclusion of these various steps forms the basis of the agreement, which is next prepared in written form for use during labor negotiations.

Combining Productivity Bargaining Results with Operational Systems. Implementing and maintaining a productivity agreement becomes primarily a job of showing both supervisors and workers how the agreement benefits them. A worker displaced by a new work method, for example, may be given the opportunity to learn a new, higher-paid skill.

Work method changes must be implemented with careful instruction in every step for every supervisor or worker affected. Increased benefits, and their dependence on increased productivity, should be emphasized.

SUGGESTED FURTHER READING

Hawkins, K., "Productivity Bargaining: A Reassessment," *Industrial Relations Journal,* Spring 1971.

Llewellyn, D. T., "Incomes Policy: The Wider Issues," *Industrial Relations Journal,* September 1970.

McKersie, R. B., "Productivity Bargaining," *Personnel Management,* September 1966.

Robinson, D., *Wage Drift, Fringe Benefits, and Manpower Distribution,* OECD, Paris, 1968.

Towers, B., T. G. Whittingham, and A. W. Gottschalk, eds., *Bargaining for Change,* G. Allen, London, 1972.

Walton, R. F., and R. B. McKersie, *A Behavioral Theory of Labor Negotiations,* McGraw-Hill, New York, 1965.

PRODUCTIVITY LINKING

Areas for use in Cost Control:

FINANCIAL MOTIVATIONAL MANAGEMENT
ORGANIZATIONAL AND OPERATIONAL SYSTEMS
INDUSTRIAL APPLICATIONS

Productivity linking is a labor payment system that links all wage increases to productivity increases, with a minimum standard rate to protect workers during a recession or during a period of raw material or equipment disruption. Use of the method reduces labor costs by limiting wage increases in relation to output increases.

Although used at present primarily in small industrial applications, some economists recommend adaptation of the method on a nationwide scale, called a high wage economy, as a means of controlling inflation. In the current situation, if wages rise 20 percent and productivity increases 5 percent, a 15 percent rate of inflation results. Productivity linking would link wage increases to productivity increases (in this case, it would limit increases to 5 percent), and, provided government spending did not exceed its income, inflation should become zero.

SUGGESTED FURTHER READING

Secretan, L., "More Pay for More Production," *The Financial Times,* London, Aug. 20, 1974.

PRODUCT LIABILITY PREVENTION

Areas for use in Cost Control:

ORGANIZATIONAL AND OPERATIONAL SYSTEMS
MATERIALS AND EQUIPMENT MANAGEMENT
INDUSTRIAL APPLICATIONS

Product liability prevention is the control of production quality for lower liability, and the accompanying costs, to purchasers. Use of the method has been accelerated by recent legal trends to hold the manufacturer responsible for damage caused by defective production.

Product liability control involves the following:

1. Control is companywide and continuous.

2. Materials and production methods are examined in relation to possible damage to product users, as well as in relation to cost and other factors.

3. Purchaser feedback on production is closely monitored and corrective action is taken where necessary.

4. Quality loss prevention, quality appraisal, and quality failure costs are determined periodically.

5. *Quality motivation* programs are operated at all phases of production.

6. Product service programs are strengthened.

SUGGESTED FURTHER READING

Lapedes, D. N., ed., *Yearbook of Science and Technology,* McGraw-Hill, New York, 1974.

PRODUCT SCREENING

Areas for use in Cost Control:

ORGANIZATIONAL AND OPERATIONAL SYSTEMS
INDUSTRIAL APPLICATIONS

Product screening is the elimination of proposed products that would prove not economically feasible for one or more reasons. Reasons might include too costly production, insufficient market, and excessive competition. Successfully eliminating such products *before* they reach production and marketing is, of course, essential in reducing wasted expenditures. Several methods can be used in screening.

Checklists are ideal for most screening operations. The following is a typical checklist:

1. Does projected sales volume exceed minimum company objectives?

2. Does projected per-unit profitability exceed minimum company objectives?

3. Does projected product growth fit into company growth needs and plans?

4. Does projected product fit into company image?

5. Is projected product compatible with the rest of the company's line?

6. Is capital available for production?

7. If not, how costly will needed capital be to obtain?

8. Is the company technologically capable of economic manufacture of the product?

9. Are plant and labor force adequate to add the product to current manufacturing?

10. If not, can they be rapidly acquired at an economical cost?

Product indexes rate proposed products on a scale, usually of 0 to 10. Usually factors similar to those set out in the checklist are evaluated, although other factors, such as effect on other production and degree of competition, may be added.

Matrix charting can be used to visually evaluate the proposed product (see Fig. 87).

	Factor weight	0	1	2	3	4	5	6	7	8	9	10	Weighted evaluation
Sales volume	20						×						100
Profit margin	25								×				175
Exclusivity	15				×								45
Technical capability	15						×						75
Physical capability	15										×		135
Line compatibility	10		×										10
Total	100												540

Figure 87. Product screening matrix chart.

Here, product factors are weighted according to importance and rated on a scale of 0 to 10. By multiplying the rating by the weighted factor, rated evaluations are obtained. Results should be compared with alternate proposed products and minimum acceptable company-objective ratings.

SUGGESTED FURTHER READING

Bass, F. M., C. W. King, and E. A. Pessemier, eds., *Application of the Sciences in Marketing Management,* Wiley, New York, 1968.
Kotler, Philip, *Marketing Management,* Prentice-Hall, Englewood Cliffs, N.J., 1972.

PROFIT CENTERS

Areas for use in Cost Control:

ORGANIZATIONAL AND OPERATIONAL SYSTEMS

INDUSTRIAL APPLICATIONS

Profit centers are collecting points for all expenditures grouped under a single head, such as "Product A Machine Hour Cost," "Product B Direct Labor Cost," or "Product C Overhead Cost." Some companies prefer this method of cost organization, since it allows more flexibility than costing by department alone. Other companies compile cost rates separately, both by department and by profit center.

SUGGESTED FURTHER READING

Dickey, R. I., *Accountant's Cost Handbook,* Ronald, New York, 1960.
Hart, H., *Overhead Costs,* Heinemann, London, 1973.

PROFIT PLANNING

Areas for use in Cost Control:

ORGANIZATIONAL AND OPERATIONAL SYSTEMS

MATERIALS AND EQUIPMENT MANAGEMENT

INDUSTRIAL APPLICATIONS

BUSINESS AND COMMERCIAL APPLICATIONS

Profit planning is evaluation of current profits, setting profit goals, and implementing these goals through cost reductions and increased efficiency. Specific methods of achieving the goals are set out in writing at the start of the program, as are timetables for goal achievement.

The first step is to set clearly defined goals rather than meaningless ones. For example, to just say, "We should increase profits," will not provide a goal that can be used in planning.

J. R. Katzenbach of McKinsey & Co., Inc., has developed a method to test goal definition. Reverse the goal statement, he says. If the reverse sounds ridiculous, the goal is probably not useful. For example, if a goal is expressed as, "We should have less wasted time," the reversal would read, "We should have more wasted time." On the other hand, if the goal is expressed, "We should reduce wasted time by 10 percent," the reverse would read, "We should not reduce wasted time by 10 percent." The latter phrase is not ridiculous when reversed, since it may provide a standard of measurement such as, "Wasted time should be reduced *more* than 10 percent."

Quantitative methods, particularly computerized ones, have sophisticated profit planning. A company can, for example, test alternate strategies, with their effects on costs and profits, and such criteria as greatest profit/cost ratio of several alternative projects; profit changes that would result from marketing, distribution, and other changes; and the impact of inventory control changes.

Line management and employee participation are essential to the success of profit planning. Line management should be involved in goal setting as well as in implementation of cost reduction and increased efficiency programs, since their knowledge of what savings can be effected are the most practical and essential, and since no program can operate without their cooperation.

Individual employees may be less concerned with the planning stage, although some companies have found it worthwhile to include at least one worker from each department in general planning sessions. As with line management, they have knowledge of everyday possibilities of cost reduction and increased efficiency.

Once a program is begun, the company profit goals should be broken down into departmental goals, and these should be subdivided until each worker knows precisely what his or her own working area goals are. For example, a goal for a single piece of machinery and its operation might be to decrease material waste by 10 percent and to reduce rejected production by 15 percent without slowing production time. Employee and line-management performance should be readily visible, with goals and results, divided by worker and area, charted in a public display area for comparison by all.

Studies indicate that profit planning can reduce overhead costs by 25 to 30 percent. Labor and material cost increases have been completely offset by productivity increases stemming from profit planning. The method, as described above, must be used continuously to attain this sort of success, however. Periodic cost reduction campaigns are not enough. Profit consciousness must become a permanent way of life at all levels of operation.

SUGGESTED FURTHER READING

Ansoff, H. I., *Corporate Strategy,* McGraw-Hill, New York, 1965.
Argenti, John, *Corporate Planning,* G. Allen, London.
Batty, J., *Corporate Planning and Budgetary Control,* MacDonald, London, 1970.
Mann, R., ed., *The Arts of Top Management,* McGraw-Hill, New York, 1970.

PROFIT SHARING

Areas for use in Cost Control:

FINANCIAL MOTIVATIONAL MANAGEMENT
ORGANIZATIONAL AND OPERATIONAL SYSTEMS
INDUSTRIAL APPLICATIONS
BUSINESS AND COMMERCIAL APPLICATIONS

Profit sharing is a form of *incentive payment* (*see* **Incentive Payment Systems**) in which workers are paid a portion of company profits as a means of motivating them to increased productivity, thus reducing labor costs. The technique also provides an amount of psychological motivation, since it creates an atmosphere of cooperation between labor and management.

SUGGESTED FURTHER READING

Robertson, D. J., *Growth, Wages, Money,* Cambridge, Cambridge, Mass., 1961.

PROGRAM BUDGETING

Areas for use in Cost Control:

ORGANIZATIONAL AND OPERATIONAL SYSTEMS
INDUSTRIAL APPLICATIONS
BUSINESS AND COMMERCIAL APPLICATIONS

Program budgeting is the addition of a second dimension to an operating budget (see Table 44), dividing budgeted costs by both company areas (such as departments)

Table 44. Typical Program Budget

Production Budget

Project, department	Product A	Product B	Product C	Total
Assembly	$50,000	$20,000	$40,000	$110,000
Welding	5,000	2,500	4,200	11,700
Painting	6,000	2,750	—	8,750
Packaging	—	—	3,200	3,200
Total	$61,000	$25,250	$47,400	$133,650

and work areas (such as projects). Use of the method allows a more precise pinpointing of the source and cause of cost deviations from the budgeted amounts for better control of such costs.

SUGGESTED FURTHER READING

Argenti, J., *Management Techniques,* G. Allen, London, 1970.

PROGRAM EVALUATION AND REVIEW TECHNIQUE (PERT)

Areas for use in Cost Control:
ORGANIZATIONAL AND OPERATIONAL SYSTEMS
INDUSTRIAL APPLICATIONS
BUSINESS AND COMMERCIAL APPLICATIONS

Program evaluation and review technique (PERT) is another version of **critical path analysis.** It differs in giving three time estimates for each activity—one pessimistic, one optimistic, and one likely. If, for example, a specific project requires a bank loan, the length of the time it will take to have the loan approved may be anywhere from two days to three months. Recording this on a *critical path chart* may delay the project if the time is recorded as "two days" and workers and materials are planned for that time. Using PERT, however, three time estimates are made, and a later starting time will be planned to allow sufficient time for approval of the loan.

While PERT is a more expensive technique in itself than CPA, the method can save the money spent through the unplanned-for delays that can occur when CPA is used.

SUGGESTED FURTHER READING

Deverell, C. S., *Business Administration and Management,* Gee & Co., London, 1966.

PROGRAMMED INSTRUCTION

Areas for use in Cost Control:
PSYCHOLOGICAL MOTIVATIONAL MANAGEMENT
INDUSTRIAL APPLICATIONS
BUSINESS AND COMMERCIAL APPLICATIONS

Programmed instruction is a method of teaching and training that uses teaching machines, programmed texts, and computer-controlled learning. It can reduce costs of training employees, or of teaching them new ideas, because it does a much more thorough job of training in less time than conventional methods. The reason for this is its provision for *feedback.* That is, information is presented step by step; questions are asked about what has just been described, and the student cannot proceed to the next step until he or she has learned the correct answer to the last question. Material may be presented visually on a teaching machine or via programmed texts with answer sheets.

Two main types of programmed instruction materials are now in general use:

1. Branching programmed instruction
2. Linear programmed instruction

Branching Programmed Instruction. Branching techniques were devised to provide flexibility in the speed of operation of the teaching. In these techniques, the machine tells the employee immediately not only whether the answer to a question was right or wrong, but also why, and then returns to the original question to have the employee select a new answer if the answer was wrong. In complex branching programs, the repeated question may be slightly rephrased to emphasize areas that the employee does not yet understand.

Linear Programmed Instruction. The simplest linear method was designed by B. F. Skinner, the behavioral scientist. He divided information into small blocks and then asked questions linking one subject block to the next. He emphasized conditioning the behavior of the student through repetition and trying to make sure that the student could answer each question correctly.

SUGGESTED FURTHER READING

George, F. H., *Cybernetics in Management,* Pan Books, London, 1970.
Kempner, Thomas, ed., *A Handbook of Management,* Weidenfeld and Nicolson, London, 1971.

PROMOTION ANALYSIS

Areas for use in Cost Control:

PSYCHOLOGICAL MOTIVATIONAL MANAGEMENT
FINANCIAL MOTIVATIONAL MANAGEMENT
ORGANIZATIONAL AND OPERATIONAL SYSTEMS
INDUSTRIAL APPLICATIONS
BUSINESS AND COMMERCIAL APPLICATIONS

Promotion analysis is the evaluation of information about promotion, used both as a motivational tool and as a basis for increasing internal promotion as a means of reducing labor costs. Factors that are determined and assessed in an individual operation include:

1. Ratio of total supervisory recruits to needed management at all levels
2. Recruitment attrition ratios
3. Company promotion rate
4. Competitor's promotion rate
5. Promotion rates by function

Ratio of total supervisory recruits to needed management at all levels. If 15 new managers are needed at various levels annually, is the quantity of total supervisory recruits adequate to "feed" this number upward, allowing for attrition? Or is expensive, outside recruitment commonly used to fill senior managerial positions?

Recruitment attrition ratios. What percentage of supervisory recruits leave the company? Why do they leave? Would they be more apt to stay if promotion was faster?

Company promotion rate. What is the average rate of promotion of supervisory recruits? Once each two years? Once each four years?

Competitor's promotion rate. How does the company's promotion rate compare with that of major competitors? If it is considerably better, this offers both psychological and financial motivation for the supervisory recruit to join, and stay with, the company.

Promotion rates by function. How do various promotion rates by function compare? In one company, for example, supervisory recruits in production were promoted on an average of once each 18 months—primarily because the bulk of top production management was reaching retirement age, allowing for constant upward movement all along the line. In the accounting department, made up primarily of management in the 30-to-40 age bracket, promotion averaged once each six years. While supervisory recruits in the production department had a low attrition rate, accounting recruits were more apt to transfer to other departments or to move to a new company with a better chance for promotion.

SUGGESTED FURTHER READING

Mann, R., ed., *The Arts of Top Management,* McGraw-Hill, New York, 1970.

PROMOTION QUESTIONNAIRE

Areas for use in Cost Control:

ORGANIZATIONAL AND OPERATIONAL SYSTEMS
PAPERWORK DESIGN AND FLOW SYSTEMS

INDUSTRIAL APPLICATIONS
BUSINESS AND COMMERCIAL APPLICATIONS

The promotion questionnaire is a simple scale device used to determine the least costly person to promote among alternative candidates. The scale (see Fig. 88) was developed by Frank A. Heller, Tavistock Institute, for use in research of decision making and styles of leadership.

Figure 88. Promotion questionnaire scale. (Frank A. Heller, *Managerial Decision-Making,* Tavistock Publications, London, 1971.)

In using the scale, both the employee being considered for promotion and the supervisor whose position he or she will fill mark the length of time they estimate it will take the employee to acquire the skill to do the job effectively. The results of the employee's self-rating and the manager's rating are averaged in each case. These are used as a rough comparison of employees potentially able to fill the position.

SUGGESTED FURTHER READING

Heller, Frank A., *Managerial Decision-Making,* Tavistock Publications, London, 1971.

PUNCTUALITY BONUS

Areas for use in Cost Control:
PSYCHOLOGICAL MOTIVATIONAL MANAGEMENT
FINANCIAL MOTIVATIONAL MANAGEMENT
ORGANIZATIONAL AND OPERATIONAL SYSTEMS
INDUSTRIAL APPLICATIONS
BUSINESS AND COMMERCIAL APPLICATIONS

A punctuality bonus is a share of reduced costs stemming from prompt work attendance that is paid to the employee. *See also* **Absenteeism Control.**

SUGGESTED FURTHER READING

Marsh, A. I., and E. O. Evans, *The Dictionary of Industrial Relations,* Hutchinson, London, 1973.

PURCHASE ACCOUNTING

Areas for use in Cost Control:
ORGANIZATIONAL AND OPERATIONAL SYSTEMS
PAPERWORK DESIGN AND FLOW SYSTEMS
INDUSTRIAL APPLICATIONS
BUSINESS AND COMMERCIAL APPLICATIONS

Purchase accounting is a method used to make sure that:

1. Only goods authorized are purchased.
2. Only goods and services purchased and received are paid for.
3. Payment is made in accordance with agreed and/or contractual terms.

Forms. Forms used in purchase accounting include Purchase Orders, Receipt of Goods Forms, Invoices, and Statements. In addition, a Purchase Journal and a Ledger are kept.

The *Purchase Order* is a form requisitioning and authorizing the purchase of goods. The buyer presents this to the company supplying the goods or service.

The *Receipt of Goods Form* is sometimes a copy of the invoice and sometimes a separate form. It is prepared by the supplier and signed by the buyer when goods are delivered to prove delivery.

The *Purchase Invoice* is a form completed by the supplier and usually given to the buyer at the time goods are delivered. The *Invoice* details the shipment items, as well as their cost. The buyer will check this form against her or his *Purchase Order* before posting the amount to the *Purchase Journal*. Generally, separate journals are maintained for the purchase of raw materials and for general expenses or overhead. Goods returned must be credited against the recorded invoice amounts in the *Purchase Journal*.

Statements are forms prepared by the supplier, usually monthly, informing the buyer of the total amount owed—or a statement of the status of his account—at the time of preparation. Invoices and Statements are posted to *a Purchase Ledger,* as the amount of all Invoices less the *Credit Statements* should equal the money due recorded on the monthly (or other) Statement. Entry is by the supplying company and includes terms of purchase, such as cash discounts for prompt payment of statements.

Discounts. Three types of discounts are generally used:

1. Trade
2. Quantity
3. Prompt cash payment

Trade discounts are those given to persons trading in the goods by a supplier who sells both retail (to the general public) and wholesale.

Quantity discounts are those given purchasers buying in bulk.

Prompt Cash Payment or *Cash* discounts are those given for payment of a bill within a specified time, usually seven days.

SUGGESTED FURTHER READING

Standingford, Oliver, ed., *Newnes Encyclopedia of Business Management,* Newnes, London, 1967.

PURCHASE BY USE

Areas for use in Cost Control:

ORGANIZATIONAL AND OPERATIONAL SYSTEMS
INDUSTRIAL APPLICATIONS
BUSINESS AND COMMERCIAL APPLICATIONS

Purchase by use is the method of paying only for the amount of use of a piece of equipment or other asset. For example, a firm may pay for salesmen's cars by the miles the vehicle is driven. Or, in an office, payment for a copier may be based on the number of copies made. Use of the technique reduces costs for equipment that is not in continual use by limiting payment to actual use of the asset.

SUGGESTED FURTHER READING

Weinberg, Sidney, *Profit through Quality,* Gower Press, London, 1969.

PURCHASE RESEARCH

Areas for use in Cost Control:

ORGANIZATIONAL AND OPERATIONAL SYSTEMS
INDUSTRIAL APPLICATIONS
BUSINESS AND COMMERCIAL APPLICATIONS

Purchase research is a technique that systematically searches for the quality and quantity of needed goods at the best price, as well as analyzing eventual use of such goods and suggesting more efficient and/or less expensive methods of use. Study of the following may be included in purchase research:

1. *Materials used in production*—new materials, alternate materials, higher- or lower-quality materials

2. *Price*—including satisfactory supply at best price, market trends, and economic trends

3. *Capital equipment decisions*—whether to buy, manufacture, or subcontract

4. *Work study and measurement*

5. *Operations research*—a method of replacing equipment parts

6. *Assessment of material cost* in relation to its use

Purchasing employees who have studied these areas can provide the following cost reduction purchasing services:

1. Recommend an economic intercompany system of supply.
2. Set up a purchasing system for continuous supply of goods required.
3. Buy ahead when it is expected that suppliers will be short or when prices are likely to rise.
4. Be aware of new materials and work methods.
5. Be aware of new suppliers.
6. Be able to forecast supply price changes.
7. Be able to forecast market changes.

SUGGESTED FURTHER READING

Standingford, Oliver, ed., *Newnes Encyclopedia of Business Management,* Newnes, London, 1967.

PURCHASING

Areas for use in Cost Control:

ORGANIZATIONAL AND OPERATIONAL SYSTEMS
PAPERWORK DESIGN AND FLOW SYSTEMS
INDUSTRIAL APPLICATIONS
BUSINESS AND COMMERCIAL APPLICATIONS

Purchasing needed raw materials, supplies, and equipment is a vital area for cost reduction since it involves the spending of large sums.

PURCHASE REQUISITIONING

The process is started with *purchase requisitioning,* the authorization of the company (through an approved official) to buy the needed goods. Quality, quantity, and date needed are specified on a *Requisition Form,* which must be signed by an authorized person.

The Requisition Form should also be numbered for accounting control. In the case of goods that are needed periodically, a *Repeating Requisition Form* may be established, where goods are ordered regularly according to a predetermined schedule.

A section to include *Purchase Order* number, date ordered, and supplier's name and address should be included in the form's design for best control.

ORDERING

Selection of supplier in purchasing depends on several factors:

1. Quality of goods
2. Price of goods
3. Availability of goods
4. Service offered by supplier
5. Payment terms offered by supplier
6. Reliability of supplier

It may be less costly, for example, to order slightly more expensive goods from a supplier who offers terms of 60 days than to buy less expensive goods from a supplier who ships only C.O.D. In the same way, suppliers offering discounts for prompt payment may be cheaper overall than companies without discounts, even if the basic goods cost is more.

Quotation Request Forms are often used to determine suppliers' prices for goods.

Quotations are compared and the supplier offering the best advantage to the buyer is chosen. The next step is preparation of a *Purchase Order*. Careful form design is needed, since the Purchase Order serves as a legal contract. Factors to be included are:

1. Name and number of form
2. Name and address of supplier
3. Name and address of buyer
4. Date of order
5. Description of goods
6. Quantity of goods
7. Production specifications of goods
8. Price of goods
9. Delivery destination
10. Delivery date
11. Terms of payment
12. Cost of transportation, if any
13. Discounts, if any
14. Signature of purchasing officer

Form design and flow should be planned for simplicity of handling, avoiding unnecessary and costly duplication. For example, a company might prepare copies of purchase orders for the following:

1. Supplier
2. Purchasing file
3. Receiving department
4. Inspection of goods
5. Accounting department
6. Requisitioning department

Often it is possible to combine use of copies. In the example given above, one copy may be used for items 3, 4, and 5. In this way, the accounting department receives notice of the need to pay and is assured that the goods have been received and inspected prior to payment. In combinations of this kind, the form should have added space for notation of handling by the Receiving and Inspection departments.

Purchase Orders or *Contracts* often list conditions and terms to protect the buyer. These may include:

1. Definition of terms
2. Time limits on acknowledging an order and/or supplying goods
3. Substitutions permitted in goods

4. Minimum quality of goods
5. Guarantee of goods
6. Delivery terms
7. Ownership of property
8. Terms for rejection of goods
9. Loss or damage in transit
10. Terms of payment and/or discounts
11. Insurance of goods in transit
12. Patent infringement
13. Subcontracting or assignment of order
14. Bankruptcy
15. Indemnity

PURCHASING RECORDS

One key area in reducing purchasing cost is that of recordkeeping. The following trade lists should be maintained for rapid consultation:

1. Suppliers' names and addresses, including what goods are supplied by each
2. Prices of goods last purchased in each area
3. Purchases made, listing items, prices, and suppliers
4. Material specifications required
5. Dates of purchases

In addition, the following records give the status of purchases in process, ensuring time and cost control:

1. File of contracts outstanding by deadline dates
2. Receiving book, detailing deliveries
3. Invoice book, detailing invoices processed
4. Codes for use on *Requisitions, Quotation Requests,* and *Purchase Orders* to indicate department and material for accounting use
5. Order register for purchases in progress but not yet received
6. Departmental breakdown of purchasing costs

PURCHASING TECHNIQUES

Purchase Research. This method involves systematically searching for the quality and quantity of goods needed at the best price. Purchasing costs and their results are also examined, and changes in materials purchased or methods used may be suggested. *See also* **Purchase Research.**

Value Analysis. Also called "value engineering," this technique reduces costs by analyzing the value of goods purchased in relation to their use, systematically substituting designs, components, or materials of lower cost but giving the minimum performance required. *See also* **Value Analysis.**

Standardization. This technique requires establishment of a normal or usual material, component, or work method to be used in a specific product or series of products. Cost advantages stem from volume-buying possibilities as well as from greater labor familiarity and capability in using the goods. *See also* **Standardization.**

Simplification. This technique reduces costs by reducing the items stocked, allowing bulk purchasing. *See also* **Simplification.**

Purchasing Evaluation. No matter which purchasing techniques are used, they should be evaluated as to cost effectiveness periodically. Evaluation should determine volume, time required, and money saved. Generally, three methods of evaluation are used:

1. *Survey Evaluation,* or answering questions about costs, organization, volume of work, etc.
2. *Checklist Evaluation,* or measuring results against a list of purchasing activities
3. *Statistical Scoring,* or comparing results with past costs and/or production figures

See also **Purchasing Evaluation.**

SUGGESTED FURTHER READING

Bull, George, ed., *The Director's Handbook,* McGraw-Hill, London, 1969.

Standingford, Oliver, ed., *Newnes Encyclopedia of Business Management,* Newnes, London, 1967.

PURCHASING BY LIFE

Areas for use in Cost Control:

ORGANIZATIONAL AND OPERATIONAL SYSTEMS
INDUSTRIAL APPLICATIONS
BUSINESS AND COMMERCIAL APPLICATIONS

Purchasing by life is a technique used to determine the most economical purchase of equipment or other assets that are constantly in use and that are not likely to be outdated in the near future. Cost divided by life provides a means of comparing such assets and determining which will be the least costly over the asset's use life. For example, if a company is considering the purchase of an electric typewriter, it might compare available models (see Table 45). Although typewriter B costs the most initially, its cost per year is least.

Table 45. Purchasing by Life Comparison

Machine	Total cost	Estimated life	Cost per year
A	$675	5 years	$135
B	$805	7 years	$115
C	$520	4 years	$130

SUGGESTED FURTHER READING

Weinberg, Sidney, *Profit through Quality,* Gower Press, London, 1969.

PURCHASING EVALUATION

Areas for use in Cost Control:

ORGANIZATIONAL AND OPERATIONAL SYSTEMS
INDUSTRIAL APPLICATIONS
BUSINESS AND COMMERCIAL APPLICATIONS

Purchasing evaluation is a technique used to measure the effectiveness of purchasing cost reduction methods. Evaluation should determine volume of work handled, time required to complete work, and money saved. Methods of evaluation include:

1. *Survey Evaluation*—answering predetermined questions about costs, organization of work, volume of work, etc.

2. *Checklist Evaluation*—measuring results against a list of purchasing activities (see Table 46).

3. *Statistical Scoring*—comparing results with past costs and/or production figures.

Table 46. Sample Evaluation Checklist

1976 Purchasing Evaluation Checklist

	Less than 1975	Same as 1975	Greater than 1975
1. Requisitions received			√
2. Bids requested			√
3. Purchase orders sent	√		
4. Cost/purchases			√
5. Number items purchased and stocked	√		
6. Purchasing time/order	√		
7. Number items standardized			√
8. Number items simplified			√

Costs can be directly compared with previous figures, but evaluation of volume and qualitative aspects of purchasing requires more research and analysis.

Volume evaluation includes such factors as:

1. Number of requisitions
2. Number of bids requested
3. Number of orders placed
4. Value of orders placed
5. Number of invoices received
6. Value of invoices received
7. Telephone calls placed
8. Personal supplier visits made
9. Number of other correspondence items

Quality of purchasing can be evaluated using the following factors:

1. Number of requisition deadlines met

2. Production cost saved through material or method change, standardization, and/ or simplification

SUGGESTED FURTHER READING

Standingford, Oliver, ed., *Newnes Encyclopedia of Business Management,* Newnes, London, 1967.

QUADRATIC PROGRAMMING See Mathematical Programming.

QUALITY IMPROVEMENT CAMPAIGN

Areas for use in Cost Control:

PSYCHOLOGICAL MOTIVATIONAL MANAGEMENT
ORGANIZATIONAL AND OPERATIONAL SYSTEMS
MATERIALS AND EQUIPMENT MANAGEMENT
INDUSTRIAL APPLICATIONS

The quality improvement campaign involves organizing and operating a campaign to reduce controllable worker production defects and the accompanying cost of wasted time and materials. Workers and supervisors are motivated to eliminate such defects by being persuaded that each worker is part of the overall production and quality team and can and should work to improve production quality. Intercompany publicity and attention are used, and the goals should be personalized for each employee, the individual worker being shown what he or she should do and how he or she might do it.

Some of the methods used to conduct a quality improvement campaign include:

1. Slogans, displayed on "giveaways," near elevators, etc.
2. Posters
3. Contests
4. Quality-connected incentive payments
5. Letters or campaign bulletins mailed to the employees' homes by the company president
6. Features in the company newspaper or magazine
7. Design of a "quality" cartoon character, used throughout the company in various cartoon applications
8. Displays of wasted material from rejected, poor-quality production
9. Self-rating sheets
10. Displays to provide employees with better understanding of how the firm's products are ultimately used
11. Display of contest prizes
12. Quality suggestion boxes and awards

If the quality improvement campaign is to provide lasting results, each worker must also be provided with a list of factors required to maintain quality, including illustrations of correct work methods where useful. Such a list may be printed on pocket-sized plastic cards with commonly used measurement or conversion tables on the opposite side.

Training or retraining should be provided for employees whose work quality is substandard.

The campaign results should be visible plantwide, since such results measure quality improvement.

New work methods, tools, etc., that improve quality should be permanently incorporated into company operating policies. These new methods should be written and distributed companywide for more extensive application.

Quality "scoring" introduced during a contest may be continued permanently as a constant measurement of quality performance.

SUGGESTED FURTHER READING

Juran, J. M., ed., *Quality Control Handbook,* McGraw-Hill, New York, 1962.

QUALITY INSPECTION

Areas for use in Cost Control:

ORGANIZATIONAL AND OPERATIONAL SYSTEMS
INDUSTRIAL APPLICATIONS

Quality inspection of manufactured goods is a technique used to determine the acceptability or unacceptability of the product to the eventual purchaser. Quality inspection reduces costs by preventing unacceptable goods being sold and returned, as well as by pinpointing quality problems (and the accompanying cost of wasted labor and materials) for attention before waste costs become exorbitant.

Use of quality inspection involves the following steps:

1. Establish minimum quality standards acceptable to purchasers of the product.

2. See that product specifications match the purchaser's quality needs. Such specifications may be set needlessly high, costing more than necessary, or they may be set too low.

3. Establish and implement quality measurement methods for incoming raw materials.

4. Establish and implement quality measurement methods for production.

5. Inspection checks should include product handling, packaging, warehousing, and shipment.

6. Quality records should indicate any unacceptable percentage of production and its causes.

7. Make very careful checks of new items in production.

8. Regularly schedule calibration of testing equipment.

In addition to normal quality checks, the inspector may be able to make cost-reducing suggestions in the following areas:

1. Estimate of production rate potential
2. Suggestions for improving the production rate through improved work methods
3. Suggestions for improved equipment use

SUGGESTED FURTHER READING

Weinberg, Sidney, *Profit through Quality,* Gower Press, London, 1969.

QUALITY PROTECTION

Areas for use in Cost Control:

ORGANIZATIONAL AND OPERATIONAL SYSTEMS
INDUSTRIAL APPLICATIONS

Quality protection is the technique of checking quality of materials and supplies purchased. Use of the method reduces costs by eliminating unsuitable-quality materials before they are used in production and labor is wasted. Usually a random sampling of incoming materials and supplies are tested against predetermined minimum standards, since testing of all materials would be too costly to be economically feasible. If a shipment contains some substandard materials, the entire shipment may then be tested to determine whether to return the materials for credit or keep the portion that is acceptable.

SUGGESTED FURTHER READING

Argenti, John, *A Management System for the '70's,* G. Allen, London, 1972.
Weinberg, Sidney, *Profit through Quality,* Gower Press, London, 1969.

QUALITY SURVEY

Areas for use in Cost Control:

ORGANIZATIONAL AND OPERATIONAL SYSTEMS
DATA RETENTION—FILES AND RECORDKEEPING
MATERIALS AND EQUIPMENT MANAGEMENT
INDUSTRIAL APPLICATIONS

A quality survey, also called "quality audit," combines information about the quality-related aspects of functional design specifications, production design specifications, known production problems and solutions, inspection schedules and accuracy, equipment accuracy and efficiency, and employee production attitudes, accuracy, and efficiency. Such data are compiled and tabulated to determine areas where costs can be reduced through improved quality control.

A quality survey may be performed by management consultants who will have an objective view of operating procedures. A survey committee, consisting of top company management, line-management representatives, and the consultant can then determine a course of action to correct quality defects, eliminating the cost of the accompanying waste of time and materials.

If an outside consultant is not used, engineering, production, and sales managerial staff should be appointed to conduct the survey. The survey committee procedure outlined above is used.

SUGGESTED FURTHER READING

Juran, J. M., ed., *Quality Control Handbook,* McGraw-Hill, New York, 1962.

QUARTERING

Areas for use in Cost Control:

ORGANIZATIONAL AND OPERATIONAL SYSTEMS
INDUSTRIAL APPLICATIONS
BUSINESS AND COMMERCIAL APPLICATIONS

Quartering is the practice of deducting a quarter of an hour's pay for each predetermined unit of time (usually three minutes) that an employee is late for work.

SUGGESTED FURTHER READING

Marsh, A. I., and E. O. Evans, *The Dictionary of Industrial Relations,* Hutchinson, London, 1973.

QUESTIONNAIRE STUDY See Personnel Attitude Measurement.

QUEUEING THEORY

Areas for use in Cost Control:

ORGANIZATIONAL AND OPERATIONAL SYSTEMS
MATERIALS AND EQUIPMENT MANAGEMENT
INDUSTRIAL APPLICATIONS
BUSINESS AND COMMERCIAL APPLICATIONS

Queueing theory is mathematical evaluation providing optimal service to customers while reducing service costs as much as possible. The calculations might be used, for example, to determine the minimum number of salesclerks needed to provide adequate service in a retail store. Probability rates of demand for services, servicing rates, etc., are made from a sampling of historic demands or by other forecasting techniques.

Cost reduction can be further increased by scheduling such services to reduce employee idle time, such as beauty shop service scheduling, to make sure all work hours are as nearly filled as possible. Additionally, labor involved in providing the service should be reduced to the acceptable minimum through such devices in stores as self-service goods selection and multiple-service counters operated by one employee; or such arrangements as a cashier who takes payment from two lines of customers, one on either side of the work position, absorbing the time lag that occurs as customers find their money, count their change, etc.

SUGGESTED FURTHER READING

Morse, P. M., *Queues, Inventories, and Maintenance,* Wiley, New York, 1958.

RANDOM-ACCESS FILE CARDS

Area for use in Cost Control:

DATA RETENTION—FILES AND RECORDKEEPING

Random-access file cards are data storage facilities used to retain information for on-line use in a computerized system. Costs can be reduced through both immediate availability of information and decreased storage space required. For example, as many as 1,200 pages can currently be reproduced on a two-inch plastic square. This plastic "card" is stored in the computer file. When information from it is required, a viewer magnifies the copy up to 50,000 times. *See also* **Electronic Data Processing.**

SUGGESTED FURTHER READING

Lefkovitz, D., *File Structures for On-Line Systems,* Spartan/Macmillan, London, 1969.
Martin, J., and A. R. D. Norman, *The Computerized Society,* Prentice-Hall, Englewood Cliffs, N.J., 1970.

RANDOM OBSERVATION See Sampling.

RANKING See Personnel Performance Appraisal.

RATE CUTTING

Areas for use in Cost Control:

ORGANIZATIONAL AND OPERATIONAL SYSTEMS
INDUSTRIAL APPLICATIONS

Rate cutting is the reduction of wages paid, particularly piece rate wages, for a specific production step where a new, faster work method has been implemented, or where original ratings have set the wage rate too high. Although the technique reduces wage costs, management will usually meet trade union objections to rate cuts. If the cuts are justifiable, they can often be made in a trade-off agreement, in exchange for granting a desired labor benefit, during labor negotiations.

SUGGESTED FURTHER READING

Maynard, H. B., ed., *Industrial Engineering Handbook,* 3d ed., McGraw-Hill, New York, 1974.
ASME Work Standardization Bulletin, American Society of Mechanical Engineers, New York.

RATIONALIZATION

Areas for use in Cost Control:

ORGANIZATIONAL AND OPERATIONAL SYSTEMS
INDUSTRIAL APPLICATIONS
BUSINESS AND COMMERCIAL APPLICATIONS

Rationalization is the conscious combination of operational steps to eliminate material, labor, and/or labor waste, thus reducing costs. For example, uneconomical product lines may be discontinued while profitable lines are expanded. Processes may be automated to increase production per overhead dollar, or production may be switched to up-to-date equipment as slower equipment that produces less is discarded.

SUGGESTED FURTHER READING

Burnham, T. H., and G. O. Hoskins, *Elements of Industrial Organization,* Pitman, London, 1965.

READY RECKONERS

Areas for use in Cost Control:

ORGANIZATIONAL AND OPERATIONAL SYSTEMS
PAPERWORK DESIGN AND FLOW SYSTEMS
INDUSTRIAL APPLICATIONS
BUSINESS AND COMMERCIAL APPLICATIONS

Ready reckoners are simple devices used to perform repetitive calculations. In the case of simple calculations, such devices are faster, and therefore less costly, than calculating machines. For example, ready reckoners can be used to convert other systems of measure to metric measurement. Or percentage reductions or increases can be quickly calculated. Many inexpensive ready reckoners are commercially available, but they can usually be made to fit exact requirements.

SUGGESTED FURTHER READING

Longman, H. H., *How to Cut Office Costs,* Anbar Publications, London, 1967.

RECYCLING

Areas for use in Cost Control:

ORGANIZATIONAL AND OPERATIONAL SYSTEMS
MATERIALS AND EQUIPMENT MANAGEMENT
INDUSTRIAL APPLICATIONS
BUSINESS AND COMMERCIAL APPLICATIONS

Recycling is the reuse of raw materials already used one or more times in production by processing to make them suitable for such use. Cost reductions result in several areas. Materials previously used and discarded can be sold for recycling, saving product costs for the end user. The product's manufacturer, or other industries, can, at the same time, use lower-cost but acceptable-quality recycled materials over and over. This is particularly important in light of declining (and thus, more costly) world supplies of raw materials.

Industry, business, and the consumer must cooperate if recycling is to be successful. Industry must be willing to use recycled materials and must develop facilities, where they do not already exist, to process such materials. Business, a large consumer of many recyclable goods, such as packing cases and cartons and packaging materials, must make special efforts to sell such materials back to industry for reuse. Individual consumers can provide material for reuse and should be required by governments to separate reusable items, such as paper goods, for refuse collection. Governments, like business, can then sell the reusable materials as well as ensure maximum use of them.

Facilities and processes for recycling have been more thoroughly developed in some areas than in others. Processes already operative are discussed here by industry.

Paper. Repulped paper can provide content for paper and paperboard products up to 100 percent of total content. De-inking processes, making newspaper reusable, are also operative. The primary problem is the separating of paper goods from other refuse by businesses, consumers, and governments, and its channeling back into industry.

Textiles. Waste textile materials are best recycled into other industries. Discarded cloth can be processed into thread, padding and stuffing, roofing felt, and cleaning cloths.

Synthetic cloth waste is more difficult to recycle than natural materials because the variety of fiber content cannot be economically sorted. Processes have been developed to produce active carbons from such waste, however, and these are currently being refined.

Wool wastes are generally repulled and respun, usually to be mixed with some percentage of new wool.

Metals. Metals are recycled basically by repeating the original production process. Sorting of metals is a primary problem, as is processing metal compounds containing ferrous metals.

New copper recovery techniques are particularly efficient, spurred by the very rapid decline in supplies of copper.

Nonferrous metals require good security during storage, reprocessing, and delivery because of their high value.

Chemical and electronic devices have been developed to aid in the complex task of sorting aluminum wastes, although hand sorting is still heavily used.

Scrap tin is best used in alloys, such as some bronze alloys. Collection of industrial and household tinplate can greatly increase the amounts of the material made available for reuse. Other areas, such as tin waste in soldering, have no economical means of scrap collection at this point.

Lead recovered from used pipe and sheet, fittings, automobile batteries, electrical cables, bullets, and industrial discard is reprocessed into both soft and antimonial lead.

About 5 percent of total material used for both platinum and mercury is reprocessed scrap. Available reprocessing techniques make the complete turnaround with little or no waste.

Ferrous scrap from iron and steel were leaders in recycling. For example, estimates of pig iron reuse are about 4 million tons annually; and the steel industry spends about $25 million a year on research, including that aimed at obtaining optimum reuse of the material. Reconstituted steel—scrap steel sheeting stamped without resmelting—is one economical recycling technique that has been developed. Scrap is cut into small pieces, heat-treated to welding temperature, and rolled directly into steel sheets.

Glass. Waste glass, called *cullet,* is remelted and mixed with new glass in proportions of up to 30 percent. Not only does the recycled glass reduce costs; it also aids the liquefaction. Industrial cullet is reused by the plant producing it after crushing to 3-inch size. Glass wastes collected externally must be separated by color for some applications. Magnetic separators are used to remove metal objects before the glass is crushed.

Waste glass can be used in glass paper, road-surfacing aggregates, and glass-reinforced plastics, as well as in glass manufacture.

Coal. Slag—wastes remaining once coal is mined—is being recycled into civil engineering applications, including highway and other foundations as well as filling.

Sand. Waste sand from clay production can be used in some concrete grades. As with coal slag, a primary problem is reuse near the mining site, since transportation costs quickly rise above the materials' reuse values.

Plastics. Thermoplastic wastes are sorted for content, sawed or ground to small size, and melted into an extruder. Filters strain out impurities during the molten phase. Recycled plastics are generally mixed with virgin grades, depending on the end application. Recycling processes for thermosetting materials are still in experimental stages, although a great deal of research is being channeled into this area. Current waste plastics that are recycled are largely industrial; consumers' plastics wastes can provide much-needed new raw material supplies if suitable collecting and refining methods can be developed.

Rubber. This industry was another forerunner in recycling, and both industrial and commercial rubber scrap is recycled by crushing, grinding, and melting. Low grades of rubber commonly contain reused materials. In fact, current needs for reused rubber consume about one-third of total scrap available.

Food. Many waste by-products from food processing can be recycled for other industrial uses. Residual mustard meal, for example, is used in animal feed. Commercially usable oil is also an extractable mustard waste. Scrap chocolate nut, as well as syrup mixtures not of acceptable quality for reuse in candy, is also used in animal feed, as are crushed crackers and cookies. Fruit of a quality unusable for canning or jams may be used in ice cream or in animal feed. Stones and seeds can be used to polish metals. Low-quality vegetables are used as animal feed or fertilizer.

Tobacco. Tobacco wastes that cannot be used because of their low quality are collected to earn rebates on taxes and, in the case of imported tobaccos, customs fees. Vacuum cleaners are often used to collect waste tobacco in processing areas. Tobacco stems may be pulped and rolled into sheets for cigar coverings. Ordinary paper-manufacturing equipment can be used.

Leather. Scrap leather may be used in fertilizer, while fleshings are commonly collected and sold to glue manufacturers. Hair is recycled into such goods as felt and plaster as a binding agent.

Wood. Waste products generally make up to 30 percent of total volume used. These may be pulped for bonded or fabricated building sheet and sound-insulation sheet. Some wastes, such as sawdust, may be used as an energy source to power manufacturing processes.

Water. Newer manufacturing plants are being designed to clean and reuse water where possible, as much as a means of reducing the cost of meeting newly required environmental laws as to provide adequate supplies of water. In many cases, laws defining limits of permissible water pollution do not apply to self-contained water systems, and "polluted" water can be reused where it does not affect product quality (as it might in food processing, for example) and where it is not returned to the public water or sewage system. Industrial areas particularly active in developing water recycling and reconditioning include textiles, paper, and power generation.

CONTRACTED RECYCLING OR WASTE SALES?

When equipment or other factors make recycling too costly for the volume of waste produced by a single manufacturer, it may wish to contract the process, using the lower-cost raw materials that result. The waste may also be sold to the recycling contractor, who will process it and sell it to other producers. Some consulting firms are beginning to specialize in advising which course of action will bring the greatest cost reduction, as well as in detailing all possible areas of recycling within a given operation.

RECOVERY METHODS AND EQUIPMENT

Some recovery methods and types of recovery equipment are used in multiple recycling areas. Although new methods and equipment appear regularly, some of the basics include the following:

1. *Magnetic separators.* These are used in removing metals from other materials. Glass, plastics, and rubber are a few common applications. A magnetic pulley or end section on a rotary screen may be used. Wastes pass by the separator on a short conveyer belt, and the magnetic pulley passes over the wastes, removing metal scrap and discarding it in a separate container or onto a separate conveyer belt. In a magnetic drum separator, wastes are fed into the drum, and end magnetic sections of the drum remove the metal scrap as it rotates, discharging the scrap into a separate container.

2. *Hand raking.* Wastes are placed on a conveyer belt and workers separate various types of scrap as the wastes move past.

3. *Dry fluid bed.* Mixed solids and metals in solution are separated as wastes and passed through an inclined sintered-bronze-based trough. Low-pressure air fluidizes a medium of magnetite or iron powder, providing a bed of a density midway between the densities of wastes to be separated. Wastes are then fed into the trough. Less dense scrap floats to the top while more dense wastes sink to the bottom. The bottom wastes are vibrated up the trough's incline and onto a screen which removes the accompanying medium. Vibrations forcing a flow in the opposite direction remove the upper layer of wastes in the same way. Copper and plastic can be separated by this method, as can copper and aluminum. Materials are usually shredded prior to separation to provide uniform-sized particles.

4. *Pinched sluice.* Metals can also be separated from plastics, dust, etc., with use of the pinched sluice. The equipment has an inclined shallow and tapered porous deck trough. Wastes are fed onto the deck and fluidized by a continuous stream of air. Heavy-density scrap settles to the bottom and is removed through a slot in the bottom of the trough, while lighter-density wastes are emitted at the end of the trough.

5. *Swarf processing.* This removes and purifies oil from machine tool residues, leaving dry material wastes for reuse. Wastes are fed by conveyer to a pulverizer. They pass through a screen to a centrifuge, where oil is removed, leaving dried waste or "swarf." Oils are drained into a purification tank.

6. *Metal separators.* These divide ferrous from nonferrous wastes. Temperatures are set to selectively melt one metal, which runs out of the unit, leaving the other material. Oxidation of ferrous metals is avoided since temperatures are sufficient only to remove metals with a lower melting point. Alloys may go through several stages, removing zinc first, for example, then aluminum, and so on.

7. *Baling.* Baling is the compression of wastes for greater handling convenience. Desired compression varies depending on reuse requirements. Textile wastes, wood chips, steel, and tin, for example, require different degrees of compression. Wastes are fed into a hopper and compressed by a baling ram operating in a repeating cycle. When the desired tightness is reached, the bale is wired vertically and horizontally.

8. *Can-crushing equipment.* The equipment punctures faulty cans, removing contents for reuse if possible, and then crushes the cans.

9. *Glass-crushing equipment.* This equipment sorts glass wastes (cullet) as to color and type and crushes the wastes to sizes varying from 1 to 3 inches. Small units are specially designed for glass bottle crushing.

10. *Shredding equipment.* This equipment reduces the bulk of wastes as well as rendering them into a somewhat uniform size for further processing. Series of hammers on a fast-rotating shaft, passing between star wheels, disintegrate the wastes. Wastes are fed into the unit by conveyer.

11. *Electrical cable stripping equipment.* This equipment reclaims nonferrous metals. Waste cable is fed between spiked rollers and forced onto a flared cutting blade, removing steel armor.

12. *Screening equipment.* Screening equipment sizes wastes for further processing. Wastes are fed into a revolving drum, falling through various-sized meshes. Shaker table models vibrate wastes along various-sized screens to remove smaller particles.

In addition, many types of construction equipment, such as hoists, clamshells, and grapples, are used in moving and separating waste materials.

SUGGESTED FURTHER READING

Bennet, A., and T. Schoeters, "Recycling Scrap Glass," *The Financial Times,* July 28, 1974, London.
—— and ——, "Scrap Metal Reclaimed," *The Financial Times,* London, Aug. 1, 1974.
Grad, F. P., *Environmental Law: Sources and Problems,* Matthew Bender, New York, 1971.
Neal, A. W., *Industrial Waste,* Business Books, London, 1971.
World Health Organization, *Treatment and Disposal of Wastes,* Report No. 367, 1970.
Wright, N. F., *The Producer and the Reclaimer,* National Industrial Recovery Association, London, 1972.

REFLATION

Areas for use in Cost Control:

ORGANIZATIONAL AND OPERATIONAL SYSTEMS
INDUSTRIAL APPLICATIONS
BUSINESS AND COMMERCIAL APPLICATIONS

Reflation is economic expansion of an operation in order to reduce cost factors, such as employee loss (and subsequent costs of hiring and training replacements) during a deflationary trade situation. One of the primary methods of providing such expansion, since the deflation of trade has been accomplished by monetary inflation in recent years, is to borrow the large sums of money required. As inflation lowers the real value of money when it is paid back in the future, the costs of such expansion are also reduced. *See also* **Inflation Accounting; Index Linking; Inflation Cost Control.**

SUGGESTED FURTHER READING

Keegan, William, "Reflation," *The Financial Times,* London, July 11, 1974.

REINSURANCE

Areas for use in Cost Control:

ORGANIZATIONAL AND OPERATIONAL SYSTEMS
BUSINESS AND COMMERCIAL APPLICATIONS

Reinsurance is a technique that is used to reduce capital investment costs of insurance companies and that has now extended to other areas, including raising loan capital and investment guarantees.

Reinsurance operates through a spreading of costs to provide tax advantages to larger, well-established firms and increased capital for smaller, developing firms. Tax laws provide an immediate write-off privilege for initial costs involved in selling an insurance policy, including sales, commission, and setup cost, even though the purchase price of the policy will be received by the company over a period of many years with little or no additional expense costs involved. In small companies without a need for massive write-offs, such a practice removes capital that should be available for use as stockholders' funds. The general effect of such circumstances is to limit expansion (new sales) to enable the firm to pay adequate stock dividends and maintain or increase company stock value in the market. However, using reinsurance, the small company sells a portion of the assured risk (sale) to a larger company which needs large write-offs, lowering its capital expenditure yet increasing its volume of sales.

SUGGESTED FURTHER READING

Gilling-Smith, Dryden, "Easing New Business Strain," *The Financial Times,* London, June 12, 1974.

RELATIVE ALLOCATION OF FACILITIES TECHNIQUE

Areas for use in Cost Control:

ORGANIZATIONAL AND OPERATIONAL SYSTEMS
MATERIALS AND EQUIPMENT MANAGEMENT
INDUSTRIAL APPLICATIONS

The relative allocation of facilities technique (RAFT) determines the economical and efficient plant layout of very complex manufacturing processes (20 to 40 activity centers) by computerized evaluation of the following:

1. Activity flow paths and variations
2. Space requirement variations
3. Material and material handling variations
4. Process locations that are fixed because of structural or equipment constraints

Inputs of data relating to the frequency and cost of various forms of movement and work, depending on location, are evaluated and optimal layout is determined.

The technique can be used on complex departmental or branch, as well as plant, layouts.

SUGGESTED FURTHER READING

Buffa, E. S., *Modern Production Management,* Wiley, New York, 1969.

RELEVANCE ANALYSIS

Areas for use in Cost Control:

ORGANIZATIONAL AND OPERATIONAL SYSTEMS
INDUSTRIAL APPLICATIONS
BUSINESS AND COMMERCIAL APPLICATIONS

Relevance analysis studies the pattern of relevant factors in a cost or other problem to determine when specific things can be made to happen and/or when and how events will affect specific projects. This **time-series analysis** technique is usually computerized to produce a *relevance tree* or other logical pattern order of relevant factors to be considered.

SUGGESTED FURTHER READING

Smith, P. I. S., *Think Tanks and Problem Solving,* Business Books, London, 1971.

RELEVANT COSTING

Areas for use in Cost Control:

ORGANIZATIONAL AND OPERATIONAL SYSTEMS
INDUSTRIAL APPLICATIONS

This newer **costing** technique is designed to match costs and income. Costs are carried forward as assets only when they will affect costs or income in the future. In this way, problems of both **direct costing** and *absorption costing* are overcome. **Fixed costs,** in this method, are treated as unexpired costs when future production will be at a maximum peak with sales high enough to require both total future production plus current inventories; when increased variable production costs are likely; and when future sales would be lost if it were not for current inventory.

The primary fault of the method is the inability to predict future sales and production accurately to use as a basis for fixed cost asset valuation.

SUGGESTED FURTHER READING

Hart, H., *Overhead Costs,* Heinemann, London, 1973.
Horngren, C. T., *Cost Accounting: A Managerial Emphasis,* Prentice-Hall, Englewood Cliffs, N.J., 1967.

REMOTE CONTROL RULES

Areas for use in Cost Control:

PSYCHOLOGICAL MOTIVATIONAL MANAGEMENT
ORGANIZATIONAL AND OPERATIONAL SYSTEMS
INDUSTRIAL APPLICATIONS
BUSINESS AND COMMERCIAL APPLICATIONS

The remote control rules technique is the use of written work rules that are given to employees and tell them specific tasks to be done and specific methods of accomplishing such tasks. Method developer A. W. Gouldner states that such rules form a mental bent and/or bond of obligation to follow the instructions on the part of the employee, thus increasing the individual's output in accordance with the wording of the rules and reducing labor costs as well as material and equipment wastage costs. Such rules may also substitute for instructions normally given by a supervisor, or they may reinforce instructions given by a superior. For example, a rule detailing a method of equipment operation makes it impossible for employees to excuse their incorrect, and perhaps wasteful, method of operation by saying that they did not know the correct method.

Remote control rules may also be used by management as a method of informal bargaining for greater employee cooperation. For example, if work output has increased, a supervisor may relax rules forbidding employees to talk to their coworkers or to smoke at the desk.

SUGGESTED FURTHER READING

Gouldner, A. W., *The Functions of Rules,* The Free Press, Glencoe, N.Y., 1954.

REMOTE CONTROL SUPERVISION

Areas for use in Cost Control:

ORGANIZATIONAL AND OPERATIONAL SYSTEMS
MATERIALS AND EQUIPMENT MANAGEMENT
INDUSTRIAL APPLICATIONS
BUSINESS AND COMMERCIAL APPLICATIONS

Remote control supervision is the extension of supervisory scope through the use of closed-circuit television, interarea communications systems, and, in the case of mechanical supervision, remotely operable equipment controls. Patterned on plant and store security systems that allow one guard to watch several areas via closed-circuit television, these kinds of equipment permit the supervisor to manage two or more areas, reducing supervisory costs. As in security systems, primary areas to be supervised should be channeled to the central screen in the closed-circuit bank. Secondary areas are seen on peripheral screens, and such areas may be televised on a sequenced basis, pictorial coverage of many areas being rotated on a few peripheral screens.

Good communications systems are necessary when supervising human labor from a remote location, and must allow two-way discussions as required.

Remote supervision of multiple pieces of automated equipment requiring little physical labor or control also extends supervisory scope and reduces operating costs.

SUGGESTED FURTHER READING

Radke, Magnus, *Manual of Cost Reduction Techniques,* McGraw-Hill, New York, 1972.

REPLACEMENT CONTROL

Areas for use in Cost Control:

ORGANIZATIONAL AND OPERATIONAL SYSTEMS
INDUSTRIAL APPLICATIONS
BUSINESS AND COMMERCIAL APPLICATIONS

Replacement control is an **operations research** technique used to determine the best time to replace equipment, tools, plant, employees, etc. The technique reduces costs by replacing these assets before their use becomes more costly—in terms of wasted production or poor-quality production—than their replacement.

Use of the technique involves studying cost factors, including:

1. Cost of new or replacement value
2. Scrap value of old equipment or materials
3. Maintenance cost for the old equipment
4. Changeover cost
5. Depreciation allowances, or other tax advantages
6. Employee severance pay
7. New-employee recruiting, hiring, and training costs
8. Labor savings in new operation

Various alternatives are studied, all factors involved being considered. Cost figures are prepared and converted to discounted cash flows. Replacement is made when it becomes less costly than operation with the old equipment.

SUGGESTED FURTHER READING

Wicks, C. T., and G. A. Yewdall, *Operational Research,* David & Charles, London, 1971.

REPLACEMENT COST ACCOUNTING

Areas for use in Cost Control:

ORGANIZATIONAL AND OPERATIONAL SYSTEMS
DATA RETENTION—FILES AND RECORDKEEPING
MATERIALS AND EQUIPMENT MANAGEMENT
INDUSTRIAL APPLICATIONS
BUSINESS AND COMMERCIAL APPLICATIONS

Replacement cost accounting is the substitution of replacement cost values for fixed currency cost values when evaluating assets such as plant or equipment. Use of the method reduces tax and other costs by deduction of depreciation based on this higher replacement—cost value of an asset. First developed in the Netherlands, the technique makes allowance for technological as well as inflation-connected and other price changes.

For example, if a piece of equipment cost $10,000, historic accounting methods would probably depreciate this at $1,000 a year over a period of 10 years. In replacement cost accounting, all price changes at the close of the accounting period are considered. Assume that the average price rise due to inflation for the period was 7½ percent, or 15 percent annually; and that the average price rise due to technological advancement was 10 percent, or 20 percent annually. Valuation of the equipment would then be adjusted by 17½ percent, for a total of $11,750. Depreciation for the last year of the period would then be $1,175 rather than $1,000.

In subsequent years, adjustments are made to the adjusted value of the preceding accounting period.

SUGGESTED FURTHER READING

Brittan, Samuel, "Living with Inflation: The Key Points," *The Financial Times,* London, May 13, 1974.

Guide to Current Purchasing Power Accounting, Price, Waterhouse, and Co., New York, 1974.
Morris, Richard, "Replacement Cost Accounting," *Accounting and Business Research,* January 1975.

REPORT WRITING AND COST CONTROL

Areas for use in Cost Control:

ORGANIZATIONAL AND OPERATIONAL SYSTEMS
PAPERWORK DESIGN AND FLOW SYSTEMS
DATA RETENTION—FILES AND RECORDKEEPING
INDUSTRIAL APPLICATIONS
BUSINESS AND COMMERCIAL APPLICATIONS

All areas of cost reduction are dependent on adequate information and effective communication of that information. Management reports may be used to convey necessary knowledge about a work area *up* to top management for decision making or *down* to subordinates for implementation of cost reduction or other decisions. To be effective, such a report must be well organized and clearly written—readable and understandable. It should use illustrations, charts, graphs, and tables where these will increase reader understanding, but not just for effect. Paper and printing method should be chosen for their contribution to report readability as well as for cost.

CONSIDERING THE AUDIENCE

Before writing a management report, it is essential to determine the audience for which it is intended. If top management will use the information, the report will need to be presented differently from a presentation for line-supervisory readership. It may help to consider several specific individuals who will use the report and, while writing, to ask yourself if they would find the material useful for the purpose intended, would understand specific phrasing or terminology, etc.

Information *not* needed by the readers and users of the report should be eliminated, no matter how much it interests the report writer.

REPORT TYPES

Reports of all types are used by management, but the most effective of these include:

Work progress reports to top management. These are periodic summaries of work progress, prepared by the head of a department. All significant work areas should be covered and unneeded detail should be avoided.

Forecasts to top management. Usually issued quarterly, these reports by department heads forecast work trends for their areas.

Customer reports. Content is prepared by top management to report to customers on company developments and achievements, providing knowledge of products and/or services available.

Work reports within the department. Here, work supervisors or skilled workers report to the head of the department on work progress under their supervision. Such reporting may be done verbally, too, of course. But regular written reports summarizing all progress are needed so the department head can be sure that work is being adequately carried out.

Sales reports. Several of these may be needed: reports to top management by the sales department to detail volume; reports to sales personnel to provide information and incentives; reports to production, planning, purchasing, etc., to coordinate activities; and reports to customers to emphasize the company's size and success.

Technical reports. These detail information to solve a particular technical work or customer problem.

Instructional/operational reports. Such reports are made by managers to subordinates outlining decisions and/or policies along with steps for implementation. Follow-through procedures must be established to make sure the new procedures are being carried out as instructed.

REPORT CLASSIFICATION

Some companies develop intricate numbering systems for reports, while others seem to ignore any logical means of classification. Generally, a department code should be established, such as *P* for production, *A* for administration, and *T* for technical. These letters may then be followed by the date of the report and a sequence number (see Fig. 89), providing easy reference and filing data for future use.

```
       P   10/6/76  1821
      /      /          \
 (Dept.)  (Date)   (Sequence)
```

Figure 89. Typical report classification system.

The subject of the report should not be expressed in numbered codes, but should be stated concisely and in bold print at the head of the first page (see Fig. 90).

```
P   10/6/76  1821


          DRILL  PRESS  OPERATION

```

Figure 90. Typical report classification and head.

Report pages should be numbered consecutively, using roman numerals. Tables, figures, and charts should follow the same rules.

REPORT ORGANIZATION

Good organization is the most essential factor in writing an effective report. Again, the reader and how he or she will use the report should be the focal point for organization. The start of the report should catch the interest of the reader, the body should report important facts in sequence, and the close should draw conclusions inherent in the information.

Using an outline as a first step may help in organizing the report body material into sequential order.

Other methods include a four-step organization technique:

1. *Set a goal or goals.* Who is the reader? What do you want to tell the reader? Where will the report be used? When? Why?

2. *Accumulate and evaluate information.* Use only data that relate to the goal to be reached by the report. For example, if the objective is to report the number of X machines in use, omit reference to their maintenance schedules.

3. *Draw conclusions for reaching the report goal.* Suggestions for improvements should be included here. For instance, if a report shows that 24 X machines were used in 1973, 30 X machines in 1974, and 36 X machines in 1975, the report may suggest that XY machines (a larger model) could be substituted for more efficient use in this growing-need area.

4. *Summaries* may be used at the end of the report, depending on overall length. While the additional emphasis is useful, particularly in longer reports, summaries sometimes encourage the reader to skip over necessary information in the report body.

REPORT WRITING

The easiest method of writing is usually to follow the sequence of the report: title, contents, lead, introduction, body, and conclusion.

The *title* should be short and concise. Avoid long or unnecessary words. If possible, keep the title to five words or (preferably) less. Be careful to avoid words with double meanings. The title should explain the report's contents first and attract attention only after this. Key words, indicating contents, should be used in the title to facilitate filing and reference.

Contents are necessary if the report is more than a very modest length. All areas, including headings and subheadings, should be included. Illustrations, charts, graphs, etc., may be included or they may form an additional contents listing.

Section numbering may be used. One style of this is used in McGraw-Hill Book Company handbooks. Subject areas are listed in the contents, as are specialized subjects within these areas. For example, in the 3d edition of the *Maintenance Engineering Handbook,* Section 1 is "Organization and Administration of the Maintenance Function." Eight chapters are listed in the contents for this section, including "Considerations in Using Outside Contractors." This seventh chapter is, therefore, numbered 1-7.

Divisions in the contents may also be made in simple decimal format. Usually not more than three divisions are made. Thus, if a head in the report is *Typing Pool,* a subhead is *Equipment,* and a further subhead is *Electric Typewriters,* this might have the number 1.1.1. in the contents.

The *lead* is usually a brief summary of the most important facts and conclusions in the report. Its purpose is to provide an idea of the contents and, more importantly, to make the reader interested in studying the report. If the lead is not strong, the user may read no further.

Immediately following this, the goal of the report should be clarified and the source of report data stated.

The *body* of the report presents all pertinent data in sequential order. Supplementary detail may be noted in footnotes and added in appendices.

Writing should use the simplest words and phrasing possible. Content should be clear and to the point without the addition of unnecessary opinions.

Data and ideas should be tied together by words that show relationships.

Heads and subheads make report reading easier by giving the reader an idea of what information comes next.

Vocabulary should be simple, and special terms should be explained when it is necessary to use them.

Examples can be used to clarify content where necessary, as can illustrations, graphs, tables, etc.

Conclusions are used to interpret the data in the body of the report. Each area reported should be covered separately by a conclusion and/or suggestion for improvement. More detailed summary of body material is sometimes included at this point. This may detract from the report itself, however, and should be used only in the case of very long reports.

Use of bibliographies, footnotes, addendums, and indexes will depend on company policy and complexity of the report. If they are needed for clarity, use them.

ILLUSTRATIVE MATERIAL

Photos, sketches, charts, graphs, tables, and other illustrations should be used to clarify report content. These must be placed, in sequence, near the copy referring to their subject matter. References to illustrations, by illustration number, help the reader make the association.

Short tables, examples, formulas, etc., may be set off within the body copy without numbering or special reference. For example:

The formula for determining the indexed value of such equipment is:

$$\frac{\text{Cost} \times \text{current index} - \text{index at cost}}{\text{Index at cost}}$$

Tables should be used to group three or more items of information. Comparisons of two or more factors may also be presented in tabular form. For report purposes, tables should be small enough to be easily read on a standard-size single sheet. Larger tables should be avoided if possible, or, if absolutely necessary, used in the addendum material.

Measurement or other units must be clearly indicated at column heads, and units within a column (and preferably within a table) must be consistent. Footnotes may be used where special conditions exist for one or a few items within the table.

Numbers should be aligned vertically on the decimal point.

Table layout should be uniform where possible. Vertical positioning is easier to read and understand and should be preferred.

Graphs and drawings are usually prepared by draftsmen from rough sketches prepared by the report writer.

Photographs are effective if printed but are costly for normal report use. If the photograph can be used for several reports, however, the cost factor will disappear. In addition, new and more sophisticated offset equipment is capable of reproducing photographs without halftones.

REPORT REPRODUCTION

Choice of method of reproducing reports will depend on use, number of copies required, and budget.

For a very few copies for internal use, copy typed with a carbon ribbon and photocopied should be adequate.

Newer offset printing methods offer the greatest possibilities. Paper plates may be typed, but typed copy photographed onto plastic plates costs only a few cents and can be used to print 5,000 or more professional-looking reports. For even better appearance, copy can be typeset or computer-typeset, rather than using typewritten material.

Letterpress printing may be used for runs of 2,000 or more reports, although offset methods may prove economical and just as satisfactory in appearance.

SUGGESTED FURTHER READING

Hayakawa, S. I., *Language in Action and Thought,* G. Allen, London.
Ironman, Ralph, *Writing the Executive Report,* Heinemann, London, 1966.
Korzybski, Alfred, *Science and Sanity: An Introduction to Non-Aristotelian Systems and General Semantics,* Science Press, Lancaster, Pa.

RESEARCH AND DEVELOPMENT COST CONTROL

Areas for use in Cost Control:

ORGANIZATIONAL AND OPERATIONAL SYSTEMS
MATERIALS AND EQUIPMENT MANAGEMENT
INDUSTRIAL APPLICATIONS

Research and development can be the lifeblood of a company, as it develops new products or more up-to-date and/or more economical means of producing current products. But what about the cost of the R&D program itself? How can the executive tell whether or not a specific project is worth pursuing? And once a project has begun, who determines the necessary budget? Since R&D expenditures vary from 1.5 to 3.4 percent of the Gross National Product in countries around the world, R&D cost control can mean good-sized cost reductions.

INITIATING A PROJECT

Before authorizing a project, ask yourself if:

1. *The timing of the project is right.* When the research is finished, will it be economically useful? A project studying oil products may be interesting, for example, but given current energy problems and prices, a project researching possible alternatives to oil-based power would be more timely. **Technological forecasting** is one technique to determine the timeliness of an R&D project.

2. *The project would fit into current company structure.* If, for example, the company processes frozen foods, an R&D project involving new printing techniques would be of little value in the current situation. New staff, plant, etc., would be needed to move into this field. Development of faster-freezing methods, on the other hand, would be of great interest and use.

3. *The project is aimed at solving a major problem.* Research for its own sake may be interesting to scientists. But in business it is not economical to use R&D unless it is aimed at solving business problems.

4. *The project's results fit in with the company's objectives.* For example, if a food processing company wants to branch into new areas, an R&D project might be launched to design a new type of equipment for heating preprocessed food in the home. Such a project would offer the diversification the company wants yet is closely aligned with current production, giving company management at least rudimentary knowledge of the new area.

5. *Scientists in the company have sufficient expertise to handle a specific project.* If not, is the project important enough for the firm to add new staff?

Cost Control and Reduction. Cost of a research project may include:

1. *Salaries.* These are estimated by multiplying the work force required times salary level for each of the various staff grades used.

2. *Personnel benefits.*

3. *Equipment,* if it must be specifically purchased for the project. Leasing of equipment, such as computer time rental, should be included.

4. *Materials and supplies.*

Usually, overheads such as rent, lighting, and heat, are not added into project cost, since they exist as part of departmental operation rather than applying to separate projects. Companies with large research departments will find it to their advantage to draw up a table of unit costs for each item in all of the above categories.

Timing of costs should also be taken into consideration. If a project will cost $80,000, but half of this sum will not be needed for one year, the money can be invested, with interest offsetting project costs. Alternatively, the money can remain as working capital in general company accounts until it is needed.

Speed at which the project is to be completed will also affect the cost. This is particularly true in the current inflationary economy where materials purchased now may be considerably less expensive than those purchased in another year. In a year when the inflationary rate exceeds the rate of interest paid on deposited money, purchase of materials needed in a project's future years may be the best course of action to reduce costs.

REVIEWING A RESEARCH PROJECT

Once a research project becomes operational, it is necessary to review it periodically. Costs can be reduced here by introducing a simplified system using as little clerical and computer time as possible to do a thorough job. Cost reduction areas that should be examined are:

1. *Possibility of automating some aspects of the project.* Equipment that can be turned on and off by an electronic timer, mathematical work using a computer, electronic measurement of chemicals or other supplies—these can be handled less expensively by machinery than by scientists.

2. *Elimination of duplicated work.* Does every scientist know what the others are doing, or is he or she repeating steps already completed?

3. *Layout of laboratory, equipment, and supplies. These should be conducive to easy working.*

4. *Evaluation of project progress and results. This should be continuous,* preferably with data fed into a computer for accessibility.

PROJECT CONTROL

Staff assigned to the project must have a complete knowledge of the project's goal, as well as a detailed set of plans for its completion. Individual tasks are allocated by project leaders according to special skills of the workers, deadlines for project completion, and facilities available. In addition, all staff members should be encouraged to contribute better ways of working, lower-cost ideas, and comments on problem areas in the general project plan.

The project leader will continuously measure progress against the *strategy diagram,* altering timing, methods, working hours, and materials as necessary. *See also* **Critical Path Analysis.**

Control forms are used to measure *work performed* against *time allotted* (see Fig. 91).

Monthly reports by the project leader will keep management informed on time and cost control—whether or not time and costs are on schedule, and if not, where they stand.

USING PROJECT RESULTS

Once a project is completed, effective communication of the results is essential to achieve optimum benefit. Since each project has a goal—the solution of some problem—the goal must be clearly presented along with the problem's solution and necessary data to back up that solution. Written reports, including comparative tables; conferences; seminars; personal discussions; printed material (magazine articles, pamphlets); and films are some of the methods used to communicate results of research. Scientists should be reminded to present reports and seminars in nontechnical language when communicating with management. Such reports should be brief and clearly written.

SUGGESTED FURTHER READING

Beattie, C. J., and R. D. Reader, *Quantitative Management in R & D,* Barnes & Noble, Cranbury, N.J., 1971.

Bright, J. R., *Research, Development, and Technological Innovation,* Irwin, Homewood, Ill., 1964.

Chorfas, D. N., *Managing Industrial Research for Profits,* Cassell, London, 1967.

Davies, D., and C. McCarthy, *Introduction to Technological Economies,* Wiley, New York, 1967.

Yovits, M., ed., *Research Program Effectiveness,* Gordon and Breach, New York, 1966.

Research Control Form					
Activity	Employee	Jan.	Feb.	Mar.	Apr.
Project Planning:					
Time allotted (in days)	CTN	20			
	FJS	18			
Time taken (in days)	CTN	20			
	FJS	20			
Total over or below allotment:		−2			
Project Design:					
Time allotted (in days)	CTN	−	20		
	FJS	−	22		
Time taken (in days)	CTN	−	20		
	FJS	−	22		
Total over or below allotment:		−2	−		
Equip. Lab. Set up Study:					
Time allotted (in days)	CTN	−	−	20	
	FJS	−	−	20	
Time taken (in days)	CTN	−	−	21	
	FJS	−	−	20	
Total over or below allotment:		−2	−	−1	

Figure 91. Typical research control form.

RESOURCE ALLOCATION

Areas for use in Cost Control:

ORGANIZATIONAL AND OPERATIONAL SYSTEMS
INDUSTRIAL APPLICATIONS
BUSINESS AND COMMERCIAL APPLICATIONS

Resource allocation uses graphic calculations, linear programming, or simulation to facilitate decision on resources required for each step of a project. Graphic calculations—charts, graphs, tables, etc.—are most commonly used. For example, charts may show that 200 workers are needed for the first week of a project, 300 for the second and third weeks, and 200 for the fourth week (see Fig. 92).

To complete the project on schedule, it will be necessary to hire 300 men *unless* the *critical path* can be rearranged to distribute the need for workers evenly. In other words, actual working resource allocation problems are set out on paper and solved prior to the project's beginning, cutting costs. This technique is a necessary second step, following other types of **network planning and analysis.**

SUGGESTED FURTHER READING

Beattie, C. J., and R. D. Reader, *Quantitative Management in R & D,* Barnes & Noble, Cranbury, N.J., 1971.

Figure 92. Resource allocation graph.

RESOURCE APPRAISAL

Areas for use in Cost Control:

ORGANIZATIONAL AND OPERATIONAL SYSTEMS
PAPERWORK DESIGN AND FLOW SYSTEMS
MATERIALS AND EQUIPMENT MANAGEMENT
INDUSTRIAL APPLICATIONS
BUSINESS AND COMMERCIAL APPLICATIONS

Resource appraisal is the evaluation of current company assets, including labor and working methods, to determine areas where cost reduction and other changes are needed. The nature of such cost reductions and other changes is based on information from the resource appraisal.

A questionnaire, distributed to top management, is used in gathering the necessary information, and suitable questionnaire design is essential to the success of the technique. A guide to the preparation of such questionnaires has been developed by the P-E Consulting Group, who established a checklist of information areas to be covered. Before questionnaire preparation is undertaken, each of these items is evaluated as to information availability:

1. Readily available at daily, weekly, or monthly intervals
2. Available on an annual, semiannual, or quarterly review basis
3. Available only after irregular review
4. Not available

The information areas, and their subdivisions, normally evaluated by these criteria include:

Product Evaluation:

1. Identification of volume/mix constraints
2. Sales mix/maximum profit ratios
3. Relationship of product quality to marketing policy
4. Managerial requirements
5. Design/material cost relationship
6. Product position in life cycle

Management Evaluation:

1. Company management performance
2. Recruiting policies/future needs
3. Turnover ratios
4. Development program availability and use
5. Financial compensation/industrywide levels

Personnel Evaluation:

1. Training programs
2. Financial compensation/industrywide levels
3. Turnover, evaluated by each skill
4. Labor and/or labor union relations status

Production Evaluation:

1. Sales/capital ratio now
2. Sales/capital ratio historically
3. Sales/employee ratio now
4. Sales/employee ratio historically
5. Raw material waste now
6. Raw material waste historically
7. Stock turnover now
8. Stock turnover historically

Sales and Marketing Evaluation:

1. Sales/fixed asset ratio now
2. Sales/fixed asset ratio historically
3. Sales/salesperson ratio now
4. Sales/salesperson ratio historically
5. Sales promotion cost/sales increase ratios
6. Product price/competitive product price
7. Product market value/product cost plus ratio
8. Selling costs/product unit
9. Distribution costs/product unit
10. Sales trends by outlet type
11. Sales trends by geographical area
12. Sales trends by product group

Physical Asset Evaluation:

1. Value/life expectancy of plant
2. Value/life expectancy of equipment
3. Plant size related to needs
4. Plant location related to market locations
5. Use of plant and equipment/capacity ratio

Areas that are not easily measured by existing data should be thoroughly reviewed, as should areas with unsatisfactory performance, as these resource areas are primary targets for cost reduction.

SUGGESTED FURTHER READING

Lock, D., ed., *Management Techniques,* Directors Bookshelf, London, 1972.

RESPONSIBILITY ACCOUNTING

Areas for use in Cost Control:

ORGANIZATIONAL AND OPERATIONAL SYSTEMS
PAPERWORK DESIGN AND FLOW SYSTEMS

INDUSTRIAL APPLICATIONS
BUSINESS AND COMMERCIAL APPLICATIONS

Responsibility accounting is a technique to control costs at their starting point. This means that all levels of personnel are brought into budgeting and **budgetary control,** since each staff member is responsible for controlling and reducing costs for all work done in the individual's area. Additionally, all managerial staff are collectively responsible for group costs.

In this technique areas of responsibility, called "responsibility centers," and cost standards are determined. Review and measurement of cost control effectiveness on the part of the individual managers are used to determine the standard of performance. Standards on which individual performances are judged include:

1. Volume of production within given responsibility area
2. Gross profit or effect of production within given specific area
3. Actual costs traceable to the responsibility area

SUGGESTED FURTHER READING

Edge, C. G., *A Practical Manual on the Appraisal of Capital Expenditure,* Canadian Society of Industrial and Cost Accountants, 1964.
Kempner, Thomas, *A Handbook of Management,* Weidenfeld and Nicolson, London, 1971.
Merrett, A. J., and Allen Sykes, *The Finance and Analysis of Capital Projects,* Longmans, London, 1966.

RESPONSIBILITY CENTERS

Areas for use in Cost Control:

ORGANIZATIONAL AND OPERATIONAL SYSTEMS
INDUSTRIAL APPLICATIONS
BUSINESS AND COMMERCIAL APPLICATIONS

Responsibility centers are clearly defined areas of cost responsibility assigned to individual members of the managerial staff as their areas of costs to be controlled. Such an area generally coincides with the individual's other responsibilities, such as production control or sales control. *See also* **Responsibility Accounting.**

SUGGESTED FURTHER READING

Batty, J., *Corporate Planning and Budgetary Control,* MacDonald, London, 1971.

REVALUATION ACCOUNTING

Areas for use in Cost Control:

ORGANIZATIONAL AND OPERATIONAL SYSTEMS
INDUSTRIAL APPLICATIONS
BUSINESS AND COMMERCIAL APPLICATIONS

Revaluation accounting, also called replacement value accounting, reduces tax costs by basing accounts on real value in terms of purchasing power or replacement cost. *See also* **Inflation Accounting.**

SUGGESTED FURTHER READING

Batty, J., *Management Accountancy,* MacDonald, London, 1971.

REVERSAL TECHNIQUE

Areas for use in Cost Control:

ORGANIZATIONAL AND OPERATIONAL SYSTEMS
BUSINESS AND COMMERCIAL APPLICATIONS

The reversal technique is a deliberate reversal of a work method, which often decreases working time and labor cost. Some experts have gone so far as to say that the solution of any problem is some form of the problem's opposite. Others, such as Harold Longman of Unilever, say that the technique often provides better ways of dealing with office problems. For example, if a clerk is filing by number, most systems use a left-to-right number sequence. Sorting and filing are more rapidly done using a right-to-left sequence, however, since the eye naturally falls to the right-hand digit first.

If a company cannot hire adequate clerical help at a low salary level, for instance, it might reverse the problem and hire a smaller number of very competent clerical employees at adequate salary levels.

Or, if an office does not have enough space for its files, perhaps the problem should be reversed by decreasing any unnecessary filed material to reduce the space required.

SUGGESTED FURTHER READING

Longman, H. H., *How to Cut Office Costs,* Anbar Publications, London, 1967.

RICARDO TECHNIQUE

Areas for use in Cost Control:

ORGANIZATIONAL AND OPERATIONAL SYSTEMS
INDUSTRIAL APPLICATIONS
BUSINESS AND COMMERCIAL APPLICATIONS

The Ricardo technique is the substitution of labor for equipment when the real cost of wages decreases in an inflationary situation. Devised by economist and self-made millionaire, David Ricardo, the technique is based on the fact that when the cost of raw materials rises faster than prices, the real cost of wages drops and human labor is more economical than machinery.

SUGGESTED FURTHER READING

Bannock, G., R. E. Baxter, and R. Rees, *A Dictionary of Economics,* Penguin, Baltimore, 1974.

RIGHTS ISSUES

Areas for use in Cost Control:

ORGANIZATIONAL AND OPERATIONAL SYSTEMS
INDUSTRIAL APPLICATIONS
BUSINESS AND COMMERCIAL APPLICATIONS

Rights issues are offers of company shares to persons already owning stock. The method is often considered the least costly initially in raising financing. Shareholders are commonly offered the right to purchase new shares in a specified proportion to their current holdings.

SUGGESTED FURTHER READING

Clarkson, G. P. E., and B. J. Elliot, *Managing Money and Finance,* Gower Press, London, 1969.
Samuelson, J. M., and F. M. Wilkes, *Management of Company Finance,* Nelson, London, 1971.

RISK MANAGEMENT

Areas for use in Cost Control:

ORGANIZATIONAL AND OPERATIONAL SYSTEMS
MATERIALS AND EQUIPMENT MANAGEMENT
INDUSTRIAL APPLICATIONS
BUSINESS AND COMMERCIAL APPLICATIONS

Risk management is the reduction of insurance costs through four basic methods:

1. *Avoidance*—the elimination of work or work methods that constitute a risk
2. *Assumption*—in-company holding of a risk
3. *Reduction*—handling a risk (such as fire or theft) to reduce its frequency
4. *Transfer*—passing risks to an insurer

Studies show that a company may reduce its insurance costs by as much as 20 percent or more with use of these methods. Two types of operation are used: an in-company *risk management* department or use of a *risk management* consulting firm. If the latter is chosen, it may be best to use a firm not brokering insurance and thus without interest in the degree of *transfer* used.

A rule of thumb devised by Keith Shipton Developments, London, to determine the efficiency level of current insurance programs is that *a company should recover at least 60 percent of its premiums in claims.* If the figure is lower than this, risk management can be beneficially applied to operational systems.

Greater attention should be focused on company assets most responsible for income. For example, if the production area of a plant has high fire or arson risks, controls should be added to lower the element of such risk. Sprinkler systems and/or fire-fighting equipment may be installed and should be continuously checked and kept ready for use. Plant security should be strengthened to control arson. *See also* **Security and Cost Control.**

Human assets should be protected as well. For example, all top-level executives should not fly on one plane. The risk of dollar loss (through managerial ability) to the firm is too large.

Valuable inventories should not be stored in one location, and warehouses should contain firewalls where possible to lower the overall risk.

Computer security is another important area, since industrial espionage is often conducted through computer personnel. In addition, programming controls are needed, since incorrect programming when applied to invoicing, inventories, etc., can cost a company vast sums. *See also* **Computer Security.**

Safety equipment and its correct use are another area that can reduce risk costs when properly controlled.

Cost reduction from the use of risk management generally falls into one of three areas:

1. *Lower insurance premiums,* due to decreased risks. For example, a warehouse fitted with an operable sprinkler system will cost considerably less to insure.

2. *Decreased costs of uninsured losses,* due to decreased risks, such as less shoplifting loss because of increased security.

3. *In-company insurance,* where a firm establishes its own insurance operation to absorb some losses. "Premiums" are "paid" to the company to the insurance division—to itself, in effect—and are returned to operating funds if the loss occurs. In addition to insurance cost reductions from use of this technique, the method also carries some tax advantages. *See also* **In-Company Insurance.**

SUGGESTED FURTHER READING

"Risk Management: A Financial Times Report," *The Financial Times,* London, July 8, 1974.

ROLE PLAYING

Areas for use in Cost Control:

PSYCHOLOGICAL MOTIVATIONAL MANAGEMENT
ORGANIZATIONAL AND OPERATIONAL SYSTEMS

Role playing, also called reality practice and the problem approach, is an executive training technique that reduces operating costs by having management practice decision-making and other operating procedures in hypothetical situations. Problems presented may include personnel, operational, equipment, financing, and organizational problems. *See also* **Gaming.**

SUGGESTED FURTHER READING

Bavelas, A., "Role Playing and Management Training," *Sociatry,* no. 1, 1947.
Bennis, W. G., *Changing Organizations,* McGraw-Hill, New York, 1966.
Tannenbaum, R., I. R. Weschler, and F. Massarik, *Leadership and Organization,* McGraw-Hill, New York, 1961.

ROLL-ON, ROLL-OFF FERRIES

Area for use in Cost Control:

INDUSTRIAL APPLICATIONS

Roll-on, roll-off ferries are constructed to allow loaded trucks to drive directly on and off them to provide short-distance sea transportation. Use of the method reduces shipping costs primarily through reduction of goods' handling, since products are loaded only at the production point and unloaded at the selling point.

SUGGESTED FURTHER READING

Magee, J. F., *Physical Distribution Systems,* McGraw-Hill, New York, 1967.
Murphy, G. J., *Transportation and Distribution,* Business Books, London, 1972.

ROTA LABOR SYSTEMS

Areas for use in Cost Control:

PSYCHOLOGICAL MOTIVATIONAL MANAGEMENT
FINANCIAL MOTIVATIONAL MANAGEMENT
ORGANIZATIONAL AND OPERATIONAL SYSTEMS
MATERIALS AND EQUIPMENT MANAGEMENT
INDUSTRIAL APPLICATIONS

Rota labor systems are repetitive schedules of shift working to make maximum use of plant and equipment while minimizing adverse employee reaction to working during unusual and unsocial hours. Use of the method reduces costs, since fixed overheads are spread over a greater level of production—that is, plant and equipment can be used up to 24 hours a day, seven days a week. In addition, bonuses paid to workers for unsocial hours are reduced when such hours are occasional rather than constant, and bonuses are spread more evenly among workers, providing wider financial incentives.

Temporary rota systems may be used to meet seasonal production increases, eliminating the need for capital expansion costs.

Various rota systems can be developed, assigning individual workers to periodic rotation (see Table 47). A worker in Rota 1 of Table 47, for example, would work five day shifts, have one day off; work seven afternoon shifts, have one day off; work seven night shifts, have two days off; work one day shift; and then repeat the schedule. Shifts may be divided into from one to seven groups, depending on hours and production required. Complete rota labor systems tables are listed in the suggested reading material and many other industrial texts.

SUGGESTED FURTHER READING

Clay, M. J., and B. H. Walley, *Performance and Profitability,* Longmans, London, 1965.

Table 47. Typical Seven-Shift Rota Chart

Rota	S	M	T	W	Th	F	Sa	S	M	T	W	Th	F	Sa	S	M	T	W	Th	F	Sa	S	M	T
1	D	D	D	D	D	O	A	A	A	A	A	A	A	O	N	N	N	N	N	N	N	O	O	D
2	D	D	A	A	A	A	A	A	A	A	O	N	N	N	N	N	N	N	O	O	D	D	D	D
3	A	A	A	A	A	A	O	N	N	N	N	N	N	N	O	O	D	D	D	D	D	D	D	A
4	A	A	O	N	N	N	N	N	N	N	O	O	D	D	D	D	D	D	D	O	A	A	A	A
5	N	N	N	N	N	N	N	O	O	D	D	D	D	D	D	D	A	A	A	A	A	A	A	O
6	N	N	N	O	O	D	D	D	D	D	D	D	O	A	A	A	A	A	A	A	O	N	N	N
7	O	O	D	D	D	D	D	D	D	A	A	A	A	A	A	O	N	N	N	N	N	N	N	N

D = day shift   S = Sunday   Th = Thursday
A = afternoon shift   M = Monday   F = Friday
N = night shift   T = Tuesday   Sa = Saturday
O = day off   W = Wednesday

SALE AND LEASE-BACK

Areas for use in Cost Control:

ORGANIZATIONAL AND OPERATIONAL SYSTEMS
MATERIALS AND EQUIPMENT MANAGEMENT
INDUSTRIAL APPLICATIONS
BUSINESS AND COMMERCIAL APPLICATIONS

Sale and lease-back is a technique used primarily to obtain medium-term capital. The method can also reduce the cost of maintenance of equipment or other assets since the lease-back may transfer the repair and/or maintenance responsibilities to the purchaser.

To use the technique, the company sells the asset to raise capital and leases it back on a long-term basis. A renewal option is usually included in the lease to protect the original owner, who is now renting the asset. A reduction in tax costs can also occur when using the method, since the asset's rent is fully deductible.

SUGGESTED FURTHER READING

Batty, J., *Management Accountancy,* MacDonald, London, 1971.

SALES ACCOUNTING

Areas for use in Cost Control:

ORGANIZATIONAL AND OPERATIONAL SYSTEMS
PAPERWORK DESIGN AND FLOW SYSTEMS
INDUSTRIAL APPLICATIONS
BUSINESS AND COMMERCIAL APPLICATIONS

Sales accounting is a method used to make certain that:

1. All goods sold and shipped to a customer are charged to that customer, reducing lost payment costs.
2. Payment for goods is prompt, reducing bad debt cost.
3. Details about goods and customers are maintained.

Both a *Sales Ledger* and a *Sales Journal* are used, data being recorded from the *Sales Invoice.*

The *Sales Journal* records daily sales, with itemizing of date, customer, invoice reference or number, and cost of goods invoiced. Sales are usually totaled daily, and this total is transferred to the *General Ledger.* Some firms use extra copies of invoices in lieu of the *Sales Journal.* Copies are filed by invoice number and later posted to individual customers' accounts in the *Sales Ledger.*

The *Sales Ledger* records each transaction—sale or payment—with the individual customer. Credit memorandums to a customer are also entered. Individual ledger accounts should contain the customer's name and address and terms of business (discounts, for example), as well as sale and payment data. The ledger should be noted where special efforts have been necessary to collect payment, and such a customer may, in the future, buy only on a C.O.D. basis. Sales statistics for forecasting and other marketing studies can be obtained from the Sales Ledger.

SUGGESTED FURTHER READING

Davidson, S., *Handbook of Modern Accounting,* McGraw-Hill, New York, 1970.

Gillespie, Cecil, *Accounting Systems: Procedures and Methods,* Prentice-Hall, Englewood Cliffs, N.J., 1971.

Standingford, Oliver, ed., *Newnes Encyclopedia of Business Management,* Newnes, London, 1967.

SALES CONCENTRATION

Areas for use in Cost Control:

ORGANIZATIONAL AND OPERATIONAL SYSTEMS
INDUSTRIAL APPLICATIONS
BUSINESS AND COMMERCIAL APPLICATIONS

Studies show that about 30 percent of customers purchase 70 to 80 percent of production. Using sales concentration, consumer types that make up this 30 percent are defined and all marketing and sales programs are targeted for these groups. Overall sales and marketing costs are reduced, since efforts are not expended in areas with minimal returns.

SUGGESTED FURTHER READING

Radke, Magnus, *Manual of Cost Reduction Techniques,* McGraw-Hill, New York, 1972.

SALES/OPERATIONS PLANNING AND CONTROL (SOPC)

Areas for use in Cost Control:

ORGANIZATIONAL AND OPERATIONAL SYSTEMS
MATERIALS AND EQUIPMENT MANAGEMENT
INDUSTRIAL APPLICATIONS
BUSINESS AND COMMERCIAL APPLICATIONS

Sales/operations planning and control (SOPC) is the use of a comprehensive information system to plan goals and ways to meet them, carry out the plan, and follow up action to ensure that results are accurate in five major areas:

1. *Cost reduction* of inventory holding, labor, distribution, etc.
2. *Maximum use of equipment*
3. *Maximum use of plant*
4. *Efficient inventory control*
5. *Customer service* that facilitates competitiveness, including shipment reliability, product service, etc.

Planning. Planning methods to meet company objectives in these areas are the first step in SOPC. All data affecting company performance, such as outstanding orders, sales forecasts, cost records, and production records, are evaluated, and needed action in each area is incorporated into an overall plan. Plan time can coincide with production lead time, or it can be for a predetermined operational period.

Performance. Overall SOPC plans are delegated by responsibility area, and each area manager draws up working schedules for completion of his or her section of the plan. Performance of this work is assigned to subordinates according to these schedules, through known management techniques. In many cases, performance may be accelerated through computerization.

Follow-up. Results of execution of the plan are reported by area of responsibility, and those parts of the plan not completed satisfactorily receive immediate management attention and action.

SUGGESTED FURTHER READING

Greene, James H., *Operations Planning and Control,* Irwin, Homewood, Ill., 1967.
Lock, D., ed., *Management Techniques,* Directors Bookshelf, London, 1972.
Ramlow, Donald H., and Eugene H. Wall, *Production Planning and Control,* Prentice-Hall, Englewood Cliffs, N.J., 1967.

SALESPERSON MOTIVATION

Areas for use in Cost Control:
PSYCHOLOGICAL MOTIVATIONAL MANAGEMENT
FINANCIAL MOTIVATIONAL MANAGEMENT
WORK PLACE MOTIVATIONAL MANAGEMENT
INDUSTRIAL APPLICATIONS
BUSINESS AND COMMERCIAL APPLICATIONS

Cost reduction, so often dependent on large-scale production and sales, can often be as greatly effected through salesperson motivation as through greater motivation of production workers. Ways to motivate salespeople to greater performance not only differ from other worker motivation but also differ among individual salespeople, as the result of personality and attitude differences. For example, one study shows that salespeople working for an aggressive, expanding company are more likely to be motivated by promotion potential in successful job performance than are salespeople with large, more established firms. Large-firm salespeople, on the other hand, are more easily motivated by benefit plans than are small-company salespeople.

BELIEVABILITY

Looking at these motivational factors, we can see that company reputation and product quality are important motivators. In other words, a salesperson can sell more effectively when he or she feels that the product and company represented have something to offer the customer and when his or her "sales pitch" has believability.

The salesperson also needs training to help take advantage of the company's or product's advantages. In the same study, as many as 23 percent of the salespeople interviewed said that adequate training and product knowledge motivated them to greater productivity.

In addition to company and product image, good customer service can motivate salespeople. In a comparison of management and sales attitudes,[1] 32 percent of sales personnel felt that more after-sales service should be provided to customers, while 90 percent of management felt that too much service was already offered. For the salesperson, satisfactory service means a pleased customer and greater possibility of future sales.

Improving the company image, product quality, and after-sales service, then, can be strong sales force motivators, plus improving the company.

FINANCIAL MOTIVATION

A very large percentage of salespeople say payment is of key importance to them. In other words, they assume it will be satisfactory. Payments above this "satisfactory" level will have some motivational effect, but a far greater negative effect results if payment falls below the satisfactory point.

In addition to the question of amount of payment, the method of payment is a factor in sales force motivation.

Straight salary plans do not provide adequate motivation in most cases, and their use is not recommended for increasing sales. Even for an in-store clerking position, a minimal bonus or commission added to a base salary will encourage better attention to customers.

Salary plus commission provides good motivation for the salesperson, since income is directly related to sales. Most salespeople prefer a base salary of 50 to 70 percent with commissions forming the balance of their earnings. Commission scales vary according to the product sold, of course, but care should be used to plan a steady or increasing commission scale. Commissions that decrease after a certain volume is reached tend to discourage really top-quality salespeople. Nor do they make sense from a management point of view, since overheads decrease as volume increases, and there should be more— not less—money available for commissions.

Commission only plans also offer good motivation, but there is less opportunity to attract good salespeople who want something to rely on during a slow week or until their clientele is established. Paperwork is less cumbersome and less costly in this type of plan, however, and there will be no stockpiling of orders to ensure maximum commission one week with no orders the following week. Little salesperson supervision is required, because if sales are not made, payments are not required.

Salary plus bonus plans award lump payments for good performance. These may or may not be related to the total sales volume. Usually they are given to motivate sales of specific products or to obtain a predetermined number of new customers in a specific period. The plan may be a form of profit sharing, with the bonus based on current profits.

PROMOTION INCENTIVES

Chances for promotion also serve as motivators. Younger salespeople are most likely to be motivated by the promise of senior positions in exchange for superior selling. Care should be taken in using this motivator, however, since top salespeople do not necessarily make good managers.

[1]Douglas Smallbone, *How to Motivate and Remunerate Your Salesmen,* Staples Press, London, 1971.

CHALLENGE AND RESPONSIBILITY

The actual work, challenge, and responsibility are excellent motivators. The average salesperson personality enjoys these, and management should make sure that challenges are set and the employee is offered adequate responsibility. The challenge of trying to beat other sales records during a sales campaign is the major reason they are so effective. But somewhat the same effect can be achieved by setting goals for salespeople—goals that will make them stretch performance if reached. Bulletins of sales volume of various salespeople should be visible—on bulletin boards, for example. These may be expressed as percents of individual goals reached to increase competitiveness that would fall off if dollar figures were used.

Salespeople can be reminded of their own past performance as motivation. For example, if a salesperson sees sales drop 15 percent, he or she will know that something in the selling approach is being poorly used. Commission reports are a way to automatically provide sales records. Where these are not used (with straight salary plans, for example), special reports should be issued periodically.

Helping the salesperson to acquire a positive attitude about the work and the product should also improve his or her performance, since a person works harder both consciously and unconsciously for something he or she believes will happen.

JOB SECURITY

Job security becomes a great motivator as the salesperson ages. It is more important generally to salespeople who will accept straight salary payments and less important to those who sell for commissions. Use of job security as a motivator relies on a negative use of fear with the salesperson being made to fear loss of his or her job if sales are not increased.

PROBLEM SOLVING

Another type of challenge, solving customers' problems, motivates salespeople. It also provides customer satisfaction. Management can best use this motivator by hiring salespeople who are interested in solving customers' problems, and then making sure that these workers have enough product and/or industry knowledge to do the job. For example, if a food service publication's space salesman is approaching a china manufacturer, he or she needs to know how and when the publication can best serve the client. If an upcoming issue will feature disposable dinnerware, for example, this would not be a good issue to carry the manufacturer's ads. But if it were to feature fine restaurant design, advertising would be well placed. The salesperson would, then, need to know the contents of upcoming issues, as well as statistical breakdowns of the types of readers.

PRAISE

According to studies, praise from customers motivates a salesperson more than praise from company management. Management can, however, facilitate this by providing adequate training and product knowledge and by passing along any praise of the salesperson that is made to management.

Praise, when deserved, is an important factor in improving the salesperson's mental attitude, resulting in greater productivity.

WORK SURROUNDINGS

Work surroundings are more important motivators for in-store salespeople. Traveling salespeople, seldom in the office, are less affected by the work atmosphere. Older salespeople are more apt to be motivated by an improved atmosphere. Private office space, pleasant furnishings, good lighting, good lounge and cafeteria facilities, etc., are areas that can be improved to increase motivation through the work surroundings.

SUGGESTED FURTHER READING

Apsley, J. C., *Sales Manager's Handbook,* Dartnell Corp., Chicago, 1965.
Compensation of Salesmen, Dartnell Corp., Chicago, 1967.
Haas, Kenneth B., *How to Develop Successful Salesmen,* McGraw-Hill, New York, 1963.
Smallbone, Douglas, *How to Motivate and Remunerate Your Salesmen,* Staples Press, London, 1971.
Smyth, R. C., "Financial Incentives for Salesmen," *Harvard Business Review,* January–February 1968.

SAMPLING

Areas for use in Cost Control:

ORGANIZATIONAL AND OPERATIONAL SYSTEMS
INDUSTRIAL APPLICATIONS
BUSINESS AND COMMERCIAL APPLICATIONS

Sampling is the selection at random of a number of statistics as a means of predicting the whole statistical picture without actually computing all figures involved. Sampling is often used as a means of learning public opinion of or need for a certain product before it is produced and marketed, for example. Thus, the extent of the probable market can be ascertained at a relatively low cost.

To be accurate, sampling must cover a minimum number—500 to 1,000, depending on the end goal of the project. Quality of questionnaires and/or interviewing is also essential to accurate sampling, since biased questions will give a biased rather than a true result. Questionnaires and interviewing should be handled by professionals in this area, where possible.

The most important sampling techniques include:

1. *Stratified Sampling.* This divides the population into various levels, then samples and compares the results of each with others. For example, sampling strata may be divided by such standards as annual income, age, job type, and place of residence.

2. *Systematic Sampling.* Also called *Quasi-random Sampling,* this takes every fourth, fifth, fifteenth, or other predetermined number in a list, such as the telephone book.

3. *Multistage Sampling.* This plan chooses specialized sample strata and samples within those areas. For example, a company considering the manufacture of a new printing press would obtain lists of owners of printing companies (stage 1) and draw samples (stage 2) from those lists.

4. *Quota Sampling.* This is the choice of people by predetermined average types. For example, in a sampling of 500, quotas might be set to interview 250 women and 250 men, with further breakdowns as to age, area of residence, etc.

5. *Random Sampling.* Random sampling gives everyone an equal chance of being questioned, as when interviewers stop people on the street to ask questions.

SUGGESTED FURTHER READING

Deming, W. E., *Sampling Techniques,* Wiley, New York, 1963.
Standingford, Oliver, ed., *Newnes Encyclopedia of Business Management,* Newnes, London, 1967.

SANDWICH TECHNIQUE

Areas for use in Cost Control:

PSYCHOLOGICAL MOTIVATIONAL MANAGEMENT
INDUSTRIAL APPLICATIONS
BUSINESS AND COMMERCIAL APPLICATIONS

The sandwich technique consists of telling an employee some unfavorable comments about his or her work by "sandwiching" them between favorable comments. In this way, the worker is made aware of the faults in his or her performance, yet good morale and motivation are maintained.

SUGGESTED FURTHER READING

Bittel, L. R., *What Every Supervisor Should Know,* McGraw-Hill, New York, 1974.

SCALAR TECHNIQUE

Areas for use in Cost Control:

ORGANIZATIONAL AND OPERATIONAL SYSTEMS
INDUSTRIAL APPLICATIONS
BUSINESS AND COMMERCIAL APPLICATIONS

The scalar technique is the hierarchal grading of work by responsibility and authority required, and the delegation by an employee of work graded below his or her level to an employee of the suitable level. The technique is based on the *scalar principle,* developed by J. D. Mooney, and it can reduce labor costs by ensuring that work is done only by the employee level (and expense) necessary. In other words, when the technique is applied, a vice-president's costly time is not spent stamping envelopes.

SUGGESTED FURTHER READING

Mooney, J. D., *The Principles of Organization,* Harper & Row, New York, 1954.
Pollard, H. R., *Developments in Management Thought,* Heinemann, London, 1974.

SCANLON PLAN

Areas for use in Cost Control:

FINANCIAL MOTIVATIONAL MANAGEMENT
ORGANIZATIONAL AND OPERATIONAL SYSTEMS
INDUSTRIAL APPLICATIONS
BUSINESS AND COMMERCIAL APPLICATIONS

The Scanlon plan is a system to distribute cost reduction savings to both the company and its employees in return for improved work performance which provides worker participation in the operation of the company. Devised by the late Joseph Scanlon, the method is based on McGregor's "Theory Y," which states the following:

1. Physical and mental effort in work is natural.
2. Threats of punishment and control are not the only motivation. Workers will direct their work efficiently if they share company goals.
3. Sharing work goals leads to worker growth and satisfaction.
4. Workers can learn to seek responsibility.
5. On the average, employee capacity is not fully used.

The Scanlon plan involves setting goals that all company employees can share through two factors: increased productivity and/or cost reduction savings, and company control.

SHARED SAVINGS

Cost reduction and increased-productivity goals are set for the company as a whole. Cost savings are shared by the company and employees, providing financial motivation for workers to reach these savings goals. Usually 50 to 75 percent of savings are shared by workers, with the exception of top management. Such payments are paid monthly, following the accounting period closure, providing a more immediate and more effective reinforcer than annual bonuses or payments.

PARTICIPATION

At the same time, workers participate in company operation. A series of committees is formed at every level of operation, and regularly scheduled meetings are held to discuss ways of increasing productivity and reducing costs. Each worker participates in a meeting at some level. Ideas are channeled upward for consideration and eventual adoption, when suitable.

SUGGESTED FURTHER READING

Lesieur, F. G., ed., *The Scanlon Plan,* Wiley, New York, 1958.

McGregor, D., *The Human Side of Enterprise,* McGraw-Hill, New York, 1960.

SCATTER GRAPH

Areas for use in Cost Control:

ORGANIZATIONAL AND OPERATIONAL SYSTEMS

INDUSTRIAL APPLICATIONS

The scatter graph technique is a **cost analysis** method, used in separating fixed and variable elements in mixed costs. *See also* **Overhead Cost Control.**

Cost data for several periods of time are charted (See Fig. 93), and a line is drawn

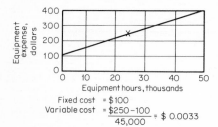

Fixed cost $= \$100$

Variable cost $= \dfrac{\$250-100}{45,000} = \$0.0033$

Figure 93. Typical scatter graph.

midway between high and low points. The fixed cost element is the low point; the variable cost element is the average between the points, with the fixed cost subtracted, divided by the number of time units used. *See also* **Fixed Costs; Variable Costs.**

SUGGESTED FURTHER READING

Solomons, D., *Studies in Cost Analysis,* Sweet and Maxwell, London, 1968.

Blecke, Curtis J., *Financial Analysis for Decision Making,* Prentice-Hall, Englewood Cliffs, N.J., 1966.

SCENARIO WRITING

Areas for use in Cost Control:

ORGANIZATIONAL AND OPERATIONAL SYSTEMS

INDUSTRIAL APPLICATIONS

BUSINESS AND COMMERCIAL APPLICATIONS

Scenario writing is the writing of imaginary logical events relating to a specific project as a means of determining when specific things can be made to happen and/or when and how events will affect the project, costs, problem, etc. Used as a method of **time-series analysis,** the written scene starts from the current cost or other problem and imagines the sequence of action, including crisis points and points of decision. Use of the method details possible important decisions and alternate solutions to cost or other problems, giving the user a better "feel" of the situation before action is required.

SUGGESTED FURTHER READING

Kahn, H., *Thinking About the Unthinkable: A Study of the Problems of Thermonuclear Strategy,* Avon Books, New York, 1964.

SCHLOSBERG THEORY

Areas for use in Cost Control:

PSYCHOLOGICAL MOTIVATIONAL MANAGEMENT
INDUSTRIAL APPLICATIONS
BUSINESS AND COMMERCIAL APPLICATIONS

The Schlosberg theory states that mild fear, risk taking, mild frustration, and the need for problem solving motivate workers to increased efficiency, thus reducing labor costs. This does not necessarily apply to *all* mild fears, problems, frustrations, etc., and when such fears, frustrations, and problems increase greatly in intensity, performance efficiency drops off sharply. Rather, sufficient of these elements to provide work excitement and to arouse work curiosity should be provided if productivity is to be increased.

SUGGESTED FURTHER READING

Pribram, K. H., ed., *Adaptation,* Penguin, Baltimore, 1969.
Schlosberg, H., "Three Dimensions of Emotion," *Psychological Review,* vol. 61, 1954.

SCOTT GRAPHIC RATING SCALE

Areas for use in Cost Control:

ORGANIZATIONAL AND OPERATIONAL SYSTEMS
INDUSTRIAL APPLICATIONS
BUSINESS AND COMMERCIAL APPLICATIONS

The Scott graphic rating scale is used to evaluate employee performance, detailing areas where efficiency can be increased to reduce labor costs. The method differs from other rating scale techniques in that:

1. The supervisor rating an employee does not use quantitative methods, but rather places a simple check mark at the level of performance that he or she feels best describes the employee's work.

2. If an employee's performance falls somewhere between two standards, the supervisor can place the check mark between performance levels to indicate this, ensuring that discrimination can be as fine as the supervisor wishes.

Figure 94 shows a typical response scale to measure one area of performance. In evaluating performance, each rating scale is ranked from 0 to 10. For example, if the

Figure 94. Typical Scott graphic rating response scale.

supervisor places a check mark on the major division mark of *low* on the response scale in Fig. 94, the employee receives three points. Points are determined for all response scales used. In one comparison, these may include:

1. Volume of work
2. Quality of work

3. Reliability
4. Learning ability
5. Initiative
6. Work knowledge
7. Cooperativeness
8. Ability to communicate

Total scores of employees, as well as totals of individual response scales, are evaluated by management to point up areas where efficiency increases are needed.

SUGGESTED FURTHER READING

Whisler, T. L., and S. F. Harper, *Performance Appraisal,* Holt, New York, 1962.

SCRAMBLED MERCHANDISING

Areas for use in Cost Control:

ORGANIZATIONAL AND OPERATIONAL SYSTEMS
BUSINESS AND COMMERCIAL APPLICATIONS

Scrambled merchandising is the sale of multiple lines of products in one outlet, including unconventional products and brands, to increase traffic and sales with no additional cash outlay other than the goods' cost. Some retailers find that this method increases sales volume as effectively as a moderate advertising program yet costs considerably less. A variation of the technique is *discount merchandising,* where a wide variety of goods with a low profit margin is offered from one store. Decreased profit margins are covered with increased sales volume, providing greater operational profits.

SUGGESTED FURTHER READING

Kotler, Philip, *Marketing Management,* Prentice-Hall, Englewood Cliffs, N.J., 1972.

SECONDING

Areas for use in Cost Control:

ORGANIZATIONAL AND OPERATIONAL SYSTEMS
INDUSTRIAL APPLICATIONS
BUSINESS AND COMMERCIAL APPLICATIONS

Seconding is a Japanese technique in which workers are temporarily transferred to a subcontractor during slack periods. Use of the technique reduces recruiting, hiring, and training costs, as well as offering a cost advantage on work performed by subcontractors, since a lower contract rate usually accompanies seconding.

SUGGESTED FURTHER READING

Dore, R., *British Factory, Japanese Factory,* G. Allen, London, 1973.

SECURITY AND COST CONTROL

Areas for use in Cost Control:

ORGANIZATIONAL AND OPERATIONAL SYSTEMS
MATERIALS AND EQUIPMENT MANAGEMENT
INDUSTRIAL APPLICATIONS
BUSINESS AND COMMERCIAL APPLICATIONS

Security is the protection of business property, including information, both in the plant and/or office and in transit. Costs are reduced through the use of security by a reduction of materials, supplies, products, and information that are pilfered or stolen. Additionally, insurance costs may be reduced when adequate security provisions are made.

One study, made by Professor Leon Radzinowicz, a well-known criminologist at Cambridge University, indicates that as many as 7 percent of women and 29 percent of men carry out one or more indictable crimes during their lifetimes, and percentages are rising. This means that as many as one in four employees, for example, may be prone to pilfering from their employer.

In addition to public and employee thefts of money, supplies, or information, there are industrial information thefts (*see* **Industrial Espionage Prevention**), shoplifting, and computerized information theft (*see* **Computer Security**).

Cost of the security system itself is much lower when the system is designed and built into a plant or office. Alarms, locks, theft-resistant doors and windows, and closed-circuit television surveillance are all much cheaper to install when the property is built than when added as an afterthought. Proper use of security devices and plans, once installed, is just as essential to successful security control. Employees should be trained to use these devices and held accountable for their use.

HIRE OR LEASE SECURITY PERSONNEL?

Whether to hire and train security personnel or lease a guard service is another primary decision in implementing a security system. Cost of training and benefits can generally be avoided by renting the service, but security personnel are not then under the direct control of the company. In renting a guard service, great care should be taken to investigate the agency's hiring, checking, and training programs to make sure they meet standards the company would use if hiring its own guard staff. Some firms feel that a company employee feels more loyalty toward his or her own employer, and these firms prefer to hire security staff even if the cost is a bit more.

PERSONNEL AND SECURITY

A good measure of security can be installed through careful company hiring practices for *all* staff. References should be carefully checked to eliminate candidates with a history of pilfering office supplies or worse. Some companies require applicants to take lie detector tests to eliminate security risks. When the employee will be in contact with some government-contracted work and must have a security clearance, official investigation of the applicant's private life may be necessary.

An additional security checkup should be made of any employee to be promoted as an added measure of ensuring that a responsible person is going into the more responsible job.

Pay and benefits, including pensions, affect security, too, since employees are less inclined to steal when their financial rewards are adequate.

Disgruntled employees may be especially poor security risks. If they feel the company is not giving them a "fair deal" in some area, they may be more likely to steal to "get even." Grievances should be settled, or the employee dismissed, to clear this area of security risk.

PHYSICAL SECURITY DEVICES

Physical devices are the backbone of any security system. These include the following:

Control equipment at any point involving the handling of cash. In banks, for example, a bulletproof screen between teller and customers offers the employee protection and perhaps courage to reach for an alarm during a holdup. Electronic devices, such as videotape machines, can be used to photograph such locations for proof of any crime and identification of the thief.

Radio or telephone reporting equipment. This allows the guard to report in frequently, with a missed report signaling the need for action.

Locks, safes, and other security devices. They should be of top quality, and keys, combinations, etc., should be carefully controlled. Double and triple locks are useful.

Armored cars and larger vehicles. These are useful in moving cash or valuable assets, such as gold or platinum. Armed guards usually accompany the vehicle in transit.

Electronic devices. Such devices are used to control access and to provide warnings of a break in security. Some new electronic locks are designed to provide access to the individual user, and only his or her handprint will unlock the device. Other electronic equipment may be geared to open only when the device has a record of the pattern of the eye retina of the user, which is particularly useful for employee access. Closed-circuit television allows one guard to monitor several areas at once. Videotaping can provide identification of thieves.

Alarm systems should be specifically designed for the plant or office. Regular inspections and tests offer a good measure of control. Several alarm systems installed in one office or plant will increase the degree of protection possible.

Costs can be limited by protecting only those parts of an operation that need security. In an office, for example, only the safe may need a high degree of security, while good door and window locks provide adequate protection for office equipment.

Some electronic systems are both invisible and silent. An electronic or infrared eye or a combination of such units may be interrupted as an intruder enters, for example. No alarm rings, and he or she continues to work on the safe. The guard or police, however, are signaled and have time, as the thief works, to reach the location.

Wiring across windows, door contacts, and roof wiring are all used in electronic systems. A cut, broken, or shorted wire signals guards or police. Contact mats can be placed under carpeting in an access area. Switched on, weight on the mat signals for help.

Ultrasonic devices emit unheard (because of frequency) sound patterns into a room. Interruption of the pattern—any human movement in the entire room—signals guards or police.

Seismic electronic devices can detect any pressure on metal or building-wall structures.

SECURITY TECHNIQUES

Common sense and proper use of security devices are key points in implementing a security system.

Money and valuable materials should not be handled in public if possible. Bank deposits should not follow a pattern, and employees carrying money should be provided with protection. Armored-car routes and timing should be regularly altered.

Guard schedules and routes should also be regularly changed. Guard dogs, trained to attack intruders on the guard's command, are often used to provide additional security.

Information that would help a thief—alarm wire layouts, guard schedules, and safe or vault location diagrams—should be particularly controlled.

In transportation of goods, hitchhikers (including women) should be avoided.

FIRE SECURITY

Protection from fire is especially important in relation to cost control. Insurance seldom covers 100 percent of physical assets lost, and business lost because operations were suspended can add to the bill. In addition, insurance rates are lower for property with certain fire-protection devices, such as sprinkler systems.

Building materials are one area for security. Wood and fiberboard products are less secure, of course, than are concrete blocks or bricks. Drywall, a less expensive substitute for plaster, does not burn and can provide some protection.

Plastics (wall paneling, furniture, lighting fixtures, piping) where used should be made of fire-resistant grades, as should foam insulation. Such synthetic materials should also have low noxious-odor ratings, since some grades do not burn rapidly but give off poisonous fumes.

Reinforced-cement roof spans and supports not only provide fire protection but are lower in cost than suitable alternatives such as steel.

Equipment and materials used in an operation should be viewed from a fire security attitude. For example, welding activities and flammable materials should be widely separated. Combustible materials, such as oil, should be cleaned from floors and other surfaces as quickly as possible.

Fire walls can limit the area damaged and reduce insurance premiums in most cases. Open floor plans which eliminate the use of these need the protection of sprinkler systems or other devices.

A fireproof vault should house business records, including computerized data, to ensure their safety in case of fire. Usually, smaller fireproof safes or cabinets are located in work areas to allow easy storage and removal of current records, with one major unit housing seldom used material. Specially designed cabinets are advisable for microfilmed or magnetic-tape records, which are ruined at lower temperatures than would affect paper records.

SUGGESTED FURTHER READING

Berkovitch, I., "Check the Man—Not His Pass," *Security Gazette,* November 1973.
Currer-Briggs, Noel, ed., *Security Attitudes and Techniques for Management,* Hutchinson, London, 1968.

SELECTIVE DISTRIBUTION

Areas for use in Cost Control:

ORGANIZATIONAL AND OPERATIONAL SYSTEMS
INDUSTRIAL APPLICATIONS
BUSINESS AND COMMERCIAL APPLICATIONS

Selective distribution is a technique that can reduce sales and servicing costs, shipping costs, and accounting costs, as well as concentrate interest in a product or service. Use of the method entails selling a branded product or service through limited outlets. Success of selective distribution depends on:

1. A product or service suitable for or adaptable to selective distribution
2. Choice of the best outlets
3. Provision of merchandising aids for chosen outlets

Product or Service. Selective distribution was first used for prestigious retailing of branded products. A perfume manufacturer, for example, might allow only one outlet for every 50,000 or 100,000 persons living in a city. Or, only one high-quality store in each town or city might be chosen. Sale of products that could claim an association with professional use are sometimes limited to professional application. Some hair care products, for example, cannot be purchased in a store and can be used only by a professional beautician in a hairdressing salon.

Selective distribution of branded services or of combinations of services and products has also become relatively common, partially through franchising. One English hairdresser, for example, will train operators in selected salons in his methods. In exchange for fees, his methods of service are then sold via these selected shops worldwide.

To be suitable for, or adaptable to, such selective distribution, the product or service should be something that can be given a prestigious or exclusive image, and it should be a branded product or service. Such exclusiveness can be added to an already produced plain product or service. The product may be glamorized with packaging design, advertising-image improvement, and the fact that it is obtainable on a "limited" basis.

A service can be made more prestigious through public-relations-image improvement and through use of any unique aspects of the service. Again, the haircut is a good example. To an American, a styled cut by a European-trained stylist sounds much more glamorous than a trip to the barber.

Outlet Choice. Outlets should be chosen for:

1. Prestige value
2. Potential sales volume

High-quality, multiple-store chains, for example, are a better choice than are single-unit, very exclusive stores.

Prestige value of the outlet should match the prestige value of the product or service, and advertising should be geared to this level. The principle can be applied to low-cost as well as expensive products if outlets are ample for sales needs. A baking company, for example, may offer selective distribution of a special style of sandwich bun to one fast-food chain and one supermarket chain. Advertising would be geared to the XYZ Hamburger, the only place to get Toasty Buns when eating out, and the X&Z Supermarket, the only place to buy Toasty Buns to use at home.

Merchandising. Sales per outlet increase when selective distribution is used. Outlet managers are more interested in selling a product or service when they can offer it exclusively in their area. They benefit from the producer's advertising, and their own ads help the producer. A supermarket manager is more apt to advertise "Toasty Buns—X&Z's Special Sandwich Bun for You" than to feature products the homemaker can buy at any competitor's store. In-store displays, consumer advertising, and public relations programs can be geared to help outlets with marketing.

New Products or Services Only. Use of selective distribution is best limited to new products or services, since a switch to this method would alienate outlets not chosen. Such limitation also allows suitable brand-name choice, "image" packaging, and advertising programs oriented to selective distribution.

SUGGESTED FURTHER READING

Palamountain, J. C., *The Politics of Distribution,* Harvard, Cambridge, Mass., 1955.
Stacey, N. A., and A. Wilson, *The Changing Pattern of Distribution,* Pergamon, New York, 1965.

SENSITIVITY TRAINING

Areas for use in Cost Control:

PSYCHOLOGICAL MOTIVATIONAL MANAGEMENT
INDUSTRIAL APPLICATIONS
BUSINESS AND COMMERCIAL APPLICATIONS

Sensitivity training educates management personnel to be more aware of their subordinates' needs, wants, reactions, emotions, and personalities to help in communicating with them and in motivating them to increased production and/or efficiency, thus reducing labor costs.

Group training sessions are usually conducted by an accredited organization such as National Training Laboratories, Washington, D.C., and may be limited to all management membership or a cross-sectional-group membership. Sessions conducted by business organizations, such as the American Management Association, are generally limited to business participants. Some experts feel that experience with a group representing various occupations and personalities is more suitable when the goal is learning better ways to understand and motivate employees.

Games to develop awareness are used. For example, moving around a circle, each participant may tell the kind of "box" he or she feels the rest of the group has put him or her in, and the "labels" on the box. Others comment individually on the kind of "box" they have designed for the individual. Fantasizing, visualizing, and projecting games are also used.

Fears, emotions, and hopes are discussed individually. Relationships between two or more members of the group are dissected and examined. Conversations are blunt and honest.

Groups are usually limited to 12 or fewer participants, although some groups may combine with others for minimal large-group experience.

SUGGESTED FURTHER READING

Saylor, R. W., "Notes on Sensitivity Training," *Nation's Schools,* Chicago, November 1970.

SEPARABLE PROGRAMMING See Mathematical Programming.

SEPARATING OUT DEVIATIONS

Areas for use in Cost Control:

BUSINESS AND COMMERCIAL APPLICATIONS
INDUSTRIAL APPLICATIONS

This technique subdivides work, separating out anything not part of the normal routine. The sorting may be done as a first step, or the worker may do the separating as he or she completes the task. These special problems, once separated out, are handled by personnel trained to work with difficult problems, speeding "normal" work and reducing labor costs. In business and commercial applications, for example, a clerk may be sending out travel brochures in response to an advertisement for tours to Italy. If one response asks for information about Spain, it is set aside to be dealt with by the other clerk. Industrial applications work in much the same way, with production line workers discarding components that are not standard. The cost reduction factor can be great, since normal workloads move faster and more efficiently with this technique, yet special problems are dealt with economically.

SUGGESTED FURTHER READING

Bittel, Lester, *Management by Exception,* McGraw-Hill, New York, 1964.

SEQUENCING

Areas for use in Cost Control:

ORGANIZATIONAL AND OPERATIONAL SYSTEMS
MATERIALS AND EQUIPMENT MANAGEMENT
INDUSTRIAL APPLICATIONS
BUSINESS AND COMMERCIAL APPLICATIONS

Sequencing is the scheduling of customers wanting service to reduce operating costs for the company providing the service. The sequence of each servicing job and the length of time required to complete the sequence are evaluated, as is total probable service demand. Demands for servicing are then scheduled to eliminate idle employee time. Commercial examples might include TV repair shops making appointments to service customers' sets. Industrial applications include grouping of tasks to provide even workloads for all employees in a given sequence of work.

SUGGESTED FURTHER READING

Churchman, C. W., R. L. Ackoff, and E. L. Arnoff, *An Introduction to Operations Research,* Wiley, New York.

SEQUENTIAL ANALYSIS

Areas for use in Cost Control:

ORGANIZATIONAL AND OPERATIONAL SYSTEMS
INDUSTRIAL APPLICATIONS

Sequential analysis is a **mathematical statistics** method used to reduce quality-control costs by determining the minimum number of inspections of production items needed to provide acceptable quality, and then implementing that system. Complex mathematical calculations are used to compute the minimum number. The method is especially useful in high-cost sampling or testing, such as plastics flame-retardancy tests where the product is destroyed as it is tested.

SUGGESTED FURTHER READING

Wicks, C. T., and G. A. Yewdall, *Operational Research,* David & Charles, Newton Abbot, England, 1971.

SERIAL ORGANIZATION

Areas for use in Cost Control:

PSYCHOLOGICAL MOTIVATIONAL MANAGEMENT
ORGANIZATIONAL AND OPERATIONAL SYSTEMS
MATERIALS AND EQUIPMENT MANAGEMENT
INDUSTRIAL APPLICATIONS

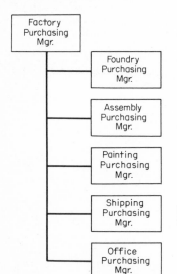

Figure 95. Typical serial organization chart.

Serial organization is the division of work and responsibility by the stage of manufacture. Figure 95 shows a Serial Organization Chart.

Cost advantages of the system stem from the fact that production performance can be better controlled, goals are more easily defined and achieved, and employees may be motivated through greater job variety, since they can see the results of their work when it is organized by stage of manufacture. The close proximity of each stage of work not only makes workers feel more involved, but it also helps them visualize company goals for their areas, lowering communications problems. While related to **functional organization,** serial organization specializes by general type of work rather than the more limiting specific job.

SUGGESTED FURTHER READING

Ammer, D. S., *Materials Management,* Irwin, Homewood, Ill., 1968.

SERVICE CONTRACTS

Areas for use in Cost Control:

ORGANIZATIONAL AND OPERATIONAL SYSTEMS
INDUSTRIAL APPLICATIONS
BUSINESS AND COMMERCIAL APPLICATIONS

Service contracts are legal agreements between employer and employees as to the minimum length of employment, salary, and other factors and are used to reduce the cost of key personnel turnover. For example, if a service contract is drawn for a five-year period, and the employee leaves prior to that time, he or she may forfeit all bonus or incentive payments, pension benefits, etc.

SUGGESTED FURTHER READING

Davis, William, *Money Talks,* Coronet Books, London, 1974.

SHAREHOLDER SERVICING COST CONTROL

Areas for use in Cost Control:

ORGANIZATIONAL AND OPERATIONAL SYSTEMS
INDUSTRIAL APPLICATIONS
BUSINESS AND COMMERCIAL APPLICATIONS

Since studies show that paperwork for dividend checks, annual reports, proxy statements, tax forms, Christmas cards, and other records costs more than they are worth for shareholders with a limited number of shares, some companies use repurchasing programs for holdings of all shareholders with 25 or fewer shares, thus eliminating such costs.

SUGGESTED FURTHER READING

Young, A., and D. Ellis, *The Repurchase of Common Stock,* Ronald, New York, 1971.
——— and W. Marshall, "The Repurchase of Common Stock," *Harvard Business Review,* January–February 1971.

SHORT-INTERVAL SCHEDULING

Areas for use in Cost Control:

PSYCHOLOGICAL MOTIVATIONAL MANAGEMENT
ORGANIZATIONAL AND OPERATIONAL SYSTEMS
INDUSTRIAL APPLICATIONS
BUSINESS AND COMMERCIAL APPLICATIONS

Short-interval scheduling is the planning and assigning of work in limited time blocks as a means of increasing efficiency and reducing labor costs. For example, a typist may be given forms to prepare in the next hour. Once this task is completed, he or she is given a new assignment for the next hour or two. Although the method uses more managerial time, it can greatly reduce employee time, including the following:

1. The supervisor knows what the employee is doing and whether the time used by the employee is satisfactory, too long, etc.

2. The employee is apt to be more interested in his or her work when there is an element of curiosity involved, such as wondering what the next task will be.

3. Employees with limited organizational ability operate more efficiently with someone else doing their work planning.

SUGGESTED FURTHER READING

Bittel, L. R., *What Every Supervisor Should Know,* McGraw-Hill, New York, 1974.
Smith, M. R., *Short-Interval Scheduling,* McGraw-Hill, New York, 1968.

SIMPLIFICATION

Areas for use in Cost Control:

ORGANIZATIONAL AND OPERATIONAL SYSTEMS
PAPERWORK DESIGN AND FLOW SYSTEMS
INDUSTRIAL APPLICATIONS
BUSINESS AND COMMERCIAL APPLICATIONS

Simplification is a purchasing cost control technique that reduces the items purchased and/or stocked. Multiple sizes or qualities of goods or materials used are eliminated wherever possible, one size or quality being used for all operations. This method reduces inventory labor, as well as reducing paperwork. It also facilitates use of bulk purchases, ensuring discounts. Inspection and production are simplified, as are tooling, equipment operation, and equipment maintenance.

SUGGESTED FURTHER READING

Standingford, Oliver, ed., *Newnes Encyclopedia of Business Management,* Newnes, London, 1967.

SIMULATION

Areas for use in Cost Control:

ORGANIZATIONAL AND OPERATIONAL SYSTEMS
INDUSTRIAL APPLICATIONS
BUSINESS AND COMMERCIAL APPLICATIONS

Simulation is an **operations research** technique used to represent possible results from alternate operational methods to determine whether such methods could do as good a job or better at a lower cost than current methods.

Typical sample operation situations are programmed into a computer, which compares all factors and presents the results if a specific alternate operational method is used. The best result at the least cost is then chosen and used. For example, the cost reduction possible through automating one or more phases of a production line could be determined.

The technique requires programmers and analytic scientists for operation. It is especially useful in controlling costs when building new operations or introducing new systems.

SUGGESTED FURTHER READING

Wicks, C. T., and G. A. Yewdall, *Operational Research,* David & Charles, London, 1971.

SINGLE COSTING See Output Costing.

SITE PLANNING

Areas for use in Cost Control:

ORGANIZATIONAL AND OPERATIONAL SYSTEMS
PAPERWORK DESIGN AND FLOW SYSTEMS
MATERIALS AND EQUIPMENT MANAGEMENT
INDUSTRIAL APPLICATIONS

Site planning includes both long- and short-term detailed planning and scheduling of construction-site work to control the use and cost of materials and labor. The methods can be adapted for planning in other industries.

LONG-TERM PLANNING

The long-term site plan encompasses a construction project from start to completion. Several areas are considered when drawing up the long-term plan, including:

1. *Time*—contracted completion date, holidays, weekends, daylight hours available, and weather probabilities due to time of year.

2. *Site characteristics*—site layout, ground conditions, utilities currently available, security needs, equipment needs, and labor availability in the area.

3. *Vacations and holidays.* Except for very short contracts for periods with no vacations or holidays, add 10 percent to time required to cover vacations and holidays.

Preparing the Long-Term Site Plan. Begin by forecasting availability of labor and materials for a specific job, including a detailed cost forecast. Forecasts should include alternate methods of construction and materials, so that the lowest-cost satisfactory plan can be used.

All major steps in the job should be set out, including priority of each step and materials, labor, and plant needed for each. Cost of all factors should be included.

Work flow should be laid out visually on a site map, using circles or straight lines to reduce material movement and prevent bottlenecks.

Separate time planning is useful in overall control of the project. This may start with a rough estimate of the overall project. For example, if the contract calls for completion of the project in 20 weeks (100 working days), the time breakdown might be as follows:

1. Start to damp course level—10% = 10 days
2. Damp course level to roofing-in—40% = 40 days
3. Vacation and holiday allowance—10% = 10 days
4. Emergency-time margin—10% = 10 days
5. Roofing, interior completion—30% = 30 days

Once this breakdown is estimated, detailed labor, material, and plant schedules should be prepared for the three working blocks (1, 2, and 5).

A progress record should also be prepared to record work as it is completed.

SHORT-TERM PLANNING

Just as important as the overall plan is the short-term site plan. Changes in weather conditions, labor and material supplies, etc., can be more easily controlled if a weekly or daily plan is used. These should provide planned short-term action in the following areas:

1. *Weather Conditions.* Can scheduled work be adapted to forecast weather? For example, concentrate on interior work where possible during inclement weather.

2. *Materials.* Are materials for work scheduled in hand? Or will work have to be rescheduled around available materials to avoid waiting time?

3. *Labor.* Are adequate numbers of workers on the payroll to avoid excessive overtime? Are any work areas overstaffed, reducing efficiency per worker?

4. *Plant.* Is needed equipment on site? If not, can it be obtained or leased? If not, can labor be rescheduled to avoid lost time?

5. *Subcontractors.* Is subcontracted work on schedule to avoid waiting time? If not, can labor be rescheduled to avoid lost time?

SUGGESTED FURTHER READING

Gobourne, J., *Cost Control in the Construction Industry,* Newnes-Butterworths, London, 1973.
Howorth, R., *Building Craft Foremanship,* David & Charles, Newton Abbot, England, 1972.
Programming and Progressing, MPBW Advisory Leaflet no. 14, H.M.S.O., London.
Scott, J. S., ed., *A Dictionary of Building,* Penguin, Baltimore, 1974.

SITUATIONAL DYNAMICS

Areas for use in Cost Control:

ORGANIZATIONAL AND OPERATIONAL SYSTEMS
INDUSTRIAL APPLICATIONS
BUSINESS AND COMMERCIAL APPLICATIONS

Situational dynamics is a technique used to measure managerial effectiveness in a given situation and to improve such effectiveness to maximum levels, reducing operational costs. The technique was developed by W. J. Reddin, Associate Professor of Business Administration, University of New Brunswick, Canada, as an operational tool in his **Three-D Theory.**

To implement situational dynamics, a flex map is drawn to represent the conditions as they stand, using the four basic styles of human behavior as a starting point (see Fig. 96).

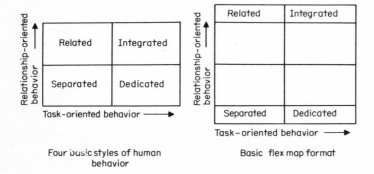

Four basic styles of human
behavior

Basic flex map format

Figure 96. Elements of flex map preparation.

The conditions or situations are then transferred to the flex map format (see Fig. 97). The name of the manager, the problem, and relevant activity should be used. In Fig. 97, for example, the head of labor relations has a problem with labor union demands as the result of increased automation of production.

Using the factors involved, the importance of action for each factor is weighted, with the sum of all factors equaling 10. In Fig. 97, for example, the labor relations head's effectiveness is the most important factor, since his or her actions will result in greater or less cost of replacing workers with machines. Union action is second most important in this case, since continued operation of the plant depends on their agreement to a settlement. Automation is involved in that its lower cost in use can offset costs of union demands. Thus, the manager may be given a rating of 5, the union a rating of 3, and automation a rating of 2 (see Fig. 98).

Related	Integrated
Labor relations head	Union demands
	Automation
Separated	Dedicated

Relationship-oriented behavior ↑
Task-oriented behavior →

Figure 97. Flex map showing a business situation.

Related	Integrated
Labor relations head ⑤	Union demands ③
	Automation ②
Separated	Dedicated

Relationship-oriented behavior ↑
Task-oriented behavior →

Figure 98. Flex map showing weighted importance of each factor.

The flex, or movement, required for maximum effectiveness is then shaded onto the map, with heaviness of shading varied according to the importance of each factor (see Fig. 99). The shaded areas are those behavioral styles where most effective control is possible, the styles increasing in value in proportion to heaviness of shading shown. The point of intersection of flex areas gives the area and pattern of possible effectiveness.

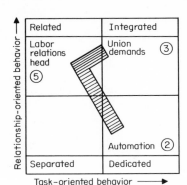

Figure 99. Flex map with shading density to show weighted importance of action.

In this case, primary activity is in the "Related" and "Integrated" behavior-style areas. The head of labor relations will move in a *task-oriented* (T.O.) direction to overcome union demands for payment to compensate for automation, tempered with a *relationship-oriented* (R.O.) movement between "Dedicated" and "Related" behavior-style areas to show a human concern for workers replaced by machinery. His or her primary target is to continue production with automation, making fair but not disproportionate pay settlements to workers displaced.

SUGGESTED FURTHER READING

Reddin, W. J., *Managerial Effectiveness,* McGraw-Hill, New York, 1970.

SKILLING

Area for use in Cost Control:

PSYCHOLOGICAL MOTIVATIONAL MANAGEMENT

Skilling is intended to increase an individual worker's motivation and production, reducing labor costs. The technique gives more responsibility to the employee. If the worker has been adding one part to a component being assembled on the line, for example, he or she may now assemble a whole section of the component. In the office, if an employee has been recording daily sales, he or she may now keep all sales records and complete weekly sales reports.

Although use of the technique usually means that additional training must be provided, it relieves employee boredom and allows greater sense of pride in work. *See also* **Deskilling.**

SUGGESTED FURTHER READING

Cemach, H. P., *Work Study in the Office,* MacLaren & Sons, London, 1969.
Larkin, J. A., *Work Study,* McGraw-Hill, New York, 1969.
Nadler, Gerald, *Work Design,* Irwin, Homewood, III., 1970.

SKILLS INVENTORY

Areas for use in Cost Control:

PSYCHOLOGICAL MOTIVATIONAL MANAGEMENT
ORGANIZATIONAL AND OPERATIONAL SYSTEMS
INDUSTRIAL APPLICATIONS
BUSINESS AND COMMERCIAL APPLICATIONS

A skills inventory is a cross-referenced recording of all available personnel skills that is used to fill job vacancies internally, providing psychological motivation for workers as they are promoted or moved into more suitable jobs and eliminating the costly search to fill the vacancy from outside the firm. Demonstrated skills of each employee are listed and cross-referenced in the skills inventory. For example, an accountant may have handled long-range forecasting programs in a previous job; or an employee being hired as a maintenance worker may have previously operated a drill press. When job vacancies occur, skill specifications from the job specification sheet are checked against the same skills in the inventory to determine whether or not there is a qualified, promotable employee suited for the job. The inventory is usually computerized.

SUGGESTED FURTHER READING

Mann, R., ed., *The Arts of Top Management,* McGraw-Hill, New York, 1970.

SLIP SYSTEM

Areas for use in Cost Control:

ORGANIZATIONAL AND OPERATIONAL SYSTEMS
PAPERWORK DESIGN AND FLOW SYSTEMS
DATA RETENTION—FILES AND RECORDKEEPING
INDUSTRIAL APPLICATIONS
BUSINESS AND COMMERCIAL APPLICATIONS

The slip system is the substitution of invoice copies for a separate and duplicated, more costly recording of the same information in an accounts receivable ledger. An extra "ledger" carbon copy of each invoice is prepared at the same time as the invoice.

This is held in an accounts receivable binder, filed by account name or number. On payment, the invoice copy is removed and transferred to a payments binder.

Statements are not sent at all unless an account is not paid regularly. Invoices act as statements and are clearly marked to indicate this. With rising postage and clerical costs, savings can be substantial. Some companies indicate that only about 10 percent of all accounts need the reminder of a statement. The clerical worker responsible for statements checks the invoice accounts receivable binder, sending statements only to customers requesting them or to accounts past due.

Control of the invoice binder is maximized by *never* removing an invoice copy unless a covering memorandum is filed in its place.

The physical makeup of the slip system should allow for easy insertion and removal of invoices.

SUGGESTED FURTHER READING

Longman, H. H., *How to Cut Office Costs,* Anbar Publications, London, 1967.
Zweig, Jeanne, *Accountant's Office Manual and Practice Guide,* Prentice-Hall, Englewood Cliffs, N.J., 1969.

SOCIOMETRY See Personnel Morale Building; Personnel Morale Measurement.

SOFTWARE FACTORY CONCEPT

Areas for use in Cost Control:

ORGANIZATIONAL AND OPERATIONAL SYSTEMS
DATA RETENTION—FILES AND RECORDKEEPING
MATERIALS AND EQUIPMENT MANAGEMENT
INDUSTRIAL APPLICATIONS
BUSINESS AND COMMERCIAL APPLICATIONS

The software factory concept reduces computer software production costs through combining program phases. For example, the output of one phase may be designed to also serve as the input of the next phase. This reduces the coding required. Automatic test data generators and dependency analysis are used to limit needed program updates to only those phases directly affected by the change. A common data base is used for related program factors so that updating of material in one program will automatically update identical material in other programs held by the same memory bank. *See also* **Electronic Data Processing.**

SUGGESTED FURTHER READING

Lapedes, D. N., ed., *Yearbook of Science and Technology,* McGraw-Hill, New York, 1974.

SOLAR POWER

Areas for use in Cost Control:

ORGANIZATIONAL AND OPERATIONAL SYSTEMS
MATERIALS AND EQUIPMENT MANAGEMENT
INDUSTRIAL APPLICATIONS
BUSINESS AND COMMERCIAL APPLICATIONS

Solar power is that developed from direct or diffused sun rays. Although the cost of commercial quantities of solar power is only beginning to meet rising costs of fossil-produced power, increased development and use are likely to reduce solar power costs, while fossil power costs will continue to rise because of decreasing world supplies.

Additional advantages are the fact that solar power is not potentially dangerous, as is cheap nuclear power, another available alternative. Once equipment is installed for operation, the company using the power can control the system's operation without government regulation and with little additional cost.

First economical use of solar power at commercial levels was solar-powered heating and air conditioning of office buildings. Research departments of Arthur D. Little, Cambridge, Massachusetts, designed the first office installation of this type, which featured a *flat-plate collector roof* to utilize the diffused New England sunlight in the installation, as well as direct rays. Flat-plate collectors absorb sun heat into a flat surface which can be made of various materials, such as metals or thermal plastics. Heat is diffused by air or water, which is circulated below the surface. Well-insulated pipes are essential for maximum heat extraction, and used still-warm water may be recirculated to the collector to intensify heat extraction. Flat-plate collectors can be designed as an integral part of the office or factory, as a tilted roof, or as a wall section facing south.

Solar-power generation of electricity on an industrial basis is not yet widespread but is becoming economically feasible. *Focusing collectors,* using reflecting panels of light-weight aluminum on plastic, curved or cupped, are rotated to catch the sun's rays and reflect them into a small collection area. Higher temperatures result from the use of focus collectors than from flat-plate collectors (about 500°C compared with 100°C) even without high-precision optical equipment. A 33-ft collector runs engines to about 10 hp. *Thermionic converters* are used for large industrial applications, collecting approximately 1500°C temperatures with high-precision focusing collectors.

Large *solar engines* for industrial use may be powered from *solar ponds* at costs much lower than other solar-power installations. Ponds 1 to 2 m in depth are lined with a black bottom and a layer of strong brine, such as magnesium chloride, to prevent heat loss into the bottom of the pool. A clear plastic dome prevents wind and other pollution of the clean water used to fill the area. Power is extracted with a *heat exchanger.*

Another promising area is the *solar cell,* a spin-off of American space programs. The cells are photovoltaic instruments used to convert the sun's rays directly into electricity. Low-cost fabrication methods have been developed for the single-crystal silicon type, which should bring equipment cost to about $25 per watt shortly, in whatever multiples desired. Fuel cost is, of course, free. The cells could be used singly or in panels to recharge batteries.

SUGGESTED FURTHER READING

Bennett, A., and Ted Schoeters, eds., "Power from the Sun," *The Financial Times,* London, July 29, 1974.
Daniels, F., *Direct Use of the Sun's Energy,* Yale Press, New Haven, 1970.
Solar Energy, Arizona University Press, Tempe, Ariz.

SPAN OF CONTROL

Areas for use in Cost Control:

PSYCHOLOGICAL MOTIVATIONAL MANAGEMENT
ORGANIZATIONAL AND OPERATIONAL SYSTEMS

The span of control refers to the number of employees for whom a single executive is responsible (see Fig. 100). Although the number varies according to the type of operation, businesses and commercial applications should generally be limited to 5 or 6 employees directly responsible to one supervisor, for optimum cost control; while 7 to 10 workers may report to one executive in routine industrial applications. At this ratio, supervisory control is adequate for increasing worker motivation and production, thus cutting operating costs.

SUGGESTED FURTHER READING

Cemach, Harry P., *Work Study in the Office,* MacLaren & Sons, 1969.

Putnam, A. O., Robert F. Barlow, and G. N. Stilian, *Unified Operations Management,* McGraw-Hill, New York, 1963.

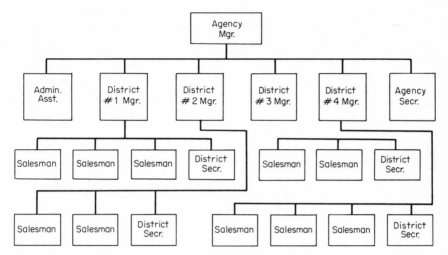

Figure 100. Typical span of control in an insurance agency.

SPECIFICATIONS

Areas for use in Cost Control:

ORGANIZATIONAL AND OPERATIONAL SYSTEMS
INDUSTRIAL APPLICATIONS
BUSINESS AND COMMERCIAL APPLICATIONS

Specifications are written orders, detailing the exact requirements of a product to be manufactured or a service to be performed and/or detailing the method of production or performance. Quality of the product or service can then be checked by comparing data *specified* with the actual product or service. Use of specifications reduces costs by providing the employee with acceptable standards for work performed, thus reducing unacceptable production and the accompanying cost of wasted labor and materials.

SUGGESTED FURTHER READING

Weinberg, Sidney, *Profit through Quality,* Gower Press, London, 1969.

SPEED READING

Areas for use in Cost Control:

ORGANIZATIONAL AND OPERATIONAL SYSTEMS
INDUSTRIAL APPLICATIONS
BUSINESS AND COMMERCIAL APPLICATIONS

Speed reading includes several methods of teaching managers to read more rapidly than they do now. Since the average manager reads about 20 percent of the working day, the use of speed reading can increase performance, reducing costs.

While degree of speedup varies, most managers can at least double their basic reading speed of 250 words per minute. A smaller proportion will quadruple it, reaching about 1,000 words per minute. Films, slides, and books are used, depending on the method of teaching. Programmed instruction and other kits are also available and may be incorporated into company management training programs. Time requirements are reasonable. A typical film class, for example, may require half an hour twice a week for six months.

Most films and other methods use the *word-grouping method,* teaching the managers to read groups of words at a glance rather than single words. Gradually, larger groups of words are highlighted and speed is eventually accelerated.

Training the eyes to follow these groups of words teaches better concentration as well as more rapid reading. Tests frequently show that at very rapid reading rates the mind absorbs the content of the written material subconsciously rather than consciously; the manager may not consciously remember what was read, but he or she can correctly answer questions about the content.

Some speed-reading instructors use a tachistoscope, a device that shows groups of words to the reader for an increasingly shorter period of time.

Costs for adding speed reading to company training are minimal, with textbooks available for $2 and up, kits for about $25, and film classes for $200 to $300.

SUGGESTED FURTHER READING

Wainwright, Gordon, "Learning to Read Faster," *The Financial Times,* London, Oct. 14, 1974.
————, *Rapid Reading Made Simple,* W. H. Allen, London.

STAFF RESHUFFLE

Areas for use in Cost Control:

INDUSTRIAL APPLICATIONS
BUSINESS AND COMMERCIAL APPLICATIONS

Staff reshuffle is reallocation of jobs, making better use of individual skills and personalities and reducing labor costs. In business and commerce, an employee hired to type invoices but who shows mathematical abilities may be moved to the bookkeeping department. Industrial applications include moving workers from one type of work, such as welding, to another, such as component assembly, if their abilities indicate that such a transfer is desirable. Since employees work harder and produce more when employed at a task that suits their skills and personalities, managerial staff should make a practice of considering company employees for other positions when a vacancy occurs.

SUGGESTED FURTHER READING

Cemach, H. P., *Work Study in the Office,* MacLaren & Son, London, 1969.
Larkin, J. A., *Work Study,* McGraw-Hill, New York, 1969.

STANDARD COSTS

Areas for use in Cost Control:

ORGANIZATIONAL AND OPERATIONAL SYSTEMS
INDUSTRIAL APPLICATIONS

Standard costs are calculated by absorbing **fixed costs** into units of production. They are sometimes called average costs. *See also* **Overhead Cost Control.**

SUGGESTED FURTHER READING

Dickey, R. I., *Accountant's Cost Handbook,* Ronald, New York, 1960.
Hart, H., *Overhead Costs,* Heinemann, London, 1973.

STANDARD COST THEORY

Areas for use in Cost Control:

ORGANIZATIONAL AND OPERATIONAL SYSTEMS
PAPERWORK DESIGN AND FLOW SYSTEMS
INDUSTRIAL APPLICATIONS
BUSINESS AND COMMERCIAL APPLICATIONS

The standard cost theory controls and reduces costs by setting a standard for every expected area of cost. These standards, recorded together, provide a basic operational budget, and actual costs are measured against the budgeted standards. *Cost and variance statements* (*see* **Cost and Variance Analysis**), together with the *budget* (*see* **Budgeting**), complete the basic paperwork required to implement the system.

Cost statements (*see* **Costing**), showing actual costs, and *variance statements* (*see* **Variance Analysis**), showing the difference between budgeted standards and actual costs, are prepared by the person responsible for the phase of work being considered. This acts as a measurement of the effectiveness of individual supervisors in controlling costs.

Standard production unit costs are determined by adding material, labor, and overheads divided by number of units. This standard unit cost figure is then used for inventory and other controls.

SUGGESTED FURTHER READING

Maynard, H. B., ed., *Industrial Engineering Handbook,* 3d ed., McGraw-Hill, New York, 1974.

STANDARDIZATION

Areas for use in Cost Control:

ORGANIZATIONAL AND OPERATIONAL SYSTEMS
PAPERWORK DESIGN AND FLOW SYSTEMS
INDUSTRIAL APPLICATIONS
BUSINESS AND COMMERCIAL APPLICATIONS

Standardization is a purchasing cost control technique that requires establishment of a normal or usual (standard) material, component, or work method in a business operation. Such standards are set by analyzing quality and performance of alternate materials, as well as by determining optimum use in regard to design, size, and work method used.

SUGGESTED FURTHER READING

Aljian, George W., *Purchasing Handbook,* McGraw-Hill, New York, 1973.
Standingford, Oliver, ed., *Newnes Encyclopedia of Business Management,* Newnes, London, 1967.

STANDARD PRICE METHOD

Areas for use in Cost Control:

MATERIALS AND EQUIPMENT MANAGEMENT
INDUSTRIAL APPLICATIONS
BUSINESS AND COMMERCIAL APPLICATIONS

The standard price method is a **stock control** technique used to value inventorial goods and stored materials and supplies. Values are based on a list of market costs of the items, even though actual cost to the company may differ from the charted figure.

The technique is popular because of its simplicity. However, inflation has forced cost variance control with a revision of charted figures once they vary by a predetermined percentage of 3 to 5 percent.

SUGGESTED FURTHER READING

Greene, J. H., *Production and Inventory Control Handbook,* McGraw-Hill, New York, 1970.
Lipman, B., *How to Control and Reduce Inventory,* Prentice-Hall, Englewood Cliffs, N.J., 1972.
Standingford, Oliver, ed., *Newnes Encyclopedia of Business Management,* Newnes, London, 1967.

STANDARD SCALES RATING See Personnel Performance Appraisal.

STANDARD TIMES AND COST CONTROL

Areas for use in Cost Control:

ORGANIZATIONAL AND OPERATIONAL SYSTEMS
INDUSTRIAL APPLICATIONS

Once standard times are determined for specific jobs, many companies accept them as permanent. However, they should be examined periodically (yearly is suggested) and corrected in relation to production conditions, methods, or other factors which have changed the time required to complete a specific task.

Redesign of work place or methods to purposely reduce standard times is another technique used to reduce labor costs.

Such changes will, of course, require written proof of change for labor purposes.

Informal comparisons of standard times with PMTS (*see* **Predetermined Motion Time Systems**) can call attention to the need for standard time adjustment, with highest-cost labor items compared first.

SUGGESTED FURTHER READING

Radke, Magnus, *Manual of Cost Reduction Techniques,* McGraw-Hill, New York, 1972.

STANDBY DESIGN

Areas for use in Cost Control:

ORGANIZATIONAL AND OPERATIONAL SYSTEMS
INDUSTRIAL APPLICATIONS
BUSINESS AND COMMERCIAL APPLICATIONS

Standby design is a technique that provides an extra, or "standby," element in an operation if that element is essential to the operation, especially if it has a lower than desirable percentage of expected reliability. For example, if a factory employing 300 men had one piece of equipment used before any production could begin, and if that equipment was not 100 percent reliable, a "standby" piece of equipment should have been available. Use of the method reduces costs because working time and production are not lost if the original element becomes inoperative.

Decisions to use standby design are usually based on cost of extra equipment and space to house it compared with rate of unreliability of the original element. Reliabilities of systems using standby design can be determined by multiplying the failure probability. Thus, if a particular piece of equipment is 70 percent reliable, a system using the original element and one standby would be 91 percent reliable ($0.3 \times 0.3 = 0.09$), while a system using the original element and two standbys would be 97.3 percent reliable ($0.3 \times 0.3 \times 0.3 = 0.027$).

SUGGESTED FURTHER READING

Buffa, Elwood S., *Modern Production Management,* Wiley, New York, 1973.
Weinberg, Sidney, *Profit through Quality,* Gower Press, London, 1969.

STATISTICAL EMPLOYMENT TECHNIQUES See Personnel Testing.

STIMULUS GENERALIZATION

Areas for use in Cost Control:

PSYCHOLOGICAL MOTIVATIONAL MANAGEMENT
FINANCIAL MOTIVATIONAL MANAGEMENT
WORK PLACE MOTIVATIONAL MANAGEMENT

Stimulus generalization is the application of a work factor similar to one to which employees have been conditioned to respond with more effective performance, in order to achieve similar favorable response and lower labor costs in a new work situation. For example, if an employee has been conditioned to respond to a financial incentive by working harder, a smaller financial incentive, an extra fringe benefit, etc., will also produce harder work. A smaller incentive may produce somewhat less increased effort.

Or if an employee has been conditioned to work harder after receiving praise from his or her supervisor, the employee will also work harder, although to a lesser degree, if the supervisor smiles or shows other signs of approval. *See also* **Behavior Control.**

SUGGESTED FURTHER READING

Eysenck, H. J., *Sense and Nonsense in Psychology,* Penguin, Baltimore, 1972.
Pavlov, I. P., *Conditioned Reflexes,* Oxford University Press, London, 1927.

STOCK CONTROL

Areas for use in Cost Control:

ORGANIZATIONAL AND OPERATIONAL SYSTEMS
PAPERWORK DESIGN AND FLOW SYSTEMS
MATERIALS AND EQUIPMENT MANAGEMENT
INDUSTRIAL APPLICATIONS
BUSINESS AND COMMERCIAL APPLICATIONS

Careful stock control assures the user that materials and supplies are not being wasted or stolen and can reduce costs of such goods and their storage. Another facet of the technique controls manufactured goods inventories from the time they are produced until purchased and shipped to the buyer. Both areas of stock control include the following basic steps:

1. *Goods receiving* and recording that receipt.

2. *Storage* of goods in good condition.

3. *Control* through recording incoming and outgoing materials and supplies, as well as the supply on hand. Control of incoming and outgoing production goods, as well as inventories of stock on hand and reserved stock, records of returned stock, and the rate of inventory turnover.

The cost of goods storage, or *inventory burden cost,* is high—usually 20 to 25 percent of the value of the goods. This figure includes the cost of the physical storage facilities, handling, distribution, taxes, insurance, obsolescence, and deterioration. Obsolescence and deterioration account for well over half of the total cost, and therefore they are especially suitable targets for cost reduction procedures.

Storage should be kept to the minimum required, and reasons for storage should include one or more of the following:

1. Stockpiling goods or materials to meet shortages from predicted industry strikes or slowdowns

2. Lack of available transport for immediate goods shipment
3. Widely fluctuating market for goods
4. Large batches required by production for economic operation
5. Seasonal materials price fluctuations
6. Quantity discounts or projected inflation-caused price increases on materials purchased large enough to offset storage costs

Physical Storage Facilities. In arranging storage areas, the following factors should be considered:

1. *Central versus Network Systems.* Choice of one large storage place or warehouse or a network of smaller storage areas is the first consideration. If only one operation is served, or if multiple operations are located near one another, a central storage place is the most economical. If branch operations are spread over a wide geographical area, however, branch areas may be preferred to allow storage near the point of use.

2. *Transportation.* Loading and unloading docks should be designed to most efficiently handle the type of transportation used, as should access facilities such as road- or rail-access features.

3. *Safety Areas* should be designed for storage of flammable or dangerous goods, including explosives, oil-based products, chemicals, gases, etc.

4. *Open Areas,* such as outdoor yards, may be used for low-cost storage for durable materials or goods not harmed by weather.

Goods Receiving. In goods receiving, incoming materials and supplies are checked against purchase orders for quantity and condition, and shipment is recorded. Purchasing and inspection departments are notified. A multiple-copy form called a *Goods Received Register* may be used for these purposes. The forms are numbered and show the date received, supplier's name and address, goods description and quantity, and transportation details. This form, combined with the supplier's invoice, and an inspection form, are used by the accounting department to make payment. In many cases it is usual for inspectors to initial each item in a column provided on the Goods Received Register to save the time and expense of handling an additional form.

In the case of industries using quantities of technical equipment, however, an *Inspection Report* form is needed. This should contain date of inspection, supplier's name and address, goods description, detail of test performance, and the inspector's signature as a release for payment.

If materials received are not satisfactory, the suppliers must be notified. A *Rejection Note* form is often used to detail goods rejected as well as the reason for dissatisfaction. The supplier may then request return of the goods or may offer credit for minor repairs that can be done by the buyer's staff to save time and transportation cost.

If materials are short or damaged, the shipping firm must be notified as well as the supplier, since they may be held responsible.

Control. Stock control requires the following steps:

1. Establishing a base inventory of goods now held, as well as a method for adding to or subtracting from this inventory. A system of checks, giving a **perpetual inventory,** will eliminate costly annual stocktaking.

2. Decisions must be made as to the amount of supplies or goods to be held, taking business conditions and quantity needed into account along with storage cost factors.

3. Coordination of purchase and delivery schedules by departmental heads and the purchasing department.

Stock control is an ideal area for **electronic data processing,** since data can be recorded and changed quite easily with such a system, often eliminating the need for extra forms and cross checks. The computer can also be programmed to give an automatic warning when stocks fall below the minimum desired level. In repeat ordering, a *computerized stock control* program can automatically instigate the required order.

ABC analysis is a useful technique for stock control. Here, goods are broken down into one of three classifications of value of goods consumed. A small percentage of items stocked will account for a large percentage of total value, and storage cost control can be more precisely applied to these items, with the saving of large areas of cost with little effort.

Delivery schedules can greatly affect the cost of stock control. Frequent deliveries from suppliers—daily, if possible—will cut storage costs, since the rate of stock turnover will be high. Infrequent deliveries, with ensuing low rate of stock turnover, raises storage costs. Even though frequent deliveries may be encouraged, however, a reserve stock of the supply should be held to prevent work stoppage in the event of late deliveries, particularly in the case of essential materials.

Use of stored goods should be controlled in much the same way as their receipt. A *Request for Goods* form should be completed and authorized by a supervisory employee. Issuing of goods should then be recorded, the clerk subtracting it from the balance of stock on hand and updating the *perpetual inventory.*

Fastest handling of stocked materials can be facilitated through the use of **popularity storage.** In this technique, easiest moved, lightest-weight items are stored nearest the point of issue, while slow-moving, heavy, or out-of-date stock is stored farther away.

Fire protection, including sprinkler systems and security measures, is also necessary for optimum cost control in storage.

Additional time and cost savers are planned storage layout and visible labeling of all stocks.

Valuing Stock. Putting a precise value on goods stored can be facilitated by:

1. Actual cost price method
2. First-in, first-out method
3. Last-in, first-out method
4. Average price method
5. Standard price method

The **actual cost price method** values stored goods from invoices recorded and is one of the most satisfactory methods when such figures are available.

The **first-in, first-out method** used the cost of goods first taken in until the quantity purchased at that time is gone, even though other shipments of the same goods may be received in the interim. Once this number is reached, cost of the next shipment is used until those quantities are gone, etc.

The **last-in, first-out method** values items according to the cost of the last items received.

The **average price method** values goods by averaging the cost of goods in stock, sometimes using weighted costs, taking quantities of items received at each price, and sometimes using a moving average of various costs of shipments received.

The **standard price method** values items according to a list of market costs of the items, even though actual cost to the company may differ from the charted figure.

SUGGESTED FURTHER READING

Bull, George, ed., *The Director's Handbook,* McGraw-Hill, London, 1969.
Standingford, Oliver, ed., *Newnes Encyclopedia of Business Management,* Newnes, London, 1967.

STOCKPILING

Areas for use in Cost Control:

ORGANIZATIONAL AND OPERATIONAL SYSTEMS
MATERIALS AND EQUIPMENT MANAGEMENT
INDUSTRIAL APPLICATIONS

Stockpiling is the acquisition of large amounts of materials and/or supplies needed for production or operation. Use of the method can reduce costs when such materials and/or supplies will rise in price in the near future as the result of inflation, natural shortages, shortages due to impending war, etc. *See also* **Inflation Cost Control.**

SUGGESTED FURTHER READING

Bull, R. J., and P. Doyle, *Inflation,* Penguin, Baltimore, 1972.
Hanson, J. L., *A Dictionary of Economics and Commerce,* MacDonald, London, 1974.

STOGDILL LEADERSHIP THEORY

Areas for use in Cost Control:

PSYCHOLOGICAL MOTIVATIONAL MANAGEMENT
ORGANIZATIONAL AND OPERATIONAL SYSTEMS

The Stogdill leadership theory is a human-relations-oriented organizational model providing an approach to the selection of managerial personnel and motivation of workers. Costs are reduced by increase of work produced by the technique. In the technique, three factors are said to be the basis for leadership selection:

1. The employee's status
2. Demands from the remainder of the business organization
3. Opinions and regard of coworkers

The effective leader uses reinforcement and learning techniques to define the work group structure and to motivate employees in work performance.

SUGGESTED FURTHER READING

Stogdill, R. M., *Individual Behavior and Group Achievement,* Oxford University Press, Fair Lawn, N.J., 1959.

STRATEGY FORMULATION

Areas for use in Cost Control:

ORGANIZATIONAL AND OPERATIONAL SYSTEMS
INDUSTRIAL APPLICATIONS
BUSINESS AND COMMERCIAL APPLICATIONS

Strategy formulation is a formalized technique of business planning and cost control. Originally patterned on governmental defense strategy, the method has the following goals:

1. Determination of market product position
2. Determination of growth possibilities
3. Detailed specification of new markets to be entered, strengths to be used, and weaknesses to be avoided
4. Constant control of production and marketing, including quality, growth, and cost control

Strategy formulation is generally divided into two major approaches, *root method* and *branch method.* In the *branch method,* strategy is built by extending current company policy into new areas. The *root method,* on the other hand, creates a completely new strategy each time growth or change is implemented.

In planning, it is essential to know what to expect from the market your business or factory serves. H. Kahn and A. J. Wiener, writing in *Daedalus,* a magazine published by the American Academy of Arts and Sciences in Boston, have predicted that the following trends will continue in Western society through 1990:

1. Increasingly sensate cultures
2. Bourgeois, bureaucratic, meritocratic, democratic, and perhaps nationalistic elites
3. Accumulation of scientific and technological knowledge
4. Institutionalization of change
5. Worldwide industrialization and modernization
6. Increasing affluence and leisure
7. Population growth
8. Decreasing importance of primary occupations
9. Urbanization and the growth of megalopolises
10. Literacy and education
11. Increased capability for mass destruction
12. Increased tempo of change

In planning for successful growth and expansion, a company should also be aware of the fact that profitable markets will be international ones.

THE BASICS OF STRATEGY FORMULATION

To implement strategy formulation, create a master plan, tailored to suit your specific company or business. This plan must cover the type of product or service to be sold, the best way to sell the product or service, and cost and quality control for efficient implementation of the first two areas. Four steps, originally designed by the U.S. Department of Defense, have been adapted to business use in strategy formulation.

Step 1: Resources should be allocated. In this step, the company chooses potential expansion areas. These are analyzed (*see also* **Network Planning and Analysis**), and the most profitable projects are chosen. Basis for choice usually includes potential market for the product or service, relationship of the project to current operations, expenditures necessary to complete the project, including rate of return in relationship to cost, and ability of present work force to complete the project. Once projects are chosen, project goals should be carefully set out, as should methods of project implementation.

Step 2: A one-year budget should be combined with a long-range planning budget. Generally, a tentative five-year budget is set up, and yearly more precise budgets are pulled from this planning during an annual review period.

Step 3: Systems analysis, such as network analysis, should be used when formulating strategy, and a plan should be drawn up in detail (*see also* **Systems Analysis**). Kahn and Wiener's list of future trends and technological advances set out earlier in this section should give a great deal of insight into the problem of deciding on specific new project goals and planning strategies necessary to reach those goals. Network diagrams for any project undertaken will aid control of time and costs. Both **program evaluation and review technique** (**PERT**) and **critical path analysis** (**CPA**) are usable network diagrams for this purpose.

Step 4: A strategic formulation center to review projects and suggest new projects is a useful addition. Care should be taken to build in cost control factors as well as consideration for growth. This is best done by using graphic network analysis such as that explained in **resource allocation.** This form of network analysis allows a visual presentation of both time and cost required for any project under consideration, while other forms of network analysis are limited to one or more chartings of time elements.

STRATEGY FORMULATION IN PRACTICE

As strategy changes from theory to a reality for a project or for a company, several factors should be considered:

1. *Know your industry and market.* If a company makes office equipment, it is not enough to "think" that customers will be interested in an automated typewriter, for example. Market studies must be carried out to determine their interest, as well as what price they would be willing to pay. If possible, find out whether competing companies are working on this project. It may be that a firm will *have* to offer such a product to remain competitive; or if production cost will be so high that sales are questionable, it may be better to wait and see how a competitor's product is received.

2. *Markets should be defined in detail.* What sort of people buy the product? Where do they live? Do they use the product at home or at work? Do they use a large quantity of the product? As these questions are answered, it will be possible to see the largest potential segment of the market, and product development should be aimed at this segment. If, for example, a company manufactures china, it may find several potential market areas: institutional—hotels, restaurants, hospitals, schools, etc.; home use; and specialty china uses—fondue pots, etc. Any of these can be potential markets, but one manufacturer cannot cater to the tastes of all three. It will, instead, need to decide which market offers the largest potential in order to gear the operation to it.

3. *Product timing is an essential factor.* The institutional china manufacturer, for example, has been hurt by the growing use of disposable paper and plastic dishware. However, with increased cost of plastics (made from oil) and paper products, as well as ecological pressure, less disposable ware may be used in the future, again making institutional china a more profitable area.

4. *It is necessary to understand the supply and demand cycle.* A new product is announced, and the demand for it becomes great. After a time, demand slacks off—the market may be saturated. For best profitability, a manufacturer must be in production well ahead of the initial heavy demand and must be able to anticipate the drop in demand by having dropped production. Some industries, of course, have a more stable cycle of demand. Cotton yard goods demand continues rather steadily, while a novelty item, such as the hula hoop, was in heavy demand for only one or two seasons.

5. *Research and development departments should work on projects to lower costs of current technology,* as well as on ideas for new production.

6. *Worldwide distribution,* with its huge potential market, offers many cost-control advantages. In publishing and selling a children's book, for example, costs will be much less per copy if 100,000 copies are sold than if 10,000 copies are sold. Widening geographical markets will become an increasingly important factor in cost control.

With these factors in mind, the next step is drawing up a company statement of *strategy*—a statement of the company's plans and goals, and how it intends to achieve them. This statement should be used as a guide rather than as a set of hard-and-fast rules. Each section of such a statement should be written by the executive responsible for that area of work, since writing the statement will help crystallize planning.

SUGGESTED FURTHER READING

Ansoff, H. I., *Business Strategy,* Penguin, Baltimore, 1969.
————, *Corporate Strategy,* McGraw-Hill, New York, 1965.
Tilles, S., "Strategies for Allocating Funds," *Harvard Business Review,* vol. 44, no. 1, January–
    February 1966.

STRATEGIC SPACE PLANNING

Areas for use in Cost Control:

WORK PLACE MOTIVATIONAL MANAGEMENT
ORGANIZATIONAL AND OPERATIONAL SYSTEMS
PAPERWORK DESIGN AND FLOW SYSTEMS
DATA RETENTION—FILES AND RECORDKEEPING
MATERIALS AND EQUIPMENT MANAGEMENT
BUSINESS AND COMMERCIAL APPLICATIONS

Strategic space planning is the use of preplanning techniques to determine the least costly office space that will meet required and specified standards. These standards are determined by written statements of company needs and objectives in several areas, including the following:

1. *Economic office life*—an estimate of the length of time the company's office needs will remain relatively static. Usually, this ranges from 5 to 20 years. The figure can provide a guide when leasing space, but in general 10 years should be the maximum length of lease negotiated.

2. *Current needs.* The urgency of the need for new office quarters is considered. For example, if a large new account will cause marked growth in the next several months, new office space must be found quickly to ensure maximum operational efficiency.

3. *Facility needs.* Needs for Telex, cafeteria, conference rooms, training quarters, mail room, rest rooms, etc., must be determined.

4. *Personnel.* Growth of the company in the life period of the new quarters should be considered when determining overall space needs. If adequate space for the latter part of a 10-year period leaves excess space now, this area may be sublet to another business for a shorter period of time.

5. *Cost limits.* Good office layout and care in providing suitable lighting, wall colors, etc., have greater positive motivational effect on employees' performance than do expensive, but poorly designed, offices.

6. *Office layout.* This should facilitate easy paperwork flow and other communication. *See also* **Communication Grid Analysis; Office Layout.**

SUGGESTED FURTHER READING

Lock, D., ed., *Management Techniques,* Directors Bookshelf, London, 1972.
Ripnen, Kenneth H., *Office Space Administration,* McGraw-Hill, New York, 1974.

STRETCH-OUT TECHNIQUE

Areas for use in Cost Control:

ORGANIZATIONAL AND OPERATIONAL SYSTEMS
INDUSTRIAL APPLICATIONS
BUSINESS AND COMMERCIAL APPLICATIONS

The stretch-out technique reduces labor costs by giving employees additional, regular work without providing an increase in salary or benefits.

SUGGESTED FURTHER READING

ASME Work Standardization Bulletin, American Society of Mechanical Engineers, New York.
Maynard, H. B., ed., *Industrial Engineering Handbook,* 3d ed., McGraw-Hill, New York, 1974.

STRIKE LOSS COMPUTER

Areas for use in Cost Control:

PSYCHOLOGICAL MOTIVATIONAL MANAGEMENT
FINANCIAL MOTIVATIONAL MANAGEMENT
INDUSTRIAL APPLICATIONS

The strike loss computer is a device used by business or industry to persuade employees that a strike would cost more than they could gain, thus avoiding a strike and the resulting costs to the company (see Fig. 101). The technique was developed by the Republic Aviation Corporation, but the basic format can be adapted for all areas of business and industry.

PERSONAL STRIKE LOSS COMPUTER

Weekly take-home pay, dollars	Weekly pay loss during strike, dollars	Length of time, in weeks, needed to recover each week's loss if you strike for:					
		0¢/hr.	2¢/hr.	4¢/hr.	6¢/hr.	8¢/hr.	10¢/hr.
250	250	Never	312½	156¼	78+	39+	19+
240	240	Never	300	150	75	37+	18+
230	230	Never	287	143+	71+	35+	17+
220	220	Never	275	137+	68+	34+	17+
210	210	Never	262+	131+	65+	32+	16+
200	200	Never	250	125	62+	31+	15+
190	190	Never	237+	118+	59+	29+	14+
180	180	Never	225	112	56+	28+	14+
170	170	Never	212+	106+	53+	26+	13+
160	160	Never	200	100	50	25	12+
150	150	Never	187+	93+	46+	23	11+

Figure 101. Typical personal strike loss computer format.

SUGGESTED FURTHER READING

Hutchinson, J. G., *Management under Strike Conditions,* Holt, New York, 1966.

STRIKES AND COST CONTROL

Areas for use in Cost Control:

ORGANIZATIONAL AND OPERATIONAL SYSTEMS
INDUSTRIAL APPLICATIONS

Not only are strikes costly in themselves, but the eventual settlement of a threatened or actual strike affects many areas of operational cost control, including labor costs, work method changes, equipment and/or plant changes, marketing and pricing, customer goodwill, subcontracting rights, performance standards, and capital investment return. (See Table 48 for detailing of costs to firms not operating during a strike.) In many cases, however, management is panicked by the threat of a strike and settles before it really analyzes the costs of a strike, weighing possible gains against possible losses.

Table 48. Strike-Related Costs of Firms Not Operating During Strikes

Direct (economic) costs	Indirect (human) costs
Increases in wages and benefits	Increased labor control of company operation, including job security, allowable equipment and work methods, and negotiating strength
Legal costs	
Lost sales	

THE LENGTH OF A STRIKE AND COSTS

The first step in such an assessment is to determine the length of time a strike can continue before yearly output is affected at all. Basically, this is done by computing expected sales as a proportion of capacity of output. For example, if a plant could produce 250 tons of plastic per day if it were operating at full capacity (three shifts per day), yet sales or availability of materials limit production to 150 tons per day, depending on other factors, the plant could afford up to a 20-week strike with few additional costs. The strike would simply rearrange the timing of the 40 percent slack capacity that would not be used anyway if the plant was in full-capacity operation for the balance of the year.

Other factors that should be considered in determining the length of a strike at marginal cost include the quantity of goods inventoried at the outset. Even though the plastic manufacturer's total output would not suffer until the strike had lasted 20 weeks, customer goodwill, as well as sales, would drop sharply if inventories were not sufficient to carry through the strike period.

OPERATION DURING A STRIKE

The next discussion will concern the decision whether or not to try to operate the plant without the striking laborers (strike-related costs incurred during operation of a plant during a strike are detailed in Table 49). Strangely enough, it is easier to do this when the economy is strong than when unemployment is high. When other jobs are easily available, picketing is not as rigid, particularly after several weeks. In such a case, low-skilled, minority, and older workers are more easily hired, while pickets are more militant in defending their jobs against "scab" labor when few other jobs are available. Geographical location also affects availability of nonunion labor. In a low-wage, growing area with few unionized plants, plentiful labor supplies with no trade union affiliations would be available. In highly unionized areas with tighter worker supplies, chances of successfully operating a factory during a strike would be very low.

Production cost structure is another factor that should be considered when deciding whether or not to operate during a strike. Generally, a firm will be more anxious to continue production during strikes in operations where labor costs are a large proportion of total costs than in more automated operations. In the same way, very large fixed costs may influence a company to hire "scab" labor and continue operations.

LOSSES FROM STRIKES

Once a strike is under way, it is necessary to calculate potential losses (the costs of the strike) as a reference point for bargaining. For example, if prolonging a strike four additional weeks will cost $100,000 in lost sales, while immediate settlement will add $30,000 to annual production costs, management may decide to settle. In any case, it is

Table 49. Strike-Related Costs While Operating During Strikes

Direct (economic) costs	Indirect (human) costs
Lost sales through lower production of inexperienced, new employees	Loss of customer goodwill/confidence
Hiring and training costs of nonunion employees	Increased hostility between labor and management
Damage to company property from violence	Loss of skilled employees
Legal costs	
Severance pay for replaced workers	
Back wages for reinstated employees	
Start-up and/or shutdown costs	

essential that management know where it stands in regard to potential losses from the strike. Amount and source of such loss costs depend on the following factors:

1. *Inventory size.* Determination of length of time sales can be made from current inventories will provide a basis for cost of sales lost.

2. *Location and distribution.* Centralized operations are more easily closed and reopened.

3. *Industry conditions and specialization.* If a large manufacturer with diverse production is struck, while specialized competitors for some of the product lines are not, temporary and permanent sales loss will be proportionately greater than when similar strike conditions affect the entire industry.

4. *Goodwill loss.* Temporary and permanent loss of goodwill by the firm as a reliable source of supply is a definite strike cost although difficult to measure.

5. *Labor union conditions.* The number and nature of unions involved, as well as long- and short-term cost of meeting union demands, affect costs of strike losses.

THE DECISION: SETTLE OR CONTINUE THE STRIKE?

During bargaining, management must repeatedly make the decision whether to settle or to permit the strike to continue. Redistribution of slack time can provide a basis for determination of the length of time a strike can continue at minimal cost. Once this period has passed, however, assessment of future strike costs must be continuously updated to provide information on which to base the decision. Factors to be considered in assessing future strike costs include:

1. *Industrial effects.* Will settlement adversely affect the entire industry? This is particularly likely when an industry leader is struck.

2. *Snowball effects.* Will wage or benefit increases for one type of work lead to similar increases for other jobs? Will nonunion employees demand similar increases?

3. *Capital.* Will high settlements or continued strikes affect the level of public investment in the company? Which will provide the greater strike loss cost, and by how much?

4. *Sales and goodwill.* Will customer sales and goodwill be lost because of the strike? If so, will these losses be temporary or permanent? What dollar value can be placed on such losses?

5. *Trade-offs.* Can the company gain advantages in exchange for the loss, such as trading a greater degree of automation for increased wages for the fewer workers remaining? If so, long-term gains due to the settlement may be greater than short-term losses.

STRIKE ACCOUNTING

A firm or industry facing the possibility of a strike can best assess and control potential strike costs by establishing a *strike accounting system.* Strike accounting estimates the following *financial* losses at various stages of progression if the strike occurs:

1. Cost of lost sales
2. Increased wages' and benefits' costs
3. Mutual aid fund costs, to benefit affected firms within the industry
4. Hiring and training, or retraining, costs stemming from the strike

Other strike costs, less easily measured in dollars, include:

1. Loss of customer goodwill
2. Loss of mutual respect between management and employees
3. Costs stemming from violence during picketing, boycotting, etc.

Some efforts are being made to translate such costs into monetary terms (*see* **Human Accounting**), and if such estimates can be more accurately calculated in the future, the total strike cost picture will provide a more accurate basis for settlement decisions.

DANGER AREAS IN STRIKE COSTS

Loss of sales and other direct strike costs are not likely to be overlooked, they are so obvious. Other, more subtle strike costs from union demands offer just as many if not more dangers, and special care should be taken to consider these. They include union demands for:

1. *Limitations of subcontracting, as a means of job protection.* Such contract clauses, if accepted, may force a firm to set up uneconomical, specialized departments to do work they would rather have subcontracted.

2. *Price and/or product control.* Such factors enter negotiation when price and/or product decisions by management affect the number of workers employed.

3. *Control of equipment and/or work methods changes,* since they may decrease the number of workers employed. Special payments for workers laid off from such changes may be demanded.

4. *Control of determining work standards which may affect incentive plan payments.*

5. *Regulation of number of hours worked, number of workers, and length of workweek.*

6. *Control of new plant locations.*

7. *Continued-training provisions.*

NEGOTIATION

This list of demands to strengthen job security will undoubtedly continue to grow as "democratization" trends increase employee control of business and industry. In negotiation, cost of such demands should be weighed when making settlement-offer decisions. Trade-offs—agreements to give employees a benefit (such as increased wages, pensions, etc.) in exchange for a company benefit (plant location in a low-cost area, a greater degree of automation, etc.)—may reduce overall costs if the company can afford to take the long- rather than the short-term view.

Inflation, and the ensuing rapid rise in living costs, has renewed worker demand for equally accelerating wages. A satisfactory method of controlling labor costs stemming from inflation has not yet been developed. From the employee's point of view, wage increases tied to the *cost of living index* are desirable. From management's point of view, such a method would require a means of immediately reflecting indexed increases in price rises, real profits, and tax payments. Some steps have been taken in these areas in **inflation accounting** systems.

Benefits demands have held a central portion of the negotiations picture in recent years, and benefits will continue to be an increasing proportion of labor costs. Management must be sure such benefits are "visible" to workers, since human nature is apt to take these for granted, or even to forget about them, noticing the more obvious pay check. *See also* **Cost Control; Fringe Benefits.**

Time, as well as reason, can be a primary asset for the company in negotiation. A firm may be able to afford a 10-week strike because most production can later be rescheduled in slack time. Employees, however, may face a different set of circumstances. Union funds and unemployment benefits are usually available in only limited amounts and for limited periods, and the average worker's savings today are not large enough to supplement these for any considerable length of time. Employees should be aware of wages lost by strike (*see also* **Strike Loss Computer**). Forecasts of employee reaction to lengthening strikes should be made and seriously considered among cost-control factors, since potential violence exists when income and jobs are seriously threatened for an extended period of time.

Strike costs, both direct and indirect, then, can be reduced through accurate estimation of costs and the effects to be expected in alternative methods of reacting to labor demands. *See also* **Productivity Bargaining and Agreements.**

SUGGESTED FURTHER READING

Chandler, M., *Management Rights and Union Interests,* McGraw-Hill, New York, 1964.
Dean, Joel, *Managerial Economics,* Prentice-Hall, Englewood Cliffs, N.J., 1951.
Hutchinson, J. G., *Management under Strike Conditions,* Holt, New York, 1966.
Reynolds, L. G., *Labor Economics and Labor Relations,* Prentice-Hall, Englewood Cliffs, N.J., 1960.
Stanley, J., *The Cost-Minded Manager,* American Management Assn., New York, 1963.

STRUCTURED PROGRAMMING

Areas for use in Cost Control:

ORGANIZATIONAL AND OPERATIONAL SYSTEMS
DATA RETENTION—FILES AND RECORDKEEPING

MATERIALS AND EQUIPMENT MANAGEMENT
INDUSTRIAL APPLICATIONS
BUSINESS AND COMMERCIAL APPLICATIONS

Structured programming reduces computer software production costs through top-down design and through limitation of sequencing operations. Loop statements are used for repeated predicates. *See also* **Electronic Data Processing.**

SUGGESTED FURTHER READING

Lapedes, D. N., ed., *Yearbook of Science and Technology,* McGraw-Hill, New York, 1974.

SUBBING

Areas for use in Cost Control:

FINANCIAL MOTIVATIONAL MANAGEMENT
ORGANIZATIONAL AND OPERATIONAL SYSTEMS
INDUSTRIAL APPLICATIONS

Subbing is the making of interim payments to workers who are paid at long intervals on an incentive plan. Payment is usually estimated for time-to-date, with final payment correcting actual earnings as necessary. Primary advantage of using the method is the continuing financial motivation provided.

SUGGESTED FURTHER READING

Marsh, A. I., and E. O. Evans, *The Dictionary of Industrial Relations,* Hutchinson, London, 1973.

SUCCESS EXAMPLE TECHNIQUE

Area for use in Cost Control:

PSYCHOLOGICAL MOTIVATIONAL MANAGEMENT

The success example technique is the use of a successful example to persuade an employee to use a work method or piece of equipment that will increase efficiency and/or reduce costs. For example, if a secretary does not want to switch to an electric typewriter that would increase typing speed up to 20 percent, the supervisor might tell about one of the other secretaries who was also hesitant but who now likes the electric typewriter better than a manual machine.

SUGGESTED FURTHER READING

Bittel, L. R., *What Every Supervisor Should Know,* McGraw-Hill, New York, 1974.

SUGGESTIBILITY See Hypnosis.

SUPERSESSION

Areas for use in Cost Control:

ORGANIZATIONAL AND OPERATIONAL SYSTEMS
MATERIALS AND EQUIPMENT MANAGEMENT
INDUSTRIAL APPLICATIONS
BUSINESS AND COMMERCIAL APPLICATIONS

Supersession reduces operating costs by replacing a specific piece of equipment with new equipment that does the same work more rapidly. The results of a study of time costs should be weighed against additional equipment costs in making decisions as to whether to apply supersession or not.

SUGGESTED FURTHER READING

ASME Work Standardization Bulletin, American Society of Mechanical Engineers, New York, 1971.

Maynard, H. B., ed., *Industrial Engineering Handbook,* 3d ed., McGraw-Hill, New York, 1974.

SUPERVISION METHODS AND COST CONTROL

Areas for use in Cost Control:

PSYCHOLOGICAL MOTIVATIONAL MANAGEMENT
ORGANIZATIONAL AND OPERATIONAL SYSTEMS
INDUSTRIAL APPLICATIONS
BUSINESS AND COMMERCIAL APPLICATIONS

Much of the level of productivity achieved in a company depends on the type of supervision practiced individually and collectively by the firm's management. No one method of supervision is best in all cases. When the most effective method of supervision *for that particular installation* is used, work output increases and labor costs are reduced.

Three basic types of supervision are generally used:

1. Autocratic
2. Democratic
3. Laissez-faire

Autocratic. This authoritarian type of supervision is most effective when used with groups of workers not particularly capable of organizing their own work and in need of a very structured working atmosphere to increase output. In some studies, even more capable employees are shown to have increased productivity when a switch was made from democratic to autocratic supervisory techniques, although company morale was considerably lowered in these cases, resulting in a higher rate of costly turnover.

Democratic. Where employees are capable of some work organization, democratic supervision methods are most effective. Improved motivation, morale, and employee participation are keys to top efficiency in this group. A single supervisor can oversee more workers in a group of this quality, since employees are able to assume greater individual responsibility.

Laissez-Faire. In this type of supervision, employees are capable of complete self-organization and self-supervision. Any formal "supervisor" serves basically as a figure-head. Formal supervisors should be eliminated from groups capable of self-management as an unnecessary cost.

SUGGESTED FURTHER READING

Applewhite, P. B., *Organizational Behavior,* Prentice-Hall, Englewood Cliffs, N.J., 1965.

Argyle, M., G. Gardner, and F. Cioffi, "Absenteeism and Labor Turnover," *Human Relations,* vol. 11, 1958.

SUPERVISOR PROGRAMS See Executive Programs.

SUPERVISORY TRAINING

Areas for use in Cost Control:

PSYCHOLOGICAL MOTIVATIONAL MANAGEMENT
ORGANIZATIONAL AND OPERATIONAL SYSTEMS

INDUSTRIAL APPLICATIONS
BUSINESS AND COMMERCIAL APPLICATIONS

Supervisory training is the operation of a formal company program to develop the use of management skills, increasing operating efficiency and productivity and reducing operating costs. Line-management employees usually have not had formal training in these skills, as top and middle management usually have. Often they have been promoted from among the workers with little more than the knowledge of their supervisor's behavior to serve as a guide for optimum performance on their jobs. In costs and output, they can be the weak link if they are not properly trained, since upper management may make the operating decisions but line management must implement them. The quality of work, the control of waste and other costs, the supervision of workers and maintenance—all of these vital areas, and more, come under the direct control of the supervisor. His or her adequate training is essential to maximize profits.

SUPERVISOR SELECTION

Line management has been traditionally chosen for work skill. The fastest and most organized typist was promoted to a position as supervisor of the typing pool, for example. An exceptionally good press operator was promoted to foreman. Speed and skill abilities, however, do not ensure performance as a supervisor. The supervisor needs to know the work processes thoroughly, including work methods that achieve the greatest output. But the ability to communicate work instructions to workers and to motivate them to better performance is more important than skills with the physical mechanics of the workers' jobs. Intelligence and initiative in reducing waste and other costs are more important than speed on a machine that subordinates will operate.

Selection of supervisors should be made from among current employees *if* a suitable applicant is available. A job description detailing necessary qualifications should be posted, advertising available positions. Qualifications should include:

1. Knowledge of work and work methods used
2. Ability to supervise and organize
3. Ability to communicate effectively
4. Ability to get along with others, and particularly with types of persons he or she would supervise (including attitudes toward minority groups, modes of dress, hair styles, etc.)
5. High level of personal motivation

OUTLINING TRAINING PROGRAMS

Few applicants will be suitable in every respect. Once selected, weaknesses of the supervisor are the areas where training should be concentrated. For example, if the supervisor has difficulty communicating work instructions to employees, development should be stressed in this area. If his or her knowledge of work and work methods is not adequate, these should be taught.

Social adjustments should be covered in training, too. Particularly in smaller, one-industry communities, the supervisor and his or her family will have close friends among workers he or she will now be supervising. These friendships cannot be closely maintained if the supervisor is to be able to exercise discipline at work. In training, the company should offer formal recognition of this problem and should help bridge the gap by making sure the new supervisor and his or her family are introduced to other supervisors. The company may also assist the supervisor in buying a home in a new neighborhood and encourage him or her to join clubs or groups that will be useful in work but which are not associated with the workers.

Training objectives, for both the company and the individual supervisor, should be set at the level of performance desired. The supervisory trainee should participate in deciding his or her own training goals and should be made aware of the reasons for and importance of company training objectives.

The supervisory trainee can be best motivated during training by being shown how the training can aid in both career performance and advancement.

In setting up the overall formal program for supervisory training, two main areas should be emphasized:

1. Management technique—knowledge and use
2. Knowledge of specialty areas within the company and their availability and specific applications for the individual supervisor

Most companies find that training-time cost should be divided between the company and the supervisor, so that each is putting something into and taking something out of the program. A two-hour class, then, may begin one hour before normal working hours finish, with company and supervisor each contributing one hour of their time.

Training should use visual aids wherever possible, as these, when well prepared, speed the learning process and hold trainee attention.

Discussion should be heavily emphasized, particularly in the latter half of the training program, so that supervisors can apply newly learned techniques to actual work problems encountered on the floor during the rest of the day. Being able to apply techniques to familiar work situations and problems facilitates rapid learning more than "thinking" about their hypothetical application in unfamiliar work circumstances.

Specialists, such as the head of the computer operations section, should be used as teachers to instruct supervisors in available services, their benefits, and their use.

EMPHASIS IN SUPERVISORY TRAINING

A great deal of the specific content of the two types of training programs outlined above will depend on the nature of the individual business or industry. Work methods to be studied, for example, will be quite different in a company manufacturing small machine tools from those to be used in an insurance company's regional office. Most companies do have some common areas that deserve particular emphasis, however. These areas include:

Discipline. Discipline should be handed out by the same person who gives the worker his or her instructions. Repeated discipline problems with a single worker, however, should be referred to the next person in the management hierarchy.

Supervisors should be taught to discipline workers fairly, and only for justifiable reasons, when the offense is outlined in company policy. Reprimands should *always* be made in private, since public embarrassment of the worker is likely to increase his or her hostility toward the supervisor and the job. Once the reprimand is made, the supervisor must be careful not to mention it to others. The reprimand should not be constantly brought up to the worker, unless there is fresh cause for complaint.

The supervisor should invite, and be willing to consider, constructive criticism from the employee when the reprimand is given.

Young supervisors, particularly, need to establish firm discipline, which can be relaxed in special cases, to maintain control.

Supervisors should encourage employees to approach them with their problems at all times. If a worker feels free to discuss problems, fewer discipline problems are likely to occur. Once problems are presented, the supervisor should do his or her best to help the employee solve them.

Company policy must be thoroughly explained during training, since an understanding of every detail is essential to supervisory discipline administration.

Employment Legislation. Employment legislation as it affects work should also be taught in detail to supervisors. Periodic one-session brush-up courses are available for *all* levels of management, and as more legislation is enacted, this will be made plain. Worker safety, working place safety, cleanliness, lighting, ventilation, heating, etc.; health and sanitary conditions; unemployment conditions and benefits; total hours of employment (in some cases); minimum age of employment; and antiprejudicial employment are major areas where legislation affects the supervisor's implementation of his or her subordinates' work. Written, easily understood summaries of all legislation of this type should be provided each supervisor and discussions should be held to make sure he or she has read the material and understands it.

Labor Contracts. In unionized firms, it is essential that the supervisor understand the terms of contracts and the effect his or her actions may have on that contract. Benefits, wages, vacation rights, notice in case of layoff or dismissal, benefits on dismissal, and appeal rights in the case of unfair dismissal are major areas to be covered.

Worker Training. Company-, government-, or privately-sponsored training programs to help workers improve or replace their skills should be emphasized in supervisory training so that the supervisor can communicate facts about these programs to workers when applicable.

Reports and Paperwork. These should be dealt with in detail when supervisors are being trained. Supervisors should be taught the reason for and the importance of each form. Methods of minimizing paperwork, yet providing adequate records, should be emphasized. The need for a logical order of paperwork, in preparation and in storage, should also be stressed.

Charts, graphs, and other visual presentation use should be explained, and examples in use at the supervisor's level should be provided.

Planning. Planning for any business or industry includes supervisory knowledge of a basic planning guide: knowledge of the company work goal, including amount of output and costs per unit; knowledge of work methods and/or product design, materials, and equipment; and knowledge of timing schedules.

Work and vacation schedules must be planned around this basic knowledge, and each supervisor should be taught the mechanics of this process.

Group Psychology. This is an especially useful tool to the supervisor, although the subject is too wide to be hastily covered during a general training session. Periodic brush-up courses, taught by experts in the field, should instruct all levels of management in new and the most useful techniques for motivating and controlling groups. (*See also* **Behavioral Control; Gestalt Techniques.**)

SUGGESTED FURTHER READING

Being a Supervisor in an Office, Industrial Society, London.
Being a Supervisor in a Factory, Industrial Society, London.
Bowen, C. M., *Developing and Training the Supervisor,* Business Books, London, 1971.
The Supervisor and Cost Control, American Management Assn., New York, 1966.

SUPPLIER RATING

Areas for use in Cost Control:

ORGANIZATIONAL AND OPERATIONAL SYSTEMS
INDUSTRIAL APPLICATIONS
BUSINESS AND COMMERCIAL APPLICATIONS

Supplier rating, also called vendor rating (*see* **Vendor Rating Formula**), is the rating of materials and equipment suppliers by the quality, cost, and delivery of goods supplied. All aspects are compared and the supplier providing acceptable quality goods, acceptable delivery, and the lowest possible cost is chosen. Arbitrary scales of 1 to 9, or A, B, C, D ratings, are set up to accomplish actual rating.

SUGGESTED FURTHER READING

Weinberg, Sidney, *Profit through Quality,* Gower Press, London, 1969.

SUPPLIES RATIONING

Areas for use in Cost Control:

ORGANIZATIONAL AND OPERATIONAL SYSTEMS
MATERIALS AND EQUIPMENT MANAGEMENT
INDUSTRIAL APPLICATIONS
BUSINESS AND COMMERCIAL APPLICATIONS

Supplies rationing estimates the amount of supplies needed by an employee periodically (weekly or monthly). These are issued and further supplies cannot be drawn without a special requisition signed by one or more responsible management employees. Such rationing systems include office, cleanup, safety, and other supplies. Paperwork is minimal once the level of need for each job is established. Studies indicate that supplies rationing can reduce consumption of supplies by 60 percent or more.

SUGGESTED FURTHER READING

Radke, Magnus, *Manual of Cost Reduction Techniques,* McGraw-Hill, New York, 1972.

SUPPORTIVE MANAGERIAL BEHAVIOR

Areas for use in Cost Control:

PSYCHOLOGICAL MOTIVATIONAL MANAGEMENT
ORGANIZATIONAL AND OPERATIONAL SYSTEMS

Supportive managerial behavior is supervisory leadership that motivates subordinates by establishing and maintaining in them a sense of pride and involvement in their work. Use of the technique reduces costs through increased work efficiency.

SUGGESTED FURTHER READING

Brown, W., *Exploration in Management,* Penguin, Baltimore, 1965.
Likert, R., *New Patterns for Management,* McGraw-Hill, New York, 1961.

SYNECTICS

Areas for use in Cost Control:

ORGANIZATIONAL AND OPERATIONAL SYSTEMS
INDUSTRIAL APPLICATIONS
BUSINESS AND COMMERCIAL APPLICATIONS

Synectics is the use of a group of employees, working independently of the company, to solve company problems such as how to increase productivity and/or efficiency or reduce costs. A small group of employees are chosen, with choice usually based on intelligence, emotional maturity, cooperativeness, and knowledge of the work problem areas.

Training of the Group. The group is trained in synectic methods of problem solving. These methods include the following steps:

1. Thorough examination of the work problem is made.
2. Information is accumulated as necessary for all areas of the work problem.

3. Explanation is given (by experts) of any problem aspects not understood by the group.
4. The whole problem is phrased in analogy form.
5. The analogy form is examined and evaluated without referring to the problem in its natural form.
6. Evaluations of the analogy and evaluations of the problem in its natural form are compared, and similarities in possible solutions are noted.

SUGGESTED FURTHER READING

Armand, R., R. Lattes, and J. Lesourne, *The Management Revolution,* Denoel Press, Paris, 1970.
Crosby, Andrew, *Creativity and Performance in Industrial Organization,* Tavistock Publications, New York, 1968.
Gordon, W. J. J., *Synectics: The Development of Creative Capacity,* Harper, New York, 1961.

SYNTHETIC LEVELING

Areas for use in Cost Control:

FINANCIAL MOTIVATIONAL MANAGEMENT
PSYCHOLOGICAL MOTIVATIONAL MANAGEMENT
ORGANIZATIONAL AND OPERATIONAL SYSTEMS

Synthetic leveling is the comparison of the actual skill, effort, conditions, and efficiency required by an employee to do a specific unit of work with standard degrees of these factors determined through **work study and measurement.** The technique is used in **performance rating** and may be used to determine wages paid the individual when **incentive payment systems** are used. In such a case, costs are reduced by limiting wage payment in proportion to actual work done.

Synthetic leveling can also provide psychological motivation for the employee to work harder in order to receive a better "ranking."

SUGGESTED FURTHER READING

Maynard, H. B., ed., *Industrial Engineering Handbook,* 3d ed., McGraw-Hill, New York, 1974.
Morrow, R. L., *Time Study and Motion Economy,* Ronald, New York, 1946.
Mundel, M. E., *Motion and Time Study,* Prentice-Hall, Englewood Cliffs, N.J., 1955.

SYSTEM 4

Areas for use in Cost Control:

PSYCHOLOGICAL MOTIVATIONAL MANAGEMENT
FINANCIAL MOTIVATIONAL MANAGEMENT
WORK PLACE MOTIVATIONAL MANAGEMENT
ORGANIZATIONAL AND OPERATIONAL SYSTEMS
INDUSTRIAL APPLICATIONS
BUSINESS AND COMMERCIAL APPLICATIONS

System 4 uses the results of quantitative research to improve performance of the work force, thus reducing labor costs. Designed by Rensis Likert, of the University of Michigan, the systems approach allows management to optimize their company's human assets through better organizational, operational, and motivational techniques, using research as their basis rather than subjective personal judgments.

Likert divides management of human assets into four levels of effectiveness, beginning with the lowest, *System 1,* and moving through the most effective, *System 4.* Table 50 sets out the differences in organizational and performance characteristics in these four systems.

Table 50. Typical Organizational and Performance Characteristics of Management Systems 1–4*

Organizational variable	System 1	System 2	System 3	System 4
1. Leadership processes used				
Extent to which superiors have confidence and trust in *subordinates*	Have no confidence and trust in subordinates	Have condescending confidence and trust, such as master has to servant	Substantial but not complete confidence and trust; still wishes to keep control of decisions	Complete confidence and trust in all matters
Extent to which superiors behave so that subordinates feel free to discuss important things about their jobs with their immediate superior	Subordinates do not feel at all free to discuss things about the job with their superior	Subordinates do not feel very free to discuss things about the job with their superior	Subordinates feel rather free to discuss things about the job with their superior	Subordinates feel completely free to discuss things about the job with their superior
Extent to which immediate superior in solving job problems generally tries to get subordinates' ideas and opinions and make constructive use of them	Seldom gets ideas and opinions of subordinates in solving job problems	Sometimes gets ideas and opinions of subordinates in solving job problems	Usually gets ideas and opinions and usually tries to make constructive use of them	Always gets ideas and opinions and always tries to make constructive use of them

2. Character of motivational forces

	System 1	System 2	System 3	System 4
Manner in which motives are used	Fear, threats, punishment, and occasional rewards	Rewards and some actual or potential punishment	Rewards, occasional punishment, and some involvement	Economic rewards based on compensation system developed through participation; group participation and involvement in setting goals, improving methods, appraising progress toward goals, etc.
Amount of responsibility felt by each member of organization for achieving organization's goals	High levels of management feel responsibility; lower levels feel less; rank and file feel little and often welcome opportunity to behave in ways to defeat organization's goals	Managerial personnel usually feel responsibility; rank and file feel relatively little responsibility for achieving organization's goals	Substantial proportion of personnel, especially at high levels, feel responsibility and generally behave in ways to achieve the organization's goals	Personnel at all levels feel real responsibility for organization's goals and behave in ways to implement them

3. Character of communication process

	System 1	System 2	System 3	System 4
Amount of interaction and communication aimed at achieving organization's objectives	Very little	Little	Quite a bit	Much with both individuals and groups

Table 50 (*Continued*). Typical Organizational and Performance Characteristics of Management Systems 1–4

Organizational variable	System 1	System 2	System 3	System 4
Direction of information flow	Downward	Mostly downward	Down and up	Down, up, and with peers
Extent to which downward communications are accepted by subordinates	Viewed with great suspicion	May or may not be viewed with suspicion	Often accepted but at times viewed with suspicion; may or may not be openly questioned	Generally accepted, but if not, openly and candidly questioned
Accuracy of upward communication via line	Tends to be inaccurate	Information that boss wants to hear flows; other information is restricted and filtered	Information that boss wants to hear flows; other information may be limited or cautiously given	Accurate
Psychological closeness of superiors to subordinates (i.e., how well does superior know and understand problems faced by subordinates?)	Has no knowledge or understanding of problems of subordinates	Has some knowledge and understanding of problems of subordinates	Knows and understands problems of subordinates quite well	Knows and understands problems of subordinates very well

Organizational variable	System 1	System 2	System 3	System 4
4. Character of interaction-influence process				
Amount and character of interaction	Little interaction and always with fear and distrust	Little interaction and usually with some condescension by superiors; fear and caution by subordinates	Moderate interaction, often with fair amount of confidence and trust	Extensive, friendly interaction with high degree of confidence and trust
Amount of cooperative teamwork present	None	Relatively little	A moderate amount	Very substantial amount throughout the organization
5. Character of decision-making process				
At what level in organization are decisions formally made?	Bulk of decisions at top of organization	Policy at top, many decisions within prescribed framework made at lower levels	Broad policy and general decisions at top, more specific decisions at lower levels	Decision making widely done throughout organization, although well integrated through linking process provided by overlapping groups
To what extent are decision makers aware of problems, particularly those at lower levels in the organization?	Often are unaware or only partially aware	Aware of some, unaware of others	Moderately aware of problems	Generally quite well aware of problems

Table 50 *(Continued).* Typical Organizational and Performance Characteristics of Management Systems 1–4

Organizational variable	*System 1*	*System 2*	*System 3*	*System 4*
Extent to which technical and professional knowledge is used in decision making	Used only if possessed at higher levels	Much of what is available in higher and middle levels is used	Much of what is available in higher, middle, and lower levels is used	Most of what is available anywhere within the organization is used
To what extent are subordinates involved in decisions related to their work?	Not at all	Never involved in decisions; occasionally consulted	Usually are consulted but ordinarily not involved in the decision making	Are involved fully in all decisions related to their work
Are decisions made at the best level in the organization so far as the motivational consequences (i.e., does the decision-making process help to create the necessary motivations in those persons who have to carry out the decisions?)	Decision making contributes little or nothing to the motivation to implement the decision, usually yields adverse motivation	Decision making contributes relatively little motivation	Some contribution by decision making to motivation to implement	Substantial contribution by decision-making processes to motivation to implement

	System 1	System 2	System 3	System 4
6. Character of goal setting or ordering				
Manner in which usually done	Orders issued	Orders issued, opportunity to comment may or may not exist	Goals are set or orders issued after discussion with subordinate(s) of problems and planned action	Except in emergencies, goals are usually established by means of group participation
Are there forces to accept, resist, or reject goals?	Goals are overtly accepted but are covertly resisted strongly	Goals are overtly accepted but often covertly resisted to at least a moderate degree	Goals are overtly accepted but at times with some covert resistance	Goals are fully accepted both overtly and covertly
7. Character of control processes				
Extent to which the review and control functions are concentrated	Highly concentrated in top management	Relatively highly concentrated, with some delegated control to middle and lower levels	Moderate downward delegation of review and control processes; lower as well as higher levels feel responsible	Quite widespread responsibility for review and control, with lower units at times imposing more rigorous reviews and tighter controls than top management

Table 50 *(Continued).* Typical Organizational and Performance Characteristics of Management Systems 1–4

Organizational variable	*System 1*	*System 2*	*System 3*	*System 4*
Extent to which there is an informal organization present and supporting or opposing goals of formal organization	Informal organization present and opposing goals of formal organization	Informal organization usually present and partially resisting goals	Informal organization may be present and may either support or partially resist goals of formal organization	Informal and formal organization are one and the same; hence all social forces support efforts to achieve organization's goals
Extent to which control data (e.g., accounting, productivity, cost, etc.) are used for self-guidance or group problem solving by managers and non-supervisory employees; or used by superiors in a punitive, policing manner	Used for policing and in punitive manner	Used for policing coupled with reward and punishment, sometimes punitively; used somewhat for guidance but in accord with orders	Largely used for policing with emphasis usually on reward but with some punishment; used for guidance in accord with orders; some use also for self-guidance	Used for self-guidance and for coordinated problem solving and guidance; not used punitively

*Rensis Likert, *The Human Organization*, McGraw-Hill, New York, 1967.

Likert theorizes that historically when management wished to cut costs, it moved left toward System 1 in its approach to employees. When the economic picture has been good, it was more apt to move toward System 4. The System 4 approach, he says, is the correct approach at all times, since the better management-employee relationship, employee participation in decisions and profits, and increased worker responsibility lead to greater productivity, reduced costs, reduced wastes, higher earnings, etc.

HUMAN-ASSET MANAGEMENT CHECK

One way to check the current human-asset management approach of a specific company is to use the scale provided under each item in Table 50. Marks from 1 to 5 for each of the four systems are provided. For example, in rating the "extent to which superiors have confidence in *subordinates*," a company that feels its attitude is about midway on the System 2 scale would mark the table as shown in Fig. 102.

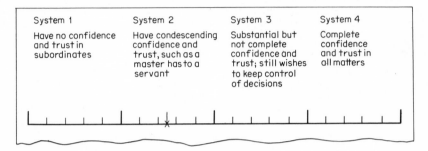

Figure 102. Typical rating on a Likert systems chart.

Ratings for all aspects will reflect the overall company approach to human assets, indicating areas where greater employee participation could be used to increase performance.

A second rating may be taken, marking the scales in the same way, to indicate the type of management system desired. The resulting scale, when compared with the first rating, will indicate areas where improvement goals are planned and/or under way, as well as areas where improvement is needed.

MOVING TOWARD SYSTEM 4

Once a current rating of the management system is established, the next step to increase performance is to implement characteristics in the System 4 approach. It is important that all aspects of operation move toward, and reach, the System 4 level. For example, if most decisions are made by top management (System 1), it would be unrealistic to expect employees to act responsibly and to believe that the company had complete confidence and trust in them in all matters (System 4).

Methods used in implementing the System 4 approach are discussed here by operational area, and many scientifically based techniques in each area are discussed separately, in alphabetical order, throughout the book.

Leadership. The System 4 approach requires that management have complete confidence in employees, that employees feel free to discuss job problems and factors with their superiors, and that employee ideas be considered, used, and acknowledged when they are constructive. Recruiting and hiring policies are important in implementing these factors, as is a sound training program. To be able to trust employees, the company must know that they all have the quality and training to make them worthy of trust.

Once these programs are strengthened, stress should be placed on supervisors' giving employees as much responsibility as they are individually capable of handling. Training of supervisors to teach the importance and effects of such measures is advisable, particularly for companies tending toward System 1 ratings in leadership.

Additional cost savings result from implementing a System 4 approach in leadership because employees' increased responsibility means less need for supervision, decreasing the number and cost of line supervisors required.

Motivation. Financial incentives, psychological motivation, and work place motivation are all based on employee participation in the System 4 approach. Employees, or their representatives, are included in discussion of possible incentive payment systems, quotas and goals, new and improved work methods, etc. They are equally involved in decision making in these areas. Having had a say in deciding the company's goals and being given a financial and/or personal interest in reaching them, employees will act more responsibly in their work efforts to reach these goals.

Most aspects of System 4 serve as psychological motivation, since the approach gives the individual worker a greater feeling of personal involvement and value.

Communication. In the System 4 approach, communication channels should be completely open, with communication moving up from workers to management, down from management to workers, sideways among coworkers, and around to provide feedback at all levels. Workers should be encouraged to question communications down, and management should have a keen understanding of subordinates' problems. Again, training of management is usually necessary to implement effective communication.

Interaction. For companies with lower systems ratings, interaction will present major difficulties. Supervisors will need training in cooperating *with* subordinates, rather than using separation, fear, and mistrust as tools to get the work done. In some cases, where supervisors cannot adapt to the cooperative approach, replacement may be necessary. Newly hired supervisors should be vetted as to their attitudes.

Decision Making. The System 4 method involves employees, or their representatives, in policy, goal, and work method decisions. A good example is productivity bargaining (*see* **Productivity Bargaining and Agreements**), where employees discuss work methods that could be used to increase productivity and have an equal voice in final decisions. Generally, workers should be involved in any decisions that affect them. Thus, in a decision to replace some element of human labor, technical employees would be included to provide background knowledge and advice. Workers to be replaced would discuss retraining or transfer possibilities. With the security of such involvement, employees are habitually more cooperative in implementing decisions.

Objectives. As in decision making, objectives are set by group participation in System 4 to motivate workers in better implementation of the goals. Acceptance of goals at all levels must be real, not merely superficial. Bargaining similar to productivity bargaining can be used effectively.

Control. Control is implemented by the worker responsible in System 4. Thus, production-level workers are trained in control techniques for all work that is primarily their responsibility. A typist who has been given the responsibility for checking his or her own work for errors, for example, is trained in methods to avoid and/or correct errors, bringing the work to an acceptable standard. As in leadership, control at this grass-roots level decreases time and cost of supervision in control.

SYSTEM 4's DIRECT EFFECT ON COST CONTROL

Using the scientifically based approach of System 4 to reduce costs results in greater employee cooperation and implementation of the goal. Several studies, of the improvement of performance and the reduction of costs as System 4 was implemented, were combined by Likert (see Fig. 103). These include studies by the Institute for Social Research and other groups. Moving from left to right on Fig. 103's time scale, the shaded area shows growing performance improvements and reduced cost results as System 4 is adopted,

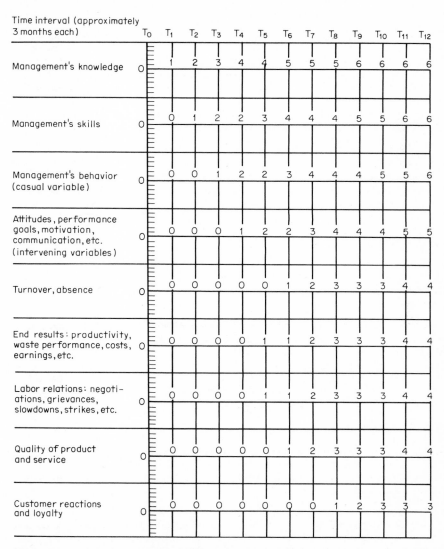

Figure 103. Improvement of performance and cost reduction as System 4 is adopted. (Rensis Likert and S. E. Seashore, "Making Cost Control Work," *Harvard Business Review,* vol. 41, no. 6, 1963.)

SUGGESTED FURTHER READING

Likert, Rensis, *The Human Organization,* McGraw-Hill, New York, 1967.
————, *New Patterns in Management,* McGraw-Hill, New York, 1961.
————and S. E. Seashore, "Making Cost Control Work," *Harvard Business Review,* vol. 41, no. 6, 1963.

SYSTEMS ANALYSIS

Areas for use in Cost Control:

ORGANIZATIONAL AND OPERATIONAL SYSTEMS
INDUSTRIAL APPLICATIONS
BUSINESS AND COMMERCIAL APPLICATIONS

Systems analysis is the transferring of work to a computer to reduce costs, increase efficiency, etc. The technique requires design of a data processing system that will provide management with required operational data, eliminating all superfluous matter and finding the most economical sources of required data. Systems analysis consists of determining what information is needed, where to get it, how often to get it, and what format is to be used for reporting it. This information is then programmed into the computer, which, in turn, will produce the data as required.

SUGGESTED FURTHER READING

Argenti, J., *Management Techniques,* G. Allen, London, 1970.
Clifton, H. D., *Systems Analysis for Business Data Processing,* Auerbach Publications, New York, 1971.

TASK BONUS SYSTEM

Areas for use in Cost Control:

FINANCIAL MOTIVATIONAL MANAGEMENT
ORGANIZATIONAL AND OPERATIONAL SYSTEMS
INDUSTRIAL APPLICATIONS

A task bonus system is a form of incentive payment based on the amount of standard working time saved. Use of the system reduces costs through increased production.

SUGGESTED FURTHER READING

Marsh, A. I., and E. O. Evans, *The Dictionary of Industrial Relations,* Hutchinson, London, 1973.

TAX COST CONTROL

Areas for use in Cost Control:

ORGANIZATIONAL AND OPERATIONAL SYSTEMS
DATA RETENTION—FILES AND RECORDKEEPING
INDUSTRIAL APPLICATIONS
BUSINESS AND COMMERCIAL APPLICATIONS

Tax cost control contains many basic aspects of tax laws and their application that are useful background information for the executive who wants to reduce tax costs. Discussions of these areas, which follow, should not be substituted for use of a competent tax adviser, however. Tax laws, claims, and response to claims are extremely complicated. Wording to establish business intent is essential, as is a knowledge of previous decisions that can be cited as precedents.

Areas frequently used for tax reduction include:

1. *Capital gains;* lighter tax rates are applied to capital gains than to taxable corporate income.
2. *Percentage depletion allowances for oil.*
3. *Farm or other write-offs.*
4. *Tax-exempt bond holding.*
5. *Lighter tax rates on some essential production,* such as tree and cattle production.

Other areas for tax control depend on the structure of the business and the laws relating to those specific structures.

Corporation. Taxes on corporate income are often called double taxes, since the money is taxed at the corporate level and again as individual income when received by shareholders as dividends. Current corporate United States taxes are 22 percent of taxable income, plus a surtax of 26 percent on taxable income in excess of $25,000. Minimum tax on income from tax-preference areas is 10 percent. Main areas available for tax cost control include the following:

Capital debt rather than share financing. Interest payable on bank debts, for example, is deductible, while dividends to shareholders are not. Thus, a company having net income of $100,000 before debt or dividend payment of $15,000 would pay nearly $4,200 less if financing were by bank loan rather than by issue of stock.

Distribution of assets to stockholders is not taxable at the corporate level when such distribution in kind is used in partial or complete liquidation. Marketable assets are distributed to shareholders as tenants-in-common. No gain or loss may be recognized by the company.

A parent company can purchase a liquidated subsidiary's assets at a fair market price above the assets' original depreciation value without paying tax on the appreciation. The purchase cost can then be used as the basis for cost depreciation.

Contributions to companies by shareholders or others are not taxable if they are genuine contributions. Such contributions are less likely to be exempted from corporate income tax when contributed by shareholders in a closely held corporation, however.

Income that would be taxed can be reinvested in the company to capitalize increased production, avoiding taxation.

Dividends in the form of stock can be paid tax-free to common stock shareholders. Exceptions include offering property in lieu of stock or distribution of stock to discharge preferential dividends. The law also does not apply if the proportional interest in the company is altered by the method or if there is another type of stock outstanding.

Gains or losses on stock exchanged for new stocks of equal value are not taxed if the exchange is for the purpose of reorganization, mergers, etc. Genuineness of need to reorganize, merge, etc., must be proved.

Professional service organization—doctors, lawyers, etc.—organized under state professional association or corporation statutes can be treated as corporations for tax purposes. This may be especially advantageous when they fall under the Subchapter S treatment of small business corporations.

Multiple corporations can be formed in some circumstances, providing a $25,000 exemption from the surcharge for each. However, a business reason showing the need for multiple corporations must be proved. Groups of corporations allowed only one exemption under any conditions are:

1. Parent corporations with 80-percent-owned subsidiaries.

2. Corporate groups 80 percent owned by five or fewer persons, ownership to include stock attributed to those persons, or overlapped ownership of 50 percent at lowest rate of percentage of ownership in any corporation in the group.

Accumulated corporate earnings may be held, rather than distributed. Shareholders may then pay capital gains rather than personal income tax. A special tax (maximum of 38½ percent) is added if such holding is for the purpose of shareholders' avoiding personal income tax payment, but shareholders in the 70 percent tax bracket may still find it advantageous. The holding tax is not paid if earnings are not distributed for justifiable business purposes.

Partnerships. No income taxes are levied against partnerships, although joint income records are filed. Each partner pays taxes on his or her income or capital gains from the partnership at the United States individual tax rate. Additionally, individuals in partnerships are personally liable for debts incurred by the business.

Small Business Corporations. A tax code change in 1958 allows small businesses the advantage of being a corporation (no personal debt liability, for example) without paying corporate taxes. Taxes are paid by shareholders when income is distributed to them. Application must be made by the company to the government for this tax status. All shareholders must consent to the method at the time of the application. New shareholders may terminate the method thereafter by affirmatively objecting to it. Termination also results from unanimous withdrawal of consent by shareholders. Once the method is terminated, a new application cannot be filed for five years. Qualifications a business must have for small business corporation status include the following:

1. No more than 10 shareholders.
2. No nonresident alien shareholders.
3. Not more than 80 percent of gross receipts derived from outside the United States.
4. Only one class of stock, unless others are designated as debt.
5. Cannot be a member of an affiliated group.
6. All shareholders (other than estates) must be individuals.

Tax-free income such as interest from tax-exempt bonds remains tax-free on distribution to shareholders rather than being converted to dividend income.

Deductions of up to 10 percent of $2,500, whichever is greater, are allowable for pension funds. Pension expense beyond this amount is considered taxable dividend income on the shareholders' personal tax returns.

Ordinary loss treatment, rather than the smaller-advantage capital loss treatment, may be applied to the sale or exchange of small business corporation stock if:

1. The shareholder is an individual.
2. The shareholder is the original stock owner.

Losses treated in this way are limited to $25,000 per individual or $50,000 per couple. Additionally, only $500,000 of one company's stock can be so treated, and stock offerings and equity capital of the corporation may not exceed $1,000,000.

Personal Holding Companies. These companies are primarily closely held corporations with five or fewer individuals owning 50 percent or more of the stock and with 60 percent or more of their income derived from passive sources. Historically, they have provided corporate tax shelters for wealthy individuals, since income could be held rather than distributed, avoiding personal income tax payment and potential loss write-offs. Income could be later removed, paying the lighter-rate capital gains tax.

While undistributed income of personal holding companies is now taxed at 70 percent, some tax-avoidance devices are still used. These include: mineral, oil, gas, or copyright income is not classified as personal holding company income when these are the principal business; or if business deductions (15 percent or more of gross income) show that actual business is being conducted.

Up to 60 percent of a company's gross income can be sheltered. Thus, if a company has a $200,000 annual gross income from a temporary secretarial service, it can have just under $300,000 of passive income and yet be allowed to hold income without personal income tax or personal holding company tax payment. Lighter-rate capital gains taxes, rather than personal income taxes, are usually paid on these moneys when they are distributed at a later time.

SUGGESTED FURTHER READING

Internal Revenue Code, U.S. Government Printing Office, Washington, D.C.
Levin, J., *A Practitioner's Guide to the Tax Reform Act of 1969,* Practicing Law Institute, Washington, D.C., 1970.
Pechman, J., *Federal Tax Policy,* Brookings Institution, Washington, D.C., 1971.
Wolfman, B., *Federal Income Taxation of Business Enterprises,* Little, Brown, Boston, 1971.

TAXES AND MOTIVATION

Areas for use in Cost Control:

PSYCHOLOGICAL MOTIVATIONAL MANAGEMENT
FINANCIAL MOTIVATIONAL MANAGEMENT
ORGANIZATIONAL AND OPERATIONAL SYSTEMS
INDUSTRIAL APPLICATIONS
BUSINESS AND COMMERCIAL APPLICATIONS

Tax scales, accelerating in proportion to salary increases as they do in most countries, affect employees' attitudes toward their work in one of three ways. Studies show that about 60 percent of all workers are less motivated to increase their productivity output (and income) once their wages move into higher brackets. Most of the rest find that their motivation is not affected. And, surprisingly, a very small percentage of top management say that reaching top brackets motivates them to increase their earnings even more in order to maintain their current standard of living, which would otherwise be eroded by increased taxes.

Applying financial incentives to cut tax costs for employees, then, should motivate at least 60 percent of the work force to increase efficiency, lowering labor costs. These incentives can also attract qualified new employees and reduce turnover. Specific employee tax-reduction incentives include the following:

Retirement incentives. Retirement contributions by both employer and employee are tax-free except as they are payable to the employee. This means that this portion of employee income, to a maximum of 10 percent of his or her income of $2,500 (whichever is greater), is not taxed at the time of earning. Capital gains tax, a much lower rate, will be assessed when this income is distributed to the employee at retirement.

Deferred retirement. This is the practice of offering a retiring employee a lower salary for less work, to avoid higher tax brackets. At the same time, pension payments are made at full or part value. This has the effect of providing the employee with the same amount of income, less tax to pay, and less work to do. Managerial-level staff may be retained on a consulting-fee basis to create basically the same effect.

Profit sharing. This is another benefit that can be used to financially motivate an employee in lieu of highly taxable cash. Capital gains tax is paid on funds when they are withdrawn.

Stock options. These fall into much the same category. Income tax is not paid by the employee on income realized from stock appreciation; rather, capital gains taxes are paid when stock is sold.

Housing. Although uncommon in the United States, many international companies pay part of their employees' salaries in housing. When the need to live on company property can be established in the United States, as in the case of a property management employee in a supervisory capacity, or in the case of a housing development maintenance worker, such employee "income" is not subject to tax.

Meals. Food eaten on the work premises can be provided by the company as nontaxable employee "income."

Medical services. Medical services, including glasses, dental care, etc., can be provided tax-free in the same way.

Company discounts. Discounts on the company's products are not taxed when used by the employee.

Company cars. Company cars are used more extensively as a tax-free portion of income in European countries, with as many as 80 percent of mid-management employees using company cars.

Medical and hospital insurance. This insurance paid by the company also provides tax-free "income" to motivate employees.

VISIBILITY OF TAX MOTIVATORS

If tax reduction motivators are used, be sure the employees are aware of the value of their benefits. Fringe benefits lose their power to motivate if they are taken for granted or if the employee does not realize their cost. Some companies, particularly those using computerized payroll systems, provide a printed statement of the monetary value of each benefit with every pay check. The tax savings can easily be added to these figures, making such benefits more visible.

SUGGESTED FURTHER READING

Maness, B. R., and G. C. Thompson, "How Taxes Affect Executive Incentives," in M. D. Richards and W. A. Nielander, *Readings in Management,* South-Western Publishing Company, Cincinnati, 1958.
Mann, P., ed., *The Arts of Top Management,* McGraw-Hill, New York, 1970.

TAYLOR SYSTEM OF ORGANIZATION

Areas for use in Cost Control:

ORGANIZATIONAL AND OPERATIONAL SYSTEMS
INDUSTRIAL APPLICATIONS

The Taylor system organizes work responsibility by function. Thus, one worker may be supervised in various aspects of his or her work by supervisors responsible for those areas. Costs may be reduced through better knowledge used in control, since each supervisor is responsible only for his or her area of specialty. The system usually works

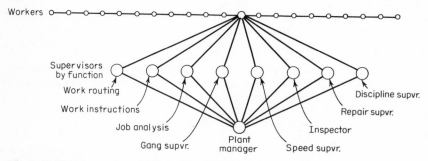

Figure 104. Taylor system of organization chart.

economically in small operations but proves too conflicting in larger firms, with several supervisors giving contradictory orders to one worker at the same time. Figure 104 shows the eight function systems developed by Taylor.

SUGGESTED FURTHER READING

Taylor, F. W., *Scientific Management,* Harper, New York, 1947.

TEAM PROGRAMMING

Areas for use in Cost Control:

ORGANIZATIONAL AND OPERATIONAL SYSTEMS
DATA RETENTION—FILES AND RECORDKEEPING
MATERIALS AND EQUIPMENT MANAGEMENT
INDUSTRIAL APPLICATIONS
BUSINESS AND COMMERCIAL APPLICATIONS

Team programming is the use of two or more programmers in computer programming to increase productivity and accuracy, reducing programming costs. Work is divided by similar types to allow each team member to program in one area. Gerald M. Weinberg, consultant for IBM, originated many facets of the method, including programmers reading each others' programs as a check for accuracy. Another variation is the use of the most qualified programmer on a team to develop "pattern" programs, which are then adapted to other areas by less skilled and lower-cost programmers.

SUGGESTED FURTHER READING

Voysey, Hedley, "Computers," *The Guardian,* Sept. 27, 1974, London.
Weinberg, Gerald M., *Psychology of Computer Programming,* Van Nostrand Reinhold Company, Cincinnati, 1971.

TEAMWORK

Areas for use in Cost Control:

ORGANIZATIONAL AND OPERATIONAL SYSTEMS
INDUSTRIAL APPLICATIONS
BUSINESS AND COMMERCIAL APPLICATIONS

Teamwork is an essential element in cost control, particularly when problems are interdepartmental. The most effective means of accomplishing such teamwork is for supervisors of all areas affected to work together on the solutions. Regularly scheduled meetings are one step of such a system, but each individual must prepare himself or herself beforehand. To do this, each should have a list of cost problems to be considered. Questions he or she may ask about the problems should include:

1. Is my department primarily responsible for this cost? If not, what part of the total responsibility do we bear?

2. What other departments or individuals are responsible for the cost? Are they represented in the meeting?

3. Have there been similar cost problems solved by our department or other departments?

4. Are the departments or individuals who must approve any possible solution included in the meeting?

Next comes the actual solving of the cost problem. Steps to be taken include:

1. Hold a meeting of all departmental supervisors involved to get ideas for possible solutions.

2. Each supervisor takes the cost problem directly to the employees who are involved with that aspect of the work. The supervisor discusses the cost problem with them and asks them for solution ideas. This not only leads to employee suggestions but also makes the employee feel valued.

3. Accumulate all suggested ideas for solving the cost problem and work them out on paper to see whether they are practical or need some minor alterations before implementation.

4. Ask suppliers involved in the cost problem area for their help. Frequently such firms employ specialists as a service to customers, and certainly they will have a wide range of practical experience from a variety of customers with similar problems.

5. Present the ideas to fellow supervisors at a second meeting. Discuss and alter the cost solutions and decide on areas in which to test them.

SUGGESTED FURTHER READING

Cost Control and the Supervisor, American Management Assn., New York, 1966.

TECHNOLOGICAL FORECASTING

Areas for use in Cost Control:

ORGANIZATIONAL AND OPERATIONAL SYSTEMS
INDUSTRIAL APPLICATIONS

Technological forecasting basically anticipates changes in scientific areas that may affect the company's product or service. Such changes may totally replace the product or service, or they may make a product obsolete because of cheaper materials, more efficient methods, etc.

From a cost reduction standpoint, technological forecasting is an essential business skill. With it, the company can anticipate or be prepared for changes, taking advantage of lower-cost possibilities as soon as they are available. Without it, a business may be caught off guard and find its product or service overpriced or completely unsalable. For example, in the 1960s, many products made of steel, wood, and glass were replaced by low-cost plastics. Natural fibers were replaced by synthetic ones, particularly in low-cost plastics. But with today's higher-priced oil (the basic feed stock of the synthetic materials), these replacements of the 1960s may themselves be replaced by an alternate material. It is the job of the technological forecaster to anticipate such changes.

METHODS OF TECHNOLOGICAL FORECASTING

Although new techniques are still being developed in this rather new field, the following are the major methods that have been used and found satisfactory:

Extrapolation. The first approach to technological forecasting is to project past and current trends into the future. These can be charted to show what future trends will be. If men's clothing, for example, has been getting gaudier, the forecaster follows that line, going one step further by suggesting more far-out styles. As this trend progresses, however, it eventually reaches a point of being ridiculous. Styles then are likely to suddenly reverse themselves, returning to an earlier and more conservative point on the scale. A good example of this was the wedgie style of women's shoes, with the thickness of the soles and heels increasing annually until they reached the point of absurdity and the style reversed itself, adopting more feminine lines again.

Environmentalistic. Various environmental factors can all affect technology and change the future of any product or service, Consider a product as basic as housing, for example. Inflation, a domestic business factor, has forced home prices to such a high level in many countries that the average working people have little or no hope of owning their own homes. While interest rates have climbed to as much as 15 percent in some areas, housing starts have dropped drastically. France has the highest mortgage interest rates (15 percent) and a fairly low home-ownership percentage (44 percent). Material and labor costs, as well as a tight money market, have compounded the problem. What is clearly needed is a change in technology to lower the cost of a home—a new, inexpensive material, for example, or new construction techniques, such as factory construction or premolded shell construction, possibly using a durable plastic or concrete.

Morphological Analysis. In this technique, technological factors are compared with natural ones, for example, comparing artificial means of locomotion with those of birds and animals. The forecaster tries to find probable ways of improving the scientific methods involved in producing the product or in the materials used.

Normative Approaches. This technique anticipates future technology by projecting probable developments of current technology. Such methods as *scenario writing, anticipations,* and *futures* are used, setting out ways in which a specific technological goal might be achieved. **Gaming** and **brainstorming** are just two offshoots of this technique.

Corporate Compatibility Screening. In the consideration of new products or services, a company should consider how the new product or service fits in with current output.

Products or services' compatibility with current output can be rated as follows:[1]

High compatibility	10
Good compatibility	8
Average compatibility	6
Poor compatibility	4
Very poor compatibility	2

APPLYING TECHNOLOGICAL FORECASTING

These techniques can be extremely effective when used to introduce a product using advanced technology features before a competing company manufactures the same product. By training research and development staffs in these methods, as well as in relevant technologies, it should be possible to overcome technical obstacles.

SUGGESTED FURTHER READING

Ayers, R. U., *Technological Forecasting and Long-Range Planning,* McGraw-Hill, New York, 1969.
Kahn, H., and A. J. Wiener, *The Year 2000,* Macmillan, New York, 1967.
Wills, Gordon, *Technological Forecasting,* Penguin, Baltimore, 1972.

TECHNOLOGY ASSESSMENT

Areas for use in Cost Control:

ORGANIZATIONAL AND OPERATIONAL SYSTEMS
MATERIALS AND EQUIPMENT MANAGEMENT
INDUSTRIAL APPLICATIONS

Technology assessment is a policy study of a proposed technology. Social impact, costs, and alternatives are examined, as well as need, market, profit, safety, and other factors. The method is used to reduce both social costs (undesirable social effects which might be caused by the new technology) and monetary costs.

The area is particularly important to business and industry since the 1972 passage of the U.S. Technology Assessment Act, under which the federal government will examine and regulate new technologies where necessary. Thus, if business does not correctly assess proposed technologies, later government assessments may impose regulations that will add to, rather than reduce, costs.

---

[1]Gordon Wills, *Technological Forecasting,* Penguin, Baltimore, 1972.

—-and A. R. D. Norman,

A series of seven steps is used by the U.S. Office of Science and Technology in technology assessment:

1. *Define the assessment task.* Problems and issues are established, along with required assessment scope.

2. *Describe relevant technologies.* The technology to be assessed, supporting technologies, and alternative technologies are defined.

3. *Develop state-of-society assumptions.* Social factors influencing the use of alternative technologies are defined.

4. *Identify impact areas.* Social factors that may be changed by a proposed technology are defined.

5. *Make preliminary impact analysis.* Changes caused by the technology and their effects on society in the long term are defined.

6. *Identify possible action options.* Programs to obtain maximum social gain from the technology are determined.

7. *Complete impact analysis.* Social changes stemming from each alternative technology are compared.

Technology assessment has been used by commercial and research organizations for several years. For example, the Stanford Research Institute assessed increasing snowfall as a means of increasing water supplies in Colorado. Using the seven steps described above, it was determined that the technology would provide the lowest-cost method of channeling additional water supplies into the area. Concurrent effects on other areas' water supplies and local agricultural and water programs, however, resulted in recommendations for legislative regulation of the technology.

Geothermal energy, pollution control, solar energy, electronic banking, and biological pesticides are some additional technologies recently assessed.

SUGGESTED FURTHER READING

Lapedes, D. N., ed., *Yearbook of Science and Technology,* McGraw-Hill, New York, 1974.

TELECOMMUNICATION DATA TRANSMISSION

Areas for use in Cost Control:

ORGANIZATIONAL AND OPERATIONAL SYSTEMS

DATA RETENTION—FILES AND RECORDKEEPING

Telecommunication Data Transmission is the transmission of computer data by the ordinary telephone systems, allowing easier shared use (and reduced costs) of computer hardware. Newer systems allow sharing of data from any connected computer by dialing the specific installation. Terminals—the device used to decode data for the user—may be audio-oriented, paper-tape readers, punched-card readers, or electronic printout screens. Voice-response terminals are least costly, since they allow use of any public telephone as a terminal.

"Picturephones," a terminal designed to decode computerized transmission of visual data such as graphs, charts, photographs, or live transmissions, use cable transmission facilities capable of carrying about 100 times today's data capacity and should further reduce data transmission cost per unit. *See also* **Electronic Data Processing; Optical Fiber Communications.**

SUGGESTED FURTHER READING

Gentle, E. C., Jr., *Data Communications in Business,* American Telephone and Telegraph Co., New York, 1965.

Martin, J., *Telecommunications and the Computer,* Prentice-Hall, Englewood Cliffs, N.J., 1969.
— and A. R. D. Norman, *The Computerized Society,* Prentice-Hall, Englewood Cliffs, N.J., 1970.

TELEPHONE METERING

Areas for use in Cost Control:

ORGANIZATIONAL AND OPERATIONAL SYSTEMS
MATERIALS AND EQUIPMENT MANAGEMENT
INDUSTRIAL APPLICATIONS
BUSINESS AND COMMERCIAL APPLICATIONS

Telephone metering is arranging to have the telephone company bill by extension as well as by individual call. Thus, all calls are charged to the extensions used in placing the calls. A call form located at each extension is used to record each call, the employee placing the call, the company and/or individual called, the reason for the call, and call duration. Forms are monitored monthly against telephone bills, and unrecorded or nonbusiness calls are charged to the individual employee.

Call information is also used in designing guidelines to reduce costs of authorized calls, such as time limits, purpose-of-call restrictions, and distance limits.

The method offers control of telephone costs yet does not hamper peak-hour-use needs by forcing employees to place calls through a switchboard which may become overloaded. Additionally, direct-dialing call costs—used in telephone metering—are reduced as much as 30 percent below operator-connected calls.

SUGGESTED FURTHER READING

Radke, Magnus, *Manual of Cost Reduction Techniques,* McGraw-Hill, New York, 1972.

TELEX SYSTEMS

Areas for use in Cost Control:

ORGANIZATIONAL AND OPERATIONAL SYSTEMS
MATERIALS AND EQUIPMENT MANAGEMENT
INDUSTRIAL APPLICATIONS
BUSINESS AND COMMERCIAL APPLICATIONS

Telex systems using punched-tape recorders to transmit messages reduce communications costs in many circumstances. For long messages to distant points particularly, Telex charges are lower than telephone costs, yet they are rapidly transmitted. They are also less costly and faster than dictating, typing, and mailing a letter. A written record of the Telexed message is provided.

Administrative employees may be provided with cost comparison figures for telephone, Telex, and mail communications of varying lengths and to various locations to serve as a cost reduction guide.

SUGGESTED FURTHER READING

Radke, Magnus, *Manual of Cost Reduction Techniques,* McGraw-Hill, New York, 1972.

TEROTECHNOLOGY

Areas for use in Cost Control:

ORGANIZATIONAL AND OPERATIONAL SYSTEMS
MATERIALS AND EQUIPMENT MANAGEMENT
INDUSTRIAL APPLICATIONS

Terotechnology is a combination of management disciplines used to ensure lowest cost and greatest efficiency of equipment during its life cycle. Equipment is designed and/or specified with regard to reliability, maintenance, performance, and replacement and the effects of these on the lifetime cost of the item. For example, one piece of equipment may be less costly initially, but an alternate machine may be less costly over its period of use because of lower maintenance costs, higher performance, etc.

Practicing terotechnology means the inclusion of various disciplines in decision making for equipment design and/or specification. Accounting and maintenance management representatives, for example, are included in the design committee or team. After comparing all costs over the useful life of a proposed piece of equipment or plant, that item with overall lowest cost and optimum performance is chosen.

SUGGESTED FURTHER READING

Terotechnology, Department of Trade and Industry, London.
"Terotechnology in Action," Trade and Industry, *The Financial Times,* Sept, 26, 1974, London.

T-GROUP See Sensitivity Training.

THEOREM-PROVING PROGRAMMING

Areas for use in Cost Control:

ORGANIZATIONAL AND OPERATIONAL SYSTEMS
DATA RETENTION—FILES AND RECORDKEEPING
MATERIALS AND EQUIPMENT MANAGEMENT
INDUSTRIAL APPLICATIONS
BUSINESS AND COMMERCIAL APPLICATIONS

Theorem-proving programming reduces the cost of computer software production by the elimination of the need for a programmer. A basic theorem is programmed into the computer. Thereafter, problems that can be stated in the same terms as this theorem can be solved without additional programming.

SUGGESTED FURTHER READING

Lapedes, D. N., ed., *Yearbook of Science and Technology,* McGraw-Hill, New York, 1974.

THINK TANKS

Areas for use in Cost Control:

ORGANIZATIONAL AND OPERATIONAL SYSTEMS
MATERIALS AND EQUIPMENT MANAGEMENT
INDUSTRIAL APPLICATIONS
BUSINESS AND COMMERCIAL APPLICATIONS

Think tanks are groups of highly intelligent, skilled, and/or creative persons used to study and evaluate business and/or technological problems and to determine possible solutions and the outcomes of those solutions. Both private industry and university-connected think tanks, such as the Rand Corporation and Tempo, are currently operating. Think tank advice on cost or other problems is usually presented in the form of background information, alternate courses of action and their probable effect, and related statistical data, from which the user then selects the best possible solution to the problem.

Feedback systems, responding to and taking best advantage of technological change, are a key element in the operation of a think tank. Transfer of technology, using discoveries in one area to benefit an unrelated area, is one example.

Systems analysis, cost analysis, gaming, and **technological forecasting** are some of the individual methods developed and used by think tanks in forward business and industry planning.

Members of a think tank represent various areas of specialization, thus providing a multidisciplinary team. Ideas from specialty areas are transferred to unrelated areas, just as technologies are.

While some companies prefer to operate their own think tanks, contracted use of a major group offers quality planning and/or research at a more economical cost for the small or medium-sized company.

SUGGESTED FURTHER READING

Chase, S., *The Most Probable World,* Harper & Row, New York.
McHale, J., *The Future of the Future,* George Braziller, Inc., New York.
Smith, P. I. S., *Think Tanks and Problem Solving,* Business Books, London, 1971.
Wall Street Journal staff, *Here Comes Tomorrow: Living and Working in the Year 2000,* Dow Jones, New York, 1972.

THREE-DIMENSIONAL COMMUNICATIONS

Areas for use in Cost Control:

PSYCHOLOGICAL MOTIVATIONAL MANAGEMENT
ORGANIZATIONAL AND OPERATIONAL SYSTEMS
INDUSTRIAL APPLICATIONS
BUSINESS AND COMMERCIAL APPLICATIONS

Three-dimensional communications is the three-way movement of information within a business:

1. *Down* from management to employees to provide needed information and motivation to increase productivity.
2. *Up* from employees to management to provide worker feedback on managerial ideas.
3. *Across*—interdepartmental sharing of information and ideas.

Three-dimensional communications provide better morale and cooperation, plus a sharing of ways to increase productivity and reduce costs no matter where they occur in the company structure.

SUGGESTED FURTHER READING

Bittel, L. R., *What Every Supervisor Should Know,* McGraw-Hill, New York, 1974.

THREE-D THEORY

Areas for use in Cost Control:

ORGANIZATIONAL AND OPERATIONAL SYSTEMS
INDUSTRIAL APPLICATIONS
BUSINESS AND COMMERCIAL APPLICATIONS

Three-D Theory ("third-dimension theory") is a technique intended to combine the two basic types of managerial behavior—*task-oriented* behavior (T.O.) and *human relations-oriented* behavior (R.O.)—in correct proportions to achieve the greatest overall effectiveness of the manager in cost reduction or other business problems.

The technique breaks down behavioral types into four styles:

1. *Integrated style:* combining of task-oriented and relationship-oriented behavior
2. *Dedicated style:* primarily task-oriented behavior

3. *Related style:* primarily relations-oriented behavior
4. *Separated style:* little task-oriented or relations-oriented behavior

The "third dimension" is added when styles are put into practice, becoming more effective or less effective, by matching the style to the business conditions and situation.

Use of the Three-D Theory teaches managers how to use two of the four behavior styles, depending on the business situation; in other words, they are taught to rate their behavioral value to the company and to match their actions to the business conditions, improving their own value.

Business situations are classified as one of five types to determine the correct *behavior style* application for the condition:

1. *Organization*—operating procedures, systems, design, assignment of work, etc.
2. *Technology*—physical aspects of completing tasks
3. *Superiors* involved in the problem or situation—their personalities, behavior patterns, and skills
4. *Coworkers* involved in the problem or situation—their personalities, behavior patterns, and skills
5. *Subordinates* involved in the problem or situation—their personalities, behavior patterns, and skills

Through use of a flex map (see Fig. 105) the situation is analyzed and the most effective behavioral styles are applied to it. Such analysis and application leads to

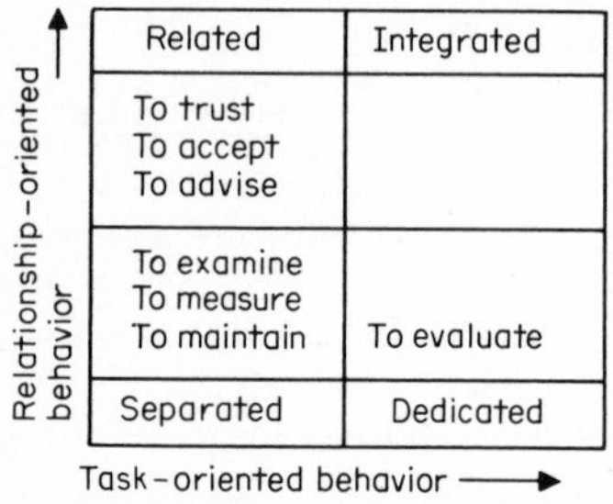

Figure 105. A flex map showing optimal managerial behavior between two department heads. (W. J. Reddin, *Managerial Effectiveness,* McGraw-Hill, New York, 1970.)

increasingly flexible, as well as effective, management. For example, in Fig. 105, the flex map shows the optimal managerial behavior between two department heads: the head of marketing and the head of sales.

Both books and management training classes can be used in learning the methods used in Three-D Theory technique. *See also* **Situational Dynamics**.

SUGGESTED FURTHER READING

Reddin, W. J., *Managerial Effectiveness,* McGraw-Hill, New York, 1970.
——, "The Tri-Dimensional Grid," *The Canadian Personnel and Industrial Relations Journal,* January 1966.

THREE-TRACK PAY SYSTEM

Areas for use in Cost Control:

FINANCIAL MOTIVATIONAL MANAGEMENT
ORGANIZATIONAL AND OPERATIONAL SYSTEMS
INDUSTRIAL APPLICATIONS
BUSINESS AND COMMERCIAL APPLICATIONS

A three-track pay system is one using three simultaneous degrees of pay increases to reflect the degree of effort made by the employee. The method is used primarily for executive compensation and reduces costs by reflecting the productivity of these employees as well as the level of their jobs. Typical annual increases for the three tracks are:

1. Fast track: 15%
2. Middle track: 9%
3. Slow track: 7%

These figures are, of course, affected by other conditions, such as an inflationary economy, when the inflation rate may be added to them.

In practice, managerial recruits start out in the faster tracks. As the limits of their ability, and thus their performance, level out, they are placed in a slower pay track. Bonuses, fringe benefits, stock options, retirement plans, etc., can be tied to the three-track system to further reflect performance level and to reduce costs when performance decreases.

SUGGESTED FURTHER READING

Mann, R., ed., *The Arts of Top Management,* McGraw-Hill, New York, 1970.

TIME AND MATERIAL CONTRACT

Areas for use in Cost Control:

ORGANIZATIONAL AND OPERATIONAL SYSTEMS
MATERIALS AND EQUIPMENT MANAGEMENT
INDUSTRIAL APPLICATIONS

A time and material contract is a purchase agreement that pays the seller's material costs plus a predetermined fee per hour of work. The method protects the seller from possible losses if materials and time costs are greater than originally estimated.

In most cases, the buyer pays too much under such a contract, since the seller may tend to make the work last as long as possible. However, on jobs that are difficult to estimate, the buyer's costs may be reduced by a time and material contract, since the seller will not be required to make unnecessary allowances for uncertainties.

SUGGESTED FURTHER READING

Ammer, D. S., *Materials Management,* Irwin, Homewood, Ill., 1968.

TIME LIFE SYSTEM

Areas for use in Cost Control:

ORGANIZATIONAL AND OPERATIONAL SYSTEMS
MATERIALS AND EQUIPMENT MANAGEMENT
INDUSTRIAL APPLICATIONS

The time life system is a **preventive maintenance** technique where equipment parts are changed periodically, based on their average operating life and before breakdown, to save maintenance and downtime costs. For example, if a piece of equipment has six parts with an expected life of three months, and an average of one part must be replaced each two weeks, maintenance costs for a three-month period will appear as follows:

Time to replace one part   = 1 hour
Time to inspect and test machine = 2 hours

    Total   = 3 hours × 6 parts = 18 hours

Using the time life system, all parts are replaced at once, at a time just short of the expected life—about once each 2¾ months in this case. Maintenance costs for the 2¾-month period appear as follows:

Time to replace one part = 1 hour × 6 parts = 6 hours
Time to inspect and test machine   = 2 hours
$\qquad$ Total   = 8 hours

Steps in establishing the time-life for each piece of equipment include:

1. Determine average working life of each machine part.
2. Group parts with similar-length life expectancies.
3. Establish replacement schedules for each group of parts with frequency of replacement falling at, or just short of, the shortest average life expectancy.

SUGGESTED FURTHER READING

Higgins, L. R., and L. C. Morrow, *Maintenance Engineering Handbook,* 3d ed., McGraw-Hill, New York, 1977.

TIME RATING

Areas for use in Cost Control:

PSYCHOLOGICAL MOTIVATIONAL MANAGEMENT
FINANCIAL MOTIVATIONAL MANAGEMENT
ORGANIZATIONAL AND OPERATIONAL SYSTEMS

Time rating is a **performance rating** technique used to measure the time required by an employee to perform a unit of work as compared with an acceptable standard time required. The rank may be given in terms of parts of a standard hour or in a percentage of the standard time required. Method and skill are not measured. Rankings that form the basis for an incentive program reduce costs by limiting payment to proportion of work accomplished.

SUGGESTED FURTHER READING

Maynard, H. B., ed., *Industrial Engineering Handbook,* 3d ed., McGraw-Hill, New York, 1974.
Morrow, R. L., *Time Study and Motion Economy,* Ronald, New York, 1946.
Mundel, M. E., *Motion and Time Study,* Prentice-Hall, Englewood Cliffs, N.J., 1955.

TIME-SERIES ANALYSIS

Areas for use in Cost Control:

ORGANIZATIONAL AND OPERATIONAL SYSTEMS
INDUSTRIAL APPLICATIONS
BUSINESS AND COMMERCIAL APPLICATIONS

Time-series analysis is a type of long-range forecasting used to determine when specific factors, such as cost reduction, can be made to happen and/or when and how events will affect specific projects. For example, a company might want to determine the soonest probable time it can fully automate production, as well as the probable cost of such automation in both equipment expenditure and labor union settlements. **Parameter analysis,** using current trends to develop such information, and the **Delphi method,** using expert advice to develop such information, are two basic time-series analysis techniques.

SUGGESTED FURTHER READING

The Delphi Method III: Use of Self-Ratings to Improve Group Estimates, The Rand Corporation, New York, 1969.
Smith, P. I. S., *Think Tanks and Problem Solving,* Business Books, London, 1971.

TRADE CREDIT TECHNIQUE

Areas for use in Cost Control:
ORGANIZATIONAL AND OPERATIONAL SYSTEMS
INDUSTRIAL APPLICATIONS
BUSINESS AND COMMERCIAL APPLICATIONS

The trade credit technique refers to delaying payment for materials purchased, since most credit terms cost less than short-term bank financing. For example, if a company buys $10,000 worth of supplies and borrows money to pay for them at 12 percent, receiving a 2 percent discount for immediate payment, net financing costs will be 10 percent per year, or about $83 per month. On the other hand, if the company will wait 90 days for payment, the lost 2 percent discount ($200) will cost less than the interest (about $250) on money borrowed to pay the account. The method reduces costs even further during an inflationary period, as the money owed devaluates.

SUGGESTED FURTHER READING
Samuels, J. M., and F. M. Wilkes, *Management of Company Finance,* Nelson, London, 1971.

TRADE DISCOUNT See Discount.

TRADE EXHIBIT COST CONTROL

Areas for use in Cost Control:
ORGANIZATIONAL AND OPERATIONAL SYSTEMS
INDUSTRIAL APPLICATIONS
BUSINESS AND COMMERCIAL APPLICATIONS

Trade exhibit cost control is the reduction of costs of exhibiting products and/or services at national and international trade fairs. Such exhibits, particularly international ones, have become extremely valuable marketing tools in new markets. Too often, however, cost reductions and maximum efficiency measures are not implemented, and the company spends more money per dollar of sales effected than is necessary. Planning, organizing, designing, and managing techniques can be applied to exhibiting, reducing such costs and increasing the efficiency of the exhibiting.

The company should begin with a careful analysis of potential markets at home and abroad. Exhibits can then be planned in the heaviest-potential market areas. For example, there would be little value in exhibiting frozen foods in an international trade fair if the majority of dealers attending were primarily from countries with a low ownership of refrigerators. If these countries' economies were improving, however, there would be a great value in exhibiting refrigerators.

Exhibits can be used as a follow-up step in assessing potential markets. Company representatives should plan to ask questions (and record the answers in writing) to evaluate attendance response to the potential of their product or service in specific markets.

Exhibiting also provides an opportunity to evaluate the competition, and planning should include a specific program in this area.

In addition to these reasons for exhibiting, company goals may include:

1. Securing product or service inquiries for salesmen to follow up later
2. Company and product publicity
3. Customer contact
4. Potential customer contact
5. Meeting competitive showings
6. Order taking

PLANNING

Deciding on the specific objectives of exhibits is the first step in planning. Once goals are chosen, the best way of reaching them should be planned, including the choice of locations to be used.

Product or service timing should be considered at the planning stage. While new products attract the most attention, production must be capable of filling orders immediately. A working model of a nonpolluting incinerator, for example, would probably attract a lot of attention at the right type of trade show. But if production were still two years off, most of that interest would be lost and/or wasted. The company would have accomplished more by featuring the current model and using a small side exhibit clearly labeled "things to come."

Choice of Events. In choosing events for exhibiting at home or abroad, consider the following questions:

1. Will attendance represent a strong potential market?
2. Will the time fit in well with the introduction of new products and/or production capabilities?
3. Does the personality of the event fit into overall marketing plans?
4. Has the event an established and successful history?
5. Are trade associations backing the event?
6. How many states/countries will be exhibiting?
7. What symposiums, conferences, etc. (in addition to exhibits), will attract attendance?
8. Do conferences or exhibits in other locations clash with this one?
9. How will attendance be structured? Trade only? Trade and public?

Exhibit Location. Location of the exhibit within the show is a key factor to success. Some companies prefer to exhibit in a national block. All exhibitors within this block may then join together to provide a national refreshment booth or lounge to attract attention at a minimal cost to each. On the other hand, companies with strong exhibits of their own may make a better impact separated from other exhibits from their own state or country.

The best location is usually on the ground floor, indoors, and in a direct-flow path from the entrance. Locations near the rest rooms, restaurants, bars, coffee stands, etc., will ensure a flow of traffic, too. Island locations, when properly designed, offer more visible area and are more effective than walled booths.

Light available at the location is a factor to be considered. Height restrictions, pillars, fire doors, etc., should be avoided.

Firms with newer and/or better products than their competitors will find exhibiting in trade blocks effective. This encourages comparison of products, and the company makes a good showing.

Companies with subsidiaries who want to exhibit will find that a joint exhibit provides greater impact (because of increased size), since booths usually cost less per square foot of exhibit space for larger areas. It may also be possible to share exhibit space and expenses with an unaligned company. For example, a frozen food company and a freezer manufacturer might prepare a joint exhibit to the advantage of both companies.

Costs to be considered in addition to the exhibit space include booth construction, product and literature transportation, company representatives' expenses, installation costs, and insurance fees. These are discussed separately in the design and organization sections.

DESIGN

Most companies will find that design is more effective when carried out by an expert. A free-lance designer can be used, as can a contractor specializing in design and building of exhibits. Very large firms that exhibit frequently may find it economical to maintain a design staff.

The designer should be hired before a space is rented, and should be involved in deciding the amount of space (and its location) possible within the given budget. This will ensure that adequate funds remain for effective exhibit construction.

Designs, to meet stated exhibit goals, should be prepared by the designer and submitted for management approval. Designer Misha Black states that the three essentials a designer should know are:

1. What is the main goal of the exhibit?
2. What main idea should viewers receive from the exhibit?
3. What action should the exhibit motivate?

The designer should know the products or services to be featured, their storage and security requirements, and their utility needs.

Costs should be estimated by the designer at the design stage and exact costs determined when construction bids are received.

Simple design to highlight products and/or services is not only cheaper than more elaborate design. It is usually more effective, since it does not detract from the product or service.

ORGANIZATION

Once the exhibit location, size, and design are planned in detail, the transportation of products and the operation of the booth must be organized.

Transportation. For national shows, transportation is usually most economical when handled as deliveries. This means allowing adequate time for the shipment to reach the show site. Special exhibit items, such as electronic equipment, audiovisual equipment, and literature, may be carried by representatives of the firm or shipped air freight.

Table 51. Typical Exhibit Customs Policy and Internal-Handling Entry Costs

Area	Customs policy	Approximate percent of entry cost for internal handling
Continental Europe	Sliding scale based on value	60–75%
U.S.S.R.	Minimal charge	80–90%
South America	No set scale; each case negotiated separately	60–70%*
Australia, England	Set fee	50%
U.S.A.	Set fee	50%

*Most companies find that money is saved by hiring a local customs negotiator to arrange the South American customs fees.

Overseas transportation presents special problems because of the slowness of sea travel and the frequency of labor problems in loading and unloading. For smaller product items, air freight is a better investment. Large items, such as trucks, should be shipped by sea well in advance of the last boat available. Arrange for a forwarding agent to pay customs fees where possible (see Table 51).

Customs documents are required, depending on method of shipment and country entered for overseas exhibits. The consulate of the country to be entered should be asked for suitable forms. Table 52 shows major documents required.

A.T.A. Carnets, obtained from local exhibition officials or transport firms, can be used to allow *temporary* duty-free admission of products, equipment, etc., in the following countries:

Austria	Hungary	Spain
Belgium	Ireland	Sweden
Bulgaria	Israel	Switzerland
Czechoslovakia	Italy	U.K.
Denmark	Netherlands	U.S.A.
Finland	Norway	West Germany
France	Portugal	Yugoslavia
Gibraltar	Romania	

When A.T.A. Carnets are used, however, products may *not* be sold at the close of the exhibit to avoid the cost of return shipment. It should be determined which method is the most economical.

Table 52. Major Documents and Invoices Required for Overseas Exhibit Product Entry

	Documents required			
Country	Sea transport	Rail transport	Road	Invoice required
European Free Trade Area (Austria, Portugal, Switzerland, Scandinavia, U.K.)	Bill of lading	International Rail Consignment	T.I.R. Carnet	EFTA Declaration
European countries	Bill of lading	International Rail Consignment	T.I.R. Carnet	Commercial invoice with statement of origin
South America	Bill of lading	International Rail Consignment	T.I.R. Carnet	Consular invoice
U.S.A.	Bill of lading	International Rail Consignment	T.I.R. Carnet	Commercial invoice *plus* consular invoice

Whether or not the goods are to be shipped home affects decisions about type of packing to be used. Although reusable crates are most economical if goods are to be returned, storage of these may prove to be a problem and an extra expense at the exhibition site.

When crates are being shipped overseas, special directions, such as "fragile" or "this side up," should be written both in English and in the host country's language.

Insurance. This is one very necessary cost. Coverage should include liability to company representatives and booth visitors as well as loss of expensive equipment or products in transit and on exhibit. Coverage may be obtained for fire, loss of smaller products, etc.

Travel and Accommodation Costs. Most companies find that it is cheaper to have a travel agent arrange transportation and accommodations for all representatives. Class of travel and hotel required should be specified. Depending on the season and location, "package" vacations may provide lower-cost rates than other available payment scales.

BOOTH CONSTRUCTION

If a designer-contractor is handling the booth, construction will automatically be included. Even when a free-lance designer is used, he or she can usually recommend a suitable booth-construction contractor. The company should make sure that constractors being considered are capable of competent work, completed on schedule. In considering these contractors, price comparisons are the next step.

If possible, a knowledgeable company representative should be on-site during booth construction to make certain that plans are followed.

Materials used in construction must meet local and national fire and safety regulations.

Prefabrication of the booth and electrical fittings may be advisable when available skills at the exhibit location are either in short supply or very expensive. In some countries, union rules must be precisely observed in construction on-site.

Only the parts of the booth visible to those attending should be "finished" with paint, fabric, wallpaper, etc.

A platform is a convenient way of hiding utility wiring, and it can provide storage if products shown are not too heavy for a display platform.

Matting that can be dyed is an inexpensive substitute for booth carpeting and often provides better wear.

Wallpaper can provide a finished look more economically and quickly than paint.

Open, island-design displays provide easier visibility of products and at the same time eliminate the cost of several walls, muslin ceilings, etc.

Special lighting effects are an inexpensive method of attracting attention. Strobe lights, colored lights, and spotlights are some possible lighting methods.

Signs should be limited and should use large wording at standing eye level. Black lettering on white or yellow backgrounds is most effective.

Any wall space should be used for visual presentation of the company message. Photographs of products or services can be effective, as can large schematic drawings.

Features that involve the visitor are especially effective. These may include displays that require the visitor to push a button or take a short (and preferably humorous) test. Free literature should be displayed where visitors can easily help themselves.

OPERATION

If a company representative is not on-site during construction, someone knowledgeable must check the display well in advance of opening time to allow for necessary corrections.

A kit of useful items should accompany the exhibit, including hammer, nails, cellulose tape, double-sided tape, masking tape, pins, screwdriver, and paper clips. These items are for use during the show, not for booth construction, when union rules might be violated.

Any display should always have at least two company representatives on hand, and more for larger exhibits. One person on each period of duty should plainly be in charge. This person will draw up a duty schedule and make sure that it is followed, as well as supervise personnel attentiveness and other behavior.

If working models or products are used, make sure that needed power, oil, etc., are stocked. Spare parts are also advised, particularly for parts that can be easily removed.

Find an interesting way to obtain data about visitors. Forms for a free gift drawing are one way, as are humorous tests with samples or prizes given for successful completion. Inquiry and order forms should be available to help personnel deal with serious inquiries.

If interpreters are needed for overseas exhibits, try to find college business students, who will charge less and will probably be more interested in the work at hand than would professional interpreters.

Events accompanying exhibits are often effective. Invitations to cocktail parties, lunches, etc., may be given to customers and selected potential customers who visit the exhibit.

Direct sales may be made from the stand, particularly in the case of consumer goods.

Free samples are ideal for inexpensive products—tastes of wine, food, etc. Miniatures of tools in the form of bracelet charms were given by one United States tool manufacturer. Trade visitors took them home to wives, daughters, and girl friends.

Literature and public relations news releases should be used to provide maximum company exposure.

The company may sponsor accompanying conferences, which are also featured in the display. Such conferences should be strongly audiovisual for best effects. Movies and demonstrations are more effective than lectures. Extra publicity can be obtained from these presentations, both at home and in exhibit-location media.

TRAVELING EXHIBITS

Permanent, traveling exhibits can reduce costs. Construction is a one-time factor, and exhibit visitors seem fascinated by the more unusual displays. Airplanes, boats, buses, trailers, railway cars, and specially built vehicles can be used. If there is not a convention or exhibit center for a specific date, the vehicle can be driven to the location of a potential area to provide demonstrations, information, etc. Consumer products can be easily exhibited in shopping or other center parking lots.

SUGGESTED FURTHER READING

Black, S., *Exhibiting Overseas,* Pitman, New York, 1971.
Exhibition Bulletin, monthly, London.

TRAINING

Areas for use in Cost Control:

PSYCHOLOGICAL MOTIVATIONAL MANAGEMENT
ORGANIZATIONAL AND OPERATIONAL SYSTEMS
INDUSTRIAL APPLICATIONS
BUSINESS AND COMMERCIAL APPLICATIONS

A well-designed formal training program can cut the cost of breaking in a new employee as much as 50 percent. Even better, production costs stay lower when workers have been trained in the correct method of doing their job. This section provides an introduction to four areas of employment training:

Industrial employee training
Clerical employee training
Sales employee training
Supervisory employee training

TRAINING INDUSTRIAL EMPLOYEES

The largest cost reductions that can be expected from training techniques are those applied to general industrial labor forces—both new employees and existing operators who are not working efficiently. Just what these training techniques should be for an individual company can best be determined through job investigation techniques, including **job evaluation** as well as **work study and measurement.** Whatever techniques are finally used, cost reduction benefits of formal industrial training include:

1. Increased productivity
2. More efficient use of labor
3. Reduction of operator break-in time

Greater production per worker can be the result of new machinery or new methods of production. If new equipment is installed, workers must, of course, be trained to use it. But in our discussion of training, we are primarily concerned with the use of new and more efficient operational methods.

The Goal of a Training Program. In training to increase efficiency of working methods, the following checklist should be considered:

1. Working place and tools should be designed for economy of motion, and the employee should be trained to use only the necessary motions.

2. Working methods for work involving several operators should be standardized.

3. Production time for a single unit should be limited to what an average operator can remember and perform. Yet, it must have enough variety to hold the operator's interest and give a feeling of pride in having completed the work.

4. Work should be physically arranged so that the employee uses both hands yet does not have to reach or stretch beyond a comfortable area. Foot controls and pedals may also be used in making best use of equipment and labor.

Formal versus Informal Training. Many companies train new employees informally. That is, the trainee watches the worker next to him to learn the job. Actually, this informal training involves three costs that can be eliminated in a formal training program:

1. Cost of materials wasted on "learning" production
2. Cost of lost wages of experienced workers and supervisors who "help" the trainee
3. Cost of lost production of experienced workers who "help" the trainee

In addition, many firms pay the new employee a lower wage—a base hourly wage perhaps—while training. But if he or she is informally trained on the shop floor, the incentive addition must also be paid. Adding all these costs together, some companies estimate that at least 50 percent of training costs are saved by switching from informal to formal training systems. Such formal systems are designed to include the following:

1. Good hiring practices
2. Good training instructors
3. Suitable training worshops
4. Effective training techniques

Good Hiring Practices. Choose those workers with the necessary mechanical aptitudes. A trainee should have a predetermined minimum intelligence, yet most firms prefer not to hire those with a very high I.Q., since they are more apt to become easily bored with the work. Generally, younger unmarried persons, particularly those who have held a number of jobs in the past three to five years, are unlikely to remain with the company long enough to make hiring them as profitable as hiring older, more settled workers.

Some companies give tests to help select employees. These may include:

1. Intelligence tests
2. Aptitude tests
3. Psychological tests
4. Medical examinations

Useful as these tests are when properly administered, it is well to remember that some of them are illegal in some states and countries when given under certain circumstances. For example, although the hiring company may still legally give intelligence tests, many governments have made it illegal for employment agencies to do so.

Application forms are another tool that can help in choosing trainees, and they should be designed to give thorough background information. Personal interviews will help round out the overall impression of applicants.

Good Training Instructors. A good training instructor should have the following characteristics:

1. Knows the manufacturing methods to be taught, as well as the company's products.
2. Is effective in presenting the "how-to" aspects of production.
3. Is young enough to be vital but old enough to be respected by the trainee. Generally, 35 to 45 is considered the best range.
4. Should like working with and teaching people.
5. Knows the background of the company.
6. Knows the firm's supervisory staff, since trainees will have to please these people.

Suitable Training Workshops. In setting up suitable training workshops, do not buy new equipment and tools. Trainees should learn on equipment as nearly like that in the plant as possible. Nor should the lighting, ventilation, and atmosphere be better than actual conditions. The best location for a training area is near the actual production department, perhaps even using one end of it. In this way, normal noise and activity become as familiar as the tools and equipment used.

Effective Training Techniques. Before setting up the training program, the following steps should be carried out:

1. Define, on paper, the various elements of the job the trainee will hold.
2. Set out the knowledge the trainee will need on the job.
3. Decide the best way to teach the trainee these job elements.

Once these steps are completed, the instructor should write a detailed instruction program, setting out both theoretical and practical instruction to be used, in sequence. Emphasis should be placed on the actual skills required—operation of the tools and equipment and handling and production of the manufactured item. Safety procedures should be included in the program and incorporated in the teaching.

The trainee should be taught the basics of any incentive plan used by the company, including how to calculate his or her own bonus. Time cards, work sheets, or any other required paperwork should be explained.

After training, the instructor should continue to make occasional follow-up checks on the trainee's work for a break-in period.

Length of training usually extends from two to three weeks, with an additional week of follow-up.

TRAINING CLERICAL EMPLOYEES

Office workers seldom receive much on-the-job training. Of course, the new employee is expected to have required skills—typing, shorthand, accounting ability—

before being hired. But every company has its own methods of working, and too often a new employee is either not introduced to these at all or else is advised to "watch" another worker.

As in industrial training, formal training methods can reduce the cost of breaking in a new employee. The first step in such training of clerical workers is to be sure that one person is responsible for the training job. This individual should begin by making sure the newcomers know something about the company, its history, its services or products, and its methods.

The new employee should be introduced to fellow workers and should be shown where to find supplies, how incoming and outgoing mail is handled, and basic telephone procedures used by the firm.

Departmental training will be needed to learn machine operation, layout of letters and forms, filing systems, etc.

Cost reductions are not limited to direct costs stemming from the output of the new employee, since inadequately prepared work may have to be done over completely if the employee is not properly trained, and since this lack of training may keep others from completing their work.

TRAINING SALES PERSONNEL

Cost control will result automatically if salespeople are trained to do the best job. Labor costs are the largest item in most budgets, and as a salesperson is trained to sell more effectively, her or his cost per dollar of sales drops.

Before hiring and training an employee for sales, be sure his or her personality is suited for the job, for no one can teach a shy, fearful person to be a good salesperson. Generally, the person who will make a good salesperson is outgoing and likes to meet people. He or she should be able to believe in the product or service, and the salary received should be at least partially dependent on the produced results.

When designing a sales training program, be aware of what your salespeople will be selling:

1. A tangible product, with the salesperson taking the initiative. Such a product might be an electric range or paper supplies.

2. A tangible product, with the buyer taking the initiative. In this case, the product is being sold in a retail store and the buyer has taken the first step by coming into the shop. True, the salesperson still has a sale to make—but she or he knows the buyer is interested in a specific product.

3. An intangible product or service. This category includes life insurance, mutual funds, etc.

Not every salesperson can sell all three types of products, and it is desirable to consider this when hiring and training. It is much easier to sell a retail product in a store, for example, since the customer makes the first move. Selling a tangible product is next easiest, while selling an intangible product or service is the most difficult.

Know the Product. The first step in sales training is making certain that the employee knows all about the product—its advantages and shortcomings. If selling an electric range with a self-cleaning oven, for example, the employee should know how the self-cleaning feature works and why the buyer should be interested in the feature.

Almost every product changes over a period of time. Automobiles are replaced annually by new models with new features, for instance. The more frequent the product change, the more essential it is to have regular training sessions to make sure the sales staff knows the product thoroughly. A fine example of this is a comparison of two trade magazine advertising salespeople. One may say to the prospective advertiser: "Our magazine is the finest in your industry—it has won six awards and has a fine editorial staff." His or her competitor, on the other hand, may have read the editorial plans for the upcoming issues and studied the current issues as well. This sales talk may begin: "In May, there will be a special issue on kitchen equipment—that's an annual feature in the magazine, and always well received. Since restaurant owners will be reading the article to learn all about new equipment available, it would be an ideal time for you to advertise your self-cleaning commercial-oven model." The second salesperson's knowledge of the product is much more likely to help make a sale than are the rather vague but flowery statements made by the first one.

Help the Buyer. Train salespeople to think about the buyer's problems that are connected with your product. Even if each of two competing salespeople has an equally fine line of products, the one who will make the sales is the one who tries to consider the buyer's needs. If a woman is buying a dress for an important dinner, for example, one shop may show her some good-quality items. But these dresses may all be unsuitable if the salesperson does not take the trouble to find out what the buyer needs. A good salesperson will ask what sort of dinner the buyer will attend and what type of people will be there and, considering the buyer's personality and appearance, will recommend suitable dresses.

A People of Their Word. Salespeople should be trained to keep their word—if you want repeat business, that is. Delivery dates, promises about the quality of the product or service, and quoted prices should be presented to prospective buyers honestly. Few firms can survive for long unless their reputation is maintained, and to customers, the salesperson *is* the firm.

The Positive Approach. As far as possible, salespeople should be trained to keep personal problems out of their working life. Sales are more likely when the salesperson believes in the product and approaches the prospective buyer in a positive frame of mind.

Follow-up. Train salespeople to check back with the customer, whether there is any prospect of another sale immediately or not. If the customer feels the salesperson is genuinely interested in whether the product or service was satisfactory, goodwill—and future sales—result.

Careful Accounting. Salespeople should be taught to record orders and billing details carefully. Make sure they know what data are needed, as well as why and how they are used.

The salespeople should also keep close track of expenses and be able to provide suitable receipts. This may be considered a petty nuisance, but a salesperson will respect the supervisor who controls expense costs. Some firms pay a bonus to salespeople who can cut expense costs below a predetermined percentage of orders.

Appearance Brush-up. Companies usually hire salespeople who present the image they want to have connected with their product or service. But occasionally someone is promoted from within the firm, or a young person is hired who has just the right personality but not quite the correct appearance. A short training session detailing the importance of good grooming, suitable clothing, and general manner expected can be a real help to such an employee.

TRAINING SUPERVISORY EMPLOYEES

Training within Industry (TWI) is a management technique used in Great Britain to train industrial foremen in essentials of supervision, but its methods are applicable everywhere. Training is concentrated in two major areas:

1. Job instructions
2. Labor relations

Job instructions training teaches the supervisor how to give instructions clearly. He or she may be given training in communications control and semantics (*see* **Cybernet-**

ics), but the main goal is to help the supervisor learn to explain working orders clearly, completely, and plainly.

Labor relations training teaches the supervisor how to prevent labor relations problems and how best to handle human relations problems that do occur. A supervisor may rebuke an employee in front of coworkers, for example, embarrassing and probably angering the employee. Or, a foreman may wait until the last minute before telling his subordinates that they will be expected to work overtime. While these incidents would be small ones if handled correctly, wasted time and money result from worker discontent and grumbling, low morale, and high turnover that often are caused by poor handling of labor relations.

Training cost of supervisors is usually low—about $250 per person, according to British figures. Usually a long-term and respected supervisor undergoes an initial supervisory training session given by a local college or an outside consultant group. The American Management Association is one organization conducting classes of this type. This supervisor, in turn, repeats the sessions for other supervisors.

See also **Booster Training; Career Trainee System.**

SUGGESTED FURTHER READING

Albright, L. E., *The Use of Psychological Tests in Industry,* Muksgard Publishing Company, Copenhagen, 1963.

Cemach, H. P., *Work Study in the Office,* MacLaren & Sons, London, 1969.

Denerly, R. A., and P. R. Plumbley, *Recruitment and Selection in a Full-Time Employment Economy,* Institute of Personnel Management, London.

Sampson, Robert C., "Train Executives While They Work," M. D. Richards and W. A. Nielander, eds., in *Readings in Management,* South-Western Publishing Company, Cincinnati, 1969.

TRAIT APPROACH

Areas for use in Cost Control:

PSYCHOLOGICAL MOTIVATIONAL MANAGEMENT
ORGANIZATIONAL AND OPERATIONAL SYSTEMS

Trait approach is a technique used to determine successful managerial personnel before they are hired. Costs are reduced by the selection of the most efficient applicants for such jobs. The technique operates on the assumption that a successful leader possesses certain good traits determined by research. Most important of these, according to a study by C. Wilson Randle, are:

1. *Position performance*—the success of the applicant in performing current work.
2. *Drive*—energy and determination to get things done.
3. *Intellectual ability.*
4. *Leadership*—others are willing to cooperate with and are motivated by the person.
5. *Administration*—the applicant can organize subordinates' work as well as his or her own, and can delegate and follow through.
6. *Initiative.*
7. *Motivation*—the person has goals and is willing to work to achieve them.
8. *Creativity*—the person is flexible, has new ideas, and can look at problems from all viewpoints.

Difficulties in using the technique stem primarily from the problem of how to measure advantageous traits once they are defined.

SUGGESTED FURTHER READING

Ghiselli, E. E., "Traits Differentiating Management Personnel," *Personnel Psychology,* no. 12, 1959.

Porter, L. W., and M. M. Henry, "Job Attitudes in Management," *Journal of Applied Psychology,* no. 48, 1964.

Randle, C. W., "How to Identify Promotable Executives," *Harvard Business Review,* no. 34, 1956.

TRANSPORTATION NETWORK AND MATRIX METHOD

Areas for use in Cost Control:

ORGANIZATIONAL AND OPERATIONAL SYSTEMS

INDUSTRIAL APPLICATIONS

The transportation network and matrix method is a means of analyzing delivery cost data to establish the lowest-cost delivery route. Relative costs are established between all points on a map of delivery points, assigning the number 1 to the lowest cost (see Fig. 106).

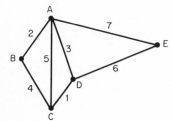

Figure 106. Transportation network chart of relative costs.

Relative cost numbers are then transferred to a transportation relative cost matrix (see Table 53). Points that can only be reached via a third point are indicated with an X.

Using the transportation relative cost matrix, routing is analyzed for possible cost reductions in overall routing. Each delivery point is tested against all other points in the network, as shown in the following equations, by adding all possible movements.

Table 53. Typical Transportation Relative Cost Matrix

	A	B	C	D	E
A	0	2	5	3	7
B	2	0	4	X	X
C	5	4	0	1	X
D	3	X	1	0	6
E	7	X	X	6	0

Unknown factors (those indicated by an X) from routes that must pass through a third point are carried into the comparisons.

AA + AB = 0 + 2 = 2
AB + BB = 2 + 0 = 2
AC + CB = 5 + 4 = 9
AD + DB = 3 + X = 3 + X
AE + EB = 7 + X = 7 + X

After the A-to-B route is compared in all possible combinations, the A-to-C route comparison is drawn up, and so on for each letter in the matrix. The lowest-link value for each route is then chosen, and a notation is made of alternate routes. A new matrix is then drawn up to show lowest-link values, at the same time clarifying X links by the lowest combination of routes (see Table 54). For example, BE could be reached by BAE (2 + 7 = 9) or by BCDE (4 + 1 + 6 = 11), in Table 53. Obviously, the BAE route is the lowest-cost route.

Table 54. Typical Lowest-Link Cost Matrix

	A	B	C	D	E
A	0	2	4d	3	7
B	2	0	4	5^{a}_{c}	9a
C	4d	4	0	1	7d
D	3	5^{a}_{c}	1	0	6
E	7	9a	7d	6	0

In analyzing the *lowest-link cost matrix* (Table 54), alternate routes may appear, such as from B to D, which has the same value whether transportation is via A or C. In such a case, selection of the alternate that offers lowest-cost routing to the next delivery point is the best choice.

From this point, comparison of total routing costs is established. All route possibilities and their accompanying point values are itemized and added. Examples of these might be:

ABCDEA = 2 + 4 + 1 + 6 + 7 = 20
ABCADEA = 2 + 4 + 5 + 3 + 6 + 7 = 27
ADCBAEA = 3 + 1 + 4 + 2 + 7 + 7 = 24

Of these three examples, the first routing would cost the least to operate.

Success of using the transportation network and matrix method to reduce transportation costs depends on the accuracy of cost figures for transportation from point to point as well as on accurate calculations of matrix and network sums.

SUGGESTED FURTHER READING

Bruce, H. J., *How to Apply Statistics to Physical Distribution,* Chilton Company, Philadelphia, 1967.
Murphy, G. J., *Transportation and Distribution,* Business Books, London, 1972.

TRANSPORTATION PROGRAMMING See Mathematical Programming.

TRAVELING REQUISITION

Areas for use in Cost Control:

ORGANIZATIONAL AND OPERATIONAL SYSTEMS
PAPERWORK—DESIGN AND FLOW SYSTEMS
MATERIALS AND EQUIPMENT MANAGEMENT
INDUSTRIAL APPLICATIONS
BUSINESS AND COMMERCIAL APPLICATIONS

The traveling requisition is a permanent requisition form maintained for each item kept in inventory. When stock reaches the order point, the inventory clerk pulls the card and sends it to the buyer. The buyer places the order, records the data, and returns the card to the inventory clerk. Use of the method reduces costs by eliminating preparation of requisitions each time materials are needed. The traveling requisition may be used as a *purchase record* and an *inventory record,* eliminating the need for preparation of these additional forms.

SUGGESTED FURTHER READING

Ammer, D. S., *Materials Management,* Irwin, Homewood, Ill., 1968.
Weiss, L. W., *Economics and American Industry,* Wiley, New York, 1961.

TURNOVER CONTROL

Area for use in Cost Control:

ORGANIZATIONAL AND OPERATIONAL SYSTEMS

According to F. J. Gaudet in *Supervisory Management Magazine,* a recent Los Angeles study shows that turnover cost per employee is at least $500. For skilled or managerial staff, the cost can be as much as the hourly rate of pay times 500. When such extras as employment agency fees, extensive training, and break-in time are combined, each managerial staff turnover can cost more than $5,000.

Breaking down turnover costs, these are the major cost areas:

Recruiting Costs. These may include advertising expense, employment agency fees, convention recruitment coverage, intercompany fees paid to employees who recommend a friend, educational facility coverage, publications for prospective employees, and all company personnel time used in the preparation or implementation of these programs.

One of the least costly methods of recruitment is that of recommendation from current staff. Usually, the cost is no more than a token honorarium of $25 or so to the employee who successfully recommends someone for employment.

Advertising in newspapers and magazines can be effective and reasonable in cost *if* the advertisements are prepared by someone who knows how to do it. Some key words are more likely to attract attention than others, for example. Content should be such that the prospective employee knows what the job has to offer and knows what will be required. Fewer answers may come from this sort of ad, but workers responding will be more suited for the position than would those responding to a vaguely worded ad. Use the company name rather than a box number. Many workers feel that "blind" advertisers have something to hide. Convention and educational facility coverage *can* be good methods of recruitment, but this cost is high. The recruiting officer is generally of management level, and both his or her time and expenses must be included (Table 55 shows typical recruitment trip cost).

Table 55. Typical Recruitment Trip Cost

Recruiting officer's salary: 4 days (1 day in transit, 3 days on site)	$400
Plane fare, round-trip	200
Hotel, meals, transportation	250
Total	$850

Whether or not recruiting trip costs are worthwhile depends largely on the number and quality of personnel hired.

Employment agency costs and effectiveness vary widely. Many large-city firms have escalated fees to as much as 15 percent of the annual salary. Yet some firms of this type still charge more reasonable fees, usually equivalent to one or two weeks' salary. Quality varies, too, with some agencies testing and checking references thoroughly while others do little or nothing.

Before using an agency, check fees and testing procedures thoroughly. In a few locations, new employees may pay the fee themselves, but this is generally undesirable and should be avoided. Employment agency use may be most economical when searching for a highly specialized employee.

Government-operated employment agencies are generally free. Testing is usually adequate, but little special effort is made to find exactly the type of person needed, so one will not be secured unless one happens along. Usually, government agencies can be best used in recruiting general or clerical labor.

Interviewing Costs. Once prospective employees are selected, it is necessary to begin a series of interviews. How many interviews are required depends partially on how the applicant was recruited. Newspaper ad applicants will require extensive testing, checking, and interviewing. Applicants reaching the company through convention or educational facility coverage, or through a reputable agency, can be directed to the person who will be their supervisor after a brief stop in the personnel department.

Interviewing should be kept to a minimum, since its costs are high (the interviewer's time, plus overhead). Table 56 shows the difference between hiring costs when inter-

Table 56. Typical Comparison of Hiring Costs in Heavy and Minimum Interviewing

Heavy interviewing—30 prospective employees		Minimum interviewing—10 prospective employees	
Personnel Dept., first interview: 30 × $2	$ 60.	Personnel Dept., first interview: 10 × $2	$20
Personnel Dept., supervisor interview, field narrowed to 10: 10 × $3	30	Floor supervisor, field narrowed to 3: 3 × $3	9
Department manager, field narrowed to 3: 3 × $3	9	Department manager, approval interview, field narrowed to 1: 1 × $3	3
Floor supervisor: 3 × $3	9	Hiring interview, personnel supervisor: 1 × $3	3
Hiring interview, personnel supervisor: 1 × $3	3		
Total	$111	Total	$35

viewing is extensive and when it is limited, assuming 15 minutes per interview. Such limitation can be accomplished by careful screening of application forms and application letters.

This case (Table 56) used such screening as a means to narrow the number of prospective employees to 10 before starting interviews. Once past the initial interview, prospects were seen by the floor supervisor (the person for whom the applicant would work) in the minimum-interviewing plan. In this way, the department head needed to interview only one person to be sure the prospective employee was satisfactory.

Hiring Costs. Reference checking, medical and psychological testing, and any necessary security checks are best limited to the one applicant who will be hired (provided the checks are positive). This policy controls moneys spent, since such checks are expensive (see Table 57).

Table 57. Typical Costs of Hiring Checks*

Reference checks:	
By letter, each	$ 2
Per average applicant	12
Medical testing, medical doctor	7
Psychological testing,	
management personnel	240
Security check	15+

*Cost Control and the Supervisor, American Management Assn., New York, 1966.

Training Costs. Cost of formal training varies widely, depending on the job filled. A few hours of instruction spread over the first week may suffice for simple jobs while specialized areas will require greater amounts of training. Experts assume a minimum of $100 in starting training, and this figure can climb to as much as $1,000 per employee when small groups and lengthy-method instruction are used, as they are in management trainee or sales trainee programs.

The **training** section gives specific cost reduction ideas for employee training.

Severance Costs. In addition to costs for the new employee, the company has severance costs, including its requirement to fulfill certain financial obligations to the employee who is leaving. These include:

Severance pay
Earned vacation pay
Severance interviews
Earned profit sharing

Little can be done to reduce these costs, which are determined by the terms of employment, with the exception of the *severance interview*. This interview is frequently skipped in smaller firms, but paperwork management may make it a worthwhile expenditure. If properly conducted, it can provide guidance as to the reasons for turnover, helping the employer to avoid the problem in the future if such knowledge is applied.

See also **Lump Hiring.**

SUGGESTED FURTHER READING

Cost Control and the Supervisor, American Management Assn., New York, 1966.

TWO-BIN SYSTEM

Areas for use in Cost Control:

MATERIALS AND EQUIPMENT MANAGEMENT
INDUSTRIAL APPLICATIONS
BUSINESS AND COMMERCIAL APPLICATIONS

The two-bin system is a method used to reduce inventory costs. One "bin" or storage area holds an amount of material equaling that needed for lead time and a safety margin. The second "bin" or storage area contains all remaining materials. When the second "bin" is empty, materials equaling the amount in the first "bin" are ordered, and use of the "bins" is reversed in order so that the older materials are used first.

Costs can be reduced by use of the method since detailed inventory records are not used. The system is particularly useful in controlling purchasing and inventorying of office supplies, as well as repair and operating materials. Production material control, with fluctuating lead times, is not suited to the method.

SUGGESTED FURTHER READING

Ammer, D. S., *Materials Management,* Irwin, Homewood, Ill., 1968.

TYPING COST CONTROL

Areas for use in Cost Control:
ORGANIZATIONAL AND OPERATIONAL SYSTEMS
PAPERWORK DESIGN AND FLOW SYSTEMS
MATERIALS AND EQUIPMENT MANAGEMENT
BUSINESS AND COMMERCIAL APPLICATIONS

Costs of typing letters, forms, and other materials can be systematically reduced through a number of methods.

Output Review. Current typing production can be measured and evaluated by having each typist make an extra carbon of each item typed for a predetermined period such as a day, a week, or a month. The typist records time not spent typing during this period. Average number of words typed per minute or hour can then be determined or estimated, as can time used on other work and wasted time. Using this review as a basis, cost-saving methods such as mechanization, better supervision and control, and more efficient work organization can be applied.

Mechanization. Several forms of mechanization have been developed to reduce typing costs. *Audio typing* consists of a dictating machine used to record material, which is later transcribed into typewritten form by a typist. Use of the method allows great freedom of work organization and limits interruptions of phone calls or visits to one, rather than two, employees. Accuracy is increased since the material can be heard repeatedly by the typist, if necessary.

Automatic typewriters, in varying degrees of sophistication, have also been developed. In some models, a tape is made of the material to be typed. This tape, when inserted into the typewriter, types the material at very rapid speeds. The method is particularly useful for form letters requiring a few personal name insertions.

Fully automated typewriters that type directly from the dictated material are also in use, although present models have limited vocabulary capacity. This restriction will undoubtedly be eliminated in the future.

Typing Pools. Use of several typists to do a large amount of work reduces costs compared with the one executive–one secretary system (*see also* **Pooling of Work**). The workload is more evenly spread, with the pool supervisor deciding priority of work and distributing it evenly. Here, typists expect to work continuously at whatever is given to them and not just on material from "their" boss or department.

Other. Use of correction paper will make typed corrections a faster process; and many companies find that carbons (unless being sent out of the company) do not need to be corrected, a practice further reducing correction time.

Acoustical booths increase accuracy and speed of audio typing, since outside office noise is reduced. Conversely, dictation noise from the recording is not so likely to disturb other workers.

Dictionaries, frequently used addresses, and a glossary of industry terms should be within arm's reach of each typist for ready reference.

See also **Typing Policy Control.**

SUGGESTED FURTHER READING

Longman, H. H., *How to Cut Office Costs,* Anbar Publications, London, 1967.

TYPING POLICY CONTROL

Areas for use in Cost Control:

ORGANIZATIONAL AND OPERATIONAL SYSTEMS
MATERIALS AND EQUIPMENT MANAGEMENT
BUSINESS AND COMMERCIAL APPLICATIONS

Some areas of typing cost control are dependent on managerial policy and the use of typing services. These include:

Limitation. Many memos, form letters, speech drafts, etc., are typed when the original handwritten draft or duplicated copy would serve the purpose just as well.

Additionally, material should not be typed until it is in finished form. Constant retyping of a speech, making minor changes each time, is a cost-waster.

Careful Dictation. This is particularly important when Dictaphones or other audio typing equipment are used, since the typist cannot ask to have a word repeated when it is mumbled or otherwise garbled. A good practice is for the person dictating material to listen to his or her own dictation at regular intervals to check it for clarity.

Form Design. Forms should be designed by management to allow for standard typewriter spacing to reduce time spent in regulating carriage alignment. Window envelopes save addressing time and are satisfactory for many uses.

Letter format should be designed to save time and costs, too. For example, a block format with heading, salutation, letter body, and closing all blocked along the left-hand margin, with double spacing between paragraphs rather than indentations, should reduce output time and cost.

Carbonset forms and second sheets are another time-saver and should be included whenever possible.

Provide Motivation. Some companies, particularly Japanese firms, hold periodic contests of typing speed and accuracy. The competitive atmosphere motivates increased work output and provides the typist with a standard to measure his or her own work by. Prizes for top performance, of course, provide an additional motivation and may be more effective than incentive payment plans, since continuing typing production is sometimes difficult to measure.

SUGGESTED FURTHER READING

Longman, H. H., *How to Cut Office Costs,* Anbar Publications, London, 1967.

UNIFORM COSTING

Areas for use in Cost Control:

ORGANIZATIONAL AND OPERATIONAL SYSTEMS
INDUSTRIAL APPLICATIONS
BUSINESS AND COMMERCIAL APPLICATIONS

Uniform costing is the technique of using *standardized* methods of:

1. Classification of accounts
2. Cost definitions
3. Account content
4. Depreciation methods
5. Data recording and reporting
6. Overhead cost allocation
7. Wage systems
8. Materials accounting

Use of the technique makes cost comparison simpler, increases operating efficiency, and aids pricing. Interfirm cost comparisons are possible via the technique and can produce extended cost controls through a greater understanding of industrywide costs.

SUGGESTED FURTHER READING

Backer, Morton, and L. E. Jacobsen, *Cost Accounting: A Managerial Approach,* McGraw-Hill, New York, 1964.
Batty, J., *Management Accountancy,* MacDonald, London, 1971.
Moonitz, Maurice, and A. C. Littleton, *Significant Accounting Essays,* Prentice-Hall, Englewood Cliffs, N.J.

UNIQUE-USER TECHNIQUE

Areas for use in Cost Control:

MATERIALS AND EQUIPMENT MANAGEMENT
INDUSTRIAL APPLICATIONS
BUSINESS AND COMMERCIAL APPLICATIONS

The unique-user technique is a method used to reduce the costs of materials or goods purchased when such costs are industry-priced. Material or goods specifications are slightly altered, giving the negotiation "unique" status and eliminating industry prices. Price may then be negotiated freely between seller and buyer. For example, retail chain stores frequently buy brand-name goods with a few specifications altered and rebranded under their "house" name at lower cost than virtually the same goods carrying the major brand name.

SUGGESTED FURTHER READING

Ammer, D. S., *Materials Management,* Irwin, Homewood, Ill., 1968.

UNITY OF COMMAND TECHNIQUE

Areas for use in Cost Control:

ORGANIZATIONAL AND OPERATIONAL SYSTEMS
INDUSTRIAL APPLICATIONS
BUSINESS AND COMMERCIAL APPLICATIONS

The unity of command technique allows only one supervisor to give orders or instructions to an employee. If other supervisors have something the employee should do, the instructions are routed via the employee's supervisor. Use of the technique limits confusion and overlapping of work, thus reducing costs.

SUGGESTED FURTHER READING

Pugh, D. S., ed., *Organization Theory,* Penguin, Baltimore, 1971.

UNITY OF DIRECTION METHOD

Areas for use in Cost Control:

ORGANIZATIONAL AND OPERATIONAL SYSTEMS
INDUSTRIAL APPLICATIONS
BUSINESS AND COMMERCIAL APPLICATIONS

The unity of direction method is the use of only one chief executive and one plan for a group of activities having the same goal. Use of the method avoids confusion and unnecessary double or overlapping performance of work, thus reducing labor costs.

SUGGESTED FURTHER READING

Pugh, D. S., ed., *Organization Theory,* Penguin, Baltimore, 1971.

UNIVERSAL PRODUCT CODING

Areas for use in Cost Control:

ORGANIZATIONAL AND OPERATIONAL SYSTEMS
MATERIALS AND EQUIPMENT MANAGEMENT
BUSINESS AND COMMERCIAL APPLICATIONS

Universal product coding is the use of electronic-sensitive coding, applied to products at time of manufacture, for rapid and low-cost checkout in self-service retail stores. The price code—a series of small lines on the bottom of the product—passes over a scanner which automatically adds the amount to the customer's bill and removes the product from inventory. Price changes, normally requiring 20 percent of supermarket work time, for example, are effected by simple changes of the price symbol in the computer data bank. Reduction of employee pilfering, fewer salesclerk hours, less clerk training, and faster and less costly accounting and inventorying are some of the areas where reduced costs are possible by using the system.

SUGGESTED FURTHER READING

Lapedes, D. N., ed., *Yearbook of Science and Technology,* McGraw-Hill, New York, 1974.

UTILITY THEORY

Areas for use in Cost Control:

ORGANIZATIONAL AND OPERATIONAL SYSTEMS
INDUSTRIAL APPLICATIONS
BUSINESS AND COMMERCIAL APPLICATIONS

Utility theory is an **operations research** technique used to determine the size and implications of a potential risk. The technique attempts to measure what a specific risk is worth to a company, so that risk costs can be reduced to the minimum possible.

Assume a company is considering three new products: Product A may earn $290,-000 a year or lose as much as $120,000; B may earn $130,000 a year or lose as much as $100,000; and C may earn as much as $50,000 a year or lose as much as $20,000. Which should be produced?

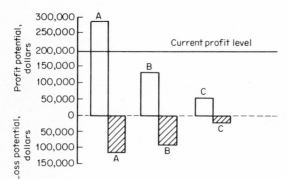

Figure 107. Utility theory chart.

A graph should be prepared showing the possible range of profit or loss, compared with current profit figures (see Fig. 107).

Looking at the example in Fig. 107, it can be seen that risks of Product A are far too great for the company to consider, since a loss would use up almost 70 percent of their current annual profits of $200,000. Product B is also too risky under most circumstances, since a loss could use half of current profits. Product C is a good risk and can increase profits by 25 percent if successful. A rule of thumb is to choose products with profit potentials of 40 percent or less of current profits and loss potentials of 10 to 20 percent or less.

SUGGESTED FURTHER READING

Wicks, C. T., and G. A. Yewdall, *Operational Research,* David & Charles, London, 1971.

VACATIONS AND HOLIDAYS

Areas for use in Cost Control:

PSYCHOLOGICAL MOTIVATIONAL MANAGEMENT
FINANCIAL MOTIVATIONAL MANAGEMENT
INDUSTRIAL APPLICATIONS
BUSINESS AND COMMERCIAL APPLICATIONS

Vacations and holidays are welcomed by employees, but they provide executives with many additional problems. In most countries, the time off from work is given with pay—even for manual labor. Vacations usually start at two weeks per year, and long-term employees may be entitled to as much as six weeks annually. In addition, there may be as many as 16 paid holidays. At the maximum, then, a company may be paying employees for more than eight weeks (assuming a five-day working week) that they do not work—before such days as sick days are counted.

FINANCIAL MOTIVATION

Originally, paid vacations and holidays were intended to be a financial motivator. But as they have become so widespread, employees tend to take them rather for granted. If you want this costly benefit to serve as a motivator, it will be necessary to think up a new approach. The following suggestions should provide financial incentives for the employee without raising the already high cost of vacations to the employer.

Vacation or holiday bonuses may be put into effect a short time before the time off occurs. A small amount is paid on top of ordinary bonus systems for as short a time as a day to a week before employees are to take their vacation. This not only provides a bit more money if the employee keeps production at top pace; it also keeps workers from falling into the common pre-holiday slump and calls attention to the fact that they are about to take a *paid-for* vacation.

Company property may be used for vacations by employees. This may be limited to managerial employees in a large firm or may be open to everyone in a smaller organization. Property, such as a remote cabin by a lake, can be written off as a company expense at tax time if it is used for company business—conferences and meetings—and, of course, the employee vacation-spot benefit. Even if employees prefer not to spend their vacation in a remote, rural area, and even if the schedule works out so that the time preferred for vacation is not available, the employees will be very much aware that the firm is supplying a vacation spot for them—an extra benefit not provided by all employers.

A vacation trip for two may be awarded to the top producer during a set, pre-vacation time period. This will not only increase the winner's production but the production of the entire staff as well. If this bonus is given annually, it should serve as a good incentive.

Holiday pay plans are essential motivators for those few companies that do not give paid vacations. In these systems, each employee has a holiday savings book. Weekly amounts are deducted from the employee's pay check, accumulating in his or her "account"; and the sum is paid when vacation time arrives. Of course, the incentive is much stronger if the company adds an equal amount or at least pays interest on the sum saved.

VACATION SCHEDULING

Some factories simply close down for a period of two weeks or a month, to fit their vacation needs. A few offices do the same, particularly in Europe. But this is not desirable for many businesses. Setting up a vacation schedule will allow you to make certain that all key people in any one area are not absent at the same time.

When employees are entitled to three or four weeks of paid vacation, they may be encouraged to split the time—particularly if their work is so important that a three- or four-week absence would create a problem. Checking the schedule, it should be possible to determine a satisfactory time for employees—yet not place too heavy a load on replacement workers.

Once the vacation schedule is drawn up, a second schedule should be started to show who will do the vacationing employee's work. The following checklist provides some sources of replacement:

1. Have a similar worker in another department cover the vacationer's essential work.

2. Divide the work among employees with lightest workloads during the vacation period.

3. Recall suitable layoffs temporarily.

4. Use temporary employees, hired either through an agency or by advertising on your own. Students may provide a source of temporary employees during the summer months, and they will work for lower hourly wages than will agency workers. But agency workers will be tested and interviewed by the agency, saving executive time. Some firms call in retired or semiretired employees for temporary vacation coverage.

Whoever replaces the vacationing employee, make sure that he or she spends some time together with the vacationer before the vacation begins. If this is impossible, the employee should write out detailed instructions for essential duties for her or his replacement.

Use the vacation period as a test for possible overstaffing. During vacations, keep a close eye on how many temporary employees are actually needed and how much of the work can be absorbed internally. This time is a perfect way to check staff levels; you may find that the work can be done just as well with one or two employees less.

THE HOLIDAY SLUMP

Both before and after a holiday or vacation, work efficiency slows down. This is particularly true with multiple holidays, which are becoming more and more popular with trade unions. Looking forward to a three- or four-day weekend, employees are apt to slow down before in anticipation and to be tired or let down at the end of the period.

One of the best ways to keep production near normal levels is to try to harness pre-holiday high spirits. This may mean planning a company social event at major holidays to encourage a feeling of togetherness. Or the supervisor may initiate more frequent breaks during working hours as a means of releasing excess anticipation. After the holiday, tighten supervision in a friendly way so that workers will know that steady production is expected. Try to schedule something special then—even if it is only free doughnuts at coffee-break time—to give workers the feeling that all the fun is not over until the next holiday.

SUGGESTED FURTHER READING

Cost Control and the Supervisor, American Management Assn., New York, 1966.

VALUE ADDED CONCEPT

Areas for use in Cost Control:

ORGANIZATIONAL AND OPERATIONAL SYSTEMS
INDUSTRIAL APPLICATIONS

The value added concept measures the costs added at each stage of production, as well as profits, and is used to measure the cost efficiency of each stage. The greater the value added, the theory states, the greater the potential sales profit and the lower the proportion of *conversion costs* (labor, administration, etc.) required.

Labor efficiency is measured by computing the percentage of total value added costs attributable to labor at various periods of time. Such wages are frequently measured as *value added per man-hour.*

Value added figures can also be used in setting production and sales goals, in budgeting, and as a negotiating point in labor bargaining.

Most European companies calculate consumer goods taxes by a value added figure (*see* **Value Added Tax Control**).

Value added can be determined by adding:

Gross profits
Depreciation
Rent, property taxes, and insurance
Wages and salaries
Benefits
Advertising and public relations
Consultant or other professional fees
Interest
Administration costs
Overheads

SUGGESTED FURTHER READING

Engineering Employers Federation, *Value Added as an Instrument of Management Discipline,* Kogan Page, London, 1972.
Wagner, H. M., *Principles of Management Science,* Prentice-Hall, Englewood Cliffs, N.J., 1970.

VALUE ADDED TAX CONTROL

Areas for use in Cost Control:

ORGANIZATIONAL AND OPERATIONAL SYSTEMS
INDUSTRIAL APPLICATIONS
BUSINESS AND COMMERCIAL APPLICATIONS

The value added tax is a tax against the value of *each* production or sales process of products and services. Varying rates may apply to different products or services, and some products or services may be zero-rated or exempt. The tax method began in Europe in the early 1970s and is spreading to other areas. Costs of the tax can be reduced by:

1. Limiting the number of processes used wherever possible
2. Eliminating dealings with any middle agent whose handling of the product incurs an additional tax
3. Reclaiming taxes for inputs on zero-rated products or services (taxes cannot be reclaimed for inputs on exempt-rated products or services)

SUGGESTED FURTHER READING

Ball, R. J., and P. Doyle, *Inflation,* Penguin, Baltimore, 1972.
Hanson, J. L., *A Dictionary of Economics and Commerce,* MacDonald, London, 1974.

VALUE ANALYSIS

Areas for use in Cost Control:

ORGANIZATIONAL AND OPERATIONAL SYSTEMS
INDUSTRIAL APPLICATIONS
BUSINESS AND COMMERCIAL APPLICATIONS

Value analysis, also called value engineering, is a technique used to reduce purchasing cost by analyzing the value of goods or services purchased in relation to their use and systematically substituting designs, components, or materials of lower cost that give the minimum performance required.

Factors of each item or service used in production that should be analyzed include:

1. Its purpose.
2. Its location of use.
3. The way it is used.
4. Can another item or service be substituted for it?
5. Can it be discarded?
6. Can material used in its manufacture be changed?
7. Can its size or shape be changed for easier manufacture?
8. Can it be improved?
9. Can alternate production methods save costs?
10. Is equipment adequate for quantities used?
11. Relationship of material, labor, and overhead cost to sales.
12. Is it available at lower cost?

Knowledge of these factors should serve as a control for costs and waste. Once cost-saving changes in use of material, equipment, or work methods have been determined, they should be implemented, beginning with those changes that will save the most money first but gradually making all acceptable and lower-cost changes in design, components, materials, and/or methods.

SUGGESTED FURTHER READING

Bull, George, ed., *The Director's Handbook,* McGraw-Hill, London, 1969.

VARIABLE COSTS

Areas for use in Cost Control:

ORGANIZATIONAL AND OPERATIONAL SYSTEMS
INDUSTRIAL APPLICATIONS

Variable costs are those that alter directly in proportion to volume of output and other measures of activity, such as production lot size, utilization of plant, and continuity of production. Costs that have a use rather than a time function generally are variable costs. *See also* **Overhead Cost Control.**

SUGGESTED FURTHER READING

Dickey, R. I., *Accountant's Cost Handbook,* Ronald Press, New York, 1960.
Hart, H., *Overhead Costs,* Heinemann, London, 1973.

VARIANCE ANALYSIS

Areas for use in Cost Control:

ORGANIZATIONAL AND OPERATIONAL SYSTEMS
PAPERWORK DESIGN AND FLOW SYSTEMS
INDUSTRIAL APPLICATIONS
BUSINESS AND COMMERCIAL APPLICATIONS

Variance analysis is a systematic checking of all budgetary cost aspects that deviate from the preset figure to see why the cost differs and to determine a means of controlling the deviation.

In practicing variance analysis, the following steps should be followed:

1. When actual costs differ from budgetary figures, determine the *cause* of the difference.

2. Once the cause of the variance is determined, the managerial employee responsible for that area of work should be asked to explain why the difference occurred and what should have been done to control it. *See also* **Responsibility Accounting.**

3. The management employee responsible for the work area of the cost difference should meet with other managerial staff to set up means of controlling such costs (of holding them to the standard figure) in the future, and such control should be immediately implemented at the point of the excess cost.

4. Reports on control of the variance should be issued to share knowledge of the problem with the entire managerial staff.

5. For deviations in budget costs which cannot be controlled by the company (such as an increase in government taxation of the firm), budgetary figures must be changed.

The most effective cost control is achieved by dividing variance analysis into two main areas of application: one concerned with profits and the other with production and costs.

PROFIT VARIANCE ANALYSIS

In applying this part of the technique, the executive must consider why the budgeted profit has not been reached and must take steps to correct this problem to come as near to the budgeted profit as possible. Profit factors to be considered in such an analysis include the following:

1. *Capital Return.* Current return should be compared with return in previous years and with return in similar companies. Reasons for upward- or downward-moving capital return should be determined. After corporate taxes, a return of 15 percent or more should be the minimum goal.

2. *Sales Profit.* Profit margins should be checked against those of previous years, considering sales volume. For example, if a company had a $100,000 profit with sales of $400,000 five years ago but this year had a $100,000 profit on sales of $600,000, sales allowances may now be too generous, prices may not be competitive, or selling and distribution costs may be excessive. Market changes and possible production changes should also be taken into consideration. The profit margin should be 10 percent or more in an efficiently operated business.

3. *Sales Ratio Compared with Capital.* Volume of sales annually should be about twice the amount of capital investment. If this is not true, determine which area is causing the problem, production or sales. Lower production inventory, better machine utilization, and better personnel utilization are the key factors used in controlling this ratio. Automation will become increasingly more important as the answer to such a problem.

4. *Government Intervention.* Increased taxation may be responsible for not reaching a budgeted profit. Although many aspects of taxation cannot be controlled by management, it is wise to know areas of cost control that do affect taxation.

5. *Sales Values.* Profit is dependent on pricing by competitors, as well as on production and sales costs. A cost-plus profit margin system of pricing may have to be discarded to meet such competition. Meeting the budgeted profit figure is then dependent on cutting production costs.

PRODUCTION AND COST VARIANCE ANALYSIS

In examining the deviation of budgeted production and cost figures, the following factors should be considered:

1. *Labor.* Determine reasons for any costs higher than budgeted. Planning required for cost control includes job specification writing to ensure having the type and number of workers needed, as well as use of a standardized pay scale to ensure payment comparable to skill required.

2. *Work Study.* This is needed in analysis of such costs to determine the most efficient use of workers, equipment, and materials. *See also* **Work Study and Measurement.**

3. *Material.* Compare cost and use of materials with previous production records when a variance occurs. Standard prices should be determined. If these cannot be met, quality of materials may be reduced; or conversely, price of the goods may be raised. If variances are caused by controllable causes, such as last-minute buying or purchase in uneconomical lot sizes, steps to correct this factor should be taken at once.

4. *Overheads.* Comparison of overhead costs with budgeted figures is difficult, since it is often impossible to determine the exact nature of an overhead. Flexible budget figures, or two-tiered budget figures, are often suggested for overhead costs by accounting experts. Analysis of a variance should try to pinpoint the source of the cost to determine the best method for its control. *See also* **Overhead Cost Control.**

As in profit variance, overhead variance may not be controllable. For example, if production consumes more time than anticipated, overhead costs will increase proportionately. These costs cannot be brought back to the budgetary figure by themselves, but can be corrected only if production efficiency meets its budgeted goals.

SUGGESTED FURTHER READING

Batty, J., *Corporate Planning and Budgetary Control,* MacDonald, London, 1970.
Veidt, Anthony, "The Men and the Boys and All That," *Car Magazine,* London, 1968.

VARIETY REDUCTION See Standardization.

VENDOR DELIVERY RATING

Areas for use in Cost Control:

ORGANIZATIONAL AND OPERATIONAL SYSTEMS
PAPERWORK DESIGN AND FLOW SYSTEMS
MATERIALS AND EQUIPMENT MANAGEMENT
INDUSTRIAL APPLICATIONS
BUSINESS AND COMMERCIAL APPLICATIONS

Vendor delivery rating is a system of evaluating suppliers' performance so that those vendors providing satisfactory delivery will be given preference when supplies are being purchased. Use of the method reduces costs, since receiving supplies on time is essential to maintaining production and sales schedules without overtime labor costs.

Vendor delivery ratings are usually given on a point scale of 0 to 100. Factors, weighted by the purchasing company's needs, may include the following:

1. Delivery time
2. Delivery quality
3. Paperwork accuracy and promptness
4. Sales literature and salesperson quality

SUGGESTED FURTHER READING

Lock, D., ed., *Management Techniques,* Directors Bookshelf, London, 1972.

VENDOR INVENTORYING TECHNIQUE

Areas for use in Cost Control:

ORGANIZATIONAL AND OPERATIONAL SYSTEMS
MATERIALS AND EQUIPMENT MANAGEMENT
INDUSTRIAL APPLICATIONS
BUSINESS AND COMMERCIAL APPLICATIONS

The vendor inventorying technique reduces company inventory costs by using the seller's facilities rather than the company's. Usual agreements, negotiated between buyer and seller, guarantee that a quantity of stocks sufficient for a predetermined period of use, are maintained by the seller for the buyer. In addition to removal of costs for the mechanics of storage (warehouse, clerks, etc.), little or no lead time is required and materials are paid for only as they are used.

SUGGESTED FURTHER READING

Ammer, D. S., *Materials Management,* Irwin, Homewood, Ill., 1968.

VENDOR RATING FORMULA

Areas for use in Cost Control:

ORGANIZATIONAL AND OPERATIONAL SYSTEMS
MATERIALS AND EQUIPMENT MANAGEMENT
INDUSTRIAL APPLICATIONS
BUSINESS AND COMMERCIAL APPLICATIONS

A vendor rating formula can be used as a guide to selecting the supplier who offers required quality material and service at the lowest possible cost. The basic formula assigns numerical value according to the importance of each factor in the company's operations, and according to past buying experience with a particular supplier.

Basic vendor rating formula:

$$\text{Price performance \%} = \frac{\text{low price (all suppliers)}}{\text{actual price}}$$

$$\text{Lead-time performance \%} = \frac{\text{shortest lead time (all suppliers)}}{\text{actual lead time}}$$

Typical numerical values used include:

Price: 40%
Quality: 35%
Delivery: 20%
Lead time: 5%

In addition to determining the efficiency of suppliers, the formula indicates the degree of favorable relationships the company has established with suppliers.

SUGGESTED FURTHER READING

Ammer, D. S., *Materials Management,* Irwin, Homewood, Ill., 1968.
Weiss, L. W., *Economics and American Industry,* Wiley, New York, 1961.

VENTURE MANAGEMENT

Areas for use in Cost Control:

ORGANIZATIONAL AND OPERATIONAL SYSTEMS
INDUSTRIAL APPLICATIONS

Venture management combines marketing, R&D, and production development to ensure that new products are designed, marketed, and produced at lowest possible cost and the greatest rate of efficiency. Interrelated factors, such as materials used, for example, can adversely affect production costs if these are not taken into consideration during the design stage of a new product. Markets should be determined prior to design completion, too, since these may affect quality and cost of materials required, production methods and costs, etc.

SUGGESTED FURTHER READING

Walley, B. H., *How to Make and Control a Profit Plan,* Business Books, London, 1969.

VERTICAL INTEGRATION

Areas for use in Cost Control:

ORGANIZATIONAL AND OPERATIONAL SYSTEMS
INDUSTRIAL APPLICATIONS
BUSINESS AND COMMERCIAL APPLICATIONS

Vertical integration is the linking of successive specialized operational steps (see Fig. 108). The technique reduces costs because it eliminates the middlemen and their profit

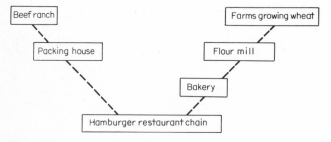

Figure 108. Vertical integration.

from any operation. For example, a nationwide hamburger chain may decide to raise its own beef, operate its own packing house, operate its own bakery, etc.

SUGGESTED FURTHER READING

Batty, J., *Corporate Planning and Budgetary Control,* MacDonald, London, 1971.
Burnham, T. H., and G. O. Hoskins, *Elements of Industrial Organization,* Pitman, London, 1965.

VERTICAL JOB LOADING

Areas for use in Cost Control:

PSYCHOLOGICAL MOTIVATIONAL MANAGEMENT
ORGANIZATIONAL AND OPERATIONAL SYSTEMS
INDUSTRIAL APPLICATIONS
BUSINESS AND COMMERCIAL APPLICATIONS

Vertical job loading is designing jobs so that work provides motivation factors to increase the employees' responsibility, achievement, growth, and recognition. Use of the method can reduce labor costs through increased productivity. Specific forms of vertical job loading include:

1. Giving employees more freedom to do their work in whatever way they please and maintaining accountability for successful completion of that work.
2. Providing complete work units to encourage the sense of achievement from successful production of a product.
3. Providing work of a difficulty in line with the employees' abilities.
4. Providing work requiring new skills or other growth factors.

SUGGESTED FURTHER READING

Herzberg, F., "One More Time: How Do You Motivate Employees," *Harvard Business Review,* vol. 46, 1968.
Vroom, V. H., *Work and Motivation,* Wiley, New York, 1964.

VERTICAL ROUND TABLE TECHNIQUE See Personnel Morale Building.

VESTIBULE TRAINING

Areas for use in Cost Control:

ORGANIZATIONAL AND OPERATIONAL SYSTEMS
INDUSTRIAL APPLICATIONS
BUSINESS AND COMMERCIAL APPLICATIONS

Vestibule training is the training of new employees in hypothetical, rather than actual, work operations. Costs can be reduced by teaching the employee needed work method data before he or she actually enters the work stream. Such instruction can utilize waste materials and supplies rather than good materials and supplies, for example. The training area must duplicate the actual work area, however, if a smooth transition is to be made at the end of the training.

SUGGESTED FURTHER READING

Bittel, L. R., *What Every Supervisor Should Know,* McGraw-Hill, New York, 1974.

VIDEOTAPED METHODS STUDY

Areas for use in Cost Control:

ORGANIZATIONAL AND OPERATIONAL SYSTEMS
INDUSTRIAL APPLICATIONS

Videotaping work methods reduces costs and improves production efficiency in several ways. In the actual observation and recording of work methods, videotaping requires little floor space and is less costly than conventional observation. Recording is precise, and replays of the observation are possible for detailed examination when setting the standard times, devising simplified work methods, etc.

Workers can be asked to view their own performance as a training method in pointing out time-consuming or fatiguing motions. Group discussions by workers and management can be more effective when videotaped methods studies are used to show employee participation.

Equipment layout that adds to production cost is more easily observed with video-tape study, as overall work-area views will show repeated trips to and from materials and supplies locations, for example.

The film used in such a study can be reused at a later date, lowering the methods' supplies costs.

SUGGESTED FURTHER READING

Lapedes, D. N., ed., *Yearbook of Science and Technology,* McGraw-Hill, New York, 1974.

VIRTUAL MEMORY SYSTEM

Areas for use in Cost Control:

ORGANIZATIONAL AND OPERATIONAL SYSTEMS
DATA RETENTION—FILES AND RECORDKEEPING
MATERIALS AND EQUIPMENT MANAGEMENT
INDUSTRIAL APPLICATIONS
BUSINESS AND COMMERCIAL APPLICATIONS

The virtual memory system is a computer hardware system designed to reduce the costs of programming. Data stored on magnetic discs in the central processor can be rapidly transferred to low-storage-capacity programming equipment which, prior to the system, was unable to transfer data at the necessary high speed. This allows use of low-cost, minimum-storage programming units for maximum programming output.

SUGGESTED FURTHER READING

Voysey, Hedley, "Computers," *The Guardian,* Sept. 27, 1974, London.

V-MASK TECHNIQUE

Areas for use in Cost Control:

ORGANIZATIONAL AND OPERATIONAL SYSTEMS
MATERIALS AND EQUIPMENT MANAGEMENT
INDUSTRIAL APPLICATIONS

The V-mask technique is a method used to measure cost or quality changes as recorded on a control or *Cusum* chart. Use of the technique provides early detection of quality problems and can thus reduce costs.

A V-shaped mask is placed on the chart with the latest factor observation placed at Θ. The point of the V lies precisely ahead of the current observation. If past observations are inside the V (see Fig. 109), cost or quality levels are acceptable. If they are outside the V, action is to be taken (see Fig. 110). The distance from Θ to the front of the V, D, and the distance between the V's arms at Θ, may vary. These are usually determined by testing various distances on past quality-control charts to calculate the acceptable level of cost or quality variance.

SUGGESTED FURTHER READING

Chatfield, C., *Statistics for Technology*, Penguin, Baltimore, 1970.
Rickmers, A. D., and H. N. Todd, *Statistics*, McGraw-Hill, New York, 1967.

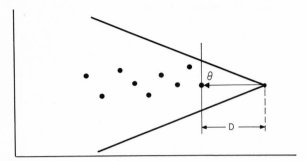

Figure 109. V-mask over acceptable cost or quality observations.

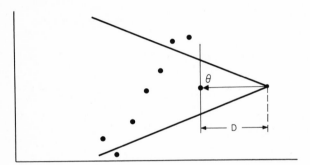

Figure 110. V-mask over unacceptable cost or quality observations.

VROOM'S THEORY OF MOTIVATION

Area for use in Cost Control:

PSYCHOLOGICAL MOTIVATIONAL MANAGEMENT

V. H. Vroom, an industrial psychologist, has developed a theory of motivation stating that the need for any goal is related to the probability that accomplishing the goal will not end all needs or wants but will free the individual to want to achieve additional goals. In addition, Vroom says, the greater the individual's desire to reach a specific goal, the more likely the person is to take definite action to do so. Thus, a management trainee who wants very badly to reach the top management level, or a specific salary level, will work very hard to do so. If employees at any level can be motivated to want something from their job—higher salary, more responsibility, greater respect, etc.—they will work harder, reducing labor and/or management costs.

Vroom, basing much of his theory on the work of social psychologist Kurt Lewin, suggests that the individual company should evaluate job satisfaction of its employees by looking at turnover and absentee rates. If employees are satisfied with their job and the goals it provides, they will be more likely to stay with the company and will be more likely to not be absent from work.

SUGGESTED FURTHER READING

Vroom, V. H., *Work and Motivation*, Wiley, New York, 1964.

WAGE FREEZE

Areas for use in Cost Control:

ORGANIZATIONAL AND OPERATIONAL SYSTEMS
INDUSTRIAL APPLICATIONS
BUSINESS AND COMMERCIAL APPLICATIONS

A wage freeze, also called a pay pause, is the holding of wages and salaries at current levels in an attempt to control labor costs. Businesses sometimes apply such a freeze temporarily when cost/profit ratios are not satisfactory, either by formal announcement of the program to all employees or by an announcement to management that no wage increases will be permitted for a predetermined time, perhaps three to six months.

Various national governments have applied a temporary wage freeze policy to entire national economies in an effort to control inflation. Such governmental policies are usually accompanied by price controls, restricting industrial and business price increases except to cover increased material costs. *See also* **Inflation Cost Control.**

SUGGESTED FURTHER READING

Ball, R. J., and P. Doyle, eds., *Inflation*, Penguin, Baltimore, 1972.

WAGES AND SALARIES

Areas for use in Cost Control:

PSYCHOLOGICAL MOTIVATIONAL MANAGEMENT
FINANCIAL MOTIVATIONAL MANAGEMENT
PAPERWORK DESIGN AND FLOW SYSTEMS
INDUSTRIAL APPLICATIONS
BUSINESS AND COMMERCIAL APPLICATIONS

Many wage and salary plans are discussed in this book under their specific headings, such as **incentive payment systems;** but this section will serve as a guideline to trends in payment methods, as well as setting out the various methods used for paying different levels of employees.

The wage or salary paid an employee is the primary motivation for the employee to do the job properly, since being able to live in a satisfactory way depends upon the money received for doing the work. People who have been steadily employed with the same company for a period of years, and who are well paid, may tend to take their wage or salary for granted. When this happens, at least a part of the motivation is lost. For this reason, anything executives can do to call the employees' attention to salary will add an incentive factor.

Job reviews, whether held every six months or annually, provide a good opportunity to call the worker's attention to the money earned. If the worker is going to receive a raise, the reasons for the raise should be pointed out. If the employee will not receive a raise, the reasons for this should be given, too. Personal contact between the worker and the supervisor is important—whether the supervisor takes the employee out for lunch or draws him or her aside for a long coffee break. Job review time is an ideal time to call attention to the cash benefits the worker receives for doing the job well.

Convenience for the employee should be a factor in the method of payment. While almost all companies today pay their employees by check, care should be taken that payments are made for timing convenience. If paydays are normally every other Friday, for example, local banking hours should be considered. If the banks close at 3 P.M., pay checks should be distributed before the lunch hour so that workers can bank their money. Checks should be handed out by the employee's immediate supervisor, not an accounting department worker who is seen only on payday. This helps the employee to realize that he or she is responsible to the supervisor, and that the supervisor is responsible to management for the worker.

TYPES OF PAYMENT

Wages are generally payments made to blue-collar workers and are hourly rates or rates tied to the output of the employee. Hourly rates are particularly suitable for work that cannot be standardized or work not suited for top-speed production, such as on intricate mechanisms; work that cannot be quality-controlled by the employee (e.g., plastics); or work that cannot be measured exactly, such as maintenance.

Salaries are set sums of payment, made weekly, biweekly, or monthly, usually to white-collar employees. These payments usually cover a greater variety of types of work, making hourly or output-connected rates impossible.

Bonuses are exceptional payments, made over and above the wage or salary in return for some extraordinary performance of work.

Incentive payments may be a part of the wage or salary or an amount in addition to the wage, set up in connection with the worker's output and giving additional money when she or he produces more.

TRENDS IN WAGES

In the United States, real earnings—that is, the amount available for purchases— were level from about 1895 until 1914 at 15.1 cents per hour. By 1929, they had jumped to 52.2 cents per hour, and in 1972 they averaged $3.74 per hour. Benefits, such as medical insurance, which were nonexistent in the late 1800s, stood at an average of 18.1 percent of the worker's wages in 1972. The gap between white- and blue-collar employees had narrowed by 1971, too, with the average white-collar worker in the United States earning $153 per week, while the average blue-collar worker received $136.

Internationally, earnings have followed a somewhat similar upward curve, but wages vary considerably from country to country, depending partially on the costs of rent, food, and clothing in each area. Table 58 gives a brief comparison of wages on an international level.

Generally, more benefits are paid in Europe than elsewhere in the world. Family allowance benefits, for example, are paid by the employer in Italy, France, and Belgium. Companies in those countries pay 8 percent of wages as an allowance for the worker with a family to support.

COST REDUCTION AND WAGES

Cost reductions can generally be made in three areas:

1. Tying wages to production, ensuring that a specific amount of work is done for every dollar paid out.

2. Hiring and training carefully, particularly when the employee is salaried, to ensure that the salary dollar is used most effectively.

3. Setting up an efficient method of payment.

Tying wages to production is done primarily through various incentive programs (*see* **Incentive Payment Systems**). Using these techniques, it is possible to more nearly predetermine what the production or service cost will be for every item manufactured. In offices and retail stores, it may be more difficult to pay on production alone, since these jobs may vary considerably from one application to another. Even so, using incentive plans or bonuses designed for these purposes can cut costs by encouraging employees to increase their production.

Table 58. Comparison of Bus Drivers' Wages, July 1, 1970[1]

Country and city	Annual wage
U.S.A., New York	$9,330
Netherlands, Amsterdam	4,810
England, London	3,116
France, Paris	3,261
Sweden, Stockholm	6,637
Brazil, Rio de Janeiro	1,051
Italy, Rome	4,293
Japan, Tokyo	2,075
Switzerland, Zurich	5,004

[1]Study by the Union Bank of Switzerland.

Good hiring and training techniques are essential, not only to cut company turnover, but also to ensure that the best worker for the money is doing a specific job. Hiring techniques are detailed under **Turnover Control** and **Training,** while training methods are set out under **Training, Booster Training,** and **Career Trainee System.**

Setting up an efficient method of payment can cut not only accounting department time but also unnecessary banking charges. The following checklist provides items that need attention in establishing such a method:

1. *Frequency of Payment.* When deciding how often workers should receive their wages or salaries, much depends on the type of workers being paid. Generally, industrial production workers and lower-grade office employees have preferred a weekly pay check. If this can be changed to a biweekly payment without undue hardship, a good deal of time (and costs) can be saved through the less frequent pay check preparation.

   Many companies pay managerial employees once a month, assuming that they will be able to budget adequately for such a method, cutting costs even further. Less common is the European management payment system that pays executive staff once a quarter. Generally, it seems advisable to divide salary levels and to pay those salaries under a predetermined amount—perhaps $15,000 a year—every two weeks, while those above this salary are paid once a month.

   Additionally, in an inflationary economy, any wage payment lag means reduced costs, since the sum due will be automatically devalued by the rate of inflation.

2. *Time of Payment.* When to pay will depend largely on the company's local banking services. If, for example, the bank will pay interest on money held in an account until the 15th of each month, the firm may find it advisable to write pay checks on the 16th. Biweekly pay checks may be changed to twice-monthly checks on the same days of the month, perhaps the 15th and the 30th, for the same reason.

3. *Method of Payment.* Almost every business now pays by check, since this facilitates a smooth flow of paperwork, as well as providing a record of the payment. Most large companies find that wage and salary payments can be handled at lower cost if check preparation is programmed through a computer.

4. *Additional Payments.* It is important that bonus and incentive payments be added to the pay checks as soon after they are earned as possible. This also holds true for overtime payments. The incentive value of staying late and earning extra money, or of producing an extra number of products to increase the pay check, drops off sharply if a long period elapses before the employee receives the additional payment. Paperwork should be set up so that supervisors report such additions to pay checks daily, and payment should be added to the next check whenever possible.

SUGGESTED FURTHER READING

Bowan, W. G., *The Wage-Price Issue: A Theoretical Analysis,* Princeton University Press, 1960.
Standingford, Oliver, ed., *Newnes Encyclopedia of Management,* Newnes, London, 1967.
Richards, M. D., and W. A. Nielander, *Readings in Management,* South-Western Publishing Company, Cincinnati, 1969.
Ross, A. M., "The External Wage Structure," in Taylor and Pierson, *New Concepts in Wage Determination,* McGraw-Hill, New York, 1957.

WAREHOUSE EQUIPMENT SELECTION

Areas for use in Cost Control:

MATERIALS AND EQUIPMENT MANAGEMENT
INDUSTRIAL APPLICATIONS

Warehouse equipment selection can reduce handling and storage costs through:

1. Choice of short-turning equipment that reduces aisle space required, such as platform trucks and outrigger lift trucks (*see also* **Warehouse Layout Design**).

2. Increased capacity of equipment, depending on ratio of decreased aisle space cost/increased efficiency cost.

Studies of efficiency at various capacity levels will show optimum equipment, as well as providing a formula for determining the amount of equipment required per ton of goods moved for future use in equipment purchasing. Such studies should determine handling cycle time per load. Cost per pound of goods handled is calculated by multiplying equipment and employee time cost times cycle time, and dividing this product by the poundage capacity of the equipment used.

SUGGESTED FURTHER READING

Magee, J. F., *Physical Distribution Systems,* McGraw-Hill, New York, 1967.
Murphy, G. J., *Transportation and Distribution,* Business Books, London, 1972.

WAREHOUSE LAYOUT DESIGN

Areas for use in Cost Control:

ORGANIZATIONAL AND OPERATIONAL SYSTEMS
INDUSTRIAL APPLICATIONS

Warehouse layout design reduces goods storage costs through the most efficient physical layout of the storage place.

Placement method is the first decision to be made. Generally, goods are stored on pallets located on the square (Fig. 111) or angularly (Fig. 112).

Although *placement on the square* has no wasted storage space as *angular placement* does (see black areas), easier movement and narrower aisles possible in angular placement may reduce handling and storage costs more than enough to pay for such wasted

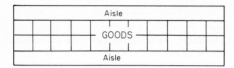

Figure 111. Storage placement on the square.

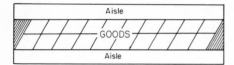

Figure 112. Angular storage placement.

space. Generally, angular placement is least expensive where the building area requires long aisles, while short aisles for storage are less costly with storage placement on the square.

Since *aisles* are wasted space, an important cost reduction factor is limiting their size as much as possible. Aisle width is determined by goods stored, equipment (such as fork-lift trucks) used in storage, and, as already noted, goods placement method. Calculation of minimum aisle width is made by adding equipment turning radius, length of pallet or goods, width of pallet or goods, and a safety clearance allowance. Outrigger lift trucks require less working area than do rider lift trucks, and these should be used where possible. Platform trucks may also save aisle space, but care must be taken to use a model with a platform larger than the maximum size of pallet to be stored.

Employee handling of such equipment affects aisle width requirements, too, and space costs saved by a very skillful driver who can turn the vehicle in the shortest possible distance will more than pay for the additional labor cost.

Pattern of goods location is the next decision in layout design. The area may be divided into zones, which are then assigned to various goods depending on size, frequency of removal, and amount of goods to be stored. Most frequently needed goods and/or largest goods should be located nearest the source of goods for maximum handling-cost reduction. *See also* **Cube/Order Index.**

Order pickup areas must also be added to the warehouse design. These may be arranged in one of three ways:

1. *Area pickup.* An employee assembles a customer's order from inventory, area by area, removing the entire order to a loading dock or shipping department.

2. *Zone pickup.* Employees in each zone deliver order components from their section to a central area.

3. *Coded pickup.* Orders are divided by zone with letter, number, or color codes on the order form. A copy of the order is sent to each zone affected, which, in return, sends goods to an assembly area.

Unless there is a reason for using method 2 or 3, such as restricted handling of government-contracted goods, the *area pickup* method will generally reduce handling and compilation costs.

SUGGESTED FURTHER READING

Magee, J. F., *Physical Distribution Systems*, McGraw-Hill, New York, 1967.
Murphy, G. J., *Transportation and Distribution*, Business Books, London, 1972.

WEAKNESS ANALYSIS

Areas for use in Cost Control:

ORGANIZATIONAL AND OPERATIONAL SYSTEMS
MATERIALS AND EQUIPMENT MANAGEMENT
INDUSTRIAL APPLICATIONS

Weakness analysis is the examination of product parts to determine the relative life span of each and subsequent reduction of quality and costs of stronger parts so that all product parts become inoperable at approximately the same time. For instance, when manufacturing an alarm clock, it is a waste of material cost to use body and parts that will last longer than the mainspring. Substitutions must, of course, be of a quality acceptable to the product's purchaser. For example, purchasers might not feel the clock was of adequate quality if a very cheap body material was used, even though this would last as long as the works.

SUGGESTED FURTHER READING

Radke, Magnus, *Manual of Cost Reduction Techniques*, McGraw-Hill, New York, 1972.

WEIGHTED COST PER THOUSAND TECHNIQUE

Areas for use in Cost Control:

ORGANIZATIONAL AND OPERATIONAL SYSTEMS
INDUSTRIAL APPLICATIONS
BUSINESS AND COMMERCIAL APPLICATIONS

The weighted cost per thousand technique is the determination of the lowest-cost effective advertising media by evaluation of cost per thousand of potential purchasers reached *and* the effect of the quality of the media on the prospects. The quality and effectiveness of the various media are used as criteria in making the choice of a particular medium. Factors to be considered include:

Percentage of total audience that are potential buyers. If a general-interest magazine has 50 percent adult female readers, for example, and the product to be sold is lipstick, divide circulation by 50 percent, and the advertising rate by this result. This figure is then multiplied by 1,000, providing the cost per thousand potential purchasers.

Personality of the media. An expensive perfume would reach more potential purchasers in a high-fashion magazine, for example, than in an inexpensive love story magazine, even though both media have primarily feminine readership. Most magazines survey reader incomes and preferences, and, using these figures, the company should estimate the percentage of readers who would be able to buy their product.

Overlap of the audience. This should be considered, too, and advertising should be placed to reach different segments of the market. If a television commercial has the cheapest cost per thousand potential buyers, for example, a company might be tempted to place all of its advertising there. But if the potential buyer sees the same advertisement a dozen times, much of the money will be wasted. One advertising study estimates that an ad's effectiveness increases each time the potential buyer sees it, up to four times.

Thereafter, the money would be better spent to reach a segment of the market that cannot be reached through television advertising.

SUGGESTED FURTHER READING

Kotler, Philip, *Marketing Management,* Prentice-Hall, Englewood Cliffs, N.J., 1972.
———, "Toward an Explicit Model for Media Selection," *Journal of Advertising Research,* March 1964.

WHITE LIST TECHNIQUE

Areas for use in Cost Control:

ORGANIZATIONAL AND OPERATIONAL SYSTEMS
INDUSTRIAL APPLICATIONS
BUSINESS AND COMMERCIAL APPLICATIONS

The white list technique is the listing of workers who are particularly efficient or productive to ensure that they are given priority on future work projects, reducing overall labor costs in proportion to the number of workers so listed and used. The method is particularly effective in work where casual labor is used, such as construction. The "list" may be an informal one, kept in the manager's head, if the company is small; or in a larger firm it may be a formal listing. The technique developed from Gilbreth's *white list cards,* which were cards testifying to a worker's performance standards and given to the worker to be used in obtaining preference when seeking work.

SUGGESTED FURTHER READING

Pollard, H. R., *Developments in Management Thought,* Heinemann, London, 1974.
Spriegel, W. R., and C. E. Myers, eds., *The Writings of the Gilbreths,* Irwin, Homewood, Ill., 1953.

WORK COUNT AND ANALYSIS

Areas for use in Cost Control:

ORGANIZATIONAL AND OPERATIONAL SYSTEMS
INDUSTRIAL APPLICATIONS
BUSINESS AND COMMERCIAL APPLICATIONS

Work count is a *work measurement* technique (*see* **Work Study and Measurement**) that shows how much of the employee's actual day is spent productively. The operation is first broken into work classifications, including:

1. *Planning and developing*
2. *Functional activities,* such as estimating or forecasting
3. *Physical activities*
4. *Waiting,* when work is dependent on a prior step in work flow
5. *Nonproductive break periods,* lunch hours, etc.

Random 15-minute samples of each employee's work are classified into these areas. After 100 or more such classification periods, a pattern should emerge showing how an employee spends his or her time.

Analysis of the work count is the next step; it includes investigation of these points:

1. Comparison of time spent by the average employee in this job with time spent by the particular employee examined.
2. Does the employee use the fastest method of work?
3. Could the job be combined with another step in the work flow for greater speed?
4. Would new equipment speed the work?

5. Can waiting time be reduced by changing the steps in the work flow?
6. Can breaks be timed to coincide with necessary waiting time?
7. Is the greatest proportion of working time spent on important facets of the work? Or is it spent on petty details?
8. Do the job factors coincide with job description factors?

Once the work count is taken and *analyzed,* an improved method of work should be established, using the study's findings, in the following steps:

1. Decentralization of work will be necessary if tasks have become overspecialized, limiting the work an employee can do.

2. Employees should be made aware of the standard of their work as compared with the average for their specific job.

3. If work standards are not available, they should be established through internal study.

4. Duplicate or unnecessary facets of the work should be eliminated. For example, copies of congratulatory letters need not be kept or filed.

5. Schedule employees' workloads to give peak-hour work to other departments with slack periods. For example, if the mail room has a slack midday period after mail has been distributed but before outgoing mail is heavy, employees may be assigned to direct mail duties, such as envelope stuffing, in the clerical pool. Work steps may be rescheduled, too, to even the departmental workload.

6. Calculate the number of employees actually needed for each task and cut any overstaffing. If the department is undermanned, use work count and analysis to show top management the need for additional employees.

SUGGESTED FURTHER READING

Cost Control and the Supervisor, American Management Assn., New York, 1966.

WORK ESTIMATION

Areas for use in Cost Control:

ORGANIZATIONAL AND OPERATIONAL SYSTEMS
MATERIALS AND EQUIPMENT MANAGEMENT
INDUSTRIAL APPLICATIONS
BUSINESS AND COMMERCIAL APPLICATIONS

Work estimation provides approximate work measurement data quickly and inexpensively, to be used where essentially correct but not precise measurement is needed (*see also* **Work Study and Measurement**). For example, the method may be used to determine the number of employees needed to work on a specific project. Use of the technique is lower in cost than more precise work measurement methods and can be substituted where precise data are not necessary.

Thee basic work estimation techniques include:

1. *Time estimation*—generally used to measure short-cycle repetitive or nonrepetitive work.
2. *Rated steady-state sampling*—used to measure long-cycle repetitive work.
3. *Analytical assessment*—used to measure long-cycle nonrepetitive work.

Time Estimation. For repetitive short-cycle work, several brief studies are made of the work done, timing the work cycle with a stopwatch. A dozen cycles may be timed, for example. These can be averaged and an extra time allowance added to determine approximate time and/or costs for the work.

The method is *not* suitable for determination of incentive payment plans or for setting standard times, which require more precise measurement.

Nonrepetitive short-cycle work can be estimated in the same way, the approximate length of time required to complete the task being averaged. If too few samples of the work are available, however, an estimate can be made by allocating times after as little as one observation of the task performed.

Rated Steady-State Sampling. This method measures approximately the time required for long-cycle repetitive work. A few random-time samples of very brief duration are taken for several jobs at one time. Job elements and cycle time are recorded for each brief random observation (usually five seconds in length) on an observation sheet until the curve steadies and a probable cycle time can be estimated. Sampling must be representative for successful estimation.

Analytical Assessment. Long-term nonrepetitive work time can be estimated using this technique. Such time is estimated by combining an average of detailed time studies from other companies for the same type of work, brief supplementary on-site time studies, and an experienced supervisor's estimate of the time required.

Mini-Work-Estimation Techniques. In addition to these three methods, quick time estimates are often made in the following ways:

1. Use of detailed time studies for similar work by other companies or for other jobs.
2. Measurement of a key job and estimation of other work by the work's proportion to the key job.
3. Rule-of-thumb estimates, such as increasing the number of employees in proportion to increased production requirements.
4. Averaging work-time estimates from several sources, such as independent contractors, supervisors, and operators.
5. Use of equipment manufacturers' estimated times.
6. Referral to old production and/or personnel records for similar work.
7. *Bracketing*—averaging the shortest and longest probable cycle times.
8. Use of mechanical tools, such as stopwatches, tape measures, cameras, and closed-circuit TVs, to monitor work.

SUGGESTED FURTHER READING

Clay, M. J., and B. H. Walley, *Performance and Profitability,* Longmans, London, 1965.

WORK FACTOR AND METHODS TIME MEASUREMENT See Predetermined Motion Time Systems (PMTS).

WORKING CONDITIONS IMPROVEMENT

Areas for use in Cost Control:

WORK PLACE

MOTIVATIONAL MANAGEMENT

The output of individuals can be increased by improving the conditions of their place of work, whether the work is done in an office or in a factory. The following checklist will help in establishing the quality of current conditions and will serve as a guide to needed improvements:

1. Is the working area arranged for usefulness? Frequently used materials, tools, and supplies should be near at hand, while the area should be free of the clutter

of seldom used items. Storage places should be positioned for convenience and some wall panelings should have multiple slots for shelves and cabinets, allowing employees to position these storage places where they choose. Most frequently used items should be located within easy reach so that workers do not have to get up.

2. Are seating arrangements designed for work tension relief? Chair backs, generally movable, should be positioned to support the back. Office equipment company representatives can show employees how to make this adjustment.

3. Are heights of assembly line, work tables, counters, and desks suitable for the average-height person?

4. Are furniture items correctly positioned? Desks should be arranged for privacy and lighting. Desks facing one another lead to distractions and poor distribution of light from any direction. Chairs should allow free movement of the legs.

5. Is the working place clean and pleasant? A coat of light, cheerfully colored paint on the walls and thorough, frequent cleaning help keep morale high. Dirty, dreary factory areas or offices discourage employees from doing their best work.

6. Does the area have good lighting? Lighting is best that comes from the front of the working area. Lighting company representatives can help test a particular working place by government standards. Direct and reflected glare are two factors that should be eliminated, since they cause strain and early tiring in the employee.

7. Are heating, cooling, and ventilation adequate? Best working conditions are at a temperature of about 68°F. Air, heat, and cooling air should be evenly distributed throughout the factory or office.

8. Is there a minimum of noise? In some factory installations, limitation of noise is almost impossible. Loud noises, however, do cause distraction; they may be controlled by dividing working areas with insulation board. Offices can be soundproofed to some degree by area dividers and carpeting.

9. Does the working place offer sufficient conveniences? These include an employee lounge with sufficient space, coat storage, clean, convenient toilet facilities with separate stalls for privacy, lunch rooms (preferably including availability of hot meals), drinking water, and vending machines with cigarettes, candy, gum, and feminine hygiene needs.

SUGGESTED FURTHER READING

Ansoff, H. I., ed., *Business Strategy*, Penguin, Baltimore, 1969.
Cemach, H. P., *Work Study in the Office*, MacLaren & Sons, London, 1969.

WORK SHARING

Areas for use in Cost Control:

PSYCHOLOGICAL MOTIVATIONAL MANAGEMENT
FINANCIAL MOTIVATIONAL MANAGEMENT
ORGANIZATIONAL AND OPERATIONAL SYSTEMS
INDUSTRIAL APPLICATIONS

Work sharing is the practice of distributing diminished workloads equally over an entire work force to avoid layoffs and to equalize employee opportunity to earn. Primary advantages of the practice are the financial motivation provided for employees by their having some work available and the psychological motivation provided by the increased job security of the technique. These advantages may be partially or wholly negated in firms with independent *sub-pay plans* (retainer paid to employees who are laid off to help them financially until recall) or in geographical areas with good governmental or private unemployment insurance coverage.

SUGGESTED FURTHER READING

Cunnison, S., *Wages and Work Allocation,* Tavistock, London, 1966.

WORK STRUCTURING

Areas for use in Cost Control:

PSYCHOLOGICAL MOTIVATIONAL MANAGEMENT
ORGANIZATIONAL AND OPERATIONAL SYSTEMS
INDUSTRIAL APPLICATIONS
BUSINESS AND COMMERCIAL APPLICATIONS

Work structuring is the practice of organizing jobs, so far as is possible while improving or maintaining production, to fit the skills, goals, and capacity of the individual employee. Primary advantage of the method is motivation from increased employee job satisfaction. *See also* **Job Enlargement; Job Enrichment.**

SUGGESTED FURTHER READING

Herzberg, F., *Work and the Nature of Man,* World Publishing, Cleveland, 1966.

WORK STUDY AND MEASUREMENT

Areas for use in Cost Control:

FINANCIAL MOTIVATIONAL MANAGEMENT
INDUSTRIAL APPLICATIONS

Work study means analyzing work with a goal of increased labor from each employee and a basis for paying wages in an amount comparable to production. Work study can be divided into two main areas—study of methods used and application of measurement. Often work study is used in determining rates paid in incentive programs (such as piece rate payments or bonus schemes), but it is also used to help any office or plant achieve better efficiency with existing staff and equipment.

STUDY OF METHODS

If work study is to be the basis of payment, then each job must be analyzed. If work study does not enter into the decision of how much salary to pay an employee, then use the following checklist as a guide to determine whether work study will be of any help to you in reducing costs for any one job:

1. Are costs of doing the job rising?
2. Has production output recently risen or fallen?
3. Is the increase in the amount of overtime needed greater than the increase in production?
4. Do employees have to move around the plant or office frequently in order to do their work?
5. Is equipment idle a good part of each day?
6. Is production frequently delayed by one specific department?

Find the Facts. Once the decision has been made to apply work study to a specific job, the first task is to define the problem and record all of the facts about it. Both *operation process charts* and *flow process charts* are commonly used.

The *operation process chart* shows graphically the steps, in sequence, of materials used, processing, and inspection for the job being surveyed. The chart records time used but not the location of work or the worker. Symbols, as shown in Fig. 113, are used to make references to the chart simpler.

○ = Operation

◱ = Delay

⇨ = Transportation

☐ = Inspection

▽ = Storage

Figure 113. Symbols used in charting.

Operations are numbered for reference and are linked together step by step. Two typical *operation process charts* are shown in Fig. 114.

Looking at the charts, it is easy to see that at least two steps in the sequence can be eliminated, thus saving costs. Steps 2 and 4 can be combined for the executive, as can steps 3 and 5. The secretary can take dictation for the policy and letter (steps 1 and 3)

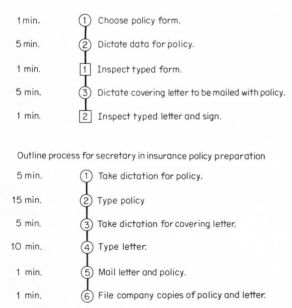

Outline process for executive in insurance policy preparation

1 min.	①	Choose policy form.
5 min.	②	Dictate data for policy.
1 min.	☐1	Inspect typed form.
5 min.	③	Dictate covering letter to be mailed with policy.
1 min.	☐2	Inspect typed letter and sign.

Outline process for secretary in insurance policy preparation

5 min.	①	Take dictation for policy.
15 min.	②	Type policy
5 min.	③	Take dictation for covering letter.
10 min.	④	Type letter.
1 min.	⑤	Mail letter and policy.
1 min.	⑥	File company copies of policy and letter.

Figure 114. Two typical outline process charts.

and type both items (steps 2 and 4) at one time, saving trips to and from the boss's office, as well as avoiding scheduling a second dictation session.

Flow process charting uses the same symbols as the *operation process chart* but adds movements and delays to operational and inspection steps. It can be used to chart the movement of workers or materials, but a separate chart for each must be drawn up (see

Fig. 115) if both are to be recorded. Time and distance, if desired, are recorded to the left of the chart.

A *multiple-activity chart* shows the amount of time used on each activity and the relationship of the worker and his or her equipment. Figure 116 is an example of this technique. Looking at the example in Fig. 116, we can see that the paint-spraying

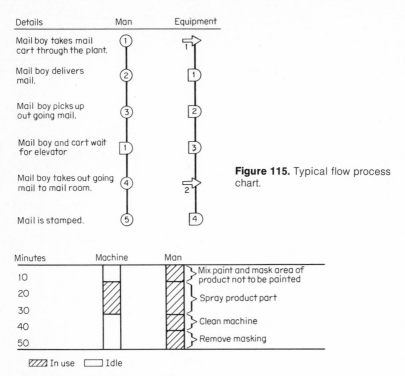

Figure 115. Typical flow process chart.

Figure 116. Typical multiple-activity chart.

equipment is idle a good part of the time. Figure 117 shows how the same machine can be used by two painters.

The *flow diagram,* another technique commonly used in work study, is a scale drawing of the work area, with locations numbered with symbols showing where activities are carried out. Directions of movement are indicated by a flow line.

A *string diagram* is a variation of the *flow diagram,* using various-colored strings moving from pins placed on the scale drawing of the work area.

EXAMINING WORK STUDY RESULTS

Once all of the aspects of a job are recorded, you must decide which steps can be improved. The following guidelines can help you analyze the records:

1. What work is done?
2. What additional work could be done at the same time?
3. Where is the work carried out?
4. Could it be done more efficiently in another location?
5. Who is responsible for the work?
6. Could it be more efficiently done by someone else?
7. Could the series of steps be shortened?

8. Could one or more of the steps be eliminated?
9. Could two or more of the steps be combined?
10. Could the actual motions involved in doing the work be more efficient?

AN IMPROVED METHOD

Recording the methods on paper, decide which steps to eliminate, which to combine, etc. Operating instructions for the new procedure should be written down and given to all employees, supervisory or labor, as they should immediately be involved in

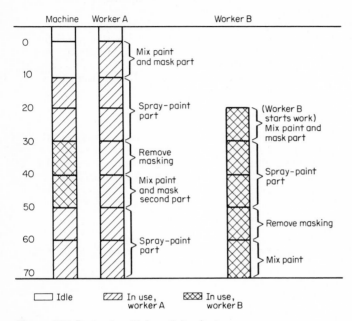

Figure 117. Revised multiple-activity chart.

installation of the new method. The following checklist will help in installing a new method of operation:

1. Check all steps of the new technique. Make sure that all needed tools and equipment are available.
2. Make certain that new materials are in place.
3. Design needed records.
4. Train employees and supervisors in the new method.
5. Request accounting department to set new wages for the method, if the work is to be done on piece rates.
6. Make sure employees have close supervision initially.
7. Check method in operation and make adjustments to technique where required.

WORK MEASUREMENT

Determining the amount of time that should be allowed for doing a specific job is another aspect of work study. Called work measurement, it is generally accomplished through one of three methods:

Time study
Synthesis
Analytical estimating

A single company may use one or all of the techniques, depending on work circumstances.

Time study is the technique of having a trained person observe a job and collect time information about that job while it is being done. For repetitive jobs, such as assembly line work, the method is especially suitable.

Synthesis requires detailing a job, using previous time studies or information. The steps of the task are outlined in order, including an estimate of the time required for each. Use of this technique assumes that someone who knows the steps and their length of time is setting up the study, since no one actually observes the work in progress. The method is best used when jobs are diverse but have several repetitive factors.

Analytical estimating is a technique used for measuring nonrepetitive work, such as maintenance work, receptionist duties, and retail sales. Using this system, workers of a cross sampling of those actually doing the task will each set down the various elements involved in their work, along with the amount of time each step takes. Several examples for each job should be collected and averaged, as there are likely to be elements within each task that the worker cannot control in a specific instance.

USING WORK MEASUREMENT STUDIES

Whatever technique is used, applying work measurement studies effectively is what reduces costs. From any of the three methods given, you will have an idea of how much time *should* be used in the job studied. This is the *standard,* against which future work will be measured. Adding a small margin to the standard as a rest allowance, this figure serves as the basis for production bonuses and piece rate scales.

SUGGESTED FURTHER READING

Cemach, Harry P., *Work Study in the Office,* MacLaren & Sons, London, 1969.
Cost Control and the Supervisor, American Management Assn., New York, 1966.
Jervis, F. R., and W. F. Frank, *An Introduction to Industrial Administration,* Harrap, London, 1970.

X METHOD

Areas for use in Cost Control:

ORGANIZATIONAL AND OPERATIONAL SYSTEMS
INDUSTRIAL APPLICATIONS
BUSINESS AND COMMERCIAL APPLICATIONS

The X method is a device used to spark creative thinking in solving cost or other business problems. Devised by G. B. Dubois, of Cornell University, the problem is split into sections. Each section is examined and possible solutions determined. If no solution seems likely for any one section, it is "X'd," or skipped over. Later, possible solutions for all sections are evaluated as a whole, usually solving the unsolved problems.

SUGGESTED FURTHER READING

Bittel, L. R., "How to Make Good Ideas Come Easy," *Factory Management and Maintenance,* March 1956.

ZAIBATSU DISSOLUTION

Areas for use in Cost Control:

ORGANIZATIONAL AND OPERATIONAL SYSTEMS
INDUSTRIAL APPLICATIONS
BUSINESS AND COMMERCIAL APPLICATIONS

The Zaibatsu dissolution technique is a movement of younger department heads, divisional managers, and other line management personnel who are relatively young, yet experienced, to top executive positions where they make all cost and other decisions. For example, a firm may replace all top executives at the age of fifty.

The method was developed by the Japanese after World War II, when government-controlled, monopolistic industries, the Zaibatsu, were broken into smaller units. The lower levels of the three- and four-tier management systems were moved into areas of responsibility, bringing an entirely youthful and vigorous management into action for the whole economy at the same time, rather than employing the traditional gradual replacement in the power structure. Use of the technique reduces administrative cost as the result of the lower salary levels of younger managerial employees, as well as spurring growth and dynamism of the firm through an influx of young and aggressive management.

SUGGESTED FURTHER READING

Broadbridge, Seymour, *Industrial Dualism in Japan,* Aldine, Chicago, 1966.
Ginzberg, Eli, *Manpower for Development,* Praeger, New York, 1971.
Komiya, Ryutaro, *Post-War Economic Growth in Japan,* University of California Press, Los Angeles, 1966.

ZERO DEFECTS

Areas for use in Cost Control:

PSYCHOLOGICAL MOTIVATIONAL MANAGEMENT
FINANCIAL MOTIVATIONAL MANAGEMENT
ORGANIZATIONAL AND OPERATIONAL SYSTEMS
INDUSTRIAL APPLICATIONS
BUSINESS AND COMMERCIAL APPLICATIONS

Zero defects is a technique that reduces operating costs by decreasing worker mistakes to zero, or as near zero as possible. A publicity campaign is conducted making fun of or belittling the worker who makes mistakes. A good-sized prize, such as a vacation trip or a color TV, is given to workers making no mistakes during the campaign. Success of the technique depends on the skill and degree of its application. A really big fuss must be made. For example, there may be a champagne kick-off lunch, daily posting of "scores," cartoon posters pointing out the bad effects or workers who make mistakes, etc.

SUGGESTED FURTHER READING

Argenti, J., *Management Techniques,* G. Allen, London, 1970.

INDEX